T0336693

Web Services Security Development and Architecture:
Theoretical and Practical Issues

Carlos Gutierrez
Correos Telecom, Spain

Eduardo Fernandez–Medina
University of Castilla–La Mancha, Spain

Mario Piattini
University of Castilla–La Mancha, Spain

INFORMATION SCIENCE REFERENCE

Hershey · New York

Director of Editorial Content: Kristin Klinger
Director of Book Publications: Julia Mosemann
Development Editor: Joel Gamon
Publishing Assistant: Sean Woznicki
Typesetter: Jamie Snavely, Sean Woznicki
Quality control: Jamie Snavely
Cover Design: Lisa Tosheff
Printed at: Yurchak Printing Inc.

Published in the United States of America by
   Information Science Reference (an imprint of IGI Global)
   701 E. Chocolate Avenue
   Hershey PA 17033
   Tel: 717-533-8845
   Fax: 717-533-8661
   E-mail: cust@igi-global.com
   Web site: http://www.igi-global.com/reference

Library of Congress Cataloging-in-Publication Data

Web services security development and architecture : theoretical and practical issues / Carlos Gutierrez, Eduardo Fernandez-Medina and Mario Piattini, editors.
      p. cm.

  Includes bibliographical references and index.
  Summary: "This book's main objective is to present some of the key approaches, research lines, and challenges that exist in the field of security in SOA systems"--Provided by publisher.

  ISBN 978-1-60566-950-2 (hbk.) -- ISBN 978-1-60566-951-9 (ebook) 1. Web
services--Security measures. 2. Computer networks--Security measures. 3.
Service-oriented architecture (Computer Science) I. Gutierrez, Carlos, 1977-
II. Fernandez-Medina, Eduardo, 1973- III. Piattini, Mario, 1966-
  TK5105.88813W427 2010
  006.7'8--dc22
                              2009026285

British Cataloguing in Publication Data
A Cataloguing in Publication record for this book is available from the British Library.

All work contributed to this book is new, previously-unpublished material. The views expressed in this book are those of the authors, but not necessarily of the publisher.

Editorial Advisory Board

Table of Contents

Section 1
Web Services Security Engineering

Chapter 1

    Sebastian Höhn, Albert-Ludwig University, Germany
    Lutz Lowis, Albert-Ludwig University, Germany
    Jan Jürjens, Open University, UK
    Rafael Accorsi, Albert-Ludwig University, Germany

Chapter 2

    Frank Innerhofer-Oberperfler, University of Innsbruck, Austria
    Markus Mitterer, University of Innsbruck, Austria
    Michael Hafner, University of Innsbruck, Austria
    Ruth Breu, University of Innsbruck, Austria

Section 2
Web Services Security Architectures

Chapter 3

    Amit Jain, University of South Carolina, USA
    Csilla Farkas, University of South Carolina, USA

Section 3
Web Services Security Standards

Section 4
Web Services Security Threats and Countermeasures

Section 5
Selected Readings

Detailed Table of Contents

Section 1
Web Services Security Engineering

Sebastian Höhn, Albert-Ludwig University, Germany
Lutz Lowis, Albert-Ludwig University, Germany
Jan Jürjens, Open University, UK
Rafael Accorsi, Albert-Ludwig University, Germany

In a service-oriented architecture, business processes are executed as composition of services, which can suffer from vulnerabilities. These vulnerabilities in services and the underlying software applications put at risk computer systems in general and business processes in particular. Current vulnerability analysis approaches involve several manual tasks and, hence, are error-prone and costly. Service-oriented architectures impose additional analysis complexity as they provide much flexibility and frequent changes within orchestrated processes and services. Therefore, it is inevitable to provide tools and mechanisms that enable efficient and effective management of vulnerabilities within these complex systems. Model-based security engineering is a promising approach that can help to fill the gap between vulnerabilities on the one hand, and concrete protection mechanisms on the other. The authors present an approach that integrates model-based engineering and vulnerability analysis in order to cope with the security challenges of a service-oriented architecture.

Frank Innerhofer-Oberperfler, University of Innsbruck, Austria
Markus Mitterer, University of Innsbruck, Austria
Michael Hafner, University of Innsbruck, Austria
Ruth Breu, University of Innsbruck, Austria

This chapter is devoted to the continuous security analysis of service oriented systems during design and operation. We present the ProSecO framework which offers concepts and a process model for the elicitation of security objectives and requirements, evaluation of risks and documentation of security controls. The goal of ProSecO is to provide the analyst at any time during design and operation with information about the security state of the system. Core ideas of ProSecO are interweaved elicitation and documentation of functional and security properties based on system models and the clear separation of business oriented and technical information. The kind of information ProsecO handles is in wide parts informal and non-executable.

Section 2
Web Services Security Architectures

Chapter 3

Amit Jain, University of South Carolina, USA
Csilla Farkas, University of South Carolina, USA

This research work proposes a Semantic-Aware Authorization Framework, called SAAF, for applying syntax independent authorization on eXtensible Markup Language (XML) documents. Our model supports secure data sharing in an open environment without the need for a centralized authority and supports application flexibility. We propose the use of data and application semantics, expressed as Resource Description Framework (RDF) ontologies, to specify security requirements for XML documents. XML documents are associated with their semantics (RDF ontologies) via mappings. We use these mappings and the corresponding RDF authorizations models to generate access control permissions for the mapped XML documents. The SAAF ensures the preservation of authorization permissions on XML data even if the syntax and the structure of the data are changed. Our method also aids the detection and removal of inconsistent authorizations on structurally different but semantically similar XML data.

Chapter 4

Nico Brehm, RepuGraph.com, Nordhausen, Germany
Jorge Marx Gómez, University of Oldenburg, Germany

The Service-oriented Architecture (SOA) paradigm mostly provides a suitable approach as to meet the requirements of flexible distributed software systems. Referring to the activities for the standardization of Web Service semantics or alternatively the introduction of intelligent search mechanisms future software architectures are supposed to integrate software components as remote services of foreign providers. If we assume that such services can be standardized e.g. as components of standard business application systems the vision of a service economy arises where services of the same type can be marketed by different providers. A service consumer on the other hand could choose the service he likes best at runtime. However, this vision is clouded by a multiplicity of risks which meet each other in the question of the specific reliability and trustworthiness of service providers in a certain context. Previous research activities picked up this problem whereby a lot of promising approaches and frameworks have been developed which concern the negotiation of trust within open network architectures like grids or peer-to-peer networks. Nevertheless, the genesis of the trust relationship between two network nodes has been neglected. This chapter presents an approach for the establishment of reputation in federated software systems where central network instances for the management of evaluations are avoided. In our approach the service providers are responsible for this task on their own. We present a novel security protocol for the message-based exchange of service evaluations that deters service providers from manipulating their own ratings.

Chapter 5

Murat Gunestas, General Directorate of Security, Turkey
Duminda Wijesekera, George Mason University, USA
Anoop Singhal, National Institute of Standards and Technology, USA

Web services are currently a preferred way to architect and provide complex services. This complexity arises due to the composition of new services by choreographing, orchestrating and dynamically invoking existing services. These compositions create service inter-dependencies that can be misused for monetary or other gains. When a misuse is reported, investigators have to navigate through a collection of logs to recreate the attack. In order to facilitate that task, we propose creating forensic web services (FWS), a specialized web service that when used would securely maintain transactional records between other web services. These secure records can be re-linked to reproduce the transactional history by an independent agency. Although our work is ongoing, we show the necessary components of a forensic framework for web services and its success through a case study.

Chapter 6

Antonio Maña, University of Málaga, Spain
Gimena Pujol, University of Málaga, Spain
Antonio Muñoz, University of Málaga, Spain

In this chapter the authors present a policy-based security engineering process for service oriented applications, developed in the SERENITY and MISTICO projects. Security and dependability (S&D) are considered as first-class citizens in the proposed engineering process, which is based on the precise description of reusable security and dependability solutions. Their process is based on the concept of S&D Pattern as the means to capture the specialized knowledge of security engineers and to make it available for automated processing, both in the development process (the focus of this chapter) and later at runtime. In particular, in this chapter the authors focus on the verification of the compliance with security policies, based on the formal specification of S&D Properties. The main advantages of the approach presented in this chapter are precisely that it allows us to define high-level policies and to verify that a secure oriented system complies with such policy (developed following the SERENITY approach). They also describe the application of the proposed approach to the verification of S&D properties in the web services (WS) environment. Concretely, they describe the use of SERENITY framework to facilitate the development of applications that use standard security mechanisms (such WS-Security, WS-Policy,

WS-Security Policy, etc) and to ensure the correct application of these standard mechanisms, based on predefined policies. Finally, the authors show how to verify that the application complies with one or several S&D policies.

Chapter 7

Deepti Parachuri, Infosys Technologies Limited, India
Sudeep Mallick, Infosys Technologies Limited, India

Security is of fundamental concern in computing systems. This chapter covers the role of security policies in Web services. First, it examines the importance of policies in web services and explains the WS-Policy standard. It also highlights the relation of WS-Policy with other WS-* specifications. Next, it covers different facets of security requirements in SOA implementations. Later, it examines the importance of security policies in web services. It also presents the basic concepts of WS-Security policy language. WS-Security policy specification specifies a standard way to define and publish security requirements in an extensible and interoperable way. A service provider makes use of security policy to publish the security measures implemented to protect the service. Security policies can also be made customizable to meet the security preferences of different consumers. Towards the end, it discusses about the governance of security polices and also future trends in security policies for web services.

Section 3
Web Services Security Standards

Chapter 8

Eduardo B. Fernandez, Florida Atlantic University, USA
Keiko Hashizume, Florida Atlantic University, USA
Ingrid Buckley, Florida Atlantic University, USA
Maria M. Larrondo-Petrie, Florida Atlantic University, USA
Michael VanHilst, Florida Atlantic University, USA

This chapter surveys the context for web services security and discusses the issues and standards at every level of architectural. The authors attempt to evaluate the status of industrial practice with respect to the security of web services. The authors look at commercial products and their supporting levels, and end with some conclusions. The authors see a problem in the proliferation of overlapping and possibly incompatible standards. Reliability is also an important aspect. They discuss some of its issues and consider its effect on security. A basic principle of security is the need to secure all levels of architecture; any weak levels will permit attackers to penetrate the system. These levels include: Business workflow level, catalog and description of web services level, communications level (typically SOAP), and storage of XML documents. There is a variety of standards for web services security and reliability and they will look at most of them.

Chapter 9

Service Oriented Architectures (SOAs) have become the defacto standard for defining interoperable architectures on the web with the most common implementation of this concept being in the form of web services. Information exchange is an integral part of SOAs, so designing effective security architectures that ensure data confidentiality and integrity is important. However, selecting a security standard for the architecture is challenging because existing solutions are geared toward access control in relatively static scenarios rather than dynamic scenarios where some form of adaptability is needed. Moreover, when services interact across different domains interoperability becomes a problem because of the lack a consistent security model to handle service interactions. This chapter presents a comparative analysis of SOA security standards. We discuss the challenges SOA security architecture designers face, in relation to an example travel agent web services scenario, and outline potential mitigation strategies.

Section 4
Web Services Security Threats and Countermeasures

In the modern electronic business world, services offered to business partners as well as to customers have become an important company asset. This again produces interests for attacking those services either to paralyze the availability or to gain unauthorized access. Though founding on decades of networking experience, Web Services are not more resistant to security attacks than other open network systems. Quite the opposite is true: Web Services are exposed to attacks well-known from common Internet protocols and additionally to new kinds of attacks targeting Web Services in particular. This chapter presents a survey of different types of such Web Service specific attacks. For each attack a description of the attack execution, the effect on the target and partly the results of practical experiments are given. Additionally, general countermeasures for fending Web Service attacks are shown.

Chapter 11

This research work proposes a threat modeling approach for Web 2.0 applications. The authors' approach is based on applying informal method of threat modeling for Web 2.0 applications. Traditional enterprises are skeptical in adopting Web 2.0 applications for internal and commercial use in public-facing situations, with customers and partners. One of the prime concerns for this is lack of security over public networks. Threat modeling is a technique for complete analysis and review of security aspects of application. The authors will show why existing threat modeling approaches cannot be applied to Web 2.0 applications, and how our new approach is a simple way of applying threat modeling to Web 2.0 applications.

Section 5
Selected Readings

Chapter 12

David G. Rosado, University of Castilla-La Mancha, Spain
Eduardo Fernández-Medina, University of Castilla-La Mancha, Spain
Javier López, University of Málaga, Spain
Mario Piatini, University of Castilla-La Mancha, Spain

Mobile Grid includes the characteristics of the Grid systems together with the peculiarities of Mobile Computing, with the additional feature of supporting mobile users and resources in a seamless, transparent, secure and efficient way. Security of these systems, due to their distributed and open nature, is considered a topic of great interest. In this article we present the practical results of applying a secured methodology to a real case, specifically the approach that define, identify and specify the security requirements. This methodology will help the building of a secured grid application in a systematic and iterative way.

Chapter 13

Rodolfo Villarroel, Universidad Católica del Maule, Chile
Eduardo Fernández-Medina, Universidad de Castilla-La Mancha, Spain
Juan Trujillo, Universidad de Alicante, Spain
Mario Piattini, Universidad de Castilla-La Mancha, Spain

This chapter presents an approach for designing secure Data Warehouses (DWs) that accomplish the conceptual modeling of secure DWs independently from the target platform where the DW has to be implemented, because our complete approach follows the Model Driven Architecture (MDA) and the Model Driven Security (MDS). In most of real world DW projects, the security aspects are issues that usually rely on the DBMS administrators. We argue that the design of these security aspects should be considered together with the conceptual modeling of DWs from the early stages of a DW project, and being able to attach user security information to the basic structures of a Multidimensional (MD) model. In this way, we would be able to generate this information in a semi or automatic way into a target platform and the final DW will better suits the user security requirements.

    M. Mujinga, University of Fort Hare, South Africa

    Hippolyte Muyingi, University of Fort Hare, South Africa

    Alfredo Terzoli, Rhodes University, South Africa

    G. S. V. Radha Krishna Rao, University of Fort Hare, South Africa

Internet protocol version 6 (IPv6) is the next generation Internet protocol proposed by the Internet Engineering Task Force (IETF) to supplant the current Internet protocol version 4 (IPv4). Lack of security below the application layer in IPv4 is one of the reasons why there is a need for a new IP. IPv6 has built-in support for the Internet protocol security protocol (IPSec). This chapter reports work done to evaluate implications of compulsory use of IPSec on dual stack IPv4/IPv6 environment.

    Subhas C. Misra, Carleton University, Canada

    Vinod Kumar, Carleton University, Canada

    Uma Kumar, Carleton University, Canada

In this chapter, we provide a conceptual modeling approach for Web services security risk assessment that is based on the identification and analysis of stakeholder intentions. There are no similar approaches for modeling Web services security risk assessment in the existing pieces of literature. The approach is, thus, novel in this domain. The approach is helpful for performing means-end analysis, thereby, uncovering the structural origin of security risks in WS, and how the root-causes of such risks can be controlled from the early stages of the projects. The approach addresses "why" the process is the way it is by exploring the strategic dependencies between the actors of a security system, and analyzing the motivations, intents, and rationales behind the different entities and activities in constituting the system.

Foreword

We live in a service oriented world where service providers provide a variety of services to the consumers. These services include healthcare and medical services, financial and baking services, telecommunication and television services, entertainment and video services, and education services. Typically a consumer may request a service from the service provider. Contracts may be negotiated between the consumer and the service provider. The service provider provides the services for which the consumer may pay n accordance with the contract. The service provider may invoke other service provides to provide certain services to satisfy the consumer. For example, a customer may request a service from an airline. The airline may have a negotiated contract with a hotel service and may invoke the hotel service provider. The airline may then provide both the airline and the hotel service to the customer.

During the past ten years with the advent of the World Wide Web, the consumer/service provider concept has been digitized and enforced via the web. This way we now have web supported services where a consumer may request a service via the web site of a service provider and the service provider provides the requested service. This service could be making an airline reservation or purchasing a book from the service provider. Such web supported services have come to be known as web services. Note that services do not necessarily have to be provided through the web. A consumer could send an email message to the service provider and request the service. Such services are computer supported services. However much of the work on computer supported services has focused on web services. An architecture that provides support for the implementation of services has come to be known as service oriented architecture (SOA). In supporting the services, it is crucial that security is enforced. For example, only authorized entities may request certain services and only authorized entities may provide certain services.

Standards groups such as W3C (World Wide Web Consortium) and OASIS (*Organization for the Advancement of Structured Information Standards*) have developed standards for SOA and security services. This book titled *Web Services Security: Standards and Industrial Practice* consists of a collection of eleven papers that provides a comprehensive view of secure web services and SOA. It is divided into four parts, each describing some aspect of secure web services, SOA and related standards. Section 1, consisting of two chapters, discusses security engineering of web services. Security engineering tasks include gathering requirements, designing the secure system, verifying and validating the system as well as certifying and accrediting the system. The chapters in Part I describe approaches for security engineering of web services including identification of vulnerability effects in web services using model-based security as well as service oriented security analysis.

Section 2, consisting of five chapters, discusses concepts in web services security architectures. In particular, security polices, security models, building federated systems using the service oriented architecture paradigm and forensics over web services are described. Section 3, consisting of two chapters, describes web services security standards. In particular some of the trends, challenges and industry practices related to standards are discussed. Section 4, consisting of two chapters, describes security threats and countermeasures. This includes a discussion of the security attacks, threat modeling and security solutions.

This book is a must for anyone who wants to get an understanding of secure services and their related standards. It can be used as a senior undergraduate or first year graduate text on secure web services. It can also be used as a references guide for a student or professor who wants to conduct research in secure web services. This book will also be invaluable to those in the industry, government and standards organization who want to learn about web services security as well as develop standards. The editors have included an excellent collection of papers that provide breadth and depth in secure services and architectures. Since secure web services is a rapidly growing field, we encourage the reader to keep up with the developments. In addition to familiarizing oneself with the security standards that are emerging, the reader should also attend various conferences in this field including the IEEE International Conference on Web Services, Services Computing Conference and the various security related workshops on web services.

Dr. Bhavani Thuraisingham
IEEE Fellow
Professor of Computer Science and
Director of the Cyber Security Research Center
The University of Texas at Dallas, USA

Bhavani Thuraisingham joined The University of Texas at Dallas (UTD) in October 2004 as a Professor of Computer Science and Director of the Cyber Security Research Center in the Erik Jonsson School of Engineering and Computer Science. She is an elected Fellow of three professional organizations: the IEEE (Institute for Electrical and Electronics Engineers), the AAAS (American Association for the Advancement of Science) and the BCS (British Computer Society) for her work in data security. She received the IEEE Computer Society's prestigious 1997 Technical Achievement Award for "outstanding and innovative contributions to secure data management." Prior to joining UTD, Dr. Thuraisingham was an IPA (Intergovernmental Personnel Act) at the National Science Foundation (NSF) in Arlington VA, from the MITRE Corporation. At NSF she established the Data and Applications Security Program and co-founded the Cyber Trust theme. She worked at MITRE in Bedford, MA between January 1989 and September 2001 first in the Information Security Center and was later a department head in Data and Information Management. Dr. Thuraisingham's work in information security and information management has resulted in over 80 journal articles, over 200 refereed conference papers and workshops, and three US patents. She is the author of nine books in data management, data mining and data security and has given over 60 keynote addresses. Dr. Thuraisingham was educated in the United Kingdom both at the University of Bristol and at the University of Wales.

Preface

The flow of today's market conditions is continuously changing. Competitive demands from traditional and non-traditional businesses, the rapid appearance and growth of new channels, the rising trend to outsource certain business processes, and the demand to comply with an ever-growing amount of new regulatory and legal requirements, are all creating an increasing demand for change. The effective and efficient management of organizational changes has traditionally been a real challenge. In order to withstand this and to show a profit in the future, organizations will need to develop their capability to sustain a constant state of change and evolution. The capability of an organization's IT systems to handle this level of change will be a major factor in its success when it comes to adapting to increasingly more dynamic marketplace environments.

Service-Oriented Architecture (SOA) is the main architectural style that IT departments are currently adopting to support the aforementioned business requirements owing to its capacity to enable the loose-coupling and dynamic integration of business services and applications, and their possible operations across trust limits.

Just as organizations' timely response to changes in the business environment is critical to their survival, so is the appropriate protection of their assets. In the field of IT systems, the main assets are information and IT services, which support the implementation of the business services and must, therefore, handle this information in a secure manner. Securing access to information is thus a critical factor for any business, and security is even more critical for IT deployments based on SOA principles.

This book's main objective is to present some of the key approaches, research lines, and challenges that exist in the field of security in SOA systems.

It is a valuable resource for senior undergraduate or graduate courses in information security which have a special focus on SOA security. It might also be useful for technologists, managers, and developers who are interested in discovering more about this topic. Its authors are noted researchers in the field of IT security engineering, methodologies, Semantic Web, Web services and SOA.

We shall first provide a general picture of security in Web services and then discuss the contents of the book.

GENERAL PICTURE OF SECURITY IN WEB SERVICES: CHALLENGES AND OBJECTIVES

As was previously mentioned, the SOA paradigm enables organizations to actually fall into line with the current changing business environment requirements. There has consequently been an increasing adoption of SOA, both in industry and academia, and as a consequence of its main implementation technology: Web services technology.

The security challenges presented by the Web services approach are highly complex and technologically advanced. On the one hand, the security challenges arising from this technology are:

- Risks that appear as a result of the publication on the Internet of a complete and well-documented interface to back office data and company's business logic. One of the main security problems associated with the adoption of WS is derived from the Internet publication of business interfaces through HTTP or HTTPS ports.
- Protecting the semantic Web by ensuring that security is preserved at the semantic level.
- Context-aware and context-based protection at the document level. Documents usually have information with different "degrees of sensitivity" which it is necessary to protect at different levels of security. Access control policies that govern access to the different security parts of the documents, and an architecture enforcing these policies, currently constitute an extremely important research area in the context of WS security.
- Service trustworthiness. Dynamic discovery and the composition of services imply that a Web service consumer may not know whether the services, either individually or as a whole, will behave as expected. How to select trustworthy Web services consequently remains a challenge.
- The unstructured and overwhelming number of WS security related literature and approaches make the developers' task of attaining a complete knowledge of all the potential WS security issues, and the standard means to address them, extremely difficult.

On the other hand, some of the main security objectives are:

- Management of security policies in a large and distributed WS environment.
- Application-level, end-to-end and just-one-context-security communications. Network topologies require that end-to-end security be maintained in all the intermediaries in the path of the message. When data is received and forwarded on by an intermediary beyond the transport layer, both the data integrity and any security information that flows with it may be lost.
- Interoperability of the requirements and on-line security elements.
- Ability to federate the full information concerning the subjects, thus permitting single sign-on environments and facilitating across-enterprise interoperability.
- Maintaining sensitive users' attributes and identity private in trust domains.

AIMS OF THIS BOOK

This book aims to provide a theoretical and academic description of Web services security issues, and practical and useful guidelines, models and techniques for implementing secure Web services-based systems in organizations.

The book covers the following topics:

- Security goals, features and requirements specification of Web services-based systems: reviews of approaches toward modelling, analyzing, validating, verifying and documenting security requirements for Web services-based systems from both theoretical and practical perspectives will be presented.

- Web services-based security architectures: theoretical and industrial approaches through which to define Web services-security architectures will be covered, and we shall also attempt to cover all potential types of threats, attacks and security requirements.
- Web services-based security standards: an in-depth review of the major international standards related to Web services security will be carried out.

ORGANIZATION OF THIS BOOK

This book is divided into four sections, each addressing a state-of-the-art topic in Web services security, and then a fifth containing selected readings. These are as follows: *Web Services Security Engineering*, *Web Services Security Architectures*, *Web Services Security Standards* and *Web Services Security Threats and Policies*.

Section 1: Web Services Security Engineering

Security engineering integrated into software development is one the major security topics developed during the last few years. Applying security engineering throughout the different steps devised by the different software development methodologies has been a major topic in both scientific and industrial literature.

This section of the book deals with this subject in Chapters 1 and 2.

The first chapter, *"Identification of Vulnerability in Web Services Using Model-Based Security"* by Sebastian Höhn, Lutz Lowis, Jan Jürjens, and Rafael Accorsi, presents an approach that integrates model-based engineering and vulnerability analysis in order to cope with the security challenges of a service-oriented architecture.

The second chapter, *"Security Analysis of Service Oriented Systems: A Methodical Approach and Case Study"* by Frank Innerhofer-Oberperfler, Markus Mitterer, Michael Hafnera and Ruth Breu, presents the ProSecO process which is aimed at defining a security model process for security requirement elicitation, security risk evaluation and security control specification, thus providing security analysts with system security state information in both design and production-time.

Section 2: Web Services Security Architectures

Web services security architectures should define the highest level organization of the IT security infrastructure necessary to meet the security requirements specified for the systems to be built by articulating the necessary security mechanisms in such a way that reusability, manageability and (internal/external) interoperability is guaranteed.

Section 2 of the book shows different architectural approaches to different security requirements, and consists of five chapters.

Chapter 3, *"Ontology-Based Authorization Model for XML Data in Distributed Systems"*, by Amit Jain and Csilla Farkas, proposes a framework that preserves authorization permissions on XML data even when its structure changes during transactions. In order for this to occur, the authors define an authorization framework that permits the specification of authorization requirements from the semantic perspective rather than on the syntactic representation of that information.

Chapter 4, "*Secure Service Rating in Federated Software Systems Based on SOA*", by Nico Brehm and Jorge Marx Gómez, deals with the establishment of reputation in federated software systems in which trust evaluation management is de-centralized.

Chapter 5, "*Forensics over Web Services: The FWS*" by Murat Gunestas, Duminda Wijesekera and Anoop Singhal describes a security Web service whose objective is to store and preserve the evidences yielded from Web services interactions thereby enabling the capability to recreate the composed Web service invocations independent of those parties with a vested interest. This forensic security service would facilitate and base later forensic investigations on a reliable infrastructure that could be used in a court of law.

Chapter 6, "*Policy-Based Security Engineering of Service Oriented Systems*", by Antonio Maña, Gimena Pujol and Antonio Muñoz, presents a policy-based security engineering process for service oriented applications based on security and dependability patterns. This chapter focuses on the verification of the compliance with security policies, based on the formal specification of security and dependability properties

Chapter 7, "*Security Policies in Web Services*", by Deepti Parachuri and Sudeep Mallick, discusses the different approaches developed in the field of security policies in Web services systems giving a brief overview for each one.

Section 3: Web Services Security Standards

Undoubtedly, the earliest and greatest effort on the subject of Web services security has been that of the definition of the security standards that accomplish all the security aspects that this type of systems must deal with. The main motivation behind this effort is the particular feature that Web services (and their security) should provide: interoperability. This quality aspect is being achieved thanks to the definition of an overwhelming number of standards generated from a diverse set of standardization bodies, consortiums, organizations, etc.

This aspect is covered by Chapters 8 and 9. Chapter 8, entitled "*Web Services Security: Standards and Industrial Practice*" by Eduardo B. Fernandez, Keiko Hashizume, Ingrid Buckley, Maria M. Larrondo-Petrie, and Michael VanHilst provides an in-depth state-of-the-art review of the existing Web services security standards and their practical implementations.

Chapter 9, entitled "*Security in Service Oriented Architectures: Standards and Challenges*" by Anne V.D.M. Kayem, reviews current Web services security standards and how they cope with the dynamic nature of the scenarios enabled by Web services technologies.

Section 4: Web Services Security Threats and Countermeasures

This last section of the book covers specific threats and policies inherent to Web services technologies. The main security threats and attacks are exemplified and the countermeasures to, fully or partially, mitigate them are shown.

Chapter 10, "*A Survey of Attacks in the Web Services World*" by Meiko Jensen and Nils Gruschka, reviews the main types of security attacks on Web services enabled infrastructures and explains the main countermeasures to allow their mitigation at an acceptable level of risk.

Chapter 11, *"Threat Modeling: Securing Web 2.0 Based Rich Service Consumers"* by Nishtha Srivastava, Sumeet Gupta, Mayank Mathur, provides an overview of security threats to Web 2.0 systems and explains security best practices to protect them.

Section 5 includes four selected readings.

Carlos A. Gutierrez, Correos Telecom, Spain
Eduardo Fernandez-Medina, University of Castilla – La Mancha, Spain
Mario Piattini, University of Castilla – La Mancha, Spain
June 2009

Acknowledgment

This book is part of the QUASIMODO (PAC08-0157-0668) and SISTEMA (PII2009-0150-3135) Projects financed by the FEDER and the Regional Science and Technology Ministry of Castilla-La Mancha (Spain).

The editors would like to thank all the people that collaborated in making this book a reality. First, we would like to thank the publishing team at IGI Global. In particular, we would like to thank Liang-Jie (LJ) Zhang who gave us the opportunity to edit this book, to Jan Travers and Joel Gamon for guiding throughout the editing process, and the members of the Editorial Advisory Board, Sushil Jajodia, Elena Ferrari, Duminda Wijesekera and Jan Jürjens, for their constant support and advice.

We also want to express our gratitude to the authors of the chapters for their insights and brilliant contribution to this book. Most of them also served as reviewers for chapters written by other authors. We wish to thank all of them for their productive and complete reviews. We would also like to thank Prof. Thuraisingham for accepting to write the Foreword of this book.

Carlos A. Gutierrez
Eduardo Fernandez-Medina
Mario Piattini
Editors

Section 1
Web Services
Security Engineering

Chapter 1
Identification of Vulnerabilities in Web Services Using Model–Based Security

Sebastian Höhn
Albert-Ludwig University, Germany

Lutz Lowis
Albert-Ludwig University, Germany

Jan Jürjens
Open University, UK

Rafael Accorsi
Albert-Ludwig University, Germany

ABSTRACT

In a service-oriented architecture, business processes are executed as composition of services, which can suffer from vulnerabilities. These vulnerabilities in services and the underlying software applications put at risk computer systems in general and business processes in particular. Current vulnerability analysis approaches involve several manual tasks and, hence, are error-prone and costly. Service-oriented architectures impose additional analysis complexity as they provide much flexibility and frequent changes within orchestrated processes and services. Therefore, it is inevitable to provide tools and mechanisms that enable efficient and effective management of vulnerabilities within these complex systems. Model-based security engineering is a promising approach that can help to fill the gap between vulnerabilities on the one hand, and concrete protection mechanisms on the other. The authors present an approach that integrates model-based engineering and vulnerability analysis in order to cope with the security challenges of a service-oriented architecture.

DOI: 10.4018/978-1-60566-950-2.ch001

INTRODUCTION

Information systems consist of a plethora of different applications, services and components. The complex interplay between these system parts is one of the main challenges for the establishment of reliable and secure service oriented architectures (SOA). Among the prominent requirements for enterprise information systems is the ability to react to changes quickly and flexibly. To this end, a SOA is deployed in many different application scenarios. It allows the orchestration of services and the implementation of complex business processes without implementing the basic functions over and over again.

Security concepts for SOA heavily rely on model-based technologies. This is due to two prominent reasons: (1) model-based mechanisms work reliably and fast even in complex industrial settings, and (2) SOA itself is a model-based architecture. The deployment and the execution of business processes in a SOA are based on executable business process models mostly written in BPEL. The description of atomic services and their composition to higher-order services is also done in BPEL-Models, together with a WSDL description of the implemented interfaces.

To this end, we propose the integration of model-based security mechanisms for SOA. Current approaches (as explained in the next chapter) neglect the fact that vulnerabilities are major source for security incidents. In classical systems, vulnerability analysis and integration of appropriate counter-mechanisms is a mainly manual task. This is possible because these systems are quite static: they are deployed once and used for longer period in time. In a SOA, systems are composed and re-composed frequently and it becomes infeasible to manually interact with specific instances of business processes or high-order services. For example, they might be part of a complex orchestration. While it might seem a strong assumption that processes and services are orchestrated for unique tasks, systems exist that

allow for dynamic integration of additional steps into existing processes (Reichert et al., 2006): by integrating individually required steps, a unique process arises that is executed exactly once.

These scenarios clearly show that security information and vulnerability information must be prepared for automated processing. If users can integrate additional process steps into existing business processes on the fly, it is inevitable to automatically evaluate the security implications. Several security properties of the resulting processes can be evaluated automatically. The following section will provide a motivation for and an overview of these mechanisms. Afterwards, we present a model-based extension for UMLsec that allows for the automated evaluation of vulnerabilities and their effects in a SOA.

Model-Based Security Analysis

Challenges for Computer Security

Attacks against computer systems, on which the infrastructures of modern society and modern economies rely, cause substantial financial damage. Due to the increasing interconnection of systems, such attacks can be waged anonymously and from a safe distance. Thus networked computers need to be secure. The high-quality development of security-critical systems is difficult. Still, many systems are developed, deployed, and used over years that contain significant security weaknesses. Causes: While tracing requirements during software development is difficult enough, enforcing security requirements is intrinsically subtle, because one has to take into account the interaction of the system with motivated adversaries that act independently. Thus security mechanisms, such as security protocols, are notoriously hard to design correctly, even for experts. Also, a system is only as secure as its weakest part or aspect. Security is compromised most often not by breaking dedicated mechanisms such as encryption or security protocols, but by exploiting weaknesses in the way

Figure 1. Model-based security engineering

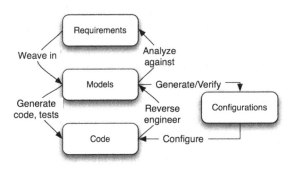

they are being used (Anderson & Long, 2001). Thus it is not enough to ensure correct functioning of security mechanisms used. They cannot be "blindly" inserted into a security-critical system, but the overall system development must take security aspects into account in a coherent way (Saltzer & Schroeder, 1975). In fact, according to (Schneider, 1998), 85% of Computer Emergency Response Team (CERT) security advisories could not have been prevented just by making use of cryptography. Building trustworthy components does not suffice, since the interconnections and interactions of components play a significant role in trustworthiness (Schneider, 1998).

State of the Art in Model-Based Security

In practice, the traditional strategy for security assurance has been "penetrate and patch": It has been accepted that deployed systems contain vulnerabilities. Whenever a penetration of the system is noticed and the exploited weakness can be identified, the vulnerability is removed. Sometimes this is supported by employing friendly teams trained in penetrating computer systems, the so-called "tiger teams". However, this approach is not ideal: Each penetration using a new vulnerability may already have caused significant damage, before the vulnerability can be removed. It would thus

be preferable to consider security aspects more seriously in earlier phases of the system life-cycle, before a system is deployed, or even implemented, because late correction of requirements errors costs up to 200 times as much as early correction (Boehm, 1981). Also, security concerns must be taken into account during every phase of software development, from requirements engineering to design, implementation, testing, and deployment. Academic approaches trying to improve security during development must be *tightly integrated* with software development approaches already used in industry (Devanbu & Stubblebine, 2000). Some other challenges for using sound engineering methods for secure systems development exist. For example, the boundaries of specified components with the rest of the system need to be carefully examined, for example with respect to implicit assumptions on the system context (Gollmann, 2000). Lastly, a more technical issue is that formalized security properties are not in all approaches preserved by refinement. Since an implementation is necessarily a refinement of its specification, an implementation of a secure specification may, in such a situation, not be secure, which is clearly undesirable. A truly secure software engineering approach thus needs to take both dimensions of the problem into account:

- it needs to integrate the different system lifecycle phases,
- it also needs to take into account the different architectural levels of abstraction of a security-critical system in a demonstrably sound, trustworthy, and cohesive way.

The approach in the second part of this chapter presents how we can cope with possible vulnerabilities arising from the refinement of the model into an actual application.

Approaching Model-Based Security

In this section, we give an overview on some approaches for secure software engineering, with an emphasis on model-based development using UML. Of course, there are also approaches for secure software engineering outside of or predating model-based development with UML (cf. for example (Anderson & Long, 2001; Devanbu & Stubblebine, 2000; Eckert & Marek, 1997; Saltzer & Schroeder, 1975; Schneider, 1998) for some examples and overviews), but because of space restrictions, we cannot consider those in detail here.

Model-Based Development

Generally, when using model-based development (cf. Figure 1), the idea is that one first constructs a model of the system. Then, the implementation is derived from the model: either automatically using code generation, or manually, in which case one can generate test sequences from the model to establish conformance of the code regarding the model. The goal is to increase the quality of the software while keeping the implementation cost and the time-to-market bounded. For security-critical systems, this approach allows one to consider security requirements from early on in the development process, within the development context, and in a seamless way through the development cycle: can first check that the systems fulfils the relevant security requirements on the design level by analyzing the model and secondly that the code is in fact secure by generating test sequences from the model. However, one can also use the security analysis techniques and tools within a traditional software engineering context, or where one has to incorporate legacy systems that were not developed in a model-based way. Here, one starts out with the source code. One then extracts models from the source code, which can then again be analyzed against the security requirements. Using model-based development, one can

also incorporate the configuration data (such as user permissions) in the analysis, which is very important for security but often neglected.

For example, in the Model-based Security Engineering (MBSE) approach based on the UML extension UMLsec (Jürjens, 2002; Jürjens, 2005a; Jürjens, 2005b), recurring security requirements (such as secrecy, integrity, authenticity and others) and security assumptions on the system environment, can be specified either within a UML specification, or within the source code (Java or C) as annotations. This way we encapsulate knowledge on prudent security engineering as annotations in models or code and make it available to developers who may not be security experts. The UMLsec extension is given in form of a UML profile using the standard UML extension mechanisms. Stereotypes are used together with tags to formulate the security requirements and assumptions. Constraints give criteria that determine whether the requirements are met by the system design, by referring to a precise semantics of the used fragment of UML. The security-relevant information added using stereotypes includes security assumptions on the physical level of the system, security requirements related to the secure handling and communication of data, and security policies that system parts are supposed to obey. The semantics for the fragment of UML used for UMLsec is defined in (Jürjens, 2005a) using so-called UML Machines, which is a kind of state machine with input/output interfaces similar to Broy's Focus model, whose behaviour can be specified in a notation similar to that of Abstract State Machines (ASMs), and which is equipped with UML-type communication mechanisms. On this basis, important security requirements such as secrecy, integrity, authenticity, and secure information flow are defined.

After an early paper on the UML extension UMLsec for secure software development (Jürjens, 2001b), a number of approaches have been developed each targeted at certain facets of model-based development of security-critical systems using UML, several of them initially presented at the workshop series CSDUML (Critical Systems Development using Modeling Languages). A general development process in this context was proposed in (Breu, R., Burger, K., Hafner, M., Jürjens, J., Popp, G., Wimmel, G. & Lotz, V., 2003; Popp, G., Jürjens, J., Wimmel, G. & Breu, R., 2003).

Security requirements modelling: (Fernandez & Hawkins, 1997) proposes a method determining role-based access rights. Use cases are extended with rights specifications and the rights of a role are derived from the use cases. The method thus enforces the design principle of least privilege. (Crook, Ince, Lin & Nuseibeh, 2002; Haley, Laney, Moffett & Nuseibeh, 2008) formulates a vision for the requirements engineering community towards providing a "bridge between the well-ordered world of the software project informed by conventional requirements and the unexpected world of anti-requirements associated with the malicious user". (Giorgini, Massacci, Mylopoulos & Zannone, 2005; Massacci, Mylopoulos & Zannone, 2007; Mylopoulos, Giorgini & Massacci, 2003) proposes an extension of the i*/Tropos requirements engineering framework to deal with security requirements. The Tropos Requirements Engineering methodology is also extended to cover security aspects in (Manson, Mouratidis & Giorgini, 2003). (Sindre & Opdahl, 2005) presents an approach to eliciting security requirements using use cases which extends traditional use cases to also cover misuse. (Fox, Mouratidis & Jürjens, 2006) uses a combination of UMLsec and Tropos to get a transition from the security requirements to the design phase. (Whittle, Wijesekera & Hartong, 2008) presents an executable misuse case modelling language, which allows modellers to specify misuse case scenarios in a formal yet intuitive way and to execute the misuse case model in tandem with a corresponding use case model. (Yskout, Scandariato, Win & Joosen, 2008) presents an approach for the transformation of security requirements to software architectures. (Arenas,

Aziz, Bicarregui, Matthews & Yang, 2008) discuss the use of requirements-engineering techniques in capturing security requirements for a Grid-based operating system. (Yu & Elahi, 2008) examines how conceptual modelling can provide support for analyzing security trade-offs, using an extension to the i* framework. (Flechais, Mascolo & Sasse, 2007) presents an approach that integrates security and usability into the requirements and design process, based on a development process and a UML meta-model of the definition and the reasoning over the system's assets.

Security patterns: (Yoshioka, Honiden & Finkelstein, 2004) proposes a UML based method that enables developers to specify several candidate system behaviours that satisfy the security requirements, using patterns, and shows an application of the method to a real implemented system, the Environmentally Conscious Product (ECP) design support system. A methodology to build secure systems using patterns is presented in (Fernandez, Larrondo-Petrie, Sorgente & VanHilst, 2006). A main idea in the proposed methodology is that security principles should be applied at every stage of the software lifecycle and that each stage can be tested for compliance with those principles. Another basic idea is the use of patterns at each stage. A pattern is an encapsulated solution to a recurrent problem and their use can improve the reusability and quality of software. (Rosado, Fernandez-Medina, Piattini & Gutierrez, 2006) compares several security patterns to be used when dealing with application security. The SERENITY approach is based on the notion of Security and Dependability Patterns (Maña et al., 2007). They include a functional description of the proposed security solution, a semantic description of the security requirements addressed by it, and descriptions of the assumptions on the context in which the pattern can be used.

Automated security verification: So far only few of the UML based approaches for secure software development come with automated tools to formally verify the UML design for the relevant security requirements. One of these is again the UMLsec approach. The UMLsec tool-support can be used to check the constraints associated with UMLsec stereotypes mechanically, based on XMI output of the diagrams from the UML drawing tool in use (Jürjens, 2005b; Jürjens & Shabalin, 2007; Shabalin & Jürjens, 2004; UMLsec group, 2009). They generate logical formulas formalizing the execution semantics and the annotated security requirements. Automated theorem provers and model checkers automatically establish whether the security requirements hold. If not, a Prolog-based tool automatically generates an attack sequence violating the security requirement, which can be examined to determine and remove the weakness. Since the analysis that is performed is too sophisticated to be done manually, it is also valuable to security experts. There is also a framework for implementing verification routines for the constraints associated with the UMLsec stereotypes. Thus advanced users of the UMLsec approach can use this framework to implement verification routines for the constraints of self-defined stereotypes. Other approaches for verifying UML models for security properties emerge. For example, (Egea, Basin, Clavel & Doser, 2007) explains an approach in which queries about properties of an RBAC policy model are expressed as formulas in UML's Object Constraint Language and evaluated over the metamodel of the security-design language, based on the rewriting logic Maude. Also, (Siveroni, Zisman & Spanoudakis, 2008) presents a tool for verifying UML class and state machine diagrams against linear temporal logic formulas using Spin, which is planned to be applied to security properties.

Model construction and development: Having a formally based design notation allows one to precisely formulate and investigate non-trivial questions that need to be solved to enable trustworthy secure software development. For example, to support stepwise development, it has been shown that within UMLsec, secrecy, integrity, authenticity, and secure information flow are preserved under refinement and the composition of system components (under suitable assumptions) (Jürjens, 2005a). Similarly, it has been shown that layering of security services (such as layered security protocols) is sound, again only under certain assumptions. The same applies to the application of security design patterns, or the use of aspect-oriented modeling techniques. Related approaches have been reported in (Santen, 2006; Santen, Heisel & Pfitzmann, 2002). To support the Security and Dependability Patterns used in the project, the SERENITY approach also provides Security and Dependability Schemes which allow the users to combine existing security solutions to more complex ones (Maña et al., 2007). Automated tools for classification, selection, and composition of security patterns support this.

Aspect-Oriented Security Modeling: (Houmb, Georg, France, Bieman & Jürjens, 2005; Ray, France, Li & Georg, 2004) propose to use aspect-oriented modeling for addressing access control concerns. Functionality that addresses a pervasive access control concern is defined in an aspect. The remaining functionality is specified in a so-called primary model. Composing access control aspects with a primary model then gives a system model that addresses access control concerns. Model-based Security Risk Assessment: (Dimitrakos et al., 2002) uses UML for the risk assessment of an e-commerce system within the CORAS framework for model-based risk assessment. This framework is characterized by an integration of aspects from partly complementary risk assessment methods. It incorporates guidelines and methodology for the use of UML to support and direct the risk assessment methodology as well as a risk management process based on standards such as AS/NZS 4360 and ISO/IEC 27002. It uses a risk documentation framework based on RM-ODP together with an integrated risk management and system development process based on UP and offers a platform for tool inclusion based on XML. In another approach (Baldwin, Beres, Shiu & Kearney, 2006; Kearney & Brügger, 2007) use

UML for risk-driven security analysis that focuses on the assessment of risk and analysis of requirements for operational risk management.

Secure business processes and Service-oriented architectures: A business process driven approach to security engineering using UML is presented in (Maña, Montenegro, Rudolph & Vivas, 2003). The idea is to use UML models in an approach centered on business processes to develop secure systems. A model-based security engineering approach for developing service-oriented architectures is proposed in (Deubler, Grünbauer, Jürjens & Wimmel, 2004). The approach is applied on a standard for service-oriented architectures from the Automotive domain (OSGi). Access control policies: (Basin, Doser & Lodderstedt, 2006; Wolff, Brucker & Doser, 2006) show how UML can be used to specify access control in an application and how one can then generate access control mechanisms from the specifications. The approach is based on role-based access control and gives additional support for specifying authorization constraints. (Koch & Parisi-Presicce, 2006; Pauls, Kolarczyk, Koch & Löhr, 2006) demonstrate how to deal with access control policies in UML. The specification of access control policies is integrated into UML. A graph-based formal semantics for the UML access control specification permits one to reason about the coherence of the access control specification. An aspect-oriented approach to specifying access control in UML is presented in (Zhang, Baumeister, Koch & Knapp, 2005). (Méry & Merz, 2007) presents an approach for the specification and refinement of access control rules, including proof rules for verifying that an access control policy is correctly implemented in a system, and preservation of access control by refinement of event systems. (Hafner, Memon & Alam, 2008) presents usage scenarios for access control in contemporary healthcare scenarios and shows how to unify them in a single security policy model. Based on this model, the SECTET (Alam, Breu & Hafner, 2007) framework for Model Driven Security is then specialized towards

a domain-specific approach for healthcare scenarios, including the modelling of access control policies, a target architecture for their enforcement, and model-to-code transformations. (Agreiter, Alam, Hafner, Seifert & Zhang, 2007) extends the SECTET approach to take into account operating system level and application level security mechanisms to realize security-critical application and services for healthcare scenarios.

Health information systems: There have been several approaches using UML for security aspects in developing health-care systems. (Blobel, Nordberg, Davis & Pharow, 2006) presents an approach based on formal models where security services can be integrated into advanced systems architectures enabling semantic interoperability in the context of trustworthiness of communication and co-operation to support application security challenges such as privilege management and access control. The approach covers domains, service delegation, claims control, policies, roles, authorisations, and access control. (Mathe et al., 2007) presents an approach based on model-based design techniques and high-level modelling abstractions which provides a framework to rapidly develop, simulate, and deploy clinical information system (CIS) prototypes. It includes a graphical design environment for developing formal system models and generating executable code for deployment.

Secure database design: An approach to designing the content of a security critical database uses the Object Constraint Language (OCL) which is an optional part of the Unified Modeling Language (UML). More specifically, (Piattini & Fernández-Medina, 2004) presents the Object Security Constraint Language V.2. (OSCL2), which is based in OCL. This OCL extension can be used to incorporate security information and constraints in a Platform Independent Model (PIM) given as a UML class model. The information from the PIM is then translated into a Platform Specific Model (PSM) given as a multilevel relational model. This can then be implemented in a particular Database

Management System (DBMS), such as Oracle9i Label Security. These transformations can be done automatically or semi-automatically using OSCL2 compilers.

Smart-card based applications: (Haneberg, Reif & Stenzel, 2002; Moebius, Haneberg, Reif & Schellhorn, 2007) present a method for the development of secure smartcard applications which includes UML models enriched by algebraic specifications, and dynamic logic for JavaCard verification. The approach is implemented in the KIV specification and verification system.

Secure information flow: (Hultin & Heldal, 2003) provides support for the use of UML with secrecy annotations so that the code produced from the UML models can be be validated by the Java information flow (Jif) language-based checker. (Seehusen & Stølen, 2006) provides an approach which can analyze secure information properties in UML sequence diagrams.

Model-Based Security Engineering with UMLsec

We now explain the idea of model-based security engineering in more technical detail at the hand of one of the approaches mentioned in the previous section, namely the UMLsec approach. We describe a simplified fragment of UMLsec. For more details and a formal semantics cf. (Jürjens, 2002; Jürjens, 2005a; Jürjens, 2005b).

UML consists of diagram types describing different views on a system:

- **Use case diagrams** describe typical interactions between a user and a computer system (or between different components of a computer system).
- **Activity diagrams** can be used e.g. to model workflow and to explain use cases in more detail.
- **Class diagrams** define the static structure of the system: classes with attributes and

operations/signals and relationships between classes.
- **Interaction diagrams**, which may be sequence diagrams or collaboration diagrams, describe interaction between objects via message exchange. Here we consider sequence diagrams; collaboration diagrams are very similar.
- **Statechart diagrams** give the dynamic behavior of an individual object: events may cause state in change or actions.
- **Package diagrams** can be used to group parts of a system together into higher-level units.
- **Deployment diagrams** describe the underlying physical layer; we use them to ensure that the physical layer meets security requirements on communication.

UML offers rich extension mechanisms in form of labels. These can be either stereotypes (written in double angle brackets such as <<*stereotype*>>) or tag-value pairs (written in curly brackets such as {tag, value}). Using *profiles* or *prefaces* one can give a specific meaning to model elements marked with these labels. Here we give the extension UMLsec of UML making use of such labels to express security requirements.

Figure 2. Exemplary use case diagram: "fair exchange"

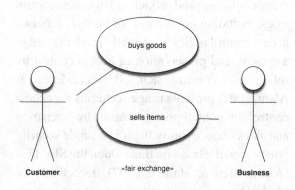

We stress that the aspects not mentioned here (such as association and generalization in the case of class diagrams) can and should be used in the context of UMLsec; they do not appear in our presentation simply because they are not needed to specify the considered security properties.

Since we are using a formal fragment of UML, we may reason formally, showing e.g. that a given system is as secure as certain components of it. This way, we can reduce security of the system to the security of the employed security mechanisms (such as security protocols). For example, we can exhibit the conditions under which protocols can be used securely in the system context. Work on refining security properties aids in verification applied within the design process.

Capturing Security Requirements with Use Case Diagrams

Use case diagrams describe typical interactions between a user and a computer system (or between different components of a computer system). We use them to capture security requirements.

To start with our example, Figure 2 gives the use case diagram describing the situation to be achieved: a customer buys a good from a business. The semantics of the stereotype <<*fair exchange*>> is, intuitively, that the actions "buys good" and "sells good" should be linked in the sense that if one of the two is executed then eventually the other one will be (where these actions are specified on the next more detailed level of specification).

Secure Business Processes with Activity Diagrams

Activity diagrams are especially useful to model workflow and to explain use cases in more detail. Following our example, Figure 3 explains the use case in Figure 2 in more detail. To demonstrate the connection between this diagram and the one in Figure 2, we give two possible diagrams. Both

are separated in two *swim-lanes* describing activities of different parts of a system (here Customer and Business). Round boxes describe actions (such as Request Good) and rectangular boxes describe the object flow (such as Order[filled]). Horizontal bars (*synchronisation bars*) describe a required synchronisation between two different strands of activity. A diamond describes the merging of two strands of activities. The start state is marked by a full circle, the final state by a small full circle within a circle. In each diagram, two tag-value pairs {fair exchange, buys goods} and {fair exchange, sells goods} are used to mark certain actions. Now any such diagram fulfills the security requirement "fair exchange", given in the diagram in Figure 2, if for both actions marked with these tag-value pairs it is the case that if one of the actions is executed, then eventually the other will be. As one can demonstrate on the level of the formal semantics, the left diagram does not fulfill this requirement because the Business may never Deliver Order. Also one can show that the right diagram does fulfill the requirement (intuitively, because the customer may reclaim the payment if the order is undelivered after the scheduled delivery date), assuming that the customer is able to prove having made the payment (indicated by the stereotype <<*provable*>>), e.g. by following a fair exchange protocol.

Preservation of Sensitivity Levels with Class Diagrams

Class diagrams define the static structure of a system. As an example, Figure 4 gives a class-level description of a key generator (such as possibly used in the above business application example). The key generator offers the method newkey() which returns a Key for which it guarantees confidentiality and integrity.* On the other hand, it calls methods random() supposed to return a random number that is required to fulfill integrity and confidentiality (as specified in the model element stereotyped <<*outgoing actions*>> added

Figure 3. Activity diagram for "fair exchange"

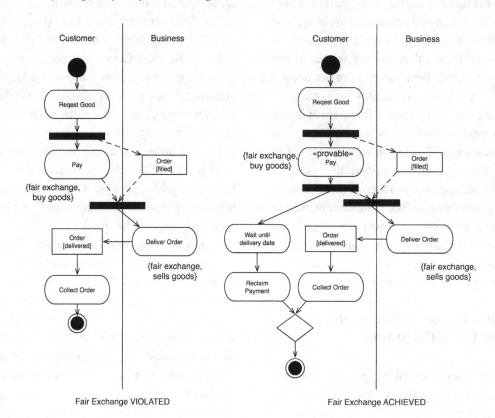

in UMLsec). Here, this requirement is however not met by the random generator. As an example, consider the Homebanking-Computer-Interface (HBCI) specifications which in an early version (in the case of the RDH procedure) required the client system to perform key generation without specifying security requirements for the used random number generators. Omissions such as this one can be detected using our modelling approach.

Here we assume that the attributes are fully encapsulated by the operations, i. e. an attribute of a class can be read and updated only by the class operations.

Security-Critical Message Exchange with Sequence Diagrams

In practice, the way security mechanisms (such as protocols) are employed in the system context offers more vulnerabilities than the mechanisms themselves. Also one sometimes has to adjust protocols to specific situations, e.g. for resource-bounded applications.

In our UML-based approach, security protocols can be specified using message sequence charts. An example is given in Figure 5. Assumptions on the underlying physical layer (such as physical security of communication links) can be expressed in implementation diagrams (cf. below), and the behavior of the system context surrounding the protocol can be stated using state charts and reasoned about as indicated below. In Figure 5, two objects in the system (a card C and a purchase

Figure 4. Class diagram for key generator

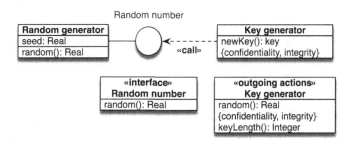

Figure 5. Sequence diagram for CEPS purchase transaction

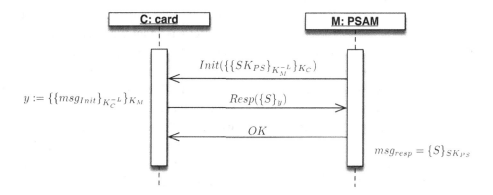

security application module (PSAM) M) exchange messages that involve cryptographic operations such as public-key encryption and signing. The encryption of the value d (or verification of signature) with the public key K is denoted by ${d}_K$, the decryption (or signing) with the private key K^{-1} by ${d}_{K^{-1}}$ (for simplicity we assume use of RSA type encryption). Thus M starts by sending to C the message Init with argument a value SK_{PS} (the session key created by the PSAM) signed with M's private key and encrypted with C's public key. C decrypts the received message with its private key and verifies the signature with M's public key. C uses the resulting session key to encrypt a secret S which is then sent back as an argument of the message Resp M decrypts the received message using the session key and sends back the message OK.

Again one can make use of a formal semantics and automated tools to reason about such protocol descriptions.

Secure State Change with Statechart Diagrams

Statechart diagrams give the dynamic behaviour of an individual object: events may cause state in change or actions. We demonstrate how this kind of diagram can be used in the context of UMLsec with an example involving guards (such as used in Java security) in Figure 6. Statechart diagrams consist of states (written as boxes) and transitions between them. The initial state is marked with a transition leading out from a full circle. Transitions between states can be labelled with events, conditions (in square brackets) and actions (preceded by a backslash). An event can be a method of the specified object called by another object (e.g. the transition labelled checkGuard in Figure 6), and the interpretation is that the transition labelled with an event is fired if the event occurs while the object is in the state from which the transition goes out. If a transition is labelled by a condition (formulated in the UML-associated object constraint language (OCL) or otherwise) then it is only fired if the condition is true at the respective moment. If a transition is labelled with an action (which can be to call a method of another object or to assign a value to a local variable), then this action is executed whenever the transition is fired.

Suppose that a certain micropayment signature key may only be used by applets originating at and signed by the site Finance (e.g. to purchase stock rate information on behalf of the user), but this access should only be granted five times a week.

The Java 2 security architecture allows the use of guard objects for this purpose which regulate access to an object. In our example, the guard object can be specified as in Figure 6 (where ThisWeek counts the number of accesses in a given week and weeklimit is true if the limit has not been reached yet). One can then demonstrate using a formal semantics that certain access control requirements are enforced by the guards.

Assumptions on the Physical Layer with Deployment Diagrams

Deployment diagrams describe the underlying physical layer; we use them to ensure that security requirements on communication are met by the physical layer. For example, Figure 7 describes the physical situation underlying a system including a client system and a webserver communicating over the Internet. The two boxes labeled Client and Webserver denote nodes in the system (i. e. physical entities). The two rectangles labeled browser and access control represent system components residing on the respective nodes. The component browser has an interface offering the method get password. The component access control calls this method over the Internet via remote method invocation. The system specification requires the data exchanged in this invocation to be guaranteed confidentiality and integrity. However, these requirements are not met by the underlying communication link (as usual, this would be treated by using encryption).

Code-level Assurance against High-Level Security Requirements

Even if specifications exist for the implemented system, and even if these are formally analyzed, there is usually no guarantee that the implementation actually conforms to the specification. To deal with this problem, we can use the following approach: After specifying the system in the

Figure 6. State chart for guard object

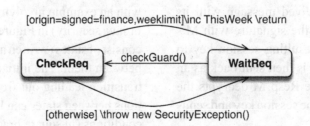

[origin=signed=finance,weeklimit]\inc ThisWeek \return

CheckReq ← checkGuard() WaitReq

[otherwise] \throw new SecurityException()

given notation (such as UMLsec) and verifying the model against the given security goals, we make sure that the implementation correctly implements the specification with techniques such as those explained below. Note that in addition it is often necessary to use dedicated tools to detect specialized weaknesses (such as buffer overflows), although this is not in scope of the current overview.

Run-time Security Monitoring: A simple and effective alternative is to insert security checks generated from the specification that remain in the code while in use, for example using the assertion statement that is part of the Java language (Bauer & Jürjens, 2008). These assertions then throw security exceptions when violated at run-time. In a similar way, this can also be done for C code. The SERENITY approach provides dynamic runtime verification mechanisms that can monitor various security properties dynamically based on event calculus (Maña et al., 2007). For example, they can monitor whether the assumptions made by a given security pattern is satisfied at the execution of the system. To achieve this, (Spanoudakis, Kloukinas & Androutsopoulos, 2007) proposes to use formal patterns that formalize frequently recurring system requirements as security monitoring patterns. Also, evolution tools record the operational data relevant for the Security and Dependability Patterns to obtain feedback that can help improving the patterns.

Model-based Test Generation: For performance-intensive applications, it may be preferable not to leave the assertions active in the code. This can be done by making sure by extensive testing that the assertions are always satisfied, for example by generating the test sequences automatically from the specifications. Since complete test coverage is often infeasible, an approach that automatically selects those test cases that are particularly sensitive to the specified security requirements is sketched in (Jürjens, 2009; Jürjens & Wimmel, 2002) (with respect to the formal semantics underlying UMLsec). Other work on testing crypto-protocols includes (Gürgens & Peralta, 2000).

Formally verifying cryptoprotocol implementations: For highly non-deterministic systems such as those using cryptography, testing can only provide assurance up to a certain degree. For higher levels of trustworthiness, it may therefore be desirable to establish that the code does enforce the security properties by a formal verification of the source code. There have recently been some approaches towards formally verifying implementations of crypto-protocols against high-level security requirements such as secrecy, for example (Bhargavan, Fournet, Gordon & Tse, 2006; Goubault-Larrecq & Parrennes, 2005; Jürjens, 2006; Jürjens & Yampolskiy, 2005). These works so far have aimed to verify implementations which were constructed with verification in mind

Figure 7. UMLsec deployment diagram

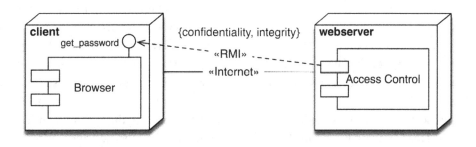

(and in particular fulfill significant expectations on the way they are programmed) (Bhargavan et al., 2006; Goubault-Larrecq & Parrennes, 2005), or deal only with simplified versions of legacy implementations (Jürjens, 2006; Jürjens & Yampolskiy, 2005). In related work, (Pironti & Sisto, 2008) investigates under which conditions it is sound to abstract from marshalling and unmarshalling operations on transmitted messages when verifying protocol specifications.

Analyzing Security Configurations

There have also been some first steps towards linking model-based security engineering approaches with the automated analysis of security-critical configuration data. For example, a tool that automatically checks SAP R/3 user permissions for security policy rules formulated as UML specifications is presented in (Höhn & Jürjens, 2008). Because of its modular architecture and its standardized interfaces, the tool can be adapted to check security constraints in other kinds of application software, such as firewalls or other access control configurations.

Application Examples

An overview on industrial applications of model-based security engineering can be found in (Apvrille & Pourzandi, 2005). We list some examples below.

German Health Card architecture: Ongoing work for the German health telematics platform using a model-driven architectural framework and a security infrastructure based on Electronic Health Records and multifunctional Electronic Health Cards is presented in (Blobel & Pharow, 2007). A security analysis of the German Health Card Architecture using UMLsec is reported in (Jürjens & Rumm, 2008).

Electronic purses: UMLsec was applied to a security analysis of the Common Electronic Purse Specifications (CEPS), a candidate for a globally interoperable electronic purse standard supported by organizations representing 90% of the world's electronic purse cards (including Visa International). Three significant security weaknesses were found in the purchase and load transaction protocols, improvements to the specifications were proposed, and it was shown that these are secure (Jürjens & Wimmel, 2001). There was also a security analysis of a prototypical Java Card implementation of CEPS. A method for the development of secure smartcard applications which includes UML models and is implemented in the KIV specification and verification system (Haneberg et al., 2002; Moebius et al., 2007) was applied to the specification of the Mondex electronic purse.

Intranet information systems: An application of UMLsec to information systems in an intranet at BMW is reported in (Best, Jürjens & Nuseibeh, 2007). There, the use of single-sign-on mechanisms was central, so the application of UMLsec was targeted to demonstrating that it was used correctly within the system context.

Biometric authentication: For a project with an industrial partner, UMLsec was chosen to support the development of a biometric authentication system at the specification level, where three significant security flaws were found (Jürjens, 2005b). It was also applied to the source-code level for a prototypical implementation constructed from the specification.

Web-based banking application: In a project with a German bank, model-based security engineering was applied to a web-based banking application to be used by customers to fill out and sign digital order forms (Jürjens, 2005a). The personal data in the forms must be kept confidential, and orders securely authenticated. The system uses a proprietary client authentication protocol layered over an SSL connection supposed to provide confidentiality and server authentication. Using the MBSE approach, the system architecture and the protocol were specified and verified with regard to the relevant security requirements.

Remaining Challenges in Model-Based Security

Given the current unsatisfactory state of computer security in practice, model-based security engineering seems a promising approach, since it enables developers who are not experts in security to make use of security engineering knowledge encapsulated in a widely used design notation. Since there are many highly subtle security requirements, which can hardly be verified with the "naked eye", even security experts may profit from this approach. Thus one can avoid mistakes that are difficult to find by testing alone, such as breaches of subtle security requirements, as well as the disadvantages of the "penetrate-and-patch" approach. Since preventing security flaws early in the system life cycle can significantly reduce costs, this gives a potential for developing securer systems in a cost-efficient way. Model-based security engineering has been successfully applied in various industrial projects. The approach has been generalized to other application domains such as real-time and dependability. Experiences show that the approach is adequate for use in practice, after relatively little training. As a consequence, model-based security engineering is now also considered an important emerging technology by industrial think-tanks. Due to space restriction, the current overview can only provide very limited detail or completeness. More comprehensive overviews on model-based security engineering and secure software engineering include (Jayaram & Mathur, 2005; Redwine, 2007). Some examples for open problems that remain:

Tracing security requirements: From a practical point of view, the construction of trustworthy security-critical systems would be significantly facilitated if one would have a practically feasible approach for tracing security requirements through the system lifecycle phases. A first step in that direction is presented in (Yu, Jürjens & Mylopoulos, 2008).

Preservation of security properties: Despite some early advances into this question (Jürjens, 2000; Jürjens, 2001a) there is so far relatively little known about the preservation of security properties when using design and analysis techniques such as the modular composition or decomposition, refinement or abstraction, or horizontal respectively vertical layering of system parts.

Security verification of legacy systems: A major open problem is to verify complex legacy implementations against high-level security properties in a practically feasible way. Again, some steps in that direction were reported above.

Security vs. other non-functional requirements / feature interaction: Another open problem is how to reconcile security requirements with other non-functional requirements, which may be orthogonal or even in conflict. First examples regarding performance properties can be found in (Maidl, Gilmore, Haenel & Kloul, 2005; Montangero, Buchholtz, Gilmore & Haenel, 2005; Woodside et al., 2009).

Model-Based Identification of Vulnerabilities

Although software, requirements, and security engineering all offer methods for improved software development, today's software still contains vulnerabilities. These vulnerabilities, once exploited, can have various effects, ranging from subtle, maybe even more theoretical ones to practically devastating consequences. In a SOA, which implements business processes on top of web services, which again build upon software, it is evident that vulnerabilities jeopardize business processes. For that reason, this section shows how vulnerabilities can be identified. A brief introduction of the basic terms and concepts is followed by a discussion of the available approaches.

Vulnerabilities are flaws in information systems that can be abused to violate the security policy. The actual abuse is called an exploit.

Vulnerability analysis aims to support avoiding, finding, fixing, and monitoring vulnerabilities (Bishop, 2005). These *vulnerability management* tasks typically require patterns, for example, to perform static or dynamic analysis of source code. Livshits (Livshits, 2006) presents an example of a practical method that uses such *vulnerability patterns*, specified as PQL queries (Martin, Livshits & Lam, 2005), to analyze Java programs for taint-style (i.e., use of unchecked input) vulnerabilities.

The *SOA* we refer to follows the OASIS SOA reference model and architecture (OASIS, 2006). The Business Process Execution Language (BPEL) is used to describe and execute the business processes. Processes in Business Process Modelling Notation (BPMN) can be translated to BPEL, e.g., through an Eclipse Plug-in developed by Google (http://code.google.com/p/bpmn2bpel/) Messages are exchanged through SOAP, and web service interfaces are defined in Web Service Description Language (WSDL). However, these standards and the WS Security standards family do not necessarily prevent software vulnerabilities from putting services at risk. We therefore refrain from a discussion of these standards and instead focus on software vulnerabilities and their model-based identification. Figure 8 shows our view on SOA layers, following, amongst others, Krafzig et al. (Krafzig, Banke & Slama, 2004) and IBM's reference architecture (Arsanjani, Zhang, Allam & Channabasavaiah, 2007). The bold arrows indicate the analysis focus: identifying vulnerabilities on the service level which result from software vulnerabilities.

The presentation layer and the hardware layer will be using the same technology as before, so we do not analyze them any further. The software layer will increasingly be implemented using managed code, meaning a decrease of buffer overflows and similar vulnerabilities. Nevertheless, previous vulnerabilities might still be present in legacy software, so we share the view and classification of Yu et al. (Yu, Aravind & Supthaweesuk, 2006)

for both the software and service layer. We differentiate between the service and the software layer by defining a service as a self-contained function which has a WSDL description and communicates through SOAP.

Business processes are executed as workflows, i.e., a set of activities performed in a certain order. The orchestration layer contains the workflow logic, typically implemented as an execution engine calling specific services in the order and with the parameters specified in a BPEL document. While before, the business process logic often was interwoven in PHP or ASP scripts of web applications, it is now separately defined in BPEL. Also, business process activities are no longer mere sections of code in a web application script, but specific services with a WSDL description and a SOAP interface. This creates new vulnerabilities in addition to the ones this section focuses on, the ones based in software applications. (Jensen, Gruschka, Herkenhöner & Luttenberger, 2007) lists some prominent examples with a description of counter measures. Regarding the services which implement the business process, two general options are available: top-down, generating services moving from the business process orchestration to the software layer, and bottom-up, wrapping existing software to be used in the service, and,

Figure 8. SOA layers and vulnerabilities

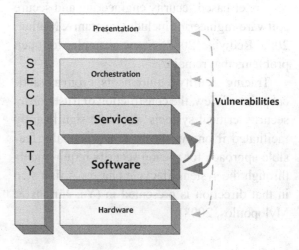

consequently, in the orchestration. Given that initial SOA projects typically start by wrapping existing software, in the following we focus on the latter.

We employ the OASIS threat model (OASIS, 2006), comprising both internal and external attackers and the threats message alteration, message interception, man in the middle, spoofing, denial of service (DoS), replay, and false repudiation. Microsoft's STRIDE (Swiderski & Snyder, 2004) with its threats spoofing, tampering with data, repudiation, information disclosure, DoS, and elevation of privilege, is covered with that model because tampering with data, information disclosure, and elevation of privilege can be achieved through, e.g., message alteration and interception.

While in theory it might seem possible to come up with a complete list of vulnerabilities, in practice this is next to impossible even for simple components. In both cases, the precondition is that a certain task or attack goal is specified. Without a task that could be disturbed or an attack that is to be prevented, the most important search parameter for the vulnerability search would be missing (Anderson & Long, 2001). However, even if a method could determine all vulnerabilities regarding a certain task or attack, this list of tasks and attacks would have to be complete. Considering the fact that for the attacker it is enough to find a single attack the defenders did not think of (Anderson & Long, 2001), the initial idea of "simply" creating a complete list of vulnerabilities in an IT system turns out to be inapplicable. Zero-day vulnerabilities continue to be found (see (Turner, 2008) for current trends in zero-day vulnerabilities), which further indicates that complete vulnerability lists are a rather unrealistic assumption. The approach presented here is not based on the notion of such a complete list of vulnerabilities but on the notion of analyzing only known vulnerabilities the existence of which has been verified. Before discussing sources of such vulnerability information in the following,

a brief description of the required information is given.

The main and mandatory detail about a vulnerability is where it is located, i.e., the name and version of the software it can be found in. Then, depending on the type of analysis, more or less information is required describing how the vulnerability can be exploited (e.g., remotely through a certain network protocol), what the direct effects are (e.g., elevation of privileges), and a severity rating (e.g., easily exploitable, severe effects on availability). The Common Vulnerability Scoring System (CVSS) (Mell, Scarfone & Romanosky, 2007) offers a widely accepted format for such descriptions (see Table 1).

Sources of Vulnerability Information

In order to determine the effects an attacker could cause by exploiting vulnerabilities, a list of known vulnerabilities that are or could be present in the IT system at hand must be obtained. Penetration testing, source code analysis, and vulnerability databases allow compiling such a list of vulnerabilities and will now be discussed regarding their SOA applicability.

Penetration Testing

Also known as "red team testing", penetration testing (Bishop, 2005; Thompson, 2005) is a hands-on approach to security analysis. Given a specific IT system, sometimes including configuration details, a team of security experts tries to attack the system and break the system's security policy by, e.g., creating attack trees and then applying tools to check that the devised vulnerabilities actually are exploitable. Regarding attack trees, tools such as (Ou, Boyer & McQueen, 2006) can support the creation of graphs, however, care should be taken to not restrict the team's focus to automatically generated graphs as attackers might come up with new ideas not covered by the graphs. Often, tools such as vulnerability scanners (see (Lyon, 2006)

Table 1. Common vulnerability scoring system

CVSS Base Score: 0 (Low) to 10 (High) (Impact Subscore 0 to 10, Exploitability Subscore 0 to 10) CVSS Temporal Score: 0 (Low) to 10 (High) CVSS v2 Vector: (AV:N/AC:L/Au:N/C:C/I:C/A:C) Published: mm/dd/yyyy		
CVSS metric group	**CVSS metric**	**CVSS values**
Base Score Metrics		
Exploitability Metrics	Access Vector	local, adjacent network, network
	Access Complexity	low, medium, high
	Authentication	none, single, multiple
Impact Metrics	Confidentiality Impact	none, partial, complete
	Integrity Impact	none, partial, complete
	Availability Impact	none, partial, complete
Temporal Score Metrics	Exploitability	unproven, proof-of-concept, functional, high, not defined
	Remediation Level	official fix, temporary fix, workaround, unavailable, not defined
	Report Confidence	unconfirmed, uncorroborated, confirmed, not defined

for a valuable list; Nessus and Microsoft's Baseline Security Analyzer mark beginning and end of the top ten) and fuzzers are separately used to scan for vulnerabilities and to check how the system reacts to various inputs. The test result is a list of attacks the team was able to perform, along with detailed information on how the attacks were carried out. Besides configuration weaknesses and other information such as improper privilege settings, a very detailed description of vulnerabilities can be obtained.

With more and more exploit toolkits (e.g., Metasploit[1]) and other tools becoming available, penetration testing no longer is the tedious, purely manual task it used to be. Also, because the test is run on the actual IT system, the results are perfectly tailored to the specific setting. This is especially beneficial when a vulnerability has to be analyzed regarding its effect on the business process.

On the other hand, this advantage is a big drawback from a different point of view. Testing the real system does not only provide precise data on vulnerabilities and exploits, it can also damage the system. This is why penetration testing is not applicable in scenarios where, e.g., IT services may not be disturbed under any circumstances.

In this case, a more theoretical approach can be used to analyze a model of the system.

Another drawback is that employing a team of security experts is expensive, sometimes prohibitively. This fact links to the additional drawback that because it is so expensive, most companies cannot afford continuous penetration tests. Therefore, it is not suitable to maintain an up-to-date list of vulnerabilities. Penetration testing still is very valuable in terms of the highly detailed and relevant vulnerability data it creates.

Source Code Analysis

Besides manual code inspection, elaborate algorithms and tools are able to find vulnerabilities in source code. Tool support started with rather simple lexical scanners (Chess & McGraw, 2004), which, for example, point out the use of *printf* function calls in C so that a human analyst can (and has to) decide whether there is a buffer overflow vulnerability or not. Far more sophisticated approaches use model-checking to show that, e.g., there is no path in the code an input string could reach a certain part of the code without being sanitized. (Livshits, 2006) presents such an approach for Java web applications. It offers a sound solution which includes pointer and reflection analysis, meaning that a call graph is constructed which allows tracing input data along functions calls including, to some extent, code or libraries which are not statically linked.

Source code analysis does not touch the actual system and thus, unlike penetration testing, will not interrupt any services. For the same reason it produces results of a slightly different quality, because the code will never run alone but always in combination with other software. To illustrate what this means, consider a web service with an input vulnerability which will crash the service as soon as an overly long input is received. If XML schema validation is in place (see (Jensen et al., 2007) for an overview of attacks that schema validation can defend against), dropping the SOAP message with the dangerous XML input, source code analysis of the web service would report a vulnerability, while penetration testing would not show it (except if XML schema validation had been disabled through an earlier attack during testing).

In general and from a practical point of view, source code analysis is more likely to yield false positives than penetration testing. This must be kept in mind when assessing the vulnerability effects as described below in the evaluation section. The forensic approach based on logging will filter the more theoretical vulnerabilities source code analysis reports. Achieving the same filtering with the model-based approach is possible yet imposes additional complexity on the model as more components must be incorporated.

Vulnerability Databases

Querying vulnerability databases to benefit from the security community's vulnerability search efforts is an approach that should always be applied. Even if a company has enough resources to perform its own penetration testing and source code analysis, it makes little sense to ignore the vulnerabilities others have found and published. Because the results of a company-internal vulnerability search can be entered into a database as well, the vulnerability identification suggested here does not specifically build upon penetration testing or source code analysis, but relies on vulnerability databases as the more general solution. So, besides company-internal databases, which vulnerability databases are available? We briefly describe some sources of vulnerability information which we did not consider, and then describe the more suitable ones.

While most databases list vulnerabilities independent of the software vendor, *Microsoft*'s vulnerability database[2] only lists vulnerabilities in Microsoft software. However, the descriptions contain all the standard entries discussed below. *SecWatch*[3] can be considered a meta search engine, it does not provide its own description scheme. In a similar manner, the *SANS Newsletter*[4] offers a brief vulnerability overview and refers to other databases for the details. The *Open Web Application Security Project (OWASP)*[5] does not list vulnerability instances but vulnerability types. It might serve as a guide for a penetration test or source code analysis, but it does not contain vulnerabilities in actual products, services, or web applications. *Milw0rm*[6] does not offer its vulnerability descriptions in a standardized format, therefore it was excluded from the comparison. The same holds true for the SecuriTeam database[7], which in addition draws many descriptions from the other databases.

The following free online databases will be compared below (in alphabetical order): *French Security Incident Response Team (FRSIRT)*[8], *Internet Security Systems (ISS) X-Force*[9], *National Vulnerability Database (NVD)*[10] with *Common Vulnerabilities and Exposures (CVE)*[11] entries, *Open Source Vulnerability Database (OSVDB)*[12], *SecurityFocus*[13] (including *Buqtraq*), and *SecurityTracker*[14].

Comparing the above-mentioned databases, it shows that the majority has a big overlap between their description schemes. All databases offer their own and unique name or id for each vulnerability, a disclosure date, and a textual vulnerability description. In addition, they all list the vulnerable software including version numbers, credits or pointers to the information source, references to related reports and descriptions in other databases, references to the affected software's vendor, and protection hints or links to such.

CVE names are included in all description schemes, thus CVE and the corresponding CVSS data can easily be obtained. FRSIRT and SecurityFocus explicitly describe the access vector in their descriptions ("remote/local" with "yes/no" values each), perhaps in order to not depend on the completeness of CVSS data. OSVDB, Secunia, and SecurityFocus each use their own vulnerability classification (see Figure 9 for an example). These specific classifications can in some cases aid in determining the effect a vulnerability's exploit could have, however, they require a customized analysis and should be considered volatile as they do not follow a widely-accepted standard such as CVSS.

In terms of vulnerability effect determination, ISS X-Force's database is particularly interesting as it contains adjusted CVSS data (CVSS temporal values filled in by the ISS team) and a "business impact" field, containing a textual description of the business impact. To give an example, CVE-2008-3466 business impact according to ISS reads: "Compromise of networks and machines using affected versions of Microsoft Host Integration Server may lead to exposure of confidential information, loss of productivity, and further network compromise. An attacker does not need to entice any kind of user interaction to trigger this vulnerability. Successful exploitation would grant an attacker the privileges of the SNA RPC service." Even though the description of effects such as loss of confidentiality also are part of CVSS data, the brief information in this field allows a quick assessment of the vulnerability and represents a promising, business-oriented extension of the description scheme.

Figure 9. OSVDB's Vulnerability Classification

Vulnerability Classification			
Location	**Attack Type**	**Impact**	**Solution**
☐ Physical Access Required ☐ Local Access Required ☐ Remote/Network Access Required ☐ Local / Remote ☐ Dialup Access Required ☐ Wireless ☐ Mobile Phone ☐ Unknown Location	☐ Authentication Management ☐ Cryptographic ☐ Denial of Service ☐ Hijacking ☐ Information Disclosure ☐ Infrastructure ☐ Input Manipulation ☐ Misconfiguration ☐ Race Condition ☐ Other ☐ Unknown	☐ Loss of Confidentiality ☐ Loss of Integrity ☐ Loss of Availability ☐ Unknown	☐ No Solution ☐ Workaround ☐ Patch ☐ Upgrade ☐ Change Default Setting ☐ Third Party Solution ☐ Discontinued Product ☐ Solution Unknown
Exploit	**Disclosure**	**OSVDB**	
☐ Exploit Available ☐ Exploit Unavailable ☐ Exploit Rumored / Private ☐ Exploit Unknown	☐ OSVDB Verified ☐ Vendor Verified ☐ Vendor Disputed ☐ Third Party Verified ☐ Coordinated Disclosure ☐ Uncoordinated Disclosure ☐ Third Party Disputed ☐ Discovered in the Wild	☐ Authentication Required ☐ Context Dependent ☐ Vuln Dependent ☐ Wormified ☐ Web Related ☐ Concern ☐ Best Practice ☐ Myth/Fake ☐ Security Software	

Identifying Vulnerabilities in Services

Vulnerable software can lead to vulnerable services, which again can lead to vulnerable business processes as, in a SOA, these are implemented as composition of services. Having obtained a list of vulnerabilities as described above, this information must now be mapped to services and, ultimately, the business process. In the following, the focus lies on mapping between software and services, as the mapping between services and business processes is directly contained in BPMN or BPEL documents.

The vulnerability databases mentioned above contain a large number of vulnerability descriptions that refer to web related vulnerabilities. Nevertheless, there are very few entries on vulnerabilities in actual web services. While there will be more such entries as more web services become available, the software currently deployed will still be used and wrapped in web services. Therefore, given the description of a software vulnerability, the question is which services build upon that software and, thus, could be affected by an exploit of the vulnerability. To answer that question, we extract the required information from vulnerability descriptions and include it in the UMLsec model of the system under analysis. This allows a model-based vulnerability identification, as Figure 10 shows.

Vulnerability descriptions always include the target software, i.e. the software the vulnerability was found in. To avoid false positives during the analysis, a preliminary check should be run regarding the current IT environment: If the software has been patched already or a newer version has been installed which does not contain the vulnerability, the vulnerability should be excluded from the list before being mapped to services. The Open Vulnerability and Assessment Language (OVAL) (MITRE, 2007) can be used to obtain the information necessary to run such a check. Figure 11 shows an exemplary OVAL definition.

Once the list of actual vulnerabilities in a specific IT system has been created, and all vulnerabilities that have been patched or removed in other ways have been excluded, the services that run on top of the affected software must be identified. This identification step can be done before, at, or after runtime, and each of these options will be discussed below.

Identification before Runtime

During service design time, it is apparent which other services and software a certain service involves. A simple approach is entering these mappings into a database. Then, each time a vulnerable service or software is to be checked for connected services, this database can be queried. However, a clear drawback of this simple approach is that it highly depends on the designer to enter each and every mapping. This can be remedied by integrating the mapping into the implementation phase. When implementing a service, the supporting services and underlying applications must be specified. In integrated development environments (IDE) such as JDeveloper[15], every

Figure 10. UML deployment diagram with software-service mapping

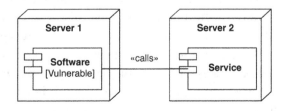

Figure 11. Exemplary OVAL definition

Definition Id: oval:org.mitre.oval:def:5883		Date: 2008-10-30
Title:	Potential Sec. Vulnerability in Java VM, JSSE, Plug-in, and Webstart. (rev.1)	
Description:	X509TrustManager in (1) Java Secure Socket Extension (JSSE) in SDK and JRE 1.4.0 through 1.4.0_01, (2) JSSE before 1.0.3, (3) Java Plug-in SDK and JRE 1.3.0 through 1.4.1, and (4) Java Web Start 1.0 through 1.2 incorrectly calls the isClientTrusted method when determining server trust, which results in improper validation of digital certificate and allows remote attackers to (1) falsely authenticate peers for SSL or (2) incorrectly validate signed JAR files.	
Version:	0	**Class:**	vulnerability
Status:	DRAFT	**Reference(s):**	CVE-2003-1229
Family:	unix		
Platform(s):	HP-UX 11	**Product(s):**	
Definition Synopsis:		

- Criteria meets HP Security Bulletin HPSBUX0301-239
  - HP Release B.11.04
  - AND VaultTS.VV-IWS-JAVA is installed
  - AND NOT Patch PHSS_28685 is installed
- OR Criteria meets HP Security Bulletin HPSBUX0301-239
  - HP Release B.11.04
  - AND VaultTS.VV-IWS-JAVA is installed
  - AND NOT Patch PHSS_28686 is installed

time such a connection is created the target can be selected from a constantly updated list of available services. Also, the programmer can select databases and other software the service will connect to. Keeping track of these assignments allows to map between vulnerable software (and services) and the services which involve those vulnerable components.

Regardless of a purely manual or partly automated approach of mapping before runtime, both the mapping between software and services and the mapping between services is covered. The manual approach will impose little additional effort during SOA creation; however, it is too cumbersome to be applied when an existing SOA is frequently changed. IDE support for service mapping is already implemented today (e.g., in JDeveloper), support for software to service mapping so far is rudimentary but, in IDEs such as Eclipse[16], can be added through plugins.

Having obtained the mapping between software and services, these links can be included in the UMLsec model. Then, each time a new vulnerability is announced, the model can be automatically analysed, resulting in an identification of the affected services. Because in a SOA, service compositions are the BPMN or BPEL equivalent of a business process, this model-based approach provides pre-runtime vulnerability identification for SOA-based business processes.

Identification at Runtime

Web Services communicate with each other through SOAP messages. A network monitor observing these messages can gather information on the hosts and ports the services are running on. The problem here is that while sometimes this information is sufficient to automatically construct a mapping table (compare Figure 12a), in other cases the network traffic only allows ambiguous conclusions (cf. Figure 12b).

Imagine a network in which each host either supports exactly one service or software. Seeing a communication between a service host and a software host, the monitor can deduce that the service depends on the software (cf. Figure 12a). Now imagine a network with only two hosts, one running all the services, and one running all the software. Unless analyzing the protocols in use allows a precise service and software identification, the monitor can only guess which service uses which software (cf. Figure 12b). So if the monitor sees traffic from different services going to a host with multiple software applications, it cannot always automatically map between services and software applications. For example, automated mapping is possible when a service queries a MySQL database with a constant, unique username. It is impossible when several services use the same username for their queries. Note that

Figure 12. Identification of the software that a service uses

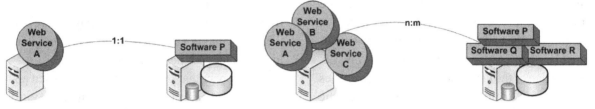

(a) Mapping one service to one software application   (b) Mapping between several services and several software apps

SQL injection vulnerabilities can easily be a source of false positives when analyzing a SOA: If the service correctly filters its input before sending it to the database, the vulnerability is not exploitable through the service. However, assuming that SQL injections cannot be executed just because software is wrapped into a service is a fallacy.

Ambiguous communication only exists when software is involved. Services communicating with each other can be identified through their unique name in SOAP messages. This means that the runtime approach can automatically identify service-to-service mappings. For software to service mappings, sometimes a human will have to resolve ambiguities. In restricted cases an automated identification will be possible, yet, in the general case, mapping at runtime might require manual intervention.

Again, as in the pre-runtime case, once the mapping of software to services is captured, it serves as input to the UMLsec model and thusly enables model-based identification of vulnerabilities in a SOA-based business process. The drawback is that here, runtime behaviour must be observed before the analysis can begin, which opens a window of opportunity for attackers. Nevertheless, the runtime approach is valuable when the previous approach is not applicable, and it can also serve to confirm the findings of the pre-runtime mapping.

Identification after Runtime

Log files offer an additional opportunity of identifying the links between services and the software they use. Depending on the network setup and the level of detail found in the logs, correlating log entries to map from services to software can be straightforward or prove rather difficult. Therefore, the applicability of this approach is high when the logs already offer detailed information, or the logging mechanisms can easily be extended to include details on services and software being invoked. In a highly complex setting, where customized logging cannot be implemented, and the logfiles at hand offer too low a level of detail, mapping after runtime requires manual involvement. Such manual resolution of mapping ambiguities might seem acceptable in a scenario with static links. However, one of the main notions behind web services is flexibility, so that the assumption of static links will rarely hold in practice.

The model-based identification of vulnerabilities after runtime can be performed through an audit of log files. To this end, one must first ensure that system records are written and stored in a secure way. Here, we assume that the storage provides confidentiality and tamper-evidence. Confidentiality means that entries stored in the log file cannot be read by unauthorized subjects and is necessary to avoid the replication and the replay of entries. Tamper-evidence means that if logfiles are manipulated, then these manipulations, e.g. deletion of entries or entry modification, are *evident* to a verifier. Technically, tamper-evidence is broken down into three subordinated properties: all the entries must be authentic, i.e. they are stored, as they have been transmitted from the logging device to the logging system. The entries must be encrypted in a forward secure way, i.e. knowledge of the key to decrypt one of the entries may not put an attacker in a position where he can decrypt all – in particular the previous – the entries. And the entries must be complete, i.e. deletion of one or more entries must be detected by the system.

These properties are achieved by secure logging protocols. Current state of the art can be distinguished into those protocols adding confidentiality and tamper-evidence to the traditional syslog and those designed for providing these functionalities from the outset based on the Schneier-Kelsey secure logging protocol scheme (Schneier & Kelsey, 1999). Thorough threat analysis has demonstrated that these protocols fail to provide the necessary guarantees, so that attackers can still manipulate with log data (Accorsi, 2008).

To our knowledge, the only secure logging protocol providing for all the necessary security properties is that proposed in (Accorsi, 2006). In this protocol suite, confidentiality is achieved using an evolving encryption scheme (Franklin, 2006): the current encryption key is newly calculated for every entry using a one-way function. An attacker that can get hold of the encryption key for one entry n is not able to calculate the key for the previous entries n-1, n-2, ... Clearly, it is possible to calculate the keys for the log entries n+1, n+2, ... This property is not overly important though, as a logging-system that has been corrupted cannot write secure and reliable log messages anyway. With regard to tamper evidence, entries are digitally signed and, therefore, cannot be modified without knowing the private key used to generate these digital signatures. In addition to this, a hash chain that connects all the entries with each other guarantees the completeness of the entries. (See (Lamport & Schneider, 1984) for details on hash-chains.) This hash chain is calculated for an entry

by applying some cryptographic hash functions to the previous entry. Only if the chain is correct from the first to the last entry one can be sure that the log file has not been tampered: a broken chain indicates that tampering has taken place.

One aspect that if often overlooked when applying hash-chains in this setting is that one must check whether the number of entries is correct. The proposed scheme is not able to detect truncation attacks where an attacker removes entries from the tail of the hash-chain. This can easily be calculated, by comparing the current cryptographic key (which is calculated by applying n-times the evolution function, with n being the total number of entries in the file) with the actual length of the log file.

Such secure logging mechanisms provide a sound basis for the evaluation of vulnerability effects. The actual evaluation takes place by means of an audit, whose goal is to correlate suspicious events recorded in the log file and check whether the emerging patterns matches to one (or more) in the vulnerability database. Such an audit can efficiently be implemented using, e.g., a pruning algorithm based on the structure of the log files (Accorsi & Stocker, 2008). Together with a normalization step, which merely correlates events, the algorithm runs in linear time and, hence, can cope with log files of industrial size. An alternative approach is proposed in (Accorsi, 2008).

In order to carry out such an automated audit, one needs a formalization of the effects of the vulnerabilities. In (Accorsi & Stocker, 2008), a Domain Specific Language based on XML is employed when expressing the effects. Specifically, this language was designed to capture the different preconditions for and postconditions arising from successful exploits. These conditions can be derived from vulnerability descriptions, so that an automated audit becomes possible. For example, CVSS entries describe the access vector to a vulnerability, which represents a precondition, and the confidentiality/integrity/availability impact, which represent postconditions. Given the log files and the pre- and postconditions, pattern matching on the log data can pinpoint vulnerable services and indicate the effects an exploit of a certain vulnerability might induce on the services and their composition. Because this composition represents the implementation of a business process, the analysis result is a list of those parts of the business process that are put at risk by vulnerabilities.

Obviously, this "after the fact" approach opens the biggest window of opportunity for attackers. However, log based audits are necessary to verify that the system works as expected. And even if this approach does not prevent a specific vulnerability from being exploited, the identification after runtime points that vulnerability out so that it can be fixed. This clearly provides better security than leaving the services and their composition vulnerable.

DISCUSSION

The current state of vulnerability analysis tools clearly shows that identification of existing vulnerabilities is crucial for every systematic approach. Although we have presented an approach that can cope with the impact of distinct vulnerabilities, still no systematic way of identifying unknown vulnerabilities exists. Furthermore, it is important to realize that WS-Security and similar standards will not reduce the number of vulnerabilities in a complex business infrastructure. Because they cause additional complexity, they much rather introduce new vulnerabilities into the computer systems.

The exact determination of the effects a vulnerability exploit can have still is an open issue. Certainly, a viable solution is to use forensic information as a reliable source of information. But it is necessary to consider the attackers' intelligence and knowledge, which might cause new, unforeseen effects. Attackers can find completely new attack paths in the system, which the system

providers did not think of, let alone protect. To this end, it is necessary to closely investigate the different effects of vulnerabilities and their categorization. Such a categorization will allow for systematic verification of the absence of certain attack paths.

Even with such verified absence of certain attack paths, what is still missing is a mechanism to protect systems from zero day exploits. The simple reason is the fact that it is impossible to verify a given computer system regarding *unknown* properties. If the zero day exploit falls into one of the well-known categories and it is proven that vulnerabilities within this category cannot cause any damage, then the new zero day exploit will not cause any damage. Newly discovered vulnerabilities that fall into a different category still impose a threat.

Another tricky aspect of the methodology proposed in this chapter is the area of conflict between generic evaluation of processes (or process patterns) and the specific effects that are observed in a specific instance of a business process. In many cases, it is hardly possible to predict the effects of exploited vulnerabilities without taking into account the specific business goals. Further analysis is required regarding the degree to which the effects of exploiting a given vulnerability depend on the business process under consideration.

REFERENCES

Accorsi, R. (2006). On the relationship of privacy and secure remote logging in dynamic systems. In *Proceedings of the international information security conference.* (pp. 329-39). Boston: Springer-Verlag.

Accorsi, R. (2008). *Automated counterexample-driven audits of authentic system records.* Thesis.

Accorsi, R., & Stocker, T. (2008). Automated privacy audits based on pruning of log data. In *Proceedings of the international workshop on security and privacy in enterprise computing.* Washington, DC: IEEE Computer Society.

Agreiter, B., Alam, M., Hafner, M., Seifert, J. P., & Zhang, X. (2007). Model driven configuration of secure operating systems for mobile applications in health care. In J. Sztipanovits, R. Breu, E. Ammenwerth, R. Bajcsy, J. Mitchell, & A. Pretschner (Eds.), *Workshop on model-based trustworthy health information systems.*

Alam, M., Breu, R., & Hafner, M. (2007). Model-Driven security engineering for trust management in SECTET. *Journal of Software, 2*(1), 47–59. doi:10.4304/jsw.2.1.47-59

Anderson, R., & Long, C. (2001). *Security engineering: A guide to building dependable distributed systems.* Hoboken, NJ: Wiley & Sons.

Apvrille, A., & Pourzandi, M. (2005). Secure software development by example. *IEEE Security and Privacy, 3*(4), 10–17. doi:10.1109/MSP.2005.103

Arenas, A., Aziz, B., Bicarregui, J., Matthews, B., & Yang, E. Y. (2008). Modelling security properties in a grid-based operating system with anti-goals. In *ARES '08: Proceedings of the 2008 third international conference on availability, reliability and security.* Washington, DC: IEEE Computer Society.

Arsanjani, A., Zhang, L. J., Allam, A., & Channabasavaiah, K. (2007, March 28). *Design a SOA solution using a reference architecture.* Armonk, NY: IBM. Retrieved April 20, 2009, from http://www.ibm.com/developerworks/library/ar-archtemp/

Baldwin, A., Beres, Y., Shiu, S., & Kearney, P. (2006). A model-based approach to trust, security and assurance. *BT Technology Journal, 24*(4), 53–68. doi:10.1007/s10550-006-0097-7

Basin, D., Doser, J., & Lodderstedt, T. (2006). Model driven security: From UML models to access control infrastructures. *ACM Transactions on Software Engineering and Methodology, 15*(1), 39–91. doi:10.1145/1125808.1125810

Bauer, A., & Jürjens, J. (2008). Security protocols, properties, and their monitoring. In *SESS '08: Proceedings of the fourth international workshop on software engineering for secure systems.* New York: ACM.

Best, B., Jürjens, J., & Nuseibeh, B. (2007). Model-Based security engineering of distributed information systems using UMLsec. In *ICSE '07: Proceedings of the 29th international conference on software engineering.* Washington, DC: IEEE Computer Society.

Bhargavan, K., Fournet, C., Gordon, A. D., & Tse, S. (2006). Verified interoperable implementations of security protocols. In *Computer security foundations workshop, 2006 19th IEEE.*

Bishop, M. (2005). *Introduction to computer security.* Reading, MA: Addison-Wesley.

Blobel, B., Nordberg, R., Davis, J. M., & Pharow, P. (2006). Modelling privilege management and access control. *International Journal of Medical Informatics, 75*(8), 597–623. doi:10.1016/j.ijmedinf.2005.08.010

Blobel, B., & Pharow, P. (2007). A model driven approach for the german health telematics architectural framework and security infrastructure. *International Journal of Medical Informatics, 76*(2-3), 169–175. doi:10.1016/j.ijmedinf.2006.05.044

Boehm, B. W. (1981). *Software engineering economics.* Englewood Cliffs, NJ: Prentice-Hall.

Chess, B., & McGraw, G. (2004). Static analysis for security. *IEEE Security and Privacy, 2*(6), 76–79. doi:10.1109/MSP.2004.111

Crook, R., Ince, D., Lin, L., & Nuseibeh, B. (2002). Security requirements engineering: When anti-requirements hit the fan. In *Requirements engineering, 2002 proceedings IEEE joint international conference on.*

Deubler, M., Grünbauer, J., Jürjens, J., & Wimmel, G. (2004). Sound development of secure service-based systems. In *Proceedings of the 2nd international conference on service oriented computing.*

Devanbu, P. T., & Stubblebine, S. (2000). Software engineering for security: A roadmap. In *ICSE '00: Proceedings of the conference on the future of software engineering.* New York: ACM.

Dimitrakos, T., Ritchie, B., Raptis, D., Aagedal, J., Braber, F. D., Stølen, K., et al. (2002). Integrating model-based security risk management into ebusiness systems development: The CORAS approach. In *I3E '02: Proceedings of the IFIP conference on towards the knowledge society.* Amsterdam: Kluwer, B.V.

Eckert, C., & Marek, D. (1997). Developing secure applications: A systematic approach. In *SEC '97: Proceedings of the IFIP TC11 13 international conference on information security (SEC '97) on information security in research and business.* Boca Raton, FL: Chapman Hall, Ltd.

Egea, M., Basin, D., Clavel, M., & Doser, J. (2007). A metamodel-based approach for analyzing security-design models. In *Lecture notes in computer science.* (pp. 420-35). Berlin: Springer.

Fernandez, E. B., & Hawkins, J. C. (1997). Determining role rights from use cases. In *RBAC '97: Proceedings of the second ACM workshop on role-based access control.* New York: ACM.

Fernandez, E. B., Larrondo-Petrie, M. M., Sorgente, T., & VanHilst, M. (2006). A methodology to develop secure systems using patterns. In *Integrating Security and Software Engineering: Advances and Future Vision*, (pp. 107-126).

Flechais, I., Mascolo, C., & Sasse, M. A. (2007). Integrating security and usability into the requirements and design process. *International Journal of Electronic Security and Digital Forensics, 1*(1), 12–26. doi:10.1504/IJESDF.2007.013589

Fox, J., Mouratidis, H., & Jürjens, J. (2006). Towards a comprehensive framework for secure systems development. In *Lecture notes in computer science,* (pp. 48-62). Berlin: Springer.

Franklin, M. (2006). A survey of keyx evolving cryptosystems. *International Journal of Security and Networks, 1*(1/2), 46–53. doi:10.1504/IJSN.2006.010822

Giorgini, P., Massacci, F., Mylopoulos, J., & Zannone, N. (2005). Modeling security requirements through ownership, permission and delegation. In *Requirements engineering, 2005 proceedings 13th IEEE international conference on.*

Gollmann, D. (2000). On the verification of cryptographic protocols: A tale of two committees. *Electronic Notes in Theoretical Computer Science, 32,* 42–58. doi:10.1016/S1571-0661(04)00094-5

Goubault-Larrecq, J., & Parrennes, F. (2005). Cryptographic protocol analysis on real C code. In *Verification, model checking, and abstract interpretation.* Berlin: Springer.

Gürgens, S., & Peralta, R. (2000). Validation of cryptographic protocols by efficient automated testing. In *Proceedings of the thirteenth international florida artificial intelligence research society conference.* AAAI Press.

Hafner, M., Memon, M., & Alam, M. (2008). Modeling and enforcing advanced access control policies in healthcare systems with sectet. In *Models in software engineering.*

Haley, C. B., Laney, R., Moffett, J. D., & Nuseibeh, B. (2008). Security requirements engineering: A framework for representation and analysis. *Transactions on Software Engineering, 34*(1), 133–153. doi:10.1109/TSE.2007.70754

Haneberg, D., Reif, W., & Stenzel, K. (2002). A method for secure smartcard applications. In *AMAST '02: Proceedings of the 9th international conference on algebraic methodology and software technology.* London, UK: Springer-Verlag.

Höhn, S., & Jürjens, J. (2008). Rubacon: Automated support for model-based compliance engineering. In *ICSE '08: Proceedings of the 30th international conference on software engineering.* New York: ACM.

Houmb, S. H., Georg, G., France, R., Bieman, J., & Jürjens, J. (2005). Cost-Benefit trade-off analysis using BBN for aspect-oriented risk-driven development. In *Engineering of complex computer systems, 2005 ICECCS 2005 proceedings 10th IEEE international conference on.*

Hultin, F., & Heldal, R. (2003). Bridging model-based and language-based security. In *Lecture notes in computer science.* (pp. 235-52). Berlin: Springer.

Jayaram, K. R., & Mathur, A. P. (2005). Software engineering for secure software - state of the art: A survey. *CERIAS and SERC SERC-TR-279, September 19Th.*

Jensen, M., Gruschka, N., Herkenhöner, R., & Luttenberger, N. (2007). SOA web services: New technologies - new standards - new attacks. In *Proceedings of the 5th IEEE european conference on web services (ECOWS).*

Jürjens, J. (2000). Secure information flow for concurrent processes. In *Lecture notes in computer science,* (pp. 395-409). Berlin: Springer.

Jürjens, J. (2001a). Secrecy-Preserving refinement. In *Lecture notes in computer science,* (pp. 135-52). Berlin: Springer.

Jürjens, J. (2001b). Towards development of secure systems using UMLsec. In *Lecture notes in computer science,* (pp. 187-200). Berlin: Springer.

Jürjens, J. (2002). UMLsec: Extending UML for secure systems development. In *UML '02: Proceedings of the 5th international conference on the unified modeling language.* London: Springer-Verlag.

Jürjens, J. (2005a). *Secure systems development with UML.* Berlin: Springer.

Jürjens, J. (2005b). Sound methods and effective tools for model-based security engineering with UML. In *Software engineering, 2005 ICSE 2005 proceedings 27th international conference on.*

Jürjens, J. (2006). Security analysis of crypto-based java programs using automated theorem provers. In *ASE '06: Proceedings of the 21st IEEE/ACM international conference on automated software engineering.* Washington, DC: IEEE Computer Society.

Jürjens, J. (2009). A domain-specific language for cryptographic protocols based on streams. *Journal of Logic and Algebraic Programming,* 54–73. doi:10.1016/j.jlap.2008.08.006

Jürjens, J., & Rumm, R. (2008). Model-Based security analysis of the german health card architecture. *Methods of Information in Medicine, 47*(5), 409–416.

Jürjens, J., & Shabalin, P. (2007). Tools for secure systems development with UML. *Int. J. Softw. Tools Technol. Transf., 9*(5), 527–544. doi:10.1007/s10009-007-0048-8

Jürjens, J., & Wimmel, G. (2001). Security modelling for electronic commerce: The common electronic purse specifications. In *I3E '01: Proceedings of the IFIP conference on towards the e-society*. Amsterdam: Kluwer, B.V.

Jürjens, J., & Wimmel, G. (2002). Specification-Based test generation for security-critical systems using mutations. In *Lecture notes in computer science*, (pp. 471-82). Berlin: Springer.

Jürjens, J., & Yampolskiy, M. (2005). Code security analysis with assertions. In *ASE '05: Proceedings of the 20th IEEE/ACM international conference on automated software engineering*. New York: ACM.

Kearney, P., & Brügger, L. (2007). A risk-driven security analysis method and modelling language. *BT Technology Journal, 25*(1), 141–153. doi:10.1007/s10550-007-0016-6

Koch, M., & Parisi-Presicce, F. (2006). UML specification of access control policies and their formal verification. *Software and Systems Modeling, 5*(4), 429–447. doi:10.1007/s10270-006-0030-z

Krafzig, D., Banke, K., & Slama, D. (2004). *Enterprise SOA: Service-Oriented architecture best practices*. Upper Saddle River, NJ: Prentice Hall PTR.

Lamport, L., & Schneider, F. (1984). The 'hoare logic' of CSP and all that. *ACM Transactions on Programming Languages and Systems, 6*(2), 281–296. doi:10.1145/2993.357247

Livshits, B. (2006, December). *Improving software security with precise static and runtime analysis*. Thesis.

Lyon, G. (2006). *Top 100 network security tools* [Web page]. Retrieved April 20, 2009, from http://sectools.org/

Maidl, M., Gilmore, S., Haenel, V., & Kloul, L. (2005). Choreographing security and performance analysis for web services. In *Lecture notes in computer science*, (pp. 200-14). Berlin: Springer.

Maña, A., Montenegro, J. A., Rudolph, C., & Vivas, J. L. (2003). A business process-driven approach to security engineering. In *DEXA '03: Proceedings of the 14th international workshop on database and expert systems applications*. Washington, DC: IEEE Computer Society.

Maña, A., Rudolph, C., Spanoudakis, G., Lotz, V., Massacci, F., Melideo, M., et al. (2007). Security engineering for ambient intelligence: A manifesto. In *Integrating security and software engineering: Advances and future vision*. (pp. 244-70).

Manson, G., Mouratidis, H., & Giorgini, P. (2003). Integrating security and systems engineering: Towards the modelling of secure information systems. In *Lecture notes in computer science*. Berlin: Springer.

Martin, M., Livshits, B., & Lam, M. (2005). Finding application errors and security flaws using PQL: A program query language. In *20Th annual ACM conference on objects-oriented programming, systems, languages and applications*.

Massacci, F., Mylopoulos, J., & Zannone, N. (2007). Computer-Aided support for secure tropos. *Automated Software Engineering, 14*(3), 341–364. doi:10.1007/s10515-007-0013-5

Mathe, J., Duncavage, S., Werner, J., Malin, B., Ledeczi, A., & Sztipanovits, J. (2007). Implementing a model-based design environment for clinical information systems. In *Workshop on model-based trustworthy health information systems*.

Mell, P., Scarfone, K., & Romanosky, S. (2007). *CVSS: A complete guide to the common vulnerability scoring system*.

Méry, D., & Merz, S. (2007). Specification and refinement of access control. *Journal of Universal Computer Science, 13*(8), 1073–1093.

MITRE. (2007). *Open vulnerability and assessment language (OVAL)*.

Moebius, N., Haneberg, D., Reif, W., & Schellhorn, G. (2007). A modeling framework for the development of provably secure e-commerce applications. In *ICSEA '07: Proceedings of the international conference on software engineering advances.* Washington, DC: IEEE Computer Society.

Montangero, C., Buchholtz, M., Gilmore, S., & Haenel, V. (2005). End-To-End integrated security and performance analysis on the DEGAS choreographer platform. In *Lecture notes in computer science,* (pp. 286-301). Berlin: Springer.

Mylopoulos, J., Giorgini, P., & Massacci, F. (2003). Requirement engineering meets security: A case study on modelling secure electronic transactions by VISA and mastercard. In *Lecture notes in computer science,* (pp. 263-76). Berlin: Springer.

OASIS. (2006, October 12). *Reference model for service oriented architecture V1.0.* Retrieved April 21, 2009, from http://docs.oasis-open.org/soa-rm/v1.0/soa-rm.pdf

Ou, X., Boyer, W., & McQueen, M. (2006). A scalable approach to attack graph generation. In *CCS '06: Proceedings of the 13th ACM conference on computer and communications security.* New York: ACM.

Pauls, K., Kolarczyk, S., Koch, M., & Löhr, K. (2006). Sectool – supporting requirements engineering for access control. In *Lecture notes in computer science,* (pp. 254-67). Berlin: Springer.

Piattini, M., & Fernández-Medina, E. (2004). Extending OCL for secure database development. In *Lecture notes in computer science,* (pp. 380-94). Berlin: Springer.

Pironti, A., & Sisto, R. (2008). Soundness conditions for message encoding abstractions in formal security protocol models. In *ARES '08: Proceedings of the 2008 third international conference on availability, reliability and security.* Washington, DC: IEEE Computer Society.

Ray, I., France, R., Li, N., & Georg, G. (2004). An aspect-based approach to modeling access control concerns. *Information and Software Technology, 46*(9), 575–587. doi:10.1016/j.infsof.2003.10.007

Redwine, S. (2007). *Introduction to modeling tools for software security.*

Reichert, M., Rinderle, S., Kreher, U., Acker, H., Lauer, M., & Dadam, P. (2006). ADEPT next generation process management technology — tool demonstration. In *Caise '06 forum.* Luxembourg.

Rosado, D. G., Fernandez-Medina, E., Piattini, M., & Gutierrez, C. (2006). A study of security architectural patterns. In *ARES '06: Proceedings of the first international conference on availability, reliability and security.* Washington, DC: IEEE Computer Society.

Saltzer, J. H., & Schroeder, M. D. (1975). The protection of information in computer systems. In *IEEE, proceedings.*

Santen, T. (2006). Stepwise development of secure systems. In *Lecture notes in computer science,* (pp. 142-55). Berlin: Springer.

Santen, T., Heisel, M., & Pfitzmann, A. (2002). Confidentiality-Preserving refinement is compositional - sometimes. In *ESORICS '02: Proceedings of the 7th european symposium on research in computer security.* London: Springer-Verlag.

Schneider, F. B. (1998). *Trust in cyberspace.* National Academy Press.

Schneier, B., & Kelsey. (1999). Security audit logs to support computer forensics. *ACM Transactions on Information and System Security, 2*(2), 159–176. doi:10.1145/317087.317089

Seehusen, F., & Stølen, K. (2006). Information flow property preserving transformation of UML interaction diagrams. In *SACMAT '06: Proceedings of the eleventh ACM symposium on access control models and technologies.* New York: ACM.

Shabalin, P., & Jürjens, J. (2004). Automated verification of UMLsec models for security requirements. In *Lecture notes in computer science,* (pp. 365-79). Berlin: Springer.

Sindre, G., & Opdahl, A. L. (2005). Eliciting security requirements with misuse cases. *Requir. Eng., 10*(1), 34–44. doi:10.1007/s00766-004-0194-4

Siveroni, I., Zisman, A., & Spanoudakis, G. (2008). Property specification and static verification of UML models. In *ARES '08: Proceedings of the 2008 third international conference on availability, reliability and security.* Washington, DC: IEEE Computer Society.

Spanoudakis, G., Kloukinas, C., & Androutsopoulos, K. (2007). Towards security monitoring patterns. In *SAC '07: Proceedings of the 2007 ACM symposium on applied computing.* New York: ACM.

Swiderski, F., & Snyder, W. (2004). *Threat modeling.* Redmond, WA: Microsoft Press.

Thompson, H. (2005). Application penetration testing. *IEEE Security and Privacy, 3*(1), 66–69. doi:10.1109/MSP.2005.3

Turner, D. (2008). *Symantec global internet security threat report: Trends for July-December 2007.*

UMLsec group. (2009). *Security analysis tool* [Web page]. Retrieved January 12, 2009, from http://www.umlsec.org

Whittle, J., Wijesekera, D., & Hartong, M. (2008). Executable misuse cases for modeling security concerns. In *ICSE '08: Proceedings of the 30th international conference on software engineering.* New York: ACM.

Wolff, B., Brucker, A. D., & Doser, J. (2006). A model transformation semantics and analysis methodology for secureuml. In *Lecture notes in computer science,* (pp. 306-20). Berlin: Springer.

Woodside, M., Petriu, D. C., Petriu, D. B., Xu, J., Israr, T., & Georg, G. (2009). Performance analysis of security aspects by weaving scenarios extracted from UML models. *Journal of Systems and Software, 82*(1), 56–74. doi:10.1016/j.jss.2008.03.067

Yoshioka, N., Honiden, S., & Finkelstein, A. (2004). Security patterns: A method for constructing secure and efficient inter-company coordination systems. In *EDOC '04: Proceedings of the enterprise distributed object computing conference, eighth IEEE international.* Washington, DC: IEEE Computer Society.

Yskout, K., Scandariato, R., Win, B. D., & Joosen, W. (2008). Transforming security requirements into architecture. In *ARES '08: Proceedings of the 2008 third international conference on availability, reliability and security.* Washington, DC: IEEE Computer Society.

Yu, E., & Elahi, G. (2008). A goal oriented approach for modeling and analyzing security trade-offs. In *Lecture notes in computer science,* (pp. 375-90). Berlin: Springer.

Yu, W., Aravind, D., & Supthaweesuk, P. (2006). Software vulnerability analysis for web services software systems. In *Computers and communications, 2006 ISCC '06 proceedings 11th IEEE symposium on.*

Yu, Y., Jürjens, J., & Mylopoulos, J. (2008). Traceability for the maintenance of secure software. In *24Th IEEE international conference on software maintenance*.

Zhang, G., Baumeister, H., Koch, N., & Knapp, A. (2005). Aspect-Oriented modeling of access control in web applications. In *Proc. 6Th int. Workshop on aspect oriented modeling, AOSD*.

ENDNOTES

* Here we use the convention that where the values are supposed to be boolean values, they need not be written (then presence of the label denotes the value true, and absence denotes false).

1   http://www.metasploit.com/

2   Microsoft http://www.microsoft.com/technet/security/current.aspx

3   SecWatch http://secwatch.org/

4   http://www.sans.org/newsletters/risk/display.php

5   Open Web Application Security Project http://www.owasp.org/

6   Milw0rm http://www.milw0rm.com/

7   SecuriTeam http://www.securiteam.com/

8   French Security Incident Response Team http://www.frsirt.com/english/

9   IBM Internet Security Systems X-Force. Alerts and Advisories, 2007. http://www.iss.net/rss.php

10 National Institute of Standards and Technology. National Vulnerability Database NVD http://nvd.nist.gov

11 Common Vulnerabilities and Exposures http://cve.mitre.org/

12 Open Source Vulnerability Database OSVDB http://osvdb.org

13 SecurityFocus. SecurityFocus Vulnerability Database, 2007. http://www.securityfocus.com/bid

14 SecurityTracker http://securitytracker.com/

15 Oracle. http://www.oracle.com/technology/products/jdev/index.html

16 The Eclipse Foundation. http://www.eclipse.org

Chapter 2
Security Analysis of Service Oriented Systems:
A Methodical Approach and Case Study

Frank Innerhofer-Oberperfler
University of Innsbruck, Austria

Markus Mitterer
University of Innsbruck, Austria

Michael Hafner
University of Innsbruck, Austria

Ruth Breu
University of Innsbruck, Austria

ABSTRACT

This chapter is devoted to the continuous security analysis of service oriented systems during design and operation. The authors present the ProSecO framework which offers concepts and a process model for the elicitation of security objectives and requirements, evaluation of risks and documentation of security controls. The goal of ProSecO is to provide the analyst at any time during design and operation with information about the security state of the system. Core ideas of ProSecO are interweaved elicitation and documentation of functional and security properties based on system models and the clear separation of business oriented and technical information. The kind of information ProsecO handles is in wide parts informal and non-executable.

INTRODUCTION

The concept of Service Oriented Architecture (SOA) lately became one of the most powerful architectural paradigms acquitting itself of IT's original promise to boost an organization's bottom line by an increase of productivity, sharpened competitive differentiation, and fostered operational effectiveness. SOA and Web services originally started as a technical trend, but soon unveiled their huge potential to businesses.

In a world where business process model innovation is the actual key differentiator, business

DOI: 10.4018/978-1-60566-950-2.ch002

processes change frequently. As a result, in the past technology constantly outpaced process (re-) engineering. With SOA and Web services emerging, organizations were suddenly given the perfect means to develop flexibility capabilities. This was possible through a highly flexible IT infrastructure which facilitated the proper alignment of IT and business processes. SOA became a top priority in many organizations and an important strategic initiative to pursue (Marks 08). The results are impressive: companies who built their strategy on flexible IT infrastructures and tightly linked IT and business shown clear gains in business results (Carter 07).

It soon became evident, that turning a business' IT into a successful SOA – one that reliably meets defined business objectives over time – requires rules and guidelines for the organization and all participants, from architects and developers to service consumers, service providers, and even applications and the services themselves (Marks 2006). These so-called "policies" should cover the complete cycle of designing, developing, deploying, maintaining and operating the IT. The process of ensuring that all efforts related to SOA meet all stakeholders' interests and enterprise requirements is called as SOA governance (WebLayers 2005). Nevertheless, security turned out to be a major challenge.

Along with all its advantages, the paradigm of SOA comes with an array of new security problems, mainly due to the "lowering" of security barriers between traditional applications. The distributed, peer-to-peer style architecture of SOA scenario and the general "statelessness" of services that may be reused in various contexts by potentially unknown clients impose a requirement of utmost flexibility on the underlying infrastructure and its security capabilities. This goes against the intuition of security experts who prefer to impose conservative and cumbersome restrictions on the use of functionality on target infrastructures - be they services or traditional applications. Fortunately, with SOA acceptance

spreading among businesses new tools, standards and technologies were developed. Their aim: guaranteeing a high level of security without diluting the benefits of SOA.

An important step towards the systematic design of secure applications is the tight integration of security in the whole development process. In too many real-world projects security is conceived a mere technical aspect and security controls are designed in an ad-hoc way. This causes major drawbacks for the resulting system.

The acceptance of SOA as a mainstream paradigm for a business IT infrastructure depends on the ability to guarantee an appropriate level of security to mission-critical businesses. The major risks can be identified along three dimensions.

First, threats originating in the social or organizational context of the system may not be adequately covered. Examples of such threats are social engineering attacks where the attacker uses human interaction to compromise the system.

Second, the realized security solutions may not be in line with the requirements. Since most security controls have an impact on factors like user flexibility, system performance and budget a thorough analysis of requirements and possible security controls is an important step in a systematic design process.

Third, compliance plays a crucial role for many security-critical systems. For instance, in the e-government and e-health area privacy protection and authentication are connected with strict legal regulations. Moreover, regulations like Basel II and the Sarbanes Oxley Act have increasing influence also on applications in e-business. As a consequence the validation of compliance requirements plays an important role in many service oriented applications. A prerequisite for such a validation are interconnected requirements and solutions.

The chapter is organized as follows. In Section 2 we present the security analysis method ProSecO, starting with the underlying functional models and followed by a step-by-step description of the security analysis process. Section 3 presents a case study from the health care domain that explains the use of the method following a practical example. In Section 4 we present a short overview of related work in the field of security analysis of service oriented systems. Finally in Section 5 a conclusion is drawn.

BACKGROUND

Information is an important asset and resource for businesses and needs to be protected like any other asset. The protection of information is usually known as information security (ISO, 2005). A basic and classical model of security objectives includes the so called CIA triad (Peltier, 2001; Bishop, 2003), which stands for confidentiality, integrity and availability. We agree with this or similar other classifications but we would like to point out that security requirements always have to be put into context with the functional system requirements.

The systems we are considering in this chapter are service oriented systems. Service oriented systems have some specific characteristics which require a tailored approach in analyzing their security. First of all, these systems connect different stakeholders which very often participate in inter-organizational workflows. This is an aspect that is different from a classical security analysis in a single organization.

The different stakeholders can be very heterogeneous, e.g. especially in B2C environments in which large corporations or service providers might collaborate with a large number of single households or consumers. While the large corporation has a top-tier technology infrastructure which is hopefully managed following best practices, the consumers or other smaller interacting parties generally just operate from a simple technological environment using commodity hard- and software.

This difference in size and infrastructure is directly related with the protection level and the security of the infrastructure from which the collaborating stakeholders operate. While a large corporation will generally have sophisticated protective and preventive measures and an information security management system in place, other stakeholders might lack a proper approach to security at all.

Stakeholders may also have various reasons, everyone pursuing different objectives for using service oriented systems. They may regard the information which they provide or process using such a system as highly valuable and therefore require strong security, while for another stakeholder throughput and efficiency might be the primary objective.

The local implementation of a specific service or the local infrastructure is not in control of the other partners. It is the responsibility of the participating stakeholders to manage their systems and provide adequate security. To support a security analysis of a service oriented system, these points have to be taken in consideration.

To summarize, some of the key points with regard to the security analysis of service oriented systems are:

- The networks of stakeholders and services are highly dynamic, both concerning stakeholder types, stakeholder instances and the workflows to be run.
- The stakeholders are heterogeneous in their organizational structure, security requirements and security infrastructure.
- There may be a high number of stakeholder instances requiring complex infrastructures and effective engineering techniques.

From these basic assumptions and characteristics we derive the following two requirements for a methodical security analysis of service oriented solutions:

- **Modularity**
  ○ Different levels of abstraction can be analyzed independently of each other (e.g., separating organizational requirements from technical requirements)
  ○ Different sub domains can be analyzed independently of each other (e.g., separating the analysis of the organizational structure of hospitals and general practitioners)
  ○ The notions of requirements, risks and controls are clearly separated and may be considered independently of each other and arriving at the implemented security controls. Security controls may range from organizational rules (e.g., four eyes principle) to technical components (encryption firewalls).
- **Traceability**
  ○ Security aspects can be traced along the levels of abstraction starting with general security objectives (e.g. which may be derived from legal regulations, contractual agreements or organizational policies) and arriving at the implemented security controls.
  ○ The analyzer is provided with aggregated information about the state of the security analysis process at any time.

The methodical approach presented in this chapter is based on earlier works of our group, which are targeted to the overall objective of developing systematic approaches for security engineering (Breu, Burger, Hafner, & Popp, 2004). As a starting base for developing a tailored approach for analyzing service oriented systems the ProSecO approach for model based security management (Innerhofer-Oberperfler & Breu, 2006, Hafner & Breu, 2008) was used.

The ProSecO approach was initially developed with the idea to support organizations in the process of security management. Special emphasis was given to a systematic analysis integrating business and technical perspectives and to make the analysis of complex infrastructures tractable. However, the above mentioned characteristics of service oriented systems required an adaptation of the original ProSecO approach.

Especially the fact, that not anymore a single organization was the object of analysis, but multiple stakeholders with their own infrastructures have to considered in the overall analysis convinced us to extend the method. The resulting method for analyzing service oriented systems described in this chapter was labeled ProSecO-SOA.

A Case Study from the Health Care Domain

The example applications for the description of the method in this chapter are health care networks. Health care networks support cooperation between stakeholders in the health care domain like hospitals, general practitioners and the patient. As running example we will use the system health@net, an Austrian initiative to develop concepts and an implementation of distributed cross-institutional health data records.

The intention behind health@net is to utilize earnings of increased quality and efficiency when different health care institutions cooperate. Traditionally, medical documents remain at the institution where they were created. Any kind of distribution of such documents has to be initiated by the author himself and is called indirect communication. A potential recipient has at least to know about the existence of the author or the document. The better approach is to establish a so called direct communication, where documents are available for authorized recipients on their simple request. In this scenario no time and space restrictions may occur, as documents are stored centralized in a Shared Electronic Health Record (SEHR). The direct communication offers a lot of interesting application areas., among them:

- automatic accounting with health insurance companies
- analysis of disease patterns (regional, national, international)
- avoidance of double medications with harmful impacts
- statistical evaluation and control of the health care system

Beside all advantages of the health information exchange several severe risks have to be considered. In general we can state that the more comprehensive a system gets, the higher the risks and impacts will become of improper usage. To gain the necessary acceptance for a healthcare network it is mandatory to establish appropriate mechanisms to reduce those risks to an adequate level. As medical information is quite sensitive and confidential the terms security and privacy play a key role.

ProSecO: A Model-Based Approach to Security Analysis

The ProSecO approach is a model based framework for information security risk management that aims at bridging the business and technical perspectives on information security risks. The framework is based on an enterprise model that forms the foundation on which security requirements, threats and risks related to IT are identified, analyzed and assessed.

ProSecO consists of the following main parts:

- an enterprise model – the functional system view – that defines relevant business and technical artifacts of an organization and their dependencies,

- a security model that defines security related concepts (i.e. requirements, threats, risks, controls) and their relations,
- a defined process which guides security analysts throughout their activities.

In most process models security requirements are treated in an unstructured way as non-functional requirements. The key idea of our method is that we put any security related aspect in the context of the functional system view (e.g., specifying which data objects have to be kept confidential or which actions are non-repudiable).

The Functional System View describes the system at different levels of abstraction ranging from business processes to the functional and technical architecture. The elements of the Functional Model (e.g., business processes, information objects, components) drive the security analysis through their interrelations. We conceive security as a process accompanying the whole lifecycle of the system. The aim of this process is

- to identify security objectives
- to elicitate security requirements
- to detect threats and evaluate risks
- to design and to implement security controls meeting the requirements and counteracting the risks

These security management related activities are condensed in the ProSecO security micro-process. Each instance of the micro-process is associated with a part of the functional model and analyzes security aspects of the associated model elements. In this respect the security analysis may focus on subsystems (e.g., concerning specific stakeholders) or on specific levels of abstraction (e.g., the business level). During systems development instances of the security micro-process are integrated with the software development process. This means that the development of functional artifacts like the software architecture is enhanced

Table 1. Functional system view

		Level of Abstraction		
		Business View	Application View	Technical View
Level of Interaction	Global View (GV)	GV Business Model	GV Software Architecture	–
	Local View (LV)	LV Business Model	LV Software Architecture.	LV Technical Infrastructure.

by security related activities with the goal to develop an adequate security solution.

As soon as the system gets productive the security micro-process is used to monitor the system as part of the organizations security management process. The goals in this phase are to detect security leaks, react to changed requirements (e.g., new legal regulations) or to adapt configurations of the security architecture.

Functional System View

The main idea behind ProSecO is the use of a model of the system under consideration to enable a systematic security analysis. This Enterprise Model or Functional System View describes the scope of analysis and contains all relevant parts of the system.

In general, our modeling approach is based on an iterative principle, i.e. the intention is to start with important elements of the business layer in order to iteratively identify dependencies and further elements. For describing the functional aspects of a service oriented system in a modular way we use two orthogonal concepts for layering – the Level of Interaction and the Level of Abstraction.

- **Level of Interaction:**
  - The Global View describes aspects related with the interaction of different stakeholders (i.e. autonomous partners in the network) at a high level of abstraction hiding the details of local technical implementations.
  - The Local View describes aspects related with the behavior and

structure of a specific stakeholder (like a hospital or a surgery). In the Local View the respective infrastructures and specific implementation is depicted.

- **Level of Abstraction:**
  - The Business View describes the business processes, processed information and the requirements at business level.
  - The Application View represents the services and components that implement the services.
  - The Technical View describes the underlying technical infrastructure.

Table 1 shows the core models along this classification. The elements that can be modeled with these core models are defined in the ProSecO-SOA Functional Meta Model. The meta-model defines the concepts to describe aspects of the core models (e.g. global business processes, local business processes, global services, local applications and local infrastructure).

The Functional Meta Model therefore reflects the classification and sections as shown in Table 1 and is split in two meta-models, the Global System Meta Model and the Local System Meta Model. Each of these parts is layered based on the levels of abstraction.

The Global and Local Functional Meta Model are linked with each other since they are just different perspectives on the same ensemble of partners and service provided in the system. The different layers in the Functional Meta Models are linked via defined dependency relations between the model elements.

Figure 1. Global functional meta-model

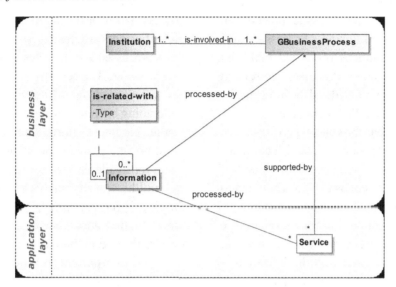

Both types of relations – the links between the Global Model and the Local Model, and the links within the Models – are crucial to support the model driven security analysis of the whole system. These relations are used as a frame to propagate security relevant information and to provide traceability throughout the models.

In the following we present the meta-model elements of the ProSecO Functional Meta Model in more detail. Figure 1 shows the Global Functional Meta-model, Figure 2 the Local Functional Meta-model. The main concepts and their interrelations are explained below, the description have partly been taken from a previous publication (Breu, Hafner, Innerhofer-Oberperfler, & Wozak, 2008).

Following the description of the concepts and relations of the meta-models, the models that have been developed during the case study will be described to provide the reader with a practical example.

Global Functional Meta-Model

The Global Functional Model describes the global aspects of the service oriented system. For this reason it is a rather abstract description of the inter-organizational workflows containing the partici-pating stakeholders, the workflows, the processes information and the involved services. Below is a more detailed description of the concepts.

Institution (Business Layer). An institution instance represents an autonomous partner in the service oriented application. In the subsequent chapters we also use the term partner role as a synonym for an institution.

Examples: In the context of health@net typical institutions are hospitals, medical practitioners, pharmacies or health insurances. Moreover you will have further involved parties like the patient itself and the provider which administrates the infrastructure.

Information (Business Layer). Information is an abstract concept to specify information types. Information classes may be related in various relation types such as association, composition or inheritance.

Examples: The main information object used in health@net is the virtual health record. This object can be split up into several elements, as illustrated in Figure 4. Other examples for information object are access policies storing concrete access rights or the access protocol logging all activities.

Global Business Process (Business Layer). A Business Process is a type of interaction between stakeholders. A Global Business Process models the interaction of institutions from an external point of view. Global Business Processes are related with the institutions involved and the information types processed during the interaction.

Example: Global business processes in health@net are 'read document', 'add document', 'update document' or 'read protocol'. Each of these processes corresponds to an institution and information objects.

Service (Application Layer). Services are executable components available in the network. Each service is associated with the information types it processes (e.g., as input or output).

Examples: To allocate the previous described business processes we need a 'read' (named 'Consumer' in health@net), 'write' (named 'Source' in health@net) and an 'audit record repository (ARP)' service. The ARP provides a user interface where patients can log in and view their personal health-record protocol.

Local Functional Meta Model

The Local Functional Meta Model describes the concepts used to model the properties of a specific stakeholder in the inter-organizational system. According to the definitions in the Global Functional System Model these stakeholders in the sequel are called institutions. As can be seen in the notes depicted in Figure 2, the Local Functional Model is inheriting concepts from the Global Functional Model.

Domain Role (Business Layer). A domain role represents an actor in the fine-grained view of an institution.

Examples: In the institution 'hospital' we have several departments, where each of it has a medical director, some physicians, nurses and other staff.

Local Business Process (Business Layer). A local business process models a fine-grained inter-

action of an institution as part of a global business process. A local business process is related with the global business process it is part of, the information types processed and the roles involved.

Examples: The security analysis for health@net was carried out while the system was still undergoing changes on a global level due to further development efforts. Therefore, on the local view, no fine-grained and stable process details were yet available. To nevertheless be able to explain the security analysis from a local view, the global processes 'read document', 'add document', 'update document' or 'read protocol' have been replicated in the local model.

Local Component (Application Layer). A local component represents an application residing on the institution's domain. A component may be related with the service it implements, may be part of other components or may depend on other components and processes information objects.

Moreover, local components are linked with the local business processes they support and the information types they process.

Examples: Local components in health@net are for example email clients, Web browsers or specific hospital software tools (KIS) and the corresponding databases.

Node (Physical Layer). A node represents technical or physical objects that are either used to store information objects (e.g., file server, USB stick, plain paper), to run applications or to transmit information. The concept of a node may be hierarchically composed and nodes may be linked with other nodes. Moreover, nodes can be linked with the components they run.

Examples: For example, the project health@ net identified several desktop PCs, the KIS (the german abbreviation for Hospital Information System) or the GIN (german abbreviation for Health Information Network) adapter, which is responsible to establish a connection to the non-public health network.

Location (Physical Layer). A location instance describes a physical location (e.g., a server room,

Figure 2. Local functional meta-model

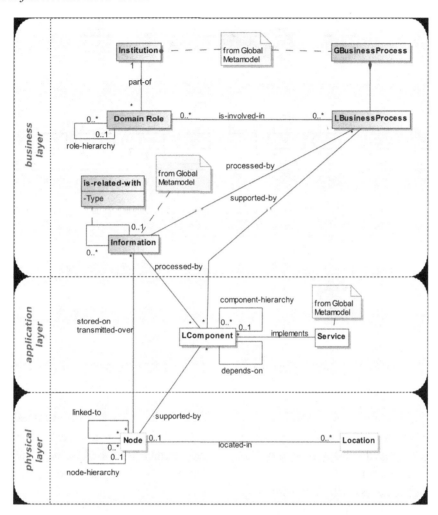

an office) and is associated with the residing nodes.

Examples: In the hospital environment we have locations like laboratories, examination rooms or technical infrastructure rooms (server rooms).

Case Study: Example Functional Models

The ProSecO Functional Meta Model defines the structure of functional model elements but does not constrain their representation. This means that Functional Models may be represented both in textual or graphical way. The ProSecO Meta-model is intended to provide a starting point for the security analysis and not a complete meta-model for the development of service oriented applications. For the latter goal the meta-model has to be enhanced by detailed structural and behavioral information. In particular, business processes may be defined based on business process notations such as BPMN (Hafner et al., 2006; OMG, 2009). Figure 3 shows as an example the Global Functional Model in the health care case study.

To outline the meaning of the Global Functional Model we concentrate on the business process 'Read Protocol'. This process is executed by a 'Patient' who wants to read the access protocol

Figure 3. Sample global functional model

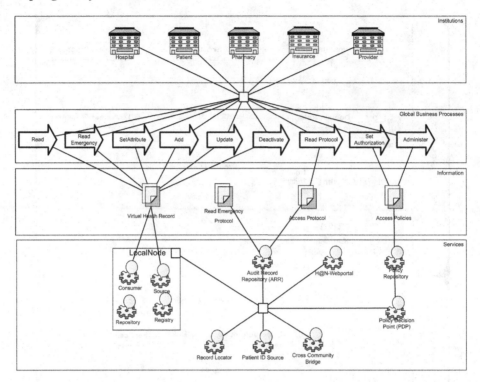

for his specific health record. In this sample global functional model every institution could execute every business process, which is indicated by the all-to-all relation between institutions and business processes. In practice access will be restricted by an access control module, which was out of scope of the current analysis.

The access control module also regulates which parts of the virtual health record (c.f. Figure 4) a user is authorized to access.

ProSecO does not require complete Functional Models as input for the security analysis. The identification of interrelationships across layers is part of the initial steps within the security analysis process and may involve only a part of the model (e.g., starting from a specific business process or an information type).

Figure 5 shows a sample schematic Local Functional Model in the health care case study. The Local Functional Model of the 'Hospital' is closely related to the Global Functional Model and

extends it with some fine grained details. Some typical hospital roles were added and services are already described in the context of concrete hardware components and locations.

The Security Model

Once a basic version of the Functional Models has been created, the security analysis can already begin. Similar to the Functional Meta-Models described in the previous section, we have defined a Security Meta-model that contains the central elements and relations of security notions.

The ProSecO Security Meta-model is shown in Figure 6. In this meta-model the class *ModelElement* acts as a placeholder for any element of the Functional Meta-models. More precisely, *ModelElement* is considered to be a supertype of all classes in the Functional Meta-models.

Security Objective. A Security Objective describes a general security goal to the system.

Figure 4. A detailed model of the information element virtual health record

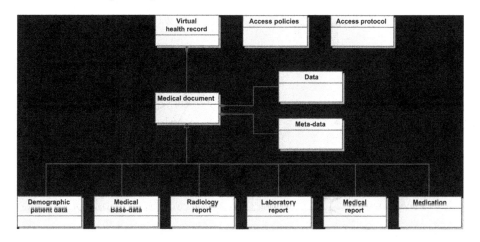

Security Objectives in many cases originate in legal requirements and general availability, integrity and confidentiality requirements. For the purpose of the Security Analysis, Security Objectives are associated with model elements of the business layer (business processes or information types).

Examples: An example security objective in the context of the presented case study is confidentiality (i.e. protection of patient data).

Security Requirement. A Security Requirement is a detailed context-dependent explication of a Security Objective. It breaks a Security Objective down in several more detailed descriptions. The context of a Security Requirement is derived from the model element for which it is defined.

Security Requirements are linked to Security Objectives to depict their paths of inheritance.

Examples: An example security requirement that could be derived from the security objective of confidentiality could be to restrict access to certain parts of the health record.

Threat. A Threat is the description of an adverse event that is considered as potentially having a negative impact. A Threat by itself is not interesting for our analysis; it only becomes relevant, if we further identify a targeted model element and a related security requirement. Once the threat has been assessed and estimated regarding its impact, it becomes a risk.

Examples: A threat could be an external hacker gaining unauthorized access to a service.

Risk. A Risk is therefore defined as a triplet consisting of a targeted model element, a related security requirement and a threat that potentially undermines the requirement, including an assessment of its severity. Moreover, every risk is evaluated in the context of the currently implemented security controls.

Examples: A risk in the case study could be a service (source), that has a requirement (restrict access), and an associated threat (external hacker gaining unauthorized access). A security control could be in place (authentication and access control) that addresses this risk already. The resulting assessment of the risk in qualitative manner could be a low probability and a high impact, resulting in a medium risk.

Security Control. A Security Control is any measure or safeguard that has been put in place to mitigate the identified risks.

Examples: A security control could be the use of strong encryption and access control.

The different states listed for the classes of Risk, BusinessSecurityObjective and SecurityRequirement (cf. upper right part of Figure 6) serve the purpose to depict the progress of the security analysis. For example, a Security Requirement reaches the state COMPLETERISKS once all

Figure 5. Sample local functional model

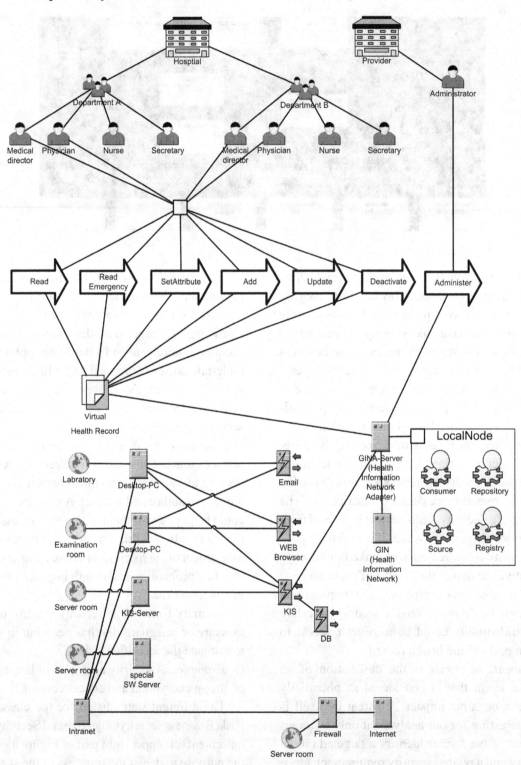

Figure 6. Security meta-model

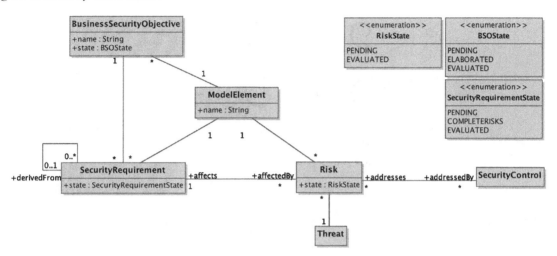

relevant threats have been identified. It reaches the state EVALUATED once the risk of all of these identified threats has been evaluated.

More detailed examples about the security elements treated in the case study will be given in the following sections, following the description of the single activities of the security analysis process. For now, the description of the Security Meta-Model serves the purpose to understand the general description of the analysis process.

Security Analysis Process

Core of the security analysis process of ProSecO are the classical actions of security analysis as described in the standard ISO/IEC 27001:2005 (ISO, 2005). These actions comprise

- elicitation of security requirements,
- identification of threats,
- evaluation of risks,
- security control engineering.

The concepts of the Security Meta-Model described in the previous section provide the inputs and outputs for all the actions of the security analysis process. In the ProSecO approach we

extend this core process in two directions. First, all the security relevant actions are performed in the context of some model element and the security related information (requirements, threats, and controls) is attached with these model elements. Second, we conceive the core process as a micro-process that is continuously executed on a defined part of the Functional Model.

To facilitate the security analysis we divide the Functional Model in submodels (domains) that will be analyzed by stakeholders which have the best knowledge about and the responsibility for modeling that specific domain. Good candidates for domains are the Global Functional Model and Local Functional Models attached to specific institutions, for large institutions it may be advisable to additionally separate abstraction levels or business processes.

Each "domain responsible" continuously executes the security micro-process on his domain which leads in the global view to a concurrent execution of security micro-processes (cf. Figure 7). Since each security micro-process may modify the state of related security information (e.g. adding new requirements and threats) and the model elements of different domains may be interrelated the micro-processes are not independent but interact with each other.

Figure 7. Responsibility domains and security micro-processes

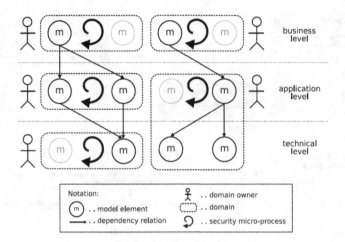

Figure 7 depicts in a schematic way domains, responsibles and the interplay of security micro–processes. Domains are defined as specific non intersecting sets of model elements. As an example, consider the network nodes of the Local Functional Model depicted in Figure 5, which could be treated as a separate domain, which is modeled and analyzed by a network administrator of the hospital. Grey model elements are those elements which are not linked with others in a dependency relation. The security analysis process is always carried out on the model elements which are linked with each other through dependency relations. A Domain Owner is the stakeholder responsible for the security analysis of a Domain. Consider for example a network administrator who will be just focusing on the security analysis of the network components.

The actions of the security micro–process are shown in Figure 8. Within the process the Security Model is elaborated, i.e. new model elements are added and security related information is created and modified. Each process is repeatedly executed and every iteration is initiated by a set of triggers. These triggers are mainly time events (e.g. the security process is executed periodically) or a state change in the Security

Model. Relevant state changes may be the creation of new model elements (e.g. new business processes or services), the identification of new requirements or threats and the implementation of security controls.

In the sequel we will describe each of the actions of the security analysis process in more detail along with the example case study.

Elaborate Functional Model

The first step in each micro-process is the *creation* – or in the case of reiterated cycles the *adaptation* – of the domain. The output of this step is a simple Functional Model which provides a starting point for the analysis. The inputs for this activity generally are gathered in interviews and workshops with the respective stakeholders and domain experts. During a reiteration of the security process, change may be incorporated in the Functional Models.

For instance, new services may be added and linked with other model elements or the technical infrastructure is changed. In this step it is not yet necessary to complete the links to other model elements.

Figure 8. The ProSecO analysis process

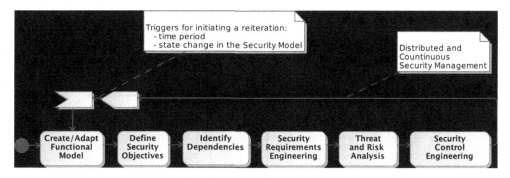

Case Study: Creating and Adapting the Functional Models

In our case study of the health care network, this activity comprised a series of interviews and discussions with the partners participating in the network in order to understand the global processes, the structure of the processed health records and the services involved. These general tasks mostly are characterized by information gathering and structuring (Alberts & Dorofee, 2002).

In the case study we followed an interative approach to refine the models accordingly and incorporate the feedback from the stakeholders. The system we have analyzed is a prototype that is evolving and therefore continuous adaptations to the functional models were needed.

Define Security Objectives

The next step in the security management process is the definition of high level, abstract security objectives to provide a starting point for the detailed security risk analysis. Security objectives can be based on legal requirements, contractual agreements or be based on business decisions. Security objectives are useful for establishing a clear goal that is understandable at all levels. Typically such a Security Objective is attached to a model element of the business level (e.g. a business process, an information object). But depending on the context of analysis it is also

suitable to attach an abstract security objective to a low level technical object (e.g. a specific service or infrastructural system).

The security objective's purpose is not only the communication of the goal of a security management effort, but it also serves as guidance on the formulation of concrete security requirements. It is possible to define many security objectives per domain.

The inputs required for this activity are a simple Functional Model of the service oriented system which provides the model elements to which security objectives can be attached. The necessary information required to define the security objectives is again gathered during interviews and workshops with compliance experts, legal advisors or domain experts. The output of the activity are security objectives which are attached to specific model elements of the Functional Models.

Case Study: Security Objectives

In the case study the definition of the security objectives started with an analysis of relevant Austrian and EU laws and regulations that the system has to comply with. This analysis was supported by interviewing domain experts having a strong legal background like the data protection officer of a hospital.

As a frame for structuring and grouping the security objectives we have used the list of general security requirements proposed by Firesmith

Figure 9. Sample security objectives

Category	Source	Identification	Authentication	Authorization	Immunity	Integrity	Availability	Intrusion Detection	Nonrepudiation	Privacy	Security Auditing	Survivability	Physical Protection	System Maintenance Sec.
Legal Requirements for the Exchange of Patient Data in Austria	Federal Act on data protection (Datenschutzgesetz)		X							X	X	X		
	Federal Act on digital signatures (Signatur Gesetz)		X			X			X					
	Federal Act on Provisions Facilitating Electronic Communications with Public Bodies (E-Government Gesetz)	X	X						X					
	Federal Act on Health telematics (Gesundheitstelematikgesetz)	X	X	X		X			X					

(Firesmith, 2003). The first group of objectives was primarily derived from national laws regulating the Health Care domain in Austria. For every one of these legal sources of security objectives, the relevant type of requirement proposed by Firesmith was highlighted to provide an overview of the range of objectives.

As an example (cf. Figure 9) we attached an extract of the security objectives relevant for health@ net. In the columns you find the general security objectives which were proposed by Firesmith (Firesmith, 2003). In each row we have relevant legal or business requirements for health@net. Each cross in the matrix symbolizes that this source has an impact on that specific security objective and is therefore of further interest.

Identify Dependencies

With the security objectives we have defined the areas of interest in the Functional Model. Each of the model elements that have a security objective attached is the root element of a separate scope called a dependency graph. The dependency graph is a non-cyclic graph of model elements. The dependencies are identified following a top-down-approach along the levels of abstraction of the Functional Meta-model. In the case of a global business process we

- identify associated local business processes
- identify the institutions and roles involved in the processes
- analyze processed information and
- the services supporting the processes
- relate the services with the implementing components
- relate these components with the hosting physical nodes and their location

Case Study: Dependencies

In the case study, the definition of dependencies first focused on the global level to get an accurate picture of the global business processes, the processed information and the involved services. After several iterations and refinements the global functional model was stabilized and the local models of the participating stakeholders were ready to be created.

For the creation of the local functional models (for every stakeholder one local functional model is created) the relevant business processes, processed information objects and invoked services were the starting point. In an iterative approach, the relevant local infrastructure was modeled, as well as local roles and additional local business process. As an example we refer to Figure 5, which depicts the exemplified local functional model of a hospital participating in the global workflow.

Security Requirements Engineering

During security requirements engineering a general security objective attached with some model element is broken down into concrete requirements based on the model element's dependency tree. Security requirements engineering is done in a top-down way where the security requirements of lower level model elements inherit the security requirements of upper level model elements.

The input for the security requirements engineering activity are the Security Objectives defined in the context of specific model elements of the Functional Model, which are then refined in more detailed security requirements defined in the context of related model elements.

Case Study: Security Requirements

Starting from the list of security objectives and their description, a refinement of the objectives in more detailed requirements was done in close collaboration with experts from the various domains as well as using checklists and standards. We followed both types of approaches, a bottom-up and top-down approach.

The first approach (bottom-up) uses general security catalogs like the Baseline Protection Manual (BSI, 2004) and EBIOS (DCSSI Advisory Office, 2005) to identify security requirements from existing knowledge bases.

The second approach (top-down) uses the knowledge of domain experts and brain-storming sessions, where individual domain requirements are worked out. In Table 2 you find an excerpt from the list of security requirements and the corresponding model elements.

As a result of the elicitation of security requirements we obtain a noncyclical graph of security requirements, where each requirement is attached with some model element and the parent-child relationships are induced by the dependency relations between the attached model elements. Note that security requirements at the same level are connected by a logical "and" which means that a parent security requirement enforces the fulfillment of all children security requirements.

Threat and Risk Analysis

While the security requirements state what properties have to be guaranteed, threats and risks state what kind of attacks may occur and what damage may be the consequence. Similarly to security requirements we associate each risk with some model element.

For a systematic threat analysis at the application or technical level again knowledge bases providing extensive threat catalogues such as the Baseline Protection Manual (BSI, 2004) EBIOS (DCSSI Advisory Office, 2005) can be used. In this respect the focal point of analysis are the model elements at the application or technical level which are exposed to attacks from outside or inside the network.

In the second step threats are elaborated to risks. Each risk evaluates a threat in the context of a model element, an attached security requirement and relevant security controls. This means that we only consider threats related to security requirements. Moreover, the evaluation is based on the current set of related security controls. For the evaluation itself we use a qualitative approach estimating the probability and the impact of the damage. For an approach which uses key figures for evaluating risks we refer to (Breu, Innerhofer-Oberperfler, & Yautsiukhin, 2008).

Case Study: Threat and Risk Analysis

In our case study we have made extensive use of the German Baseline Protection Manual (BSI, 2004) to elaborate the list of threats. Some of the security requirements were already very explicit and required just a reformulation of the requirements on its contrary to derive the threat.

For other security requirements a detailed list of several threats was identified. As an example

Table 2. Example list of security requirements

Security Requirement	Model Element
SR1: completeness of the health record	Virtual health record
SR2: no unauthorized altering or changing of information	All information objects
SR3: synchronized time-basis	All information objects
SR4: health documents must be assigned correctly to patients	Virtual health record

consider the list of threats in Table 3 for the security requirement *"SR1: completeness of the health record"*. The threat *"TH1: missing or incomplete test and release mechanisms"* describes the scenario that potential changes to the system may cause problems due to inadequate testing procedures.

The threats of Table 3 were identified in a similar bottom-up and top-down approach as the security requirements. Each of those threats was evaluated with a probability and impact level. For example, for the threat "missing or incomplete test and release mechanism" both values were set to high by the responsible domain experts. In the case study we have used a qualitative risk assessment approach based on three classes (low, medium, high). The risk assessment was done in workshops with the domain experts.

Security Control Engineering

In the final step of the micro-process, the security controls are chosen and documented in the security information network. Generally, security control engineering is a complex task ranging from the choice of appropriate countermeasures (including alternatives), their correctness check, analysis of cost effectiveness compared to the reduction of risks, analysis of remaining threats and the whole procurement and roll-out process.

At this place we only consider the small part of documenting implemented security controls. Each security control is related to the set of risks it reduces. Consequently, the risks have to be re–evaluated which means that the states of the related risks are re–set to pending and this state change is propagated up in the dependency graph as described above.

Case Study: Security Controls

In the case study we first identified existing controls that already addressed identified threats. For risks which were not yet mitigated new controls were proposed. Table 4 lists examples for security controls for the risk *"missing or incomplete test-and release mechanisms"*. The security controls which were proposed were taken from industry best practices like ISO 27002 (ISO, 2005).

With this new installed security controls the probability of each risk was re-evaluated by the domain experts. Comparing the risk assessment

Table 3. Sample Threats for SR1: completeness of the health record

Threat
TH1: missing or incomplete test and release mechanisms
TH2: errors in encrypted data
TH3: software errors
TH4: damaged database integrity
TH5: loss of stored data

Table 4. Sample Controls for the threat (TH1: missing or incomplete test- and release mechanisms)

Security Controls
SC1: stepwise deployment
SC2: system and integration tests
SC3: UNIT tests

before (first matrix) and after (second matrix) installing the security controls the quality and effectiveness of your controls (cf. Figure 10) can be estimated. The estimation of the risk reducing effect of a security control is based on the qualitative judgments of the domain experts.

RELATED WORK

Our work is based on our experiences in the field of Model-Based Security Engineering. In (Breu, Burger, Hafner, & Popp, 2004) and (Innerhofer-Oberperfler & Breu, 2006) we defined a software process integrating aspects of security. The approach presented in this paper reuses some of the core artifacts and the security meta-model of this security process but focuses on service oriented systems. In (Hafner, Agreiter, Breu, & Nowak, 2006) we presented SECTET, a framework for Model-Driven Configuration of Security-Critical B2B-Workflows. In this paper we rely on the SEC-TET model views but focus on security analysis rather than on software construction.

The OCTAVE (Alberts & Dorofee, 2002) method uses a three phase approach to identify and manage information security risks. This comprises the identification of critical assets, threat analysis and security strategy planning. OCTAVE provides strong support for the overall process and management aspects whereas our approach focuses on the systematic integration of modeling artifacts and security analysis. In this respect OCTAVE could perfectly be used complementarily to our approach in the sense that it describes many useful mechanisms and methods to gather and structure security relevant information in an organization which could be fed in our security analysis process and in our models.

An approach that is following a model-based risk analysis is CORAS (den Braber, Hogganvik, Lund, Stølen, & Vraalsen, 2007). CORAS uses UML models mainly for descriptive purposes to foster communication and interaction during the risk analysis process. A strength of CORAS is the underlying methodological foundation, like Failure Trees, Event Trees, HazOp and Failure Mode Effect Analysis (FMEA), that help to identify vulnerabilities and threats. To depict identified assets, sources of threats and threats CORAS uses adapted diagrams inspired by UML. Our method uses text-based representation of threats and security requirements but supports a security

Figure 10. Risk assessment before and after deployment of controls

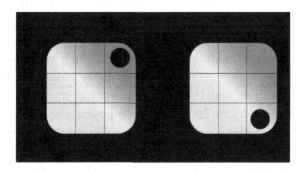

analysis process driven by the functional system properties.

Blobel and Roger-France (Blobel & Roger-France, 2001) developed an approach to design and analyze secure health information systems. They identified abstract use cases and security concepts present in such scenarios. They also follow a modular approach and provide abstract solutions for security services that can be combined to build more complex architectures. That way they provide useful blueprints to implement security services in a health information system. Our method differs in the respect that we focus much more on the underlying process and the conceptual and methodological issues related with the identification and analysis of security properties and risks inherent in a distributed health care network.

Fernandez et al. (Fernandez et al., 2007) extend their methodology to build secure systems based on security patterns covering the complete lifecycle in the style of the Rational Unified Process. In the requirements stage, security constraints are indicated in use cases, threats pertaining to specific workflow activities are identified in workflows related to use cases, and finally mitigating policies derived. The resulting conceptual models go as input into the design stage, where the engineering process is driven by architectural decisions based decision trees incorporating security concerns. The idea of this approach is similar to some extend to the SECTET approach, nevertheless – focusing on engineering aspects - it falls short on elaborating the methodological side of security analysis and risk management as when compared to ProSeccO. ProSeccO explicitly takes into account the specific needs of security-critical SOA systems through its two key concepts modularity and traceability.

Model based security engineering with UML was initially coined by Jürjens (Jürjens 2005). UMLSec supports security engineering based on UML models. It essentially provides tool-support for the analysis of UML models against security

requirements at a very technical level. The verication framework supports the construction of automated security analysis tools for UML diagrams. Behavioral UMLsec diagrams are translated to formulas in first-order logic which form the input for a theorem prover. Security analysis is confined to attacks against protocols and hence very formal and technical as opposed to the approach pursued by ProSecO aiming at security analysis and risk management in context of business objectives, basically less amenable to a formal analysis. Complementing ProSeco at the technical level on the formal side, UMLSec could be a very valuable complement to our approach. Applicability of UMLSec was demonstrated in context of an existing health information system (Jürjens & Rumm 2008), where a model-based security analysis was conducted on the German Health Card architecture and revealed some weaknesses in protocol style transactions between stakeholders. Again, this example displays the potential of UMLSec to be a valuable complement to our approach by supporting formal security analysis.

The closest to our approach is PWSSec (Gutiérrez et al 2006). PWSSec is a development process claiming to support the methodological sound development of Web services based systems starting from the business perspective. Like our approach, it supports an iterative and incremental development that supports the integration of security into Web services based systems at every stage of the development process. PWSSec covers three stages (security requirements specification, security architecture specification, and security technology). The requirements stage encompasses activities like elicitation, analysis, specification and validation of the software security requirements. Being work in progress these activities are partly based on existing methodologies or incorporate standards like OCTAVE (elicitation), composition scenarios (analysis), and SIREN (specification). A repository with security requirement templates and attack patterns supports the requirements engineering process. Similar to our approach PWSSec focuses on the traceability of requirements, architectures and solutions related to security. In addition PWSSec addresses the issue of reusability of security requirements, architectures and solutions by following a pattern based approach based on a specific Web Service Security reference architecture that the authors of PWSSec have defined. In comparison our approach is more general and focuses on a systematic analysis of any type of architecture of service oriented systems.

CONCLUSION

In the preceding sections we presented basic concepts and requirements of a framework for security analysis targeted to Service Oriented Systems. The case study which was used to describe the framework and the process of security analysis is stemming from the health care domain. The framework focuses on:

- the tight integration of security analysis with the functional view of the system
- the support of modularity concerning the chosen system context, level of abstraction and security aspects

Our approach allows analyzing the more abstract global model of a Service Oriented Systems and the different local implementations separately. By modeling the Global and Local Functional Model accordingly we provide an integrated model of the Service Oriented Systems that provides a mechanism of traceability of Security Objectives, their related Security Requirements and the associated Threats representing Risks. By partitioning the model in different domains, we provide the means for a distributed and concurrent analysis of the separate parts of a Service Oriented System.

Since we mostly presented the state of current research there are further open issues that have to be solved in future work, in particular concerning

- support of health care applications through reference models (e.g. organizational models of hospitals) and security patterns (e.g. compliance objectives, threats and business requirements)
- development of propagation rules for security related model elements along the dependencies of the Functional Model (e.g. Security Requirements of the Workflow View propagating to Security Requirements of the Application View)
- support for checking the state of a Security Model (e.g. concerning missing elements, consistency of the security related model elements)
- traceability of security related model elements (e.g. retrieving the technical threats related with a security requirement of a superior business model element)
- safeguards planning and evaluation
- information aggregation and report generation

Both the development of our method and future tool support are accompanied by our activities in the Austrian project health@net where our task is to develop and to realize security concepts for a national virtual distributed health record.

REFERENCES

Alam, M., Hafner, M., & Breu, R. (2008). Constraint based role based access control in the SECTET-framework. *Journal of Computer Security, 16*(2), 223–260.

Alberts, C., & Dorofee, A. (2002). *Managing information security risks: the OCTAVE approach.* Upper Saddle River, NJ: Pearson Education.

Bishop, M. (2003). *Computer Security: Art and Science*. Reading, MA: Addison-Wesley Professional.

Blobel, B., & Roger-France, F. (2001). A systematic approach for analysis and design of secure health information systems. *International Journal of Medical Informatics, 62*(1), 51–78. doi:10.1016/S1386-5056(01)00147-2

Breu, R., Burger, K., Hafner, M., & Popp, G. (2004). Towards a Systematic Development of Secure Systems. *Information Systems Security, 13*(3), 5–13. doi:10.1201/1086/44530.13.3.20040701/83064.2

Breu, R., Hafner, M., Innerhofer-Oberperfler, F., & Wozak, F. (2008). Model-Driven Security Engineering of Service Oriented Systems. In R. Kaschek, C. Kop, C. Steinberger, & G. Fliedl (Eds.), *Information Systems and e-Business Technologies,* (pp. 59-71). Berlin: Springer.

Breu, R., Innerhofer-Oberperfler, F., Mitterer, M., Schabetsberger, T., & Wozak, F. (2008). Model-Based Security Analysis of Health Care Networks. In *Proc. eHealth2008* (pp. 93-100). Vienna, Austria: OCG.

Breu, R., Innerhofer-Oberperfler, F., & Yautsiukhin, A. (2008). Quantitative assessment of enterprise security system. International Workshop on Privacy and Assurance. In *Proceedings of the The Third International Conference on Availability, Reliability and Security, ARES 2008*, March 4-7, 2008, Technical University of Catalonia, Barcelona, Spain (pp. 921-928). Washington, DC: IEEE Computer Society.

BSI. (2004). *IT Baseline Protection Manual*. Retrieved 11 21, 2008, from http://www.bsi.bund.de/english/gshb/index.htm

Carter, S. (2007). *The New Language of Business: SOA & Web 2.0*. Armonk, NY: IBM Press.

DCSSI Advisory Office. (2005). *EBIOS - Expression of Needs and Identification of Security Objectives*. Retrieved 11 21, 2008, http://www.ssi.gouv.fr/en/confidence/ebiospresentation.html den Braber, F., Hogganvik, I., Lund, M., Stølen, K., & Vraalsen, F. (2007). Model-based security analysis in seven steps-a guided tour to the CORAS method. *BT Technology Journal, 25*(1), 101-117.

European Commission. (2005). *eEurope 2005*. Retrieved November 21, 2008, from http://ec.europa.eu/information_society/eeurope/2005/

Fernandez, E. B., Cholmondeley, P., & Zimmermann, O. (2007). Extending a Secure System Development Methodology to SOA. In *DEXA '07: Proceedings of the 18th International Conference on Database and Expert, 2007*. Regensburg, Germany: IEEE Computer Society.

Firesmith, D. (2003). Engineering Security Requirements. *Journal of Object Technology, 2*(1), 53–68.

Gutiérrez, C., Fernández-Medina, E., & Piattini, M. (2006). PWSSec: Process for Web Services Security. In *IEEE International Conference on Web Services 2006*, Chicago, USA.

Hafner, M., Agreiter, B., Breu, R., & Nowak, A. (2006). SECTET - An Extensible Framework for the Realization of Secure Inter-Organizational Workflows. *Internet Research, 16*(5), 491–506. doi:10.1108/10662240610710978

Hafner, M., & Breu, R. (2008). *Security Engineering for Service oriented Architectures*. Berlin: Springer.

IHE. (2006, November). *IT Infrastructure Technical Framework*. Retrieved November 21, 2008, from http://www.ihe.net/Technical_Framework/

Innerhofer-Oberperfler, F., & Breu, R. (2006). Using an enterprise architecture for it risk management. In *Proceedings of the ISSA 2006 Conference*, Johannesburg, South Africa.

ISO. (2005). *ISO/IEC 15408:2005 Information technology -- Security techniques -- Evaluation criteria for IT security* (Common Criteria).

ISO. (2005). ISO/IEC 27001:2005 - Information technology -- Security techniques -- Information security management systems -- Requirements.

ISO. (2005). ISO/IEC 27002:2005 - Information technology -- Code of practice for information security management.

Jürjens, J. (2005b). Sound methods and effective tools for model-based security engineering with UML. In *Software engineering, ICSE 2005*.

Jürjens, J., & Rumm, R. (2008). Model-Based security analysis of the german health card architecture. *Methods of Information in Medicine, 47*(5), 409–416.

Marks, E. (2008). *Service-Oriented Architecture (SOA) Governance for the Services Driven Enterprise*. New York: Wiley.

Marks, E., & Bell, M. (2006). *Service-Oriented Architecture: A Planning and Implementation Guide for Business and Technology*. Hoboken, NJ: John Wiley & Sons.

NICTIZ. (n.d.). *National IT Institute for Healthcare in the Netherlands*. Retrieved 11 21, 2008, from http://www.nictiz.nl/

OMG. (2009). *Business Process Modeling Notation (BPMN) Information*. Retrieved January 6, 2009, from http://www.bpmn.org/

Peltier, T. (2001). *Information security risk analysis*. Boca Raton, FL: Auerbach.

Ramsaroop, P., & Ball, M. (2000). The Bank of Health: A Model for More Useful Patient records. *M.D. Computing, 17*(4), 45–48.

Schabetsberger, T., Ammenwerth, E., Breu, R., Hoerbst, A., Goebel, G., & Penz, R. (2006). E-Health Approach to Link-up Actors in the Health Care System of Austria. *Studies in Health Technology and Informatics*, (124): 415–420.

Shabo, A. (2006). A Global Socio-Economic-Medico-Legal Model for the Sustainability of Longitudinal Electronic Health Records. Part 1. *Methods of Information in Medicine, 45*(3), 240–245.

Web Service Security Specifications. (n.d.). Retrieved from http://www.oasis-open.org/

Weblayers. (2005). *Whitepaper: SOA Governance*, (pp. 9).

Wozak, F., Ammenwerth, E., Breu, M., Penz, R., Schabetsberger, T., Vogl, R., et al. (2006). Medical Data GRIDs as approach towards secure cross enterprise document sharing (based on IHE XDS). *Ubiquity: Technologies for Better Health in Aging Societies: Proc. MIE2006*, (pp. 377-383). Amsterdam: IOS Press.

XACML 2.0 Specification. (n.d.). Retrieved from http://oasis-open.org/

Section 2
Web Services Security Architectures

Chapter 3

Ontology–Based Authorization Model for XML Data in Distributed Systems

Amit Jain
University of South Carolina, USA

Csilla Farkas
University of South Carolina, USA

ABSTRACT

This research work proposes a Semantic-Aware Authorization Framework, called SAAF, for applying syntax independent authorization on eXtensible Markup Language (XML) documents. Our model supports secure data sharing in an open environment without the need for a centralized authority and supports application flexibility. We propose the use of data and application semantics, expressed as Resource Description Framework (RDF) ontologies, to specify security requirements for XML documents. XML documents are associated with their semantics (RDF ontologies) via mappings. The authors use these mappings and the corresponding RDF authorizations models to generate access control permissions for the mapped XML documents. The SAAF ensures the preservation of authorization permissions on XML data even if the syntax and the structure of the data are changed. Their method also aids the detection and removal of inconsistent authorizations on structurally different but semantically similar XML data.

INTRODUCTION

The rapid increase in the number of intelligent and autonomous technologies to support Internet usage created the need to represent web data and application semantics in a machine understandable way. Web data, used by humans and automated tools, exist in heterogeneous format in a distributed and open environment. Frequently, data and application

semantics are embedded in the syntax and structure of the data. While such indirect representation of semantics is usually understandable for humans, it is not the case for automated tools. Moreover, security policies that are expressed over a specific representation of the data may not be applicable if the syntax or the structure is modified. Web Services (WS), Service Oriented Architecture (SOA), and the Semantic Web are the state-of-the-art technologies supporting this distributed and open data and application paradigm. Ontologies are the building blocks

DOI: 10.4018/978-1-60566-950-2.ch003

of these technologies, providing a methodology to represent domain information and semantics in a machine understandable way. Using ontologies, syntactic data representations (such as the eXtensible Markup Language (XML), stream data, or unstructured data) can be associated with the corresponding data semantics. This enables the software applications and autonomous agents to understand and process the data intelligently without any human intervention or the need to hard code application specific semantics. WS are distributed Web applications, interacting with each other over the internet. They form a crucial component of SOA. WS operate and interact according to a set of published standards. These standards provide a way of developing decoupled software modules. Then the applications can share and process data among themselves irrespective of the heterogeneity of used languages, platforms or technologies. Current trends of Web applications indicate that WS will become a fundamental technology for Web-based applications. Web Services use XML as the basic format for data exchange. To provide security for WS applications, industry and standards committees, such as W3C and OASIS, have developed a set of standards. Security standards for XML formatted data are a fundamental component of these standards. Most of the XML security standards, however, use the syntactic and structural aspects of the XML. For example, XML access control models apply authorizations on the XML data syntax and fail to focus on the data and application semantics embedded in the syntax and structure. This can cause any change in XML format to deem the original security details invalid.

Let's consider a data sharing scenario between a Health Care Provider and an Insurance company in a Health Care domain illustrated in Figure 1. Both parties keep information about the patients in their own databases and exchange XML structured documents using WS. Here XML_1 is the message created by the Health care provider with the information pulled from its database. XML_2 represents the structure used by the Insurance Company to store the data for the shared nodes. The two XML trees have the same data but they differ in their syntax and structure. Currently authorization policies for these documents would be defined based on their syntax and structure. An access control policy for a patient data may require that a subject John is not permitted to read the illness information of the patients. Expressing this requirement would use different XPath expressions in the two XML documents. For example, element Patient/MedicalData/Illness in XML_1 may be represented as Patient/Data/HealthRecords/Diagnosis in the XML structure created by the Insurance Company (XML_2). The Web Service (WS_2) receiving the XML_1 would not know the semantics of the data and it may store and disseminate the information as XML_2. Hence the incoming XML data document is restructured and stored conforming to the target schema. This may results in accidental or intentional downgrade of for the data node "Illness" (i.e., changed from -ve to +ve access or from TopSecret to Public). In the case of a complex business workflow using WS, similar situations may arise. Furthermore, the current access control model will not be satisfactory for dynamic Web Service compositions. These compositions typically create business partners on the fly. Also periodically any of the partners may make changes to their respective storage schema for the shared data. This may also lead to inconsistent security policies that are hard to detect. As the enterprises are moving toward producing and sharing a large amount of data, leakage of sensitive data may occur very frequently. The developers of the policies must agree and incorporate data semantics to apply consistent security policies over different structured versions. Currently no automatic verification can be performed to verify that semantically equivalent components have the same access control requirements.

This research work presents a Semantic-Aware Authorization Framework (SAAF) for providing access control for RDF ontological data and

Figure 1. XML schema trees with structural and policies difference

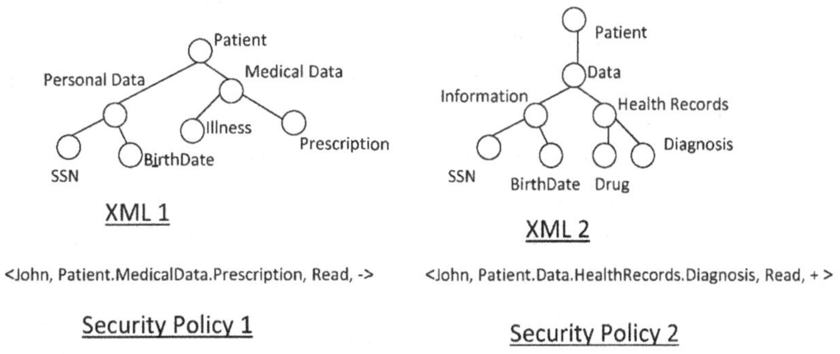

XML 1

<John, Patient.MedicalData.Prescription, Read, ->

Security Policy 1

XML 2

<John, Patient.Data.HealthRecords.Diagnosis, Read, + >

Security Policy 2

semantically annotated XML data in a syntax independent way. SAAF contains an access control model for RDF ontologies. It also consists of a data mapping method that provides the XML to RDF correspondences to semantically enhance the structural (XML) Web data. Then using these correspondences, security permissions can be provided on the XML data by deriving access control permissions from RDF authorizations. This approach removes the dependence of authorization model on data structure and syntax. By using RDF data for expressing data and application semantics, distributed applications, can be enabled to securely process heterogeneous data. This method also allows the expression of security needs of the data and applications on the metadata in a global and syntax independent manner. Automatic verification of the authorizations can also be carried out by mapping the authorizations from meta-data to the mapped Web data such as XML.

The organization of the chapter is as follows. We start with a technological background followed by the description of the research problems being targeted in this research work. The next section gives a summary of the related work. The architecture of our framework is presented in the subsequent section. The main technical contributions of the proposed Semantic Aware Authorization Framework (SAAF) are presented after our framework. Readers not interested in

the technical details may skip this section. After the technical details, we discuss future research directions. We conclude in the last section.

BACKGROUND

This section gives a brief background on the technologies behind open Web paradigms such as Web Services, Semantic Web and data authorization models.

SOA and Web Services

SOA or Service Oriented Architecture is an architectural style which allows for the modularization of software functionalities. Using this style, applications can have a loose coupling irrespective of the development platform. This provides the agility in software applications and exposes the functionality as services. Web Services utilize SOA to provide application interaction over the Web. Web Services Description Language (WSDL) (Chinnici, Moreau, Ryman, & Weerawarana, 2006), Universal Description Discovery Integration (UDDI) (Clement, Hately, Riegen, & Rogers, 2005) and Simple Object Access Protocol (SOAP) (Gudgin, Hadley, Mendelsohn, Moreau, & Nielsen, 2003) are the published standards that are used for implementing Web Services. WSDL describes the input output parameters, required request format and other constraints for using a Web Service. UDDI standard allows the listing of Web Services on a registry. This way Web Services providing a service can be discovered by other applications. Finally SOAP defines how the information in the form of structured XML messages can be exchanges by Web Services. This allows the sharing of data, metadata, and security details such as signatures among Web applications.

Semantic Web and Ontologies

Semantic Web vision follows the establishment of World Wide Web and aims to enable data production and consumption in an automatic and intelligent manner. To accomplish this goal, data is annotated with its meaning (semantics). The semantics are published in the form of domain ontology. The Resource Description Framework (RDF) (Klyne & Carroll, 2004) is an ontology modeling language. RDF uses an abstract syntax for specifying the classes (concepts) and their inter-relationships..

Authorization Models for Web Data

Authorization models allow the specification of access permissions on data and information. They can be broadly categorized into three kinds of models.

1. DAC: Discretionary Access Control (DAC) model enables the owner of a resource to specify access permissions for the users over the resource. The actions can be read, write, execute, delete or any combination of these.
2. MAC: Mandatory Access Control (MAC) model reaches an access control decision by comparing the security labels of the user requesting an access to the security label of the resources being requested. The

most widely used MAC model is the Bell-LaPadula model, supporting confidentiality. Different mechanisms have been developed for comparison considering different system properties.
3. RBAC: Role Based Access Control (RBAC) model supports the expression of authorization methods based on organizational roles. Users may have several roles within an organization. Each role is associated with a set of permissions over the organizational resources.

Detailed description of the above access control models and their formal properties are given in earlier research work on access control (Ravi S. Sandhu, 1994; Sandhu, Coyne, Feinstein, & Youman, 1996). An authorization system usually uses either one of the above three models or their combinations. Our authorization model presented in this work is not tied to any one of the above. It can be used with any one of the access controls mechanisms. Our main focus is to provide a method of defining the security objects as presented in the following section.

RESEARCH PROBLEM DESCRIPTION

This section presents the detailed description of the research problem that we have targeted in this research work.

XML Evolution as Data Interchange Standard

Before the advent of XML, the data needed to be converted back and forth into the required formats by the sender and recipient. Development of XML as the de facto data interchange and storage format has eased this problem. This has enabled the wide sharing of data across heterogeneously distributed applications. The shared data is either retrieved from an XML database or an XML view of the information pulled from non-XML databases (relational, object oriented or flat files). At one hand XML usage eases the data and application interoperability problem. On the other hand it does bring up some problems from security perspective. More specifically some of the security problems that arise due to XML usage in data exchange in open environments and have been addressed in this research work can be coarsely divided into the following components:

- Addressing the problem of XML Web data security dependence on syntax and structure
- Developing mappings from XML to RDF to represent data and application semantics
- Developing authorization model for RDF

Problem of XML Security Reliance on Syntax

A crucial aspect for wide adaptation of Web based open and distributed architecture would be the secure data sharing among the interacting application and business entities. This means that the intended access control permissions on the originating data are honored by the interacting parties. Currently, XML data is secured using standard XML security techniques such as XML encryption (Boyer, Eastlake, & Reagle, 2002), XML digital signatures (Eastlake & Reagle, 2002) and XML access control models (Bertino, Castano, Ferrari, & Mesiti, 2000; Damiani, Vimercati, Paraboschi, & Samarati, 2002; Kudo & Hada, 2000) based on XML syntax and structure. Many XML security recommendations, such as SAML (Cahill & Hughes, 2005), SOAP message security (Nadalin, Kaler, Phillip, & Monzillo, 2004), and XACML (Moses, 2005) have been developed by the standard organizations and industry players, underlining the importance for XML data security in achieving high-assurance Web-based application security. However, because these methods rely on syntax and structure of protected XML document to provide access control, they can be bypassed by tampering the syntax and structure of the XML document.

Consider the Health Care System example that we have discussed in the Introduction. WS are used to support the communication between the participants, see Figure 2. The security requirement is that the access control restrictions of the shared data items must be preserved during and after sharing. Let's assume that the Insurance Company receives data from the Health Providers. The Insurance Company formats the data according to its own database schema, and assigns the locally established security classifications to the stored data items. However, the local security restriction over the shared data is less restrictive than the original security requirements. This clearly violates the security requirements that each party maintains the security requirements of the data originator. Such a violation can only be detected if the data semantics is understood and used to compare security policies.

A possible approach to ensure that security requirements of the local databases are preserved during and after the transmission is to use XML access control over the XML formatted message between the Web Services. However, using XML Access Control to secure shared XML data is not straight forward. Assume that each local database is stored in XML format. The XML data structures, XML_1 and XML_2 corresponding to the Health Care Provider and Insurance Company databases respectively, are shown in Figure 3. During data sharing, only partial data are retrieved from the provider database and is inserted into the shared message. Let's assume that the authorization policies on the shared data are sent along with the actual data. Protection needs of the original nodes of these databases cannot be expressed using XPATH expressions by identifying nodes of the XML message. For example, the patient name in the XML_1 is identified by Patients/Record/ Name. However, such path does not exist in the

Figure 2. Web service data sharing scenario

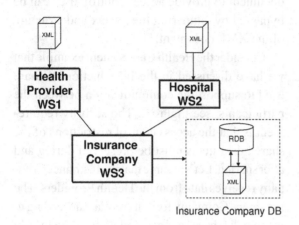

Insurance Company DB

message M_1 from the Health Care Provider to the insurance company as shown in figure (All namespaces, some headers and some body parts have been omitted for clarity). Also no such path exists in the database of the Insurance Company, XML_2. Moreover, the wild cards can not be used to identify all nodes with tag "Name" because there are different security needs for the names of the patients and names of physicians. This example shows a very optimistic scenario where some identification name is given to the tags or nodes of the shared XML messages. Very often the tag names for XML nodes may not be very meaningful and may contain names such as *g1, n1, t1*, etc. Since this syntax is perfectly valid according to the XML validation rules, the originating application would be able to process the XML with non-meaningful names. Using non-informative tag names may create a problem when there are multiple partners, such as in case of dynamic Web Services. So an administrator or a new data sharing partner, not aware of the meaning of the data tags may apply incorrect security labels. The situation to formulate the security policy can even be further complicated if the messages or databases use different tag names. For example if the tag <title> is used instead of <name> in

the Insurance Company database, it may lead to further security violations.

Several XML access control models have been developed (Damiani et al., 2002), (Bertino et al., 2000), (Kudo & Hada, 2000) to provide controlled accesses to XML formatted data. However, XML access control models are based on XML syntactic constructs without incorporating data or application semantics. The research problem that we faced here was: *Is it possible to find a standardized way to express the intended semantics of XML to be used for inter-operation and security (authorization) in open environments?*

XML-RDF Mapping Problem

One of the ways the applications processing XML data with different syntax and structure can understand its meaning is, by associating XML with its semantics represented by RDF ontologies. Several research works on semantic integration of heterogeneous systems aims to integrate data, which has similar meaning but different structures and terminologies. Mappings are created between those information sources for querying, integration and inter-operation. There are many research works that have tried to address this problem for providing querying access to disparate data available in heterogeneous formats. Some of these approaches (Lenzerini, 2002; Rahm & Bernstein, 2001) vary from structural matching, contextual matching, linguistic matching to heuristics. These mapping define how each component of XML document is associated with a component of the domain ontology. Using these mappings the security on ontology data can then be derived to create access control restrictions for XML data. This approach still provides the flexibility of enforcing authorizations using any existing XML authorization model. However usage of this method enables a uniform way of enforcing security permissions on XML data, shared in a domain using existing techniques. Hence our research objective here is:

Figure 3. Health provider & insurance company XML databases

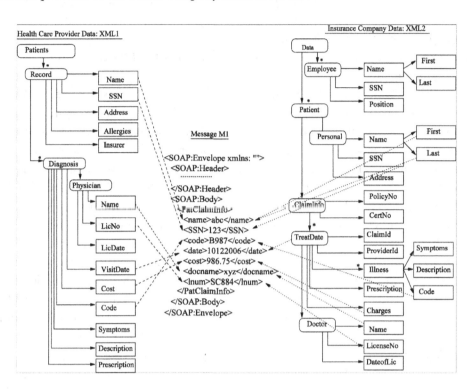

How to use the XML-RDF mappings to enforce security policies from RDF domain ontologies to secure XML data in a syntax independent way?

RDF Ontology Security Problem

Using RDF ontologies for describing semantics of associated XML data does require that RDF ontologies be assigned access control permissions in accordance with the intended authorizations on the XML data. While the existing XML security models provide fine grained authorization frameworks, the identification of the protection objects is based on XML syntax and structure only. For example lets consider an access control permission <John,/PatInfo/name,Read,+> using an existing XML access control model on the message M_1 shown in Figure 3. Here actor John is authorized to read the XML node "name", which is the child node of the root node "PatInfo". If during the data restructuring at the message destination,

node "name" is moved to another location in the document, this authorization deems invalid and ineffective in securing the newly structured XML data. So the existing authorization models may be sufficient for XML documents, they are not satisfactory for RDF for several reasons. First, the same RDF statement can be represented in several different syntactic ways (see Figure 4 for an example). This requires that different XML access control policies must be developed for each XML representation. Second, new RDF statements may be generated from the explicitly stored ones via RDF and RDFS entailments. XML syntax based access control may not be able to determine the appropriate classification of the entailed data. In addition there may be requirements that several XML nodes need to be applied associated security permission together. So either all or none of them are revealed to the user based on the user security clearance. XML access control models use XPath (Clark & DeRose, 2006) to define protection objects in XML tree. An existing data item may be inferred with a different path than existing one. To determine whether the two given XML nodes represent the same entity and if they have the different security requirements is ambiguous.

To apply security requirements on XML data based on the associated data semantics, we need a method to express access control requirements on RDF. RDF is a syntax independent ontology modeling language. Currently there are no existing access control models that can secure RDF data while considering its syntax independent model and inferencing capabilities. Here our research motivation is: *How can we express security requirements for RDF ontology data such that it is syntax independent, flexible and incorporates entailment?*

RELATED WORK

XML Security

XML is the primary standard for data exchange and storage across the applications today. There is a wide variety of research work done on XML security. Several XML access control models have been proposed (Bertino et al., 2000; Damiani et al., 2002; Kudo & Hada, 2000) to provide authorizations on XML formatted data. These models provide fine grained authorization frameworks, with different varying specifications such that the identification of the protection objects is based on XML syntax and structure. However, XML access control models are based on XML syntactic constructs without incorporating data or application semantics. Even though some of the models consider XML Schema to provide security on the valid XML documents, XML Schema dictates the structure of the XML document and does not inculcate the semantics of the XML content. Authorizations defined for a particular XML document would not work for another XML, with different structure and syntax, even if both documents correspond to the same original data.

Semantic Web Security

There are some works that define the security for Semantic Web ontologies. Qin and Atluri in (Qin & Atluri, 2003) propose a concept-level access control for Web data, where access control is defined on ontological concepts and instances of these concepts inherit the access control of the concepts they belong to. Their model also incorporates the relationships supported by the ontology. Finin et al (Reddivari, Finin, & Joshi, 2007) proposed a policy based access control model for RDF data in an RDF store. Their model provides control over the different action modes supported by the RDF store. RDF Store allows defining actions such as inserting a set of triples into the store, deleting a triple, and querying whether or not a triple is in the store. Dietzold and Auer in (Dietzold & Auer, 2006) propose another access control model for RDF Triple stores. Their model allows the specification of custom rules that can be used for securing access to the store. However, these models do not support the expression of authorization policies over RDF data triples. Kaushik et al. (Kaushik, Wijesekera, & Ammann, 2005) propose a logic based policy language for securing full or partial ontologies. While these methods can be applied to RDF databases, they do not consider RDFS and RDF entailments. These authorizations are used to provide access control over annotated Web data. Hence while extensional RDF data can be secured using these models, illegal inferences can be made, thus making the security ineffective. There is no work that addresses the access control needs of RDF data.

Semantic Integration

Information integration and inter-operation aims to integrate data in a domain having similar mean-

Figure 4. Two different XML Representation of the same RDF Statement

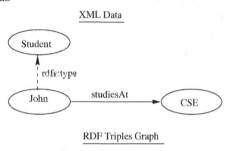

```
<rdf:Description rdf:about="http://www.cse.sc.edu/research/isl/racl#John">
    <racl:studiesAt rdf:resource="http://www.cse.sc.edu/research/isl/racl#CSE"/
    <rdfs:type rdf:resource="http://www.cse.sc.edu/research/isl/racl#Student"/>
</rdf:Description>

<racl:Student rdf:about="http://www.cse.sc.edu/research/isl/racl#John">
    <racl:studiesAt rdf:resource="http://www.cse.sc.edu/research/isl/racl#CSE"/
</racl:Student>
```

XML Data

RDF Triples Graph

ing but different structures and terminologies. It enables the creation of mappings between the disparate sources of data. Then a query on one data source should be able to search and retrieve information from another source if it contains the pertinent information. The inter schema relationships usually include an initial step of schema matching. This involves comparing the involved schemas and instances and creates correspondences between them. Several different approaches have been proposed for schema matching.

Mell and Heuser (Santos Mello & Heuser, 2005) present a bottom up approach for integrating XML data sources using ontologies. Their model integrates the local DTDs using mapping rules to create a local schema as a conceptual canonical representation for every DTD. It unifies all of these conceptual models to create a global schema for all of these models, giving an integrated view of all the represented XMLs in the domain. Based on the use of XML to convey application specific semantics, there are some engineering based works that target the induction of data semantics in XML. Authors in (Ferdinand, Zirpins, & Trastour, 2004) define XML to RDF and XML schema to OWL mappings. Both of these mappings are independent of each other. Their approach uses a set of mapping rules such as converting each xsd:complexType into an owl:Class and xsd:simpleType into an owl:DataTypeProperty. Authors in (Reif, Gall, & Jazayeri, 2005) present an automatic engineering method to map XML to RDF data and a Java module for this purpose. But they do not specify the mapping rules from XML to RDF. Framework in (Bohring & Auer, 2005) presents a set of XML to OWL conversion rules. Their proposal includes the data flow where XSD and XML are converted into OWL model and OWL instances respectively. They have also developed a tool called XML2OWL to implement their approach which creates an XSLT script to generate OWL model and instances from XML.

Web Services, Semantics and Security

With the wide usage of Web Services, several industry players and standard organizations have teamed up to recommend security standards for them. SOAP message security (Nadalin et al., 2004), SAML (Cahill & Hughes, 2005), XACML (Moses, 2005) have been developed along this goal. Specifications such as (Della-Libera et al., 2005; Web Service Enhancements (WSE 3.0), 2005) are some other initiatives taken by organizations such as IBM, Verisign, Microsoft to develop policy languages for WS security. WS SOAP message security (Nadalin et al., 2004) has security headers included in the soap messages providing information about the integrity and confidentiality etc. It provides SOAP message security through message integrity, and message confidentiality. Signatures, hash and encrypted message computed over the message are included in the SOAP message. This provides confidentiality, and integrity to the exchanged data in SOAP messages. WS security policy (Della-Libera et al., 2005) provides XML syntax for declarative security policies, determining which message parts must be present, signed, or encrypted.

Semantic Web Service seeks to include the semantics in Web Service life cycle for automatic information processing. The Web Services today use the syntactic matching for discovery, matchmaking, advertising and composition. For example a client looking for a travel service would search for keywords related to travel. These keywords are then matched at the Web Service publishing registries such as UDDI for matching service descriptions. Based on the list of available Web Services, a human can then decide which provider closely matches his/her selection criteria and avail the services. The Semantic Web Services framework uses Semantic Web ontologies based matchmaking (Paolucci, Kawamura, Payne, & Sycara, 2002) by making use of DAML-S/OWL-S ontologies. Services can then automate various tasks by getting the relevant semantic information.

Authors in (Denker, Kagal, Finin, Paolucci, & Sycara, 2003; Kagal et al., 2004) have extended semantic matchmaking to include security by proposing several security related ontologies to describe security requirements and capabilities of Web Services. Requesting agents' security requirements and Web Service security capabilities

can then be compared by an ontology reasoning engine to check for the compatibility between the request and the offer. Authors in (Agarwal & Sprick, 2005) define a capability based access control for Web Services. Their framework allows the Web Services to act as certificate authorities by including trust and delegation, removing the need for centralized trust. Though these models try to include semantics in Web Service security, they don't address the syntactic issues in data message security. SOAP messaging is a core component of Web Services. It uses the XML data model for formatting the messages exchanged between the service advertiser, consumer and provider. Being based on XML syntax, SOAP messages are vulnerable to different message integrity attacks such as XML rewriting attacks where XML data syntax can be maliciously altered to bypass security or to tamper the integrity of the message. Some solutions (Bhargavan, Fournet, Gordon, & O'Shea, 2005; Rahaman, Schaad, & Rits, 2006) have been proposed for this. These solutions also use the syntactic data checking to detect the violation of message integrity.

Our proposed framework provides a semantics-based access control model for distributed Web applications. None of the existing XML access control models utilize the semantics to express access control requirements in a syntax independent manner. Even simple modification of data structure would allow a malicious (or careless) user to violate the original access control requirements. Also syntactic variations can make access control in one XML file unusable or incorrect in a different XML structure over the same data. This work incorporates data specific semantics, represented as a conceptual model that is associated with the XML tree, to define access control requirements. The framework uses the existing access control mechanisms for XML data, such as (Bertino et al., 2000), while supporting access control specifications based on data and application semantics (such as RDF). The basis of our work is to"enforce" uniform policy requirements on semantically equivalent but syntactically different XML schema trees in distributed data sharing applications.

SYSTEM ARCHITECTURE

This research work focuses on providing authorization models for the data in open and distributed environments by linking data semantics to a syntactic representation. Restructuring of a shared XML data document may allow an application to change the authorizations on original data items, thus allowing in unauthorized data access. The proposed framework presents a novel method of data security to counter this threat. The framework proposes the addition of semantics to the XML data to detect the changes in authorizations with the change in structure. Usage of semantics provides the enforcement of consistent security permissions for the shared data across the interacting applications. This method incorporates data and application specific semantics, represented as an RDF ontology that is associated with an XML tree, to define access control requirements.

The main focus of this work is to provide security policy for XML using data semantics expressed as RDF rather than using XML syntax. Our earlier paper (Farkas, Jain, Wijesekera, Singhal, & Thuraisingham, 2006) presented our initial idea for this framework. This work also uses our previous results on expressing security policies for RDF (under revision for publishing elsewhere). The main focus of this work here is the components described in technical contribution section.

In this section we give the schematic architecture of the developed framework and briefly explain the components of the framework. Figure 5 shows the architecture for the proposed Semantic-Aware Access Control Model for assigning authorizations on XML documents. Traditionally, the data interchange has been limited to parties that agreed on an exchange protocol prior to

data exchange. XML is widely used to facilitate such exchanges, thus allowing each participant to maintain local databases in an autonomous manner such that the semantics of the exchanged data is hard-coded in the applications. This has limitations in wide distributed systems such as the Web. Applications not knowing each other before hand can not understand and process the data in a truly dynamic and automated way. To support fully autonomous and distributed systems with automatic data interchange and processing, data and applications semantics need to be expressed using a universally adapted tool and language such as RDF. With this motivation the developed framework in this research work can be divided into the following components:

Semantically Enhanced XML Data

In this component of the framework, the mappings from XML schema tree nodes to RDF components are given. We do not suggest a method to discover the mappings between XML data and RDF ontologies in this work. There are several works (see related work section) that have addressed this issue. The mappings have been derived us-

Figure 5. Semantic Access Control Architecture

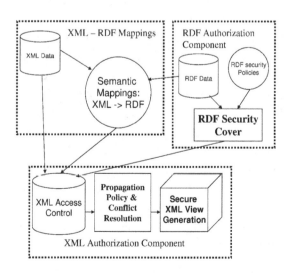

ing one or more processes such as edit distance, Natural Language Processing, linguistic parsing, entity detection, heuristics, or stemming. The approach here provides the flexibility to plug in any mapping derivation or discovery process to generate the mappings between XML and RDF. These mappings are then used to define the correspondences between XML data and its semantics in RDF data, such that they follow the pre-defined mapping properties.

Specification of an Access Control Model for RDF Ontological Data

This architectural component of the framework defines an access control model for RDF and RDF Schema data. The security policies are expressed using the policy patterns such that each pattern represents one or more triples in RDF and RDF schema. Each triple is also associated with a security label following the MAC (Mandatory Access Control) model. The policy is then enforced on the RDF data to compute a materialized view of the labeled data, called security cover. Security cover consists of the pairs of RDF objects to be protected and their respective security labels. The enforcement also takes into account the subsumption of the triples present in the database. Triples at a higher abstract level subsume the more specific triples and hence are at most as secure as the subsumed ones. The security policy also takes into consideration the entailed triples following the RDFS entailment rules. These rules can cause existing data to generate new additional data. If not addressed, this can cause problems in complex and large RDF ontological data. Also generated data needs to be assigned security classification based on the data that generated them. Our RDF authorization model takes entailment into consideration while assigning security. It pre-computes the inferred data and assigns the appropriate security labels to them and merges them into materialized view to create a comprehensive security cover.

Derivation of XML Access Control Policies from RDF Authorizations

Mappings between the XML data and its semantics in RDF data and the access control permissions defined on the RDF ontology components are used to define the access control permissions for XML data. The derived authorizations represent the security permissions on the XML data irrespective of its structure. So if the structure or the syntax of XML tags were to be changed but the meaning remained same, then the derived authorizations would still apply. This security model can be used to check for the change in permissions for semantically similar data items. Any inconsistencies during the change of XML structure can be found and corrected by the security officer. The generated XML access control permissions are derived in the form of a pair where each XML node is associated with a security label using the MAC security model. In case of distributed systems such as Web Services, more sophisticated authorizations may be required and hence the generated pairs

Figure 6. Mappings between XML and RDF ontology in a medical domain

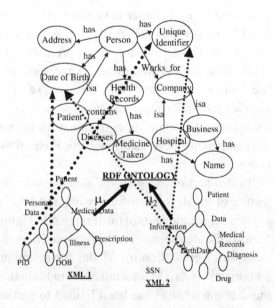

may have to go through some transformations. Additional meta policies for conflict resolution and propagation may be deployed by an access control application dealing with the large XML data documents and schemas.

Using Our Security Model to Solve the Example Problem

Figures 6 and 7 display the application of our security model. They depict how the problem presented in the earlier example can be solved by applying our authorization model. Figure 6 shows the generated mappings between the exchanged XML document and medical domain ontology. These mappings embed the data semantics for XML data nodes. Then Figure 7 depicts the derivation of consistent authorization labels for XML_1 using the mappings between XML and RDF and access control permissions on RDF data ontology. An envisioned data sharing scenario may work like this:

Figure 7. Security Labels Derivation using XML-RDF mappings

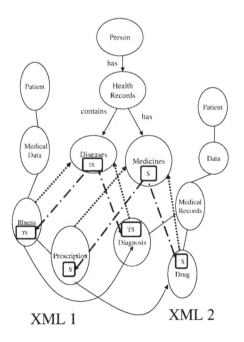

XML 1   XML 2

- The sender uses RDF domain ontologies to define their security preferences.
- The sender generates the XML to RDF mappings M_1.
- Using SAAF, the XML access control policies set XP OL_1 is generated.

The mappings M_1 and the security policies XP OL_1 are then sent along with the XML data. This can be done either by using a separate message or embedding them in the same SOAP message. At the receiver end, the received mappings and security policy are used to make sure that the original authorization permissions are maintained. They can be used to verify that the original access control permissions on the exchanged data are maintained in the following way:

- The mappings M_2 between receiver data format XML_2 and domain ontology are generated.
- Create the correspondences between M_1 and M_2 with respect to the ontology
- Use these correspondences to convert the XP OL_1 into XP OL_2 for XML_2.

TECHNICAL CONTRIBUTION OF SEMANTIC AWARE AUTHORIZATION MODEL

This section presents the main technical contents and contribution of our research work. It presents the main components presented in the architecture, involved algorithms, definitions, theorems and their proofs. Users not interested in the technical details of our framework may skip this section.

Semantically Enhanced XML Data

This section presents the correspondences between an XML document and its semantics expressed by RDF ontology. There are several works that have addressed the issue of mapping XML to RDF and

OWL ontologies for semantic data integration. For example authors in (Ferdinand et al., 2004) provide mapping rules between XML and OWL. Authors in (Battle, 2006) and (Reif et al., 2005) provide engineering tools to convert XML to RDF ontologies. However, these solutions lack the mechanisms we need to guarantee security properties. Irrespective of the methods of the mappings discovery, without the formal definition of the mapping none of the above methods can be used in our framework for providing security. In this work we assume that the semantic associations between the XML document and its metadata (RDF) are known. We define the properties of the mapping that can be used to express these associations explicitly. These mappings provide a formal semantic correspondence layer to be used in any semantic integration framework. In this section, we specify the mappings between XML schema tree and RDF ontology, followed by their properties.

Associations between XML and RDF Data

Definition 1 [XML Schema Tree]: An XML schema tree is a node-labeled directed tree T, defined as defined as (V, E, θ, L), where $v \in V$ is a node in T, $ed(v_1, v_2) \in E$ is a directed and unlabeled edge in T between v_1 and v_2 and θ is a labeling function $\theta(v) = l$, $l \in L$ where L is an infinite set of node names. Given an edge $ed(v_1, v_2)$, v_1 is the parent node of v_2 and similarly v_2 is the child node of v_1. Each node has only one parent.

Intuitively XML schema tree represents the structure of an XML document without some of the XML constraints. It contains both XML elements and attributes, which are represented using XML nodes. Attribute nodes are represented as the sub element nodes and may appear in any order if sub element nodes are already present. Tree nodes contain the XML element and attribute tags but not their values. Also the schema tree does not contain any cardinality, or type constraints. If Ele and Att are the element and attribute sets respec-

tively, then a tree node $v \in Ele \cup Att$. Labeling function θ is injective such that only one XML node is mapped to a label, assigning the node a unique label. We use the XPath (Clark & DeRose, 2006) expressions to uniquely identify the nodes in an XML schema tree. Also we assume that the leaf nodes in the XML schema tree have a built-in datatype to represent the data value and XML data document does not have ID and IDREF values and thus has no loops.

The abstract RDF syntax is a set of triples, which constitute the RDF graph (Klyne & Carroll, 2004). RDF triples include the sets of resources, R, properties, P R, URI references, U, blank nodes, B, Literals, L, and the RDF and RDFS language primitives $CT \in R$. The following holds for these sets: $R = U \cup B$, $P R \subset U$, where P R, B and L are pairwise disjoint.

Definition 2 [RDF Ontology]: An RDF Ontology can be defined as a 4-tuple $(C, P, \delta, \leq)$ where C is a set of class names, P is a set of property names such that $C \in U$, $P \in P R$, $\leq$ is the partial ordering of classes $c_i \in C$ and properties $p_i \in P$, $i = 1, ..., n$ and δ is a mapping of a property $p \in P$ to an ordered pair of classes (c_1, c_2) such that $[\delta: p \rightarrow (c_1, c_2)]$ and $c_1, c_2 \in C$. We call c_1 as the subject and c_2 the object of the property p and $[c_1, p, c_2]$ denotes the RDF triples. RDF is represented in triple format as $[s, p, v]$, where, $s \in C \cup P$, $p \in P \cup CT$, $v \in C \cup P$.

Definition 3 [XML to RDF Mappings]: Let X be the XML schema tree and O be the RDF ontology. The XML to RDF mappings are defined in the following way:

- An XML leaf node v_i is mapped to a RDF property $p \in P$, $\delta: p \rightarrow (c_1, c_2)$ such that the datatype of the leaf node element $\{R_i, a_i\}$ corresponds to the object datatype RDF Class $c_2 \in C$,
- A non-leaf node v_i with sub element nodes is mapped to a RDF class $c \in C$.

- A non-leaf node v_i with sub element nodes is mapped to a RDF property $p \in P$ such that $\mu(v_j) = c_j$, $\mu(v_k) = c_k$ and $\delta(p) = (c_j, c_k)$. Here v_j and v_k are the ancestor and descendant of node v_i, respectively.
- A pair of XML nodes (v_i, v_j) is mapped to an RDF triple [s, p, o] where $ed(v_i, v_j)$ is an unlabeled edge in XML tree and $\theta(p)$ = rdf:type, rdfs:subClassOf, or rdfs:subPropertyOf .

Intuitively the first case defines each simple type XML element with a PCDATA or built-in datatype or an attribute to be mapped to an RDF property. The second case maps any node in the XML node hierarchy to an RDF class. The third case defines the mapping of a non-leaf XML node to a property. Some XML nodes in a document fill the role of a property in a conceptual model. But a property when defined in a use case such as a data exchange is really meant to connect two classes together, where the classes are represented as the domain and range of the property. But in an XML schema tree the focus being on the structure, the XML element nodes corresponding to these classes may be anywhere along the hierarchy. Hence the third case additionally requires an ancestor and a descendant to be mapped to the domain and range of an RDF property. The fourth case defines the mapping when the properties or relationships between two XML nodes are implicitly used in the XML structure. For example two parent child XML nodes Information/Medical given in a document may most likely mean that conceptually they are related through subclass or type information. Hence in this case a pair of parent child XML nodes (v_i, v_j) is mapped to an RDF triple $t_i = [s_i, p_i, o_i]$ where property p is either rdf:type, rdfs:subClassOf or rdfs:subPropertyOf. Now we define the mappings set for XML and RDF components.

Definition 4 [XML-RDF Mapping Rule Set]: Let $X = (V, E, \theta, L)$ be an XML schema tree, $O =$ $(C, P, \delta, \leq)$ be an RDF ontology schema and $\mu: X \rightarrow O$ be a mapping function. A mapping rule set M_{xo} containing XML to RDF components' correspondences is defined as $M_{xo} = \{(x_1, r_1) \ldots (x_k, r_k)\}$ such that x_i is either an XML node $v_i \in V$ or a pair of nodes (v_i, v_j) and r_i is either an RDF class $c_i \in C$, an RDF property $p_i \in P$ or an RDF triple $t_i = [s_i, p_i, o_i]$.

XML to RDF Mapping Properties

The following are the properties of the mappings μ between XML schema tree and RDF ontology data:

Structure Preserving Classes

The procedure of an XML data sharing operation consists of pulling XML data out of the XML database and rendering it for exchange among the applications, by creating a structure. This procedure may create some extra XML elements which are not meaningful and their primary motive is for keeping the data in an exchangeable structure. These elements are not mapped to any existing RDF components since RDF ontology contains only meaningful data relevant semantics. For example the relevant patient data from Health Provider Web application may be composed in a SOAP message, enclosed between tags <SOAP:head> and </SOAP:head>. The tags have no corresponding component in RDF ontology. Several other tags such as <SOAP:enc> meant for providing administrative and security information such as XML signature, may be present in the XML document. For this purpose an RDF class spc_i is generated and added to RDF ontology such that $C = C \cup spc_i$. The mapping is done in such a way that each structure preserving XML node $v_i \in X$ is mapped to a generated structure preserving RDF class spc_j. The property p_i, $\theta(p_i)$ = st is generated to connect the structure preserving classes spc_i and spc_j. The property p_i is not mapped to any equivalence class but preserves the ontological properties of the RDF ontology schema.

Theorem 1: The XML-RDF mapping rule set M_{xo}, constructed by Algorithm 1 (Figure 8)

1. Is complete: contains one pair (v_i, c_i), (v_i, p_i) or $((v_i, v_j), [s_i, p_i, o_i])$ for every XML node v_i of the XML schema tree, i.e., each node is associated with an RDF class or property and each node pair is associated with a unique RDF triple.

2. Is consistent: does not have two pairs (v_i, r_i) and (v_j, r_j) or $((v_i, v_j), [s_i, p_i, o_i])$ and $((v_i, v_j), [s_k, p_k, o_k])$ where r_i is either an RDF property p_i or class c_i such that $v_i = v_j$, $r_i = r_j$, and i = k i.e., for an XML node there is a single corresponding RDF class or property for an XML node pair, there is a single RDF triple.

PROOF: Algorithm 1 (Figure 8) traverses XML tree in breadth first order such that every node v_i in X, including the structure preserving nodes, is

Figure 8. Algorithm 1: XML to RDF Mapping algorithm

Input: XML schema tree X = (V, E, θ, L), RDF Ontology
O = (C, P, δ, ≤), XML-RDF mapping function μ : X → O

Output: XML to RDF mapping rule set M_{xo} = {(x_1, r_1) . . . (x_k, r_k)} where x_i = v_i or
(v_i, v_j) and r_i = c_i, p_i or $[s_i, p_i, o_i]$, i = 1, . . . , k

/* Traverse X in Breadth First Search */
1   Mapping Rule set M_{xo} = {}
2   Add spc_i as the structure preserving class to RDF ontology such that
    C = C ∪ spc_i
3   Add spp_i as the structure preserving property to RDF ontology such that P = P ∪ spp_i
    where δ : spp_i → (spc_i, spc_j), θ(spp_i) = st' and spc_j is a structure preserving class
    mapped to a structure preserving XML node v_i
4   **foreach** node v_i ∈ V **do**
5   **if** ∃ μ (v_i) = c_i, c_i ∈ C & $\not\exists z_i$ ∈ M_{xo} such that z_i = (v_i, c_j) for any c_j ∈ C where i ≠ j **then**
6   Generate pair (v_i, c_i)
7   M_{xo} = M_{xo} ∪ (v_i, c_i)
8   Mark node v_i as mapped
9   **else if** ∃ μ(v_i) = p_i, p_i ∈ P & $\not\exists z_i$ ∈ M_{xo} such that z_i = (v_i, p_j) for any p_j ∈ P where i ≠ j
        and v_i is a non-leaf node **then**
10   Generate pair (v_i, p_i)
11   M_{xo} = M_{xo} ∪ (v_i, p_i)
12   Mark node v_i as mapped
13   Generate pairs (v_j, c_j) and (v_k, c_k) where δ(p_i) → (c_j, c_k) and v_j, v_k are ancestor
            and descendant of v_i respectively
14   **if** $\not\exists (v_j, c_m)$, (v_k, c_n) ∈ M_{xo} where m ≠ j and n ≠ k **then**
15   M_{xo} = M_{xo} ∪ (v_j, c_j)
16   M_{xo} = M_{xo} ∪ (v_k, c_k)
17   **else if** ∃ μ(v_i) = c_i, μ(v_j) = c_j, δ(p_i) → (c_i, c_j) and θ(p_i) = "rdf:type", "rdfs:subClassOf "
        or"rdfs: subP ropertyOf" **then**
18   Generate pair $((v_i, v_j)$, $[s_i, p_i, o_i])$ where s_i = c_i, o_i = c_j
19   **if** $\not\exists (((v_i, v_j)$, $[s_k, p_k, o_k])$ ∈ M_{xo}), i ≠ k **then**
20   M_{xo} = M_{xo} ∪ $((v_i, v_j)$, $[s_i, p_i, o_i])$
21   **else**
            /* No mappings, XML structure preserving nodes*/
22   Generate pair (v_i, spc_j)
23   M_{xo} = M_{xo} ∪ (v_i, spc_j) where spc_j is the structure preserving RDF class and δ:
            spp_i → (spc_i, spc_j), θ(spc_j) = θ(v_i)

visited. Hence a mapping pair (v_i, c_i), (v_i, p_i) or $((v_i, v_j), [s_i, p_i, o_i])$ would exist for every XML node $v_i \in V$.

Every time after generating a mapping pair (v_i, r_i) or $((v_i, v_j), [s_i, p_i, o_i])$, where r_i is either an RDF class or property, the existence of the XML node v_i is checked in existing mapping pairs in mapping rule set M_{xo}. If a pair already exists for v_i, then it is not mapped. Hence each XML node is mapped exactly once, and only one pair would exist for each of them.

Specification of an Access Control Model for RDF

In the previous section we proposed the mappings between XML documents and their data semantics represented as RDF ontology. Currently there is no access control model for RDF itself. We contend that existing access control models, such as the ones developed for securing eXtensible Markup Language (XML) documents, do not provide sufficient protection for RDF data. Here we give brief background info on our previous research work (Jain & Farkas, 2006); currently under review revision elsewhere, to provide a comprehensive view of our Semantic Aware Authorization Model.

Our RDF security model incorporates RDF and RDF Schema entailments. RDF and RDFS represent the Universe of Discourse (Hayes & McBride, 2004) for all the resources that can be represented in an RDF interpretation. RDF protection objects are represented as RDF-patterns in the security policies that are mapped to RDF and RDF Schema statements in the database to determine their security requirements. We develop methods to assign security classifications to entailed statements and to detect unauthorized inferences. We define a two-level conflict resolution strategy. Simple conflict resolution addresses the problem when more than one security policy pattern can be mapped to the same RDF statement, resulting in conflicting classification. Inference conflict resolution addresses inconsistencies that

occur due to entailment. Our RDF access control models can

- Control access to explicitly stored RDF and RDFS statements
- Assign security classifications to the newly generated RDF and RDFS statements,
- Check for unauthorized inferences due to entailment and
- Be independent of the type of database management model used for storing RDF.

RDF is conceptualized as a directed, labeled graph. It is represented using triples. Set of triples constitute the graph. Intuitively, RDF Schema defines the meaning for the nodes and edges of the RDF instance. Figure 9 shows an example of RDF instance and its schema in RDF graph representation and Figure 10 represents the same data in triple format (URIs have been abbreviated for simplicity). The triples are represented as $t = [r, p, v]$ where r is a resource, p is a property and v is the value. The triple format can also represent one element and two elements of the triple by using"'-'" as the empty placeholder for the element that is not present in the triple. For example a class resource called Student can be represented as [Student,-,-]. This triple shows only the resource Student and does not include any associations with any properties or their values. Location of the resources in the triple is also important. For example [Student,-,-] is different from [-,-, Student] since in the first triple Student is a subject while in the later case it is an object, as the triples really represent the association of a resource with the property and its value.

Current XML access control models do not fully address these problems. Our model (Jain & Farkas, 2006) allows the access control policies to be applied on the RDF and RDFS triples using a security policy independent of the RDF data stores and their actions (Reddivari et al., 2007; Dietzold & Auer, 2006). The primitive model is based on Mandatory Access Control (MAC) model, but

Figure 9. Example RDF schema and instance data in graph format

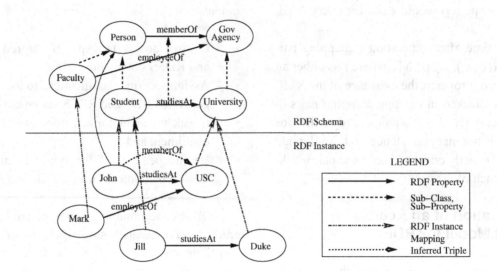

this can be adapted to other distributed security models with appropriate changes. The security policies provide a flexible way of representing RDF security objects to be protected. For example, all instances of a schema triple, all triples with a given property, and triples about a resource or property. Intuitively, a pattern in a security policy may represent any elements (resource, property, value) of the triple. Each element may be a constant (i.e., a particular value (class)), a variable (i.e., ranges over the values (classes)) or empty. Each RDF-pattern is associated with a

Figure 10. RDF triple format (a) RDF schema triples (b) RDF instance triples

[memberOf, rdfs:domain, Person]
[memberOf, rdfs:range, GovAgency]
[Student, rdfs:subClassOf, Person]
[University, rdfs:subClassOf, GovAgency]
[Faculty, rdfs:subClassOf, Person]
[studiesAt, rdsf:subPropertyOf, memberOf]
[studiesAt, rdfs:domain, Student]
[studiesAt, rdfs:range, University]
[employeeOf, rdfs:domain, Faculty]
[employeeOf, rdfs:range, GovAgency]

(a)

[John, studiesAt, USC]
[Jill, studiesAt, Duke]
[Mark, employeeOf, USC]
[Jill, rdf:type, Student]
[John, rdf:type, Student]
[Duke, rdf:type, University]
[USC, rdf:type, University]
[Mark, rdf:type, Faculty]

(b)

security classification. RDF patterns are mapped to the RDF and RDFS statements to determine the security classifications of the statements. If more than one pattern can be mapped to the same RDF statement, the most restrictive classification is selected. We define a subsumption relation between RDF-patterns and require that subsuming patterns have to be at most as restrictive as their subsumed patterns.

The conflict resolution strategies ensure that the security labeling is always deterministic and consistent. We also address the scenario where the entailment rules may generate new statements. We present entailment of new data triples from entailment rules and existing data statements. We define a procedure to automatically assign classification to a new statement as the lowest-upper bound of the labels of the statements, used to generate the new statement. The new statement and its security classification are evaluated to detect unauthorized inferences. The RDF Access Control Model, as

shown in the Figure 11, primarily consists of three components:

1. RDF Database and Security Cover
2. RDF Security Policy and Protection Objects
3. RDF Security Policies Database
4. RDF Querying Engine and Security Monitor

RDF Database and Security Cover

This is the data store component of the system which consists of native RDF database for storing RDF and RDFS data triples. The database contains the original RDF and RDFS triples as well as the generated security cover. The data store provides data access, manipulation and querying API for querying and updating data. There are several native RDF and RDFS storage systems available. The triple stores themselves have the user level

Figure 11. RDF access control architecture

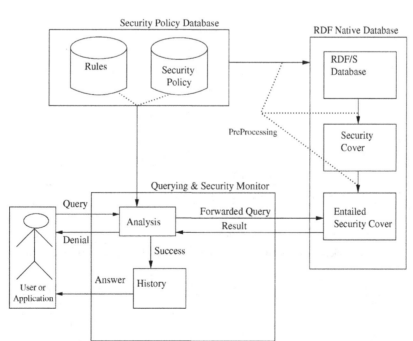

75

and admin level security provided for ontology loading and additions.

RDF Security Policy and Protection Objects

RDF security policy specifies the security requirements on the RDF data. In our authorization model each security policy consists of a set of RDF patterns and corresponding security labels. Each RDF pattern defines the security classification for a group of triples. Pattern mapping from the patterns of the policy to the RDF triples identifies RDF and RDFS database triples that conform to a specific pattern. Such triples inherit the security label of the pattern and represent the security objects in RDF format that need to be protected using the security policy. Since abstract RDF syntax is a set of triples, we use RDF patterns in triple format to represent RDF statements and data triple in security objects.

RDF Security Policies Database

This component consists of the RDF security policies and conflict resolution strategies. Since our security policy can be represented in the form of logical facts or in RDF format, this can be either

a logical knowledge base or an RDF database. It also consists of RDF entailment rules or customized business rules that are used for generating additional RDF and RDFS data from the existing one in the triple base. These rules again either can be in the form of logical rules and may be stored in RDF format.

RDF Querying Engine and Security Monitor

This component implements one of the querying standards available for querying RDF and RDFS data such as SPARQL (Prud'hommeaux & Seaborne, 2008) or RDQL (Seaborne, 2004), selected based on the RDF store used for data storage. It consists of a user interaction and an analysis module. The user interaction module receives the user queries and forwards them to the underlying database for the query results. If query results are found, then the resulting RDF and RDFS data triples are returned. The returned triples also have their security labels from the security cover. Security Monitor checks the results for security violations. If a violation is found, then the query is rejected. Otherwise the history for the user is retrieved from the user history module and aligned with the retrieved result. This updated result is again checked for the security violation.

Table 1. Example RDF patterns

Security Pattern	Interpretation	Example
[r, p, v]	All elements of the triple are specified as constants (Ground Pattern)	[John,studiesAt,USC]
[r, ?x, v]	Subject and object are specified as constants and property a variable.	[John,?x,USC]
[r, p, ?x]	Subject and property are specified as constants and object is variable	[John,studiesAt,?x]
[?x, p, v]	Property and object are specified as constants and subject is variable	[?x,studiesAt,USC]
[r, ?x, ?y]	Subject is specified as constant and property & objects as variable	[John,?x,?y]
[?x, p, ?y]	Property is specified as constant and subject & object as variable	[?x,studiesAt,?y]
[?x, ?y, v]	Object is specified as constant and subject & property are variables	[?x,?y,USC]
[?x, p, -]	Subject is a variable, property is a constant & object is empty	[?x, studiesAt, -]
[?x,?y, ?z]	All elements are variables	

If a violation is found, the query is denied otherwise the results are returned to the user and the history is updated.

If all components of the triple are data constants, we say that it is a ground RDF-pattern. RDF and RDFS statements are ground patterns. For example [John, studiesAt, USC] is a ground RDF-pattern. Table 1 shows some of the possible patterns in our model, where any of the [r,p,v] can be a variable, a data constant or an empty element as defined above.

Derivation of XML Access Control Policies from RDF Ontologies

This section presents the derivation of access control policies for XML data. The policies are derived using the semantic mappings generated using the mapping between XML and its semantics. These authorization policies for XML data can be used for checking the consistency of already present security authorizations of XML data. The policies can also be used for applying new access control permissions over the data. This would enable us to resolve the inconsistencies of security policies over semantically similar but syntactically different XML data. This approach allows the use of existing access control mechanisms.

The derived XML authorizations need to be consistent with respect to the XML data as well as the RDF ontological data. This new set of security derivations would also be required to have the properties such as completeness, consistency and soundness. Also other meta policies such as conflict resolution rules and policy fixing in case of an error need to be developed.

Theorem 2: Let SP_o denotes the access control policy of the RDF ontology. If SP_o is complete and consistent, then the XML access control policy $XP\,OL_o$, generated by Algorithm 2 (Figure 12) is complete and consistent.

PROOF: We give this proof using the method of contradiction.

1. Complete: Let's assume that XML access control policy $XP\,OL_o$ is not complete, i.e., $\exists\ v_i \in X$ such that there is no $(v_i, sl_i) \in XP\,OL_o$ where X is the XML schema tree and sl_i is the security label assigned to XML node v_i by Algorithm 2 (Figure 12). Then there would not be any mapping from v_i to either an RDF class c_i or RDF property p_i since every present XML node in the mapping rule set is assigned a security label by Algorithm 2 (Figure 12). But from the completeness property of Algorithm 1 (Figure 8), every v_i (including the structure preserving XML nodes) is mapped to an RDF class or property. Hence a security label is generated for every XML node. This contradicts our earlier assumption. Hence the XML authorization policy $XP\,OL_o$ must be complete.

2. Consistent: Lets assume that there are two pairs $(v_i, sl_i), (v_i, sl_j) \in XP\,OL_o$ such that $i = j$, i.e., an XML node is assigned more than one security label. Since RDF security policy SP_o is consistent such that each RDF class or property is given only one security label, v_i must be mapped to two RDF components r_i and r_j by mapping function μ, i.e., $\mu(v_i) = r_i$ and $\mu(v_i) = r_j$. But from the properties of the Algorithm 1 (Figure 8), XML to RDF mapping rule set M_{xo} is consistent such that $\nexists\ (v_i, r_i), (v_i, r_j) \in M_{xo}$ where $r_i = r_j$. This contradicts our earlier assumption. Hence $XP\,OL_o$ must be consistent.

The SAAF accepts an XML document, a domain RDF ontology describing the conceptual model and RDF access control policy. In addition the mapping rule set between XML and RDF ontologies is also used. An authorization policy, applicable to the XML document can then be constructed. Additional Meta policies, containing propagation policy and conflict resolution

Figure 12. Algorithm 2: XML tree security policy generation from RDF data

---

Input: RDF Ontology $O = (C, P, \delta, \leq)$, RDF Security CoverSC $= \{s_1, \ldots, s_k\}$ where s_i
$= (t_i, sl_i)$, $i = 1, \ldots, k$; XML to RDF mapping rule set $M_{xo} = \{(x_1, r_1)$.
$\ldots (x_k, r_k)\}$ where $x_i = v_i$ or (v_i, v_j) and $r_i = c_i, p_i$ or $[s_i, p_i, o_i]$, $i = 1, \ldots, k$

Output: XML Access Control Policy $XPOL_o = \{(v_1, sl_1) \ldots (v_n, sl_n)\}$, where $sl_i \in [L_i, H_i]$
is the security label of XML node v_i

```
1   XPOLo = {}
2   foreach Node vi Є X do
3     if ∃ (vi, ci) Є Mxo then
4       if ∃(ti, sli) Є SC where ti = [si,pi, oi] and ci corresponds with either si or oi then
5         zi = (vi, sli)

6     else if ∃ (vi, pi) Є Mxo then
7       if ∃(ti, sli) Є SC where ti=[si,pi,oi] and pi corresponds with either si,pi or oi then
8         zi = (vi, sli)

9     else if ∃ ((vi, vj), [si, pi, oi]) Є Mxo then
10      if ∃ (ti, sli) Є SC where ti = [si, pi, oi] then
11        zi = (vi, sli)
12        zj = (vj , sli)

      /* Structural XML tags are classified public */
13    else if ∃ (vi, spci) where spci is the structure preserving RDF class then
14      sli = slpub, where slpub is the public security classification
15      zi = (vi, sli)

16    else
        /* Unmapped XML tags are given highest security labels    */
17      sli = sldef, where sldef is the default highest security classification
18      XPOLo = XPOLo ∪ (vi, sli)

19    if ∄zk Є XPOLo where zk = (vi, slk), i ≠ k then
20      XPOLo = XPOLo ∪ (vi, sli)
```

---

may be used to aid complex security policies. We consider the Multi Level Security for our access control model here. More advanced access control models can be similarly expressed by the model for example Discretionary Access Control (DAC) and Role Base Access Control (RBAC) by making required changes in the algorithms and the security model.

In our model, the access control requirements for the XML nodes may not follow current XML access control requirements, such as increasing restrictions traversing down the XML tree. Stoica et al. (Stoica & Farkas, 2002) have addressed this problem. The resulting security policy for XML tree is stored as a set of pairs of XML node identifiers using XPATH and their security clas-

sifications. Certainly this representation is not the best from implementation perspective. Hence this can be used as an input for several existing XML access control architectures to create a final policy in a tree, table or tuples format, suitable for implementation.

Limitations and Issues

One of the limitations of our security model is its dependence on the mappings between Web data and RDF ontologies. The correctness of the generated XML security policy relies on the XML to RDF mappings generated by other methods. Hence the generated policies need to be checked for the consistency. None of the existing mapping generation framework is fully automatic and requires human assistance in several steps. To enforce the security properties on the generated policies, the mappings may need to be modified manually. Hence our model would require human assistance as well.

FUTURE WORK

We plan to implement our framework by using Web Service architecture for distributed P2P settings and integrate it with a metadata searching mechanism to develop the Semantic Aware Authorization platform. Web Ontology Language OWL (McGuinness & Harmelen, 2004) is an ontology language that extends RDF. It provides a modeling language for defining the semantics of a domain by providing additional vocabulary along with a formal semantic model. OWL has more features for expressing meaning and semantics than XML, RDF, and RDF-S. Hence it thus goes beyond these languages in its ability to represent machine interpretable content on the Web. So an access control model to secure OWL ontology data needs to be aware of OWL relationships and semantics. This would be a natural extension to RDF Access control model presented in this research work. This has been left as a future work.

Mapping several inter-domain RDF ontologies to a global ontology would allow our technique to be used across a broader spectrum and inter-domain applications. Also at this time we have considered the equivalence mappings. In some instances the mappings may be more complex and may include fuzzy matching, 'part of ' or unidirectional mapping. Also domain specific semantic mapping rules may be written to guide the mapping process, resulting in a more profound set of mappings. We plan to address these issues in our future work. Our future work also includes formal definition of semantically equivalent XML documents based on specific applications

addressing ontological inferences and enhanced conflict resolution.

A basic requirement of the open Web today is interoperability. So far client and server policies are represented in XML syntax and may require a server to process each of them differently if they have different syntax but enforce the same security requirements. Using our access control model, security policies for different Web Services can be compared for consistency. The security policies, expressed in XML format, can be compared with each other using the corresponding RDF security ontology. Automated policy verification using subsumption is another area where several policies written using different domain ontologies can be aligned to a higher level enterprise global policy.

CONCLUSION

Most of the methods to support secure data sharing in the Web Services environment define security objects based on data syntax and structure. For the Web based paradigms to be successful, the security methods have to incorporate data and application semantics in defining security objects. By using semantic-aware security model many security vulnerabilities which depend on data syntax tampering can be caught.

In this work, we proposed the RDF for representing domain information. However, there is no suitable security model available for securing RDF data. An RDF security model should consider its characteristics such as abstract syntax and entailment in developing access control mechanisms. Semantic Web Services use the ontologies for various tasks such as composition, discovery and matchmaking. This underscores the importance of ontology security. Use of various domain ontologies for information discovery in enterprise applications and tools, further highlights the importance of RDF security.

In this research work, we have proposed a Semantic-Aware Access Control Framework for providing authorizations on XML data in distributed environments. This work semantically enhances the XML data by mapping it to RDF ontology. The XML to RDF mappings would provide the necessary correspondence and enhance the XML data with its semantics. Then the authorizations can be defined on the data semantics represented as the RDF ontologies and can be converted into XML access control policies using the XML-RDF mappings. Using this method provides a consistent way of specifying authorizations on syntactically different data which has the similar meaning. Also the security verifications can be done automatically by having applications interpreting the data semantics and the security policies.

RDF security model allows the identification of RDF security objects to be protected. It expresses the RDF security policies that not only secure the existing data but also entailed RDF statements that may be generated using inference. It also follows the defined model properties such that default security policy as well as the conflict resolution policies. Simple conflict resolution addresses inconsistencies that may occur due to the mapping of more than one pattern to the same RDF statement. Inference conflict resolution detects unauthorized inferences, where a higher security statement can be inferred from lower security statements.

ACKNOWLEDGMENT

This research work was partially supported by the National Science Foundation grant, NSF IIS 0237782.

REFERENCES

Agarwal, S., & Sprick, B. (2005). Specification of Access Control and Certification Policies for Semantic Web Services. In K. Bauknecht, B. Pröll, & H. Werthner (Eds.), *EC-Web* (Vol. 3590, pp. 348-357). Berlin: Springer.

Battle, S. (2006). Gloze: XML to RDF and back again. In *First Jena user conference*.

Bertino, E., Castano, S., Ferrari, E., & Mesiti, M. (2000, May). Specifying and Enforcing Access Control Policies for XML document sources. *World Wide Web (Bussum)*, *3*, 139–151. doi:10.1023/A:1019289831564

Bhargavan, K., Fournet, C., Gordon, A. D., & O'Shea, G. (2005). An Advisor for Web Services Security Policies. In *SWS '05: Proceedings of the 2005 Workshop on Secure Web Services*, (pp. 1-9). New York: ACM Press.

Bohring, H., & Auer, S. (2005). Mapping XML to OWL Ontologies. In K. P. Jantke, K.-P. Fähnrich, & W. S. Wittig (Eds.), *Leipziger informatik-tage,* (Vol. 72, p. 147-156). GI.

Boyer, J., Eastlake, D., & Reagle, J. (2002, July). *XML-Signature Syntax and Processing (Recommendation)*. W3C. Retrieved from http://www.w3.org/TR/xml-exc-c14n/

Cahill, C. P., & Hughes, J. (2005, March). *Security Assertion Markup Language (SAML) v2.0*. Retrieved from http://docs.oasis-open.org/security/saml/v2.0/saml-core-2.0-os.pdf

Chinnici, R., Moreau, J.-J., Ryman, A., & Weerawarana, S. (2006, March). *Web Services Description Language (WSDL) 2.0*. Retrieved from http://www.w3.org/TR/wsdl20/

Clark, J., & DeRose, S. (2006, June). *XML Path Langauage (XPath) 2.0* (W3C Recommendation). Retrieved from http://www.w3.org/TR/xpath/

Clement, L., Hately, A., von Riegen, C., & Rogers, T. (2005, February). *Universal Description, Discovery and Integration (UDDI) V3.0.2*. Retrieved from http://uddi.org/pubs/uddi-v3.0.2-20041019.htm

Damiani, E., di Vimercati, S. D. C., Paraboschi, S., & Samarati, P. (2002). A fine-grained access control system for XML documents. *ACM Transactions on Information and System Security, 5*(2), 169–202. doi:10.1145/505586.505590

Della-Libera, G., Gudgin, M., Hallam Baker, P., Hondo, M., Granqvist, H., Kaler, C., et al. (2005, July). *Web Services Security Policy Language (WS-SecurityPolicy) V1.1 specification*. Retrieved from ftp://www6.software.ibm.com/software/developer/library/ws-secpol.pdf

Denker, G., Kagal, L., Finin, T. W., Paolucci, M., & Sycara, K. P. (2003). Security for DAML Web Services: Annotation and Matchmaking. In D. Fensel, K. P. Sycara, & J. Mylopoulos (Eds.), *International Semantic Web Conference* (Vol. 2870, p. 335-350). Berlin: Springer.

Dietzold, S., & Auer, S. (2006, June). Access Control on RDF Triple Stores from a Semantic Wiki Perspective. In C. Bizer, S. Auer, & L. Miller (Eds.), (Vol. 183).

dos Santos Mello, R., & Heuser, C. A. (2005). BInXS: A Process for Integration of XML Schemata. In O. Pastor & J. F. e Cunha (Eds.), *Caise*, (Vol. 3520, p. 151-166). Berlin: Springer.

Eastlake, D., & Reagle, J. (2002, October). *XML Encryption Syntax and Processing* (Recommendation). W3C. Retrieved from http://www.w3.org/TR/xmldsig-core/

Farkas, C., Jain, A., Wijesekera, D., Singhal, A., & Thuraisingham, B. (2006, May). Semantic-Aware Data Protection in Web Services. In *Proceedings of the IEEE Web Services Security Symposium,* (pp. 52-63). West Lafayette, IN: CERIAS.

Ferdinand, M., Zirpins, C., & Trastour, D. (2004). Lifting XML Schema to OWL. In N. Koch, P. Fraternali, & M. Wirsing (Eds.), *Web engineering - 4th international conference, icwe 2004, munich, germany, july 26-30, 2004, proceedings,* (pp. 354-358). Heidelberg: Springer.

Gudgin, M., Hadley, M., Mendelsohn, N., Moreau, J.-J., & Nielsen, H. F. (2003, June). *SOAP version 1.2 part 1: Messaging framework*. Retrieved from http://www.w3.org/TR/soap12-part1/

Hayes, P., & McBride, B. (2004, February). *W3C Recommendation, RDF Semantics*. Retrieved from http://www.w3.org/TR/rdf-mt/

Jain, A., & Farkas, C. (2006). Secure Resource Description Framework: an Access Control Model. In *SACMAT '06: Proceedings of the eleventh ACM symposium on Access control models and technologies* (pp. 121-129). New York: ACM Press.

Kagal, L., Paoucci, M., Srinivasan, N., Denker, G., Finin, T., & Sycara, K. (2004, July). Authorization and Privacy for Semantic Web Services. [Special Issue on Semantic Web Services]. *IEEE Intelligent Systems, 19*(4), 50–56. doi:10.1109/MIS.2004.23

Kaushik, S., Wijesekera, D., & Ammann, P. (2005). Policy-based dissemination of partial Web-Ontologies. In *SWS '05: Proceedings of the 2005 Workshop on Secure Web Services,* (pp. 43-52). New York: ACM Press.

Klyne, G., & Carroll, J. (2004, February). *W3C Recommendation, RDF Concepts and Abstract Syntax*. Retrieved from http://www.w3.org/TR/rdf-concepts/

Kudo, M., & Hada, S. (2000). XML document security based on provisional authorization. In *CCS '00: Proceedings of the 7th ACM Conference on Computer and Communications Security,* (pp. 87-96). New York: ACM Press.

Lenzerini, M. (2002). Data integration: a theoretical perspective. In *Pods '02: Proceedings of the twenty-first ACM sigmod-sigact-sigart symposium on principles of database systems*, (pp. 233-246). New York: ACM Press.

McGuinness, D. L., & van Harmelen, F. (2004, February). *OWL Web Ontology Language Overview*. Retrieved from http://www.w3.org/TR/owl-features/

Moses, T. (2005, February). *Extensible Access Control Markup Language (XACML) Version 2.0*. Retrieved from http://docs.oasis-open.org/xacml/2.0/access-control-xacml-2.0-core-spec-os.pdf

Nadalin, A., Kaler, C., Phillip, H.-B., & Monzillo, R. (2004, March). *Web Services Security, SOAP Message Security 1.1*. Retrieved from http://docs.oasis-open.org/wss/v1.1/wss-v1.1-spec-pr-SOAPMessageSecurity-01.pdf

Paolucci, M., Kawamura, T., Payne, T. R., & Sycara, K. P. (2002). Semantic Matching of Web Services Capabilities. In *Iswc '02: Proceedings of the first international semantic web conference on the semantic web* (pp. 333-347). London: Springer-Verlag.

Prud'hommeaux, E., & Seaborne, A. (2008). *SPARQL Query Language for RDF*.

Qin, L., & Atluri, V. (2003). Concept-level access control for the Semantic Web. In *Xmlsec '03: Proceedings of the 2003 acm workshop on xml security*, (pp. 94-103). New York: ACM Press.

Rahaman, M. A., Schaad, A., & Rits, M. (2006). Towards secure SOAP message exchange in a SOA. In *SWS '06: Proceedings of the 3rd ACM workshop on Secure web services*, (pp. 77-84). New York: ACM Press.

Rahm, E., & Bernstein, P. A. (2001). A survey of approaches to automatic schema matching. *The VLDB Journal*, *10*(4), 334–350. doi:10.1007/s007780100057

Reddivari, P., Finin, T., & Joshi, A. (2007, January). Policy-Based Access Control for an RDF Store. In *Proceedings of the IJCAI-07 Workshop on Semantic Web for Collaborative Knowledge Acquisition*.

Reif, G., Gall, H., & Jazayeri, M. (2005). WEESA: Web Engineering for Semantic Web Applications. In *Proceedings of the 14th International Conference on World Wide Web*, (pp. 722-729). New York: ACM Press.

Sandhu, R., Coyne, E. J., Feinstein, H., & Youman, C. (1996, February). Role-based access control models. *IEEE Computer*, *29*, 38–47.

Sandhu, R. S., & Samarati, P. (1994, September). Access control: Principles and practice. *IEEE Communications Magazine*, *32*(9), 40–49. doi:10.1109/35.312842

Seaborne, A. (2004, January 9). *RDQL - A Query Language for RDF (Member Submission)*. Tech. Rep. W3C.

Stoica, A., & Farkas, C. (2002). Secure XML Views. In E. Gudes & S. Shenoi (Eds.), *Dbsec* (Vol. 256, p. 133-146). Amsterdam: Kluwer.

Web Service Enhancements. (WSE 3.0). (2005, November). Retrieved from http://msdn.microsoft.com/webservices/webservices/building/wse/default.aspx

Chapter 4
Secure Service Rating in Federated Software Systems Based on SOA

Nico Brehm
RepuGraph.com, Nordhausen, Germany

Jorge Marx Gómez
University of Oldenburg, Germany

ABSTRACT

The service-oriented architecture (SOA) paradigm mostly provides a suitable approach as to meet the requirements of flexible distributed software systems. Referring to the activities for the standardization of Web Service semantics or alternatively the introduction of intelligent search mechanisms future software architectures are supposed to integrate software components as remote services of foreign providers. If the authors assume that such services can be standardized e.g. as components of standard business application systems the vision of a service economy arises where services of the same type can be marketed by different providers. A service consumer on the other hand could choose the service he likes best at runtime. However, this vision is clouded by a multiplicity of risks which meet each other in the question of the specific reliability and trustworthiness of service providers in a certain context. Previous research activities picked up this problem whereby a lot of promising approaches and frameworks have been developed which concern the negotiation of trust within open network architectures like grids or peer-to-peer networks. Nevertheless, the genesis of the trust relationship between two network nodes has been neglected. This chapter presents an approach for the establishment of reputation in federated software systems where central network instances for the management of evaluations are avoided. In the authors' approach the service providers are responsible for this task on their own. The authors present a novel security protocol for the message-based exchange of service evaluations that deters service providers from manipulating their own ratings.

DOI: 10.4018/978-1-60566-950-2.ch004

INTRODUCTION

Today the SOA concept is accepted as one of the most important instruments for the construction of integrated software systems. As an integral core concept of distributed applications Web Services (a common way to implement a SOA) are driving further software developments and advancements and they are widely spread in the area of integrated software systems engineering. Lately when aspects like the openness of software systems or their sustainable interoperability were frequently discussed more from a marketing-oriented point of view, those features seemed to be claimed as essential rather by the seller- than by the buyer-side. Thus, software market actors talked about exceptional extras, surpluses, added values and additional future benefits of software systems being equipped with service interfaces. Since business application systems have been established as major sources for competitive advantages enterprises are now running far more than only a few programs in parallel. As those software systems support users in their every-day work and business processes do not stop at artificial borders set by the organizational structure of enterprises, today the effort of software projects is shifting from the development of business functionality towards the construction of integrated business solutions where services (and Web Services in particular) play an important role.

Taking a look at current service-based integration methods in practice, however, similarities to old-dated green field software engineering models become obvious were developers created software independently. Then the consideration of existing foreign software artifacts as possible components of new solutions was clouded by major technical incompatibility problems. We have to admit, that well-understood software engineering concepts of nowadays like object-orientation and component frameworks still do not allow a comparison between modern software engineering and well-established industrial engineering disciplines.

However, the development of reusable software components is already supported by matured implementation platforms. Technologies can be considered as standardized and widely accepted and specialized design concepts for "industry-like" software components engineering are available.

At its main idea the concept of SOA goes one step further. Assumed that there are reusable software components already existing also the operation responsibility of those components is shifted to the component provider-side. That means that a service in a SOA can be seen as software component which can be used without dependencies to other components the service consumer has to care about. Following the vision of a marketplace for software components the SOA concept might also serve as basis for an automated mediation between consumers and providers in future software industries where software is not only developed in a collaborative and competitive manner but also software operation and management tasks are shared by a set of market competitors.

If the functionality of software services can be standardized it is possible to compare them according to their non-functional attributes as e.g. the price, the performance or the trustworthiness of the associated provider e.g. as regards to the non-misuse of input information.

The chapter describes how quality attributes of services can be measured by service consumers and how those measurements can be used for the establishment of trust in service markets. The shown concept of a decentralized reputation architecture is based on service evaluations that are given by service consumers and managed by service providers. Firstly we give an insight into the main concepts of existing trust models and the characteristics of federated systems as basis for service marketplaces. Then we describe the new concept of an architecture for the management of service ratings as basis for the establishment of trust. Therefore we introduce a novel security protocol called Service Evaluation Protocol

(SEP). Subsequently we show an extended point of view towards the SOA paradigm with a focus on a reputation-based mediation between service consumers and service providers. Finally we give a statement about the future application of the shown concept as well as some ideas about further improvements.

BACKGROUND

In this paragraph we give definitions of the most important terms used in this chapter as well as a short discussion on the relationships between these terms. Starting from federated software systems and the role of SOA as structural design pattern we show how security and trust can be considered as part of those systems. Finally the term reputation as it is used in the presented concept will be substantiated in relation to the quality of services.

Federated Software Systems and SOA

A federated software system is characterized by the following attributes:

- Distribution of software elements (services) in a network
- Heterogeneity of provided services (through different implementations with different functional or non-functional characteristics)
- Autonomy of providers (through their independent self-administration and their latitude to offer services with specific idiosyncratic characteristics)

SOA is a styling pattern for the structuring of software functionality with different owners (Estefan et al., 2008). SOA aims at the minimization of direct dependency relationships between distributed software elements. System-internal

relationships do not exist directly between two software elements but between a software element and a capability description of another software element in terms of a requirements specification. Both, requirements specifications of potentially available software elements as well as specifications of factually provided software elements refer to the functional and non-functional attributes of those. A software element which provides functionality through a well-defined interface which is reachable over a network via the exchange of messages by an open or a defined group of users is called *service*.

A federated software system can be based on a SOA in order to make use of the inherent characteristics coming along with the concepts of a loose coupling and the minimization of direct dependency relationships. On the other hand in a federated system the participants agreed on a collaborative behavior towards a common objective. The combination of both approaches allows the collaborative operation, management and usage of complex software systems in which the different participants are not dependent from each other. This can be compared to a software market where different components (services) of an overall system are provided by different companies (service providers) in a competitive manner but with the addition of benefiting from network effects caused by the compatibility among services. Providers do not have to provide the overall system on a competitive basis but single parts (services) are marketable. On the other hand utilizing companies (service consumers) are not dependent to only one provider of a service but several service instances of the same type are available. Furthermore such a service market for complex software systems can react on functional as well as non-functional requirements changes of service consumers.

As an example for such a federated software system based on SOA the theoretical approach of a Federated Enterprise Resource Planning (FERP) system (Brehm, Marx Gómez & Rautenstrauch, 2006; Brehm, Lübke & Marx Gómez, 2007; Brehm

& Marx Gómez, 2007) can be mentioned here. A FERP system is an ERP system which consists of system components that are distributed within a computer network. The overall functionality is provided by an ensemble of allied network nodes that all together appear as a single ERP system to the user. Different ERP system components can be developed by different vendors.

Security Extensions

Enhancing the described approach of a federated software system based on SOA a lot of research and technique level problems accrue. If the goal is to connect different enterprises to one single software system, a characteristic issue is standardizing and disclosure of the underlying system architecture (Brehm & Marx Gómez, 2007). Besides, in connection with the common use of distributed applications, several security problems exist. The most important security objectives in the case of distributed business application systems are:

- Resource protection (e.g. integrity and authenticity of system configurations)
- Confidentiality of transmitted data
- Integrity of transmitted data
- Authenticity of communication partners
- Anonymity of communication partners against unauthorized parties
- Non-repudiation of transactions
- Availability of Services
- Reliability (trustability) of communication partners

A security model for federated software systems based on SOA must consider these requirements (Brehm & Marx Gómez, 2005). In this chapter we focus on the trustability of communication partners and service providers in particular. However, because the mentioned security objectives are normally dependent on each other, trust management models like the one proposed in the main part of this chapter

implicate confidentiality, integrity, authenticity, and availability requirements.

Trust Extensions and Quality of Service (QoS) Considerations

When we use the term trust in this chapter we refer to the definition by Grandison (2003) who stated that trust is the quantified belief by a trustor with respect to the competence, honesty, security and dependability of a trustee within a specified context. A competent entity is capable of performing the functions expected of it or the services it is meant to provide correctly and within reasonable timescales. As stated by Maarof & Krishna (2002) trust can be classified into three categories which are

- objective trust which expresses an absolute reliability based on the experience to trust others,
- subjective trust which can be seen as a mental state that influences the behavior of individuals, and
- *reputation* which is based on the evaluation of past activities.

This work focuses on the establishment of trust relationships based on reputation and for the definition of this term we refer to Ostrom (1998) who stated that reputation is the perception that an agent creates through past actions.

In contrast to the majority of approaches where the term trust refers to the problem of proofing the identity of a participant in a federated network by trusting others who are capable of giving those proofs (Federated Identity Management), we focus on the problems related to the disclosure of the competence and cooperativeness of service providers towards the delivery of a specified service quality (QoS).

Related Work

Current approaches for the disclosure of QoS-related information are concentrated on the use of a central (neutral) monitoring instance for all network participants (Carter, Bitting & Ghorbani, 2002; Maximilien & Singh, 2001; Maximilien & Singh, 2002; Maximilien & Singh, 2004; Maximilien & Singh, 2005) which, however, is directed against our motivation of an open market model where technical and organizational barriers to participate in such a market are minimized. Having a central instance which is responsible for the management of QoS information, a pure monopoly would be created and this instance could control the price-performance ratio of accesses to this QoS information without considering concurrent offerings of market competitors (Brehm et al., 2008). A concurrent provision of access points to QoS information in a competitive manner could improve the average quality characteristics towards their trustability. Those concepts are already known from the areas of peer-to-peer networks and agent systems. Decentralized rating models as proposed in (Zacharia, 1999; Abdul-Rahman & Hailes, 2000; Yu & Singh, 2001; Yu & Singh 2002; Sabater & Sierra, 2002; Sen &. Sajja, 2002; or Carbo, Molina & Davila, 2002) do not consider a central instance for the collection of ratings. Those approaches assume that ratings of peers can be requested from neighbored peers before a service is used. Normally the accuracy of reputation measurements increases depending on the number of requested neighbor peers. The major difference to the approach proposed in this chapter is that the requesting client receives comprehensive and up-to-date reputation information directly from the provider who is concerned to be investigated before a service is going to be used. Thus, the costs for the management and storage of ratings can be assigned to the Web Service providers themselves. Trusted third parties (Evaluation Processing Authorities, see next paragraph) can exist in an unlimited number in the network. They can offer the creation of evaluation summaries (reputation reports) as service by following different business models.

DECENTRALIZED REPUTATION ARCHITECTURE FOR FEDERATED SOA-BASED SOFTWARE SYSTEMS

Based on the described targets, the following paragraphs present an alternative solution of a decentralized reputation architecture for federated software systems based on SOA. The concept is predicated on a novel security protocol which is discussed in detail after the architecture description.

Architecture Overview

The architecture consists of the three main elements (1) service consumer, (2) service provider and (3) a trustworthy inspection authority called Evaluation Processing Authority (EPA). There is a communication connection between service consumers and service providers which is used for the submission of evaluations. Such an evaluation (rating) is sent directly to the service provider it is referred to. Furthermore this communication connection is necessary for the externalization of evaluation summaries which are sent to a requesting service consumer by a service provider. Additionally, there is a second communication connection between service providers and EPAs. An EPA is responsible for the aggregation of evaluations for service providers who collected evaluations from different service consumers. This architecture is shown in Figure 1.

Because of the possibility evaluations are manipulated by service providers a security protocol has been developed in order to prevent those manipulations. This protocol is described in the next paragraph.

Figure 1. Reputation architecture overview

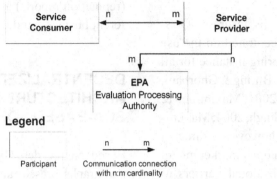

Service Evaluation Protocol (SEP)

In is paragraph we describe the Service Evaluation Protocol (SEP) which aims at the evaluation of services as basis for the establishment of trust. This protocol features a secured way for service consumers in order to evaluate the quality of services (QoS). In order to abandon central instances where evaluations have to be stored and accessed as data records, the providers themselves are supposed to administer the ratings which refer to their own services. The application of security mechanisms hinders service providers from manipulating their ratings respectively. Therefore, evaluation data is going to be processed by EPAs. The fact that also service consumers can manipulate their evaluations, e.g. by dealing dishonestly with service evaluations, is not considered in this work.

For the functional description of the protocol first of all the environment requirements are stated. Subsequently, the applied security algorithms are listed. Afterwards the communication partners and their responsibilities within the considered network are introduced and described in detail.

Prerequisites and Applied Security Algorithms

Basic prerequisite for a secured evaluation process and a secured evaluation summary processing is the existence of a public key pair for each partici-

pant. For the originality proof of public keys we assume the existence of a public key certificate which was issued by a trustworthy Certificate Authority (CA) in the run-up to a participation in the network. For the protection of secret keys we point to the necessity to equip data storage mediums with security features according to the particular use case scenario. In this context, the use of smart cards could be necessary in order to safeguard the authorized-only access to secret keys. The following security algorithms are applied in the protocol:

- Asymmetric crypto-algorithm for encryption $e(PK,M)$ and decryption $d(e(PK,M),SK) = M$; ($PK_P \rightarrow$ public key of participant P and $SK_P \rightarrow$ secret key of participant P, $M \rightarrow$ Message)
- Digital signature technique with signature $SIG = s(SK_P,M)$ and verification $M = v(SIG, PK_P)$
- (Pseudo) random number generator with output r_g, whereas g is the participant who generated the (pseudo) random number
- Message digest (hash) function $h(M)$

Participants and Protocol Elements

The following instances (participants) have to be considered in order to describe the functionality of the protocol:

- Service consumer SC who gives (sends) an evaluation E_S that refers to the service S
- Service provider SP who receives an evaluation E_S of his own service S
- Evaluation processing authority EPA which represents a trusted third party for a set of service consumers. On request an evaluation summary SUM_S of all previous evaluations of a service S is created by an EPA. Simultaneously an archive ARC_{EPA} of all evaluations E_{1-n} of various services is managed by the EPA including all evaluations which have been processed by the EPA in the context of the creation of evaluation summaries.

Public Key Certificates of the Participants

All participants possess a certificate $CERT_P$ which gives an access to the public key PK_P of the respective participant. Furthermore, the integrity of the assignment between the public key and the unique identity Id_P of participant P is ensured.

Structure of an Evaluation

An evaluation E_S consists of two parts, an identification part (header) and a rating part (body) which includes the actual evaluation content EC_E in an encrypted form. The header element consists of the following subparts:

- Public key certificate of the service consumer $CERT_{SC}$ who created the evaluation
- Public key certificate of the EPA, $CERT_{EPA}$ the evaluation content EC_E in the body part is encrypted for
- Signature $s(SK_{SC}, h(ECI_E))$ of the hash value $h(ECI_E)$ of the evaluation content identification element ECI_E of the evaluation E_S

Note: Because the evaluation content data is encrypted it is not assumable that the signer is informed about the meaning of the evaluation content data to be signed. Because the signature assures both the authorship as well as the integrity of the evaluation content data, firstly the cleartext or respectively its hash value is signed before the encryption is performed. The signature has been created by the service consumer SC and serves as proof of originality of the evaluation content data ECD_E in relation to a specific service S.

The body element of an evaluation encapsulates the evaluation content EC_E which includes a mapping between the evaluated service, the service provider and the evaluation content data. The evaluation content consists of the following elements:

- Evaluation content identification ECI_E which in turn includes the following elements:
  1. Identification of the service provider Id_{SP} who provides the service
  2. Identification of the service Id_S the evaluation refers to
  3. Hash value of the combination of a (pseudo) random number r_{SC} which has been created before and the hash value $h(ECD_E)$ of the evaluation content data

Note: This combination of hash values is aimed at the assurance of the integrity of the evaluation content identification on the one hand and on the other hand at the detection of replay-attacks where evaluation content data blocks of different evaluations of the same service consumer are exchanged. By the combination of an evaluation content identification block with a random number evaluation contents can be uniquely identified.

- Evaluation content container ECC_E which includes the **encrypted** evaluation content data ECD_E of the evaluation E_S that was encrypted for an EPA by applying the function $e(PK_{EPA}, ECD_E)$. The encryption is supposed to hinder a service provider *SP* to read evaluations after having received them and later on to differentiate between "good" and "bad" evaluations in order to selectively forward evaluations to the *EPA*.

In Figure 2 the structure of an evaluation is shown.

Structure of an Evaluation Summary

An evaluation summary SUM_S of a service S consists of two main parts, a verification part (header) and an evaluation summary content part (body). The header element consists of the following subparts:

- Certificate of the *EPA CERT$_{EPA}$* which created the evaluation summary
- Signature $s(SK_{EPA}, h(ESC_{SUM}))$ of the hash value $h(ESC_{SUM})$ of the evaluation summary content ESC_{SUM} which proofs the originality of the evaluation summary content

The body element encapsulates the evaluation summary content ESC_{SUM} which consists of the following elements:

- Identification of the service Id_S which is used for the creation of a relation between the actual evaluation summary content data and the service
- Identification of the provider Id_{SP} which is used for the creation of a relation between the service provider *SP* and the service *S*
- Evaluation summary content data $ESCD_{SUM}$ which represents the aggregated overall evaluation of all considered evaluation content data blocks $ECD_{E1} ... ECD_{En}$ of the service consumer's evaluations for service *S* in **cleartext**

Note: The term cleartext referres to a non-encrypted value of the overall evaluation.

The interrelationship between the considered evaluations E_S of a service S and the evaluation summary SUM_S of this service becomes obvious by the following formal descriptions in (I), (II), and (III) whereas

1. ECD_i describes the evaluation content data of an evaluation $(i \in [1,n])$,
2. C_j describes an evaluation criterion $(j \in [1,m])$ of a service type,
3. v_j describes the value referring to an evaluation criterion (the concrete evaluation of a service consumer referring to the evaluation criterion),
4. SM_C describes the summary of all concrete evaluations of service consumers referring to an evaluation criterion,
5. f_C describes the function (algorithm) for the summarization of concrete evaluations referring to an evaluation criterion. Note: An example for such a function is the calculation of the mean average over all available values referring to an evaluation criterion, and
6. $ESCD$ describes the evaluation summary content data as mapping between several summaries referring to the respective evaluation criteria.

$$ECD_i = \begin{pmatrix} C_1 & C_2 & ... & C_m \\ v_1 & v_2 & ... & v_m \end{pmatrix} \quad (1)$$

$$SM_{C_j} = f_{C_j}\begin{pmatrix} v_{j1} & v_{j2} & ... & v_{jn} \end{pmatrix} \quad (2)$$

$$ESCD = \begin{pmatrix} C_1 & C_2 & ... & C_m \\ SM_{C_1} & SM_{C_2} & ... & SM_{C_m} \end{pmatrix} \quad (3)$$

A function f_C for the summarization of evaluation content values is not restricted to a simple mean average calculation mechanism but it represents the application of an aggregation algorithm which is dependent to the respective evaluation

Figure 2. Structure of an evaluation

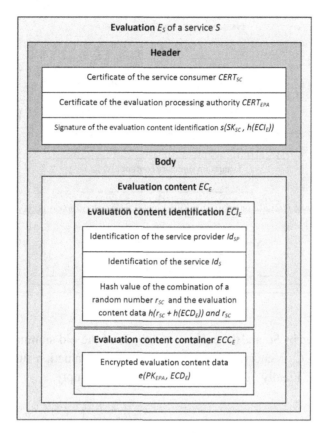

criterion. The structure of an evaluation summary is shown in Figure 3.

Functionality of the Protocol

As to describe the functionality of the protocol we differentiate between (1) the creation and submission of and evaluation (rating) by a service consumer, (2) the creation of an evaluation summary by an *EPA*, and (3) the transfer of an evaluation summary by a service provider. These three sub-functions of the protocol are described in the following sections.

Creation and Submission of an Evaluation (Rating)

Step 1: SC to SP: Init(Id$_S$)

Procedure: *SC* informs *SP* about the intension to create and submit an evaluation which is supposed to be related to service *S* with the identification *Id$_S$*.

Step 2: SP to SC: CERT$_{EPA}$

Procedure: *SP* chooses an *EPA* and sends the certificate of the *EPA* to *SC*. Alternatively the *EPA* can be negotiated between *SP* and *SC*. Therefore further communication steps would be necessary which are neglected here.

Step 3: SC to SP: E$_S$

Procedure: *SC* creates an evaluation *E$_S$*. Therefore the generation of a random number *r$_{SC}$* is necessary. Furthermore the evaluation content

Figure 3. Structure of an evaluation summary

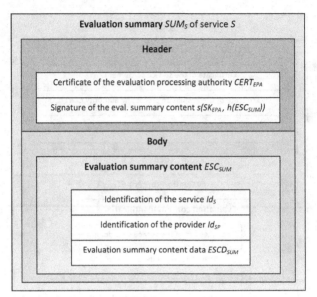

identification ECI_E is signed by SC and the evaluation content container ECC_E is encrypted using the public key of the EPA. Finally SC sends the evaluation E_S to SP.

Creation (renewal) of an Evaluation Summary

The creation of a new evaluation summary $SUM_{S(t+1)}$ always refers to an old evaluation summary $SUM_{S(t)}$. This is necessary because evaluations can be considered only once in a summary. In this manner service providers are prevented from a "trial and error" use of evaluations by means of requesting to consider evaluations multiple times.

Step 1: SP to EPA: $(E_{1S}, E_{2S}, E_{3S}, ..., E_{nS})$, $SUM_{S(t)}$

Procedure: SP sends a set of new evaluations $(E_{1S}, E_{2S}, E_{3S}, ..., E_{nS})$ that were encrypted for the EPA and the current evaluation summary $SUM_{S(t)}$ at the particular time t which represents the set of evaluations that have been included in the current (old) summary. With this request the EPA is instructed to create a new evaluation summary including the new evaluations in addition

those of the old summary. In the case that there is no old evaluation summary existing at time t, $SUM_{S(t)}$ is empty.

Step 2: EPA to SP: $SUM_{S(t+1)}$

Procedure: Initially the EPA decrypts all evaluation content container $ECC_{E1} ... ECC_{En}$ of all new evaluations. For an evaluation E_S the decryption function looks as follows:

$$ECC_E = d(SK_{EPA}, e(PK_{EPA}, ECC_E))$$

Afterwards the EPA verifies the signatures of all evaluation content identification blocks $ECI_{E1} ... ECI_{En}$ as well as the signature of $SUM_{S(t)}$ by reconstructing the hash values $h(r_{SC} + h(ECC_E))_{E1} ... h(r_{SC} + h(ECC_E))_{En}$ by considering the random number r_{SC} which is also included in an evaluation.

Note: The signature of the evaluation refers to the hash value of the evaluation content container in combination with a random number. This combination serves as protection mechanism against evaluation content reasoning attacks which are known from crypto-analysis approaches (e.g. dictionary attacks).

If one of the evaluation signatures is invalid the respective evaluation will be not considered for inclusion in the new evaluation summary. If the signature of the evaluation summary content ESC_{SUM} of $SUM_{S(t)}$ is invalid, the same evaluation summary $SUM_{S(t)}$ will be returned to SP. In this case $SUM_{S(t)} = SUM_{S(t+1)}$. Alternatively an exception could be thrown. If the signature of an evaluation content identification is valid the EPA checks if the evaluation E_{iS} was already considered in other evaluation summaries by a search in the archive ARC_{EPA}. In order to reduce the amount of data to be managed by the ARC_{EPA} only the hash values of evaluations that have been considered in evaluation summaries can be stored. If E_{iS} was not considered for inclusion, yet, the hash value of E_{iS} is added to the archive. Thus, future attempts to consider this evaluation in newer evaluation summaries will fail. After this the evaluation E_{iS} will be included in $SUM_{S(t+1)}$ by executing all functions f_{Cj} whereas the aggregation function f_{Cj} has to be described separately for the specific use case. This procedure is repeated for each evaluation E_{1S} ... E_{nS}. Subsequently the EPA signs the new evaluation summary content ESC_{SUM} in order to proof the originality. Based on this the EPA creates the new evaluation summary $SUM_{S(t+1)}$.

$$SUM_{S(t+1)} = SUM_{S(t)} + E_{1S} \ldots E_{nS}$$

Finally, the new evaluation summary $SUM_{S(t+1)}$ is sent to SP. SP renews his old summary by overwriting it with the new summary. Thus, the new value of $SUM_{S(t)}$ is from now on the value of $SUM_{S(t+1)}$ which was received as result of the last evaluation summary renewal request.

Note: SP must be forced to send several evaluations in the course of an evaluation summary creation. Because an evaluation can be considered for inclusion only once the problem of dropping evaluations in case of deterioration can be avoided. For instance if a minimum of 100 evaluations (e.g. 90 positive and 10 negative) evaluations are sent and the new evaluation summary is worse than the old one, though the new summary can be dropped, also the 90 positive evaluations are not useable anymore.

Request for an Evaluation Summary

Step 1: SC to SP: Get(Id$_S$)

Procedure: SC requests the current evaluation summary $SUM_{S(t)}$ of service S from SP.

Step 2: SP to SC: SUM$_{S(t)}$

Procedure: SP sends $SUM_{S(t)}$ to SC. SC verifies the signature of the EPA and checks the originality of the evaluation summary content

$$v(PK_{EPA}, s(SK_{EPA}, h(ESC_{SUM}))) == h(ESC_{SUM}) ?$$

Extending the Conventional SOA Paradigm

So far we described an abstract architecture of a decentralized reputation model as well as the security protocol functionality which was proposed for the transfer of evaluations and evaluation summaries. For the inclusion of this reputation architecture in a SOA an extension of the conventional SOA paradigm is necessary. This extended concept is shown in Figure 4.

Contrary to the conventional SOA concept service providers publish (1) a reference to an extended service description which includes the evaluation summary of the service. Assumed that the provided service is an instance of a standardized service type such extended descriptions include information that is useful for competitive comparisons because service providers point to the average consumer satisfaction of their service. The service registry delivers reference information about providers of a specific service type (2-discover). These references point to different extended service descriptions of different service providers. A service consumer can request these

Figure 4. Extended SOA paradigm with reputation focus

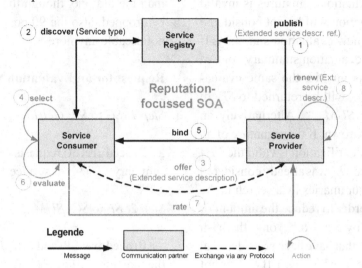

extended service descriptions (3-offer) from several service providers in order to compare the evaluation summaries for services of the same type (4-select). Here, also service level agreements (SLA) or other forms of functional and non-functional assurances could be included. After having selected a provider the respective service can be used referring to the conventional SOA concept (5-bind).

After service usage, a subjective evaluation of the actual service quality is created by the service consumer *(6-evaluate)*. Here, the assured quality features of the offering (3) could be involved as set of evaluation criteria. The result of this subjective evaluation process is sent to the service provider *(7-rate)* which can include this evaluation in a new version of his extended service description *(8-renew)* for further usages by other service consumers.

Prototype

We tested the proposed architecture in a simplified prototype implementation as an extension of a complex FERP system prototype. A discussion on the architecture of the FERP system prototype

is given in (Brehm & Marx Gómez, 2007). The evaluation of a Web Service is performed by a Web Service client (WS client) according to the sequence diagram in Figure 5. In this example, the response time of a Web Services is measured by clients after the service usage. After having received the response to a Web Service operation call the WS client calculates the difference between the moment of receiving the SOAP-response message (Timestamp B) and the moment the SOAP-request message was sent to the WS provider. After the receipt of the SOAP-response message an evaluation process is initiated automatically whereas the measured response time is taken into consideration. In our prototype a subjective performance rating (response time valuation) can be specified in a configuration file where different response time ranges can be assigned to evaluations of a scale from 1 to 10 (e.g. 2s=10, 3s=9, 4s=8 …) whereas 10 is the best and 1 the worst evaluation.

The result of this evaluation process is an XML-based evaluation which leans on the specifications of SEP (encrypted content). This evaluation is sent to the Web Service by calling the specified operation "rate" which is implemented by each rateable

Figure 5. Sequence diagram of an integrated response time measurement mechanism based on SEP in a simple prototype implementation

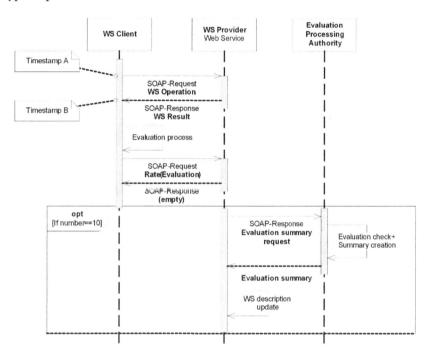

Web Service. This evaluation will be stored in an archive. After every 10th evaluation the WS provider sends an evaluation summary request to the EPA. Such a request contains ten evaluations plus the actual evaluation summary. After checking all evaluations as well as the evaluations summary (signature check and archive check, see SEP) a new evaluation summary is generated and sent back to the WS provider. Finally the provider renews his Web Service description. In our prototype we used an extended Web Service description which includes a reference to the WSDL file of the Web Service. Therefore we created our own description language called Web Service Secure Marketing Language (WSSML) which allows a specification of Web Services also on the marketing level. Here also Web Service usage prices can be specified (as e.g. 1 Cent per operation call or 10$ per month).

FUTURE RESEARCH DIRECTIONS

In order to use SEP for Web Services we propose the application of XML Signatures and XML Encryption according to the description above. Figure 6 shows a simplified signed evaluation summary as example XML tree. The summary includes identifiers of an evaluated Web Service and the respective provider. Furthermore there are objective and subjective attributes. For the aggregation of all evaluation values the average value has been calculated by a trusted party (EPA). In order to provide more statistical information this example also includes the standard deviation.

For an extension of SEP we point to (Jurca, Binder & Faltings, 2007) where a concept for the coupling of ratings and the factual usage of Web Services is described. This concept is based on the generation of a signed identification number by a service provider as rating permission for a service consumer. This identification number

Figure 6. Example for a simplified evaluation summary as XML tree

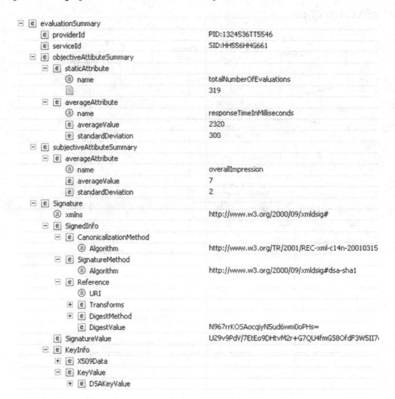

can be included in the header element of a SOAP message in case of SOAP-based Web Services. In order to give an evaluation (rate) this identification number has to be used as authorization token.

The proposed decentralized reputation architecture for federated software systems based on SOA underlies a number of problems which mostly result from the peculiarities of reputation systems in general. In particular missing incentives for the creation of evaluations by service consumers, the affinity to positive evaluations, the creation of false (dishonest) evaluations, the creation of more evaluations than service consumers are permitted to, whitewashing of service providers by a change of their identity, the problem of quality fluctuations as well as the opportunity to discriminate service providers have to be named here. For further discussions we point to (Jøsang, Ismail & Boyd, 2007) and (Jurca, Binder & Faltings, 2007).

CONCLUSION

In this chapter we described a new protocol for a secured trust management model which is based on evaluations of service consumers regarding the trustability of services. The protocol describes how these evaluations can be stored on the provider-side in order to decrease the organization expenditures on the consumer-side and to avoid central network instances which are responsible for the management of service evaluations. Because the necessary security mechanisms refer to a message-based exchange strategy conventional connection-oriented protocols like SSL or VPN are not useful in this context. We motivated the example scenario of a federated system where services wrap business software components. The protocol uses digital signatures and encryption algorithms in order to secure authenticity, integrity and confidentiality of evaluations which are exchanged as messages. The protocol has to be seen as an extendable model whereas various adoptions are imaginable. Trustworthiness and reputation attributes could be bound to the service description by different PKI-based security functions, integrated within future service provision frameworks of service providers.

Despite of the disadvantages or challenges of reputation systems in general the use of such systems might be justified by a look to the factual acceptance of similar models as part of today's electronic marketplaces as e.g. at Ebay.com or Amazon.com.

REFERENCES

Abdul-Rahman, A., & Hailes, S. (2000). Supporting Trust in Virtual Communities. In *Proceedings of the Hawaii's International Conference on Systems Sciences*, Maui, Hawaii.

Brehm, N., Lübke, D., & Marx Gómez, J. (2007). Federated Enterprise Resource Planning (FERP) Systems. In P. Saha (Ed.), *Handbook of Enterprise Systems Architecture in Practice* (pp. 290-305). Hershey, PA: IGI Global.

Brehm, N., Mahmoud, T., Marx Gómez, J., & Memari, A. (2008). Towards Intelligent Discovery for Enterprise Architecture Services (IDEAS). *Journal of Enterprise Architecture*, *4*(3), 26–36.

Brehm, N., & Marx Gómez, J. (2005): Secure Web service-based Resource Sharing in ERP Networks. *International Journal on Information Privacy and Security (JIPS)*.

Brehm, N., & Marx Gómez, J. (2007). Web Service-based specification and implementation of functional components in Federated ERP-Systems. In *10th International Conference on Business Information Systems*, Poznan, Poland.

Brehm, N., Marx Gómez, J., & Rautenstrauch, C. (2006). An ERP solution based on web services and peer-to-peer networks for small and medium enterprises. *International Journal of Information Systems and Change Management (IJISCM)*.

Carbo, J., Molina, J., & Davila, J. (2002). Comparing Predictions of SPORAS vs. a Fuzzy Reputation Agent Sys-tem. In *Third International Conference on Fuzzy Sets and Fuzzy Systems*, Interlaken, (pp. 147–153).

Carter, J., Bitting, E., & Ghorbani, A. (2002). Reputation Formalization for an Information-Sharing Multi-Agent Sytem. *Computational Intelligence*, *18*(2), 515–534. doi:10.1111/1467-8640.t01-1-00201

Estefan, J. A., Laskey, K., McCabe, F. G., & Thornton, D. (2008). *Reference Architecture for Service Oriented Architecture Version 1.0*. Public Review Draft 1, OASIS Service Oriented Architecture Reference Model TC. Retrieved January 19, 2009, http://docs.oasis-open.org/soa-rm/soa-ra/v1.0/soa-ra-pr-01.pdf

Grandison, T. (2003). *Trust Specification and Analysis for Internet Applications*. Ph.D. Thesis, Imperial College of Science Technology and Medicine, Department of Computing, London.

Jøsang, A., Ismail, R., & Boyd, C. (2007). A Survey of Trust and Reputation Systems for Online Service Provision Decision Support Systems. *Decision Support Systems*, *43*(2), 618–644. doi:10.1016/j.dss.2005.05.019

Jurca, R., Binder, W., & Faltings, B. (2007). Reliable QoS Monitoring Based on Client Feedback. In *16th International Conference on the World Wide Web*, Banff, Alberta, Canada.

Maarof, M. A., & Krishna, K. (2002). An hybrid trust management model for multi agent systems based trading society. In *Proceedings of the International Workshop on Communication Software Engineering IWCSE'2002*, Marrakech, Morocco.

Maximilien, E. M., & Singh, M. P. (2001). Reputation and endorsement for web services. *ACM SIGecom Exchanges*, *3*(1), 24–31. doi:10.1145/844331.844335

Maximilien, E. M., & Singh, M. P. (2002). Conceptual model of web service reputation. *SIGMOD Record*, *31*(4), 36–41. doi:10.1145/637411.637417

Maximilien, E. M., & Singh, M. P. (2004). Toward autonomic web services trust and selection. In *Proceedings of the 2nd international Conference on Service Oriented Computing*. New York: ACM Press.

Maximilien, E. M., & Singh, M. P. (2005). Agent-based trust model involving multiple qualities. In *Proceedings of the 4th international Joint Conference on Autonomous Agents and Multiagent Systems*. Utrecht, Netherlands: ACM Press.

Ostrom, E. (1998). A Behavioral Approach to the Rational-Choice Theory of Collective Action. *The American Political Science Review*, *92*(1), 1–22. doi:10.2307/2585925

Sabater, J., & Sierra, C. (2002). Reputation and Social Network Analysis in Multi-Agent Systems. In *Proceedings of the First International Joint Conference on Autonomous Agents and Multiagent Systems (AAMAS-02)*, Bologna, Italy, (pp. 475–482).

Sen, S., & Sajja, N. (2002). Robustness of Reputation-based Trust: Booblean Case. In *Proceedings of the First International Joint Conference on Autonomous Agents and Multiagent Systems (AAMAS-2002)*, Bologna, Italy, (pp. 288–293).

Yu, B., & Singh, M. P. (2001). Towards a Probabilistic Model of Distributed Reputation Management. In *Proceedings of the Fourth Workshop on Deception, Fraud and Trust in Agent Societies*, Montreal, Canada, (pp. 125–137).

Yu, B., & Singh, M. P. (2002). An Evidential Model of Distributed Reputation Management. In *Proceedings of the First International Joint Conference on Autonomous Agents and Multiagent Systems (AAMAS-02)*, Bologna, Italy, (pp. 294–301).

Zacharia, G. (1999), *Collaborative Reputation Mechanisms for Online Communities*. Master thesis, Massachusetts Institute of Technology.

Chapter 5
Forensics over Web Services:
The FWS

Murat Gunestas
General Directorate of Security, Turkey

Duminda Wijesekera
George Mason University, USA

Anoop Singhal
National Institute of Standards and Technology, USA

ABSTRACT

Web services are currently a preferred way to architect and provide complex services. This complexity arises due to the composition of new services by choreographing, orchestrating and dynamically invoking existing services. These compositions create service inter-dependencies that can be misused for monetary or other gains. When a misuse is reported, investigators have to navigate through a collection of logs to recreate the attack. In order to facilitate that task, the authors propose creating forensic web services (FWS), a specialized web service that when used would securely maintain transactional records between other web services. These secure records can be re-linked to reproduce the transactional history by an independent agency. Although their work is ongoing, they show the necessary components of a forensic framework for web services and its success through a case study.

INTRODUCTION

Web services are becoming a popular application of SOA (Service Oriented Architecture) within organizations, being used for many financial, government and military purposes. They do so by seamlessly integrating web services of different organizations over the Internet using choreographies, orchestrations, dynamic invocations, brokers etc.; and are now extending their way to include transactions that involve more than two participants, a.k.a. multiparty activities. These service-level compositional techniques create complex inter-dependencies between web services belonging to different organizations that can be exploited due to some localized or compositional flaws. Therefore, such exploits/attacks (Vorobiev & Jun, 2006; Demchenko, Gommans, & Oudenaarde, 2005; Singhal, Winograd, & Scarfone, 2006) can affect multiple servers and organizations, resulting in financial loss or infrastructural damage. Investigating such incidents would require that dependencies between service invocations be retained

DOI: 10.4018/978-1-60566-950-2.ch005

in a participating party neutral and secure way so that the alleged activity can be undeniably recreated while preserving evidence that could lead to and support appropriate prosecutorial activity. Material evidence currently extractable from web servers such as log records, XML firewall alerts from end point services, and the like, do not have any forensic value because defendants can rightfully claim that they did not send that message, and plaintiffs can fabricate or alter the log record to deceive the court. We describe a participant neutral, non-refutable solution, a forensically valid evidence gathering mechanism for SOA, through this chapter.

BACKGROUND

Two conceptual elements base current web services: (1) Use of XML (eXtensible Markup Language), SOAP (Simple Object Access Protocol), and WSDL (Web Service Definition Language) as basic building material; (2) Complex applications built upon long-running, sometimes transactional executions created from basic elements using choreography, orchestration and compositional methods.

Basic Paradigm

XML format underlies entire web service architecture and its artifacts. All schemas, definition files, and messages transmitted are formed by the means of XML. WSDL, a XML based definition file, defines the interface of a web service in order for the service to be invoked by other services in accordance with the specifications of internal executions. SOAP, a XML based protocol, defines the metadata of the messages to be exchanged between services. Operations are defined in WSDL documents and they are the only mechanisms that can be employed for web services to communicate with each other. SOAP messages are defined and exchanged as incoming and outgoing messages through the operations. WSDL proposes four types of operations:

- **Notification:** One message is sent to many receivers, such as broadcasting.
- **One-Way:** The message is sent and no response is expected, such as Fire-and-Forget.
- **Request-Response:** A typical RPC structure: The message is sent from sender to receiver and response is pushed back to the sender.
- **Solicit-Response:** Request is sent without any data and the response is expected.

Although there are four proposed operation types, the message exchanges can be defined in two ways, in summary, One-Way and Request-Response—this is so since notification and solicit-response can both be represented by one-way and request-response types, respectively.

Composition Paradigm

The message exchange patterns (MEP) described above form the base for the entire web service paradigm. These simple MEPs construct collaboration scenarios using the appropriate composition models. While defining a composition, two issues arise: first, how it is designed and second, what pattern it employs.

Design Types

Selecting the target provider services can be accomplished either statically or dynamically, that is, in design-time or run-time. Design-time selections entail a-priori determination while run-time selections can introduce the opportunity to switch between web services among selected domains.

Static Composition: Static compositions propose web services to be selected and determined through the business applications at design-time. Currently, most web service implementations are static. A designer makes the selection manually based on description files (WSDL) published on the web. The designed application logic is deployed into either a business process engine as a process file or into any web service container in hard code. Unless any changes are applied to the logic the web services consumed through the application never change.

Dynamic Composition: Unlike static composition, a designer selects a domain of web services rather than a particular collection of web services. The logic itself selects a specific web service at run-time by asking any filter database residing at the site of the consumer or global Quality of Services residing on the Internet.

Static web service composition introduces less anonymity than the dynamic counterpart, thus satisfying with less effort through any forensic examination. Because dynamic composition imposes much more burden in terms of revealing the activity and its actual performance at run-time, this increases the need to have a comprehensive platform that preserves evidence in regard to activities through the entire architecture.

Patterns

Some authors (Khalaf, Mukhi, & Weerawarana, 2003) categorize web service composition from another perspective, that is, its patterns. According to these patterns, web services can be composed either of their typical pattern (hierarchical) or of a little more complex one (conversational).

Hierarchical Composition: Through this pattern, the consumer web service calls another composite web service, passing the input parameter and receiving the result. Other than this request-response activity no other call is employed to the same instance at the target. The complexity of the composition is hidden in this pattern since the target system never allows change of its internal state other than atomic calls.

Conversational Composition: This pattern is mostly used when web services need to interact with each other more than once throughout the same instances at both sides in order to accomplish the ultimate task. In these scenarios, the target system, unavoidably, makes its internal state mutable, thus causing overlapping instances to be created within parties to the composition.

From the forensics point of view, representing and recreating the activities in the latter pattern is much more difficult than the former one. Figure 1 illustrates the comparison between the two patterns. In the hierarchical pattern the nested instance of an external web service completely finishes before returning the result while many interactions between instances can survive in the conversational pattern. Although describing what happened exactly during execution in the hierarchical pattern is reasonable, this may not be the case with the conversational pattern.

Composition Standards and Languages

Although there are so many standards and specifications for web services, through the chapter state-of-the-art orchestration and choreography specifications are discussed specifically. BPEL (Business Process Execution Language) is a language for business process modeling. WS-BPEL and BPEL4WS are its two popular implementations for web service architecture. They can define both abstract and executable processes. They are two effective tools to realize orchestration of composite web services from a central point. Conversely, WSCI and WS-CDL create a global view of multi-party choreographies of web services from their individual description files. These languages enable collaborative processes that are recruiting multiple web services, and facilitate interactions between them from a global, high-level perspective rather than an individual service's request-respond perspective.

Figure 1. Hierarchical and conversational patterns. Adapted from (Khalaf, Mukhi, & Weerawarana, 2003)

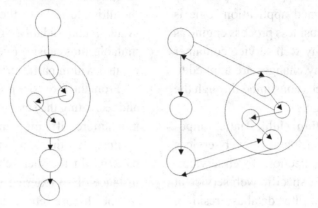

Hierarchical Pattern   Conversational Pattern

WEB SERVICE ATTACKS

There are many attacks on web services, such as WSDL/UDDI scanning, parameter tampering, replays, XML rewriting, man-in-the-middle, eavesdropping, routing detours, etc. In addition to these web service attacks, dynamic service selection, choreography, orchestration, and composition increase the ways of exploiting web services, such as application and dataflow attacks (Vorobiev & Jun, 2006; Demchenko, Gommans & Oudenaarde, 2005; Singhal, Winograd, & Scarfone, 2006).

We now show the details of a sample cross-site scripting (XSS) attack used to illustrate the capabilities of FWS. A typical XSS (Du, 2006) attack may inject a malicious script to harm a web service that dynamically builds some of its information.

1. Attacker updates MET_WS database with "regionID=234;description="Heavy Rain <script>document.write('<img src=http://attacker_IP:9999?c='+ document.cookie + '>'); </script>""

2. According to the Choreography model, MET_WS fires regional messages to update WEA_WS updateRegion

(..ID="234";Description=".+mal-script+..")

3. POR_WS sends weatherRequest(ID="234")

4. WEA_WS sends weatherRespond(ID="234";Description=".+mal-script+..")

5. Portal Web Application emits the mal-script in html form to requesting browsers.

6. Vulnerable browsers run the mal-script and send cookie information to Attacker's Fish Net Application.

7. Attacker retrieves sensitive information from cookies.

Figure 2 shows an attacker with stolen credentials injecting some malicious data and invoking an update operation on a meteorology service that stores this script (including instructions to steal cookies from web browsers). Meteorology Web Service (MET_WS) gets infected with malicious data and delivers the data ignorantly to the Weather Web Service (WEA_WS), firing the updateRegion message. WEA_WS, accordingly to their choreography, passes malicious data to Portal Web Service (POR_WS), among other legal information. Then a web application, say *Portal Web Application*, invoking a weatherRequest operation at WEA_WS retrieves this malicious data and publishes the weather information to its

Figure 2. A cross-site scripting (XSS) attack using web services

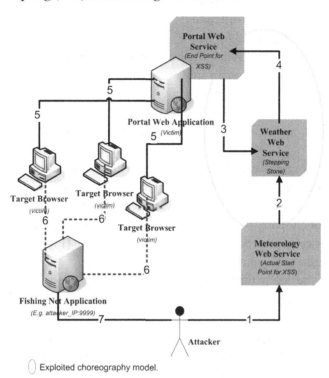

subscribers in an html form, thereby making the subscribers download the mal-script and send their personal information stored in cookies to the attacker's *Fishing Net Application*. Consequently, a *Fishing Net Application* managed by the *Attacker* can obtain sensitive user information as shown in Figure 2. An attacker, aware of choreography among web services, exploits this model and has Portal Web Application delivered malicious data to its members using web services in this choreography model.

The stated XSS attack shows how the business logic of a web service can be used to attack a server that depends upon other web services. In this scenario, *Portal Web Service* can claim that *Weather Web Service* sent the malicious content, whereas the actual source was *Meteorology Web Service*. This illustrates the need to have a mechanism that irrefutably points to the source of malice.

CHALLENGES IN FORENSICS OF WEB SERVICES

As a branch of forensics, digital forensics looks for the legal evidence on computer systems. Digital forensic examinations are performed in the direction of specific methodologies regarding the digital environment and type of evidence under search. For example, volatile medium (e.g. memory) examination would have different priorities from a database forensic examination. Forensics may address many needs including but not limited to gathering evidence for legal cases, data recovery, debugging and performance. The basic two questions should-be answered are "What happened?" and "What is the exact sequence of events?". To answer these questions digital forensics try to discover the current state of the digital artifact, which is, sometimes a database, a log file, a floppy disk, or even a mobile device (Mandia, & Prosise, 2001).

Unlike traditional forensics implementations, applying forensics to web service infrastructures introduces novel problems such as need for neutrality and comprehensiveness. The reliability issue, conversely, has always been the case for any forensics examination from the very beginning.

Neutrality

Web services are owned by organizations, that is, they have equal rights in the court of law when any dispute between parties turns into a law suit. Any log records residing at one party's site would have no forensic value under these circumstances since any alteration on the records might have been employed in favor of that site. Many forensics investigations through traditional systems have been held based on one site's records. For traditional systems, these actions may be thought reasonable since investigators take the advantage of inquiring users and establish human factors to corroborate evidence. In service oriented architectures, both sites would be automated and retain their own records. Both records would be under question by the opponent party, thus showing the need to have a neutral party capturing and preserving evidence based on interactions between parties.

Comprehensiveness

As described earlier, web service compositions may span over many web services of many organizations. Such interdependent services create long information flows. Thus, malicious data may stream over many web services. From forensics point of view, besides neutrality, the evidence gathered should be comprehensive enough so that investigation can reach every related end point to reveal what party performed what action during any executing composition. Incomplete evidence might point to any impeccable web service node as the source of malicious activity, thus misleading the investigators through the examination.

Reliability

Yet another important principle that any evidence should feature is reliability. In the court of law, judicial fellows want to be convinced of the evidence, especially when this comes from a digital source. Because impersonation and replay attacks do occur in web services, cryptographic mechanisms would help to protect ownership information passed around in messages by signing them digitally. Such a requirement, of course, would entail web services lying on a state-of-the-art cryptography platform such as Public Key Infrastructure (PKI).

OVERVIEW OF FWS

In order to facilitate and base forensic investigations on reliable infrastructure that can convince judicial systems, we propose designing *Forensic Web Services (FWS)* that preserve appropriate evidence to recreate the composed web service invocations independent of the parties with a vested interest. This would have a greater chance of being accepted in a court of law. FWS will provide on-line forensic capabilities to other web services as a web service itself. To gain these capabilities, FWS would be integrated with web services that require their services – referred to as customer web services of FWS. In order to do so, FWS provides a centralized service access point to its customer web services. This information, retained by FWS acting as a trusted third party, can be directly given to forensic examiners. Previous proposals to monitor web services (Cruz, Campos, M.L.M., Pires, & Campos, L. M., 2004) and generating evidence (Herzberg & Yoffe, 2007; Kremer, Markowitch, & Zhou, 2002; Robinson, Cook, & Shristava, 2005) have been for business purposes. The evidence produced has failed in either being considered neutral or comprehensive, thus not addressing the needs and standards of forensic examinations.

FWS uses the *Trusted Third Party (TTP)* notion that sits in between any two transactions. To obtain the services of a FWS system, all web services sign-up with a forensic web service. In order to create comprehensive evidence of an attack scenario, all relevant FWS agents must cooperate by providing relevant pair-wise transactional evidences stored with them. The following actions are necessary for FWS systems to function as required:

- A new web-service called stack, WS-Evidence layer, will be designed.
- A new XML schema for the messages used in WS-Evidence specification and records to be stored in FWS servers will be created.
- A specific agent (*EvidenceModule*) will be designed (Gunestas, Wijesekera, & Elkhodary, 2009) to re-route all transactional messages of member web services of the FWS framework through FWS servers.
- The underlying layer to WS-Evidence will be proposed to provide a trust base and cryptographic services.
- Algorithms running on FWS will be designed to manage the WS-Evidence protocol to generate pair-wise evidence (*deliver*) and to generate comprehensive evidence (*collectDependents*) for revealing global composition instances spreading over the web services in a specifically defined scope.

The Forensic Web Service Framework provides evidence generation in twofold; *pair-wise evidence generation* and *comprehensive evidence generation*:

Pair-Wise Evidence Generation

This refers to collection of transactional evidence that occurs between pairs of services at service invocation times. Figure 3 illustrates a non-

repudiation protocol based on SELP (Herzberg & Yoffe, 2007). The TTP receives the messages. After validating and proper storing, the TTP passes them to their ultimate targets. Since our messaging system is based on XML and SOAP we use the message format of $<\#session|\#message|\#signature_K(\#session|\#message/sequence|\#message/envelope))>$, where # refers to the points in XML format, | refers to concatenation of elements, and / points to the sub parts of elements, to exchange between sending web service, FWS, and receiving service. Here the session element identifies a WS-Evidence conversation, and message corresponds to an element carrying the actual upper layer message along with its sequence number (message/sequence) in the conversation, such as, for example: sequence number 2 corresponds to a response message if message exchange pattern type (MEPType) is two-way and the protocol is SELP (soon to be described). Each endpoint, either sender or receiver, signs the session, message/sequence, and message/envelope parts of the message in the signature element of the message. As described through the steps below, a typical two way (request-response) message exchange would be monitored and stored to be used in further investigations directly or to build comprehensive evidence.

1. The evidence module in the Sender side intercepts the request of an envelope and pauses the message context.
2. Creates and sends a CreateSessionRequest to the receiver web service for the target operation.
3. The evidence module in the receiver side receives the message and creates and sends a response message back to the sender. It also creates a session.
4. Sender's evidence module builds TwoWay1st ($<\#session|\#message|\#signature_{Sender-K}(\#session|"1"|\#env)>$) from the message context paused and sends it to TTP.

Figure 3. Pair-wise evidence generation protocol (deliver process in two-way mode)

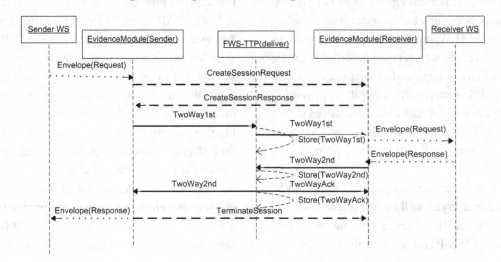

5. The TTP recieves TwoWay1st, stores the message, forwards it to the receiver, and starts a timer.

6. Receiver's evidence module intercepts the message, processes, validates and extracts the actual envelope to release it to the expected receiver operation.

7. Receiver application prepares a response message and sends it back to the sender.

8. Receiver's evidence module intercepts the response envelope, builds a TwoWay2nd (<#session |#message |#signature$_{Receiver-K}$(#session|"2"|# env)>) message and sends it back to the TTP. If the response TwoWay2nd cannot reach the TTP before timing out, then, Failure (<#session|#message |#signature$_{TTP-K}$ (#session|"-1"|# env)>) is signed by the TTP; it is stored and sent back to the Sender.

9. The TTP forwards TwoWay2nd to the sender; it also creates, signs, stores, and sends TwoWayAck (<#session|#message|#signature$_{TTP-K}$ (#session|"3" |#env)>) to the receiver.

10. Sender's evidence module intercepts the message, processes (e.g. validates) and extracts the actual envelope releasing it to

the expected application. It also creates and sends a TerminateSession to the receiver web service for related session, thus, terminating the session.

Comprehensive Evidence Generation

On demand, FWS compose pairs of transactional evidence collected at services invocation times and reveal global views of complex transactional scenarios that occurred during specified periods. They provide these views to forensic examiners. Listing 1 (Figure 4) shows the 'collectDependents' algorithm (the core component of this process), that is inspired by King and Chen's (2003) dependency graph algorithm. 'collectDependents' algorithm (see our previous work (Gunestas, Wijesekera, & Singhal, 2008) for details of the algorithm) runs recursively, traversing over many FWS stations, thus, collecting FWS records that are related to each other. Therefore, it helps in building a GRAPH that contains log records as edges and web services as nodes. See how it works through the Case Study described in the next section.

Figure 4. Listing 1: Comprehensive evidence generation (collectDependents Algorithm)

```
←!– Starts extracting values (timeThreshold, nodeThreshold, etc.) →
←!– from DependentsBagIn and initializes creating the →
←!– WebServiceNodes and LogRecordEdges instances of GRAPH →
1. baseTime = startTime - timeThreshold
2. for each logRecordIndex LRI ∈ FWS {
3.     timeThreshold=timeTreshold - (startTime - LRI.timeStamp)
4.     startTime=LRI.timestamp
5.     for each webServiceNode WS ∈ GRAPH {
6.         if (SenderWS | ReceiverWS ∈ LRI & LRI ∉ GRAPH &
               R.timestamp ≥ baseTime & WS.nodeLevel ≤ WS.nodeThreshold) {
7.             Add LRI as edge into GRAPH
8.             if (LRI's partner web service PWS ∈ GRAPH) {
9.                 PWS.nodeLevel=WS.nodeLevel+1
10.                PWS.nodeThreshold=nodeThreshold
11.                Add the PWS into GRAPH }
12.            if (LRI's PWS ∈ this.FWS & LRI's PWS ∈ GRAPH) {
13.                NeighbourFWS = getFWS(PWS)
14.                NeighbourFWS.collectDependents(DependentsBagIn)
15.                Merge DependentsBagOut into GRAPH}}}}
16. return GRAPH in DependentsBagOut format
```

A CASE STUDY: THE XSS ATTACK

Now, we show how any agent can use FWS to create comprehensive evidence for the XSS attack described earlier. Through the Case Study, we assume that FWS-1 owns POR_WS (Portal Web Service), GEO_WS (Geocoding Web Service), and so many others, while FWS-2 owns WEA_WS (Weather Web Service) and MET_WS (Meteorology Web Service), along with other many services. Figure 5 lists sample log records available at FWS-1 and FWS-2 in LRI (Log Record Index) format. Arrows illustrate how the *collectDependents* algorithm reveals activities dependent to each other spanning over many web services and FWS stations. The bold records refer to log records linked to each other and used to build the dependency graph as edges between web service nodes. Each record applies the LRI format ({OrderNo| Timestamp| SessionID| status| fwsttp| Sender| Receiver}).

Assume that an official decides to generate a digital evidence bag of this incident using the above parameters--please remember the "collectDependents" algorithm in Listing 1 (Figure 4) and the parameters to draw the dependency scope in the examination: *rootWS=POR_WS, startTime=17, nodeThreshold=3,* and *timeThreshold=16*. The examiner first defines the *rootFWS* by querying from FWS-Registry and sets FWS-1 as the root, thereby invoking the *collectDependents* process at FWS-1. We now apply the algorithm of Listing 1 (Figure 4) to this example through the following steps.

Step 1: FWS-1 first retrieves LRIs in Figure 5, and starts traversing on LRIs in decreasing time order. In this example, this order spans LRIs from time 17 to time 1 because of *timeThreshold* value 16. The algorithm skips LRIs in times 17 and 14 because they do not contain POR_WS as any other partner in their records. It finds an LRI with time 13 related to POR_WS, adds the LRI as *LogRecordEdge*, and adds the partner web service, WEA_WS, as the dependent *WebServiceNode* because it has yet to be included in the graph created so far.

Step 2: Because WEA_WS is registered to another FWS, FWS-2, this process assigns the FWS-2 as neighbor FWS and invokes the *collectDependents* process with *rootWS=WEA_WS, startTime=13, timeThreshold=12, logRecordEdges,* and *webServiceNodes* already in the graph.

Figure 5. Log Record Indexes in FWS-1 and FWS-2

LRIs in FWS-1	LRIs in FWS-2
...	...
1|234|Response|FWS-1|TRE_WS|VRE_WS.vresPT.ReserveVehicle	1|234|Response|FWS-1|TRE_WS|VRE_WS.vresPT.ReserveVehicle
2|2134|Request|FWS-2|WEA_WS|GEO_WS..getLongtitute	**2|2134|Request|FWS-2|WEA_WS|GEO_WS..getLongtitute**
3|2134|Response|FWS-2|WEA_WS|GEO_WS..getLongtitute (7)	**3|2134|Response|FWS-2|WEA_WS|GEO_WS..getLongtitute** (5)
4|2164|Response|FWS-1|TRE_WS|HRE_WS.hresPT.ReserveHotel	4|2164|Response|FWS-1|TRE_WS|HRE_WS.hresPT.ReserveHotel
6|21572|Request|FWS-1|TRE_WS|ARE_WS.aresPT.ReserveAirline (6)	**5|2196|Request|FWS-2|MET_WS|WEA_WS..updateRegion**
9|21572|Response|FWS-1|TRE_WS|ARE_WS.aresPT.ReserveAirline	7|34563|Request|FWS-2|VRE_WS|HRE_WS.hresPT.HotelLocation (4)
10|34534|Request|FWS-2|POR_WS|WEA_WS..weatherRequest	8|34563|Response|FWS-2|VRE_WS|HRE_WS.hresPT.HotelLocation
12|22534|Request|FWS-1|TRE_WS|VRE_WS.vresPT.ReserveVehicle	**10|34534|Request|FWS-2|POR_WS|WEA_WS..weatherRequest**
13|34534|Response|FWS-2|POR_WS|WEA_WS..weatherRespond (2)	11|34567|Response|FWS-2|VRE_WS|HRE_WS.hresPT.HotelLocation
14|34523|Request|FWS-1|WEA_WS|GEO_WS..getLongtitute (1)	12|22534|Request|FWS-1|TRE_WS|VRE_WS.vresPT.ReserveVehicle (3)
17|34523|Response|FWS-1|WEA_WS|GEO_WS..getLongtitute	13|34534|Response|FWS-2|POR_WS|WEA_WS..weatherRespond
...	14|34523|Request|FWS-1|WEA_WS|GEO_WS..getLongtitute
...	...
...	17|34523|Response|FWS-1|WEA_WS|GEO_WS..getLongtitute

Step 3: FWS-2 retrieves the LRIs and starts from the LRI with time 13. It ignores LRI 13 because it is already in the graph and LRIs with time 12 and 11 because of irrelevancy.

Step 4: FWS-2 adds the LRI in time 10 because the partners are already in the graph. The records in 8 and 7 are ignored because of their irrelevancy to the graph. FWS-2 adds the LRI in time 5 because one of its partners is included in the graph. The other partner MET_WS is added to the graph with a higher node level 3. Because MET_WS is registered to FWS-2 there is no need to call another FWS to collect its dependents.

Step 5: After ignoring 4, the records in time 3 and 2 are added because of their relevancy to WEA-WS.

Step 6: FWS-2 returns to FWS-1 since there remains no record to traverse.

Step 7: FWS-1 continues to process from LRI with time 12. It ignores LRIs with time 10, 3, and 2 although they are relevant, but they are already

in the graph. It also ignores other records because they are unrelated to the graph.

The case study described above shows how the FWS framework could be helpful for revealing dependencies between web services through composition models and scenarios as illustrated in Figure 6. Arrows refer to Log Records as edges in a graph; and circles refer to Web Services as nodes. The figure depicts how the web service choreography instance through the Case Study could be represented. This figure is also a result of a typical digital evidence bag document that constitutes a graph which points to dependencies among the source (MET_WS) and the victim (POR_WS) of malicious activity/path, as well as a possible stepping stone (WEA_WS) through the incident. The scenarios can be improved; and FWS could be applied to more complex attacks. For the sake of clarity, a simple scenario has been implemented through this chapter.

Figure 6. The dependency graph for the case study

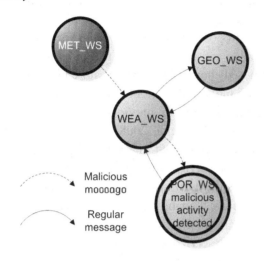

Malicious
message

Regular
message

PROMISES OF FWS

Organizations that are tightly integrated to each other through web transactions and processes can benefit from FWS in many ways. Firstly, organizations need to hold some of their partner web services accountable when their mal-acts affect one's own efficiency, consistency, availability, etc. Secondly, the detailed explanation of the malicious activity may impact the severity of punishments or collectible monetary compensation. We show that undeniable logging of critical information exchanges are an effective way to meet these two needs. FWS can monitor the systems non-refutably; those records retained by the system

would have forensic value in courts of law; which has not been the case so far. Hereafter, we propose to provide more refined evidence regarding the activities that occur on web service architectures. In the next step, we propose to extend the system in order to maintain the instance correlations through both hierarchical and conversational compositions.

Monitoring Web Services Interactions

Through the FWS framework, the WS-Evidence layer (see Figure 7) routes the interactions to pass over FWS stations on the way of their ultimate targets (remember the protocol in Figure 3). As described in our previous study (Gunestas, Wijesekera, & Elkhodary, 2009), handler-chain architecture (Srinath, Chathura, Jaliya, Eran, Ajith, & Deepal, 2006) is used to ease and standardize client side workload on deployment of agents (e.g. *EvidenceModule*). Our prototype implementation uses Axis2, where Axis2 allows services to engage modules placing their own *handlers* to retain their own control over messages. A module can utilize the extensible message handling mechanism of Axis2 to craft and process messages through *In-Flow* and *Out-Flow* pipes towards Axis2 channels – all business layer messages on their way to the transport layer and all transport layer messages in the opposite direction. According to the selected protocol (remember the steps describing Figure 3),

Figure 7. WS-evidence stack

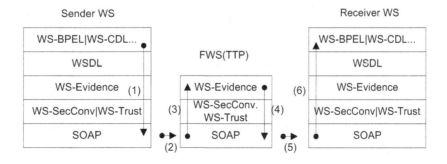

original messages are routed to deliver process at FWS-TTP through Out-Flow pipe in WS-Evidence message format and processing WS-Evidence messages, original application messages are extracted and passed to application logic through In-Flow pipe. This function underlies the entire forensic functionality of the FWS described below. The below figure depicts how WS-Evidence is applied for a message through web services and their existing stacks. It primarily supports SELP (Herzberg & Yoffe, 2007) protocol. Flows 1 and 6 shows the activity performed by the agents; flows 2 and 5 show the wire communication at SOAP level; and 3 and 4 represent inputs and outputs in FWS-TTP. Therefore, FWS-TTPs can monitor the activities between interacting web service pairs.

Forensics over Web Service Architectures

Capturing the interdependent activity makes little sense from the forensics perspective if the capturing procedure is not comprehensive. Finding the dependent interactions and web services with respect to a specific point in the scope of a certain composed execution of web services seems an exhaustive task. As a response to this challenge FWS proposes a protocol in order for evidence modules and FWS stations to run in the layer proposed above. FWS stations store interactions to ease the task that should be performed by the algorithms (see our previous work (Gunestas, Wijesekera, & Singhal, 2008) for design) to collect records of dependent interactions spanned over many web services during the actual execution. Figure 8 illustrates typical message flows earning forensics capabilities to web services. Ellipse boxes refer to the member domain of any FWS. Every web service registered to any FWS utilizes its evidence modules to route its messages over FWS stations to reach their ultimate goals (dashed lines); every FWS can call each other's services through some investigation algorithms such as "collectDependents" (solid bold lines). Some central services for registry and security purposes, for example, would inevitably be called through the framework at any time (solid lines).

Figure 8. The FWS framework and message flows

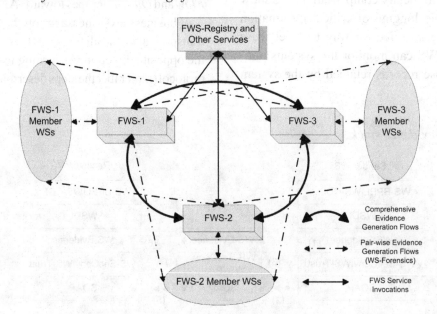

Revealing Global Composition Instances

Many studies/specifications offer composition models to handle business transactions and other cross organizational activities over web services. To the best of our knowledge, there is no framework offered that is proposing to recreate the composition instances from the events logged in a neutral way. FWS can interleave the instances of global / composed executions of web services using a global unique identifier as shown in Figure 9. We envision, with little extension to our design published so far, that it would be possible to reveal and represent composition executions on an instance basis. This capability would be based on following two functions; verification of orchestration processes and choreography instances.

Orchestration Process Verification

Given an orchestration process model of a web service, the FWS framework can detect whether the process behaved as expected. When such checks are applied to web services based on the instances revealed above, the results would reveal some forensic information, such as, for example, the fact that deviation from expected behavior happens with respect to some certain messages. Either the abstract process model or executable process model could be used in order to represent the behavioral interface of the process.

Choreography Instance Verification

Given a choreography model, FWS could detect deviations from the expected set of choreography instances and represent them. Deviating points in the choreography instance should successfully be addressed along with actual identities of sources for deviations to realize any forensic examiner's ultimate goal. Figure 9 illustrates sample interleaved instances and a deviated instance. In order to interleave the sessions, FWS records envision maintaining/discovering a "global unique identifier," referring to each separate execution and thus facilitating to interleave each set of records that belong to specific executions of any global composition. FWS records are designed to keep dependency information along with instance correlation information; therefore, allowing revealing if there is any deviation from the expected instance of global execution.

RELATED WORK

There is no distributed forensic framework for investigating inter-related web services designed so far. However, the work cited hereafter shares

Figure 9. Interleaved and deviated instances

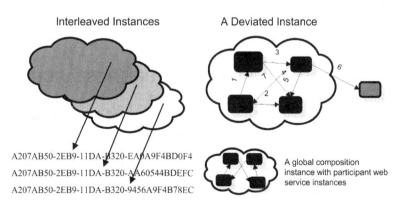

some common features with FWS objectives or methods.

WS-NRExchange (Robinson, Cook, & Shristava, 2005) influenced the model employed through FWS for pair-wise evidence generation with some differences. They provide a framework to support fair non-repudiable B2B communications on the basis of a trusted deliver agent notion. It implements the Coeffey and Saidha (1996) protocol to provide non-repudiation in their work. However, the framework is designed to run with other protocols as well. They only propose delivering evidence to the related parties, but not preserving them in trusted agents for further usage. Furthermore, choreographed, composed services are ignored. Although their work was not designed for forensics, we use relevant parts in the pair-wise evidence generation.

Herzberg et al. (2007) introduces the notion of having an Evidences Layer for e-commerce transactions. They propose this layer to be at the bottom of the e-commerce stack and on top of a transport layer (such TLS/SSL, or TCP/IP). They introduce two protocols to generate and deliver evidence to involved parties in message exchange: the first is the *Simple Evidence Layer Protocol* and the second is the *optimistic* one. They employ notaries in the first protocol while generating and delivering evidence. FWS use the layering approach of Herzberg (2007) in the web service stack with minor changes, such as adding the time stamping point; and use their SELP as the pair-wise evidence generation protocol. Like others, the Herzberg et al. (2007) approach was not designed for forensics.

FWS also implement trusted third parties for pair-wise evidence generation, as Coffey and Saidha et al. (1996) suggest. Although inline TTPs are immature for business transactions, they add value to forensics evidence. Onieva (2003) gives the intermediary usage perspective in the implementation of inline TTPs for e-commerce transactions. They also support multi-recipient cases through these intermediaries, but not for forensics. Bilal (2005) uses BPEL for non-repudiation protocol implementation in web services but does not use TTP, thereby lacking the capability to handle message content.

WSLogA (Cruz, Campos, M.L.M., Pires, & Campos, L. M., 2004) tracks web service invocations by logging service invocations using SOAP intermediaries. Therefore, it captures the external behavior of service invocations. The main purpose of WSLogA is to provide feedback to business organizations by comprehensively logging services usage records. However, it does not address any distributed collection mechanism necessary to gather comprehensive forensic evidence over services sharing multiple servers.

FWS has been influenced by many studies on network forensics, of which two are described herein. Wang and Daniels (2005) use IDS alerts to generate an evidence graph for network forensic analysis. *Local reasoning* and *global reasoning* help in defining malicious activity in individual hosts and networks, respectively. Unlike Web Server Nodes in FWS, they use hosts as nodes in their graphs.

ForNet (Shanmugasundaram, Memon, Savant, & Bronnimann, 2003) is another distributed forensic framework that uses logs from routers in a network to run agents that provide their log records to ForNet servers. Unlike Wang and Daniels (2005), ForNet uses succinct information related to all regular network packets that is adequate in tracing the actual source of packets even when they are spoofed. Although not designed for Web Services, my work has been inspired by the design of ForNET.

FUTURE RESEARCH DIRECTIONS

As mentioned during the case study collection of dependent messages and services might traverse over multi-TTPs, that is, the need may arise to make FWS framework scalable all over the internet. In order to achieve this task, WS-Trust and SAML based federation and delegation mechanisms should be reified over FWS framework.

We have already mentioned two types of basic evidence based on service level agreements (SLA): (1) Evidence of Violation and (2) Evidence of Availability in our previous work (Gunestas, Wijesekera, & Elkhodary, 2009). Many different types of Evidence of Violation could be generated given the SLAs and FWS framework, on the other hand. Using a predefined format for SLAs, such as WSLA (Keller, & Ludwig, 2003), a generic algorithm would be helpful to create evidence of violations in the case of a real unexpected behavior of one of the endpoints. Some existent SLA monitor/detection mechanisms (Sahai, 2002) also would evidently run over FWS framework.

De Pauw (2007) publishes an experimental work on semantic correlation among web service messages. Implementing such a work on FWS records would lead forensic examiners to reveal dynamically dependent web services and their run-time executions. Such evidences would be helpful to reveal dynamically exploited complex transactions.

Another possible contribution would be generating evidence for previously known mis-use patterns. In this case, rules defining the misuse patterns direct mining algorithms on FWS framework. It may sometimes feature a signature (e.g. a set of messages in specific order) frequently becoming evident among the FWS records. Association rule mining techniques would help in search for such misuse patterns.

Examiners may need to know instance level dependency among web service invocations. Although there is effort (De Pauw, 2007) to correlate instances, the results are not expected %100 true. Therefore, a mechanism measuring the accuracy using probabilistic work would lead the decision makers in the way of achieving strong judgments.

Although we have designed an agent using Axis2's extensible handling mechanism, as of writing, there is no actively running adapter module working for evidence-mindful web services. An industrial effort would be grateful if they could materialize the "Evidence as Service" concept, which means zero-effort in integration and zero-alteration in business logic at endpoints.

CONCLUSION

Composed, choreographed or stand-alone web services span many application and legal domains. Consequently, any vulnerability in one service can be exploited to affect more than one service. Once a complaint is launched with respect to an alleged attack, it is necessary to investigate the incident and determine the source of attack.

We propose a framework referred to as Forensic Web Services that provides this capability as a service to other web services by logging service invocations. Our design shows how collected logs can provide the capability to produce a bag of digital evidence in order to expose the attack from its logs. The chapter also described how FWS could be utilized as a powerful forensics tool to reveal non-refutable evidence.

REFERENCES

Bilal, M., Thomas, J. P., Thomas, M., & Abraham, S. (2005). *Fair BPEL processes transaction using non-repudiation protocols.* Paper presented at the 2005 IEEE International Conference on Services Computing.

Coffey, T., Saidha, P. (1996). Non-repudiation with mandatory proof of receipt. *ACMCCR: Computer Communication Review, 26.*

Cruz, S. M. S., Campos, M. L. M., Pires, P. F., & Campos, L. M. (2004). *Monitoring e-business Web services usage through a log based architecture.* Paper presented at the IEEE International Conference on Web Services.

De Pauw, W., Hoch, R., & Huang, Y. (2007). *Discovering Conversations in Web Services Using Semantic Correlation Analysis.* Paper presented at the IEEE International Conference on Web Services, ICWS 2007.

Demchenko, Y., Gommans, L., de Laat, C., & Oudenaarde, B. (2005). *Web services and grid security vulnerabilities and threats analysis and model.* Paper presented at the The 6th IEEE/ACM International Workshop on Grid Computing.

Du, W. (2006). *Cross-Site Scripting (XSS) Attack Lab.* Laboratory for Computer Security Education, Syracuse University, Syracuse, NY.

Gunestas, M., Wijesekera, D., & Elkhodary, A. (2009). *An Evidence Generation Model for Web Services.* Paper presented at the IEEE International Conference on System of Systems Engineering (SoSE '09).

Gunestas, M., Wijesekera, D., & Singhal, A. (2008). *Forensic Web Services.* Paper presented at the Fourth Annual IFIP WG 11.9 International Conference on Digital Forensics.

Herzberg, A., & Yoffe, I. (2007). *The Delivery and Evidences Layer* (No. Report 2007/139). Retrieved from Cryptology ePrint Archive.

Keller, A., & Ludwig, H. (2003). The WSLA Framework: Specifying and Monitoring Service Level Agreements for Web Services. *Journal of Network and Systems Management, 11*(1), 57–81. doi:10.1023/A:1022445108617

Khalaf, R., Mukhi, N., & Weerawarana, S. (2003). *Service-Oriented Composition in BPEL4WS.* Paper presented at the Twelfth International World Wide Web Conference, Budapest, Hungary.

King, S. T., & Chen, P. M. (2003). *Backtracking Intrusions.* Paper presented at the 2003 Symposium on Operating Systems Principles (SOSP).

Kremer, S., Markowitch, O., & Zhou, J. (2002). An Intensive Survey of Non-repudiation protocols. *Computer Communications, 25*(17), 1606–1621. doi:10.1016/S0140-3664(02)00049-X

Mandia, K., & Prosise, C. (2001). *Incident Response: Investigating Computer Crime.* New York: McGraw-Hill, Inc.

Onieva, J. A., Jianying, Z., Carbonell, M., & Lopez, J. (2003). *Intermediary non-repudiation protocols.* Paper presented at the IEEE International Conference on E-Commerce.

Robinson, P., Cook, N., & Shrivastava, S. (2005). *Implementing fair non-repudiable interactions with Web services.* Paper presented at the Ninth IEEE International EDOC Enterprise Computing Conference.

Sahai, A., Machiraju, V., Sayal, M., van Moorsel, A., & Casati, F. (2002). Automated SLA Monitoring for Web Services. In *Proceedings Management Technologies for E-Commerce and E-Business Applications: 13th IFIP/IEEE International Workshop on Distributed Systems: Operations and Management, DSOM 2002, Montreal, Canada, October 21-23,* (pp. 28-41).

Shanmugasundaram, K., Memon, N., Savant, A., & Bronnimann, H. (2003). *ForNet: A Distributed Forensics Network.* Paper presented at the Second International Workshop on Mathematical Methods, Models and Architectures for Computer Networks Security, St. Petersburg, Russia.

Singhal, A., Winograd, T., & Scarfone, K. (2007). *Guide to Web Services Security.* NIST Special Publication 800-95

Srinath, P., Chathura, H., Jaliya, E., Eran, C., Ajith, R., Deepal, J., et al. (2006). *Axis2, Middleware for Next Generation Web Services.* Paper presented at the International Conference on Web Services (ICWS '06).

Vorobiev, A., & Jun, H. (2006). *Security Attack Ontology for Web Services*. Paper presented at the Second International Conference on Semantics, Knowledge and Grid (SKG '06).

Wang, W., & Daniels, T. E. (2005). *Building evidence graphs for network forensics analysis*. Paper presented at the 21st Annual Computer Security Applications Conference.

ADDITIONAL READING

Agrawal, R., Gunopulos, D., & Leymann, F. (1998). Mining process models from workflow logs. In *Advances in Database Technology — EDBT'98* (pp. 467-483).

Apache Axis2 Architecture Guide. (2006). The Apache Software Foundation.

Barbon, F., Traverso, P., Pistore, M., & Trainotti, M. (2006). *Run-Time Monitoring of Instances and Classes of Web Service Compositions*. Paper presented at the Web Services, 2006. ICWS '06. International Conference on.

Baresi, L., Ghezzi, C., & Guinea, S. (2004). *Smart monitors for composed services*. Paper presented at the Proceedings of the 2nd international conference on Service oriented computing.

Barros, A., Dumas, M., & Oaks, P. (2005). *A Critical Overview of WS-CDL*: BPTrends.

BEA. *Specifying SOAP Handlers for a Web Service*: BEA WEBLOGIC WORKSHOP HELP.

Beeri, C., Eyal, A., Milo, T., & Pilberg, A. (2007). *Monitoring business processes with queries*. Paper presented at the Proceedings of the 33rd international conference on Very large data bases.

Bianculli, D., & Ghezzi, C. (2007). *Monitoring conversational web services*. Paper presented at the 2nd international workshop on Service oriented software engineering: in conjunction with the 6th ESEC/FSE joint meeting.

Bilal, M., Thomas, J. P., Thomas, M., & Abraham, S. (2005). *Fair BPEL processes transaction using non-repudiation protocols*. Paper presented at the Services Computing, 2005 IEEE International Conference on.

Bucchiarone, A., & Gnesi, S. (2006). *A Survey on Services Composition Languages and Models*. Paper presented at the International Workshop on Web Services Modeling and Testing (WS-MaTe 2006).

Butler, M., Hoare, T., & Ferreira, C. (2005). A Trace Semantics for Long-Running Transactions. In *Communicating Sequential Processes* (pp. 133-150).

da Cruz, S. M. S., Campos, M. L. M., Pires, P. F., & Campos, L. M. (2004). *Monitoring e-business Web services usage through a log based architecture*. Paper presented at the Web Services, 2004. Proceedings. IEEE International Conference on.

De Pauw, W., Krasikov, S., & Morar, F. J. (2006). *Execution patterns for visualizing web services*. Paper presented at the Proceedings of the 2006 ACM symposium on Software visualization.

Dwibedi, R. (2005). XPath injection in XML databases. from http://palisade.plynt.com/issues/2005Jul/xpath-injection/

Gruschka, N., Gruschka, N., Jensen, M., & Luttenberger, N. (2007). *A Stateful Web Service Firewall for BPEL*. Paper presented at the Web Services, 2007. ICWS 2007. IEEE International Conference on.

Holgersson, J., & Soderstrom, E. (2005). *Web service security - vulnerabilities and threats within the context of WS-security*.

Jensen, M., Gruschka, N., & Luttenberger, N. (2008). *The Impact of Flooding Attacks on Network-based Services.* Paper presented at the Availability, Reliability and Security, 2008. ARES 08. Third International Conference on.

Jian, Y. (2005). []: IEEE Computer Society Press.]. *Monitoring the Macroscopic Effect of DDoS Flooding Attacks, 2,* 324–335.

Jianyin, Z., Sen, S., & Fangchun, Y. (2006). *Detecting Race Conditions in Web Services.* Paper presented at the Telecommunications, 2006. AICT-ICIW '06. International Conference on Internet and Web Applications and Services/Advanced International Conference on.

Johnson, M. W. *Monitoring and Diagnosing Applications with ARM 4.0:* IBM Corporation.

Juric, M. B. (2006). *Business Process Execution Language for Web Services* (Second Edition ed.). Birmingham, UK: Packt Publishing.

Kremer, S., Markowitch, O., & Zhou, J. (2002). An Intensive Survey of Non-repudiation protocols. *Computer Communications, 25*(17), 1606–1621. doi:10.1016/S0140-3664(02)00049-X

Liu, F., Wang, G., Chou, W., Fazal, L., & Li, L. (2006). *TARGET: Two-way Web Service Router Gateway.* Paper presented at the Web Services, 2006. ICWS '06. International Conference on.

Nishchal, B., & Kazerooni, S. (2007). *Web Services Vulnerabilities:* Security Compass.

Onieva, J. A., Jianying, Z., Carbonell, M., & Lopez, J. (2003). *Intermediary non-repudiation protocols.* Paper presented at the E-Commerce, 2003. CEC 2003. IEEE International Conference on.

Pistore, M., Bertoli, P., Barbon, F., Shaparau, D., & Traverso, P. (2004). *Planning and Monitoring Web Service Composition.* Paper presented at the ICAPS'04 Workshop on Planning and Scheduling for Web and Grid Services.

Rahaman, M. A., Schaad, A., & Rits, M. (2006). *Towards secure SOAP message exchange in a SOA.* Paper presented at the Proceedings of the 3rd ACM workshop on Secure web services.

Rembert, A. J. (2006). *Comprehensive workflow mining.* Paper presented at the Proceedings of the 44th annual Southeast regional conference.

Roth, H., Schiefer, J., & Schatten, A. (2006). *Probing and Monitoring of WSBPEL Processes with Web Services.* Paper presented at the E-Commerce Technology, 2006. The 8th IEEE International Conference on and Enterprise Computing, E-Commerce, and E-Services, The 3rd IEEE International Conference on.

Rouached, M., Gaaloul, W., van der Aalst, W., Bhiri, S., & Godart, C. (2006). Web Service Mining and Verification of Properties: An Approach Based on Event Calculus. In *On the Move to Meaningful Internet Systems 2006: CoopIS, DOA, GADA, and ODBASE* (pp. 408-425).

Rouached, M., & Godart, C. (2006). *Analysis of Composite Web Services Using Logging Facilities.* Paper presented at the Second International Workshop on Engineering Service-Oriented Applications: Design and Composition (WESOA'06).

Sahai, A., Machiraju, V., Sayal, M., van Moorsel, A., & Casati, F. (2002). Automated SLA Monitoring for Web Services. In *Management Technologies for E-Commerce and E-Business Applications: 13th IFIP/IEEE International Workshop on Distributed Systems: Operations and Management, DSOM 2002, Montreal, Canada, October 21-23, 2002. Proceedings* (pp. 28-41).

Stamos, A. (2005). *Attacking Web Services.* DC: The OWASP Foundation.

Vorobiev, A., & Jun, H. (2006). *Security Attack Ontology for Web Services.* Paper presented at the Semantics, Knowledge and Grid, 2006. SKG '06. Second International Conference.

Yuhong, Y., Pencole, Y., Cordier, M. O., & Grastien, A. (2005). *Monitoring Web service networks in a model-based approach.* Paper presented at the Web Services, 2005. ECOWS 2005. Third IEEE European Conference on.

Zaha, J. M., Dumas, M., ter Hofstede, A. H. M., Barros, A., & Decker, G. (2008). Bridging Global and Local Models of Service-Oriented Systems. *Systems, Man, and Cybernetics, Part C: Applications and Reviews . IEEE Transactions on, 38*(3), 302–318.

Zhou, J., & Gollman, D. (1996). *A fair non-repudiation protocol.* Paper presented at the Proceedings of the 1996 IEEE Symposium on Security and Privacy.

Chapter 6
Policy–Based Security Engineering of Service Oriented Systems

Antonio Maña
University of Málaga, Spain

Gimena Pujol
University of Málaga, Spain

Antonio Muñoz
University of Málaga, Spain

ABSTRACT

In this chapter the authors present a policy-based security engineering process for service oriented applications, developed in the SERENITY and MISTICO projects. Security and dependability (S&D) are considered as first-class citizens in the proposed engineering process, which is based on the precise description of reusable security and dependability solutions. The authors' process is based on the concept of S&D Pattern as the means to capture the specialized knowledge of security engineers and to make it available for automated processing, both in the development process (the focus of this chapter) and later at runtime. In particular, in this chapter they focus on the verification of the compliance with security policies, based on the formal specification of S&D Properties. The main advantages of the approach presented in this chapter are precisely that it allows us to define high-level policies and to verify that a secure oriented system complies with such policy (developed following the SERENITY approach). They also describe the application of the proposed approach to the verification of S&D properties in the web services (WS) environment. Concretely, the authors describe the use of SERENITY framework to facilitate the development of applications that use standard security mechanisms (such WS-Security, WS-Policy, WS-Security Policy, etc) and to ensure the correct application of these standard mechanisms, based on predefined policies. Finally, they show how to verify that the application complies with one or several S&D policies.

DOI: 10.4018/978-1-60566-950-2.ch006

INTRODUCTION

The popularization of open and distributed computing environments like mobile and ubiquitous computing, service oriented computing, ambient intelligence and sensor networks among others, indicates an irreversible trend towards distributed computing. This trend, along with the ever-growing number and importance of the computer-supported aspects of our daily lives, has raised the demands for security and dependability and has exposed the limitations of the current security and dependability solutions. Moreover, we exposed the limitations of current security engineering and software engineering methodologies and tools. In particular, the shift toward service-oriented computing increases the emphasis on relationships, negotiations, and agreements. This brings particular challenges for the area of security and dependability, which are traditionally very difficult to manage and measure. Additionally, it introduces accountability and liability issues, which are topics widely debated.

According to the conclusions of the ESFORS group of experts the state of the art of development processes for secure systems in open communication environments has to be considerably improved. Such improvements should include methods for precise specification of security policies and requirements, as well as the automated tools for classifying, selecting, adapting, and reorganizing existing security services, for integrating them into software systems under development, and last but not least for verifying the compliance of systems with security regulations and policies. Furthermore, special specification for the expression of security requirements have to be integrated into existing modelling languages to support rigorous treatment of security issues throughout the entire development process.

Although, security is an essential aspect in computing and communication, it has been traditionally overlooked and considered supplementary instead of a core element in the design and development of such systems. This concern has implied consequences and has been undermined the users' confidence in computer systems. Corporate scandals and breakdowns like the recent loss of 45 Million credit and debit card numbers and other personal data by the TJX Corporation, which have flourished in the last years, highlights the need for stronger compliance regulations for publicly listed companies.

One of the most significant regulations in this context is the Sarbanes-Oxley Act, developed in 2002, which defines significant tighter personal responsibility of corporate top management for the accuracy of reported financial statements. Last case shows how many of the best known initiatives for enhancing the security of computer systems have been based on guidelines, recommendations, best practices, certification, compliance and similar approaches lacking the necessary rigour and precision that one would expect when dealing with "security". Other relevant examples are: Common criteria, Federal Information Processing Standards (FIPS), traditional security patterns, Gramm-Leach-Bliley Act (GLBA), Federal Information Security Management Act (FISMA), and Health Insurance Portability and Accountability Act (HIPAA). In some cases other compliance frameworks, such as Control Objectives for Information and related Technology (COBIT), or standards as National Institute of Standards and Technology (NIST) inform on how to comply with the regulations.

The fact that all these regulations and policies are expressed informally or semi-formally make practically impossible to rigorously verify that an application complies with a specific regulation. In fact, several initiatives have been launched with the goal of verifying that applications comply with certain security policies. However, in these proposals, the concept of "security policy" refers to a set of low-level restriction. However, one common drawback of all these approaches is that they are strongly related with the low-level details (language, OS, development framework, etc.) of the application to be checked.

In this chapter, we present a framework for the verification of the compliance with security policies, based on the SERENITY model of secure and dependable systems. Concretely, we focus on its application to the Service-Oriented Computing. The main advantages of this approach are precisely that it allows us to define high-level policies and to verify that an application complies with a given policy, with the only requirement that it has been developed following the SERENITY approach. This framework has been created to address the wide range of heterogeneous AmI (Ambient Intelligence) scenarios that makes it very well-suited for open and distributed computing paradigms such as Service-Oriented Computing. Finally, we highlight the fact that this approach constitutes a first step towards automated software certification.

BACKGROUND

Currently, the lack of security is the main impediment to the adoption of WS in open scenarios. Existing security solutions for WS are still based on technology that has been used for several years to secure e-commerce sites. In fact, until recently, the most common approach was to use elements like standard firewalls, Secure Sockets Layer Encryption, and ad-hoc gateways for authentication and authorization. The WS-Security specification has represented an important advance in the standardization of mechanisms supporting security for WS. This initiative describes enhancements to the Simple Object Access Protocol (SOAP) to provide protection of messaging. WS-Security provides a general-purpose mechanism for associating security tokens with messages and describes how to encode binary security tokens such as X.509 certificates. Although WS-Security does not address security issues such as authorization or access

control, it represents a useful initiative to support other security services. In this research area we should mention the work on Web Services-Based Security Requirement Elicitation of the group at the University of Castilla-La Mancha (Gutierrez, Fernandez-Medina & Piattini, 2007)

WS-Security is a suite composed by different specifications of mechanisms and formats. Among other relevant mechanisms specifications we highlight: (i) WS-Addressing, which defines a set of abstract properties and a set of XML structured information that is suitable to be linked to a SOAP message to reference a WS. (ii) WS-Secure Conversation, which defines the standard way to provide security at message level, by means of the definition of basic mechanisms for the exchange of secure messages.

Among the format specifications WS-Security defines a set of standard extensions to the SOAP protocol: (i) WS-Policy provides a flexible and extensible grammar to express capabilities, requirements and general characteristics of a WS. (ii) WS-Security Policy defines a standard set of assertions that represents common ways to describe how to protect messages. (iii) WS-Trust addresses the definition of methods to issue, renew and validate security tokens.

A number of works exist about S&D properties and policies such as access control or security configuration management. In general, a computer security policy defines the security-related goals and assets of an organization's information systems. Policy definitions range from informal to highly formal. In the latter case we can find many examples of formal description of policies, especially related to confidentiality and access control. Examples of these are the Bell-La Padula model (Bell & La Padula, 1973), which supports multilevel confidentiality, the Chinese Wall (Brewer & Nash, 1989), Multilevel security (MLS) (Davidson, 1996), mandatory access control (MAC) (Loscocco, Smalley, Muckelbauer, Taylor, Turner & Farrell, 1998), and role-based access control (RBAC) (Ferraiolo & Kuhn, 1992).

Integrity is also the focus of other policy models such as Biba (1977), and Clack-Wilson (1987), among others.

On the other hand, verifying informal policies such as regulations, certifications criteria, etc. represent a bigger challenge due to their broad scope and informal nature. It is important to highlight that many of the best known initiatives for enhancing the security of computer systems have been based on informal specifications (e.g. Common Criteria (1999), FIPS (2001), Sarbanes-Oxley (2002), HIPAA (1996), etc.). In this field, we includes the particular case of the traditional security patterns (Schumacher, Fernandez, Hybertson, Buschmann & Sommerlad, 2005), which are semi-formal because of their UML diagrams relation.

Currently, there are some initiatives that are focused on the verification of the compliance to a policy. This is the case of the MASTER (2008) project, which by means of observing the application of several security controls tries to ensure that an application complies with a given policy. In this line, we find proposals based on recording log archives for the purpose of network auditing and to ensure compliance with various regulations. Despite of it is not directly related with the verification of compliance, the MOBIUS project (Askarov, Hedin & Sabelfeld, 2008) has produced mechanisms for runtime verification of applications. However, this verification is done at a lower level, and therefore, the policies are also defined at low-level. The main objective of MOBIUS is to develop guarantees for the safety and security of Java applications for mobile devices.

Regarding security properties, we can find in the literature several fields of research. Researches on formalization and analysis of security protocols are relevant for our proposal, because this verification requires the formal definition of the target properties. Within the different formal methods proposed in this research field, we can find different formalisms proposed to support the verification of security properties. Among them,

some relevant research lines are based on process algebras, model checking, epistemic logics, inductive theorem proving in higher-order logic, strand spaces and distributed temporal protocol logic. In a most recent research line, Gürgens, Ochsenschäger and Rudolph propose in (Gürgens, Ochsenschlager & Rudolph, 2005) a framework for the formalization of security properties that is partly used in our proposal. This framework allows the specification of a wide variety of security properties and requirements with formal semantics in terms of security properties of a single discrete model of the system. Precisely, we use that framework at a lower level and, over this, we make use of a framework based on higher order logic to help security administrators (who we assume, have no specific training in formal methods) to produce and understand the definition of S&D properties. Additionally, our proposal allows the reasoning about the properties to find the relations among them.

The SERENITY Model of Secure and Dependable Systems

Along this section we review several basic concepts of the SERENITY project due to a complete description of the SERENITY model is out of the scope of this chapter. A further description of this project can be found on (Spanoudakis, Maña, Kokolakis, Rudolph, & Lotz, 2009). SERENITY is a research project founded by the European Commission, in its Sixth Framework Programme (SerenityProject, 2006) and (Maña, Rudolph, Spanoudakis, Lotz, Massacci, Melideo & López-Cobo, 2006). The objective of SERENITY is to provide a framework for the automated treatment of security and dependability issues in AmI scenarios. To achieve this goal the members of the SERENITY consortium have identified two key aspects: Capturing the specific expertise of the security engineers in order to make it available for automated processing; and providing means to perform run-time monitoring of the functioning

Figure 1. Simplified conceptual model showing relations between Serenity artefacts

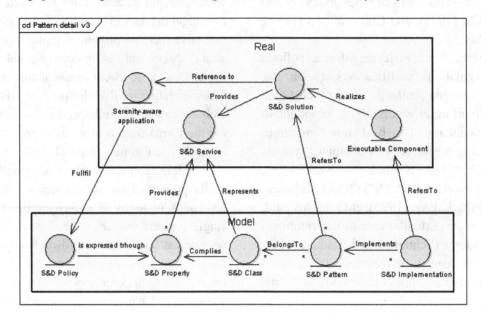

of the security and dependability mechanisms (S&D mechanisms).

One of the main SERENITY results is the set of modelling artefacts used to capture the security expertise. These artefacts represent S&D Solutions using semantic descriptions at different levels of abstraction. The main key of using different artefacts, each one for covering an abstraction level, is that doing this it is possible to cover completely both development and life cycles of secure applications. The main artefacts are shown in the conceptual UML model presented in Figure 1:

- An S&D Property is an interpretation of a security or dependability quality such as confidentiality, integrity, availability, etc. S&D Properties are defined formally using the language presented in section *Goals and Architecture of S&D Properties Language*. A reference to the S&D Properties provided must be included in the specification of each S&D Solution. The definition referenced by the S&D Solution aims to express S&D Properties in a way that is appropriate

for Security Administrators and System Developers (Maña & Pujol,2008).

- S&D Policies are detailed descriptions of the S&D Properties that must be applied to the different types of information resources in a specific environment. This artefact can be used to capture and enforce enterprise-wide policies, and also security regulations.
- S&D Solution is a general term that we use to refer to well-defined mechanisms that provide one or more S&D Properties.
- S&D Patterns are detailed descriptions of abstract but specific S&D Solutions. These descriptions contain all the information necessary for the selection, instantiation, adaptation, and dynamic application of the security solution represented in the S&D Pattern. In particular, they include the pattern semantics, which is related to the semantics of the security properties provided, the preconditions and restrictions imposed by the solution, the way to adapt the pattern interface to the class interface, etc.

- S&D Classes represent abstractions of a security service that can be provided by different S&D Solutions. All solutions belonging to an S&D Class are characterized by providing the same S&D Properties and complying with a common interface. The main purposes of introducing this artefact are to facilitate the dynamic substitution of the S&D Solutions at run-time, and to support the development process. All S&D Patterns belonging to this S&D Class will be selectable by the framework at run time.

- S&D Implementations represent the components that realize the S&D Solutions and therefore contain the specific features of that component (e.g. additional restrictions). These components are made accessible to applications throughout the Serenity Runtime Framework (SRF). An S&D Pattern will usually have more than one S&D Implementation. All these S&D Implementations must conform to the S&D Pattern but may also have differences (such as the operating system they run on).

- Finally an Executable Component (EC) is the actual implementation of an S&D Pattern. ECs are represented by S&D Implementations. These elements are not used during the development phase. Instead, they are the functional realization of S&D Solutions that is used at run-time. An Executable Component works as a standalone executable S&D Solution ready to provide security and dependability services to applications.

Due to the inherently unpredictable and dynamic nature of AmI environments, a flexible and runtime adaptable solution is required to provide security in such scenarios. SERENITY provides two frameworks to support the security and dependability of applications operating in AmI scenarios.

On the one hand, the SERENITY Development Framework includes tools for developing S&D Solutions and supports the development of SERENITY aware applications. The main characteristic of these applications is that they rely on SERENITY's S&D Solutions for the provision of S&D. On the other hand, the SERENITY Run-Time Framework (SRF) is responsible for dealing with S&D Solutions referenced by the SERENITY-aware applications at run-time (by means of what we call S&D Requests). These requests, once processed by the SRF, result in the selection of the S&D Solutions that may be used by the application. The SRF uses a set of mechanisms for context evaluation. In this way, the SRF knows the current and the past device context conditions. The provision of security solutions by the SRF is explained in more detail in (Maña, Sanchez, Serrano & Muñoz, 2006).

The process for developing SERENITY-aware applications deals with S&D issues from the very early engineering phases. SERENITY-aware applications contain calls to the SRF requesting it to provide references to ECs. These calls are called S&D Requests. Then, at runtime the SRF processes these requests, selects the best available EC to fulfil the request, activates it and returns a handler to the application. From that moment on the application can access the EC directly without the intermediation of the SRF. ECs are deactivated when context changes make them no longer suitable or by explicit request from the application.

The SERENITY Semantic Approach for S&D Properties

Our work in the definition and verification of the compliance of security policies is based on the formal framework for the definition of properties developed in SERENITY. This framework is based on the hypothesis that there will be different interpretations of the S&D properties; which in turn requires the ability to allow the definition of different interpretations that express subtle differences of security properties. There are many reasons supporting this assumption; for instance, legislation, cultural, etc. Under this assumption, and in order to guarantee the interoperability of systems based on different interpretations of the properties and on policies fulfilling those properties, we need to be able to exploit the relations between those properties. We must emphasize that the goal of this framework is not to reason about systems or solutions to verify whether they meet certain properties, but to reason about properties themselves to guarantee interoperability of these properties and of the policy complying with them.

A central element of the framework is a language to support: (i) the definition of the semantics of different S&D properties; (ii) the analysis of these definitions in order to find relations between S&D properties; and (iii) the use of the relations found in order to flexibly select S&D Solutions suitable for fulfilling the requirements of the system developers.

Identification of S&D Properties

We mentioned that the SERENITY approach regarding S&D properties is based on the idea that is not foreseeable, nor desirable, to establish a standard and fixed list of properties with a uniform definition for every property. This new approach introduces several new problems related to the identification, specification, publication and interoperability of these S&D Property definitions. This approach means that there will be many different properties defined by different entities. Therefore, the first problem to solve, before we address the ways to precisely define properties and the ways to use these definitions, is the way to univocally identify properties. Our proposal is based on the use of a domain-based scheme as our starting point for the identification of S&D properties. In this scheme, each domain corresponds to

an entity or organization that provides definitions for one or more S&D properties.

Evidently, not all organizations need to define their own S&D properties; in many cases it will be enough to rely on the definitions provided by external entities such as standardization bodies and public authorities. The main advantage of the domain-based approach is that it allows for different S&D properties definitions to coexist and to be managed independently. The domain establishes a namespace that facilitates the identification of the corresponding S&D properties and supports the mechanisms for locating and retrieving the information related to the property. Two possible examples of S&D properties are: Confidentiality. uma.es, which corresponds to the definition of the S&D Property Confidentiality in the domain of the University of Malaga (UMA) and Confidentiality.lcc.uma.es, which in turn corresponds to the definition of the same property in the subdomain of the Computer Science Department ("Lenguajes y Ciencias de la Computacion" – lcc) included in the UMA domain.

Goals and Architecture of S&D Properties Language

Our goal for the property specification language was to support (i) the definition of the semantics of different S&D properties; (ii) the analysis of these definitions to find relations between S&D properties; and (iii) the use of the relations found to flexibly select S&D Solutions suitable for fulfilling the requirements of the system developers. To achieve those goals we decided to split the specification in two different layers, each one with its own language.

On the one hand, in order to be able to create formal and precise definitions for S&D properties, to compare them and reason about them, S&D experts need a language that has no room for ambiguity and that is precise and flexible. For these reasons we have defined the Formal S&D

Figure 2. Architecture of the S&D Properties languages

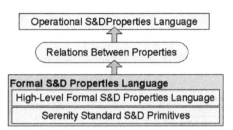

Properties Language (FPL) This language is based on High Order Logic (HOL). In particular, we use the (Bertot & Castéran's, 2004) proof assistant, which allows not only the representation of the S&D properties, but also to prove the relation between the properties. FPL is also subdivided in two parts:

- The Standard S&D Primitives which provide an extensible standard set of the basic elements needed to describe what can happen in a given system (e.g. send, receive, store, etc.), and the basic sets we need, like a set of users, a set of data, etc. We use the concept of world to represent a possible state of a system: A world is simply a sequence of actions (a trace). With this strategy, the Standard S&D Primitives are based on the theory of formal languages.
- The High-Level Formal S&D Properties Language uses the Standard S&D Primitives to define security properties. This is the starting point of a parallel work, in which we are currently working on the definition of a standard set of primitives that allow capturing a wide range of different definitions of the most important security properties.

On the other hand, in order to select S&D solutions to fulfil their requirements, system developers do not need to know the formal definition of the properties. Once the required property is identified all they need to know are the relations between properties. Relations found are then expressed in the Operational S&D Properties Language. The OPL describes S&D Properties using an XML specific format.

Consequently, the architecture of the S&D Property Language of Serenity is composed of two layers as shown in Figure 2.

S&D Policy Description

The major advantage of the approach presented in this chapter is precisely that we can verify that an application complies with an S&D policy, with the only requirement that it has been developed following the SERENITY approach. This can be useful even if it does not use SERENITY to provide runtime support.

Applications developed following the SERENITY approach, called Serenity-aware applications, are designed to make use of the security and dependability mechanisms provided by SERENITY. For this purpose, the developer includes references to S&D solutions in the applications' source code. As has been introduced in previous sections, security solutions are well defined mechanisms that provide one or more S&D Properties such as confidentiality, integrity, availability, etc. Here, an important point is the aforementioned semantically point of view of the S&D properties, which allows several interpretation of the same property to coexist and introduces the possibility of relating the properties.

The S&D properties and the S&D Policies are closely related because the latter are expressed in terms of the former. That is, S&D Policies contain information about the S&D Properties that must be ensured for each type of information asset. These rules are composed by one or several types of objects and the S&D properties that must fulfil be applied to that object.

The developer adds to the application source code a reference to an S&D Solution at development time. With this action, the developer adds

Figure 3. Partial schema of S&D policy

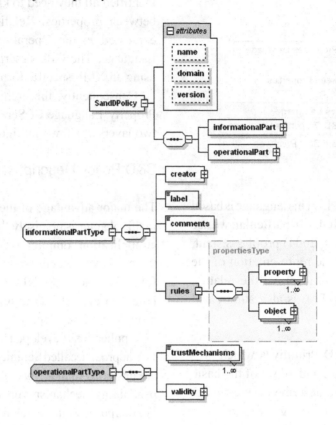

useful information to verify the compliance to the policy. In this sense, when the developer adds an S&D solution, he adds an "abstract check point" that relates a computational asset to an S&D Artefact, and therefore to a set of S&D Properties. As the S&D policy is composed by rules that relate properties and objects, applications contain all the information required for the verification of compliance to a policy.

Currently, focusing on their syntax, S&D Policies are digitally signed XML documents. Next figure depicts a general view of the structure of the S&D Policy specification language. At this level, an S&D Policy is composed by:

- S&D Policy: This field includes the policy name, domain, version, the informationalPart (described below) and operationalPart (described below).

- InformationalPart section contains the creator field, a label with the main objective of the policy, and a field describing rules. These rules relate properties to types of computational assets.
- The operationalPart section is composed by two elements: a list of trust mechanisms, and the artefact validity period of time.

Assurance and Compliance of WS-Oriented Systems to of S&D Policies

Assurance and compliance are important aspects of every information system. However, when we focus on Service-based Systems these terms are not so popular. In fact, assurance and certification of service-based systems is a difficult task, especially in the future open scenarios in which services will be assembled dynamically to provide more flexibility to the systems based on them. Currently, security and dependability (S&D) assurance is strictly intertwined with development process. Assurance is mainly carried out during analysis and coding phases, putting heavy constraints on the needed design documentation and models. In this way, assurance results are only valid for the system and its environment planned at design time, making this approach unsuitable for systems that are meant to continuously evolve (examples range from open source, to open services, including highly dynamic coalitions and long lived systems). In this section we describe the application of the proposed approach to the verification of compliance with S&D Policies in web services (WS). Concretely, we describe the use of the elements described in previous sections to facilitate the development of service-oriented applications.

A key aspect of service oriented computing is that applications become distributed and, moreover, they become composed of parts that ¿the? application developers and owners may not control (e.g. this happens when a WS-application uses an externally provided WS). In these cases, it is not possible to guarantee the availability and correct operation of the externally provided components of the application. In fact, it is not possible to guarantee reliability and continuous operation of the application unless the application is fitted with mechanisms to allow the externally provided components to be selected and replaced when appropriate at runtime. Consequently, in this setting, taking into account the lack of knowledge about the specific components that will be part of the application at runtime, it is extremely difficult with current technologies and standards to address the verification and certification of compliance of WS-oriented applications without strongly limiting the capabilities for selection and replacement of externally provided components. One additional aspect is that the application of the security-related standards for WSs remains a complex and error-prone task due to the inherent

complexity of the standards and the elements that they rely on (PKIs, SOAP, WSDL, WS-Security, WS-Policy, WS-Security Policy, etc.). Furthermore, the optimal solution may change depending on the operational context.

Therefore, two main scenarios have to be addressed in this environment. On the one hand, ensuring that applications comply with specific S&D Policies at runtime is an important challenge to address. On the other hand, WS-applications need to use different security mechanisms that can be described as S&D Patterns, thus facilitating its correct use and the flexibility to use the most suitable security solutions available at runtime. In this chapter we focus on the first of the scenarios, although the proposed solution does also support the second scenario.

Ensuring Compliance of Service-Oriented Systems with Dynamic Selection of Services

In the service-oriented scenarios, services are characterized as S&D solutions and are described by means of a set of S&D Artefacts (S&D Classes, S&D Patterns and S&D Implementations). In fact, the specific WSs themselves are considered SERENITY's Executable Components and therefore they are described as S&D Implementations, while the other artefacts provide support for applications in order to use these components.

Figure 4 shows the SERENITY model of running systems. In this model there is a security management component called SERENITY Runtime Framework (SRF), which is responsible for monitoring the context and performing the selection of the most appropriate S&D solutions to attend an S&D Request coming from an application. In our case, this component can be realized by a component on the same security domain as the application or even by a WS. In any case we assume that the communications between the application and the SRF are appropriately secured using the mechanisms described in (Maña,

Figure 4. SERENITY runtime model

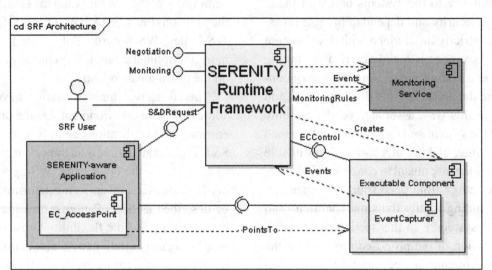

(Presenza, Piñuela, Serrano, Soria & Sotiriou, 2007). One interesting aspect of SERENITY is the monitoring of the system operation. This is achieved with inclusion of a monitoring service and the requirement for all Executable Components (those realizing the solution in practice) to support the monitoring activity by implementing specific EventCapturers. The description of the specific set of EventCapturers that an Executable Component has to provide is part of the S&D Pattern. It is mandatory that all Executable Components realizing such S&D Pattern include the specified EventCapturers. When the system is in operation, Executable Components send events to the SRF, which in turn redirects than to an appropriate monitoring service. In this way, SERENITY follows the emerging trend towards supporting transparency in distributed components, which is the key to establish the necessary trust in these components and in the systems that use them.

Currently, WS-based applications that allow a certain degree of dynamic selection and replacement of the WSs rely on a discovery or directory service to locate the services they need (using UDDI or some other mechanism). However, the selection and access to the WS ignores security aspects. In our architecture, the SRF provides a security-aware selection of the services. Therefore, instead of contacting the usual directory service, applications request services to the SRF by means of S&D Requests. These requests are extremely flexible and allow developers to choose the degree of freedom given to the SRF in the selection process. S&D Requests can be as generic as requesting an S&D service (such as a Access Control service), more restricted by requesting any implementation of a particular solution (e.g. RBAC), or very specific by requesting a specific implementation (e.g. Oracle RBAC). Please note that, although in the latter case there is no dynamic selection or replaceability, the model still provides advantages since on the one hand provides means for monitoring the operation of the WS and on the other hand the use of S&D Requests constitutes the basis for the verification of compliance of applications with S&D Policies.

Consequently, in the application code, calls to the discovery service are replaced by calls to the SRF, while direct calls to the WSs are replaced by calls to WS implemented in the form of SERENITY Executable Components.

In order to verify that an application complies with an S&D Policy we must consider that

S&D Policies are described on the basis of S&D Properties. Then, S&D Requests contain references to S&D Artefacts, which in turn refer to the S&D Properties they provide. Therefore, in order verify that an application complies with an S&D Policy we must verify that all S&D Artefacts used by the application (which can be discovered by inspecting the S&D Requests contained in the application code) refer to the properties defined in the S&D Policy.

The proposed model has two important advantages. On the one hand, it supports the dynamic replaceability of the S&D solutions needed by the application, and the monitoring of the correct execution of these solutions. On the other hand, it allows us to verify the compliance of the application to a policy even if we do not know a priori which WSs are going to be available and selected at runtime.

In order to illustrate the proposed model and the relation of the different components of the system we complement this section with the following example in which we show (i) a Serenity-aware application containing an S&D

Figure 5. Serenity-aware application

```
Import java.io.IOException;
import java.io.Serializable;
import java.net.UnknownHostException;
import java.util.Map;
import java.util.TreeMap;
import serenity.applicationSupportLibrary.*;

public class SerenitySimpleApplication extends SerenityApplication {

        protected static Map<String, Serializable> argsListE = new TreeMap<String, Serializable>();
        protected static Map<String, Serializable> argsListD = new TreeMap<String, Serializable>();
        public static SerenityExecutableComponent_AP myEC = null;
        byte[] eb,db = null;

        public SerenitySimpleApplication() {
                SRF_AP_AccessPoint mySRF = new SRF_AP_AccessPoint(this);

    try {
        myEC = new SerenityExecutableComponent_AP(mySRF, "P:DESEncrypt.uma.es",null,null);
                        argsListE = new TreeMap<String, Serializable>();
        argsListE.put("Text", "This is a string test");

        Thread.sleep(5000);
        eb = myEC.callOperation("Encrypt", argsListE);

        if(eb != null) {
                System.out.println("Encryption success!");
        }
        else {
                System.out.println("Encryption failed");
                myEC.close();
                System.exit(0);
        }
        System.out.println("String test encrypted succesfully " + new String(eb,"UTF-8"));
        argsListE.put("ciphertext", eb);
        db = myEC.callOperation("Decrypt", argsListE);

        if(db != null) {
                System.out.println("Decryption success!");
                System.out.println(new String(db,"UTF-8"));
        }
        else {
                System.out.println("Decryption failed");
                myEC.close();
                System.exit(0);
        }

        myEC.close();
        }
        public static void main(String[] args) {
                @SuppressWarnings("unused")
                SerenitySimpleApplication serenapp = new SerenitySimpleApplication();
                System.exit(0);
        }
    }
```

Request; (ii) the S&D Pattern requested by that S&D Request; and (iii) the S&D policy complied by the application.

Figure 5 shows a very simple Serenity-aware application, which uses the DES encryption protocol (represented by the DESEncrypt.uma.es S&D Pattern) to protect the confidentiality of a string. There are two points to highlight:

- The S&D Request (call to the SRF) to request the selection of an Executable Component implementing the DESEncrypt. uma.es S&D Pattern. The S&D Artefact (in this case S&D Pattern) requested is included as a parameter of this S&D Request.
- The calls to the operations of the Executable Component. In this specific application

these calls encrypt and decrypt the string. In order to verify the S&D policy compliance by the application this two points are checked and compared with the information provided by the S&Policy.

The S&D Policy is expressed on the basis of the S&D Request, which contains an S&D Artefact that in turn refers to an S&D Property. In order to verify that the application complies with the policy, we need to check the information of the S&D Pattern to verify that the S&D Property provided is the same as the S&D Property mandated by the S&D policy. Figure 6 shows the *DESEncrypt.uma.es* S&D Pattern specification, in which we can see that the S&D Property provided is *EncryptProperty.uma.es*.

Figure 6. S&D pattern DESEncrypt.uma.es

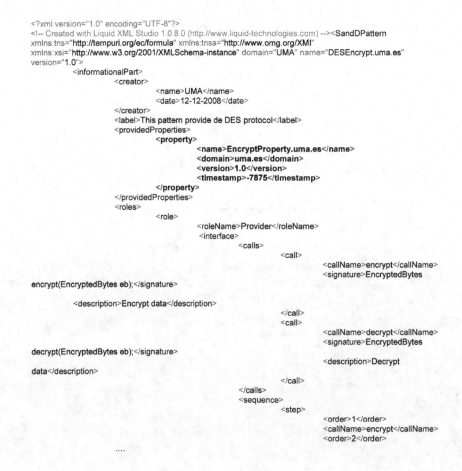

Finally, the Figure 7 shows the S&D policy, including the information of the rules that the application will have to comply with. These rules are composed by the descriptions of the object and an S&D Property that should be applied to it.

To summarize, the example shows that the information required for verifying that the SERENITY-aware application complies with a S&D policy, is available from the application, the S&D Requests it contains, the S&D Artefacts contained in these requests and the specification of the S&D Policy.

CONCLUSION

In this chapter, we have introduced the work developed in SERENITY and MISTICO projects, focused on the engineering process for service-oriented applications. One of the advantages of our framework is that provides tools to verify that an application complies with a policy, with the only

requirement that it has been developed following the SERENITY approach, even if it does not use SERENITY to provide runtime support. SERENITY defines a complete model to solve security problems in open distributed scenarios such as mobile, ubiquitous and service oriented computing, ambient intelligence and sensor networks. In previous sections, we have shown the application of the concept and realization of S&D properties in the web service environment. More concretely, we have proposed the use of our security framework to facilitate the development of applications that use standards security mechanisms (such WS-Security, WS-Policy, WS-Security Policy, etc) and to ensure the correct application of these standard mechanisms.

Currently, the verification of the compliance of a S&D Policy proposed is semi-automatic, as is explained in the previous sections, the application code includes the information to check if the policy is complies. The future work is focused in the development of an automatic tool to check the

Figure 7. S&D policy EncryptPolicy.uma.es

```xml
<?xml version="1.0" encoding="UTF-8"?>
<S_and_DPolicy xmlns="http://tempuri.org/ec/S_and_DPolicy">
        <Name>EncryptPolicy.uma.es</Name>
        <Domain>uma.es</Domain>
        <Version>0.1</Version>
        <InformationalPart>
                <Creator>uma.es</Creator>
                <Label>This policy ensure that the communication is encrypted with the DES
protocol</Label>
                <Comments></Comments>
                <Rules>
                        <Rule>
                        <!-- This rule is applicate over all the object of the Type: byte[] -->
                                <Property>
                                        EncryptProperty.uma.es
                                </Property>
                                <Object>
                                        byte[]
                                </Object>
                        </Rule>
                </Rules>
        </InformationalPart>
        <OperationalPart>
                <TrustMechanism>signed by uma.es</TrustMechanism>
                <Validity>
                        <ValidityFrom>12-12-2008</ValidityFrom>
                        <ValidityUntil>12-12-2009</ValidityUntil>
                </Validity>
        </OperationalPart>
</S_and_DPolicy>
```

application and verification of the compliance of a S&D policy. Another open issue is improving the description of the S&D Policies (and the associated xml file) in order to make it more flexible and generalized.

REFERENCES

Askarov, A., Hedin, D., & Sabelfeld, A. (2008). Cryptographically-masked flows. *Journal of Theoretical Computer Science, 402*(2-3), 82–101. doi:10.1016/j.tcs.2008.04.028

Bell, D. E., & La Padula, L. J. (1973). *Secure Computer Systems: Mathematical Foundations*, (MITRE Technical Report 2547, Vol. I, ESD–TR–73–278–I). Bedford, MA: The MITRE Corporation.

Bertot, Y., & Castéran, P. (2004). Interactive Theorem Proving and Program Development. In *Coq'Art: The Calculus of Inductive Constructions*. Berlin: Springer-Verlag.

Biba, K. J. (1977). *Integrity Considerations for Secure Computer Systems*, (Technical Report TR-3153). Bedford, MA: MITRE Corp.

Brewer, D. F. C & Nash, M.J. (1989). The Chinese Wall security policy. *Security and Privacy, 1989 Proceedings., 1989 IEEE Symposium on (1989)*, Oakland, CA (pp. 206-214).

Clark, D. D., & Wilson, D. R. (1987), A Comparison of Commercial and Military Computer Security Policies. In *Proceedings of IEEE Symposium on Security and Privacy,* (pp. 184–194).

Common Criteria Editorial Board (2006). *Common Criteria for Information Technology Security Evaluation*, Version 3.1.

Congress of the United States of America. (2002). *Sarbanes-Oxley Act of 2002*. Available from http://www.access.gpo.gov/

Congress of the United states of America.(1996). *Health Insurance Portability and Accountability Act of 1996*. Available from http://www.hhs.gov/ocr/hipaa/

Davidson, J. A. (1995). *Asymmetric isolation*. Paper presented at Computer Security Applications Conference, 1996, 12th Annual (pp. 44-54), San Diego, CA.

EU 6 Framework Program (2006). *SERENITY Project*. Retrieved from http://www.serenity-project.org/

EU 7 Framework Program (2008). *MASTER Project*. Retrieved from www.master-fp7.eu

Extended Backus-Naur Form (EBNF). (1996). Retrieved from http://www.iso.ch/iso/iso_catalogue/catalogue_tc/catalogue_detail.htm?csnumber=26153

Ferraiolo, D. F., & Kuhn, D. R. (1992). *Role Based Access Control*. Paper presented at 15th National Computer Security Conference, (pp. 554-563).

Gürgens, S., Ochsenschlager, P., & Rudolph, C. (2005). On a formal framework for security properties. *Computer Standards & Interfaces, 27*, 457–466. doi:10.1016/j.csi.2005.01.004

Gutierrez, C., Fernandez-Medina, E. & Piattini M. (2007). Web Services-Based Security Requirement Elicitation. *IEICE transactions on information and systems, 90*(9), 1374-1387.

Information Technology Laboratory. National Institute of Standards and Technology (2001). *Federal information Processing Standards Publication FIPS*. PUB 140-2. Security Requirements For Cryptographic Modules.

Loscocco, P. A., Smalley, S. D., Muckelbauer, P. A., Taylor, R. C., Turner, S. J., & Farrell, J. F. (1989). The Inevitability of Failure: The Flawed Assumption of Security in Modern Computing Environments. In *Proceedings of the 21st National Information Systems Security Conference,* (pp. 303-314).

Maña, A., Presenza, D., Piñuela, A., Serrano, D., Soria, P., & Sotiriou, D. (2007). *Specification of SERENITY Architecture*, (Serenity Public Report A6.D3.1.)

Maña, A., & Pujol, G. (2008). Towards Formal Specification of Abstract Security Properties. In *Proceedings of The Third International Conference on Availability, Reliability and Security,* Barcelona, Spain. Washington, DC: IEEE Computer Society Press.

Maña, A., Rudolph, C., Spanoudakis, G., Lotz, V., Massacci, F., Melideo, M., & López-Cobo, J. M. (2006). *Security Engineering for Ambient Intelligence: A Manifesto.* In P. Giorgini & H. Mouratidis (Eds.) *Integrating Security and Software Engineering.* Hershey, PA: IDEA Group.

Maña, A., Sánchez, F., Serrano, D., & Muñoz, A. (2006b). *Building Secure Ambient Intelligence Scenarios.* Paper presented at Eighteenth International Conference on Software Engineering and Knowledge Engineering (SEKE06), San Francisco Bay, USA.

Schumacher, M., Fernandez, E., Hybertson, D., Buschmann, F., & Sommerlad, P. (2005). *Security Patterns-Integrating Security and Systems Engineering.* Hoboken, NJ: John Wiley & Sons.

Spanoudakis, G., Maña, A., Kokolakis, S., Rudolph, C., & Lotz, V. (2009). *The Serenity Book.* Berlin: Springer-Verlag.

Chapter 7
Security Policies in Web Services

Deepti Parachuri
Infosys Technologies Limited, India

Sudeep Mallick
Infosys Technologies Limited, India

ABSTRACT

Security is of fundamental concern in computing systems. This chapter covers the role of security policies in Web services. First, it examines the importance of policies in web services and explains the WS-Policy standard. It also highlights the relation of WS-Policy with other WS-* specifications. Next, it covers different facets of security requirements in SOA implementations. Later, it examines the importance of security policies in web services. It also presents the basic concepts of WS-Security policy language. WS-Security policy specification specifies a standard way to define and publish security requirements in an extensible and interoperable way. A service provider makes use of security policy to publish the security measures implemented to protect the service. Security policies can also be made customizable to meet the security preferences of different consumers. Towards the end, it discusses about the governance of security polices and also future trends in security policies for web services.

1. INTRODUCTION

Web services emerged as a successful standard for creating interoperable solutions across various industries. Main reason for success of Web services is that they are well-suited to realize service-oriented systems (Thomas Erl, 2005). XML-based technologies such as SOAP, XML Schema and WSDL provide standards to build interoperable Web services.

DOI: 10.4018/978-1-60566-950-2.ch007

The WS-Policy (WS-Policy Spec, 2006) and WS-Policy Attachment (WS-Policy Attachment Spec, 2007) specifications extend this foundation and offer mechanisms to represent the capabilities and requirements of Web services as Policies. In order for Web services to become successful, they must be secured from malicious individuals who constantly try to compromise them. An effective and flexible way of managing security for Web services is to use security policies (WS-Security Spec, 2006). A Web service security policy is a specification describing security measures that are used to protect the Web service from security attacks. Security policy is a declarative XML format for programming how web services implementations construct and check WS-Security headers. Using XML for security policies helps web services in conforming to general principles while building secure systems. Coding security checks as XML metadata allows interoperability (Karthikeyan Bhargavan, Cedric Fournet, & Andrew D. Gordan, 2008).

This chapter details out different security issues in Web services and role of security policies in web services. Section 2 explains policies and relation of policies with other WS-* Specifications. Section 3 talks about the security issues in web services and role of security issues in web services. Section 4 deals with the Governance of security policies. In the end, we present the future trends in security policies for Web services.

2. BACKGROUND ON POLICIES IN WEB SERVICES

Policies are defined as information which can be used to modify the behavior of a system. There are two reasons for using policies in Web services for developing interoperable business processes. Firstly, policies permit managing Web services at a higher level where details of composition are separated from the behavior of Web services. Secondly, policies help in creating interoperable and adaptive service systems. Policies also address issues like how to deal with Web service unreliability, and how to substitute a Web service with an equivalent one?

There are many ways to associate policies with Web services. A simple scenario for application of policy is *"Consumer sends a service request to Provider. If the service request conforms to Provider's policy for requests, then Provider accepts the request, else it returns a fault status."* This situation exists, for instance, where Provider requires Consumer to assign a unique identifier to

its request, in accordance with WS-Reliability. If it receives a request with no suitable identifier, then it will return a fault status. Provider may publish its policy in one or more number of ways, UDDI, WSDL, HTTP, LDAP, DNS or in SQL or SAML request/response messages. Policies can also be included in SOAP headers.

2.1 Understanding WS-Policy and its Associated Standards

The Web Services Policy Framework provides a general purpose model and corresponding syntax to describe the policies of a Web Service. Web Services Policy is a machine-readable language for representing the capabilities and requirements of a Web service. Policies can be programmatically accessed at runtime by service requestors. Polices specify the requirements and restrictions to access a service provided by a service provider. The WS-Policy framework provides extensions to govern the assembly and structure of policy description documents and also associate policies to Web services. WS-Policy frameworks consist of three specifications

- WS-Policy
- WS-Policy Attachments
- WS-Policy Assertions

WS-Policy framework is also part of WS-Security (WS-Security Spec, 2006) framework. WS-Security policy specification (introduced later in the chapter) defines a set of policy assertions for use in WS-Security framework.

- **Policy assertions:** The service properties expressed by a policy description are represented by *policy assertions*. A policy description is comprised of one or more policy assertions. Policy assertions comprise of service characteristics, preferences, capabilities, requirements and rules. Assertions indicate domain-specific (e.g., security, transactions) semantics and are expected to be defined in separate, domain-specific specifications.

- **Policy alternatives:** Policy assertions can be grouped into *policy alternatives*.
- **Policy assertion type:** Policy assertions can be further categorized into policy assertion types. *Policy assertion types* associate policy assertions with specific XSD schemas.
- **Policy vocabularies:** Represent collection of policy types within a given policy.
- **Policy subject and Policy scope:** A policy can be associated with a web service, message or any other resource. *Policy subject* is the one for which the policy is intended for. A single policy can have more than one subject and the collection of policy subjects is called *policy scope*.
- **Policy expressions:** *Policy expression* is the XML statement used to express a policy assertion in a manner so that it is programmatically processed.
- **Policy attachments:** Policy expressions are bound to policy scopes using *policy attachments*.
- **Policy:** A *policy* is a collection of policy alternatives.

2.2 Associating Policies to Web Services

Web services policies are used by Services administrators in the following scenarios (Anderson, A. 2006):

- A service provider could publish policy to describe about its services for example service provider could publish security policy to describe its security measures.
- Service providers publish their policies to let developer's program consumer services or client applications that conform to them.

- Consumer services could compare their own policies with those of potential providers to ensure compatibility.
- Providers and consumers could select compatible policy options to use with each other.
- Services could use policies to verify that transactions conform to agreed-upon policies.
- Third-party service brokers or agents could use policies to match consumers with compatible providers.
- Services can link with each other to provide consumers with more powerful composite services that incorporate the policies of all involved.

There are many ways of associating policies with Web services:

- **Announcement:** These policies define how a Web service acts as a component in a composite Web service. What kind /format of messages it accepts and what kind of formats it require?
- **Selection:** This helps consumer in selecting the Web service. Consumer may publish its policy like he is interested in Web service which adheres to specific policy.
- **Compatibility:** Policies define rules for interaction between services. Interaction between services would need conformance of policies with each other.
- **Agreement:** How two services agree on policies to use?
- **Verification:** The receiving Web service must verify that the message's contents and other behaviors associated with this transaction conform to the agreed-on policies.
- **Composition:** Composing multiple Web services to meet the requirements of a single consumer.

2.3 Design Time and Run Time Policies

Policies can be applied at various stages of service development lifecycle. Policies are of two types- Design time policies and Run time policies.

- **Design Time Policies:** Rules which are used to govern a service's life prior to deployment are known as Design Time Policies. For example, Enterprise architecture team can write rules for the proper development of web services. Policies can be rules that ensure that services are interoperable, and secure. These rules would govern the use of various Web service standards such as SOAP and WS-Security. Another example of Design Time Policy can be rules to describe an approval process that must occur before a service is deployed.
- **Run Time Policies:** Run time policies describe the desirable behavior of a service during service execution. An example of a run time policy would be a service level agreement that was negotiated by service consumer who is consuming the service and provider of service. Run time policies can be thought of as SLA's. An example of run time policy is "An SLA that promises a 1 second response time may cost a penny per invocation while an SLA that promises 0.5 second response time may cost 2 cents."

2.4 Use and Role of Policy in SOA Governance

SOA Governance is the ability to ensure that services are well planned and coordinated. Policies set goals on design, creation and composition of services. Without policies, there is no Governance. Enforcing policies assist in catching errors before they occur and help in reducing the reoccurrence of these issues. There are policies that all services must adhere to from an enterprise perspective. This then proceeds down through the enterprise, all of the way to the granular policies that a project team might implement, from the perspective of the division or business unit, department, or team. Enterprise Services Polices need to be produced with enterprise quality and adhere to standards and policies in order to ensure business continuity, reduce integration costs and complexities, limit corporate liabilities, and ensure security. In order to achieve this, Enterprise Policy Governance is a must.

3. SECURITY POLICY IN WEB SERVICES

3.1 Security Issues in Web Services

Security is of fundamental concern in computing systems. Web Services are distributed and decentralized systems which provide services to clients. Owing to their nature, Web services face the security problems that are common to communication systems. Some of the major inherited security issues that Web services technologies must address are authentication, authorization, confidentiality, data integrity, non-repudiation, privacy, trust, auditing, intrusion detection and availability (Zoran Stojanovic & Ajantha Dahanayake, 2004). SOA security requirements are more complex due to:

- Major security threats due to easier access to SOA implementations
- Loosely coupled nature of interaction, requiring flexible means of handling heterogeneous implementations.
- Dynamic interaction between services necessitates dynamic security mechanisms.

Loose coupling nature of SOA will require decentralization of conventional security mechanisms so that the interactions between service providers and service requestors carry security information. These necessitate additional security features like message level security, distributed credential management functions like single sign-on, message content inspection, interoperability of different security systems and federation and delegation requirements for trust and policies. Additional security requirements for Web services are outlined below:

- **Single Sign-On:** As web services are distributed, it is impractical for each system to maintain each others authentication rights, hence need for Single sign on arises. With single sign on, one system authenticates a user and this state of authentication can be used by other systems.
- **Malicious Invocations:** Invocation of services can be done with malicious data, which may otherwise appear to be harmless to security systems like firewalls.
- **Parameter Tampering** is one example of malicious invocation. In parameter tampering attacker can invoke the service using manipulated parameter options to retrieve unauthorized information.
- **Recursive Payloads:** Attacker can break an XML parser by creating file with thousands of nested elements.
- **Oversized Payloads:** Attacker can send large files and attempt to manipulate the parser to create denial of service scenarios.
- **Repeated Invocations:** A repeated set of invocations by attacker on a service can lead to denial of service or loss of availability.
- **Schema Poisoning:** XML parser uses XML schema to interpret Web service messages. Attacker may modify the XML schema file.
- **WSDL Scanning:** An attacker might cycle through the various command and string combinations to discover unintentionally related or unpublished application program interfaces.
- **Routing Detours:** Attackers can attack the routers and can insert malicious code to reroute the confidential file.
- **External Entity Attacks:** XML can build documents dynamically by pointing to a Uniform Resource Identifier (URI) where the actual data exists. These external entities may not be trustworthy, as an attacker could replace the data being retrieved with malicious data.
- **Replay Attacks:** Attackers execute the same validated and processed command multiple number of times resulting in data inconsistency or reduce availability of services with delays.
- **XML Morphing:** Malicious morphing can transform an XML document and its contents into something completely different than its source intended. This can cause unexpected or inappropriate behavior of previously legitimate messages.
- **SQL or XQuery Injection:** Under such attacks the attacker would send specially crafted inputs with SQL keywords embedded that would alter the semantics of the query. As a result the attacker might succeed in making the server execute query that he isn't permitted to do.
- **Delegation and Federation:** Delegation is the capability of a service or an organization to transfer security rights and policies to another trusted service or organization. Federation is a special case when the transferee service is a peer and not child.

The core Web services specifications are: XML, SOAP, WSDL, and UDDI. These specifications constitute the basic building blocks of Web services, but none of these Web services standards address security issues (Carlos Gutiérrez, Eduardo Fernández-Medina, & Mario Piattini, 2004).

- **XML and SOAP:** These specifications do not say anything about how to obtain integrity, confidentiality and authenticity of the information that they represent and transport respectively.
- **UDDI and WSDL:** UDDI specification does not have answers for security issues like:
  - Is the UDDI registry located in a trustworthy location?
  - How can we be sure that the published data have not been maliciously manipulated?
  - Was the data published by the business is correct?
  - Can we trust the business that published the services?
  - Are the services available at any moment?
  - Are the transactions that are produced from the execution of the business services correct?

World Wide Web Consortium (W3C) and the Organization for the Advancement of Structured Information Standards (OASIS) provide Security standards to make Web services secure.

3.2 Role of Security Policies in Web Services

Policies allow parameters to be adjusted after deployment without recompilation at runtime. Web services can be secured by using different available security options such as WS-Security, Security Assertion Markup Language (SAML), and so forth. Security Policy (WS-Security Policy) is also part of the configuration data, which is used to govern how WS- Security is applied to incoming and outgoing messages. Separation of application code from security policy provided by WS-Security Policy helps in easy identification of security related information for auditing

and reviewing. If you want to write any kind of security for credentials, confidentiality requirements or privacy requirements, there's no way for these systems to interoperate without programmers sitting down and talking to each other and then writing that in code. WS-Security policy gives you a framework for all these things to be automated. A service provider makes use of security policy to publish the security measures implemented to protect the service. Security policies can also be made customizable to meet the security preferences of different consumers. As an example, suppose the security measure is access control. The provider's security policy may provide access to all the features of a service, whereas a particular consumer may need access to only few features (George Yee, & Larry Korba, 2005). In such scenarios, need for customizable security policies arise.

Web services possess XML-based language specifications to implement security policies. WS-Policy and WS-Security Policy (WS-Security Policy Spec, 2007) are used to express Web service security policies. WS-Policy may be applied to express security requirements for Web services in general whereas WS-Security Policy contains the policy elements applicable to WS-Security. WS-Security Policy specification defines standard ways to secure messages exchanged between Web services and clients. WS-Security policy language can be used to publish security requirements and constraints on a Web service using the WSDL specification. That is, using WS – security policy language, we can drive a Web service security engine to secure out going messages in a standard way and instruct the verification of incoming messages in a standard, defined way.

3.3 Demystifying WS – Security Policy

In this section, we define policy assertions for the security properties of Web services. These assertions are primarily designed to represent the security characteristics defined in the WSS: SOAP Message Security, WS-Trust and WS-SecureConversation specifications, but they can also be used for describing security requirements at a more general or transport-independent level. WS-Security Policy language is built on top of WS–Policy framework. WS-Policy Attachment specification defines a set of policy subjects that can be put in places where we can attach or apply security policies. We can attach security policies either at service-level, operation-level or even at message-level. WS-Security Policy specification also defines how security assertions defined in the specification can be attached to policy subjects and possible policy subjects for each of those assertions.

Web services can be secured by using different available security options such as WS-Security, Security Assertion Markup Language (SAML), and so forth. But how will the users of the web service know about the security requirements of a web service. The WS-Policy framework strives to provide a mechanism for exchanging requirements, not just security requirements, between a Web services client and a Web service provider. WS-Security policy is used to define the security requirements of a web service. WS-Security specification provides various options to secure a web service, but how will the client wanting to use the web service know about the requirements (data which the client should send to the service). WS-Security policy specification provides various assertions to specify the requirements of a WS-security enabled web service like

- A security token of a specific type (e.g. UsernameToken) is required.
- Encryption is required, and provides public key that the client will need to encrypt a message sent to this Web service.
- A signature is required

3.3.1 Security Assertion Model

There are 5 main security assertion models defined in security policy language

3.3.1.1 Security Binding Assertion

Security binding mechanisms are for securing message exchanges. Security binding assertion defines which security mechanisms are used by the service or client such as the keys being used, algorithms, etc. Common properties used by other assertions are also defined in the security binding assertion. Security characteristics and the assertions describing conditions and scope provide enough information to secure messages between an initiator and a recipient. Three security binding assertions are identified primarily by the style of protection encryption used for protection of the message exchange.

3.3.1.1.1 Transport Binding Assertion
Transport binding assertion is used in scenarios when the message protection and security is provided by secure transport medium like HTTPS. This assertion indicates that the message is protected using the means provided by the transport. In transport binding assertion, we can define a transport token through which we can constrain messages to be exchanged only through a defined medium. This binding has one binding specific token property - Transport Token. WS-Security policy specification defines a HTTPS token as transport token that defines messages which are transmitted over HTTPS.

3.3.1.1.2 Asymmetric Binding Assertion
Asymmetric binding is suited for when both parties, i.e. client and the service, possess security tokens. In Asymmetric binding assertion, initiator or client will use its private key to sign and the recipient's public key to encrypt. Recipient or the Web service will use its private key to decrypt and initiator's public key to verify the signature. Asymmetric binding defines which tokens are used by

the initiator and the recipient by setting Initiator Token and Recipient Token properties.

3.3.1.1.3 Symmetric Binding Assertion

When Symmetric binding is used, first encrypted key is derived using the recipient's security token, defined using either encryption token assertion and signature token assertion or protection token assertion. Then this encrypted key is used to secure the message back and forth between the recipient and the initiator. This binding facilitates the need to secure the messages between anonymous clients and the server. Only the server has to possess a security token.

3.3.2 Protection Assertions

Protection assertions are used to identify what is being protected and the level of protection provided. There are mainly two types of protection token assertions-Integrity Assertions and Confidentiality Assertions.

3.3.2.1 Integrity Assertions

Integrity assertions defines whether a SOAP message must be digitally signed, what specifically in the message needs to be signed, and how it is to be signed, and what algorithms must be used:

- SignedParts Assertion: The SignedParts assertion is used to specify the parts of the message outside of security headers that require integrity protection (to be signed). It defines whether body should be signed and which soap header elements should be signed.
- SignedElements Assertion: The Signed Elements assertion is used to specify arbitrary elements in the message that require integrity protection using Xpath expressions.

3.3.2.2 Confidentiality Assertions

Confidentiality assertion defines that a sender or receiver of Web services messages needs to encrypt some specific part of a SOAP message. For instance, it allows the sender (or receiver) of a message to specify that parts of a message must be encrypted with a certain algorithm.

- Encrypted Parts Assertion: The EncryptedParts assertion is used to specify the parts of the message that require confidentiality/encryption.
- Encrypted Elements Assertion: The EncryptedElements assertion is used to specify arbitrary elements in the message that require confidentiality protection using XPath expressions.

3.3.3 Token Assertions

These assertions specify the type of the tokens to be used to protect the messages. Token assertions also define two important properties about the tokens used to protect the message.

- **Token Inclusion:** This attribute indicates whether binary tokens can be included in the message.
- **Derived Keys:** This Boolean property specifies whether derived keys should be used.

Some of the token types defined in the WS - Security Policy specification are: Username Tokens, X509 Tokens, Issued Tokens, SecureConversation Tokens, SAML Tokens, Https Tokens etc.

3.3.4 Supporting Token Assertions

These tokens define additional tokens to augment the claims provided by the token which is used to generate the message signature. There are four types of supporting tokens.

- **Supporting Tokens:** Supporting tokens are additional tokens to be included in the security header and may optionally include additional message parts to sign and/or encrypt.
- **SingedSupporting Tokens:** Signed tokens are included in the "message signature". Signed supporting tokens should be signed using the primary token used to sign the message.
- **EndorsingSupporting Tokens:** If endorsing supporting tokens are defined in the security policy, the message signature generated by signing the elements defined in the security policy, should be signed again using the endorsing supporting tokens generating a second signature. In simple words, these tokens sign the message signature. So we get an additional signature element which is the signature of the original message signature.
- **SignedEndorsingSupporting Tokens:** If signed, endorsing supporting tokens are defined in the security policy, the signed endorsing supporting tokens should be signed using the primary token and the message signature should also be signed again using the signed endorsing supporting tokens. In simple terms, the supporting token is covered by the message signature and the message signature again is signed using the supporting token.

3.3.5 Protocol Assertions

WS-Security Policy Specification defines two assertions WSS: SOAP Message Security Options and Trust assertion that are used to provide SOAP message security and trust related options.

3.3.5.1 WSS: SOAP Message Security Options

WSS Version specifies which version of the Web Services Security specification should be fol-

lowed, 1.0 or 1.1. WSS 1.1 enables an encrypted key to be generated by the client and can be reused by the server in the response to the client. This saves the time required to create a Symmetric Key during the course of response, encrypt it with the client public key (which is also an expensive RSA operation), and transmit the encrypted key in the message (it occupies markup and requires Base64 operations). Enabling WSS 1.1 also enables encrypted headers.

Web Services Security (WSS): SOAP Message Security, is an open standard published by OASIS that defines mechanisms for signing and encrypting SOAP messages. WSS: SOAP Message Security has two types of assertions Wss10 assertion and Wss11 Assertion. The Wss10 assertion allows you to specify which WSS: SOAP Message Security 1.0 options are supported and the Wss11 assertion allows you to specify which WSS: SOAP Message Security 1.1 options are supported.

3.3.5.2 WS-Trust Assertion

In Web services, the trust between a service requester and a service provider is established by exchanging information between the two parties in an expected and defined manner. The WS-Security specification defines the basic mechanisms to securely exchange messages using security tokens. The WS-Trust specification builds on this model by defining how such security tokens are issued and exchanged. WS-Trust defines a set of interfaces that a secure token service may provide for the issuance, exchange, and validation of security tokens. It is designed to support the creation of multiple security token formats to support authentication and authorization mechanisms. An issuing security token service takes an input request and typically proof of identity and responds with a token that the service requester has requested. Trust policy is used to describe the expected behavior (in terms of security) of the service requester and service provider.

Table 1. Suggested policy attachment points for the assertions

Policy Subject	WSDL attachment points	Suggested Assertions
Message	wsdl:binding/wsdl:operation/wsdl:input wsdl:binding/wsdl:operation/wsdl:output wsdl:binding/wsdl:operation/wsdl:fault	Supporting Token Protection
Operation policy subject	wsdl:binding/wsdl:operation	Supporting Token
End point policy subject	wsdl:binding wsdl:port	Security binding Supporting token

3.3.2 Policy Subjects

Policy subjects are the attachment points for policies. WS Policy attachment defines various policy subjects. The table below describes, suggested policy attachment points for the assertions defined in WS-Security Policy specification.

Table 2 talks about different assertions of WS-security policy and its association with WS-Security.

3.4 Security Policies in General

Apart from the discussed WS-Policies, there are many other general security policies. We would discuss some of them in detail. Independent of technology type, security mechanisms are configured and administered through changes to security policies (Bret Hartman, Donald J.Flinn, Konstantin Beznosov, & Shirley Kawamoto, 2003).

- **Authentication policies** define which authentication protocols should be used and what authentication parameters are used.
- **User attribute assignment policies** specify the security attributes that are assigned to authenticated users.
- **Message protection policies** specify authenticity, confidentiality, and integrity protection of the messages traveling between system components.
- **Authorization policies** are responsible for defining who have access to a particular resource.
- **Audit policies** determine which events must be recorded in the audit log and under what circumstances.
- **Credentials delegation policies** specify how intermediates use received credentials for making calls and accessing other resources on behalf of the client.

Table 2. WS security policy assertions and its association with WS security

WS-Security Policy Assertion	Association with WS-security
Security binding assertion	Defines which security mechanisms are used by the service or client such as the keys being used, algorithms, etc.
Protection assertions	Defines whether a SOAP message must be digitally signed or encrypted, what specifically in the message needs to be signed or encrypted, and how it is to be signed or encrypted, and what algorithms must be used for signing or encryption
Token Assertions	Specifies which type of tokens to be used to protect the messages like username token, SAML token etc
SOAP Message Security assertion	Defines what mechanisms are used for signing and encrypting SOAP messages.
Trust assertion	Specifies which mechanisms are used to issue security tokens

3.5 XACML

eXtensible Access Control Markup Language (XACML Spec., 2005) is an XML Schema for representing authorization and entitlement policies. XACML specifies rules on who, what, when, and how to access information. WS-Security Policy is for publishing or making available the security requirements of a web service, whereas XACML is for actually checking whether or not a given client should be allowed. XACML provides an XML schema for a general policy language, which is used to protect any kind of resource and make access decisions over these resources. XACML standard not only gives the model of the policy language, but also proposes a processing environment model to manage the policies and to conclude the access decisions.

XACML has five components to handle access decisions:

- **Policy Administration Point (PAP):** PAP is the repository for the policies and provides the policies to the Policy Decision Point (PDP).
- **Policy Enforcement Point (PEP):** PEP is actually the interface of the whole environment to the outside world. It receives the access requests and evaluates them with the help of the other actors and permits or denies the access to the resource.
- **Policy Decision Point (PDP):** PDP is the main decision point for the access requests. It collects all the necessary information from other actors and concludes a decision.
- **Policy Information Point (PIP):** PIP is the point where the necessary attributes for the policy evaluation are retrieved from several external or internal actors.

3.6 Security in REST Based Services

Web services security standards like WS-Security, WS-Security policy are associated with SOAP. They don't talk about other web services communications like REST. REST based services are on increase with take off of WEB2.0. REST uses HTTP transport protocol. It's argued that REST does not require additional security standards like for SOAP. HTTP infrastructure is sufficient for reliable messaging and security in REST based services. REST can be considered as safe as HTTP. REST based Web Services should be modelled as resources which use HTTP GETs, POSTs, PUTs, and DELETEs. But in practice, REST based services use HTTP GETs with parameters being passed in QueryStrings for almost all scenarios (create, update, read and delete).

ACL's are generally applied to REST methods to secure REST based services. Theoretically, GET method has no side effects as it is for only retrieving information, whereas POSTs, PUTs, and DELETEs change the resource representations. In this case, we can apply ACL's for POSTs, PUTs and DELETEs and restrict the users on changing the resource representations. This approach of using ACLs to restrict access is effective if developers have followed REST principles. But as mentioned above, many REST based services use GETs to change the resource representations. Usage of GET method raises many security threats like SQL injection, malicious invocations, parameter tampering etc. All the standard web application security techniques are applicable to REST based services (Security for REST Web Services, 2006). Few of the web application security techniques are

- Validating the size of parameters on the QueryString
- Validating the content of parameters on the QueryString
- Examining parameters in the QueryString for known attacks such as SQL Injection

- Applying regular expressions (RegEx's) to QueryString parameters QueryStrings and Web Application Security

Logging and Auditing is very simple in REST based services. HTTP infrastructures can store the information in the HTTP query strings. Since all information is present in the method and the URI, URI's can be replayed to check the executed transaction.

3.7 Interoperability Issues

Once the enterprise or the particular project decides to have secure web services, they would need to devise policies for ensuring adherence to the security requirements. Since services are designed and implemented to cater to wider consumer community, operating on different implementation platforms, the topic of interoperability assumes prime importance. While designing security for web services, one of the critical policies would be to ensure compliance with WS-I Basic Security Profiles and the specific token profiles.

For example the WS-I Basic Security Profile 1.1 has stipulations such as the following:

- Basic security profile includes rules and restrictions for security header parts and has portions for security header format, structure, datatypes, security tokens (username, binary, REL, SAML, X.509, Kerberos tokens), encryption, signature, implications for message body, message attachments,
- The portions of the message header and body to be encrypted or signed, the usage of a particular security token are not dictated by the profile. However, the security header details related to the encryption and signing should appear in an order consistent with the sequence of these operations so that the processing at the receiver's end would result into the retrieval of the original intended input.

- It also lays down rules with respect to the number of security headers that a message can have and that it depends upon the number of actors (final recipients and intermediaries which act upon the message).
- It also lays down restrictions with respect to timestamp information that could be included in the security header.
- It also puts restrictions on the number of security token references to one, that could be used to refer to the security tokens included in the security header.
- It restricts the way the path information about any attached certificates (specifically X.509) is to be included in the security header

This ensures that application of security tokens, security mechanisms such as signature and encryptions and interpretation of the security headers in general happen uniformly by all the intended recipients (actors) of the web services. It also ensures that web services security implementation by the different vendors and platforms (Java and .Net component platforms) work seamlessly.

Besides having policies for interoperability of secure web services it is also important that the security policies applicable to a web service be coded in a structure form in order to enable automated discovery and retrieval of policy related information. The security policy is a part of the contract which any potential service consumer has to fulfill before it can avail the service. In order to enable declaration of service security policies in an unambiguous manner a standard such as the WS-SecurityPolicy need to be adopted. This standard has been explained in detail in the earlier sections. WS-SecurityPolicy would have assertions about the needed confidentiality, integrity and authentication requirements for a service.

For example, the assertions about the need to include a particular security token during invocation of a service are specified in the WS-SecurityPolicy compliant document. These assertions details would in turn contain token inclusion information which are compliant with the corresponding token profile as given by WS-I. The need to include UsernameToken for authentication before use of service is specified in the WS-SecurityPolicy document of the service as a UsernameToken assertion. So once a potential service consumer has access to the WS-SecurityPolicy document, it can ensure that all invocations of the service include a UsernameToken information in the security header of the request. Secondly, the default version of the token as specified in the WS-SecurityPolicy v1.0 standard is nothing but the UsernameToken as specified in WS Security: UsernameToken Profile 1.0. However, if the service is to be compliant with WS-I Basic Security Profile 1.1, then refer to UsernameToken Profile is v1.1.

Similarly, Basic Security Profile 1.1 defines three token types X.509v3, x.509PKI Path v1 and PKCS7. While the former is to used for formatting X.509 tokens, the latter two are to be used for specifying the certificate path for X.509 certificates. This way a combination of the WS-SecurityPolicy documents along with the Security Profiles published by WS-I ensures interoperability of security. The profiles are testable and hence can be used to implement interoperability security policies in the design and deployment environments.

Additionally, there needs to be policies for secure exchange of security policy documents between service provider and consumer in order to ensure that malicious changes are not affected to the original design causing disruptions in the web services calls.

3.8 Security Policy Infrastructure

Design time SOA policy enforcement could be done by creating policies in the development environments such as IDEs. The design, development and testing of the services and their compliance with standards such as WS-I Basic

Security Profile, etc., can be ensured before final deployment. This WS-I profiles makes the base security standards unambiguous to a large extent and are testable. Hence compliance could be automated. The policies of an existing service implementation could be retrieved from service registry and repositories (R&R) while designing and implementing a service consumer adhering to the required service contracts. The infrastructure would involve IDEs, Source code and build repositories, Policy repositories, Service R&R, Policy Enforcement infrastructure.

3.8.1 SOA Management

Run time SOA policy enforcement enables checking if service invocation and operation is in line with the run time policies. SOA management infrastructure, service dashboards, etc. enable monitoring of service ecosystem. Different types of attacks on service end points such as XML Injection, execution of rogue services exposing enterprise in unauthorized manner or seeking confidential information from service consumers can be detected by the SOA management and monitoring infrastructure. Adequate run time policies need to be defined to counter such attacks and deployed in the SOA management infrastructure.

3.8.2 XML Security Gateways

XML Security Gateways act as a proxy or intermediary between the actual service endpoint and the endpoint visible to the service consumer. All messages to and from the actual service pass through the gateway. This additional layer introduced is delegated with the responsibility of identity management, execution of cryptographic algorithms, authorization workflow management, security policy enforcements, audit logging, message transformation, obviate threats such as SQL or XML injections, payload corruption, attacks causing buffer overflow, etc. The OWASP XML

Security Gateway Evaluation Criteria Project (XSGEC) defines an open standard for evaluating XML Security Gateways.

3.8.3 Service Registry and Repository

Policies are part of service contracts and provide information about the conditions under which a service could be invoked. Service registries and repositories (R&R) is the place where such information is stored. Storage and access to policy files, their attachment to services, grouping of policies, and application of policies to service categories/groups are some of the features provided by Service R&R.

3.8.4 SOA Identity and Authorization Workflow Management Devices

These enable SSO and access control to service endpoints and implement open standards such as SAML, XACML, specifications set from the Liberty Alliance, WS-Federation, and WS-Trust.

3.9 Federated Identity

Federated Identity is a system that allows individuals to use the same user name, password or other personal identification to sign on to the networks of more than one enterprise in order to conduct transactions. With federated identity companies can share applications without needing to adopt the same technologies for directory services, security and authentication. Besides facilitating single sign on (SSO), identity federation allows sharing of service providers and identity managers (providers) to share attributes about a user (service consumer). It also enables exchange of security token across multiple security domains. Standards such as SAML, Liberty Alliance ID-FF, WS-Trust and WS-Federation have been adopted by various vendors for accomplishing Federated Identity Management (FIM) in an interoperable

manner. However, a prerequisite to such federation is the existence of agreements among the various service providers and identity providers to exchange attribute information among them, create new trust domains, define new identification mechanisms based on existing set of user identity attributes (deemed to be relevant for a particular business transaction), define access control based on federated identity information being exchanged and such other issues. It also involves taking consent from the user to share his/her attribute information with other providers and enable the user's participating in different identity federation networks. None of these aspects are defined by the standards and hence need to be settled and negotiated out of band. Businesses (service providers, identity providers) need to be have well defined identity federation policies for handling these issues.

4. SOA AND SOA GOVERNANCE

Any software component can be elevated to the status of a service once it has been mandated to be used by a larger user community in by and large standalone or loosely coupled manner. The potential user community may be known during the conceptualization of the service but the exact users are not known. In such a situation the conditions and restrictions under which the service could be availed need to be spelt out in a clear and concise manner. Standards such as WS-SecurityPolicy help in specifying the security policies applicable to a service as envisaged by the service designer. This ensures that the business functionality exposed by the service takes care of the security concerns of the data exposed and transactions initiated. The required policies (which are part of the larger service contract) need to be defined even before the service is implemented and deployed. The inputs to the definition of these policies come from the different aspects such as:

- **SOA:** The SOA lays the service abstraction layers and classifies the services based on different criteria. The service being designed ideally should be categorized and classified to belong to one or more classes according to service classification strategy. The classes are made in terms of differing security concerns, nature of service consumers, operation domain (external or internal to an enterprise), nature of operation (simple query or transactions) and such other factors. The conceptualization of these classes need to be done with great care and is a prime SOA governance concern. More often than not, the classification goes a long way in determining the security policies that are applicable to a newly conceptualized service.

- **Enterprise architecture and the SOA infrastructure:** These include various factors such as the nature of the IT infrastructure, IT systems portfolio, the geographical distribution, communication infrastructure, the security domains that exist in an enterprise, the security of the available communication channels (intranet versus extranet), the feasibility of implementing a secure channel over existing communication channels (for example, the feasibility of using a WS-Security/Kerberos Tokens based SSO solution over an extranet based communication channel), the number of security (identity) domains and trust zones to be traversed during the a business transaction using multiple service implementations exposed by various underlying enterprise IT systems, the existing security infrastructure for access control, SSO, etc. These issues determine the security architecture to be used for deployment and usage of a web service in the large. The security architecture and its governance by and large determine the feasible security policies to be applicable for a service

implementation. The compliance to these policies is determined through SOA design and run time governance using SOA management platforms, existing enterprise audit systems.

- **Enterprise security policies:** enterprise security policies and guidelines go a long way in determining the web services security policies. Enterprise security audit, business entity classification by security needs, policies for B2B, B2C and A2A secure communication need to be considered while designing the web services security policies.

- **Rogue services:** This is a category of services which are not governed and is a result of uncontrolled proliferation of services, acquisition of pre-packaged service portfolio or built out of malicious intent. These services present imminent threat to the service ecosystem by exposing critical business data and transactions without proper checks and balances. Being outside the scope of security audit and compliance they pose a great deal of security to the business. Having proper SOA governance and security policies in place ensure that service message traffic monitoring devices could be installed to automatically detect adherence/violation of the policies by the services being orchestrated over the network and in a way allow detection of rogue services not adhering to the policies or conforming to the existing SOA governance mechanisms.

5. CONCLUSION

In this chapter, we have examined role of security policies in SOA implementations. As part of this exercise, we have looked into policies in web services and there relation with other WS -* standards. We have also looked into policy enforcement points and publishing strategies. Next we have examined the various security requirements in SOA implementations. We have identified new categories of security requirements introduced by loosely coupled SOA architecture.

We looked into the role of security policies in web services and discussed the importance of security policies in SOA implementations. We then looked at the basic concepts of WS-Security policy language. WS security policy specification specifies a standard way to define and publish security requirements in an extensible and interoperable way. We have also discussed general security policies like authorization, authentication, audit policies etc. We then talked about XACML- a standard that can be used in conjunction with SAML or WS-security to enforce access control to web services. Web services are not only SOAP based there are REST based services too. Web services security standards like WS-Security, WS-Security policy are associated with SOAP. They don't talk about other web services communications like REST. We present security for REST services.

We also addressed how interoperability issues are catered using Policies. Since services are designed and implemented to cater to wider consumer community, operating on different implementation platforms, the topic of interoperability assumes prime importance. While designing security for web services, one of the critical policies would be to ensure compliance with WS-I Basic Security Profiles and the specific token profiles. We then talk about policy infrastructures.

Standards such as WS-SecurityPolicy help in specifying the security policies applicable to a service as envisaged by the service designer. This ensures that the business functionality exposed by the service takes care of the security concerns of the data exposed and transactions initiated. The required policies (which are part of the larger service contract) need to be defined even before the service is implemented and deployed.

REFERENCES

Anderson, A. (2006). Web services policies. *Security & Privacy*, *4*(3), 84–87. doi:10.1109/MSP.2006.81

Erl, T. (2005). *Service-Oriented Architecture*. Delhi, India: Dorling Kindersley (India) Pvt. Ltd.

Gutiérrez, C., Fernández-Medina, E., & Piattini, M. (2004). A Survey of Web Services Security. In *ICCSA 2004*, (LNCS Vol. 3043, pp. 968 977). Berlin: Springer-Verlag.

Hartman, B., Flinn, D. J., Beznosov, K., & Kawamoto, S. (2003). *Mastering Web Services Security*. Indiana: Wiley Publishing, Inc.

Security for REST Web Services. (2006, February 20). *Security for REST Web Services*. Retrieved December 11, 2008, from http://radio.weblogs.com/0111797/2006/02/20.html

Spec, X. A. C. M. L. (2005, February 1). *eXtensible Access Control Markup Language (XACML)*. Retrieved November 20, 2008, from http://docs.oasis-open.org/xacml/2.0/access_control-xacml-2.0-core-spec-os.pdf

Stojanovic, Z., & Dahanayake, A. (2004). *Service-Oriented Software System Engineering*. Hershey, PA: Idea Group Publishing.

WS-Federation Spec. (2003, July 18). *WS- Federation Specification*. Retrieved November 20, 2008, from http://www.ibm.com/developerworks/library/specification/ws-fed/

WS-Policy Attachment Spec. (2007, September 4). *Web Services Policy Attachment*. Retrieved November 20, 2008, from http://www.w3.org/TR/ws-policy-attach/

WS-Policy Spec. (2006, April 25). *Web Services Policy 1.2 - Framework (WS-Policy)*. Retrieved November 20, 2008, from http://www.w3.org/Submission/WS-Policy/

WS-Security Policy Spec. (2007, July 1). *WS-Security Policy 1.2*. Retrieved November 20, 2008, from http://docs.oasis-open.org/ws-sx/ws-securitypolicy/200702/ws-securitypolicy-1.2-spec-os.html

WS-Security Spec. (2006, February 1). *WS-Security*. Retrieved November 20, 2008, from http://www.oasis-open.org/committees/download.php/16790/wss-v1.1-spec-os-SOAPMessageSecurity.pdf

Yee, G., & Korba, L. (2005). Negotiated Security Policies for E-Services and Web Services. In *Proceedings of the IEEE International Conference on Web Services (ICWS'05)*, (pp. 605 - 612). Washington, DC: IEEE Computer Society. Bhargavan, K., Fournet, C. & Gordan, A.D. (2008). Verifying Policy-Based Web Services Security. In *ACM conference on Computer and communications security*, (Vol. 30, pp. 268-277). New York: ACM.

Section 3
Web Services Security Standards

Chapter 8
Web Services Security:
Standards and Industrial Practice

Eduardo B. Fernandez
Florida Atlantic University, USA

Keiko Hashizume
Florida Atlantic University, USA

Ingrid Buckley
Florida Atlantic University, USA

Maria M. Larrondo-Petrie
Florida Atlantic University, USA

Michael VanHilst
Florida Atlantic University, USA

ABSTRACT

This chapter surveys the context for web services security and discusses the issues and standards at every level of architectural. The authors attempt to evaluate the status of industrial practice with respect to the security of web services. They look at commercial products and their supporting levels, and end with some conclusions. They see a problem in the proliferation of overlapping and possibly incompatible standards. Reliability is also an important aspect. They discuss some of its issues and consider its effect on security. A basic principle of security is the need to secure all levels of architecture; any weak levels will permit attackers to penetrate the system. These levels include: Business workflow level, catalog and description of web services level, communications level (typically SOAP), and storage of XML documents. There is a variety of standards for web services security and reliability and the authors will look at most of them.

INTRODUCTION

Web services are software components defined by their interfaces that can be accessed on the In-ternet and incorporated into applications. Another definition is: "self-contained modular business applications that have open, Internet-oriented, standard-based interfaces" (Alonso, Casati, Kuno & Machiraju, 2004, p. 124). Web services commu-

DOI: 10.4018/978-1-60566-950-2.ch008

nicate using XML (Extensible Markup Language) messages that typically follow the Simple Object Access Protocol (SOAP) standard. They are becoming more and more the fundamental building blocks of distributed systems. Their value comes from their increasing use in commercial systems and the fact that they are already the basic building blocks of computational grids such as the Global Information Grid. Web services are a realization of a more abstract architectural style called Service-Oriented Architecture (SOA). This chapter surveys the context for web services security, considers appropriate architectural levels, and discusses the issues and standards at each level. We try to evaluate the status of industrial practice with respect to the security of web services. We examine the relevant levels one by one and consider their security. We look at commercial products and supporting levels, and end with some conclusions.

Reliability is another important aspect and we discuss some of its issues and consider its effect on security. To provide a complete perspective, we consider each of the architectural levels or layers involved in satisfying security requirements.

Many aspects of web services become clearer and more general if we discuss them in the context of SOA. We discuss some basic aspects of the SOA approach in Section 2.

While web services introduce a variety of new useful functions, they increase the complexity of the system where they are used. Because of this complexity, web services can be subject to a variety of attacks. The fact that web services are being used for many sensitive areas, e.g. financial and military applications, provides a strong motivation for attackers. We look systematically at security and reliability issues indicating the standards that apply to each architectural layer (Section 3). A cornerstone of any defense against threats is a secure software methodology and we look at some of these in Section 4.

There is a large variety of standards for web services. This variety is bewildering for product developers and users. We have studied the current status of all relevant standards. By relevant we mean the most important general standards and all the standards that refer to security or reliability. We have summarized this study in a set of tables (Section 5).

As an important practical aspect of this study we have kept track of products in the market that support web services security. We present a partial catalog of the products available at the time of this writing (Section 6). While not comprehensive, this catalog gives a good idea of what is available. We have used product descriptions in the past to develop security patterns. We use them now to provide a study and analysis of the current state of these products and tools, including not just security but development and composition aspects.

We believe in the value of patterns to build architectures and we provide an overview of some of the patterns used in SOA (Section 7). A pattern is a reusable solution to a recurrent systems problem. Their use has grown consistently in software development, being now adopted by many vendors and developers. We have proposed the idea of expressing standards as patterns and use these patterns to understand and compare the standards (Fernandez & Delassy, 2006). These patterns are also useful to evaluate existing products by checking if they include specific patterns.

In order to use patterns effectively we need catalogs. To organize catalogs we need a good classification of patterns. We have produced a multidimensional classification (VanHilst, Fernandez & Braz, in press), and we are extending it (Washizaki, Fernandez, Maruyama, Kubo & Yoshioka, submitted). We proposed the concept of Misuse (attack) patterns in order to describe complete attacks (Fernandez, Pelaez & Larrondo-Petrie, 2007) later we have made their description more precise (Fernandez, 2009) These topics are not discussed here, the reader is referred to the corresponding papers.

Validation and Certification approaches are important to improve trust in any product. We describe here some of the existing approaches.

Governance is another new concept for web services, also briefly considered here. We discuss these two aspects in Section 8.

A final section presents some conclusions and possible future work.

Service-Oriented Architecture (SOA)

We define SOA as an architectural style in which a system is composed from a set of loosely coupled services that interact with each other by sending messages. In order to interoperate, each service publishes its description, which defines its interface and expresses constraints and policies that must be respected in order to interact with it. A service is thus a building block for service-oriented applications. In this architectural style, applications are built by coordinating and assembling services. A service is a logical representation of a business activity that has a specified outcome. A key principle about services is that they should be easily reusable and discoverable, even in an inter-organizational context. Furthermore, the channels of communication between the participating entities in a service-oriented application are much more vulnerable than in operating systems or within the boundaries of an organization's intranet, since they are established on public networks. The complexity of the software used to handle web services adds to the total complexity.

SOA has been adopted as a main direction by IBM and Microsoft among others. It is a high-level architectural approach that attempts to glue and unify disjoint pieces of software. SOA can be implemented using ad hoc architectures, CORBA (Common Object Request Broker Architecture), Jini, web services, or other distributed architectures. A mail service is a basic type of SOA (with only one service). SOA can be seen as the generalization of client-server architectures.

Three basic roles are involved in service architectures:

- *Keeper of repositories of services*—An institution that provides public catalogs of services.
- *Provider or keeper of services*—A site that stores the service code and data. They may be the same as the keepers of repositories or the creators of services, but could also be specialized institutions. They may or may not own the services they keep.
- *Consumer of (Client)*—Any institution that uses services in its applications.

What is important is the use of explicit interfaces defining some services without showing the implementation of these services. These are the standard concepts of information hiding and encapsulation from object-oriented design. A schema describes the service and its physical binding. A service resides in an abstract hosting environment called a *container*. Clients and servers can use any technology and don't need to know the technology of the services they use. Service descriptions include the schema and an address to find the service.

Individual services can be combined to produce new composite services that introduce new levels of reuse and allow the dynamic reconfiguration of business systems (Arsanjani, Borges & Holley, 2004). Semantic integration of services is an ideal, not accomplished yet.

SOA Communication

Communication can be performed by:

- Asynchronous messages. Send a document to a service and receive an answer later.
- Synchronous operation using a Broker (Buschmann, Meunier, Rohnert, Sommerland & Stal, 1996) (proxies handle asynchronous messages).

Sender and receiver must agree on document structure and meaning. A message includes a

Figure 1. SOA architectural layers

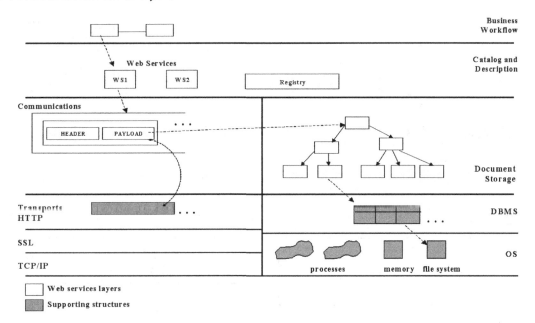

header (describing routing and security information) and an envelope (carrying the message contents). A contract defines the meaning of header and envelope for the entities that exchange messages.

Services can be used in two basic ways:

- Remote Procedure Call (RPC) style—A message invokes a service with some parameters and the response is sent back over the same connection. This is a synchronous approach.
- Document style—A complete document (or parts of it) is manipulated. This is a coarser-grained asynchronous approach.

In general, the document style is more efficient, more extensible, and more scalable. However, the RPC approach is more prevalent today because it is similar to earlier, more familiar approaches. The fact that data is exchanged for business purposes and between different entities means that, in addition to the usual requirements of security, accountability is an important factor.

SOA Architectural Layers

Figure 1 shows the layers of a SOA. We notice that SOA adds three layers to a standard client-server architecture. Another view is described by the layers proposed in (Zdun, Hentrich, & van der Aalst, 2006).

The usual quality attributes apply to SOA; that is, we need security, reliability, usability, testability, and portability. Accountability is also important. Interoperability is reached through standards. Our concern here are security and reliability but all these attributes may be important is specific applications.

Web Services Security and Standards

Figure 2 summarizes the main general standards that apply to each layer, while Figure 3 shows most of the security standards. We describe each layer in some detail.

Figure 2. Layers and web services standards

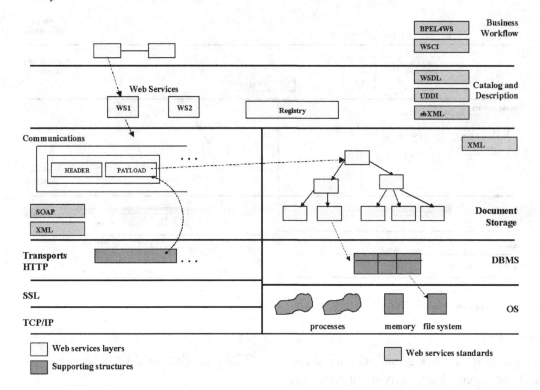

Threats

A catalog of threats can be found in (Morrison & Hirsch, 2006). They include: message alteration, message reading, falsified messages, man-in-the-middle attacks, principal spoofing, forged claims, message replay, and denial of service.

We have developed a systematic method to enumerate threats for applications (Fernandez, VanHilst, Larrondo-Petrie & Huang, 2006). This method can be applied to SOA in general or to specific applications using SOA. This approach analyzes the activities in each use case to analyze the ways they can be misused.

Business Workflow Level

The highest level of the architecture is the business workflow level. Web services workflow initially was defined by languages such as electronic business XML (Lee, 2005) and RosettaNet.

A more recent standard for the workflow level is BPEL (Business Process Execution Language), developed by IBM, BEA, and Microsoft ("Business Process," 2002). BPEL provides a language for the formal specification of business processes and business interaction protocols (called as a whole "web services choreography"). This extends the Web services interaction model and allows web services to perform business transactions. It combines ideas from XLANG (XML business process Language) and WSFL (Web Services Flow Language), two early business languages. Some systems use XML databases and other products to handle XML documents according to business workflow. Other related standards produced by these three vendors include WS-Transaction, WS-Coordination, and WS-Reliable Messaging. On its part, W3C has developed other standards for web services choreography, the Web Service Choreography Interface (WSCI).

Figure 3. Layers and security standards

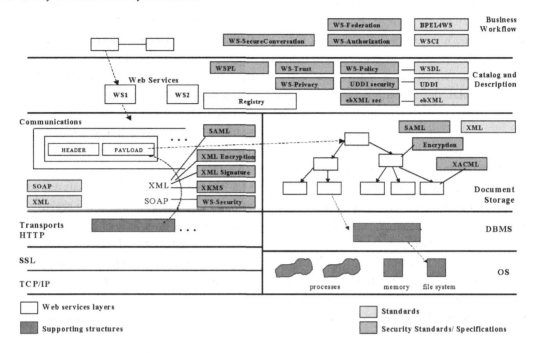

The organizations responsible for ebXML, BPEL, WSCI, or related standards have defined some security standards or recommendations for security specifications. For ebXML, OASIS (Organization for the Advancement of Structured Information Standards) has recommendations for the catalog and description level and RosettaNet in its RosettaNet Implementation Framework (Yendluri, 2000) defines messages including authentication, authorization, encryption, and non-repudiation. The Security Considerations for the BPEL, briefly mentioned at the end of the specification, strongly recommend that business process implementations use WS-Security (see below) to ensure there have not been any modifications of messages during transit or while residing in destinations. WS-Security is a broad description of a framework indicating how to secure Web services including a family of WS-* standards and specifications including those related to federation such as WS-Federation, WS-Authorization, and WS-SecureConversation. WS-Security notes that

business process implementations are subject to various forms of denial-of-service attacks and that should be taken into consideration. Although this is the workflow level, they are concerned with authorization and low-level security. There is no security defined at the semantic level.

There is a lack of consensus over how to handle Web services workflow, choreography, and transactions. Therefore, the industry has been divided into two camps--one that's behind the W3C's WSCI and another that's supporting BPEL. Co-authors of BPEL include BEA, IBM, and Microsoft. These are overlapping and competing languages, which makes it harder to evaluate their effect on the security of future systems. This lack of common standards may have a bad overall effect not just on security but also on the interoperability of web services. As we see below, diverging standards are also a problem at other levels.

Registry and Description Level

Web services descriptions are defined using the Web Service Description Language (WSDL), another standard. WSDL is a static interface definition. A WSDL definition has two parts or stages:

- An abstract part, called the port type where WSDL describes a Web service in terms of the messages it sends and receives.
- A physical or concrete part that defines the protocol specific bindings you use to access the Web service (Vinoski, 2003). A binding specifies transport and wire format details for one or more interfaces. An endpoint associates a network address with a binding. And finally, a service groups endpoints together that implement a common interface (Moreau, Chinnici, Ryman & Weerawarana, 2006).

The standards are evolving towards describing web services security policies using WS-Policy, a high level specification allowing organizations to specify the specific requirements of their web services for privacy and security, and then referring to this policy from the WSDL (Rosenberg & Remy, 2004). More policy-related specifications include WS-Privacy and WS-Trust.

There are two primary e-business registries providing registration, management, and discovery information needed to conduct e-business, the Universal Description, Discovery and Integration (UDDI) specification and ebXML registry. Both act as a focal point to organize information interactions, enable the discovery of trading partners, and register web service descriptions such as WSDL documents. In addition they classify XML schemas, Document Type Definitions (DTDs), and trading partner profiles. (Chiusano, 2003) describes the associations and compatibility of UDDI and ebXML.

The UDDI directory specifies a metadata aggregation service. These metadata aggregation services are useful repositories in which organizations can publish services they provide, describe the interfaces to their services and enable domain-specific taxonomies of services.

The UDDI committee has defined some general security guidelines with few details (Lee, 2005). These policies include:

- Only authorized individuals can publish or change information in the registry
- Changes or deletions can only be made by the originator of the information
- Each instance of a UDDI registry can define its own user authentication mechanism

The paucity of security specifications for UDDI and WSDL indicates a misunderstanding of their importance for security. The exposure of too many details could help hackers and their lack of integrity would severely affect the use of web services.

An ebXML registry provides a mechanism by which XML artifacts can be stored, maintained, and automatically discovered. ebXML provides companies with a standard method to exchange business messages, conduct trading relationships, communicate data in common terms, and define and register business processes.

On its part, the ebXML committee defined in May 2001 detailed security specifications for registries (Lee, 2005). These requirements apply to authentication, integrity, and confidentiality. They specify, among other things, that each request must be authenticated and any known entity can publish or view what has been published.

Their security model (described in UML syntax) does not reflect the classical security models but they have defined a rather ad hoc model which mixes model and implementation aspects. The ebXML committee presents a case study showing how to use the UDDI Business Registry to search for an ebXML Registry/Repository. Although it is possible to discover a UDDI registry from within an ebXML registry the OASIS/ebXML committee has not yet produced a technical paper on this (Chiusano, 2003),

UDDI is focused exclusively on this discovery aspect, while ebXML Registry is focused on both discovery and collaboration, due to its focus on storing and maintaining XML artifacts. (Chiusano, 2003) believes that UDDI has a much more prominent following than ebXML Registry for discovery of businesses, their web services, and the technical interfaces they make available.

The Communications Level

The Simple Object Access Protocol (SOAP) defines the following level. Actually there are other approaches that do not use SOAP, e.g., Representational State Transfer (REST), but they have not gained general acceptance.

SOAP security is defined by the SOAP Security Extensions. These extensions have been defined by the W3C XML Encryption Working Group (Lawrence & Kaler, 2004). One of these standards, XML Encryption, defines a process for encrypting and decrypting messages considering the granularity of the message contents. This can be as small as one element (including start/end tags) or apply to the element content (between the start/end tags). Super-encryption is possible, where the whole message with parts encrypted can be encrypted again, as is done when Secure Sockets Layer (SSL) is used for secure transmission over HTTP. A variety of encryption algorithms can be used, including the Advanced Encryption Standard (AES). Another standard from W3C for SOAP also specifies digital signatures (XML Signature). A SOAP message includes a header and a payload. Security Assertion Markup Language (SAML) defines authentication and authorization assertions. SAML assertions can be included in the header or in the payload of a SOAP message. SOAP APIs are not standardized, so moving from

one to another requires changes in your application. More importantly, SOAP APIs don't hide underlying transport details from applications. This might not be a problem if all Web services used only HTTP (Vinoski, 2003).

XML Encryption protects the secrecy of the message. A Public Key Infrastructure (PKI) can be used to provide authentication, digital signatures, and key distribution. This PKI could be based on *XML Key Management Specification* (XKMS), intended for the integration of PKI and digital certificates. For example, digital signature processing can be delegated to a web service in order to simplify the PKI structure. XKMS is an open standard that applies to any vendor PKI approach. The XKMS uses two specialized standards:

- *XML Key Registration Service* (X-KRSS), for the registration of key pairs and location of keys for later use.
- *XML Key Information Service* (X-KISS), that defines validation and location information associated with a key. This standard can be complemented or replaced by *XML Trust Assertion Service Specification* (XTASS) (Lee, 2005), which provides some higher-level functions, e.g., validation using SAML.

The WS-Security standard is an enhancement to SOAP to describe how to provide message integrity, confidentiality, and authentication (Hashizume, Fernandez & Huang, submitted; WS-Security, 2002; Security in, 2002). XML Signature is the foundational technology for WS-Security (Rosenberg & Remy, 2004). WS-Security defines security tokens that can be used for claims of authentication or proof of some right. These claims can be endorsed with evidence from a trusted party. Specifically, security tokens may include X.509 certificates and Kerberos tickets. SAML assertions can be used to specify the content of message headers and thus they complement this standard. However, SAML is not mentioned in the WS-

Security document. At this point, WS-Security and SAML work together: WS-Security defines how you insert the information into a SOAP envelope, and SAML defines what the security information is. SAML is a security token format that is used for carrying authentication and authorization information, while WS-Security is a mechanism for carrying security tokens like SAML in a SOAP message (Rosenberg & Remy, 2004).

Similarly for the XML Encryption and XML Signature standards, the WS-Security document indicates that their specifications can be combined; the problem is again that there are some overlaps. Another objection is the fact that WS-Security requires a well-defined sender-receiver pair; it doesn't have a way to handle a variety of business partners whose identities are not known in advance. This is an important business use; for example, when dealing with contractors.

The OASIS standards group recently formed a technical committee to develop XML protocols for digital signatures and cryptographic time stamping in a Web services transaction. This work appears to overlap W3C's XML digital signatures. According to OASIS, XML standards such as XML Signatures and XML Encryption will play a role in the new OASIS standards. The OASIS digital signature standard will be more application-oriented and focuses specifically on the use of the technology within a Web services context (Hashizume & Fernandez, submitted). This is another example of the overlap in the process of web services standardization.

In practice, many systems still use SSL to secure this layer but this should change when web services are more used for documents because SSL is too coarse and cannot protect portions of documents. SSL is considered a secure protocol where, so far, few vulnerabilities have been found.

There are two standards for reliable messaging: WS-Reliable Message and WS-Reliability. Both have similar objectives, patterns for them and a

comparison are given in (Buckley, Fernandez, Rossi & Madjadi, 2009).

The Document Storage Level

One can (and should) use domain-based security according to document contents. There is already a good amount of research on XML security and a standard, XML Access Control Markup Language (XACML) is a language that can define authorization rules for each element of an XML document or for whole documents. XACML is intended to provide a way to express access control policies in a variety of environments, using a single language. A rule has a subject (requesting entity), a right (read, write, etc.), an object (the document element), and a condition (for example, day of the week when access is permitted). XACML also describes an enforcement mechanism, where a request is evaluated and a decision is returned. In other words, XACML is an expression of an extended access matrix together with an enforcement mechanism.

Similarly as for transmission, each element of a document can be encrypted according to the XML Encryption standards mentioned above. Finally, the document schemas, DTDs and Document Object Models (DOMs) can also be used to provide security (Bertino, Castano, Ferrari, & Mesiti, 2000). Because documents may contain links to other documents, the security constraints applied to a document must consider also the security of these links. However, these aspects are mostly at the research stage and just starting to be considered in products.

Secure Systems Development Methodologies

Most of the approaches to produce secure software are based on analyzing code. While this is a reasonable approach, it will not have a strong impact in future systems. We believe that we need to emphasize the modeling aspects of software development. We show here some secure methodologies but we consider first general approaches to develop SOA software, followed by some ways to build secure SOAs.

In general a software development methodology should be able to accommodate refinement throughout the development life cycle in an iterative and incremental approach. The methodology should consist of phases that span from the conception of the need for the web service, to the construction of the web service and finally its deployment (Papazoglu, 2008). Security should be applied at all stages.

The following methodologies can be used to build systems using web services:

Service-Oriented Architecture (SOA) Model

IBM has produced a service-oriented analysis and design process for modeling, analyzing, designing, and producing a SOA that includes business analysis, processes, and goals (Arsanjani, 2004; Zim03]. This approach applies techniques for deployment, monitoring, management, and governance to support the full SOA life cycle and relies on Java and WebSphere. Apparently this approach was refined recently in a method called SOMA (Arsanjani, Ghosh, Allam, Abdollah, Ganapathy & Holley, 2008).

Framework for Web Services Implementation Technical Committee (FWSITC) was created with the purpose of facilitating implementation of web services by defining a practical and extensible methodology (Lee, 2005). There are several mechanism that are used to implement web services, which can include fault-tolerance, replication, security, reliability and availability.

Business Process Transformation (Feuerlicht & Meesathit, 2005) is a web services develop-ment methodology that serves as a framework for business process analysis and service design, and produces service specifications expressed in Web Services Flow Language (WSFL) and service usage interfaces expressed in WSDL. The WSFL service specification describes interaction flows between a set of web services that implement a business process.

Extreme Model-Driven Design (XMDD) is a methodology and a design environment for services (Steffen & Narayan, 2007).

None of these methodologies considers security in detail. Some approaches are tailored specifically for web services security:

Our group has proposed a general secure systems development methodology that can be used for web services (Fernandez, Larrondo-Petrie, Sorgente & VanHilst, 2006). This approach covers the complete lifecycle and applies security at all stages. It uses patterns and applies them to the different architectural levels of the system. A variant of the methodology was oriented towards SOA and MDA (Delessy &Fernandez 2008).

PWSSec (Process for Web Services Security) enables the integration of specific stages into the traditional phases of web services-based systems development providing them with security (Gutierrez, Fernandez-Medina & Piattini, 2006). This process can be applied in the development of new web services-based systems or in existing systems. PWSSec is composed of three stages: WSSecReq (Web Services Security Requirements) (Gutierrez,Fernandez-Medina&Piattini, 2007), WSSecArch (Web Services Security Architecture) and WSSecTech (Web Services Security Technologies). The main purpose of the WSSecReq stage is to produce security requirements. A set of security threats over the system is identified in this stage. The WSSecArch stage is intended to allocate the security requirements identified in the previous stage into a security architecture. The WSSecTech identifies the set of web services security standards that will implement the architectural security mechanisms identified in the WSSecArch stage.

Serenity S&D patterns. This approach makes emphasis in the later stages using S&D patterns, that include possible implementations. The S&D patterns are general security-oriented patterns but may include web service implementations (Sanchez-Cid & Maña, 2008). The approach includes monitoring aspects.

Another approach is IBM's Business-driven application development (Nagaratnam, Nadalin, Hondo, McIntosh & Austel, 2005). This is a general approach with emphasis on SOA aspects. It includes also monitoring aspects.

The specification of high-assurance web services is addressed in (Atkinson, Brenner, Falcone & Juhasz, 2008), although they do not define the later stages.

Kaiser proposed a policy-based approach that could be used for security policies (Kaiser, 2007).

THE CURRENT STATUS OF WEB SERVICES STANDARDS

We have classified these web services standards into eight groups: XML, Messaging, Description and Discovery, Security, Reliable Messaging, Business Process, Transaction, and Management Specifications. Each group identifies several standards that have similar objectives.

There are some standards that are composed by many parts such as XML Schema that has three parts: primer, structure, and datatypes. Usually primer contains basic information to have a better understanding of the standard. The second part may be the framework or core that includes the main structure of the standard, and the other parts may be extended features. There are other standards that depend on others such as WS-Security that uses XML Encryption and XML Digital Signature. Even some other standards may overlap or conflict to each other such as ebXML and UDDI standards that define similar functionalities.

XML Specifications

XML Specifications provides information about XML such as structure, schema, and namespaces. XML has also extended specifications that complement XML functionalities. (See Table 1)

Messaging Specifications

This group includes specifications that enable entities to exchange XML messages in a distributed environment. (See Table 2)

Description and Discovery Specifications

These specifications aim to describe Web Services in terms of location, operation, interfaces, and policies, and publish this information in order to be publicly accessed. (See Table 3)

Security Specifications

These security specifications describe how to secure communication between applications through integrity, confidentiality, authentication, and authorization. (See Table 4)

Reliable Messaging Specifications

These specifications guarantees the delivery of messages even when the system or network fails. (See Table 5)

Business Process Specifications

Business Process Specifications are the highest level specifications that specify business process and participants involve in a transaction.(See Table 6)

Table 1.

Standard	Date	Publisher	Status	Description	Source
XML 1.1 (eXtensible Markup Language)	Set 2006	W3C	Recommendation	It is derived from SGML. It allows its users to create their own tags, enabling the definition, transmission, validation and interpretation of data between applications and between organizations (Bray, Sperberg-McQueen, Maler, Yergeau & Cowan, 2006)	W3C
XML Namespaces	Aug 2006	W3C	Recommendation	They provide a simple method for qualifying element and attribute names used in XML documents by associating them with namespaces identified by URI references (Bray, Hollander, Layman & Tobin, 2006).	W3C
XML Schema Part 0: Primer	Oct 2004	W3C	Recommendation	It is a non-normative document intended to provide an easily readable description of the XML Schema facilities (Fallside & Walmsley, 2004)	W3C
XML Schema Part 1: Structures	Oct 2004	W3C	Recommendation	It offers facilities for describing the structure and constraining the contents of XML documents (Thompson, Beech, Maloney & Mendelsohn, 2004).	W3C
XML Schema Part 2: Datatypes	Oct 2004	W3C	Recommendation	It defines facilities for defining datatypes to be used in XML Schemas as well as other XML specifications (Biron & Malhotra, 2004).	W3C
XPath 2.0	Jan 2007	W3C	Recommendation	It is a language for addressing parts of an XML document (Berglund, Boag Chamberlin, Fernández, Kay, Robie, & Siméon, 2007)	W3C
XQuery	Jan 2007	W3C	Recommendation	It is a query language that is designed to query collections of XML data (Boag, Chamberlin, Fernández, Florescu, Robie, & Siméon, 2007).	W3C
XML Information Set	Feb 2004	W3C	Recommendation	It provides a set of definitions for use in other specifications that need to refer to the information in an XML document (Cowan & Tobin, 2004)	W3C
XInclude	Nov 2006	W3C	Recommendation	This specification introduces a generic mechanism for merging XML documents (as represented by their information sets) for use by applications that need such a facility (Marsh, Orchard & Veillard, 2006)	W3C
XLink	June 2001	W3C	Recommendation	It allows elements to be inserted into XML documents in order to create and describe links between resources (DeRose, Maler & Orchard, 2001).	W3C
XPointer Framework	March 2003	W3C	Recommendation	The framework is intended to be used as a basis for fragment identifiers for any resource (Grosso, Maler, Marsh & Walsh, 2003).	W3C
XPointer xmlns() Scheme	March 2003	W3C	Recommendation	It is intended to be used with XPointer Framework to o allow correct interpretation of namespace prefixes in pointers (DeRose, Daniel, Maler & Marsh, 2003)	W3C
XPointer xpointer() Scheme	Dec 2002	W3C	Working Draft	It is intended to be used with the XPointer Framework to provide a high level of functionality for addressing portions of XML documents (DeRose, Maler & Daniel, 2002)	W3C

Transaction Specifications

Transaction specifications provide coordination mechanisms when interoperability is needed between different domains. (See Table 7)

Management Specifications

These specifications describe how to manage and access web services or other resources located remotely on their networks. (See Table 8)

Web Services Security in Commercial Products and Tools

A large number of products and tools exist on the market, which are designed with the objective of giving greater levels of functionality while conforming to industry standards and specification. We show here some of the existing security products.

Table 2.

Standard	Date	Publisher	Status	Description	Source
SOAP 1.2 Part 0: Primer	April 2007	W3C	Recommendation	It is a non-normative document intended to provide an easily understandable tutorial on the features of SOAP Version 1.2 (Mitra & Lafon, 2007)	W3C
SOAP 1.2 Part 1: Messaging Framework	April 2007	W3C	Recommendation	It is a lightweight protocol intended for exchanging structured information in a decentralized, distributed environment (Gudgin, Hadley, Mendelsohn, Moreau, Nielson, Karmarkar & Lafon, 2007a).	W3C
SOAP 1.2 Part 2: Adjuncts	April 2007	W3C	Recommendation	It defines a set of adjuncts that MAY be used with the SOAP messaging framework such as SOAP encoding, SOAP RPC representation and so on (Gudgin, Hadley, Mendelsohn, Moreau, Nielson, Karmarkar & Lafon, 2007b).	W3C
WS-Notification	Oct 2006	OASIS	Standard	It is the base specification on which all the other specifications in the family depend. It consists of three specifications: WS-BaseNotification, WS-BrokeredNotification and Ws-Topics.	IBM, OASIS
WS-BaseNotification	Oct 2006	OASIS	Standard	It defines the normative Web services interfaces for two of the important roles: NotificationProducer and NotificationConsumer roles. It includes standard message exchanges to be implemented by service providers that wish to act in these roles, along with operational requirements expected of them (Graham, Hull & Murray, 2006).	IBM, OASIS
WS-BrokeredNotification	Oct 2006	OASIS	Standard	It defines the Web services interface for the NotificationBroker. A NotificationBroker is an intermediary which, among other things, allows publication of messages from entities that are not themselves service providers (Chappell & Liu, 2006).	IBM, OASIS
WS-Topics	Oct 2006	OASIS	Standard	It defines a mechanism to organize and categorize items of interest for subscription known as "topics" (Vampenepe, Graham & Niblett, 2006).	IBM, OASIS
WS-Addressing 1.0 - Core	May 2006	W3C	Recommendation	It provides transport-neutral mechanisms to address Web services and messages. Specifically, this specification defines XML elements to identify Web service endpoints and to secure end-to-end endpoint identification in messages (Gudgin, Hadley & Rogers, 2006a).	W3C, IBM
WS-Addressing 1.0 - SOAP Binding	May 2006	W3C	Recommendation	It defines the binding of the abstract properties defined in WS-Addressing 1.0 - Core to SOAP Messages (Gudgin, Hadley & Rogers, 2006b).	W3C
WS-Addressing 1.0 - WSDL Binding	May 2006	W3C	Candidate Recommendation	It defines how the abstract properties defined in WS-Addressing 1.0 - Core are described using WSDL (Gudgin, Hadley, Rogers & Yalçinalp, 2006a)	W3C
WS-Addressing 1.0 - Metadata	Sept 2007	W3C	Recommendation	It defines how the abstract properties defined in Web Services Addressing 1.0 - Core are described using WSDL, how to include WSDL metadata in endpoint references, and how WS-Policy can be used to indicate the support of WS-Addressing by a Web service (Gudgin, Hadley, Rogers & Yalçinalp, 2006b).	W3C
WS-Transfer	Sept 2006	W3C	Member Submission	It describes a general SOAP-based protocol for accessing XML representations of Web service-based resources (Alexander, Box, Cabrera, Chappell, Daniels, et al., 2006a).	W3C
WS-Eventing	March 2006	W3C	Member Submission	It describes a protocol that allows Web services to subscribe to or accept subscriptions for event notification messages (Box, Cabrera, Critchley, Curbera, Ferguson, et al., 2006).	IBM
WS-Enumeration	March 2006	Microsoft, BEA, CA	Member Submission	It describes a general SOAP-based protocol for enumerating a sequence of XML elements that is suitable for traversing logs, message queues, or other linear information models (Alexander, Box, Cabrera, Chappell, Daniels, et al., 2006b).	W3C
SOAP Message Transmission Optimization Mechanism	Jan 2005	W3C	Recommendation	It describes an abstract feature and a concrete implementation of it for optimizing the transmission and/or wire format of SOAP messages (Gudgin, Mendelsohn, Nottingham & Ruellan, 2005).	W3C

Table 3.

Standard	Date	Publisher	Status	Description	Source
WS-Policy 1.5 - Framework	Set 2007	W3C	Recommendation	It provides a general purpose model and corresponding syntax to describe the policies of a Web Service (Vedamuthu, Orchard, Hirsch, Hondo, Yendluri, et al., 2007a).	W3C
WS-PolicyAttachment 1.5	Set 2007	W3C	Recommendation	It defines two general-purpose mechanisms for associating policies, as defined in Web Services Policy 1.5 - Framework, with the subjects to which they apply. It also defines how these general-purpose mechanisms may be used to associate policies with WSDL and UDDI descriptions (Vedamuthu, Orchard, Hirsch, Hondo, Yendluri, et al., 2007b).	W3C
WS-Discovery	April 2005	Microsoft, BEA, Intel	Draft	This specification defines a multicast discovery protocol to locate services (Beatty, Kakivaya, Kemp, Kuehnel, Lovering, et al., 2005).	Microsoft
WS-MetadataExchange 1.1	Aug 2006	BEA Systems, IBM, Microsoft, and SAP	Public Draft	Web services use metadata to describe what other endpoints need to know to interact with them (Balinger, Bissett, Box, Curbera, Ferguson, et al., 2006).	IBM
UDDI 3.0.2 (Universal Description, Discovery, and Integration)	Feb 2005	OASIS	Standard	It defines a set of services supporting the description and discovery of (1) businesses, organizations, and other Web services providers, (2) the Web services they make available, and (3) the technical interfaces which may be used to access those services (Clement, Hately, von Riegen & Rogers, 2004).	OASIS
ebXML Registry Services and Protocols 3.0	May 2005	OASIS	Standard	It provides a set of services that enable sharing of content and metadata between organizational entities in a federated environment (Fuger, Najmi, & Stojanovic, 2005a).	OASIS
ebXML Registry: Information Model 3.0	May 2005	OASIS	Standard	It defines the types of metadata and content that can be stored in an ebXML Registry (Fuger, Najmi, & Stojanovic, 2005b).	OASIS
WSDL (Web Service Description Language) 1.1	March 2001	W3C	Note	It is an XML-based language for describing Web services and how to access them. It specifies the location of the service and the operations (or methods) the service exposes (Christensen, Curbera, Meredith, & Weerawarana, 2001).	W3C
WSDL 2.0 Part 0: Primer	June 2007	W3C	Recommendation	This primer is only intended to be a starting point toward use of WSDL 2.0, and hence does not describe every feature of the language (Booth & Liu, 2007).	W3C
WSDL 2.0 Part 1: Core	June 2007	W3C	Recommendation	It defines the core language which can be used to describe Web services based on an abstract model of what the service offers. It also defines the conformance criteria for documents in this language (Chinnici, Moreau, Ryman & Weerawarana, 2007).	W3C
WSDL 2.0 Part 2: Adjuncts	June 2007	W3C	Recommendation	It specifies predefined extensions for use in WSDL 2.0: message exchange patterns, operation safety, operation styles, and binding extensions for SOAP and HTTP (Chinnici, Haas, Lewis, Moreau, Orchard & Weerawarana, 2007).	W3C
WSDL 2.0 SOAP 1.1 Binding	June 2007	W3C	Working Group Note	It describes the concrete details for using WSDL 2.0 in conjunction with SOAP 1.1 protocol (Vedamuthu, 2007)	W3C
WSRF 1.2 Primer (WS-Resource Framework)	May 2006	OASIS	Committee Draft	It defines a generic framework for modeling and accessing persistent resources using Web services (Banks, 2006).	OASIS
WS-Resource 1.2	April 2006	OASIS	Standard	It describes the relationship between a Web service and a resource in the WS-Resource Framework (Graham, Karmarkar, Mischkinsky, Robinson & Sedukhin, 2006).	OASIS
WS-ResourceProperties 1.2	April 2006	OASIS	Standard	It standardizes the means by which the definition of the properties of a WS-Resource may be declared as part of a Web service interface (Graham & Treadwell, 2006).	OASIS
WS-ResourceLifetime 1.2	April 2006	OASIS	Standard	It defines two means of destroying a WS-Resource: immediate destruction and time-based, scheduled destruction (Srinivasan & Banks, 2006).	OASIS

Table 4.

Standard	Date	Publisher	Status	Description	Source
AVDL 1.0 (Application Vulnerability Description Language)	May 2004	OASIS	Specification	It describes a standard XML format that allows entities (such as applications, organizations, or institutes) to communicate information regarding web application vulnerabilities (Bialkowski, & Heineman, 2004).	OASIS
DSS 1.0 (Digital Signature Services)	April 2007	OASIS	Standard	It defines the XML syntax and semantics for the Digital Signature Service core protocols, and for some associated core elements (Pope, Carlos & Drees, 2007).	OASIS
SAML 2.0 (Security Assertion Markup Language) Core	March 2005	OASIS	Standard	It defines the syntax and semantics for XML-encoded assertions about authentication, attributes, and authorization, and for the protocols that convey this information (Cantor, Kemp, Philpott & Maler, 2005).	OASIS
SAML 2.0 (Security Assertion Markup Language) 2.0 Binding	March 2005	OASIS	Standard	It defines protocol bindings for the use of SAML assertions and request-response messages in communications protocols and frameworks (Cantor, Hirsch, Kemp, Philpott & Maler, 2005).	OASIS
SAML 2.0 (Security Assertion Markup Language) 2.0 Profiles	March 2005	OASIS	Standard	It defines profiles for the use of SAML assertions and request-response messages in communications protocols and frameworks, as well as profiles for SAML attribute value syntax and naming conventions (Hughes, Cantor, Hodges, Hirsch, Mishra, et al., 2005).	OASIS
SAML 2.0 (Security Assertion Markup Language) 2.0 Metadata	March 2005	OASIS	Standard	It defines an extensible metadata format for SAML system entities, organized by roles that reflect SAML profiles (Cantor, Moreh, Philpott & Maher, 2005).	OASIS
SAML 2.0 (Security Assertion Markup Language) 2.0 Authentication Context	March 2005	OASIS	Standard	It defines a syntax for the definition of authentication context declarations and an initial list of authentication context classes for use with SAML (Kemp, Cantor, Mishra, Philpott & Maler, 2005).	OASIS
SAML 2.0 (Security Assertion Markup Language) 2.0 Security and Privacy	March 2005	OASIS	Standard	This non-normative specification describes and analyzes the security and privacy properties of SAML (Hirsch, Philpott & Maler, 2005).	OASIS
SPML 2.0 (Service Provisioning Markup Language)	April 2006	OASIS	Standard	This specification defines the concepts and operations of an XML-based provisioning request-and-response protocol (Cole, 2006).	OASIS
WS-Security 1.1 Core	Feb 2006	OASIS	Standard	It enhances SOAP messages in order to provide integrity and confidentiality. It also provides a general-purpose mechanism for associating security tokens with message content (Lawrence & Kaler, 2004).	OASIS
WS-Security: X.509 Certificate Token Profile 1.1	Feb 2006	OASIS	Standard	It describes how to use X.509 Certificates with the WS-(Lawrence & Kaler, 2006a).	OASIS
WS-Security: Username Token Profile 1.1	Feb 2006	OASIS	Standard	It describes how to use the Username Token with the WS-Security (Lawrence & Kaler, 2006b).	OASIS
WS-Security: SAML Token Profile 1.1	Feb 2006	OASIS	Standard	It describes how to use Security Assertion Markup Language (SAML) V1.1 and V2.0 assertions with WS-Security (Lawrence & Kaler, 2006c).	OASIS
WS-Security: Kerberos Token Profile 1.1	Feb 2006	OASIS	Standard	It describes how to use Kerberos tickets (specifically the AP-REQ packet) with WS-Security (Lawrence & Kaler, 2006d).	OASIS
XACML 2.0 (Extensible Access Control Markup Language) Core	Feb 2005	OASIS	Standard	It expresses policies for information access (Moses, 2005a).	OASIS

continued on the following page

Table 4. continued

Standard	Date	Publisher	Status	Description	Source
XACML 2.0: Core and Hierarchical role based access control (RBAC) profile	Feb 2005	OASIS	Standard	It defines a profile for the use of XACML in expressing policies that use role based access control (RBAC) (Anderson, 2005a).	OASIS
XACML 2.0: Hierarchical resource profile	Feb 2005	OASIS	Standard	It provides a profile for the use XACML with resources that are structured as hierarchies (Anderson, 2005b).	OASIS
XACML 2.0: Multiple resource profile	Feb 2005	OASIS	Standard	It provides a profile for requesting access to more than one resource in a single XACML Request Context, or for requesting a single response to a request for an entire hierarchy (Anderson, 2005c).	OASIS
XACML 2.0: Privacy policy profile	Feb 2005	OASIS	Standard	It describes a profile of XACML for expressing privacy policies (Moses, 2005b).	OASIS
XACML 2.0. SAML 2.0 profile	Feb 2005	OASIS	Standard	It defines a profile for the use of SAML 2.0 to carry XACML 2.0 policies, policy queries and responses, authorization decisions, and authorization decision queries and responses. It also describes the use of SAML 2.0 Attribute Assertions with XACML (Anderson & Lockhart, 2005).	OASIS
XACML 2.0: XML Digital Signature profile	Feb 2005	OASIS	Standard	It uses XML-Signature Standard in order to provide authentication and integrity protection for XACML schema instances (Anderson, 2005d).	OASIS
XML Digital Signature	June 2008	W3C	Recommendation	It specifies XML syntax and processing rules for creating and representing digital signatures (Eastlake, Reagle, Solo, Hirsch & Roessler, 2008).	W3C
XML encryption	Dec 2002	W3C	Recommendation	It specifies a process for encrypting data and representing the result in XML (Imamura, Dilaway & Simon, 2002).	W3C
XKMS 2.0 (XML Key Management Specification)	June 2005	W3C	Recommendation	It specifies protocols for distributing and registering public keys, use in conjunction with the XML Signature (Hallam-Baker & Mysore, 2005a).	W3C
XKMS 2.0 (XML Key Management Specification) Bindings	June 2005	W3C	Recommendation	It specifies protocol bindings with security characteristics for the XKMS (Hallam-Baker & Mysore, 2005b).	W3C
XrML 2.0 (Extensible Rights Management Language)	March 2002	Content-Guard		It is based on XML and describes rights, fees and conditions together with message integrity and entity authentication information ("eXtensible rights", 2002).	XrML.org
XCBF 1.1 (XML Common Biometric Format)	August 2003	OASIS	Standard	It defines XML codings for Common Biometric Exchange File Format (Larmouth, 2003).	OASIS
WS-Federation Language 1.1	Dec 2006	IBM, BEA, Microsoft, RSA, VeriSign, etc	Public Draft	Mechanisms to allow different security realms to federate. Allows brokering trust of identities, attributes, authentication between participating Web services (Lockhart, Andersen, Bohren, Sverdlov, Hondo, et al., 2006)	IBM, BEA
WS-Federation: Active Requestor Profile 1.1	July 2003	IBM, BEA, Microsoft, RSA, VeriSign	Public Draft	It defines how federation mechanisms defined in WS-Federation are used by active requestors such as SOAP-enabled applications (Bajaj, Della-Libera, Dixon, Hondo, Hur, et al., 2003).	IBM, BEA
WS-Federation: Passive Requestor Profile	July 2003	IBM, BEA, Microsoft, RSA, VeriSign	Public Draft	It describes how WS-Federation can be utilized used by passive requestors such as Web browsers to provide Identity Services. limited to the HTTP protocol (Bajaj, Dixon, Dusche, Hondo, Hur, et al., 2003).	IBM, BEA
WS-SecureConversation 1.3	March 2007	OASIS	Standard	This specification defines extensions that build on WS-Security ("WS-Security appnotes," 2002) to provide a framework for requesting and issuing security tokens, and to broker trust relationships (Nadalin, Goodner, Gudgin, Barbir & Granqvist, 2007a).	OASIS

continued on the following page

Table 4. continued

Standard	Date	Publisher	Status	Description	Source
WS-SecurityPolicy 1.2	Jul 2007	OASIS	Standard	It indicates the policy assertions for use with WS-Policy which apply to WS-Security, WS-Trust and WS-SecureConversation (Nadalin, Goodner, Gudgin, Barbir & Granqvist, 2007b).	OASIS
WS-Trust 1.3	March 2007	OASIS	Standard	It defines extensions that build on WS-Security to provide a framework for requesting and issuing security tokens, and to broker trust relationships (Nadalin, Goodner, Gudgin, Barbir & Granqvist, 2007c).	OASIS

Table 5.

Standard	Date	Publisher	Status	Description	Source
WS-ReliableMessaging 1.1	June 2007	OASIS	Standard	It describes a protocol that allows messages to be transferred reliably between nodes implementing this protocol in the presence of software component, system, or network failures (Davis, Karmarkar, Pilz, Winklewr & Yalçinalp, 2007).	OASIS
WS-Reliability 1.1	Nov 2004	OASIS	Standard	It is a SOAP-based protocol for exchanging SOAP messages with guaranteed delivery, no duplicates, and guaranteed message ordering (Iwasa, Durand, Rutt, Peel, Kunisetty & Bunting, 2004).	OASIS
WS-RM Policy Assertion 1.1	June 2007	OASIS	Standard	It describes a domain-specific policy assertion for WS-ReliableMessaging that that can be specified within a policy alternative as defined in WS-Policy Framework (Davis, Karmarkar, Pilz & Yalçinalp, 2007).	OASIS

Table 6.

Standard	Date	Publisher	Status	Description	Source
WS-BPEL 2.0	April 2007	OASIS	Standard	It is a language for specifying business process behavior based on Web Services (Alves, Arkin, Askary, Barreto, Bloch, et al., 2007).	OASIS
Web Services Choreography Interface 1.0	Aug 2002	W3C, Sun, Intalio, BEA	Note	It is an XML-based interface description language that describes the flow of messages exchanged by a Web Service participating in choreographed interactions with other services (Kavantzas, Burdett, Ritzinger, Fletcher, Lafon & Barreto, 2005).	W3C
WS-Choreography 1.0	Nov 2005	W3C	Candidate Recommendation	It is an XML-based language that describes peer-to-peer collaborations of participants by defining, from a global viewpoint, their common and complementary observable behavior; where ordered message exchanges result in accomplishing a common business goal (Arkin, Askari, Fordin, Jekeli, Kawaguchi, et al., 2002).	W3C

WEB SERVICES SECURITY PRODUCTS

- **Actional - Actional XMS:** This XML Firewall provides access control to web services, while filtering SOAP messages based on their content. Some supported standards include XML Signatures, SAML (Security Assertion Markup Language), WS-Security 1.0, SOAP and WSDL.
- **BEA - BEA WebLogic Enterprise Security:** WebLogic Enterprise Security

Table 7.

Standard	Date	Publisher	Status	Description	Source
WS-Coordination 1.1	July 2007	OASIS	Standard	It describes an extensible framework for providing protocols that coordinate the actions of distributed applications (Feingold & Jeyaraman, 2007)..	OASIS
WS-BusinessActivity 1.1	July 2007	OASIS	Standard	It provides the definition of two Business Activity coordination types: AtomicOutcome or MixedOutcome, that are to be used with the extensible coordination framework described in the WS-Coordination specification (Freund & Little, 2007).	OASIS
WS-AtomicTransaction 1.1	April 2007	OASIS	Standard	It provides the definition of the Atomic Transaction coordination type that is to be used with the extensible coordination framework described in WS-Coordination (Little & Wilkinson, 2007).	OASIS
WS-Context 1.0	April 2007	OASIS	Standard	It provides a definition, a structuring mechanism, and service definitions for organizing and sharing context across multiple execution endpoints (Little, Newcomer & Pavlik, 2007).	OASIS

Table 8.

Standard	Date	Publisher	Status	Description	Source
WS-Management 1.0	Feb 2008	DMTF	Specification	It describes a general SOAP-based protocol for managing systems such as PCs, servers, devices, Web services and other applications, and other manageable entities ("Web services," 2008).	DMTF
WS-Management Catalog	June 2005	Intel, Dell, Microsoft, Sun and others	Specification	It describes the default metadata formats used for the WS-Management Protocol (Arora, Cohen, Davis, Dutch, Golovinsky, et al., 2005).	OASIS
WS-ResourceTransfer 1.0	Aug 2006	IBM, HP, Microsoft	Draft	It is intended to form an essential core component of a unified resource access protocol for the Web services space (Reistad, Murray, Davis, Robinson, McCollum, et al., 2006).	IBM
Management Using Web Services (MUWS)1.1 Part 1	Aug 2006	OASIS	Standard	It provides the fundamental concepts for management using Web services (Bullard & Vanbenepe, 2006a).	OASIS
Management Using Web Services (MUWS)1.1 Part 2	Aug 2006	OASIS	Standard	It provides specific messaging formats used to enable the interoperability of MUWS implementations (Bullard & Vanbenepe, 2006b).	OASIS
Management of Web Services (MOWS)1.1	Aug 2006	OASIS	Standard	It addresses management of the Web services endpoints using Web services protocols (Wilson & Sedukhin, 2006).	OASIS

provides access control to applications based on policies ("BEA WebLogic," 2009). It includes policy-based delegation management, authentication with single sign-on, consolidated auditing, and dynamic-role and policy-based authorization with delegation. It supports SAML and WSDL 1.1 standards.

- **Cerebit – InnerGuard:** InnerGuard provides access control to applications (including web services), based on policies ("InnerGuard," 2006). Its features include policy management and enforcement, identity management, privacy, provisioning and PKI capabilities. It conforms to the SOAP standard.

- **DataPower XS40 XML Security Gateway and XS40 XML Firewall:** DataPower provides an XML Firewall that parses, filters, validates schemas, decrypts, verifies signatures, transforms, signs and encrypts XML message flows ("WebSphere DataPower," 2004). It includes an XML Security Gateway that can be used to control access to web services. DataPower supports WS-Security, SOAP 1.2 and the SAML standards.

- **Digital Evolution XML VPN:** The XML VPN allows service consumers to securely connect to authorized web services ("Integrated SOA," 2004). These web services expose consumers to applications as local services. It provides central policy, rights management and transaction auditing services. It supports the WS-Security standard.

- **Entrust Secure Transaction Platform:** Uses a set of security services that provide security capabilities that enable secure transactions ("Entrust Secure," 2004). These services provide a foundation for integrating authentication, authorization, digital signatures, and encryption into transactions. These trust services are provided through web services interfaces to allow for integration and deployment. It supports SAML, XACML, XML Digital Signatures, XML Encryption, XKMS, and WS-Security.

- **Forum XWall Web Services Firewall:** Forum XWall is a web services firewall equipped with data authentication as well as XML intrusion prevention to protect against XML viruses, data corruption and denial of web service attacks ("Forum

Sentry," 2009). It offers data level authentication, XML intrusion prevention and interoperability enforcement that protects enterprises against XML viruses, denial of web service attacks and unauthorized data access. It supports WS-I Basic Profile, XML 1.0, SOAP 1.1/1.2 and WSDL standards.

- **Forum Sentry Web Services Security Suite:** Forum Sentry enables trusted information sharing using XML data and web services across different security domains and business processes ("Forum Sentry," 2009). It supports XML Digital Signature, XML Encryption, WS-Encryption, WS-Digital Signatures, WSDL 1.1/1.2, WS-Security, SAML, XKMS and WS-I Basic Profile standards.

- **Forum Presidio OpenPGP Security Gateway:** Forum Presidio is a content exchange platform that allows enterprises to comply with government information and privacy regulations without complexity with the use of the ubiquitous OpenPGP standard ("FTP data," 2009). Forum Presidio can be used as a legacy-to-XML security bridge for a smooth migration to XML web services.

- **GXS Technology:** GXS technology controls the use of web services according to the SOAP and WSDL standards. The current interfaces complement one or more additional protocols used for bulk data transfer. Current development work involves the use of WS-Security for the GXS Trading Grid Business Services APIs, as well as SAML.

- **IBM Tivoli Identity Manager and Tivoli Access Manager:** Tivoli Identity Manager is a policy-based user management system ("IBM application," 2009) Tivoli Access Manager is a policy-based access control system that provides authentication and authorization APIs that allow integration with application platforms such as J2EE. It supports WS-Federation and SAML standards.

- **IONA Artix:** Artix is an extensible Enterprise Service Bus (ESB). It enables an enterprise to integrate and expose its applications as web ("Progress Software," 2009). Its security features include a role based access control mechanism, authentication, support of WS-Security, SSO, LDAP plug-in, Active Directory Plug-In and SAML.

- **Microsoft Trust Bridge:** This product allows different organizations using the Windows operating system to exchange user identities and interoperate in heterogeneous environments ("Microsoft aims," 2002). It uses XML web services protocols that include Kerberos, and WS-Security.

- **Netegrity TransactionMinder:** TransactionMinder provides centralized authentication, policy-based authorization, and audit for web services transactions (Devdass & Gandhirajan, 2008). By intercepting requests made to web services, it analyzes them and communicates with its Policy Server. Netegrity conforms to the SOAP, WSDL, SAML and XML Digital Signature standards.

- **Oracle Web Services Manager** provides a means for governing the interactions with shared services through security and operational policy management and enforcement to ensure service reuse remains under control ("Oracle web," 2009).

- **Oracle Management Pack for SOA** provides management service for applications and infrastructure in a service-oriented architecture (SOA). Administrators are able to associate events and activities for all components across the SOA environment. This aids in resolving performance and availability issues. It includes a set of services and system level dashboards that can

be used by administrators to view service levels for key business processes, and SOA infrastructure components from a central location ("Oracle management," 2009).

- **Oracle Service Registry** provides a standard base interface for SOA runtime infrastructure that dynamically discovers and binds to deployed service end points. It helps to bridge the gap between the design time and runtime environments through automated synchronization with Oracle Enterprise Repository and Oracle SOA Suite.

- **Oracle Enterprise Repository** provides a base for delivering governance throughout the service-oriented architecture (SOA) lifecycle. It acts as the single source for information surrounding SOA assets and their dependencies. It provides a communication channel for the automated exchange of metadata and service information between service consumers, providers, policy decision points, and additional governance tooling.

- **Progress Actional for Active SOA Policy Enforcement:** Actional for Active SOA Policy Enforcement separates the SOA policy lifecycle from the service lifecycle to centralize the creation and management of SOA policies ("Progress Actional," 2009). It provides security and compliance while ensuring distributed SOA policy enforcement. This allows security and compliance experts to author policies, then apply them consistently across the SOA. This helps to guarantee good coverage for reduced risk. It conforms to the WS-Security standard.

- **Reactivity Gateway, Reactivity Manager and Reactivity Gatekeeper:** The Reactivity Gateway enforces XML web services security policies ("Reactivity web," 2007). The Reactivity Manager is used to define policies. It conforms to

SAML 2.0, XML Digital Signature, and WS-Security 1.0 standards.

- **Rohati's Transaction Networking System (TNS):** TNS is a network-based entitlement control (NBEC) system; that extends control across an enterprise's applications and resources ("Rohati products," 2008). It enables enterprises to authenticate sessions and authorize each transaction based on business context. It supports the XACML standard.

- **Sarvega - XML Guardian Gateway:** XML Guardian Gateway filters incoming and outgoing XML or SOAP messages based on security policies ("Validation testing," 2004). It conforms to XML encryption and XML signature standards.

- **Securent Entitlement Management:** Entitlement Management provides deployment, management, and auditing application security ("Securent overview," 2007). It separates fine-grained authorization policy from core application logic and delivers it as a XACML standard based service.

- **SecureSpan™ XML Firewall** combines the capabilities of the SecureSpan XML Accelerator and Data Screen with identity and message level security to address portal and B2B SOA security ("XML firewall," 2008). The SecureSpan XML Firewall includes support for directories, identity, access control, Single Sign-On (SSO) and Federation services. The SecureSpan XML Firewall also provides architects with policy controls for specifying message and element security rules. Key storage, encryption and signing operations can be handled in FIPS 140-2 certified acceleration hardware onboard the appliance or centrally through Safenet's Luna HSM. The SecureSpan XML Firewall includes compliance with WS* and WS-I security protocols including WS-Security, WS-SecureConversation, WS-SecurityPolicy, WS-Trust, WS-Secure

Exchange, WS-Policy and WS-I Basic Security Profile. The SecureSpan Firewall also supports SAML 1.1 and 2.0.

- **SOA Software Policy Manager** is part of a suite of products for SOA Governance ("SOA Software").

- **Sun Microsystems Identity Management:** Sun Identity Management controls user identities across a variety of applications ("Sun identity," 2008). It provides provisioning and secure access, to ensure ongoing compliance and enable federation for sharing beyond boundaries. It supports Service Provisioning Markup Language (SPML).

- **Vordel XML Gateway:** XML Gateway uses a network device for offloading processor intensive tasks from applications running in general purpose application servers. The Vordel XML Gateway performs application networking by routing traffic based on content or on sender, and performs XML content screening. It supports SSL, WS-Security, WS-Trust XML, SOAP, and SAML 2.0.

- **Vordel XML Firewall:** XML Firewall shields XML applications from attacks ("Vordel XML," 2007). The XML Firewall forms an integral component of an enterprise's SOA security infrastructure and can be deployed as part of a strategic architecture of XML firewalls, gateways and run time governance products. It complements other application security and network security products by providing the XML data screening. It supports SOAP and XML Schemas and WS-I Basic Profile.

- **Xtradyne's WS-DBC:** The Web Services Domain Boundary Controller (WS-DBC) is an XML Firewall. It provides protection against malformed messages and malicious content, encryption/decryption of XML messages, XML digital signatures, as well as providing authentication, authorization,

Table 9. Web services security features

Functionalities or Standards	Actional	Actional Enforcement	BEA WebLogic	Cerebit	DataPower	Digital Evolution	Entrust	Forum Presidio	Forum Vulcon	Forum Xwall	GXS Technology
XML schema validation	X	X			X						
XML Encryption	X				X	X	X				X
XML Signature	X				X	X	X				X
WS-Security		X			X	X	X				X
Web Services access control			X	X		X	X	X		X	X
User Authentication	X	X	X	X	X	X	X	X		X	X
Audit	X		X	X				X	X		X
Alert	X			X					X		
Content Inspection	X								X	X	X
Conformance validation	X					X	X	X			
Integrity checks										X	

and auditing ("Xtradyne XML," 2005). It supports WS-Security, SAML WSDL and XML Digital Signature.

WEB SERVICES SECURITY FEATURES

Table 9 describes the security features of the web services security products.

Patterns Used in SOA

We present below some patterns that are used in SOA. We give partial descriptions for some of them.

SOA Composition

Composition can be done point-to-point (small homogeneous systems). For large architectures it is better to use an Enterprise Service Bus (ESB), connecting the services (Ferguson & Stockton, 2005; Zdun, Hentrich, & van der Aalst, 2006). The ESB supports point-to-point and publish/ subscribe styles of communication. Components connect to the bus through their interfaces. Sometimes adapters are needed. A Broker pattern connects to remote services (Buschmann, Meunier, Rohnert, Sommerland & Stal, 1996). Message transformation patterns such as Normalizer or Envelope Wrapper can be used by the bus to integrate services. The Adapter and Façade (Gamma, Helm, Johnson & Vlissides, 1994) are important for integration.

An ESB usually includes portal services and in this case we have an MVC (Model View Controller) architecture (Buschmann et al., 1996), where the services define the model, while servlets and JSP or ASP provide the controller. Controllers build the views displayed by the portals (Ferguson & Stockton, 2005). A SOA Registry (repository, catalog) provides service description, naming, location, and binding.

Interfaces and Contracts

Service Interface and Adaptor pattern (Zdun et al., 2005). Isolates the server application from its clients using an adaptor in the client.

Service Contract pattern (Zdun et al., 2005). There should be a contract between the service provider and its clients. This contract includes aspects such as communication protocols, message types and their signatures, message formats, sequencing requirements, service-level agreement, directory service, requirements about guaranteed delivery, notification, etc.

Bridge (Gamma et al., 1994)

Decouple an abstraction from its implementation so that the two can evolve independently. This is a basic pattern for components and web services (Stal, 2006).

Adapter*AKA:* Wrapper (Gamma et al., 1994)

Intent: Convert the interface of a class into another interface expected by clients.

To match objects to relational databases we need additional patterns. In classification, the Adapter belongs to the Adaptation view that also includes the microkernel and the virtual machine (Avgeriou & Zdun, 2005).

Abstract Factory (Gamma et al., 1994)

Intent: Provide an interface for creating families of related objects without specifying concrete classes.

Façade (Gamma et al., 1994)

Intent: Provide a unified higher-level interface to a set of interfaces in a subsystem.

Applicability: Use Façade when you want to provide a simple interface to a complex object-oriented subsystem or you want an entry point to a layer in a layered system.

Wrapper Facade (Schmidt, Stal, Rohnert & Buschmann, 2000)

The Wrapper Façade encapsulates the functions and data from existing non-object-oriented interfaces in a higher-level, more concise, portable, and cohesive object-oriented interface.

Container

This pattern describes the container structure of components (Kobryn, 2000). This representation of components can describe J2EE and .NET components by proper specialization. It includes a Factory pattern to create instances of a component, a Proxy pattern (Remote Proxy) for remote access to the component objects, a Persistence Service to make the component contents persistent. Another model for a Container is given in (Voelter, Schmidt & Wolff, 2002). A component may have several interfaces, see Extension Interface Pattern (Schmidt et al., 2000). The separation of interfaces and implementation can be described by a Bridge pattern (Stal, 2006).

Interceptor (Schmidt et al., 2000)

Allows services to be added transparently to a framework and triggered automatically by specific events.

Secure versions of some of these patterns are described in (Fernandez & Larrondo-Petrie, 2006). More component patterns are given in (Voelter et al., 2002). We have produced a variety of patterns for web services security (Fernandez, 2009)

Validation, Certification, and Governance of Web Services Security and Reliability

Systems that support critical systems must be certified to show that they comply with some requirements. This certification must be part of the development process. Certification may be based on testing and formal proofs (model checking) for parts of the system.

A development method can be evaluated against the stated goal of covering all stages of the development life cycle using a matrix of concerns vs. development stages (VanHilst, Fernandez & Braz, in press). For each concern, the method must include appropriate strategies to address that concern in each stage. Similarly, for each stage, there must be an appropriate response to each concern. The coverage analysis can also evaluate the method's response to the specific issues of legacy, COTS, and outsourced components at the points where they occur (or first appear) in the overall development life cycle. The methodology also needs to be applied to some complex systems and it should show that they can be made more secure according to some qualitative metric (there are no quantitative measures of security).

An important question is the level of security reached by a particular approach. We cannot prove general security properties of a complete system produced this way. However, if we have applied a systematic approach we expect to eliminate in this way a large variety of threats. A qualitative analysis can be performed to show that we have stopped or mitigated all the identified threats (Braz, Fernandez & VanHilst, 2008). There will still be threats based on the actual code but those can be handled by other means.

The distributed and possibly heterogeneous nature of SOA makes governance a complex task. SOA appliances can be used to collect metadata and provide analysis and management (Varadan, Channabasavaiah, Simpson, Holley & Allam,, 2008). SOA requires cooperation and coordination between business and information technology (IT) as well as among IT departments and teams for smooth functioning. This cooperation and coordination is provided by SOA governance which lays out the rules and policies around service creation, service discovery, service identification and reuse. It defines the service-level agreements (SLAs) for how services should perform, so that both the consumers and the providers know their limitations and expectations. In summary, governance gives the providers and the consumers the same view of the service's quality. Since SOA extends interactions beyond the enterprise boundary, the governance of SOA must interact with similar groups in other organizations to achieve a common set of standards for communication across the enterprise boundary (Mitra, 2005).

Governance means establishing and enforcing how a group agrees to work together in co-ordination. Specifically, governance is the establishment of:

- Chains of responsibility to assign duties and rights to people
- Measurement to gauge effectiveness
- Policies to guide the organization to meet its goals
- Control mechanisms to ensure compliance
- Communication to keep all required parties informed

In other words, we can say that governance determines what decisions are to be made, who should be making the decisions and what policies should be considered before making any decisions. In practice, SOA governance guides the development of reusable services and establishes how the services should be designed and developed and how those services should change over time. It establishes agreements between the providers of services and the consumers of those services, telling the consumers what they can expect and the providers what they're obligated to provide. SOA governance is a set of practices that is applicable throughout the various stages of a service-oriented architecture such as service definition, service deployment lifecycle, service versioning, service migration, service registries, service message model, service monitoring, service ownership, service testing and service security. SOA governance ensures that all of the independent efforts whether in the design, development, deployment or operations of a service should come together to meet the enterprise SOA requirements.

SOA governance is enacted by an SOA center of excellence (COE) which is a board of knowledgeable SOA practitioners who establish and supervise policies to help ensure an enterprise's success with SOA. The COE establishes policies for identification and development of services, establishment of SLAs, management of registries, and other efforts that provide effective governance. Governance policies can be enforced through a combination of an enterprise service bus (ESB) and a service registry. A service can be exposed so that only certain ESBs can invoke it. Then the ESB/registry combination can control the consumers' access, monitor usage, measure SLA compliance, and so on. This way, the services focus on providing the business functionality and the ESB/registry focuses on aspects of governance.

CONCLUSION

The security of web services has been its weak point and the cause of its rather slow adoption. Work is needed to make this security predictable and systematic during the development of new applications. The methodologies and patterns discussed here go in that direction and we expect they will make a significant contribution but we need more patterns and the methodology needs to be tested in real environments. Following existing standards is fundamental to provide certification and interoperability.

Many of the web service products and tools discussed offer several of the same features; also many conform to a few of the most common web services standards such as SOAP, XQUERY and XML. However, the problem being faced is how to select the right web services product or tool which best suit a designer's needs. This is very hard to determine at present since many companies do not explicitly state the features and standards which are supported by their products or tools, more over it is very time consuming to acquire this information. Additionally many products may only conform to a few standards; for example from this survey it is observed that many products are not compliant with WS-Reliability standard among others. A possible solution in overcoming this problem is using web service patterns in the implementation and design of web services products and tools.

Web services can be used in critical applications but careful adherence to a systematic process is necessary to assure quality. Applications developed in non-systematic ad hoc ways will not be able to provide the required levels of security and reliability. In particular, web services can be extremely valuable in military and other critical applications because these involve heavily distributed systems with security and reliability being basic requirements. Again the adherence to standards is fundamental and we tried here to provide a complete and current overview to help designers and researchers.

ACKNOWLEDGMENT

This work was supported by DISA from the US Department of Defense, in a grant administered by Pragmatics, Inc. The comments of the reviewer of the chapter were very useful to improve it.

REFERENCES

Alexander, J., Box, D., Cabrera, L. F., Chappell, D., Daniels, G., et al. (2006a). *Web Services Transfer (WS-Transfer)*. W3C. Retrieved April 20, 2009 from http://www.w3.org/Submission/WS-Transfer/

Alexander, J., Box, D., Cabrera, L. F., Chappell, D., Daniels, G., et al. (2006b). *Web Services Enumeration (WS-Enumeration)*. W3C. Retrieved April 20, 2009 from http://www.w3.org/Submission/WS-Enumeration/

Alonso, G., Casati, F., Kuno, H., & Machiraju, V. (2004). *Web services: Concepts, architectures and applications*. Berlin: Springer.

Alves, A., Arkin, A., Askary, S., Barreto, C., Bloch, B., et al. (2007). *Web services business process execution language version 2.0. OASIS*. Retrieved April 20, 2009 from http://docs.oasis-open.org/wsbpel/2.0/OS/wsbpel-v2.0-OS.html

Anderson, A. (2005a). *Core and hierarchical role based access control (RBAC) profile of XACML v2.0. OASIS*. Retrieved April 20, 2009 from http://docs.oasis-open.org/xacml/2.0/access_control-xacml-2.0-rbac-profile1-spec-os.pdf

Anderson, A. (2005b). *Hierarchical resource profile of XACML v2.0*. OASIS. Retrieved April 20, 2009 from http://docs.oasis-open.org/xacml/2.0/access_control-xacml-2.0-hier-profile-spec-os.pdf

Anderson, A. (2005c). *Multilple resource profile of XACML v2.0*. OASIS. Retrieved April 20, 2009 from http://docs.oasis-open.org/xacml/2.0/access_control-xacml-2.0-mult-profile-spec-os.pdf

Anderson, A. (2005d). *XML Digital Signature profile of XACML v2.0*. OASIS. Retrieved April 20, 2009 from http://docs.oasis-open.org/xacml/2.0/access_control-xacml-2.0-dsig-profile-spec-os.pdf

Anderson, A., & Lockhart, H. (2005). *SAML 2.0 profile of XACML v2.0*. OASIS. Retrieved April 20, 2009 from http://docs.oasis-open.org/xacml/2.0/access_control-xacml-2.0-saml-profile-spec-os.pdf

Arkin, A., Askari, S., Fordin, S., Jekeli, W., Kawaguchi, K., et al. (2002). *Web services choreography interface (WSCI) 1.0*. W3C. Retrieved April 20, 2009 from http://www.w3.org/TR/wsci/

Arora, A., Cohen, J., Davis, J., Dutch, M., Golovinsky, E., et al. (2005). *The WS-management catalog*. Dell. Retrieved April 20, 2009 from http://www.dell.com/downloads/global/corporate/standards/ws_management_catalog.pdf

Arsanjani, A. (2004). *Service-oriented modeling and architecture*. Technical report, SOA and Web services Center of Excellence, IBM. Retrieved April 20, 2009, from http://www.ibm.com/developerworks/webservices/library/ws-soa-design1/

Arsanjani, A., Borges, B. & Holley, K. (2004). Service-Oriented Architecture. *DM Direct*. (6), 32.

Arsanjani, A., Ghosh, S., Allam, A., Abdollah, T., Ganapathy, S., & Holley, K. (2008). SOMA: A method for developing service-oriented solutions. *IBM Systems Journal*, 3(47), 377–396.

Atkinson, C., Brenner, D., Falcone, G., & Juhasz, M. (2008). Specifying high-assurance services. *Computer, IEEE*, 8(41), 64–71.

Avgeriou, P., & Zdun, U. (2005). Architectural patterns revisited: A pattern language. In *Proceedings of EuroPLoP*, (pp. 1-39).

Bajaj, S., Della-Libera, G., Dixon, B., & Hondo, M. Hur, M., et al. (2003). *WS-federation: active requestor profile version 1.0*. Armonk, NY: IBM. Retrieved April 20, 2009 from http://download.boulder.ibm.com/ibmdl/pub/software/dw/specs/ws-fedact/ws-fedact.pdf

Bajaj, S., Dixon, B., Dusche, M., Hondo, M., Hur, M., et al. (2003). *WS-federation: passive requestor profile version 1.0*. Armonk, NY: IBM. Retrieved April 20, 2009 from http://download.boulder.ibm.com/ibmdl/pub/software/dw/specs/ws-fedpass/ws-fedpass.pdf

Balinger, K., Bissett, B., Box, D., Curbera, F., Ferguson, D., et al. (2006). *Web Services Metadata Exchange (WS-MetadataExchange) 1.1*. Retrieved April 20, 2009 from http://specs.xmlsoap.org/ws/2004/09/mex/WS-MetadataExchange.pdf

Banks, T. (2006). *Web services resource framework (WSRF) – primer v1.2*. OASIS. Retrieved April 20, 2009 from http://docs.oasis-open.org/wsrf/wsrf-primer-1.2-primer-cd-02.pdf

BEA WebLogic enterprise security version 4.2, SP02 documentation. (2009). Oracle/BEA. Retrieved April 20, 2009 from http://e-docs.bea.com/wles/docs42/index.html

Beatty, J., Kakivaya, G., Kemp, D., Kuehnel, T., Lovering, B., et al. (2005). *Web Services Dynamic Discovery (WS-Discovery)*. Redmond, WA: Microsoft Corporation. Retrieved April 20, 2009 from http://specs.xmlsoap.org/ws/2005/04/discovery/ws-discovery.pdf

Berglund, A., Boag, S., Chamberlin, D., Fernández, M. F., Kay, M., Robie, J., & Siméon, J. (2007). *XML Path Language (XPath) 2.0*. W3C. Retrieved April 20, 2009 from http://www.w3.org/TR/xpath20/

Bertino, E., Castano, S., Ferrari, E., & Mesiti, M. (2000). Specifying and enforcing access control policies for xml document sources. *World Wide Web (Bussum)*, *3*(3), 139–151. doi:10.1023/A:1019289831564

Bialkowski, J., & Heineman, K. (2004). *Application vulnerability description language 1.0*. OASIS. Retrieved April 20, 2009 from http://www.oasis-open.org/committees/download.php/7145/AVDL%20Specification%20V1.pdf

Biron, P. V., & Malhotra, A. (2004). *XML Schema Part 2: Datatypes Second Edition*. Retrieved April 20, 2009 from http://www.w3.org/TR/2004/REC-xmlschema-2-20041028/

Boag, S., Chamberlin, D., Fernández, M. F., Florescu, D., Robie, J., & Siméon, J. (2007). *XQuery 1.0: An XML Query Language*. Retrieved April 20, 2009 from http://www.w3.org/TR/xquery/

Booth, D., & Liu, C. K. (2007). *Web Services Description Language (WSDL) Version 2.0 Part 0: Primer*. W3C. Retrieved April 20, 2009 from http://www.w3.org/TR/wsdl20-primer/

Box, D., Cabrera, L. F., Critchley, C., Curbera, F., Ferguson, D., et al. (2006). *Web Services Eventing (WS-Eventing)*. W3C. Retrieved April 20, 2009 from http://www.w3.org/Submission/WS-Eventing/

Bray, T., Hollander, D., Layman, A., & Tobin, R. (2006). *Namespaces in XML 1.0 (second edition)*. *World Wide Web Consortium*. Retrieved April 20, 2009, from http://www.w3.org/TR/REC-xml-names/

Bray, T., Paoli, J., Sperberg-McQueen, C. M., Maler, E., Yergeau, F., & Cowan, J. (2006). *Extensible markup language (xml) 1.1 (second edition)*. Retrieved April 20, 2009, from http://www.w3.org/TR/xml11/

Braz, F., Fernandez, E. B., & VanHilst, M. (2008). Eliciting security requirements through misuse activities. In *Proceedings of the 2nd Int. Workshop on Secure Systems Methodologies using Patterns (SPattern'07), in conjunction with the 4th International Conference on Trust, Privacy & Security in Digital Busines (TrustBus'08)*, (pp. 328-333).

Buckley, I., Fernandez, E. B., Rossi, G., & Madjadi, S. (2009, July). Web Services reliability patterns. In *21st International Conference on Software Engineering and Knowledge Engineering (SEKE'2009)*.

Bullard, V., & Vanbenepe, W. (2006a). *Web services distributed management: Management using web services (MUWS 1.1) part 1*. OASIS. Retrieved April 20, 2009 from http://www.oasis-open.org/committees/download.php/20576/wsdm-muws1-1.1-spec-os-01.pdf

Bullard, V., & Vanbenepe, W. (2006b). *Web services distributed management: Management using web services (MUWS 1.1) part 2*. OASIS. Retrieved April 20, 2009 from http://www.oasis-open.org/committees/download.php/20575/wsdm-muws2-1.1-spec-os-01.pdf

Buschmann, F., Meunier, R., Rohnert, H., Sommerland, P., & Stal, M. (1996). *Pattern-oriented software architecture: A system of patterns*. New York: Wiley.

Business process execution language for web services. (2002). Armonk, NY: IBM. http://www.ibm.com/developerworks/webservices/library/specification/ws-bpel/

Cantor, S., Hirsch, F., Kemp, J., Philpott, R., & Maler, E. (2005). *Bindings for the OASIS Security Assertion Markup Language (SAML) V2.0*. OASIS. Retrieved April 20, 2009 from http://docs.oasis-open.org/security/saml/v2.0/saml-bindings-2.0-os.pdf

Cantor, S., Kemp, J., Philpott, R., & Maler, E. (2005). *Assertions and Protocols for the OASIS Security Assertion Markup Language (SAML) V2.0*. OASIS. Retrieved April 20, 2009 from http://docs.oasis-open.org/security/saml/v2.0/saml-core-2.0-os.pdf

Cantor, S., Moreh, J., Philpott, R., & Maler, E. (2005). *Metadata for the OASIS security assertion markup language (SAML) V2.0*. OASIS. Retrieved April 20, 2009 from http://docs.oasis-open.org/security/saml/v2.0/saml-metadata-2.0-os.pdf

Chappell, D., & Liu, L. (2006). *Web Services Brokered Notification 1.3 (WS-Brokered Notification)*. OASIS. Retrieved April 20, 2009 from http://docs.oasis-open.org/wsn/wsn-ws_brokered_notification-1.3-spec-os.pdf

Chinnici, R., & Haas, H. Lewis, A. A., Moreau, J.-J., Orchard, D. & Weerawarana, S. (2007). *Web Services Description Language (WSDL) Version 2.0 Part 2: Adjuncts*. W3C. Retrieved April 20, 2009 from http://www.w3.org/TR/wsdl20-adjuncts/

Chinnici, R., Moreau, J.-J., Ryman, A., & Weerawarana, S. (2007). *Web Services Description Language (WSDL) Version 2.0 Part 1: Core Language*. W3C. Retrieved April 20, 2009 from http://www.w3.org/TR/wsdl20/

Chiusano, J. (2003). *UDDI and ebXML registry: a co-existence paradigm, Booz Allen Hamilton*. Retrieved April 20, 2009 from http://lists.oasis-open.org/archives/regrep/200304/pdf00000.pdf

Christensen, E., Curbera, F., Meredith, G., & Weerawarana, S. (2001). *Web Services Description Language (WSDL) 1.1*. W3C. Retrieved April 20, 2009 from http://www.w3.org/TR/wsdl

Clement, L., Hately, A., von Riegen, C., & Rogers, T. (2004). *UDDI Version 3.0.2, UDDI Spec technical committee draft*. OASIS. Retrieved April 20, 2009 from http://www.uddi.org/pubs/uddi_v3.htm

Cole, G. (2006). *OASIS service provisioning markup language (SPML) version 2*. OASIS. Retrieved April 20, 2009 from http://xml.coverpages.org/SPMLv2-OS.pdf

Cowan, J., & Tobin, R. (2004). *XML Information Set* (2nd Ed.). W3C. Retrieved April 20, 2009 from http://www.w3.org/TR/xml-infoset/

Davis, D., Karmarkar, A., Pilz, G., Winkler, S., & Yalçinalp, Ü. (2007). *WS-ReliableMessaging (WS-1 ReliableMessaging) version 1.1.* OASIS. Retrieved April 20, 2009 from http://docs.oasis-open.org/ws-rx/wsrm/wsrm-1.1-spec-os-01.pdf

Davis, D., Karmarkar, A., Pilz, G., & Yalçinalp, Ü. (2007). *Web services reliable messaging policy assertion (WS-RM Policy) version 1.* OASIS. Retrieved April 20, 2009 from http://docs.oasis-open.org/ws-rx/wsrmp/200702/wsrmp-1.1-spec-os-01.pdf

Delessy, N., & Fernandez, E. B. (2008). A pattern-driven security process for SOA applications. In *Procs. of the Third International Conference on Availability, Reliability and Security (ARES 2008)*, Barcelona, Spain, March 4-7, (pp. 416-421).

DeRose, S., Maler, E., & Daniel, R. (2002). *XPointer xpointer() Scheme.* W3C. Retrieved April 20, 2009 from http://www.w3.org/TR/xptr-xpointer/

DeRose, S., Maler, E., & Orchard, D. (2001). *XML Linking Language (XLink), Version 1.0.* Retrieved April 20, 2009 from http://www.w3.org/TR/xlink/

DeRose, S. J., Daniel, R., Maler, E., & Marsh, J. (2003). *XPointer xmlns() Scheme.* W3C. Retrieved April 20, 2009 from http://www.w3.org/TR/xptr-xmlns/

Devdass, R., & Gandhirajan, A. (2008). *Securing web services using TransactionMinder.* Retrieved April 20, 2009 from http://www.developer.com/lang/article.php/3108551

Eastlake, D., Reagle, J., Solo, D., Hirsch, F., & Roessler, T. (2008). *XML signature syntax and processing* (2nd Ed.). W3C. Retrieved April 20, 2009 from http://www.w3.org/TR/xmldsig-core/

Entrust secure transaction platform. (2004). Entrust. Retrieved April 20, 2009 from http://www.entrust.com/web-services-security/.

eXtensible rights markup language (XrML) 2.0 specification. (2001). ContentGuard. Retrieved March 12, 2009 from http://www.xrml.org/get_XrML.asp

Fallside, D. C., & Walmsley, P. (2004). *XML Schema Part 0: Primer,* (2nd Ed.). Retrieved April 20, 2009 from http://www.w3.org/TR/2004/REC-xmlschema-0-20041028/

Feingold, M. & Jeyaraman. (2007). *Web services coordination (WS-Coordination) version 1.1.* OASIS. Retrieved April 20, 2009 from http://docs.oasis-open.org/ws-tx/wstx-wscoor-1.1-spec-errata-os.pdf

Ferguson, D. F., & Stockton, M. L. (2005). Service-oriented architecture: Programming model and product architecture. *IBM Systems Journal, 4*(44), 753–780.

Fernandez, E. B. (2009). Security patterns and a methodology to apply them. In G. Spanoudakis & A. Maña (Eds.), *Security and Dependability for Ambient Intelligence.* Berlin: Springer.

Fernandez, E. B., & Larrondo-Petrie, M. M. (2006). Developing secure architectures for middleware systems. In *Proceedings of XXXII Conferencia Latinoamericana de Informática (CLEI 2006).*

Fernandez, E. B., Larrondo-Petrie, M. M., Sorgente, T., & VanHilst, M. (2006). A methodology to develop secure systems using patterns. In H. Mouratidis and P. Giorgini (Eds.), *Integrating security and software engineering: Advances and future vision,* (pp. 107-126). Hershey, PA: Idea Group.

Fernandez, E. B., Pelaez, J. C., & Larrondo-Petrie, M. M. (2007). Attack Patterns: A New Forensic and Design Tool. In *IFIP International Federation for Information Processing: Advances in Digital Forensics III.* 242/2007, (pp. 345-357). Boston: Springer.

Fernandez, E. B., VanHilst, M., Larrondo-Petrie, M. M., & Huang, S. (2006) Defining security requirements through misuse actions. In S. F. Ochoa & G.-C. Roman (Eds.), *International Federation for Information Processing Advanced Software Engineering: Expanding the Frontiers of Software Technology* (pp. 123-137). Berlin: Springer.

Feuerlicht, J. G., & Meesathit, S. (2005). Towards software development methodology for web services. In H. Fusita, & M. Mejri (Eds.), *New trends in software methodologies, tools and techniques: Proceedings of the fourth SoMeT-W05,* (pp. 263-277). Amsterdam: IOS Press.

Forum Sentry SOA gateway. (2009). Forum Systems. Retrieved April 20, 2009 from http://www.forumsys.com/products/soagateway.php

Freund, T., & Little, M. (2007). *Web services business activity (WS-BusinessActivity) version 1.1.* OASIS. Retrieved April 20, 2009 from http://docs.oasis-open.org/ws-tx/wstx-wsba-1.1-spec-errata-os.pdf

FTP data security and compliance. (2009). Forum Systems. Retrieved April 20, 2009 from http://www.forumsys.com/products/ftpgateway/features.php.

Fuger, S., Najmi, F., & Stojanovic, N. (2005a). *ebXML registry services and protocols version 3.0.* OASIS. Retrieved April 20, 2009 from http://docs.oasis-open.org/regrep/v3.0/specs/regrep-rs-3.0-os.pdf

Fuger, S., Najmi, F., & Stojanovic, N. (2005b). *ebXML registry information model version 3.0.* OASIS. Retrieved April 20, 2009 from http://docs.oasis-open.org/regrep/v3.0/specs/regrep-rim-3.0-os.pdf

Gamma, E., Helm, R., Johnson, R., & Vlissides, J. (1994). *Design patterns –Elements of reusable object-oriented software.* Upper-Saddle River, NJ:Addison-Wesley.

Graham, S., Hull, D., & Murray, B. (2006). *Web Services Base Notification1.3 (WS-Base Notification).* OASIS. Retrieved April 20, 2009 from http://docs.oasis-open.org/wsn/wsn-ws_base_notification-1.3-spec-os.pdf

Graham, S., Karmarkar, A., Mischkinsky, J., Robinson, I., & Sedukhin, I. (2006). *Web services resource 1.2 (WS-Resource).* OASIS. Retrieved April 20, 2009 from http://docs.oasis-open.org/wsrf/wsrf-ws_resource-1.2-spec-os.pdf

Graham, S., & Treadwell, J. (2006). *Web Services Resource Properties 1.2 (WS-ResourceProperties).* OASIS. Retrieved April 20, 2009 from http://docs.oasis-open.org/wsrf/wsrf-ws_resource_properties-1.2-spec-os.pdf

Grosso, P., Maler, E., Marsh, J., & Walsh, N. (2003). *XPointer Framework.* W3C. Retrieved April 20, 2009 from http://www.w3.org/TR/xptr-framework/

Gudgin, M., Hadley, M., Mendelsohn, N., Moreau, J.-J., Nielson, H. F., Karmarkar, A., & Lafon, Y. (2007a). *SOAP Version 1.2 Part 1: Messaging Framework* (2nd Ed.). W3C. Retrieved April 20, 2007 from http://www.w3.org/TR/soap12-part1/

Gudgin, M., Hadley, M., Mendelsohn, N., Moreau, J.-J., Nielson, H. F., Karmarkar, A., & Lafon, Y. (2007b). *SOAP Version 1.2 Part 2: Adjuncts* (2nd Ed.). W3C. Retrieved April 20, 2009 from http://www.w3.org/TR/soap12-part2/

Gudgin, M., Hadley, M., & Rogers, T. (2006a). *Web Services Addressing 1.0 – Core.* W3C. Retrieved April 20, 2009 from http://www.w3.org/TR/ws-addr-core/

Gudgin, M., Hadley, M., & Rogers, T. (2006b). *Web Services Addressing 1.0 – SOAP Binding.* W3C. Retrieved April 20, 2009 from http://www.w3.org/TR/2006/REC-ws-addr-soap-20060509/

Gudgin, M., Hadley, M., Rogers, T., & Yalçinalp, Ü. (2006a). *Web Services Addressing 1.0 - WSDL Binding*. W3C. Retrieved April 20, 2009 from http://www.w3.org/TR/ws-addr-wsdl/

Gudgin, M., Hadley, M., Rogers, T., & Yalçinalp, Ü. (2006b). *Web Services Addressing 1.0 – Metadata*. W3C. Retrieved April 20, 2009 from http://www.w3.org/TR/ws-addr-metadata/

Gudgin, M., Mendelsohn, N., Nottingham, M., & Ruellan, H. (2005). *SOAP Message Transmission Optimization Mechanism*. W3C. Retrieved April 20, 2009 from http://www.w3.org/TR/soap12-mtom/

Gutierrez, C. A., Fernandez-Medina, E., & Piattini, M. (2006). PWSSec: Process for web services security. In *IEEE Proceedings of the International Conference on Web Services*, (pp. 213-222).

Gutierrez, C.A., Fernandez-Medina, E., & Piattini, M. (2007, September). Web services-based security requirements elicitation. *IECE Trans. Inf. & Syst. E (Norwalk, Conn.)*, *90-D*(9), 1374–1387.

Hallam-Baker, P., & Mysore, S. H. (2005a). *XML key management specification (XKMS 2.0) version 2.0*. W3C. Retrieved April 20, 2009 from http://www.w3.org/TR/xkms2/

Hallam-Baker, P., & Mysore, S. H. (2005a). *XML Key Management Specification (XKMS 2.0) Bindings Version 2.0*. Retrieved June 28, 2005 from http://www.w3.org/TR/xkms2-bindings/

Hashizume, K. & Fernandez, E. B. (submitted). *The XML Signature pattern*.

Hashizume, K., Fernandez, E. B. & Huang, S. (submitted). *The WS-Security pattern*.

Hirsch, F., Philpott, R., & Maler, E. (2005). *[Saml05f] OASIS, Security and Privacy Considerations for the OASIS Security Assertion Markup Language (SAML) V2.0*. OASIS. Retrieved April 20, 2009 from http://docs.oasis-open.org/security/saml/v2.0/saml-sec-consider-2.0-os.pdf

Hughes, J., Cantor, S., Hodges, J., Hirsch, F., Mishra, P., et al. (2005). *Profiles for the OASIS Security Assertion Markup Language (SAML) V2.0*. OASIS. Retrieved April 20, 2009 from http://docs.oasis-open.org/security/saml/v2.0/saml-profiles-2.0-os.pdf

IBM application security software and services. (2009) IBM. Retrieved April 20, 2009 from http://www-01.ibm.com/software/tivoli/governance/security/application-security.html.

Imamura, T., Dilaway, B., & Simon, E. (2002). *XML encryption syntax and processing*. W3C. Retrieved April 20, 2009 from http://www.w3.org/TR/xmlenc-core/

InnerGuard. (2006). Cerebit. Retrieved April 20, 2009 from http://www.cerebit.com/Product_innerGuard.htm

Integrated SOA governance - Improving business efficiency. (2004). SOA Software. Retrieved April 20, 2009 from http://www.soa.com

Iwasa, K., Durand, J., Rutt, T., Peel, M., Kunisetty, S., & Bunting, D. (2004). *Web services reliable messaging TC WS-Reliability 1.1*. OASIS. Retrieved April 20, 2009 from http://docs.oasis-open.org/wsrm/ws-reliability/v1.1/wsrm-ws_reliability-1.1-spec-os.pdf

Kaiser (2007). Toward the realization of policy-oriented enterprise management. *IEEE Computer, 8*(40), 57-63.

Kavantzas, N., Burdett, D., Ritzinger, G., Fletcher, T., Lafon, Y., & Barreto, C. (2005). *Web services choreography description language version 1.0*. W3C. Retrieved April 20, 2009 from http://www.w3.org/TR/ws-cdl-10/

Kemp, J., Cantor, S., Mishra, P., Philpott, R., & Maler, E. (2005). *Authentication Context for the OASIS Security Assertion Markup Language (SAML) V2.0*. OASIS. Retrieved April 20, 2009 from http://docs.oasis-open.org/security/saml/v2.0/saml-authn-context-2.0-os.pdf

Kobryn, C. (2000). Modeling components and frameworks with UML. *Communications of the ACM, 10*(43), 31–38. doi:10.1145/352183.352199

Larmouth, J. (2003). *XML Common Biometric Format*. OASIS. Retrieved April 20, 2009 from http://www.oasis-open.org/committees/tc_home.php?wg_abbrev=xcbf

Lawrence, K., & Kaler, C. (2004). *Web services security: SOAP message security 1.1 (WS-Security 2004)*. Retrieved 1 February 2006, from http://www.oasis-open.org/committees/download.php/16790/wss-v1.1-spec-os-SOAPMessageSecurity.pdf

Lawrence, K., & Kaler, C. (2006a). *Web Services Security: X.509 Certificate Token Profile 1.1*. OASIS. Retrieved April 20, 2009 from http://www.oasis-open.org/committees/download.php/16785/wss-v1.1-spec-os-x509TokenProfile.pdf

Lawrence, K., & Kaler, C. (2006b). *Web Services Security: SAML Token Profile 1.1*. OASIS. Retrieved April 20, 2009 from http://www.oasis-open.org/committees/download.php/16768/wss-v1.1-spec-os-SAMLTokenProfile.pdf

Lawrence, K., & Kaler, C. (2006c). *Web services security: username token profile 1.1*. OASIS. Retrieved April 20, 2009 from http://www.oasis-open.org/committees/download.php/16782/wss-v1.1-spec-os-UsernameTokenProfile.pdf

Lawrence, K., & Kaler, C. (2006d). *Web services security: Kerberos token profile 1.1*. OASIS. Retrieved April 20, 2009 from http://www.oasis-open.org/committees/download.php/16788/wss-v1.1-spec-os-KerberosTokenProfile.pdf

Lee, E. (Ed.). (2005). *Web Service Implementation Methodology*. OASIS. Retrieved April 20, 2009 from http://www.oasis-open.org/committees/download.php/13420/fwsi-im-1.0-guidlines-doc-wd-publicReviewDraft_files

Little, M., Newcomer, E., & Pavlik, G. (2007). *Web services context specification (WS-Context) version 1.0*. OASIS. Retrieved April 20, 2009 from http://docs.oasis-open.org/ws-caf/ws-context/v1.0/wsctx.html

Little, M., & Wilkinson, A. (2007). *Web services atomic transaction (WS-AtomicTransaction) version 1.1*. OASIS. Retrieved April 20, 2009 from http://docs.oasis-open.org/ws-tx/wstx-wsat-1.1-spec-os/wstx-wsat-1.1-spec-os.html

Lockhart, H., Andersen, S., Bohren, J., Sverdlov, Y., Hondo, M., et al. (2006). *Web services federation language (WS-Federation) version 1.1*. Armonk, NY: IBM. Retrieved April 20, 2009 from http://download.boulder.ibm.com/ibmdl/pub/software/dw/specs/ws-fed/WS-Federation-V1-1B.pdf?S_TACT=105AGX04&S_CMP=LP

Marsh, J., Orchard, D., & Veillard, D. (2006). *XML Inclusions (XInclude) Version 1.0 (2nd Ed.)*. W3C. Retrieved April 20, 2009 from http://www.w3.org/TR/xinclude/

Microsoft aims to bridge your trust with new strategy. (2002). Retrieved April 20, 2009 from http://articles.techrepublic.com.com/5100-10878_11-1054084.html

Mitra, N., & Lafon, Y. (2007). *SOAP Version 1.2 Part 0: Primer* (2nd Ed.). W3C. Retrieved April 20, 2009 from http://www.w3.org/TR/soap12-part0/

Mitra, T. (2005). *A case for SOA governance*. Armonk, NY: IBM. Retrieved April 20, 2009 from http://www.ibm.com/developerworks/webservices/library/ws-soa-govern/

Moreau, J. J., Chinnici, R., Ryman, A., & Weerawarana, S. (2006). *Web services description language (WSDL) version 2.0 part 1: Core language.* Candidate recommendation, W3C. Retrieved April 20, 2009 from http://www.w3.org/TR/wsdl20/

Morrison, K. S., & Hirsh, F. (2006). *WS-I security challenges: threats and countermeasures,* WS-I Working Group Draft. Retrieved April 20, 2009 from http://www.ws-i.org/Profiles/BasicSecurity/SecurityChallenges-1.0.pdf

Moses, T. (2005a). *eXtensible access control markup language (XACML) version 2.0.* OASIS. Retrieved April 20, 2009 from http://docs.oasis-open.org/xacml/2.0/access_control-xacml-2.0-core-spec-os.pdf

Moses, T. (2005b). *Privacy policy profile of XACML v2.0.* OASIS. Retrieved April 20, 2009 from http://docs.oasis-open.org/xacml/2.0/access_control-xacml-2.0-privacy_profile-spec-os.pdf

Nadalin, A., Goodner, A., & Gudgin, M. Barbir, A. & Granqvist, H. (2007a). *WS-SecureConversation 1.3.* OASIS. Retrieved April 20, 2009 from http://docs.oasis-open.org/ws-sx/ws-secureconversation/v1.3/ws-secureconversation.html

Nadalin, A., Goodner, A., & Gudgin, M. Barbir, A. & Granqvist, H. (2007b). *WS-SecurityPolicy 1.2.* OASIS. Retrieved April 20, 2009 from http://docs.oasis-open.org/ws-sx/ws-securitypolicy/v1.2/ws-securitypolicy.html

Nadalin, A., Goodner, A., & Gudgin, M. Barbir, A. & Granqvist, H. (2007c). *WS-Trust 1.3.* OASIS. Retrieved April 20, 2009 from http://docs.oasis-open.org/ws-sx/ws-trust/v1.3/ws-trust.html

Nagaratnam, N., Nadalin, A., Hondo, M., McIntosh, M., & Austel, P. (2005). Business-driven application security: from modeling to managing secure applications. *IBM Systems Journal, 44*(4), 847–867.

Oracle management pack for SOA. (2009). Oracle. Retrieved April 20, 2009 from http://www.oracle.com/technologies/soa/management-pack-soa.html, 2007.

Oracle web services manager. (2009). Oracle. Retrieved April 20, 2009 from http://www.oracle.com/appserver/web-services-manager.html

Papazoglou, M. P. (2008). *Web services: Principles and technology.* Old Tappan, NJ: Pearson/Prentice Hall.

Pope, N., Carlos, J., & Drees, S. (2007). *Digital Signature Service Core Protocols, Elements, and Bindings Version 1.0.* OASIS. Retrieved April 20, 2009 from http://docs.oasis-open.org/dss/v1.0/oasis-dss-core-spec-v1.0-os.pdf

Progress Actional SOA governance. (2009). Progress Software. Retrieved April 20, 2009 from http://www.actional.com/solutions/soa-governance/

Progress Software IONA Artix. (2009). Progress Software. Retrieved April 20, 2009 from http://www.iona.com/products/artix/welcome.htm

Reactivity web services management. (2007). Cisco Systems. Retrieved April 20, 2009 from http://www.cisco.com/cdc_content_elements/acquisitions/reactivity/download/reactivity_uc_web_services_management.pdf

Reistad, B., Murray, B., Davis, D., Robinson, I., McCollum, R., et al. (2006). *Web services resource transfer (WS-RT) version 1.0.* HP, Intel, IBM & Microsoft. Retrieved April 20, 2009 from http://download.boulder.ibm.com/ibmdl/pub/software/dw/specs/ws-rt/ws-rt-spec.pdf

Rohati products oveview. (2008). Rohati. Retrieved April 20, 2009 from http://www.rohati.com/products/index.php

Rosenberg, J., & Remy, D. (2004). *Securing Web Services with WS-Security: Demystifying WS-Security, WS-Policy, SAML, XML Signature, and XML Encryption.* Sams.

Sanchez-Cid, F., & Maña, A. (2008). SERENITY pattern-based software development lifecycle. In *Proceedings of the 19th International. Conference on Database and Expert Systems Application (DEXA),* (pp. 305-309). Washington, DC: IEEE.

Schmidt, D., Stal, M., Rohnert, H., & Buschmann, F. (2000). Patterns for concurrent and networked objects. In *Pattern-oriented software architecture,* (vol. 2). Hoboken, NJ: J. Wiley.

Schumacher, M., Fernandez, E. B., Hybertson, D., Buschmann, F., & Sommerlad, P. (2006). *Security Patterns: Integrating security and systems engineering.* Hoboken, NJ: J. Wiley.

Securent overview. (2007). Securent. Retrieved April 20, 2009 from http://www.securent.com/products/overview/

Security in a web services world: a proposed architecture and roadmap. (2002). Retrieved April 20, 2009 from http://www-106.ibm.com/developerworks/webservices/library/ws-secmap/

Software, S. O. A. Inc. (n.d.). Retrieved from http://www.soa.com/

Srinivasan, L., & Banks, T. (2006). *Web Services Resource Lifetime 1.2 (WS-ResourceLifetime).* OASIS. Retrieved April 20, 2009 from http://docs.oasis-open.org/wsrf/wsrf-ws_resource_lifetime-1.2-spec-os.pdf

Stal, M. (2006). Using architectural patterns and blueprints for Service-Oriented Architecture. *Software IEEE, 2*(23), 54–61. doi:10.1109/MS.2006.60

Steffen, B., & Narayan, P. (2007). Full life-cycle support for end-to-end processes. *IEEE Computer, 40*(11), 64–73.

Sun identity management. (2008). Sun. Retrieved April 20, 2009 from http://www.sun.com/software/products/identity/ds_solutions_your_environment.pdf

Technology, G. X. S. *A service oriented network for high performance B2B.* (2006). GXS Technology. Retrieved April 20, 2009 from http://www.gxs.com/products/technology/tradingGrid_tech.htm

Thompson, H. S., Beech, D., Maloney, M., & Mendelsohn, N. (2004). *XML Schema Part 1: Structure,* (2nd Ed.). Retrieved April 20, 2009 from http://www.w3.org/TR/2004/REC-xmlschema-1-20041028/

Validation testing report: Sarvega XML Guardian Gateway & XML Speedway Accelerator. (2004). Retrieved April 20, 2009 from http://www.itslabs.com/tests/its04003.jhtml

Vampenepe, W., Graham, S., & Niblett, P. (2006). *Web Services Topics 1.3 (WS-Topics).* OASIS. Retrieved April 20, 2009 from http://docs.oasis-open.org/wsn/wsn-ws_topics-1.3-spec-os.pdf

VanHilst, M., Fernandez, E. B., & Braz, F. (in press). A multidimensional classification for users of security patterns. *Journal of Research and Practice in Information Technology.*

Varadan, R., Channabasavaiah, K., Simpson, S., Holley, K., & Allam, A. (2008). Increasing business flexibility and soa adoption through effective soa governance. *IBM Systems Journal, 47.*

Vedamuthu, A. S. (2007). *Web Services Description Language (WSDL) Version 2.0 SOAP 1.1 Binding.* W3C. Retrieved April 20, 2009 from http://www.w3.org/TR/wsdl20-soap11-binding/

Vedamuthu, A. S., Orchard, D., Hirsch, F., Hondo, M., Yendluri, P., et al. (2007a). *Web Services Policy 1.5 – Framework.* W3C. Retrieved April 20, 2009 from http://www.w3.org/TR/ws-policy/

Vedamuthu, A. S., Orchard, D., Hirsch, F., Hondo, M., Yendluri, P., et al. (2007b). *Web Services Policy 1.5 – Attachment*. W3C. Retrieved April 20, 2009 from http://www.w3.org/TR/2007/REC-ws-policy-attach-20070904/

Vinoski, S. (2003). Integration with web services. *IEEE Internet Computing, 7*(6), 75–77. doi:10.1109/MIC.2003.1250587

Voelter, M., Schmid, A., & Wolff, E. (2002). *Server component patterns: Component infrastructures illustrated with EJB*. West Sussex, UK: Wiley.

Vordel, X. M. L. *Firewall: Threat protection for XML applications*. (2007). Vordel. Retrieved April 20, 2009 from http://www.vordel.com/products/vx_firewall/index.html

Washizaki, H., Fernandez, E. B., Maruyama, H., Kubo, A. & Yoshioka, N. (submitted). *Precise classification of software patterns*.

Web services for management (WS-Management) 1.0. (2008). Distributed Management Task Force. Retrieved April 20, 2009 from http://www.dmtf.org/standards/published_documents/DSP0226_1.0.0.pdf

WebSphere DataPower XML Security Gateway XS40. (2004). IBM. Retrieved April 20, 2009 from http://www-01.ibm.com/software/integration/datapower/xs40/

Wilson, K., & Sedukhin, I. (2006). *Web services distributed management: management web services (WSDM-MOWS) 1.1*. OASIS. Retrieved April 20, 2009 from http://www.oasis-open.org/committees/download.php/20574/wsdm-mows-1.1-spec-os-01.pdf

WS-Security appnotes. (2002). IBM and Microsoft. Retrieved April 20, 2009 from http://www-106.ibm.com/developerworks/webservices/library/ws-secapp

XML Firewall and VPN. (2008). Layer7 Technologies. Retrieved April 20, 2009 from http://www.layer7tech.com/products/page.html?id=70

Xtradyne, W. *S-DBC - the XML firewall*. (2005). Xtradyne. Retrieved April 20, 2009 from http://www.xtradyne.com/products/ws-dbc/xml-firewall-intro.htm

Yendluri, P. (2000). *RosettaNet Implementation Framework (RNIF) 2.0*. Retrieved from http://www.rosettanet.org/rosettanet/Doc/0/TA0508V-V3E7KLCRIDD1BMU6N38/RNIF2.1.pdf

Zdun, U., Hentrich, C., & van der Aalst, W. M. P. (2006). A survey of patterns for Service-Oriented Architectures. *International Journal of Internet Protocol Technology, 3*(1), 132–143.

Chapter 9
Security in Service Oriented Architectures:
Standards and Challenges

Anne V.D.M. Kayem
German Research Center for Artificial Intelligence (DFKI GmbH), Germany

ABSTRACT

Service Oriented Architectures (SOAs) have become the defacto standard for defining interoperable architectures on the web with the most common implementation of this concept being in the form of web services. Information exchange is an integral part of SOAs, so designing effective security architectures that ensure data confidentiality and integrity is important. However, selecting a security standard for the architecture is challenging because existing solutions are geared toward access control in relatively static scenarios rather than dynamic scenarios where some form of adaptability is needed. Moreover, when services interact across different domains interoperability becomes a problem because of the lack a consistent security model to handle service interactions. This chapter presents a comparative analysis of SOA security standards. The authors discuss the challenges SOA security architecture designers face, in relation to an example travel agent web services scenario, and outline potential mitigation strategies.

1. INTRODUCTION

A Service Oriented Architecture (SOA) can be defined as an approach to distributed computing that allows loosely coupled components to interact seamlessly. On the Internet, in particular, the SOA concept has emerged as a simple but effective way of addressing the communication requirements of loosely coupled, standards-based, and protocol-in-

DOI: 10.4018/978-1-60566-950-2.ch009

dependent distributed components that often belong to different domains (Papazoglou & Van den Heuel, 2007). Yet, this quality of seamless communications in an open environment raises issues pertaining to data security, privacy, and trust. Service providers need security protocols that allow them to design architectures to protect the services and information they make available to clients (users), while users want firm guarantees of privacy. The problem is made more complex by the fact that task delegations, third party interactions and service compositions can occur between services with different security constraints and/or implementations (Cover, 2002 & Tang et al., 2007).

Composing an offered service requires the SOA to process and spread confidential data to the participating services in ways that enforce the security requirements of all the participants. However, in these cases, decomposing the security requirements of the individual participating services and composing security guarantees does not necessarily result in an overall secure system (Epstein & Matsumoto, 2006; Hutter & Volkamer, 2006; Sidharth & Liu, 2007; Alonso & Larrucea, 2008).

Implementations of Web Services have successfully manifested the SOA concept, and cases of interacting services are handled by negotiation models that establish some form of trust between the participating services (Cover, 2002 and Kleijnen & Raju, 2003). A web service is generally modeled around three key service components namely, the service provider, the client (Requester), and the registry. The service provider publishes available web services in a registry that clients (requesters) can query. Direct communications between a service provider and service requester are handled, by the semantic matchmaker.

Research in securing SOAs has aimed at, and continues to seek, ways of enforcing policies that overcome the challenges of protecting information from exposure during service execution (Sidharth & Liu, 2007; Crispo, et al., 2007; Thuraisingham et al., 2007). Each standard, model, and/or framework targets aspects of message security like confidentiality, integrity, and availability but fails to provide a method of dynamically excluding malicious and/or compromised services from the execution process (Epstein & Matsumoto, 2006; Sidharth & Liu, 2007; Alonso & Larrucea, 2008).

The aim of this chapter is to present a comparative analysis of the state of the art in security standards, models, and frameworks for SOAs. We use an example of a travel reservation web

services scenario to discuss the challenges that SOA security architecture designers continue to face in spite of the existing security standards. The example of a travel-reservation web service is aimed at illustrating a case of interacting, but distributed, web services that work together to yield a required result. In such a case, the interacting web services need to operate in ways that enforce pre-set security policies (Buecker et al., 2007; Hutter & Volkamer, 2006). Each of the challenges evoked is supported by an example of an attack possibility as well as a proposition of potential mitigation strategies.

The rest of the chapter is structured as follows. In Section 2, we briefly explain the concept of web services since they are a practical example of an implementation of the SOA paradigm, and continue to give an example of a travel reservation scenario in order to portray a case of interacting services. The section concludes with an overview of SOAs and the impact of security standards in guiding secure SOA design. Section 3, gives a comparative analysis of SOA security standards while Section 4, presents the challenges they face and proposes potential mitigation strategies. We present some ideas for future research in Section 5 and offer concluding remarks in Section 6.

2. BACKGROUND

In order to facilitate the understanding of the rest of the chapter, this section explains the architecture and terminology underlying Service Oriented Architectures (SOAs). For simplicity, we use the concept of web services to explain how self-contained and self-describing components interact to provide a service. This is due to the fact that web services are a practical manifestation of how SOAs can be built successfully. Moreover, web services are composed of self contained, self-describing functions that can be published, located, and programmatically invoked over the Internet. We begin with a discussion of the basic architecture of a web service, and use an example of a travel agent web service to illustrate how SOAs can be implemented. Our discussion continues with a consideration of SOA security architectures and why a formal method of designing them is a growing necessity.

2.1 Web Service Architecture and Terminology

A web service is a self-contained, modular application that can be described, published, located, and invoked over a network like the Internet (Alonso et al., 2004). Typically web services are constructed on the basis of an architecture that involves three types of components: the *service requestor*, the *service provider*, and the *service registry or service broker* (Alonso et al. 2004; Crampton et al., 2007; Huhns & Singh, 2005).

The service provider advertises services in the service registry from where the service requestor finds suitable services. A simple architectural model of a web service is shown in Figure 1. It shows that three fundamental operations namely, *publish, find,* and *bind* are needed to describe the interactions between the basic components. *Service providers publish* services to a *service broker (service registry).* While, s*ervice requesters find* the services they require using a *service broker* and *bind* to the services. In the following subsections we look at some XML (eXtensible

Markup Language) standards and protocols for describing web services, in order to pave the way for the example of a travel-reservation web service that we give in Section 2.2.

2.1.1. XML: eXtensible Markup Language

The eXtensible Markup Language (XML) and XML schema are popular tools for designing SOA security architectures, and web services in particular, because they provides a very extensible means for specifying document structures through a comprehensive type definition language (Chandramouli, 2003). XML provides standards for representing, interchanging, and presenting both meta data and complex content models in a platform-independent fashion. The messages as well as the files/data that define the web services for consumption are formatted as XML. Figure 2 shows an example of a simple XML document:

There are two different kinds of information in this example: **markup**, like "<contact-info>" and "<phone>"; and text (also known as **character data**), like "Micheal Koner" and "(49) 421 555-4567". The markup describes the structure of the document, while the text is the document's content. Individual pieces of information like *name, company, and phone* are surrounded by tags enclosed by angle brackets. It is also possible to have elements that are contained within other ele-

Figure 1. A simple Web service architecture

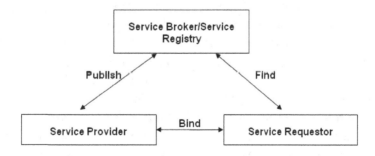

Figure 2. An example of an XML document

```
<?xml version="1.0"?>

<contact-info>
<name>Micheal Koner </name>
<company>AT&amp;T</company>
<phone>(49) 421 555-4567</phone>
</contact-info>
```

ments such as <contact-info> which contains the <name>, <company>, and <phone> elements.

As the example shows, an advantage of writing web services in XML is that the text files are human-readable which facilitates the debugging process. An added advantage of using XML is that the XML parsers are very commonplace in all modern programming languages, so applications that are written to interact with Web services do not need to parse the raw XML files directly.

2.1.2. Simple Object Access Protocol (SOAP)

The Simple Object Access Protocol (SOAP) is a unidirectional messaging protocol that supports interactions between web services (Gudgin et al., 2007). SOAP relies on the Extensible Markup Language (XML) as its message format because XML facilitates sharing structured data between information systems on the Internet. In addition to XML, SOAP messages rely on protocols like HTTP and TCP/IP to handle message negotiations and transmissions between web services. Figure 3 shows an example of the structure of a SOAP message based on XML. Each SOAP message is structured into three parts – the *envelope, header* and *body*.

The SOAP envelope is the root element of a SOAP message and its role is to define an XML document as SOAP message. In its most basic form, a SOAP Envelope contains a SOAP Body

that contains the actual data that is being transmitted. Sometimes there is a SOAP Header (within the Envelope and before the Body) that contains extra information, but the header is optional.

Although a SOAP message is a text file in standard XML format, it is often very difficult to create or interpret a SOAP message manually because there are very specific ways that all namespaces and element attributes need to be defined. Luckily, there are a large number of tools and programming libraries available that can create and interpret SOAP messages, so the complexity is abstracted away by the technology that is used for the implementation.

2.1.3. Web Services Description Language (WSDL)

The Web Services Description Language (WSDL) is an XML-based language that provides a model for describing Web Services (Chinnici et al., 2007). WSDL defines services as collections of network endpoints or ports. Every application that provides a web service uses a WSDL file to describe which services are available and how they should be called. In the WSDL file, the Service provider defines the methods that are available for consumption by other applications. For example, a Web service may have a method called *GetContactInformation* that returns the contact information of a particular person. Other information that is contained in the WSDL file includes:

Figure 3. An example of an SOAP message based on XML

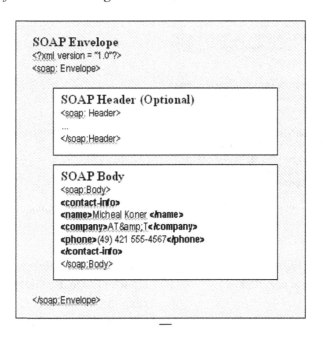

the specific name used to make a request to the method, the parameters that must be used in the request, the format of the value or values that are returned if the request is processed successfully and the protocol that should be used to call the method. Additionally, the WSDL file contains information on how the SOAP messages should be formatted, such as the namespaces to use, the order and structure of the parameters, and even what extra information may be required in the SOAP Header element or the HTTP header.

Figure 4 shows a simplified fragment of a WSDL document. In this example the <portType> element defines "ContactTerms" as the name of a port and *"getTerm"* as the name of an operation. The "getTerm" operation has an **input message** called *"getTermRequest"* and an **output message** called *"getTermResponse"*. The **<message>** elements define the **parts** of each message and the associated data types. Compared to traditional programming, ContactTerms is a function library; *"getTerm"* is a function with *"getTermRequest"* as the input parameter, and *"getTermResponse"* as the return parameter.

2.1.4. Universal Description Discovery and Integration (UDDI)

UDDI, which is the short form of Universal Description Discovery and Integration, is a standard for providing a catalog of services that have been made available by any number of different applications. It is like a registry of service providers and uses WSDL to describe interfaces to web services. Service requestors can look up service information in the UDDI registry, and the registry returns the necessary details for connecting to that service.

Although UDDI is an aggregator of all the available services a provider has to offer, its usage is optional because the only real advantage in using it is that it eases the management of complex web services that involve multiple providers. For example, many of the more organized corporate environments that have a lot of internal Web service providers have UDDI registries, because UDDI makes it very easy to change the provider of a Web service. As long as all clients use UDDI to locate the Web service instead of going directly

Figure 4. A snippet of a WSDL file based on XML

```
<message name="getTermRequest">
  <part name="term" type="xs:string"/>
</message>

<message name="getTermResponse">
  <part name="value" type="xs:string"/>
</message>

<portType name="ContactTerms">
  <operation name="getTerm">
    <input message="getTermRequest"/>
    <output message="getTermResponse"/>
  </operation>
</portType>
```

to the providing server, the SOAP calls are automatically directed to the new provider.

2.1.5. Web Services Inspection Language (WSIL)

The Web Services Inspection Language (WSIL) is an XML format both for assisting in the inspection of a site for available services and for specifying the set of rules for how inspection related information should be made available to web services for consumption. Like UDDI, WSIL uses WSDL to describe interfaces to web services. While similar in scope to the Universal Description Discovery and Integration (UDDI) specification, WSIL is a complementary, rather than a competitive, model to service discovery. As opposed to the centralized approach that UDDI favors, WSIL approaches service discovery in a decentralized fashion, where service description information can be distributed to any location using a simple extensible XML document format

WSIL is a little like a business card in the sense that it represents a specific entity, its services, and contact info, and is typically delivered directly by whom it represents. The low functionality and lightweight nature of WSIL leaves the processing for the developer to implement. Although UDDI and WSIL are both mechanisms for Web services

discovery, their models are quite different. Deciding whether to use UDDI or WSIL depends on the situation. In many cases, it may be advantageous to use both. As we show in Section 2.2 (see Figure 5), WSIL can be used to "point" to UDDI repositories and the service descriptions therein.

2.2 An Example of a Web Service

We envision a travel-reservation scenario in which a customer (user) uses a *Requestor* application to search for different travel itineraries available with respect to his/her travel requirements. In this case three applications *(Requestor, Travel Agent, Itinerary Broker)* participate in satisfying the request.

The *Requestor* application invokes a *Travel Agent Application* with a message containing the customer's travel requirements. The *Travel Agent* will analyze the request to decide whether or not it is valid and if it is, the *Travel Agent* will then proceed to check the feasibility of the customer's travel requirements by transmitting the customer's list of travel requirements to the *Itinerary Broker*. The *Itinerary Broker* will select the records that correspond to the expected response and will then return the results directly to the *Requestor* application. Once the *Requestor* application has received all the required information, an *"ac-*

Figure 5. An example of the architecture supporting a travel agent Web service

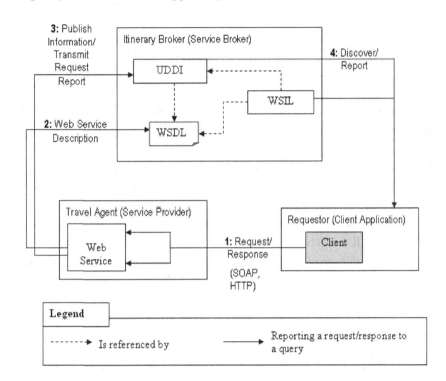

knowledgement" message is sent to the *Travel Agent*. This process chain is important for security issues because it simplifies protecting message exchanges and communications.

As shown in Figure 5, the *Travel Agent* service provider hosts a web service and makes it accessible using protocols like SOAP and HTTP. The web service is described by a WSDL document that is stored in a special repository at the *Itinerary Broker*. WSDL documents may be referenced by the UDDI business registry and WSIL documents. The WSIL document helps to integrate travel itineraries that originate from different distribute sources if the requestor application requires services from several sources.

In our example, each component of the travel-reservation web service has it own basic security requirements that need to be satisfied to guarantee an overall secure web service. The guarantees of security are enforced by monitoring, either manually or with an autonomic manager, the behavior of the system to decide if the requirements of the individual components are being met. When significant deviations from expected behavior are observed, the security manager can outline a plan for reconfiguring the component to ensure that it meets the security composition guarantees of the overall service.

It is worth noting that the inherently distributed architecture of a web service implies that different components of the same service can be spread across different machines and coordinated to perform a common task. Since this involves transmitting information across different domains often with varying security constraints establishing security and trust guarantees is a growing concern for designers and users of SOA architectures. In the next section we consider some of the reasons why establishing security in SOA architectures is challenging.

2.3 SOA Security

One of the main attractions of SOAs is that they provide high-level mechanisms that make building web applications less effort-intensive than it is the case traditionally. However, embedding security into SOAs requires choosing from a wide selection of standards, often without a clear distinction as to which is preferable (Viega & Epstein, 2006).

The role of SOA security standards is to meet the demand for uniformity amongst developers in order to facilitate interoperability between services belonging to different domains. Unfortunately, standards do not address all the details required to build secure systems, and typically deal with process and management issues as opposed to technical ones. One of the reasons for this is that standards are typically defined before a technology matures. The other reason is that the costs involved in complying with the standard keep people from adopting it. For instance, if the specifications of a standard change frequently, developers might be reluctant to adopt it because of the costs in time and resources needed to keep service security updated. Moreover, interoperability is still an issue in the development of secure SOAs because of the lack of a consistent security model across different interacting platforms. For instance, when SOA is implemented using multiple coordinated web services, a user should be able to switch from one to the other service implementation without worrying about whether the supporting security mechanisms need an update or offer the same guarantees of security. Therefore, creators of SOA security standards need to ensure that the standards provide the necessary tools required for achieving common assurance levels in an interoperable manner.

It is also worth noting that since changes in interoperable systems can occur dynamically security systems, that can adapt and evolve automatically to changing conditions in a system, are needed. In the next section we discuss SOA

security standards in order highlight the importance of designing an SOA security framework to monitor the behavior of a web service and adjust its operation to cope with perceived changes.

3. SOA SECURITY STANDARDS

In this section we present three methods that are generally combined to design SOA security architectures. We look at the ways in which these methods are combined to provide effective security in SOAs, highlighting the pros and cons of each approach. In particular we focus on methods that are used to ensure data confidentiality and integrity in SOAs. Since web services are the most common implementation of SOAs in each case we make a note of the implementation standard that is used in the web service environment.

3.1 Authentication, Authorization, and Single Sign-On

Since SOAs are information exchange intensive, protecting data and guaranteeing the authenticity of the source of the data are important concerns. Authenticity, basically involves establishing ways of providing integrity of origin of an information request or verifying the identity of a requester. In implementations of web services, authenticity is provided by using XML-Digital Signatures to sign SOAP messages. The main advantage of authentication is that it allows a system to establish some form of non-anonymous communication between the interacting parties (Hafner & Breu, 2008).

Authentication is generally a part of security policies in any SOA architecture and occurs before a request can be evaluated to determine whether or not to grant or deny access to information. In SOA, authentication occurs at the application layer instead of depending on the transport and HTTP layer authentication schemes. The reason for doing this is that applications are unable to retrieve context information (requester passwords, login, and authorization level) from the transport layer.

Since authentication is handled by the application layer, problems of interoperability typically arise in distributed heterogeneous environments like SOAs because it involves handling different applications that generally implement propriety solutions. Therefore, designing effective authentication schemes for securing SOAs, where application interactions involve conflicting security expectations, is challenging.

Additionally, accessing the individual components of interacting services typically requires some form of authentication at each component. In complex services that involve several components this would imply a need for several passwords which is tedious to manage both on the security administrator's end and the user's end. Single sign-on is a good solution to this problem because it allows a user to sign-on (log on) to a system once and gain access to all the components of the system without being prompted to log on again when access to each one is needed. Single sign-on can be defined simply as an authentication property used to control access to multiple, related, but independent software systems (Gross, T., 2003). The reverse property, single sign-off, allows a user to use a single sign off action to disconnect completely from the whole system.

One of the key benefits of using single-sign on is that it reduces number of passwords required to log-on to a system and so is easier to manage both on the user's end and the security manager's end. A major drawback of this authentication approach is that it provides access to many resources once a user has passed the initial authentication phase (Gross, T., 2003). So, if the authentication credentials end up in the hands of a malicious user, the negative impact of any malicious actions he/she carries out on the system will be more wide-spread than if several passwords were used. Web service standards like the Security Markup Assertion Language (SAML) are still to come up

with an effective solution to the single sign-on problem (Kemp et al. 2005). Some suggestions to addressing this weakness focus on protecting user credentials by combining them with strong authentication methods like smart cards.

Authorization, on the other hand involves ensuring that only the users who have been authenticated and additionally, have been granted the permission to view data get access to the information. Ways of doing this include the use of passwords and cryptographic keys. In implementations of web services, access authorizations that require cryptographic keys are handled by the XML-Encryption standard. In general authorization is enforced through an access control model (Boehm et al, 2008; Lopez et al., 2004; Jaeger, 2001). Traditional approaches for access control include discretionary, mandatory, and role-based models (Lopez et al., 2004; Jaeger, 2001).

3.2 Role and Policy Based Access Control

Role-based access control (RBAC) is an access control approach that operates by assigning users roles that define the scope of operations they can carry out within an organization's information system (Liu and Chen, 2004). The permissions to perform certain operations are assigned to specific roles. Members of staff (or other system users) are assigned particular roles, and through those role assignments acquire the permissions to perform particular system functions.

Since users are not assigned permissions directly, but only acquire them through their role (or roles), management of individual user rights becomes a matter of simply assigning appropriate roles to the user; this simplifies common operations, such as adding a user, or changing a user's department.

RBAC differs from access control lists (ACLs) used in traditional discretionary access control systems in that it assigns permissions to specific operations with meaning in the organization, rather than to low level data objects. For example, an access control list could be used to grant or deny write access to a particular system file, but it would not dictate how that file could be changed. In an RBAC-based system, an operation might be to create a 'credit account' transaction in a financial application. The assignment of the permission to perform a particular operation is meaningful, because the operations are granular with meaning within the application. RBAC has been shown to be particularly well suited to separation of duties (SoD) requirements, which ensure that two or more people must be involved in authorizing critical operations (Sohr et al., 2008). An underlying principle of SoD is that no individual should be able to provoke a breach of security through dual privilege (Li, N. & Wang, Q., 2008). By extension, no person may hold a role that exercises audit, control or review authority over another, concurrently held role.

The policy-based access control (PBAC) on the other hand extends RBAC to provide a powerful and flexible means of protecting data with security policies. Administrators define security policies that are based on the value of individual data elements, and the server enforces these policies transparently (Ventuneac et al., 2003). Once an administrator defines a policy, it is automatically invoked whenever the affected data is queried through applications, ad hoc queries, stored procedures, views, and so on.

In comparison to RBAC, using PBAC simplifies security administration and the application development process because it is the server, not the application that enforces security. This allows developers to concentrate on implementing business functionalities while administrators focus on defining a security policy to enforce confidentiality and integrity across the entire server.

3.3 Access Control Mechanisms for SOAs

Service based systems are by nature dynamic because they involve multiple services that interact in ways that cannot be predicted apriori. The security of these systems depends on that of the individual services involved so some form of dynamic access control is needed. Dynamic access control depends on attributes like time, context, and delegation of access rights that are important in deciding what authorizations to grant a user when he/her role changes. Handling these role changes statically is challenging because of the complexity of large systems so dynamic approaches are preferable.

One of the key issues in enforcing dynamic access control in SOAs is the fact that a considerable number of changes may be needed when a user's role changes. Role based access control (RBAC) (Al-Kahtani and Sandhu, 2003 & Li and Karp, 2007), which assigns privileges to roles and subjects to roles, helps to alleviate this problem. The rights associated with a role typically depend on the subject concerned and so managing roles in a way that prevents overlapping privileges can be difficult to enforce.

In order to address the problem of role explosion (Blaze et al., 1996 & Li and Karp, 2007), Policy Based Access Control (PBAC) emerged as a method by which each subject is assigned a set of attributes. Each request issued by a subject is checked by a policy engine to verify that the attributes associated with the subject permit him/her to issue the request. The request is only authorized if it does not violate the policy. The authentication, attribute, and authorization fields in SAML (Security Markup Assertion Language) certificates were designed to support PBAC models.

While RBAC and PBAC models are effective in handling the access rights management problem in identification based access control systems they fail to address the problems of access control in dynamic environments. This difficulty stems from the fact that the access control specifications differ across domains. Manually checking all the criteria required to guarantee an overall secure system can be time-consuming and so a security administrator might decide to perform an "approximate" verification check on the basis the probability of a user discovering a loophole and exploiting it is minimal.

More recently, Crampton et al. (2007) have come up with suggestions on how identity based cryptography (IBC) can be used to support web services. Crampton et al. suggest that IBC improve on conventional certificate-based approaches to securing web services because it provides five key attributes, namely simplified public key distribution, efficient provision of cryptographic services, role-based signatures, role-based encryption, and semantic public keys. Additionally, Li and Karp (2007) have also proposed a system for the purpose of security compositions that can be implemented with the existing web services security standards to help address the problem of dynamic user role changes.

We note however, that while these extensions go a long way towards facilitating access control management in dynamic environments like those that are based on SOAs, they still lack the quality of adaptability. Therefore, the security system continues to rely on manual management which can be a hindrance in scenarios where real-time constraints make autonomic security schemes an attractive alternative to addressing performance issues.

3.4 Security Assertion Markup Language and WS-Security

The Security Assertion Markup Language (SAML) defines methods for specifying trust assertions in XML (Cover, 2002 & Hu et al., 2003). SAML assertions are essentially statements that service providers use to make access control decisions.

The three types of statements provided by SAML include: *authentication statements, attribute statements,* and *authorization decision statements*.

The *authentication statement* asserts to the service provider that the user has indeed been authenticated by the identity provider. Other information about the authenticated user such as time of authentication, method of authentication and authentication context can also be disclosed in an authentication statement. The *attribute statement* indicates the properties of a subject, while the *authorization statement* states whether or not a user is permitted to access a particular resource. In SAML, assertions applied to a user can be attached to a message and so can be transported from point to point without the need to reformulate the assertions at each point. The SAML standard includes the following fields that are used to grant rights of access to a resource, in an authorization statement:

- *Decision:* This determines whether access is granted or denied. Typically this field is pre-set to ``granted".
- *Resource:* This is the resource to which the authorization decision applies. In our case, the resource is the travel-reservation web service, and this field is used to encode the URL of the web service end point reference.
- *Subject:* This is the user or web service that is authorized to access the resource. Each subject is presented with a public key certificate and the SOAP request to the web service must be signed by the private key corresponding to the public key.
- *Action:* These are the actions that a subject is authorized to perform on a resource.
- *Evidence:* This is the information used to support a claim that an authorization is valid. This field contains a copy of the certificate that represents the rights being granted to the delegator. The evidence field allows the system to reconstruct the

delegation chain even across subjects from different organizations.

The SAML authorization assertion is typically run between the policy enforcement point (PEP) and the policy decision point (PDP) with the support of the eXtensible Access Control Markup Language (XACML - *seeFigure 6*) (Hu et al., 2003, & Moses, 2005). Moreover, PEP also uses SAML to request attribute assertions from the policy information point (PIP).

Apart from SAML, WS-Security can also be used to secure SOAP messages. In a WS-Security specification a common format, that involves using XML Encryption and XML Signatures, is defined for securing SOAP messages (Hafner & Breu, 2008; Nadalin et al., 2007). Additionally, the WS-Security specification also provides methods of exchanging security tokens through SOAP headers. Since WS-security offers message-level security, each message can be encrypted or signed independently thereby ensuring end-to-end security. However, although WS-Security provides message protection the security granularity can cause performance issues because each message needs to be processed separately and different security tokens may be used within the same message or from message to message (Crampton et al., 2007 & Nadalin et al., 2007).

3.5 eXtensible Access Control Markup Language (XACML)

The eXtensible Access Control Markup Language (XACML) is a declarative language for specifying access control policies in XML and a processing model describing how to interpret the policies (Hu et al., 2003; Moses, 2005; & Newcomer, 2002). In XACML a core schema is defined with a namespace that can be used to express access control and authorization policies for XML objects. XACML supports a broad range of security policies (Chandramouli, 2003 & Hu et al., 2003), and uses a standardized syntax for

formatting requests so that a valid response to an access request is expressed as either one of *Permit, Deny, Indeterminate,* or *Not Applicable.*

As illustrated in Figure 6, XACML's standardized architecture for this decision-making uses two primary components: the **Policy Enforcement Point** (PEP) and the **Policy Decision Point** (PDP). The PEP constructs the request based on the user's attributes, the resource requested, the action specified, and other situation-dependent information retrieved from the **Policy Information Point** (PIP). The PDP receives the constructed request, compares it with the applicable policy and system state through the **Policy Access Point** (PAP), and then returns one of the four replies specified above to the PEP. The PEP then allows or denies access to the resource. The PEP and PDP components may be embedded within a single application or may be distributed across a network.

XACML provides a policy set that is used to make the PEP and PDP work. The policy set is a container that holds either a policy or other policy sets, plus links to other policies. Each individual policy is defined by a set of rules. XACML also includes methods of combining these policies and policy sets, allowing some to override others. This is necessary because the policies may overlap or conflict. For example, a simple policy-combining algorithm is "Deny Overwrites", which causes the final decision to be "Deny" if any policy results in an "Overwrite". Conversely, other rules could be established to allow an action if any of a set of policies results in "Allow". Conflicts are resolved through policy-combining algorithms.

Determining what policy or policy set to apply is accomplished using the "Target" component. A target is a set of rules or conditions applied to each subject, object, and operation. When a rule's conditions are met for a user (subject), object, operation combination, its associated policy or policy set is applied using the process described above.

The associated access control data for a given enterprise domain can be encoded in an XML

Figure 6. Underlying XACML access control model (Verma, 2004)

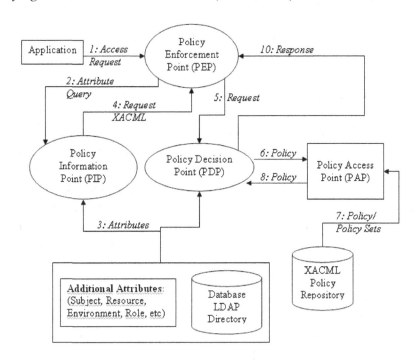

document, and the conformance of data to the enterprise access control model can be obtained by validating the XML document against the XML schema that represents the enterprise access control model using XML parsers. These XML parsers are based on standard application programming interfaces such as the Document Object Model (DOM), and the parser libraries are implemented in various procedural languages to enable an application program to create, maintain, and retrieve XML-encoded data.

The flexibility XACML allows users to specify access control policies by combining single rules to form a policy, so, encoding the security requirements of a service is simplified in comparison to SAML. However, XACML lacks a formal specification language for expressing historical constraints, so encoding constraints to avoid assigning conflicting permissions is challenging. For instance, the need for historical constraints arises when a security administrator needs to avoid granting a user a combination of access rights

that conflict with the security policy definitions of interacting web services.

Another of the drawbacks that XACML faces is that domain constraints are based on the semantic information pertaining to an enterprise context. Since grammar-based languages like XACML cannot deal with content-based constraints, XACML is insufficient for a complete specification of the RBAC model for an enterprise that contains content-based domain constraints. An example is not allowing more than one user to be assigned to the role of "security administrator" (role cardinality constraint) and not allowing the roles "viewer" and "uploader" to be assigned to the same user (separation-of-duty constraint).

3.6 Policy Driven SOA Security

In SOA security architectures security enforcement requires giving consideration to integrating different security policies that operate independently. Security policy integration, also referred to as *policy composition* allows different security policies to operate seamlessly across domain boundaries. Policy composition is very important in situations in which administrative tasks are managed by different non collaborating entities in a dynamic scenario. Policy combinations can result in conflicts between security policies and these conflicts need to be resolved to avoid generating an insecure state.

McLean (1988) introduced the algebra of security which is a Boolean algebra that makes it possible to reason about the problem of policy conflicts that arise when different policies are combined. Although, McLean's approach detects conflicts between security policies, it does not include a method of resolving the conflicts or handling security policy interactions. The notion of metapolicies to coordinate policy interactions was proposed by Hosmer (1992) and later extended by Elliot Bell (1994 to formalize the combination of two policies with a function called a *policy combiner*. The *policy combiner* provides ways of combining policies from different interacting services and also presents a formal method of resolving conflicts when they arise. However, this solution like the ones proposed by Woo and Lam (1993), Bertino et al. (1999), Li et al. (1999), Jaeger (2001), and Jajodia et al. (2001), assume that the security policies being combined have similar constraints. This assumption is limiting in dynamic scenarios where security policies with varying constraints are combined and where the role of a user can change during a service execution process (Bonatti et al. 2000).

In order to address these issues, Bonatti et al. (2002) propose that the design of a security policy composition framework has to be structured with the following considerations:

- *Heterogeneous Policy Support:* Allows the security policy framework to be flexible in the sense that it supports various policies that are expressed with different languages and mechanisms.

- *Support of Unknown Policies:* Allows the security policy framework to support policies that were not completely defined semantically or known when the composition algorithm was defined.
- *Controlled Interference:* Since merging security policies may create negative effects, policy composition needs to incorporate a method of verifying that the combination of different policies retains the access rights implemented by each individually.
- *Expressiveness:* The policy composition framework needs to allow for different combinations of policies without needing to change the input rule set or introducing ad-hoc extensions.
- *Support of different abstraction levels:* Policy compositions need to highlight the difference between components and their interplay at different levels of abstraction.
- *Formal Semantics:* Policy declaration languages need to be declarative, implementation independent and based on a formal semantic to avoid ambiguity.

Using the above properties as a guideline, Bonatti et al. (2002) proposed an algebra for combining security policies together with its formal semantics. In the Bonatti et al. approach, once the policies have been composed through the algebraic operators a translation policy is then used to convert the policy expressions into logic programs. This logic programming formulation can then be used to enforce access control dynamically.

4. SOA SECURITY: CHALLENGES AND MITIGATION STRATEGIES

The discussions of the preceding sections showed that SOAs are appealing for enterprise applications because they present a language independent way of supporting business process interaction.

The discussion of security design patterns for SOAs, highlighted the fact that a lot of effort has gone into developing tools for mitigating security vulnerabilities in SOAs. A growing source of vulnerabilities in SOAs arises primarily from their ability to allow for application interactions and compositions with services that have conflicting security constraints. In this section, we look at some of the vulnerabilities created due to dynamic run-time selection and composition of services.

4.1 Service Composition

A key feature of SOA is that it enables loose coupling of individual services. In web services in particular, the Web Services Business Process Execution Language (WSBPEL) (Hafner and Breu, 2008; OASIS WSBPEL, 2008), is used to describe service composition and to technically orchestrate their interactions. A composition consists of multiple invocations of services, often spread across different domains, in a particular order. Interacting services can be combined in either one of two ways, *Orchestration* or *Choreography*.

- *Orchestration:* This describes the order in which the services are to be executed and how the services interact with each other by exchanging messages (information flow). In the web services context, an orchestration is an executable process in a machine readable format which is usually an XML language. By executable, we mean that the process is controlled by a *Workflow Management System* (WfMS) (Hafner and Breu, 2008; & Farkas and Huhns, 2008).

- *Choreography:* This is a non-executable business protocol that describes the sequence of interaction activities (control flow) between business partners in terms of message exchange behavior of each of the parties involved in the protocol. Choreography is not limited to messages

exchanged with the WfMS executing the workflow but involves the viewpoint of all the peers participating in the process. In essence choreography can be seen as a virtual workflow that emerges through interactions of executable processes.

Service Composition Attack: A service composition attack occurs when one or more of the services participating in a composition are compromised. In a typical service composition scenario, a business process receives requests that it satisfies by invoking the necessary services required to respond to the service requestor. Since business processes communicate with other services, in the web service context, this procedure relies heavily on the WSDL description of the web services invoked by the composite web service. Although developed and managed independently, services have dependencies that arise when they are used as part of system-wide workflows. In general, the interacting services have no information about their status, or any changes that that might have occurred to the services. Therefore, if anyone of the services is compromised, all the workflows involved in the composition are at risk.

Example: The travel reservation web service scenario in Figure 5 (see Section 2.2) offering travel booking services to users may involve service compositions from different parties. In this case, the messages (e.g. request for hotel reservations, renting cars, sightseeing trips, etc) and documents (e.g. costs for combined hotel bookings, etc) are sent from one service to the next triggering some automated processing. Since these transactions typically carry private data like credit card numbers and other personal information, if one of the services is compromised, the content can be used for other unauthorized purposes or can be modified before it is consumed by authorized users. Therefore, a method of securing service compositions is needed to guarantee security in SOA environments.

Mitigation Strategies: Encrypting or signing service information individually could be used to secure the transactions, but this approach results in an additional cost in time and resources to enforce security.

Another alternative to mitigating security composition attacks is to use software-based deception to deploy intelligent software that can be used to mislead an attacker (Farkas and Huhns, 2008). However, in order to adopt both strategies in SOAs the languages used to design and implement SOAs need to be extended to enable a deeper semantic understanding. This will help reduce the number of false positive detections and the potential overhead that is likely to result from detection failures.

Work on semantic analysis of messages in an SOA is still at a budding stage so distributed network defense techniques seem to be a better choice. Distributed network defense systems can be designed to initiate, grow, and maintain a trust and reputation layer that can serve as a guide during compositions.

Anomaly detections approaches for securing SOAs include supporting SOAs with security frameworks that are designed along the autonomic computing paradigm. The SOA could be considered as being a managed component whose security behavior is constantly monitored using the autonomic framework. As shown in Figure 7, the autonomic framework, that would support the SOA security framework, is structured in the form of a feedback control loop that comprises six modules (sensor, monitor, analyzer, planner, executor, and effector) and a knowledge base. The Monitor module would record changes in behavior and would compare all values to a maximum value in a knowledge base, significant changes would be reported to an Analyzer module that determines which parameters need to be changed and by how much. Finally the Planner and Executor module are called to decide on how and when to carry out the required changes. Changes are triggered by an Effector, behavioral observations are recorded by a sensor that then transmits the data to the Monitor.

4.2 Service Transactions

Transaction management has been widely studied in the area of database management and has successfully been applied to guarantee correct execution of distributed transactions (Verma, 2005; OASIS WS-Coordination, 2008; OASIS WS-Atomic Transaction, 2008; & OASIS WS-BusinessActivity, 2008). However, one of the key differences between SOA applications and standard transactions is that in SOAs several compensating services may exist. The idea of using compensating services in SOAs, is aimed at increasing the robustness of the SOA system and allows new approaches to be used to verify correctness and security of service executions.

Service Transaction Attack: A service transaction attack occurs when the service-level dependencies that arise during the service composition process are exploited by a malicious user. Since standard transaction management techniques are not used in SOAs, preventing threats that arise due to service-level dependencies is challenging because cooperating services have no information about the workflows and so cannot determine when a global execution is faulty.

Example: Threats that service transactions face include, service invocation overload, and information starvation. As mentioned in Section 4.1, these threats exploit the fact that cooperating services typically have no information about the workflows, and the workflows have no information about the characteristics of the services, their status, or any modifications that have been made during the execution process (Hafner and Breu, 2008 & Farkas and Huhns, 2008).

Mitigation Strategies: The main concern in preventing service transaction attacks is to verify that the interacting transactions do not result in insecure states. Since multiagent approaches are typically used for implementing web services,

Figure 7. The autonomic computing feedback control loop

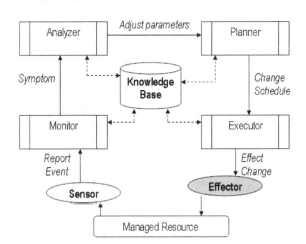

one possibility might be to record independent versions of the system (Farkas and Huhns, 2008). Each version can then be checked to ensure that the interacting transactions have not created an insecure system. In order to do this successfully, each service participating in a transaction is wrapped or "agentized" and integrated into a flexible platform that can handle multiple versions. A centralized approach would include a preprocessing algorithm to receive the input data (demand or request) and would select the best service composition to perform the task without information exposure.

The drawbacks of the multiagent approach are that the preprocessing algorithm might be flawed and its maintenance would be difficult in the SOA environment where new services are added and removed at random.

4.3 Attacks on SOAP Messages

Since web services are the most popular implementation of SOAs and SOAP is the basic protocol for transmitting messages in web services, we consider an example of a *replay attack* that involves SOAP message transmissions (Sidharth and Liu, 2007 & Viega and Epstein, 2006).

Replay Attack: This sort of attack can occur on SOAP messages in the replay attack that is similar to the ``network ping of death''. In this case the attacker issues repetitive SOAP message requests in order to overload the web service and prevent it from responding to other requests without performance delays. This type of attack will not be picked up by the intrusion detection service because the IP address being used as well as the network packet behavior and HTTP request structure are all valid.

Example: As shown in Figure 8, a valid XML-based transaction can be used to provoke a denial of service attack in our travel agent web service scenario.

Mitigation Strategies for the Replay Attack: One way of addressing the issue of replay attacks is to use a Byzantine type algorithm, where the unaffected services come to an agreement to exclude the malicious service from the composition. We can assume that, in an SOA scenario, the number of malicious nodes will generally always be much smaller than the benign nodes and so the benign nodes will be able to reach a consensus.

Figure 8. A case of a replay attack on the travel reservation Web service

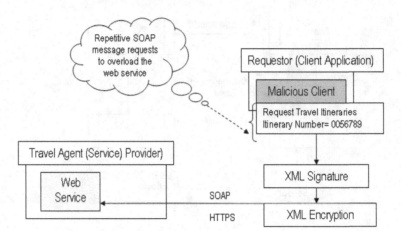

4.4 Attacks Leveraging WSDL Vulnerabilities

When SOAs are implemented using web services, another weakness they face is the *profiling attack*. Openings for profiling attacks are typically created when services of varying security levels are integrated. In these cases, the key issue is that of determining whether or not the security frameworks in the individual services were properly constructed, and whether integrating a less secure service with a more secure one does not weaken the overall security of the system.

Profiling Attack: In this case, an attacker can enumerate SOAP messages in a WSDL file and use the information gained to determine the input and output parameters of each method. Using this information the attacker can then make requests to generate SOAP faults that phish for information (Sidharth and Liu, 2007).

Example: The case shown in Figure 9 helps to highlight how weaknesses in WSDL can be exploited to provoke an attack in our travel agent web service. In this case the WSDL file stores all the critical information about the current itineraries. The web service is responsible for sharing this information on the Internet via an interface named *setCurrentItineraries* that can be defined in a WSDL file.

A closer look at this piece of code from the WSDL file shows that an attacker can look at all the methods in the WSDL file and can formulate SOAP requests that generate faults both to create errors in query responses and also get more information about the web service. This could occur if the attacker modifies the type of ``depart date'' from date to integer.

Mitigation Strategies for the Profiling Attack: In order to address profiling attacks, a security administrator in an SOA can simply design the service to prevent access to the code and implement some form of information flow control algorithm that prevents users from revealing information to unauthorized parties. However, the question of how to implement information flow control in a manner that always guarantees a secure system state in dynamically composed services remains a challenge.

4.5 Discussions

In considering existing SOA security standards, we noted that the principal focus has been on access control and how to prevent unauthorized access to data. While existing standards have come a long way in solving these issues, the inherently open nature of SOA environments indicates that access control is not enough to guarantee unauthorized

Figure 9. An example of an attack that exploits the weaknesses in a WSDL document

```
<element name = "setCurrentItineraries">
<complexType>
<sequence>
<elementname = "depart date" type = "xsd: date" />
<elementname = "trip cost" type="xsd:double" />
</sequence>
</complexType>
</element>
```

access to data. For instance, problems of inference and covert channels cannot be addressed by these existing access control tools alone. Additionally, the dynamic nature of SOA environments implies that security contexts can change during a transaction requiring that security constraints be adjusted. These adjustments are difficult to predict and hard-code into the security algorithms that support the architectures, so SOA security standards need to be extended to handle situations that require some form of adaptability.

We noted also in Section 2, that since web services are registered on the UDDI/WSIL server using a standard format (e.g. Business Entity, tModel, etc.), a set of application program interfaces (API) can be used to help in querying the registry. While this facilitates access for the users, it also has the drawback of making an attacker's job simpler because attackers can use the APIs to query the UDDI registry for specific information on a given user. The APIs work with HTTP or SOAP and extract the information from the already published WSDL file. A simple program using SOAP on a TCP/IP client enumerates or invokes the API to extract the information. This information can then be used to track all the queries that a user makes as well as the information that the user extracts. Partial information extractions can also be used to send phishing emails to the user.

In all of the above cases, the main concern is one of tracking and preventing illegal flows of information in SOAs. This problem is challenging because there is no central control and each one of the services participating in a composition, is unaware of the global impact of their executions. Perhaps a good way of establishing a globally visible picture of the effects of transaction executions would be to design some form of global distributed snapshot of a system's executions.

Researchers have also begun to explore the possibility of using language-based security approaches to specifying information flow control policies in systems (Schneider et al., 2000; & Sabefeld and Myers, 2003). In information flow security, the basic idea is to model the security system to ensure that interacting services do not execute transactions that will result in information exposure to unauthorized parties. Since access control policies suffer from the problem of Trojan Horses and other information leakages via hidden channels, standard security policies are unable to handle cases of information flow (Hutter and Volkamer, 2006). An added point worth noting is that in SOAs, there is no central authority available to fix security labels and control access globally. Interacting parties each have individual perceptions about how the data they provide will be used in executing a transaction. One of the methodologies for regulating secure transaction execution in SOAs is to use type-based information flow to control the security of dynamically computed data and its proliferation to other services (Hutter and Volkammer, 2006; & Hutter, 2006). Therefore, using language-based techniques for dynamic composition of services during transaction executions is a good way of regulating security in these scenarios.

5. FUTURE RESEARCH DIRECTIONS IN SOA SECURITY

In the discussions in Section 3, we noted that several standards exist for securing information in SOAs, but that they better suited to relatively static scenarios. We noted also that SOAs typically involve dynamic scenarios in which service interactions occur across multiple domains. In these dynamic scenarios, handling security composition guarantees requires a mechanism that automatically decides on how to combine the security requirements of the participating services to ensure an overall secure system.

Section 3.6 briefly outlined some of the strategies that have been proposed for handling security policy combinations and we pointed out that policy combination algebras and/or languages still need to be evolved to handle dynamic scenarios. One possible area of future work in SOA security standards is to find a way of addressing this concern. In Section 4.1 we pointed out that the autonomic computing paradigm presents a good way of building frameworks that incorporate predictive algorithms for enforcing security in dynamic scenarios. The autonomic model will allow a system monitor its behavior and adjust parameter settings to cope with perceived changes in the SOA environment.

As mentioned in Section 4.5, information flow security is another aspect that requires being addressed. We noted that conventional access control mechanisms are not equipped to deal with problems of information flow like inference and convert channels. Language-based information flow control tries to tackle this problem by using a number of strategies that include static analysis and type-based information flow control. These analyses can be done statically on source code or dynamically at run time. Deciding on which approach is best suited for a given context and how these approaches behave when they are combined with systems that use different security models and constraints, is an area for future work.

6. CONCLUSION

Throughout this chapter our focus has been on SOA security standards and the challenges that they face specifically in dynamic scenarios. We noted that while a wide variety of security standards exist for protecting SOAs, their principal focus has been on access control in relatively static scenarios. Increasingly, however, scenarios that involve dynamic service compositions and interacting transactions create openings for violations of data confidentiality and integrity that these access control mechanisms are not equipped to handle.

We highlighted a number of security snares that SOAs, and web services in particular, face pointing out why the vulnerabilities exist and emphasizing their impact with examples based on the travel reservation web service scenario that we outlined in Section 2 (see Figure 5). In each case we noted that even when current standards include tools that can be used to prevent the vulnerability; the open nature of SOAs and the property of loose coupling indicate that problems like inference and covert channels still remain. The mitigation strategies we proposed are centered on two main themes – *predictive models* and *fault tolerance*. We noted however, during our discussion in Section 5 that each of the mitigation strategies proposed has inherent weaknesses that will need to be addressed in order to provide meaningful security in SOAs in general and dynamic SOA compositions in particular.

ACKNOWLEDGMENT

I would like to gratefully acknowledge the extensive comments that Dieter Hutter made on an earlier draft of this chapter. Without his feedback and invaluable insights, this chapter would likely not have matured. Special thanks also to the reviewers and editors for their patience in reviewing and editing the chapter to fit within the context of the book.

REFERENCES

Al-Kahtani, M. A., & Sandhu, R. (2003). Induced Role Hierarchies with Attribute-Based RBAC. In *Proceedings of the 9th ACM Symposium on Access Control Models and Technologies*, (pp. 142-148). New York: ACM Press.

Alonso, G., Casati, F., Kuno, H., & Machiraju, V. (2004). *Web Services: Concepts, Architectures, and Applications*. Springer-Verlag, Berlin.

Alonso, R., & Larrucea, X. (2008) ISOAS: Through an Independent SOA Security Specification. In *Proceedings of the 7th International Conference on Composition-Based Software Systems*, (pp. 92-100). Washington, DC: IEEE Computer Society.

Bertino, E., Jajodia, S., & Samarati, P. (1999). A Flexible Authorization Mechanism for Relational Data Management Systems. *ACM Transactions on Information Systems*, *17*(2), 101–140. doi:10.1145/306686.306687

Blaze, M., Feigenbaum, J., & Lacy, J. (1996) Decentralized Trust Management. In *Proceedings of the IEEE Symposium on Security and Privacy*, (pp. 164 - 173). Washington, DC: IEEE Computer Society

Boehm, O., Caumanns, J., Franke, M., & Pfaff, O. (2008). Federated Authentication and Authorization: A Case Study. In *Proceedings of the 12th International IEEE Enterprise Distributed Object Computing Conference*, (pp. 356 - 362). Washington, DC: IEEE Computer Society.

Bonatti, P., De Capitani Di Vimercati, S., & Samarati, P. (2000). A Modular Approach to Composing Access Control Policies. In *Proceedings of the 7th ACM Conference on Computer and Communication Security (CCS 2000)*, (pp.164 - 173). New York: ACM Press.

Bonatti, P., De Capitani Di Vimercati, S., & Samarati, P. (2002). An Algebra for Composing Access Control Policies. *ACM Transactions on Information and System Security*, *5*(1), 1–35. doi:10.1145/504909.504910

Buecker, A., Ashley, P., Borrett, M., Lu, M., Muppidi, S., & Readshaw, N. (2007). *Understanding SOA Design and Implementation*. Redmond, WA: IBM Redbooks.

Chandramouli, R. (2003). A Policy Validation Framework for Enterprise Authorization Specification. In *Proceedings of the 19th Annual Computer Security Applications Conference*, (pp. 319 - 328). Washington, DC: IEEE Computer Society.

Chinnici, R., Moreau, J., Ryman, A., & Weerawarana, S. (2007). *Web Services Description Language (WSDL), v2.0*. June 2007, from http://www.w3.org/TR/wsdl20/

Clement, L., Hately, A., Riegen, C. V., & Rogers, T. (2004). *Universal Description Discovery and Integration (UDDI), version 3.0.2*. OASIS Standard 200502. Retrieved from http://www.uddi.orge/pub/uddi-v3.htm

Cover, R. (2002). *Web Services Inspection Language (WSIL)*. Retrieved from http://xml.coverpages.org/wsil.html

Crampton, J., Lim, H. W., & Paterson, K. G. (2007). What can Identity-Based Cryptography Offer to Web Services. In [New York: ACM Press.]. *Proceedings of SWS*, *07*, 26–36. doi:10.1145/1314418.1314424

Crispo, B., Nair, S. K., Djordjevic, I., & Dimitrakos, T. (2007). Secure Web Service Federation Management Using TPM Virtualization. In *Proceedings of the 2007 ACM workshop on Secure Web Services*, (pp. 73-82). New York: ACM.

DeLooze, L. (2008). Providing Web Service Security in a federated Environment. [Washington, DC: IEEE Educational Activities Department.]. *IEEE Security and Privacy, 5*(1), 73–75. doi:10.1109/MSP.2007.16

Elliott Bell, D. (1994). Modeling the Multipolicy Machine. In *Proceedings of the New security Paradigm Workshop*, (pp. 2-9). Washington, DC: IEEE Computer Society Press.

Epstein, J., Masumoto, S., & McGraw, G. (2006). Software security and SOA: Danger, Will Robinson. [Washington, DC: IEEE Educational Activities Department.]. *IEEE Security and Privacy, 4*(1), 80. doi:10.1109/MSP.2006.23

Farkas, C., & Huhns, M. N. (2008). Securing Enterprise Applications: Service-Oriented Security (SOS). In *Proceedings of the 10th IEEE Conference on E-Commerce Technology and the 5th IEEE Conference on Enterprise Computing, E-Commerce and E-Services,* (pp. 428-431). Washington, DC: IEEE Computer Society.

Gross, T. (2003). Security Analysis of the SAML Single Sign-on Browser/Artifact Profile. In *Proceedings of the 19th Annual Computer Security Applications Conference*, (pp. 298). Washington, DC: IEEE Computer Society.

Gudgin, M., Hadley, M., Mendelsohn, N., Moreau, J., Nielsen, H. F., Karmarkar, A., & Lafon, Y. (2007). *Simple Object Access Protocol (SOAP) version 1.2*. Retrieved from http://www.w3.org/TR/soap/

Hafner, M., & Breu, R. (2008). *Security Engineering for Service-Oriented Architectures*. Springer-Verlag: Berlin Heidelberg.

Hosmer, H. (1992). Metapolicies I. *ACM SIGSAC Review, 10*(2-3), 18–43. doi:10.1145/147092.147097

Hu, V. C., Martin, E., Hwang, J., & Xie, T. (2007). Conformance Checking of Access Control Policies Specified in XACML. In *Proceedings of the 31st Annual International Computer Software and Applications Conference* – (Vol. 02, pp. 275-280). Washington, DC: IEEE Computer Society.

Huhns, M. N., & Singh, M. P. (2005). Service-Oriented Computing: Key Concepts and Principles. *IEEE Internet Computing, 9*(1), 75–81. doi:10.1109/MIC.2005.21

Hutter, D. (2006). Possibilistic Information Flow Control in MAKS and Action Refinement. In *Energing Trends in Information and Communication Security*, (LNCS 3995, pp. 268-281). Berlin: Springer.

Hutter, D., & Volkamer, M. (2006). Information Flow Control to secure Dynamic Web-Service Composition. In *Proceedings of the 3rd International Conference on security in Pervasive Computing, SPC-2006*, York, UK, (LNCS Vol. 3934, pp.196-210). Berlin: Springer-Verlag.

Jaeger, T. (2001). Access Control in Configurable Systems. In *Secure Internet programming: security issues for mobile and distributed objects*, (LNCS, Vol. 1603, pp. 289-316). Berlin: Springer-Verlag.

Jajodia, S., Samarati, P., Sapino, M. L., & Subrahmanian, V. S. (2001). A Unified Framework for Supporting Multiple Access Control Policies. *ACM Transactions on Database Systems, 26*(2), 214–260. doi:10.1145/383891.383894

Kemp, J., Cantor, S., Mishra, P., Philpott, R., & Maler, E. (2005). *Assertions and Protocols for the OASIS Security Assertion Markup Language (SAML) version 2.0*. OASIS Standard 200503. Retrieved from http://xml.coverpages.org/ni2005-03-14-a.html

Kleijnen, S., & Raju, S. (2003). An Open Web Services Architecture. *Queue, 1*(1), 38–46. doi:10.1145/637958.637961

Krawczyk, H. (2001). The Order of Encryption and Authentication for Protecting Communications (or: How Secure is SSL?). In *Advances in Cryptology - CRYPTO 2001: 21ˢᵗ Annual International Cryptology Conference*, Santa Barbara, CA (LNCS Vol. 3934). Berlin: Springer-Verlag.

Li, J., & Karp, A. H. (2007). Access Control for the Service Oriented Architecture. In *Proceedings of the 2007 ACM workshop on Secure Web Services*, (pp. 9-17). New York: ACM.

Li, N., Feigenbaum, J., & Grosof, B. (1999). A Logic-Based Knowledge Representation for Authorization with Delegation. In *Proceedings of the 12ᵗʰ IEEE Computer Security Foundations Workshop* (pp.162-174). Washington, DC: IEEE Computer Society.

Li, N., & Wang, Q. (2008). Beyond separation of duty: An algebra for specifying high-level security policies. *Journal of the ACM, 55*(3), 12. doi:10.1145/1379759.1379760

Liu, P., & Chen, Z. (2004) An Access Control Model for Web Services in Business Process. In *Proceedings of the 2004 IEEE/WIC/ACM International Conference on Web Intelligence,* (pp. 292-298). Washington, DC: IEEE Computer Society

Lopez, J., Oppliger, R., & Pernul, G. (2004). Authentication and Authorization Infrastructures (AAIs): A Comparative Survey. *Computers & Security, 23*, 578–590. doi:10.1016/j.cose.2004.06.013

McLean, J. (1988) The Algebra of Security. In *Proceedings of the 1988 IEEE Computer Society Symposium on Security and Privacy*, Oakland, CA, (pp.2-7). Washington, DC: IEEE Computer Society.

Nadalin, A., Kaler, C., Monzillo, R., & Hallam-Baker, P. (2007). *Web Services Security: SOAP Message Security 1.1 (WS-Security 2004) OASIS Standard 200703*. Retrieved from http://www.oasis-open.org/committees/download.php/3281/WSS-OAPMessageSecurity-17-082703-merged.pdf

Newcomer, E. (2002). *Understanding Web Services: XML, WSDL, SOAP, and UDDI*. Reading, MA: Addison-Wesley Professional.

OASIS Web Services Atomic Transaction (WS-Atomic Transaction). (2008). Retrieved from http://www.oasis-open.org/committees/tc_home.php?wg_abbrev=wsbpel

OASIS Web Services Business Activity (WS-BusinessActivity). (2008). Retrieved from http://www.oasis-open.org/committees/tc_home.php?wg_abbrev=wsbpel

OASIS Web Services Coordination (WS-Coordination). (2008). Retrieved from http://docs.oasis-open.or/wstx/wscoor/2006/06

Papazoglou, M. P., & Van den Heuvel, W.-J. (2007). Service Oriented Architectures: Approaches, Technologies, and Research Issues. *The VLDB Journal, 16*(3), 389–415. doi:10.1007/s00778-007-0044-3

Parducci, B., Lockhart, H., Levinson, R., Clark, J. B., & McRae, M. (2008). *eXtensible Access Control Markup Language (XACML) version 2.0*. OASIS Standard 200502. Retrieved from http://www.oasis-open.org/committees/tc_home.php?wg_abbrev=xacml

Sabelfeld, A., & Myers, A. C. (2003). Language-Based Information Flow Security. *IEEE Journal on Selected Areas in Communications, 21*(1), 1–15. doi:10.1109/JSAC.2002.806121

Schneider, F. B., Morrisett, G., & Harper, R. (2000). A Language-Based Approach to Security. *Informatics – 10 Years Back, 10 Years Ahead, (LNCS)*. Heidelberg, Germany: Springer-Verlag.

Sidharth, N., & Liu, J. (2007). IAPF: A Framework for Enhancing Web Services Security. In *Proceedings of the 31st Annual International Computer Software and Applications Conference (COMPSAC 2007)*, (Vol. 01, pp. 23-30). Washington, DC: IEEE Computer Society.

Sohr, K., Mustafa, T., Bao, X., & Ahn, G.-J. (2008). Enforcing Role-Based Access Control Policies in Web Services with UML and OCL. In *Proceedings of the 2008 Annual Computer Security Applications Conference*, (pp. 257-266). Washington, DC: IEEE Computer Society.

Tang, K., Chen, S., Zic, J., & Levy, D. (2007). Performance Evaluation and Modeling of Web Services Security. In *Proceedings of the 2007 IEEE International Conference on Web Services (ICWS 2007)*, (pp. 431-438). Washington, DC: IEEE Computer Society.

Thuraisingham, B., She, W., & I-Ling, Y. (2007). Delegation-Based Security Model for Web Services. In *Proceedings of the 10th IEEE High Assurance Systems Engineering Symposium*, (pp. 82-91). Washington, DC: IEEE Computer Society.

Ventuneac, M., Coffey, T., & Salomie, I. (2003). A Policy-Based Security Framework for Web-Enabled Applications. In *Proceedings of the 1st International Symposium on Information and Communication Technologies*, (pp. 487-492). Dublin: Trinity College.

Verma, M. (2004). *XML Security: Control Information Access with XACML*. Retrieved from http://www.ibm.com/developerworks/xml/library/x-xacml/

Verma, M. (2005). *Web Services Transactions*. Armonk, NY: IBM Publications.

Viega, J., & Epstein, J. (2006). Why applying Standards to Web Services is not Enough. *IEEE Security and Privacy, 4*(4), 25–31. doi:10.1109/MSP.2006.110

Woo, T., & Lam, S. (1993). Authorizations in Distributed Systems: A New Approach. *Journal of Computer Security, 2*(2,3), 107-136.

ADDITIONAL READINGS

Buecker, A. Ashley, P., Borrett, M., Lu, M., Muppidi, S., & Readshaw, N. (2008). Understanding SOA Security Design and Implementation. IBM Redbooks.

Dreibelbis, A., Milman, I., Van Run, P., Hechler, E., Oberhofer, M., & Wolfson, D. (2008) Enterprise Master Data Management: An SOA Approach to Managing Core Information. IBM Press.

Hafner, M., & Breu, R. (2008). Security Engineering for Service-Oriented Architectures. Springer-Verlag, Berlin Heidelberg.

Kanneganti, R., & Chodavarapu, P. (2008). SOA Security. Manning Publications.

Pfleeger, C. P., & Pfleeger, S. L. Security in Computing. 3rd ed., Pearson Education, Prentice Hall NJ, 2003

Shah, S. (2007). Web 2.0 Security: Defending Ajax, RIA, and SOA. Course Technology PTR.

Vakali, A., & Pallis, G. (2007). Web Data Management Practices: Emerging Techniques and Technologies. IGI Publishing.

Section 4
Web Services Security Threats and Countermeasures

Chapter 10
A Survey of Attacks in the Web Services World

Meiko Jensen
Ruhr-University Bochum, Germany

Nils Gruschka
NEC Europe Ltd., Germany

ABSTRACT

In the modern electronic business world, services offered to business partners as well as to customers have become an important company asset. This again produces interests for attacking those services either to paralyze the availability or to gain unauthorized access. Though founding on decades of networking experience, Web Services are not more resistant to security attacks than other open network systems. Quite the opposite is true: Web Services are exposed to attacks well-known from common Internet protocols and additionally to new kinds of attacks targeting Web Services in particular. This chapter presents a survey of different types of such Web Service specific attacks. For each attack a description of the attack execution, the effect on the target and partly the results of practical experiments are given. Additionally, general countermeasures for fending Web Service attacks are shown.

INTRODUCTION

The rising adoption of service-orientation both in industry and academia also triggered a hype on its most prominent realization technique: the Web Services technology (Weerawarana, Curbera, Leymann, Storey, & Ferguson, 2005). Nevertheless, as with all distributed software systems, a wide spread of a particular technology also attracts individuals and organizations that try to exploit such systems

for their personal benefits. Thus, in order to cope with such general security threats, every particular technology needs a specialized, appropriate security concept in order to fend attacks and mitigate security-related business risks.

For the particular case of Web Services, a large number of security-related specifications have been released by the leading standardization organizations, each targeting a special aspect of Web Services security. These specifications cover confidentiality and message integrity issues (Nadalin, Kaler, Monzillo, & Hallam-Baker, 2006), access control

DOI: 10.4018/978-1-60566-950-2.ch010

Table 1. A list of attacks covered in this chapter

Oversize Payload	Instantiation Flooding
Coercive Parsing	Signature Wrapping
Attack Obfuscation	XML Injection
Flooding Attacks	WS-Addressing Spoofing
State Deviation	Metadata Spoofing

and authorization for Web Service invocations (Moses, 2005), reliability for guaranteed message delivery (Ferris & Langworthy, 2005), trust establishment between cooperating organizations (Nadalin, Goodner, Gudgin, & Barbir, 2007; Nadalin & Kaler, 2006) and a lot more.

Nevertheless, the field of security for Web Services includes a lot more issues than what is currently addressed by the existing standards. As an example, the number, types and impact capabilities of known attacks on Web Services raised by far during the last years (Lindstrom, 2004). Apart from general threats like malicious Internet Service Provider employees or hijacked SOAP intermediate hosts, some very skilled, Web-Service-specific attacks have been discovered.

In this chapter, we provide a survey on some of the most severe attack types disclosed yet (cf. Table 1). We give detailed descriptions on the concepts behind the attacks, discuss their potential impact in a real-world SOA, and in the end, a brief summary on appropriate countermeasures is also presented.

The chapter is organized as follows. In the next section, the basic concepts of network based attacks are presented. Then, a list of attacks on Web Services is introduced, followed by an in-depth description on each of these attacks. Each attack description covers the attack idea, the scenario requirements, the vulnerabilities that are to be exploited, and a brief example illustrating the attack concepts. The discussion of potential countermeasures was omitted intentionally in the attack descriptions, as it is briefly done in the succeeding section. More detailed countermeasures

can be found in the literature references for the specific attack types. Finally, the chapter concludes with a general statement on the chapter's topics and some future work directions.

BACKGROUND OF NETWORK ATTACKS

In Figure 1 a typical network and application processing stack for invocations of a Web Service is shown. Every incoming message is first processed by the host's TCP/IP stack. Then, the message is passed to the application server, which commonly includes the Web Service framework. Inside the Web Service framework the message is first parsed and transformed into an in-memory representation (e.g. a DOM tree). After that, the SOAP Message Processing (e.g. WS-Addressing evaluation) and the Security Processing (mainly processing WS-Security extension, e.g. decryption of encrypted message parts or signature validation) is performed. Finally, the Web Service application logic is executed with the Web Service call contained inside the SOAP body.

As shown in Figure 1, a network service can be invoked by arbitrary users including attackers (assuming the service call is not blocked by an external instance like a firewall). Such a network based attack can target on different components inside the network or application processing stack. Well known are attacks targeting the TCP/IP stack or the HTTP handling inside the application server, e.g. Ping-of-Death (Insecure.org, 1996), TCP SYN Flooding (Schuba, Krsul, Kuhn, Spafford,

Figure 1. Web Service message processing components and threat model

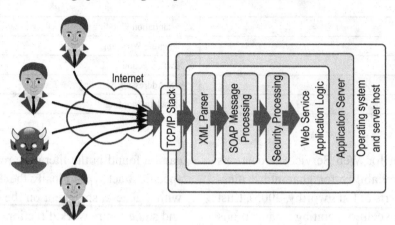

Sundaram, & Zamboni, 1997) or Cookie Poisoning (Haldar, Chandra, & Franz, 2005). Such attacks threaten all services using these components, e.g. Web applications.

Web Services are of course vulnerable to those attacks but additionally to attacks targeting on the Web Service specific processing components. Below, a number of attacks are presented which target different parts of the Web Service processing chain. E.g., the Coercive Parsing attack targets on the XML Parser.

The analysis of attacks regarding their targeted processing component is also important when developing countermeasures. Obviously, a countermeasure can only protect from attacks targeting at processing components at the same or a higher layer than the one the countermeasure is installed. As an example, a Web Service access control (performed by the Web Service Security Processing) can not protect from TCP SYN Flooding attacks.

ATTACKS ON WEB SERVICES

One of the most problematic issues of Web Services is that by default they are open to anybody within the same network. Thus, an attacker that is located within the same network as its target

Web Service can easily address, connect, and communicate with that Web Service directly. This obviously includes the Internet, but may also concern local intranets that are not accessible from the outside.

Though this issue can be addressed by several means (most prominently access control mechanisms), it is nearby impossible to prevent all kinds of attacks on Web Services completely. First of all, access control just reduces the number of potential attackers to those users who are allowed to access a particular Web Service. This does not imply that none of the legitimate users can become an attacker itself. Additionally, access control mechanisms can be circumvented or even misused by an attack.

Attacks on Web Services can roughly be classified according to their intended impact. A prominent subtype is that of the so-called Denial of Service attacks, which target at eliminating a Web Service's availability.

Denial of Service

The basic principle behind any kind of Denial of Service attack is to get the targeted system to a state where it is not able to further perform its intended task. This can for example be achieved through knowledge of a certain implementation weakness of the server-side application, causing the application to crash completely, or it can be caused by creating an enormous load on a particular limited resource of the server system. Most prominent resource types for the latter kind of attacks are CPU cycles, main memory, and network connection bandwidth. While the most common Denial of Service attacks of today reside on the network layer, targeting at bandwidth exhaustion, the more sophisticated attacks on the Web Service level aim at bringing down the computational resources of the targeted system. Such kinds of attacks are to be described in detail in the following sections.

Oversize Payload

With this type of attack, an attacker tries to exhaust the memory resources of the Web Service system by sending extremely large SOAP messages. Sending oversized protocol instances is a classic way for Denial of Service attacks, but with Web Services this procedure gets new importance as the effect is by far higher than with non-XML services.

As Web Service messages are represented as XML documents, they automatically include the whole complexity level that XML document handling arises. This leads to high memory consumption. Especially in Web Service frameworks that use a tree-based XML processing model (e.g. the well-known DOM tree model) the amount of memory required for processing a Web Service request is much higher than the request message size. This amplification factor is between 2 and 30 for common Web Service frameworks, depending on implementation details and the structure of the SOAP message. A large number of elements with small or no text content consumes more memory than few elements with large text content.

Many Web Service interface descriptions allow arbitrary large messages. In these cases, the attacker can construct an oversized SOAP message, which is completely compliant to the interface description, i.e. valid according to the services schema definition. First of all, XML data types like xsd:string or xsd:anyURI allow creating valid messages with arbitrary large text nodes. Additionally, a lot of interface descriptions include constructs that allow an unlimited number of element nodes. As stated before, such messages are even more dangerous when used during an *Oversized Payload* attack. The most common construct in this sense are unlimited lists of elements. This is defined inside the Web Service descriptions schema using the maxOccurs attribute <xsd:element maxOccurs="unbounded" ...> .

A survey of freely accessible Web Services descriptions listed on XMethods.net showed that around 45% of these Web Services include an unlimited element list.

But even if the Web Service description defines only message of limited size, the *Oversized Payload* attack can be successful. This is a result of the message processing procedures. Many Web Service frameworks perform only loose or even no syntactical checks on incoming SOAP messages. Figure 2 shows a SOAP message containing a simple *Oversized Payload* attack.

Such a message with 100.000 items was used for an experimental attack on a Web Service running Apache Axis. For processing the attack request, the system required around 50 MByte. As the serialized request message document was around 1.8 MByte, the resulting amplification factor for this attack (Jensen, Gruschka, & Luttenberger, 2008; Jensen & Gruschka, 2008) is about 28.

Coercive Parsing

Coercive Parsing attacks are targeting the XML parser and trying to induce a high resource consumption on the Web Service system. There are different types of *Coercive Parsing* attacks. The simplest form uses a message with a very deeply nested XML tree structure (see the sample attack below). For most Web Services, such a message

Figure 2. An example SOAP message for an Oversize Payload attack

```
<env:Envelope>
  <env:Body>
    <order>
      <item>12345</item>
      <item>12345</item>
      <item>12345</item>
      ...
    </order>
  <env:Body>
<env:Envelope>
```

is not valid according to the interface description. Thus, this kind of attack is only successful if the XML schema validity is not checked during reading the message from the network.

There are other forms of the *Coercive Parsing* attack, which are not subject to this restriction. The attack messages contain constructs, which according to the XML specification are valid in every XML document. Thus, the messages are always protocol compliant, independent from the Web Service description. As an example, the XML standard itself does not restrict the length of namespace prefixes nor the length of namespace URIs nor the number of prefix definitions. As the parser must store all prefix definitions during message processing, a possible *Coercive Parsing* attack consists in sending a message with a large number of needless prefix definitions.

Additionally, an attack message can contain references on (possibly large) external DTDs. The

Figure 3. Example Coercive Parsing attack

```
<soap:Envelope>
  <soap:Header />
  <soap:Body>
    <x>
      <x>
        <x>
        ...
```

parser is required to download and process these DTDs, consuming processing time and memory. The usage of DTDs is explicitly excluded for Web Services. However, a lot of XML parsers inside the Web Service frameworks support DTDs, and therefore this type of *Coercive Parsing* (which is called *Entity Expansion*) can still be successful.

As an example, a Web Service running Apache Axis was attacked using a message that contained a non-ending sequence of opening tags, as shown in Figure 3.

This message induced a full CPU load on the attacked system. The connection was not closed by the server. Thus, the attack could have been continued endlessly. Additionally, the server was only able to process the message stream with 150 Byte/s. Thus, this attack could also have been performed using connections with an extremely small bandwidth.

Attack Obfuscation

Protection of confidential information during transport from being eavesdropped is one of the major security aims. For SOAP messages, confidentiality is typically realized using the WS-Security specification. This means that message fragments containing secret information are replaced by an XML encryption element that contains the encrypted form of the original fragment together with some meta information. A typical usage is encrypting the content of the SOAP body.

While confidentiality is an important feature for most Web Services, message encryption can be misused for attacks by hiding malicious elements inside the encrypted message parts. This is called *Attack Obfuscation*. The effect of this attack is twofold. First, all intermediate systems which are not capable of XML encryption (e.g. simple XML firewall) or which are not in possession of the decryption key cannot inspect the encrypted content, and therefore are not able to detect the attack.

Secondly, before the malicious content can be detected, plenty resources are consumed for decryption. A typical tree-based procedure for handling XML encryption works as follows: the complete message is read, parsed and transformed into a DOM tree; all information needed for decryption are collected from the tree; the encrypted part is decrypted, parsed and transformed into a (new) DOM tree. Not until this point (i.e. after spending a lot of memory and processing resources) the encrypted content can be validated and a possible attack can be detected.

The following experimental attack was carried out towards a Web Service system running Apache Axis2 with Apache Rampart for WS-Security support. A SOAP message with large operation parameters (around 1 MByte) was created, and the content of the SOAP body was encrypted using WS-Security. The target Web Service system needed 90 MByte of additional memory for processing this message, resulting in an amplification factor of 90. Thus, with relatively small messages, a very large memory consumption can be induced.

Flooding Attacks

Apart from the approach of exploiting a request message's syntax in order to perform a Denial of Service effect on a certain Web Service server, it is also possible to cause a similar effect using syntactically valid requests. The key idea here is to create a large number of request messages with syntactically valid, but semantically nonsense data, and use them to flood the Web Service server. Depending on the application behind the Web Service endpoint, this approach can have two kinds of possible impacts: either the nonsense requests violate a certain semantic requirement or they are considered as valid requests, triggering a full execution of the server application behind the Web Service. Examples of these two classes will be discussed next.

State Deviation

This attack (as an example of the first class of flooding attacks) depends on a server-side application that uses more than one Web Service endpoint for providing a specific task. This is a very common approach in business process implementations, where the process workflow consists of retrieving and delivering data items from and to business partners.

As an example, consider the business process for performing an order at an online shopping system as shown in Figure 4. The process workflow consists of several input messages (triggering a new shopping session, adding items to the shopping cart, specifying billing and shipping information, and finally confirming the order) and appropriate internal actions and output messages (requesting product data and stock capacities, ordering a shipping arrangement, creating an invoice). Such a workflow can easily be realized with Web Services technology, e.g. using the Business Process Execution Language for Web Services (Jordan et al., 2007).

Due to the fact that a BPEL-based process engine performs lots of process instances (here: separate orders) at the same time, all Web Service communication endpoints need to be accessible at all times. This condition can be exploited for performing the so-called *State Deviation* attacks. The basic idea of these attacks is to send a huge amount of messages to a Web Service endpoint that is not intended to be called in the actual state of the corresponding process instance. For example, an attacker may flood the order confirmation Web Service operation for a process instance that still resides in the state of adding items to the shopping cart. Then, the state of the server application does not correspond to the state claimed in the attack messages. Thus, the process execution engine has to identify this state deviation, and reject the attack messages gracefully. As this task requires full message processing and process instance correlation operations, it is very likely to cause

Figure 4. An example for a State Deviation attack

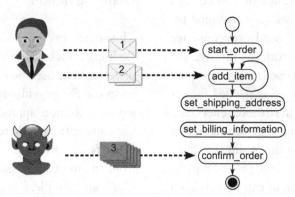

a heavy load on the process engine. An in-depth discussion and evaluation on this kind of attacks is given by Gruschka, Jensen, & Luttenberger (2007, 2008).

Additionally, the potential impact of the State Deviation attack obviously also covers the possibility for violations of execution safety. In case that the BPEL application itself can be tricked to assume that the State Deviation messages truly belong to the addressed communication session, the application logic may decide to process these messages accordingly. For the example given, this would imply having an order submitted that does contain neither a shipping address nor billing information. Additionally, once the real user tries to continue the attacked session, he may end up in a fault message, as the server-side application already closed the session context.

Instantiation Flooding

The second class of flooding attacks covers all kinds of service invocations that do not violate any technical server-side restrictions, neither syntactically nor sequentially. Thus, such an attack usually consists of completely valid service invocations that just do not serve any purpose but to create workload at the Web Service server host. Reconsidering the example from Figure 4, a flood of valid requests for the start_order operation would be an example for such an *Instantiation*

Flooding attack. For this particular scenario, the result of the attack would be that the server application (i.e. the BPEL engine) has to create and manage a new process instance for every request message. Obviously, as none of these sessions will be used for submitting a valid order, the number of running process instances at the server will increase rapidly, allocating lots of main memory. Thus, the attack may lead to a complete memory exhaustion, causing the Denial of Service effect intended by the attacker.

Another aspect of the *Instantiation Flooding* approach is that due to the validity of the attack request messages, the Web Service server triggers the full service execution for each single attack request. Depending on the intention and implementation details of the workflow, this may include outgoing Web Service calls to other hosts. This way, the workload caused by the attack messages may be spread among the whole set of server systems that are involved in the business process execution itself. Thus, the Denial of Service effect does not necessarily happen to the server directly targeted by the attacker, but may also reach other, nested servers that are utilized within the workflow (Jensen & Schwenk, 2009).

Signature Wrapping

According to the XML Digital Signature and WS-Security specifications (Bartel, Boyer,

Fox, LaMacchia, & Simon, 2002), any part of a SOAP message can be digitally signed, ensuring its originator's identity and data integrity to the server. By verifying the digital signatures within a SOAP message the server gains confidence that the signed message parts originate from a certain entity (that is in possession of a particular secret cryptographic key) and were not modified by any intermediaries since the message bypassed that originator.

Though it is a possible approach to sign the complete SOAP message as a whole, this approach has its issues in that no succeeding SOAP intermediate is able to add or remove any SOAP header information (such as WS-Addressing endpoints) without invalidating the digital signature. Thus, a better approach consists in having the digital signature enclose the SOAP message body only. An example SOAP message that illustrates this common approach is shown in Figure 5.

An important concept of WS-Security-based digital signatures on SOAP messages is that it is possible to have more than one digital signature within the same message, e.g. having different parts of the message be signed by different entities. Thus, it is possible to have more than one Signature header within the Security header element, each describing a different signature for a particular message part. In order to avoid linking problems, the WS-Security specification clearly states rules for such a scenario, prescribing that every signature metadata block must contain a direct, doubtless reference to all the message parts it covers. This referencing scheme is essential for understanding the attack approach of *Signature Wrapping*.

According to the XML Signature specification (Bartel, Boyer, Fox, LaMacchia, & Simon, 2002) the Reference element contains an attribute URI value of type xsd:anyURI that refers to the document to be signed, which in the case of SOAP messages usually is the message document itself (which is represented by an empty string). This URL reference usually refers to the document root, but it can be extended by using the *fragment* part of the URL (the part following the # character). Using this fragment token as identifier, an element within the document that is intended to be signed

Figure 5. A (simplified) sample SOAP message with signed Body element

```
<Envelope>
  <Header>
    <Security>
      <Signature>
        <SignedInfo>
          <CanonicalizationMethod Algorithm="http://...c14n11"/>
          <SignatureMethod Algorithm="http://...#dsa-sha1"/>
          <Reference URI="#myBody">
            <DigestMethod Algorithm="http://...#sha1"/>
            <DigestValue>dGhpcyBpcyBub3QgY...</DigestValue>
          </Reference>
        </SignedInfo>
        <SignatureValue>gHsDfgHHjtdd4...</SignatureValue>
      </Signature>
    </Security>
  </Header>
  <Body Id="myBody">
    <deleteUser>
      <Username>johnDoe</Username>
    </deleteUser>
  </Body>
</Envelope>
```

can be extended with an Id attribute that contains a value equal to the fragment token (the myBody token in Figure 5). This way, a URL reference of #myId refers to the single element within the same document that contains an attribute Id of value myId. Note that this identifier is required to be unique within the document.

As McIntosh & Austel pointed out (2005), this approach of referencing with Id values is vulnerable to a specific type of attack: it is possible to move a signed element within a document, without breaking the signature value. This is due to the fact that the Id referencing does not require the signed element to be placed at a particular position within the document. By itself, this issue tends to be harmless, but for the particular case of Web Service messages, it raises a severe security issue. This issue consists in that the Web Service framework takes the operation and data elements to be used for a particular Web Service invocation from the child element of the Body element as defined by the SOAP specification. This procedure is based on the message structure rather than on a particular Id attribute, thus the referencing schemes for signature validation and Web Service application logic differ.

An example of how to exploit this vulnerability is shown in Figures 6 and 7. The idea is to move the whole Body element and all of its contents to another location within the SOAP message, e.g. to a new Dummy header, and replace them with a new, attacker-defined Body element with malicious invocation information (e.g. for executing a different Web Service operation). As a result, the security logic at the Web Service server will resolve the signature reference (which now points to the element within the Dummy header), verify the digital signature, and conclude that the request is originated by an authorized entity. Thus, it delivers the SOAP message to the core Web Service framework, which will examine the child element of Body in order to determine the operation to perform. As a result, the attacker can perform an arbitrary request on behalf of someone else.

XML Injection

The idea of the *XML Injection* attack (Jensen, Gruschka, Herkenhöner, & Luttenberger, 2007) is similar to the well-known SQL Injection attacks (Anley, 2002), where a missing verification of user input data may enable the attacker to edit and rewrite an SQL statement according to his intentions. Here, the attacker does not inject SQL statements, but XML fragments.

The scenario for this kind of attacks involves a Web Service server application, and a Web Service client gathering parameters for the request from a user input (e.g. a GUI or a Web front-end). Here,

Figure 6. SOAP message structure before the Signature Wrapping attack

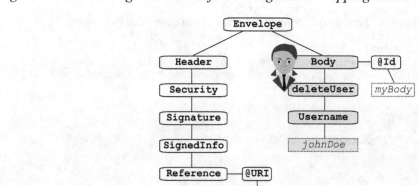

the client application is considered as a trusted terminal, i.e. the Web Service server only accepts requests that directly originate from the client application. Thus, an attacker cannot access the Web Service server interface directly, and can only influence the data fields entered at the client application's GUI.

The XML Injection approach now consists in that an attacker enters special XML fragments as data values in the client GUI's text fields. If the client application fails to verify that the entered text fragment does not contain any XML code, it may place these malicious XML contents in the outgoing SOAP messages as plain text. As a result, the XML parser at the server side will treat these newly inserted XML tags as XML elements, and process them not as character data values, but as XML elements of the SOAP message.

An example for such an attack and the resulting SOAP message is given in Figure 8. Though the contents of the CustomerName data field are intended to be plain text characters only, the client-side application fails to verify that it does not contain any XML contents. This is exploited by the attacker, who enters the string shown in Figure 9 into the appropriate input field.

As a result, the given SOAP message is sent over the network, and the server-side XML parser now identifies two occurrences of the Customer-Name element and an additional element called isPremiumMember. If the server application can be tricked this way, the attacker can perform a premium member action (e.g. order goods with premium member discount) while not being a premium member at all.

A variant of this attack consists in adding a new element (just like the isPremiumMember element above) that overwrites an existing element of the SOAP message document. By injecting a new <TotalAmount>0.01</TotalAmount> element into an online order form, the existing TotalAmount element that states the true sum of amounts as calculated by the client application may become overridden, and the attacker is charged one cent only instead of the true prices for the goods he ordered. This variant relies on the server-side condition that the message processing application can be tricked not to be alerted on the double occurrence of the TotalAmount element, and that it accepts the injected element as the truth (e.g. due to the fact that it occurred first in document order, some versions of the Microsoft

Figure 7. SOAP message structure after the Signature Wrapping attack

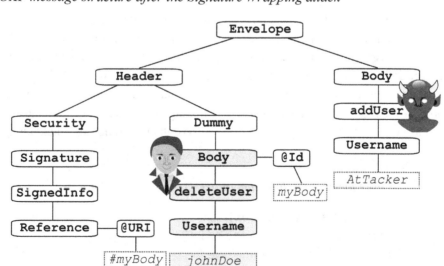

Figure 8. An example SOAP message containing an XML Injection attack

```
<Envelope>
  <Header />
  <Body>
    <createNewCustomer>
      <CustomerName>
        John Doe</CustomerName>
        <isPremiumMember>yes</isPremiumMember>
        <CustomerName>John Doe
      </CustomerName>
      <CustomerID>12345</CustomerID>
    </createNewCustomer>
  </Body>
</Envelope>
```

.NET frameworks are known to process SOAP messages this way).

WS-Addressing Spoofing

One of the main purposes of the WS-Addressing specification is to enable asynchronous Web Service invocations, where the request and response messages are not required to be transmitted using the same transportation channel (e.g. the same TCP connection). This becomes necessary for long-running service invocations, where the calculation time of the server-side application exceeds the lifetime of a single TCP connection by far.

The approach taken in the specification consists in embedding a specific ReplyTo address within the request message itself, so that once the server finishes the invocation he can contact the given reply address and deliver the result message, just like a new Web Service invocation. For the case that an error occurs during the invocation runtime or on reply message delivery, the WS-Addressing specification contains an optional FaultTo address element for stating an alternative endpoint that can be contacted in case of any problems.

The problem with this approach is that the endpoint addresses used in the ReplyTo and FaultTo headers are chosen by the requester, and are not necessarily secured against tampering by any intermediates. Though the specification itself states that it might be necessary to perform a digital signature on these header fields, the reality today is that these values are used and relied on by default, not requiring any kind of security means. For example, the installation configuration of the well-known Apache Axis Web Service Framework is to have the handling of WS-Addressing headers enabled by default.

For an attacker, this vulnerability can be exploited twofold. The first approach is to intercept and modify the ReplyTo header of a regular request message so that the results of that particular computation are sent to a Web Service endpoint in control of the attacker instead of the endpoint chosen by the original requester. This way, the attacker may gain some additional knowledge, but at least causes a Denial of Service for that particular request processing by that the reply message never reaches the requester.

Another approach an attacker may use is send-

Figure 9. Invalid input used for an XML Injection attack

```
"John Doe</CustomerName>
<isPremiumMember>yes</isPremiumMember>
<CustomerName>John Doe"
```

ing arbitrary request messages to a Web Service server with WS-Addressing enabled itself. As these messages may contain any ReplyTo or FaultTo elements of the attacker's choice, he may cause the Web Service server to contact an arbitrary URL, trying to deliver either a reply message or a SOAP fault message. This way, the attacker can cause a HTTP POST request to any URL he chooses, which is performed using the IP address of the Web Service server host. Thus, corporate firewalls secured with IP filters may become deactivated from "inside", or a Web Service server may start to order goods from online shops that falsely interpret GET parameters in URLs of HTTP POST requests. At least, the attacker can cause a high communication and processing load at the server host, which may cause a Denial of Service itself.

Metadata Spoofing

The foundations of SOA are laid upon the idea of stating communication parameters in a particular metadata format. For Web Services, this is done using the Web Service Description Language (Christensen, Curbera, Meredith, & Weerawarana, 2001), and in more advanced scenarios this may also include policy documents like WS-Security-Policy (Kaler & Nadalin, 2005). These documents are intended to contain any information necessary for a client application to perform a request for a particular service. They contain message syntax descriptions, transport bindings, security requirements, and communication endpoint addresses. The metadata is then attached to textual service descriptions, sent to developers by email, or disclosed to the public using UDDI repositories or appropriate directory websites. But by default they do not contain any security means, nor does any well-known specification attempt to ensure the integrity of these metadata documents.

As a result, if an attacker manages to spoof a metadata document for a particular Web Service, and spread this spoofed metadata document among valid users, he has many capabilities for setting up malicious activities. Examples are numerous, but two typical scenarios are to be mentioned here.

A first example consists in that the attacker modifies the WSDL of an existing service and swaps the operation identifiers (such as the wsa:Action header element values) of any two operations. As a result, every time the tricked users try to execute a submit_order operation, they create a SOAP request message that may be interpreted as a cancel_order operation at the server side.

Spoofing the WS-SecurityPolicy document, as a second example, may result in that the tricked clients automatically create and send request messages that have less or even no data encryption on particular confidential data items. This way, the attacker may eavesdrop on these unencrypted messages and gain valuable information, even though the server-side framework will reject these requests due to not fulfilling the security requirements stated in the original WS-SecurityPolicy document.

The importance of this attack vector on service-oriented architectures is very likely to rise with the existing attempts to enable automated service compositions based on service repositories and ontologies.

COUNTERMEASURES

Message Validation

The most obvious countermeasure to the attacks described here consists in performing an in-depth validation of every incoming request message's syntax at the Web Service server side. For instance, it is possible to perform a verification of the XML document's validity against an XML Schema derived from the Web Service's WSDL description (Gruschka & Luttenberger, 2006). Additionally, this verification can be combined with a strict security policy enforcement, which may already help in preventing *Attack Obfuscation* (Gruschka, Luttenberger, & Herkenhöner, 2006).

Other server-side verifications may use state information from the server application in order to determine the sequential validity of an incoming request message, fending *State Deviation* messages as well (Gruschka, Jensen, & Luttenberger, 2007).

Access Control

Though access control enforcement (Koshutanski & Massacci, 2003) does not eliminate the possible occurrence of an attack, it may reduce the number of potential attackers. This way, the overall risk of getting targeted by an attack can be mitigated, as only legitimate users are able to connect to (and thus perform an attack on) a particular Web Service.

Note that some attack types can easily circumvent the access control enforcement, for example if the access control enforcement implementation itself is vulnerable to Denial of Service attacks. Also, the access control decision may be based upon data from the particular request message itself, which may perform its attack impact even before that access-control-relevant data can be extracted (e.g. if the access control relies on the WS-Security headers of a SOAP message that already performs an *Oversize Payload* attack).

Client Puzzles

Being a specific countermeasure to Denial of Service effects, the idea of client puzzles (Aura, Nikander, & Leiwo, 2001; Leiwo, Nikander, & Aura, 2000) is to give the server application an opportunity to reduce its own load if getting close to a Denial of Service state. The idea is that every client that wants to use a particular service has to solve some computation-intensive riddles prior to being allowed to place their request. This way, the server can adapt the complexity of these riddles depending on its own utilization, and thus cause

an attacker to do a huge amount of calculations before being able to perform a common Denial of Service attack.

Signature Wrapping Countermeasures

For the particular problem of countering *Signature Wrapping* attacks, a lot of solution attempts were discussed within the Web Services community. Initially, the approach of embedding message structure information for the signed parts of a SOAP message was stated (Rahaman, Schaad, & Rits, 2006) and revised (Gajek, Liao, & Schwenk, 2007; Rahaman & Schaad, 2007), but could not be verified to completely eliminate this attack vector. Other approaches focused on defining a signature's semantics (Gajek, Liao, & Schwenk, 2007b) or circumvented the attack by using predefined positions for signed message parts (Sinha & Benameur, 2008). However, a reliable solution to this problem was not agreed upon yet.

CONCLUSION

In this chapter, we have shown that the Web Services technology used today has some severe security vulnerabilities, leaving the attending systems in a highly threatened state. First of all, the dull use of immature implementations of the Web Services specifications causes some rather simple vulnerabilities to be spread among many systems worldwide. Apart from that, some of the existing specifications themselves prescribe architectural patterns that pose vulnerabilities to any compliant implementations, and finally, even the most secure implementation is worthless if the adopters don't know how to correctly make use of it.

FUTURE WORK

In order to cope with the issues presented here, it is necessary to have an in-depth review on the numerous specification attempts around the Web Services world, evaluating their capabilities and potential risks from a security-aware point of view. Then, it becomes necessary to re-engineer and improve these specifications, and also give appropriate advice to all Web Service developers and users on how to use the new technologies in a secure, safe, and efficient way. Once these hurdles can be taken, the resulting service landscape most probably will propose great value for all of its adaptors.

REFERENCES

Anley, C. (2002). Advanced SQL injection in SQL server applications. *NGS Software Insight Security Research*.

Aura, T., Nikander, P., & Leiwo, J. (2001). *DOS-Resistant Authentication with Client Puzzles, (. LNCS, 2133*, 170–177.

Bartel, M., Boyer, J., Fox, B., LaMacchia, B., & Simon, E. (2002). *XML-Signature Syntax and Processing*. W3C Recommendation.

Christensen, E., Curbera, F., Meredith, G., & Weerawarana, S. (2001). *Web Services Description Language (WSDL)*. W3C Note.

Clark, J., & DeRose, S. (1999). *XML Path Language (XPath) Version 1.0*. W3C Recommendation.

Eastlake, D., Reagle, J., Imamura, T., Dillaway, B., & Simon, E. (2002). *XML Encryption Syntax and Processing*. W3C Recommendation .

Ferris, C., & Langworthy, D. (2005). *Web Services Reliable Messaging Protocol*.

Gajek, S., Liao, L., & Schwenk, J. (2007). Breaking and fixing the inline approach. *Workshop on Secure Web Services* (pp. 37-43). Washington, DC: ACM Press.

Gajek, S., Liao, L., & Schwenk, J. (2007). *Towards a Formal Semantic of XML Signature*. Paper presented at the W3C Workshop Next Steps for XML Signature and XML Encryption, Mountain View, USA.

Gruschka, N., Jensen, M., & Luttenberger, N. (2007). A Stateful Web Service Firewall for BPEL. In *Proceedings of the IEEE International Conference on Web Services* (pp. 142-149), Salt Lake City, UT.

Gruschka, N., & Luttenberger, N. (2006). Protecting Web Services from DoS Attacks by SOAP Message Validation. In *Proceedings of the IFIP TC-11 21st International Information Security Conference,* (pp. 171-182), Karlstad, Sweden.

Gruschka, N., Luttenberger, N., & Herkenhöner, R. (2006). Event-based SOAP Message Validation for WS-SecurityPolicy-enriched Web Services. In *Proceedings of the 2006 International Conference on Semantic Web & Web Services* (pp. 80-86), Las Vegas, NV.

Gudgin, M., Hadley, M., & Rogers, T. (2006). *Web Services Addressing 1.0 – SOAP Binding*. W3C Recommendation .

Haldar, V., Chandra, D., & Franz, M. (2005). Dynamic Taint Propagation for Java. In *Proceedings of the 21st Annual Computer Security Applications Conference,* (pp. 303-311).

Insecure.org. (1996). *Ping of Death*. Retrieved April 09, 2009 from http://www.insecure.org/sploits/ping-o-death.html

Jensen, M., & Gruschka, N. (2008). Flooding Attack Issues of Web Services and Service-Oriented Architectures. In *Proceedings of the Workshop on Security for Web Services and Service-Oriented Architectures* (pp. 117-122), Munich, Germany. Berlin: Springer.

Jensen, M., Gruschka, N., Herkenhöner, R., & Luttenberger, N. (2007). SOA and Web Services: New Technologies, New Standards - New Attacks. In *Proceedings of the IEEE European Conference on Web Services* (pp. 35-44), Halle, Germany. Washington, DC: IEEE Computer Society.

Jensen, M., Gruschka, N., & Luttenberger, N. (2008). The Impact of Flooding Attacks on Network-based Services. In *Proceedings of the IEEE International Conference on Availability, Reliability, and Security,* (pp. 509-513), Barcelona, Spain. Washington, DC: IEEE Computer Society.

Jensen, M., & Schwenk, J. (2009). The Accountability Problem of Flooding Attacks in Service-Oriented Architectures. In *Proceedings of the IEEE International Conference on Availability, Reliability, and Security,* (pp. 25-32), Fukuoka, Japan. Washington, DC: IEEE Computer Society.

Jordan, D., Evdemon, J., Alves, A., Arkin, A., Askary, S., Barreto, C., et al. (2007). *Web Services Business Process Execution Language Version 2.0 (WS-BPEL 2.0)*. OASIS Standard.

Kaler, C., & Nadalin, A. (2005). *Web Services Security Policy Language (WS-SecurityPolicy) 1.1*. OASIS Standard.

Koshutanski, H., & Massacci, F. (2003). An Access Control Framework for Business Processes for Web Services. In *Proceedings of the 2003 ACM workshop on XML security* (pp. 15-24). New York: ACM Press.

Leiwo, J., Nikander, P., & Aura, T. (2000). Towards Network Denial of Service Resistant Protocols. In *Proc. of the 15th International Information Security Conference,* (pp. 301-310).

Lindstrom, P. (2004). *Attacking and Defending Web Service*. A Spire Research Report.

McIntosh, M., & Austel, P. (2005). XML signature element wrapping attacks and countermeasures. In *Proceedings of the 2005 workshop on Secure web services,* (pp. 20-27). New York: ACM Press.

McIntosh, M., Gudgin, M., Morrison, K. S., & Barbir, A. (2007). *Basic Security Profile Version 1.0*. Web Services Interoperability Organization (WS-I).

Moses, T. (2005). *eXtensible Access Control Markup Language (XACML) Version 2.0*. OASIS Standard.

Nadalin, A., Goodner, M., Gudgin, M., Barbir, A., & Granqvist, H. (2007). *Web Services Trust Language (WS-Trust)*. OASIS Standard.

Nadalin, A., & Kaler, C. (2006). *Web Services Federation Language (WS-Federation)*. Joint whitepaper of BEA Systems, Inc., BMC Software, CA, Inc., International Business Machines Corporation, Layer 7 Technologies, Microsoft Corporation, Inc., Novell, Inc. and VeriSign, Inc.

Nadalin, A., Kaler, C., Monzillo, R., & Hallam-Baker, P. (2006). *Web Services Security: SOAP Message Security 1.1 (WS-Security 2004)*. OASIS Standard.

Rahaman, M. A., & Schaad, A. (2007). SOAP-based Secure Conversation and Collaboration. In *Proceedings of the IEEE International Conference on Web Services* (pp. 471-480), Salt Lake City, UT. Washington, DC: IEEE Computer Society.

Rahaman, M. A., Schaad, A., & Rits, M. (2006). Towards secure SOAP message exchange in a SOA. In *Proceedings of the 3rd ACM workshop on Secure web services* (pp. 77-84). New York: ACM.

Schuba, C. L., Krsul, I. V., Kuhn, M. G., Spafford, E. H., Sundaram, A., & Zamboni, D. (1996). Analysis of a Denial of Service Attack on TCP. In *Proceedings of the 1997 IEEE Symposium on Security and Privacy,* (pp. 208–223). Washington, DC: IEEE Computer Society.

Sinha, S. K., & Benameur, A. (2008). A formal solution to rewriting attacks on SOAP messages. In *Proceedings of the ACM workshop on Secure web services* (pp. 53-60). New York: ACM.

Weerawarana, S., Curbera, F., Leymann, F., Storey, T., & Ferguson, D. F. (2005). *Web Services Platform Architecture: SOAP, WSDL, WS-Policy, WS-Addressing, WS-BPEL, WS-Reliable Messaging, and More.* Upper Saddle River, NJ: Prentice Hall PTR.

Chapter 11
Threat Modeling:
Securing Web 2.0 Based Rich Service Consumers

Nishtha Srivastava
Infosys Technologies Ltd, India

Sumeet Gupta
Infosys Technologies Ltd, India

Mayank Mathur
Infosys Technologies Ltd, India

ABSTRACT

This research work proposes a threat modeling approach for Web 2.0 applications. The authors' approach is based on applying informal method of threat modeling for Web 2.0 applications. Traditional enterprises are skeptical in adopting Web 2.0 applications for internal and commercial use in public-facing situations, with customers and partners. One of the prime concerns for this is lack of security over public networks. Threat modeling is a technique for complete analysis and review of security aspects of application. The authors will show why existing threat modeling approaches cannot be applied to Web 2.0 applications, and how their new approach is a simple way of applying threat modeling to Web 2.0 applications.

INTRODUCTION

One of the major trends in the IT industry today is the adoption of Service Oriented Architecture (SOA) in building applications leading to a flexible and standardized architecture for better collaboration and sharing of data among various applications.

The evolution of Web 2.0 technologies such as blogs, wikis, podcasts, RSS, etc. has emerged as a key facilitator for creating rich service consumer ecosystems to augment the benefits of SOA including interoperability, reuse and standardization. This has expanded the reach of SOA with rich interactive controls and adoption of Web 2.0 tools and services to access content for any user at any time through any channel.

DOI: 10.4018/978-1-60566-950-2.ch011

What is Web 2.0?

Web 2.0 is a term coined by Tim O'Reilly describing changing trends for using World Wide Web (www) as a platform to facilitate information collaboration. These concepts have led to the development and evolution of web-based communities such as social-networking and video sharing sites, content generation tools and services such as wikis, blogs, podcasts, content tagging and aggregation. Other key concepts that have emerged include web syndication like RSS and Mashup applications, which combine content from more than one source for an integrated experience. Although the term Web 2.0 suggests a new version of the web, it does not refer any update to technical specifications, but to changes in the way software developers and end-users utilize the web.

Web 2.0 is basically a new way to use existing Internet technologies— such as XML and JavaScript—to enable participation, interaction, and collaboration among users, content providers, and businesses, rather than just the traditional viewing of static web pages, said Hewlett-Packard security evangelist Michael Sutton. (Lawton, n.d.)

Evolution of Web 2.0 Based Technologies and Systems

Application development has evolved over the years from purely desktop application to purely web application to what is now an application nurturing the best of the both i.e. RIAs. The result of this has blurred the line between purely desktop and exclusively web applications. Historically, the web had been a largely unidirectional, designed as a medium for print content. Web was adopted as means of content sharing and small-scale data exchange via e-mail, corporate sites, and so forth. But it was not architected as a responsive writable means to leverage as a platform and a common working place. Although client-server comput-

ing idea of separating user interfaces (UI) from business logic and data persistence was good, the UIs tight coupling restricted choice of server-side technology. To overcome these shortcomings there was a requirement to effectively utilize web as a Content Management Workplace. It was required to capture, deliver, customize, and manage web content across an enterprise/division and so evolved Web 2.0 technologies.

This evolution led to the development of functionally rich and responsive applications using web as a platform rather than the typically static pages of traditional web technologies. These applications run on some complex set of technologies such as Asynchronous JavaScript and XML (AJAX), Flash, JavaScript Object Notation (JSON), Simple Object Access Protocol (SOAP), Representational State Transfer (REST). These technologies along with cross-domain information access contributed in empowering the client. This allowed end-users to add, generate and share content onto web in real time. This facilitated co-creation of ideas by information sharing and collaborative development which led to the development and evolution of web-based communities and hosted services, such as social-networking sites, video sharing sites, wikis and blogs.

Web 2.0 and Business and Need for Security

Web 2.0 has led to creation of new business processes, communities and business models which have added substantial benefits for traditional business. While most of Web 2.0 technologies are evolutionary, it's the convergence of these technologies - along with fundamental shifts in the nature of business – which facilitated to its growth. Web 2.0 tools are better suited for content collaboration, sharing, publishing, and management of enterprise data. Wikis have already been useful in group content generation and as a lightweight project management tool.

However enterprises are skeptical in adopting Web 2.0 applications for internal and commercial use in public-facing situations.

Web 2.0 technologies, such as AJAX, expand both the attack surface and the security gaps in the application. Today, about 70 percent of malicious code in the wild is downloaded via Ajax, according to Yuval Ben-Itzhak, chief technology officer of security vendor Finjan. (Lawton, n.d.)

With lack of access control on data, social collaboration has rendered users more vulnerable. With its enormous growth implications, securing Web 2.0 based systems and service consumers is a major concern now. One of the prime concerns for these rich technologies has been implementing information security with strong user authentication and encrypted transmission over public networks.

The objective of this chapter is to threat model Web 2.0 based systems and identify possible threats and vulnerabilities associated with Web 2.0 technologies. Thereby we try to apply our threat modeling technique and share the best practices to mitigate and minimize related threats.

We discuss in this chapter how it has become so important to secure Web 2.0 applications and why current approaches are not appropriate for threat modeling Web 2.0 applications.

This chapter is intended for enterprise IT professionals such as web-developers, application administrators and stakeholders engaged in deploying Web 2.0 based services. This would also help web designers and network & system architects to secure the applications while designing. This can also render useful for researchers and student community with a good insight into threats and vulnerabilities associated with Web 2.0 technologies.

The organization of the chapter is as follows. Section 2 describes in detail the emerging problems with Web 2.0 applications. Section 3 discusses various threat modeling approaches and why those cannot be applied to Web 2.0 applications. In Section 4 we discuss the works which are related to our approach of threat modeling. In section 5 we discuss some common threats and attacks already existing/known related to Web 2.0. Finally in Section 6 we give our approach to threat model Web 2.0 applications and thereafter some best practices to keep in mind.

BACKGROUND

Advent of rich Web 2.0 applications has escalated security challenges in technology as well as user management. Web 2.0 sites inherently carry more risk than traditional web sites because they let users upload content and require scripting capabilities—which can run code or carry malware—to function properly, said Will Dorman, a vulnerability analyst at the CERT Coordination Center, part of the Carnegie Mellon University based Software Engineering Institute (Lawton, n.d.). What makes Web 2.0 security so complicated is that it covers such a broad range of applications. Some Web 2.0 applications and components and related security concerns are discussed below.

Social Networking Sites

Social networking sites encourage the users to enter certain amount of personal information. The personal information can be used to conduct a social engineering attack. Some sites may share information such as email addresses or user preferences with other companies. This may lead to an increase in spam. (Sites should include privacy policies – such as policy for handling referrals).

LinkedIn's problem isn't as much technology as the common practice of sharing of names, titles, and organizations. Through information about how people are connected, the work they do, and their positions, attacker gets an organizational chart that is typically confidential information and commits identity theft or targeted attack.

Social networking websites have opened their operating platforms to let outside developers craft fun, or functional software "widgets" that can be added to profile pages. Malicious code can be hidden in such applications. People are prone to trust social networking widgets and links from friends. People are going crazy adding applications they don't need. Hackers can write seemingly legitimate widgets that spread to enough social network members.

Fake postings on comment boards advising people to update software are ways to trick social network users into downloading malicious software that can commandeer control of machines.

Even if applications are deleted, the odds are that the data from profile pages was already copied onto an outside computer. MySpace and Facebook have no control over servers, once the content is moved from their site they have no control over that.

Social networking sites let users authenticate to the site using an email address, they open up another potential hole for an attacker. They do a lot of authentication based on unauthenticated email. A user can click onto the "forgot my password" button to reset a password, for instance.

Syndication / RSS

The Web 2.0 model of integrating partner- and customer-generated components into our web site means that administrators now have to worry not only about the security of their own web sites, but the security of those interconnected pieces. Now we've got multiple gates to defend.

The term RSS names the technology that allows a web site owner to share content among different web sites in XML format. Web publishers can post a link to the RSS feed so users can read the distributed content on the site displaying the RSS link. RSS technology is an alternative means of accessing the vast amount of information on the web. Instead of users browsing web sites for information of interest, RSS pushes that information directly to the users.

RSS can be used to deliver all kinds of content, and the most popular content is HTML-based text. However, RSS can be used to deliver more than just text. Also there are ways to include file attachments in an RSS feed. As a result, we now have exceptionally great technologies such as podcasting, which is a way of delivering audio files as RSS-item attachments. Likewise, RSS can be used to deliver video, software updates, documents, spreadsheets, and all sorts of other files. The possibilities are nearly unlimited. And therein resides the concern. Web 2.0's interconnectedness makes it easier for little snippets of information in an RSS feed to slip malware into computers.

RSS reader software heightens the potential for intrusion. RSS feeds make it possible for hackers to engage in cross-site scripting using forms on a web site that users fill in with personal information. Only a handful of the reader products let users specify the types of downloads to permit. When the cross-site scripting element is factored into the equation, all someone has to do is put a button for free sign up on an infected web site. The RSS reader does not check on the contents.

Widgets

Widgets are small applets that usually run in a web browser or on the desktop and provide a specific function such as weather reports or stock updates. The technology is used as a way to personalize a desktop or webpage to provide the information users want.

Vulnerabilities in widgets and gadgets enable attackers to gain control of user machines, and should be developed with security in mind.

Extra caution should also be taken when using interactive widgets that rely on external feeds such as RSS which may be susceptible to attacks that exploit this trust by piggybacking a malicious payload on such data.

Widgets can download and combine data from most parts of the web, which make them a powerful platform for delivering innovative services to users. The security model is initially very open to allow authors to easily create such services. The widget author may change the config.xml file of the widget in order to restrict the widget's access to protocols, hosts and ports.

Wikis/Blogs

When a website automatically posts comments to another site it is called a trackback. Essentially, Blogs and many Wiki's automatically post comments on a website's page (when comments are enabled) when one links to that particular page. In most cases, the trackbacks and comments are used to create a discussion around a particular subject. Hence why Wikis and Blogs are key to developing an internet community.

However, wiki's are also often used in development projects, and if we are not careful with the security settings, we can give away our development secrets.

Rich Internet Applications (RIAs)

The phrase "Rich Internet Applications" has become a popular term for applications that run inside our browser or on desktop and that interact with web applications or web services. RIA platforms include JavaScript (part of the AJAX umbrella), Adobe System's AIR, Microsoft's Silverlight, Java applets, and Java JFX from Sun Microsystems.

The impact of RIAs on businesses matches that of PC desktop computing.

RIA increases the liveliness of a web-based application as it combines the responsiveness of a desktop GUI with the zero-installation delivery of a web application. RIAs are a return to user interface architecture. 1970s witnessed text-based interfaces (timesharing systems, UNIX), 1980s forms-based interfaces (block-mode terminals), 1990s graphical user interfaces (Windowing systems, Windows, Apple) and object-oriented user interfaces (OS/2, Mac). And then web happened which caused a move back to forms-based interfaces and was a real setback in terms of UI

capabilities. RIAs restored the live interface and allowed UI evolution to continue. RIAs provide direct access to any part of the display at any time and real-time and asynchronous communication with the server. More and more development professionals are embracing RIAs

There are two key mechanisms that control what a RIA can do known as the "same origin policy" and the "sandbox". Without these protection mechanisms, a RIA could access anything we see on the web and could also damage our computer. (Williams, n.d.)

Browsers restrict RIAs from accessing anything that is not from the same origin. Two sites are said to be from same origin if they share the same protocol ("http"), domain ("www.xyz.com"), and port. Even if the enforcements by browser are perfect, we still have to deal with cross-site problems like cross-site request forgery and cross-site scripting (discussed later in the chapter), which bypass the policy. The sandbox is also absolutely critical for RIAs. Without it, malicious RIAs could compromise the entire operating system and the data and applications on it.

Getting these policies implemented is hard enough owing to the fact that each RIA framework has its own environment that installs into the browser, and they can all communicate through the DOM. Each plug in is responsible for enforcing its own version of the same origin and sandbox policies. There is also a lot of pressure on the developers building RIA platforms to allow even more cross-domain and cross-sandbox functionality. New use cases for sharing data and creating mashups finally stretch policies that were not intended for anything more than Web 1.0 past their breaking point.

Mashups

Mashup is an application that combines data or services from multiple web sites into one user experience. A lot of great functionality in mashups comes from using tools from multiple sources. The problem is that when the website creator embeds code written by a third party on his site, the same-origin policy no longer offers any protection, and the embedded code likely has access to information stored on the creator's site. For example, if the creator of a forum embeds a mapping application on his site, the code in the mapping application could potentially access log-in data for the forum. Mashup makers either give up security by accepting those risks and trusting third-party tools, or they give up functionality by denying themselves the use of untrusted tools. The content providers should secure their servers and validate content, which they don't always do, said HP's Sutton. (Lawton, n.d.)

Web 2.0 technologies are being used as a tool for cybercrimes. With Web 2.0, following *attack trends* came into scenario:

- Web-site vulnerabilities open the door to compromise.
- Threats spread far and wide among the most popular websites.
- Popular social networking sites became hot targets.
- Web advertising is a vehicle for delivering malware.
- Insecure web 2.0 widgets and gadgets are on the rise and being exploited.
- Malware hide under the legitimate web 2.0 applications.
- Spam replacing text content with URLs.
- The URLs becoming more varied – phishing sites are increasingly dynamic.
- Botnets (Trojan networks) and spam are interdependent and this co-perpetuating relationship between botnets and spam is a notable trend.
- Spammers adopting more targeted and more aggressive attack tactics like highly targeted spam (well-defined target lists like C-level executives who make purchase decisions), using social engineering as a

vehicle for targeted spam, spam attacks on antispam infrastructure, etc.

RESEARCH PROBLEM DESCRIPTION

What is Threat Modeling?

Threat modeling is a technique for complete analysis and review of the system or application and identifies all possible threats regardless of whether those can be exploited or not. It tries to define countermeasures to prevent, or mitigate the effects of, threats to the system. It ensures the security from possible attacks and safeguards the vulnerabilities that the application may have. Threat modeling is unique for each kind application and is based on the environment and network, it is operating in. The key to threat modeling is to determine where the most effort should be applied to keep a system secure. Any threat modeling approach has a series of steps which must be followed to safeguard the application. Threat modeling provides the foundation upon which the rest of the security system is built.

Available Threat Model Approaches

Threat modeling requires a formal and comprehensive review of any application to secure it to a desired level. In order to provide an easy way to do so many vendors have come up with their own threat modeling methodology and set of guidelines. Below mentioned are some of the widely used threat modeling approaches in the industry:

AS/NZS 4360:2004 Risk Management

First set of standards were issued in 1999 and the revised version was released in 2004. This standard is the first formal approach proposed for managing and documenting risk. Very simple in application this is an iterative and very flexible approach. It provides several set of risk tables and gives a free hand to the organization to develop and adopt their own.

Steps of the AS/NZS 4360 process are:

- **Establish Context**: Establish the risk domain, i.e., which assets/systems are important?
- **Identify the Risks**: Within the risk domain, what specific risks are apparent?
- **Analyze the Risks**: Look at the risks and determine if there are any supporting controls in place.
- **Evaluate the Risks**: Determine the residual risk.
- **Treat the Risks**: Describe the method to treat the risks so that risks selected by the business will be mitigated.

AS/NZS 4360 assumes that risk will be managed by an operational risk group, and that the organization has adequate skills and risk management resources in house to identify, analyze, and treat the risks.

OCTAVE

OCTAVE was conceptualized by Carnegie Mellon University's Software Engineering Institute (SEI) in collaboration with Computer Emergency Response Team (CERT). It uses a three-phase approach to examine organizational and technological issues. Below is a brief description of each of the phase:

- Phase 1: Build Asset-Based Threat Profiles. This step involves identification of most important assets of the organization and indentifies what is currently being done to protect them.
- Phase 2: Identify Infrastructure Vulnerabilities. In this step key operational components are analyzed for weakness

that can lead to unauthorized action against critical assets.

- Phase 3: Develop Security Strategy and Plans. This step involves identification of risk to organization's critical assets and decides whether and how to address those risks.

Trike

This methodology approaches threat modeling from a risk management perspective. Trike focuses on modeling threats from a defensive perspective, not that of an attacker. This approach can be seen in two stages first stage starts threat modeling after the requirement stage only and in the next stage after implementation model is in place weaknesses of the system are identified.

Common Vulnerability Scoring System (CVSS)

This approach prioritizes the vulnerabilities of the system and puts them across a single score so that the raw data pertaining to them can be converted into actionable information.

It basically contains three metric groups:

- **Base**: It represents the intrinsic and fundamental characteristics of vulnerability that are constant over time and user environments.
- **Temporal**: It represents the characteristics of vulnerability that change over time but not among user environments.
- **Environmental**: It represents the characteristics of vulnerability that are relevant and unique to a particular user's environment.

Microsoft's Threat Modeling Process

Microsoft has a comprehensive approach for threat modeling. The core of this approach is constant refinement of approach by repeating the steps from step 2 onwards. Following are the steps of iterative threat modeling:

- **Identify security objectives**: This is to clarify the objectives for this complete activity and determine the effort required for subsequent steps. Security objectives are goals and constraints related to the confidentiality, integrity, and availability of our data and application.
- **Create an application overview**: This step looks for a complete overview of the application so that relevant threats can be identified at later stages. Creating an application overview involves drawing end-to-end deployment scenarios, identifying roles, identifying key usage scenarios, identifying key technologies and application security mechanisms.
- **Decompose the application**: This is done for more detailing of threats. As application is decomposed in smaller portions micro level view of threats is possible. In this step, we break down our application to identify trust boundaries, data flows, entry points, and exit points. The more we know about the mechanics of our application, the easier it is to uncover threats and discover vulnerabilities.
- **Identify threats**: Knowledge gained from the previous two steps help to identify the possible threats at this level. In this step, we identify threats and attacks that might affect our application and compromise our security objectives. These threats are the bad effects that could happen to our application. We start by identifying common threats and attacks and then move on to identifying threats along use-cases and data flows.
- **Identify vulnerabilities**: Complete review of application is done after repeating the previous steps so that the areas where mistakes are made most often are identified.

In this step, you review the web application security frame and explicitly look for vulnerabilities.

We add progressively more detail to our threat model as we move through our application development life cycle and discover more details about our application design. Because key resources identified in threat modeling are also likely to be key resources from a performance and functionality perspective, we can expect to revisit and adjust our model as we balance all of our needs. This is normal and is a valuable outcome of the process. We should begin the threat modeling exercise early in our project so that the threat model influences the design of our application.

Why Existing Threat Model Approaches are Not Appropriate for Web 2.0 Apps

There is no general notion of security. For each application different aspects of security as confidentiality authenticity integrity or availability may be relevant. Though abstract security policies may be defined, the concrete security requirements are heavily influenced by the kind of attacks that are expected for the given system and the application domain. (Lotz, 1997)

All existing threat modeling approaches focus on given specific applications and apply some formal or informal methodology for threat modeling the given the application. However what makes Web 2.0 security so complicated, as stated earlier, is that it covers such a broad range of applications.

A typical Web 2.0 based systems may be polling Really Simple Syndication (RSS) feeds from multiple sites, exchanging user-generated information with various Web 2.0 functionalities like blogs, forums etc using JSON and communicating with partner's Web service over SOAP. All these services are accessed from a Rich Interface using AJAX and/or Flash. A Web 2.0

based systems can load several Java Scripts, Flash components, and widgets in the browser which can then access cross-domain information from within the browser itself. But introducing these new technologies without dynamic web security protection can lead to data loss.

There are many approaches available to secure the rich applications at various levels, for example at client-server level or at network gateways. But most of these approaches are for intermediate mitigation. For effective collaboration and to promote utilization of these rich functionalities and web as an enterprise tool, we needed to secure enterprise as well as user data. We also need to secure information sharing of user information where user input for a particular system is utilized for another application .What's essential is to implore security at application level as well as Client Communication Gateway.

Web 2.0 based systems and services are collaboratively developed by harnessing user intelligence and are involuntarily constantly under development (said to be in perpetual beta). They present new weak links for malware to attack because of lack of universal threat model governing the interim releases and conglomeration of features being added continuously. Sometimes features themselves are developed to be further matured by user's collective intelligence and they lack various security measures.

Hence it's very difficult to secure such a development system and services. We need to identify threats, attacks, vulnerabilities, and countermeasures that could affect our system, because of type of development methodology and involved technologies, kind of deployment and polled services and the communication mechanism between them, at the outset for securing the system as well as consumed services. We need to use threat modeling to model system's design for meeting security objectives, and thereby reducing risk against malware attack or security breach. Securing Web 2.0 based systems and rich service consumers, requires a comprehensive threat mod-

eling approach which should be applicable to the known usage patterns for threat modeling web application and must be expandable to adapt to new standards for classification of Web 2.0 threats vectors, attack patterns, and mitigation.

RELATED WORK

There are several existing works on threat modeling. In this section we'll discuss the works which helped in determining our approach to threat modeling Web 2.0 applications.

There was a conference on Data Protection, in December 2003, in Belgrade. An approach was suggested by Serbia and Montenegro, giving a case study of Secure Electronic Election – Electronic Voting system. For securing applications, we tend to apply security controls which are already widely in practice. But without understanding security concerns in the specific context, it will not provide adequate protection. (Obradovic, 2003)

Very correctly said, three things must be present for an attack to occur: threats, vulnerabilities and assets. Take one away and there will no attack. An attack occurs only when attacker has a motive, or reason to attack, and takes advantage of vulnerability to threaten an asset. Hence threat modeling process proposed by them includes the following steps:

- *Decompose Application*: using DFDs and UML Activity Diagrams as DFDs focus on flow of data between processes and UML Activity Diagrams focus on flow of control between processes.
- *Identify and classify information resources* in the application under consideration like Server computers, workstations and PCs, data stores, communication links (Internet links, Intranet links)
- *Determine Threats* (Threat Trees): Using STRIDE methodology to classify threats and use threat trees.

- *Rank threats* (Risk Analysis): Try to calculate threat probability, i.e., risk. Risk may be calculated as Criticality x Likelihood of Occurrence.
- *Risk Mitigation* (Techniques and Technologies): Prepare a list of Threat Mitigation Techniques

Threat modeling is the fundamental prerequisite step needed for risk analysis, which in turn provide security basis of requirements engineering process.

A similar related work was seen in (Myagmar, Lee & Yurcik, 2005). It advocates the idea that it might be tempting to skip threat modeling and simply extract the system's security requirements from "industry's best practices" or standards such as Common Criteria. However, these standards merely provide general security guidance and cannot address all of the nuances of a particular system.

Their threat modeling process consists of the following three high-level steps: characterizing the system, identifying assets and access points, and identifying threats. Characterizing the system involves creating a system model which helps in understanding every component and its interconnections, defining usage scenarios and identifying dependencies. Assets of the system are then identified followed by uncovering threats and all potential attacks that need to be either mitigated or accepted as low risk.

Although these three steps of threat modeling process are common to all type of systems, the actual execution of these steps differs depending on the type of the system.

Our approach for threat modeling Web 2.0 applications is somewhat similar to above mentioned approach. Any Web 2.0 application is a not a single application and covers a wide range of applications, hence we propose an approach which well suits the problem scenario.

EXISTING ATTACKS IN WEB 2.0

Often the terms attack, threat and vulnerability are used interchangeably. However technically these terms differ in their actual sense. Vulnerabilities are the weaknesses in a system – design flaw, software bug, etc. Whereas threats are the potential events that will have an unwelcome consequence if they become attacks. We may say that threats are the events and vulnerabilities are the causes.

With the advent of Web 2.0, cyber attacks have moved up from the network layer to the application layer. High profile websites are popular targets because they have large concentration of users and hence large amount of traffic.

Before Web 2.0, the attacks on web applications could be classified into two broad categories:

- Server-side attacks
- Communication-channel attacks

Now, with Web 2.0 in scenario, a third category of attacks have emerged – Client-side attacks. So the attacks can be classified as follows:

Client-side attacks. Because of the increasing popularity of Web 2.0, it's common for users to execute a mixture of code from the desktops, the browser and remote servers.

An Ajax application is dependent on the sandbox of whatever browser it runs in, a plug-in based RIA runtime, such as Adobe Flash or Microsoft Silverlight, uses its own security sandbox model. Desktop frameworks (like Adobe AIR, CURL, and Nexaweb's desktop client) are more permissive and provide access to local machine.

Server-side attacks. Server side attacks which have risen to the top are:

- SQL Injection (discussed in section 6)
- Cross-Site Scripting (XSS)
- Cross Site Request Forgery (CSRF)

There are two major types of web attacks that have security researchers concerned right now: Cross site scripting attacks, and cross site request forgeries. The majority of attacks use some form of cross-site scripting (XSS) or cross-site request forgery (CSRF), noted WhiteHat's Grossman. XSS exploits the trust a user has in a web site. CSRF, on the other hand, exploits the trust a web site has in a user. (Lawton, n.d.)

Cross-Site Scripting (XSS)

There are different varieties of cross-site scripting attacks, but the result is always the same: the attacker figures out a way to make unauthorized code run within a victim's browser. The code itself is usually written in HTML/JavaScript, but may also extend to VBScript, ActiveX, Java, Flash, or any other browser-supported technology. When an attacker gets a user's browser to execute his code, the code will run within the security context of the hosting web site. With this level of privilege, the code has the ability to read, modify and transmit any sensitive data accessible by the browser. A Cross-site Scripted user could have his account hijacked (cookie theft), their browser redirected to another location, or possibly shown fraudulent content delivered by the web site they are visiting.

Web sites that allow users to post their own content use filtering software to keep users from posting unsafe code to their MySpace profiles or eBay auctions. But in the case of the Samy worm, Kamkar found a way to sneak his JavaScript past the MySpace.com filters.

In a second type cross site scripting attack, the web site is tricked into running JavaScript code that is included in the URL (uniform resource locator) for a web page. Normally web designers make it impossible for these attacks to work, but a programming mistake can open the door to an attack.

Cross Site Request Forgery (CSRF)

In a cross site request forgery attack, the criminal finds a way to trick a web site into thinking that it's sending and receiving data from a user who has been logged onto the site. These kind of attacks could be used to give an attacker unfettered access to any web site that has not yet logged the victim off.

Many sites protect against this type of attack by automatically logging visitors off after a few minutes of inactivity, but if the attacker could trick a victim into visiting his malicious site just minutes after logging into, says Bank of America's web site, the bad guy could theoretically clean out the victim's bank account.

Communication channel attacks: Developers connect clients to servers with fine-grained, asynchronous services that improve responsiveness, but they also put pieces of application domain models on clients where anyone can see them. It's especially important to consider how the applications transmit data payloads and how attackers might be able to modify them. For example, in applications using Ajax calls, someone could attempt to modify JavaScript Object Notation (JSON) data payloads with new behavior or try to steal the data during its transit.

OUR APPROACH TO THREAT MODELING FOR WEB 2.0 APPLICATIONS

In usual scenarios, threat modeling is considered to be an extra step in any Software Development Life Cycle (SDLC) for assessment of security for the system. In some approaches, it appears immediately after the requirement stage wherein all the security aspects of the system under development are evaluated. Another approach is threat assessment at each step of SDLC. Adding security aspects at each SDLC stage is the usual solution given for any development project. The approach to have threat modeling at each stage is to ensure security of application in a comprehensive way protecting them from potential security exploitation and plugging the security holes that it may have.

A complete security checklist in the form of threat modeling might be an effective idea to secure the application. But in case of Web 2.0 development, standard approaches of threat modeling and having security layer at different points in application development is not possible due to *nature of Web 2.0 application development*. It can be broadly classified in two levels as mentioned:

- SaaS; procuring API's
- Collaborative; Beta; Agile development

Software as a Service (SaaS) is a software delivery model that runs on a subscription-based fee. The users do not buy the license of the software, but only the right to use it. The solution provider retains the responsibility of supporting hardware, and maintenance of the solution. Here lie the security issues. Outsourcing an application means the organization relinquishes some control. The most important thing that should be focused is control of the data.

Collaborative Development. Companies use Web 2.0 as a platform not only to communicate with customers and business partners but also as a development platform for employees, allowing them to achieve the goal of true real-time collaboration which increases productivity and provides companies with a way to more easily promote their products. In particular, the creation of online communities and blogs or wikis to initiate conversations and share knowledge is proving to be particularly interesting to companies.

For Web 2.0 development, due to the approach of agile and collaborative development a full implementation of any security model is not possible.

Informal approaches that have been shown useful in practice are based on threat identifica-tion and risk analysis where the system and its environment are investigated in detail in order to determine the kind of possible attacks, their probability and the loss in case of the attack being performed. (Lotz, 1997)

In order to make it simpler we propose a 3-dimensional security approach suitable for any kind of Web 2.0 development. These act as a checklist to ensure secure application at each stage of development.

Since Web 2.0 based systems development doesn't follow SDLC and system is collection of many Web 2.0 based services mashed up to function as a single system, such a system cannot be modeled at the outset with respect to security objectives and requirements. We cannot ascertain all threats, vulnerabilities, attacks and countermeasures for this single system. We need to model the attacks, threats and vulnerabilities onto Web 2.0 system into *System-Asset-Attacker centric* dimensions (see Figure 1).

- **System Centric**: This is based on securing the system or part of it. This can be either part of system development process or it could be addressed at later stage by decomposing the system. So it can be integrated with the software development lifecycle from the start.
- **Attacker Centric**: It starts with the analyzing goals of the possible attacker and the possible vulnerabilities in the system which an attacker can exploit. In this step the entry points and the assets of the system are secured from any kind of attack.
- **Asset Centric**: This step takes into account of any sensitive or important information like customer names with credit card numbers that the application possesses. This level of security is introduced by methods like user based access controls to the application.

Figure 1.

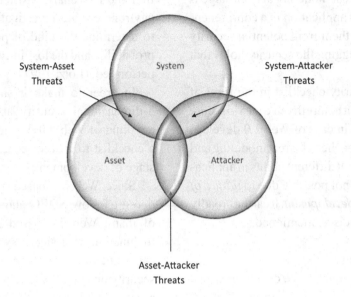

In case of web or desktop based systems disintegrating the application and looking at the three dimensions of the security is usually sufficient to secure it. In case of Web 2.0 based systems this approach doesn't hold sufficient. The boundaries where each of dimension intersect presents completely different scenario. Hence they require a different approach as mentioned below.

System – Asset

We need to secure the critical information (assets) which users provide as input to the system and which henceforth become part of the system. In other words, we need to secure information sharing of user information where user input is processed by the application or the input for a particular system is utilized for another application.

A key feature of Web 2.0 applications is that users are more readily able to upload content themselves—such as personal details (assets) to social networking sites, information for corporate blogs, etc. leading to a major shift in who defines what and how information flows in an organization. The way that users interact with Web

2.0 applications increases the risk that sensitive information will be misappropriated.

System – Attacker

We need to secure the all the entry-gates of the system through which an attacker can directly attack the system.

There are two major types of attacks on the system (Web 2.0 sites) that are of utmost concern: Cross site scripting attacks, and cross site request forgeries.

There are different varieties of cross site scripting attacks, but the result is always the same: The attacker figures out a way to make unauthorized code run within a victim's browser.

Web sites that allow users to post their own content should use filtering software to keep users from posting unsafe code to their sites. In a second type cross site scripting attack, the web site is tricked into running JavaScript code that is included in the uniform resource locator (URL) for a web page.

In a cross site request forgery attack, the criminal finds a way to trick a web site into thinking that it's sending and receiving data from a user who has been logged onto the site. These kinds of attacks could be used to give an attacker unfettered access to any web site that has not yet logged the victim off. Sites may be protected against this type of attack by automatically logging visitors off after a few minutes of inactivity.

Asset – Attacker

Sometimes instead of attacking the system, the attacker attacks the assets, on their way, which are beneficial to him. There are dangers of exposing personal information about users or the companies that they work for.

Most of the sites' problem is the common practice of sharing important assets like names, titles, and organizations. Through information about how people are connected, the work they do, and their positions, attacker gets typically confidential information and commits targeted attack.

Sometimes attacker attacks assets using social engineering like phishing attack. Phishing usually occurs when a fraudster sends an email that contains a link to a fraudulent website where the users are asked to provide personal account information. The email and website are usually disguised to appear to recipients as though they are from a bank or another well-known brand. Attacker may also redirect the user to fake websites and ask for important details like their account details, for the next password on their list of one-time passwords, etc.

Besides looking for the overlapping areas, we need to look at these dimensions individually too.

System-Centric

This stage includes securing the system or part of it. This can be either part of system or system development process or it could be addressed at later stage by decomposing the system. In case of Web 2.0 applications, the system not only in-

cludes the core application but all other systems with which it collaborates.

Securing at this level constitutes securing the code, the hardware and the technology used for the core system as well as securing the system from the vulnerabilities of the collaborating systems. Hence this step usually involves analysis of the system on the whole as well as decomposing it to the levels of collaboration and checking security.

We need to implore security at Client Communication Gateway as well as Web 2.0 application level. Client communication gateway uses software capabilities for checking file reputation before allowing user to download it. This prevents files with malicious content being further distributed.

Code needs to be secured to prevent loss of data via any code vulnerability. For example, authentication and access control should not be made in the client-side code. These should be made on the server side. Exception management should be taken care of in the code and caught exceptions should be logged.

The web way of delivering applications with mostly all application being collaboratively developed by harnessing user intelligence are involuntarily in perpetual beta. They constantly present new weak links for malware to attack because of lack of universal threat model governing the interim releases and conglomeration of features being added continuously. Sometimes features themselves are developed to be further matured by user's collective intelligence and they lack various security measures.

The system needs to be secured at the boundaries where ever it collaborates with the other systems. For this we need to decompose our concerned system, decide its boundaries with the systems it interacts and vulnerabilities which arise due to these interactions.

Asset-Centric

These represent items of value that we want to protect or that an attacker would like to get access to. Though these can be secured at system level, but it is essential to have asset centric step as securing important data is of utmost importance. Securing assets can be mainly done in two ways:

- **Securing Data & Data flow**: We need to secure information sharing of user information where user input is processed by the application or the input for a particular system is utilized for another application. The data flow in between the applications should be secured from getting leaked.
- **Defining user roles**: Each role in the system should be specified including actors (good and bad) and which assets each actor has access to. Proper Access Control Lists should be implemented for any application. Each user should be able to control his or her data with a restrictive access based on user profiles.

Attacker-Centric

It starts with the analyzing the possible vulnerabilities in the system which an attacker can exploit. In this step we need to secure against attacker tactics and vulnerabilities which may be present.

Attacker tactics. Spammers adopt more targeted and more aggressive attack tactics (like highly targeted, well-defined target lists like C-level executives who make purchase decisions), using social engineering (use specially crafted messages) that target particular user populations or interest groups, spam attacks on anti spam infrastructure, etc. One more example of attacker's tactics is the most popular phishing attack.

We need to create awareness among the users of Web 2.0 applications so that they do not get caught in the tactics used by the attackers.

Vulnerabilities. Web-site vulnerabilities open the door to compromise. Web 2.0 vulnerabilities can be classified as follows. Rest all other vulnerabilities are consequence of these two vulnerabilities.

1) Vulnerability in AJAX: most of the ***processing logic occurs on the browser client side***, instead of at the server level so JavaScript code can be embedded in HTML pages and interpreted by the web browser. Whist this allows websites to appear more dynamic and interactive, it also means that more of the business logic is exposed to the user, such as access control and session management logic.

2) Most of the data formats and protocols we're using today ***mix code and data***. Every piece of un-trusted data - every form field, every URL parameter, every cookie, and every XML parameter - might be injected a code for some downstream system.

Other vulnerabilities are:

- **User-input directly placed into SQL statement (SQL Injection)**: Attackers commonly insert single quotes into a URL's query string, or into a form's input field to insert malicious code. SQL Injection happens when a developer codes in such a way that accepts user input that is directly placed into a SQL Statement and doesn't properly filter out dangerous characters. This can allow an attacker to not only steal data from database, but also modify and delete it.
- **Lack of Input/Data Validation**: Nearly every active attack out there is the result of some kind of input from an attacker. *Secure programming is about making sure that inputs from bad people do not do bad things*. A hacker can take advantage of the

absence of input filtering and cause a web site to execute malicious code on any user's computer that views the page. Web applications take any type of input, assuming that it's valid, and process it further. Not validating input is one of the greatest mistakes that web-application developers can make.

- **Lack of Authentication and Authorization**: The lack of a usable universal authentication system for end users of social networking and collaboration sites is causing security, privacy and exposure problems. Whether in a blog or online collaborative reference resource, the authority of contributors isn't always well defined. A mechanism for uploading data based on identity/ authentication is necessary to avoid spreading malware.

- **Sensitive data**: Some sites may share user profile information with other sites or companies. This may lead to leakage of private sensitive data. Sites should include privacy policies - policy for handling referrals, etc.

Once threats and vulnerabilities are identified, those are analyzed based on their criticality and likelihood, and a decision is made by system designers whether to mitigate the threat or accept the risk involved with it. Security mechanisms are determined available to the system and developments of these mechanisms follow the general software development cycle of design, implementation, testing and maintenance.

Constructing a secure system is an iterative process. Since security mechanisms, as other refinements performed within system development introduce new components and/or data to the system which may themselves be subject to attack and have to be secured by further. (Lotz, 1997).

BEST PRACTISES

Web 2.0 applications are vulnerable to both internal and external threats. This can be evaded by implementing proper security measures against web-based attacks and providing users with threat safe environment to operate. Some of the Web 2.0 security best practices are listed below.

- **Antivirus and antispyware protection**: Deploy Web 2.0 threat protection software on the PC, along with conventional antivirus and antispyware protection. But do not rely solely on anti-virus and URL filtering. Anti-virus and URL filtering have their place in security infrastructure. But they are not adequate against today's dynamic Internet threats.

- **Data Encryption:** Employ high-quality of data encryption to ensure that non-authorized party cannot access and exploit the data. With modern data-encryption technologies with greater CPU's capacity, it's fast and inexpensive to handle data encryption in run time.

- **Data Storage:** Web 2.0 enticement to any user is the ability to contribute on web and storage of this user generated data is at risk if it sits on an unprotected server. We need to have a secure space for all work, exchange encrypted data with others allowing disk-based encryption. Alternatively we should ensure that time and again we are deleting temporary files restricting attackers to steal and exploit.

- **Input Validation:** Because of the server logic moving to the client, most input validation happens at the client side itself. Most of the attacks exploit server-side vulnerabilities by injecting malicious scripts. Input validation is an important step towards protecting web applications. Input validation and sanitation filter out all possible active or malicious content from untrusted input.

- **Don't Generate and Execute Code Dynamically:** There are several ways to generate code dynamically in a JavaScript program. One of the best-known functions is the eval() function, which allows to execute an arbitrary string as JavaScript code. However, it is very dangerous to use this function without care. Avoid the use of dynamically generated code unless absolutely necessary.

- **Partner Configurations:** Keeping a check on all the tools and partner services in Web 2.0 configuration is very tricky. Most of the supplying applications and data can be from sources that attackers can easily exploit. It's important to have a trust policy defining the partnership as well as configuration to monitor, remove, configure or reconfigure the applications and its elements.

- **Secure the network**: Operators need to employ measures to secure data transfer over the third party network when the client is not accessing from secure network. It would be better to address threats in the cloud itself. Employ a security vendor which can deliver different security applications on demand and can ensure web reputation checking active for all sessions. This ensures protection against threats in the cloud while simultaneously guarding against conventional gateway- and client-level threats.

- **Threat intelligence monitoring**: Employ services which provide continuous threat monitoring, proactive alerts, and criminal activity intelligence on the network. Cyveillance incorporated can be utilized for continuous threat monitoring for information leaks, phishing and malware attacks, counterfeiting and threat to user generated

information. Symantec's DeepSight sensor's honeypot technology can identify IP addresses linked to malicious web sites, and proactively warns consumers about accessing infected sites

- **Real time inspection by website owners:** Operators of Web 2.0 sites has a social responsibility to safeguard interest of the large concentration of users using their services. They can be an easy target for malware or any other kind of security attack. Such Organizations should employ real time monitoring of their services usage and inspect the content or file uploaded to keep a check on security exploits. Special mechanism should be incorporated by site owners to protect their business interest as well and their users' safety.

- **Secure updates and file uploads**: We need to employ measures to protect comments posted on blogs and forums as well as keep check on file uploads as this can be a very easy channel for Trojans and other malware distribution apart from email. Security administrators have to be vigilant against malware distribution for this Web 2.0 styled newer media and communication platforms. During financial transactions online, make certain that the web site does not employ perpetual cookies that can open the door to XSRF attack.

- **Content Monitoring:** A real-time content monitor should be utilized to keep a check on whatever user generated content or file has been uploaded onto the website. Logs should be generated for entire activity done by user in a session from entry to exit from the system.

- **Application Audits**: Web 2.0 applications are generally following the beta model of development as such application grows with many releases from multiple avenues. As such it becomes essential that we have a dedicated third-party vendor to check for vulnerabilities and track problems after any release.

- **Apply caution while social networking:** One should show restrain in revealing personal information or identity while social networking. It's very easy for cybercriminals or hackers to utilize the personal information for wrong things

- **Employee awareness**: Employees should be made aware of the threatening Web 2.0 attacks and safety measures to be taken; when they are working around Web 2.0 websites. This can avoid distribution of malware through browsing of un-trusted websites by employees. Moreover employees should be told about the XSRF, XSS, and viral outcomes of browsing Web 2.0 sites on company computers.

REFERENCES

Ingalsbe, (n.d.). Threat Modeling: Diving into the Deep End. *IEEE Software*, *25*(1), 28–34.

Lawton, G. G. (n.d.). Web 2.0 Creates Security Challenges. *Computer*, *40*(10), 13–16.

Lotz, V. (1997). Threat scenarios as a means to formally develop secure systems. *Journal of Computer Security*, *5*, 31–67.

Myagmar, S. Lee, A. & Yurcik, W. (2005). Threat Modeling as a Basis for Security requirements. In *Proc. Symp. Requirements Engineering for Information Security (SREIS 05)*. Retrieved from www.sreis.org/SREIS_05_Program/short30_myagmar.pdf

Obradovic, G. (2003). Threat Modeling and Data Sensitivity Classification for Information Security Risk Analysis. *Presentation at Data Protection '03*.

Swiderski, F. & Snyder, W. (n.d.). *Threat Modeling*. Redmond, WA: Microsoft Press

Threat Management –Web 2.0 Security Threats (2007, April). A Trend Micro White Paper I. Retrieved August 03, 2008 from http://us.trendmicro.com/imperia/md/content/us/pdf/threats/securitylibrary/trend_micro_web_2.0_threats_white_paper_apr07.pdf

Threat Risk Modeling (n.d.). Retrieved August 1, 2008, from http://www.owasp.org/index.php/Threat_Risk_Modeling

Williams, J. (n.d.). *The trinity of RIA security explained*. Retrieved August 09, 2008, from http://www.theregister.co.uk/2008/04/08/ria_security/

Section 5
Selected Readings

Chapter 12
Obtaining Security Requirements for a Mobile Grid System

David G. Rosado
University of Castilla-La Mancha, Spain

Eduardo Fernández-Medina
University of Castilla-La Mancha, Spain

Javier López
University of Málaga, Spain

Mario Piatini
University of Castilla-La Mancha, Spain

ABSTRACT

Mobile Grid includes the characteristics of the Grid systems together with the peculiarities of Mobile Computing, with the additional feature of supporting mobile users and resources in a seamless, transparent, secure and efficient way. Security of these systems, due to their distributed and open nature, is considered a topic of great interest. In this article we present the practical results of applying a secured methodology to a real case, specifically the approach that define, identify and specify the security requirements. This methodology will help the building of a secured grid application in a systematic and iterative way.

INTRODUCTION

Grid computing is concerned with the sharing and coordinated use of diverse resources in distributed "Virtual Organizations (VO)" (Ian Foster, Kesselman, Nick, and Tuecke, 2002). Grid manages resources and services distributed across multiple control domains (Ian Foster and Kesselman, 1999; Ian Foster et al., 2002).

Mobile computing is pervading our society and our lifestyles with a high momentum. Mobile computing with networked information systems help increase productivity and operational efficiency. This however, comes at a price. Mobile computing with networked information systems increases the risks for sensitive information supporting critical functions in the organization which are open to attack (Talukder and Yavagal, 2006).

Mobile Grid, in relevance to both Grid and Mobile Computing, is a full inheritor of Grid with the additional feature of supporting mobile users and resources in a seamless, transparent, secure and efficient way (Litke, Skoutas, and Varvarigou, 2004). Grids and mobile Grids can be the ideal solution for many large scale applications being of dynamic nature and requiring transparency for users.

Security has been a central issue in grid computing from the outset, and has been regarded as the most significant challenge for grid computing (Humphrey, Thompson, and Jackson, 2005). The characteristics of computational grids lead to security problems that are not addressed by existing security technologies for distributed systems (Ian Foster, Kesselman, Tsudik, and Tuecke, 1998; Welch et al., 2003). Security over the mobile platform is more critical due to the open nature of wireless networks. In addition, security is more difficult to implement into a mobile platform due to the limitations of resources in these devices (Bradford, Grizzell, Jay, and Jenkins, 2007).

Because of the difficulty of incorporating mobile devices into a grid environment (Guan, Zaluska, and Roure, 2005; Jameel, Kalim, Sajjad, Lee, and Jeon, 2005; Kwok-Yan, Xi-Bin, Siu-Leung, Gu, and Jia-Guang, 2004; Sajjad et al., 2005), and by adding the appearance of a new technology where security is fundamental and the advances that mobile computation has experienced in recent years, the need to define, consider and develop a methodology or process of development appears in which, within the whole software lifecycle (Anderson, 2001; Baskerville, 1993), all the requirements and security aspects related to Mobile Grid systems are analyzed and

integrated obtaining as a result a secure, robust and scalable Mobile Grid system.

In this article, we will apply the stage of security requirements analysis for obtaining a set of security requirements on a mobile grid environment for a case study of media domain where the mobile devices participate as actives resources. Using misuse cases and security use cases we obtain a vision about the threats and risks of the system and about the security requirements and mechanisms that we must use to protect to our mobile grid system.

The rest of article is organized as follows: Section II will describe some of the security requirements most important on grid environments and will identify the common attacks that can appear on a on mobile grid system. In section III, we give a brief overview of our methodology of development for mobile grid systems, we will describe the analysis stage and we will study one of the activities of this stage, the Mobile Grid Security Requirement Analysis activity. In section IV, we will present a case study and we will apply the activity of security requirements analysis for obtaining a set of security requirements for our real application. We will finish by putting forward our conclusions as well as some research lines for our future work.

SECURITY REQUIREMENTS AND ATTACKS ON A MOBILE GRID SYSTEM

Defining Security Requirements

The basic security components are comprised of mechanisms for authentication, authorization, and confidentiality of communication between grid computers. Without this functionality, the integrity and confidentiality of the data processed within the grid would be at risk.

We define the basic security requirements on grid environments, but there are many other security requirements and challenges associated with grids and mobile computing (Trusted Computing Group Administration, 2006; Vivas, López, and Montenegro, 2007) that, due to space restrictions, we do not define here:

- **Authentication:** It ensures that only valid devices and users access a given service. Authentication mechanisms and policies are supposed to constitute the basis on which local security policies can be integrated within a VO (Ian Foster et al., 1998).
- **Confidentiality:** Both privacy and intellectual property concerns require confidentiality in the use of data. Encryption is one of mechanisms used to enforce confidentiality.
- **Integrity:** It ensures that message (data) communications are not tampered with while in transit or in storage (in memory on the device, for example).
- **Authorization and access control:** In grids, local access mechanisms should be applied whenever possible, and the owner of a resource should be able to enforce local user authorization.
- **Privacy:** It is the ability to avoid information being disclosed to determined actors. Privacy also involves rules about what information can be shared among users, whether messages can be exchanged "in private," and the anonymity of users (if needed and/ or desired).
- **Non-repudiation:** It refers to the inability to falsely deny the performance of some action.

All these security requirements must be identified and analyzed in the analysis stage of our methodology from the mobile grid security use cases (MGSUC) defined in this stage and that we will explain further on.

Defining Attacks on Grid Environments

According to (Enterprise Grid Alliance Security Working Group, 2005), the following include some of the threats and risks based on the unique characteristics of an enterprise Grid:

- **Access control attacks:** defines risks with unauthorized entities, as well as authorized entities, bypassing or defeating access control policy.
- **Defeating Grid auditing and accounting systems:** includes threats to the integrity of auditing and accounting systems unique to an enterprise Grid environment. This may include false event injection, overflow, event modification, and a variety of other common attacks against auditing systems.
- **Denial of Service (DoS):** this describes an attack on service or resource availability. As an enterprise Grid is often expected to provide a better availability compared to a non-Grid environment, the following DoS threats must be considered as part of a risk assessment:
  - DoS attack against the Grid component join protocol to prevent new authorized Grid components/users from successfully joining.
  - Authorized Grid component or user is "forced" to leave the grid.
  - User or service attempts to flood the Grid with excessive workload which may cause compute, network and/or storage components to become exhausted, or the latency to access those resources significantly impacts other Grid users.
  - Altering scheduling (or other Quality of Service) priorities that have been defined for Grid components to unfairly prioritize one application/service over another.

- **Malicious code/"malware":** This describes any code that attempts to gain unauthorized access to the Grid environment, to subsequently elevate its privileges, hide its existence, disguise itself as a valid component, or propagate itself in clear violation of the security policy of the enterprise Grid.
- **Object reuse:** This describes how sensitive data may become available to an unauthorized user, and used in a context other than the one for which it was generated. In the enterprise grid context, this is a risk if a Grid component is not properly decommissioned.
- **Masquerading attacks:** describes a class of attacks where a valid Grid component may be fooled into communicating or working with another entity masquerading as valid Grid component. Such an attack could permit the disclosure or modification of information, the execution of unauthorized transactions, etc.
- **Sniffing/snooping:** involves watching packets as they travel through the network. An enterprise Grid potentially introduces additional network traffic between applications/ services, the system and grid components that should be protected. Failure to address this threat may result in other types of attacks including data manipulation and replay attacks.

In addition to these, it is also necessary to adopt the general security mechanisms applicable in any enterprise scale IT infrastructure, and includes physical security to protect against threats from humans (either malicious or accidental) as well as man-made and natural catastrophes.

OVERVIEW OF OUR METHODOLOGY

Methodology of Development

Our methodology of development (Rosado, Fernández-Medina, López, and Piattini, 2008) is a systematic process that must be iterative and incremental. An iterative approach proposes an incremental understanding of the problem through successive refinements and an incremental growth of an effective solution through several versions.

The methodology to develop a systematic process will consist of different phases; each one of them will also be divided into stages, and these, in turn, into activities and tasks. This methodology has been modified and improved with regard to a first approach (Rosado et al., 2008). In this new approach we have added two repositories (general and security) where we can include and update with artifacts, templates, patterns, elements, diagrams that are common in these environments and that we can use for future developments. Also, our methodology will be guided by specials use cases (mobile Grid use cases) with new constraints, behavior and characteristics that are compatibles with known use cases. Diagrams of mobile grid use cases will be added in our repository. A third aspect is that we build a security service oriented architecture with services, mechanisms and technologies needed for mobile grid systems.

Our methodology will initially consist of 3 phases:

- **Planning phase:** secure mobile grid system planning stage.
- **Development phase:** secure mobile **grid system analysis stage** (Figure 1, up), secure mobile grid system design stage and secure mobile grid system construction stage.
- **Maintenance phase:** secure mobile grid system maintenance stage.

Figure 1. Tasks of the "mobile Grid security requirements analysis" activity

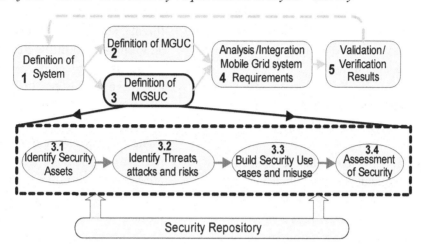

In this article, we study one of the activities of the secure mobile grid system analysis stage, the Definition of Mobile Grid Security Use Cases activity whose tasks can be seen in Figure 1 (bottom). In this activity (activity 3 of Figure 1) we identify threats and risks related to mobile grid environments which attack assets that we want to protect, and we build the diagrams of security use cases and misuse for mobile grid environments considering these assets, threats and attacks.

Secure Mobile Grid System Analysis Stage

In this subsection, we will describe the analysis stage, enumerating and describing briefly what activities are parts of this stage. This analysis stage is composed of five activities (see Figure 1):

- **Definition of Mobile Grid System.** It describes the system by adapting the previous results and limiting the reach of it to identify standards, norms and tools.
- **Definition of Mobile Grid Use Cases (MGUC).** The purpose of this activity is to build a diagram of use cases where we can identify the necessities and requirements of both users and the mobile Grid environ-

ment. There are diagrams of use cases in the general repository that we can use for building our diagram.
- **Definition of Mobile Grid Security Use Cases (MGSUC).** It builds diagrams of security use cases and misuse for identifying the security requirements of our system, analyzing the threats that the attackers can carry out and assessment risks for the mobile Grid system. We will define this activity in the next subsection.
- **Mobile Grid System Requirements Analysis.** It specifies both functional and non-functional (excluding security) requirements from MGUC. Also, it specifies security requirements from MGSUC and integrates them into a specification of requirements of the final application.
- **Validation and Verification of Results.** During the course of some designs, requirements can change at the last minute or may go undiscovered. Requirements also have a way of changing when you least expect them to, so it is always a good idea to validate them before you proceed. This activity validates the results obtained from the analysis as well as approves the analysis of the system.

Once we have described the activities of the analysis stage, we will explain activity 3, which is in charge of analyzing security requirements for the mobile grid system, and we apply the tasks of this activity in a case study.

Activity 3: Definition of Mobile Grid Security Use Cases (MGSUC)

The aim of this activity is to obtain a set of security requirements, validated and specified that we will have to use and to manage in the next stages or activities of the methodology. This analysis is centered on the specific security requirements of Grid and mobile computing (section 2.A) which are requirements with special characteristics and poorly studied. For this reason, we aim to analyze the security requirements that we can find when we build a secure mobile grid system. A set of tasks (see Figure 1) will serve as a guide for defining and specifying security requirements for mobile grid systems:

- **Task 3.1: Identify Security Assets**: The security assets for a grid with mobile devices depend on the characteristics and type of system to be built. The CPU-intensive applications will consider resources as main assets while data-intensive applications will consider data as main assets to protect.
- **Task 3.2: Identify Threats, Attacks and Risks**. The threats analysis is the process of identifying, as many risks that can affect the assets as possible. A well-done threat analysis performed by experienced people would likely identify most known risks, providing a level of confidence in the system that will allow the business to proceed. In section 2.B we defined the most important threats and attacks for these environments.
- **Task 3.3: Build Security Use Cases and Misuse**: Once we have identified the threats and vulnerabilities for Grid environments and mobile computation, we can build, using security use cases and misuse cases, a diagram of mobile Grid security use cases where threats, attacks and security are expressed and represented in the diagram indicating the assets to protect, the security objectives to achieve and the security requirements that the system must fulfill (defined in section 2.A).
- **Task 3.4: Assessment of Security**: It is necessary to assess whether the threats are relevant according to the security level specified by the security objectives. Then, we have to estimate the security risks based on the relevant threats, their likelihood and their potential negative impacts, in other words, we have to estimate the impact (what may happen) and risk (what will probably happen) which the assets in the system are exposed to. We have to interpret the meaning of impact and risk.

The aim of this activity is build diagrams of security use cases correctly defined where all security requirements of our system are represented and identified.

CASE STUDY

Our development methodology will be validated with a business application in the Media domain (see Figure 2) attempting to solve existing problems in this domain. The methodology will help us to build a Mobile Grid application, which will allow journalists and photographers (actors of media domain) to make their work available to a trusted network of peers the same instant it is produced, either from desktop or mobile devices.

With the explosion of ultra portable photo/video capture media (i.e. based on mobile phones, PDAs or solid state camcorders) everyone can capture reasonably good quality audiovisual material while on the move. We want to build a system that will cater for the reporter who is on

Figure 2. Mobile Grid computing system for media application

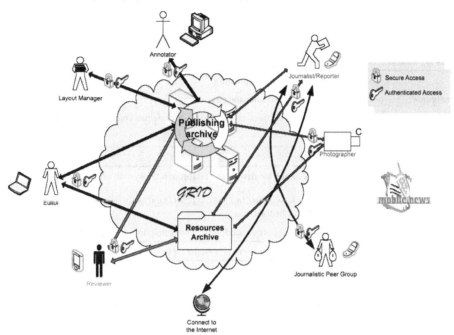

the move with lightweight equipment and wishes to capture and transmit news content. This user needs to safely and quickly upload the media to a secure server to make it easier for others to access, and to avoid situations where his device's battery dies or another malfunction destroys or makes his media unavailable.

In the media domain, both the distributions of content, and the need for rapid access to this content, are apparent. News is inherently distributed everywhere and its value falls geometrically with time. These two reasons make the need for Grid technology evident in both scenarios which represent, however, a plethora of relevant business cases which share these two common characteristics: the need for fast access to distributed content.

Following the process of analysis defined in the definition of mobile grid security use cases activity aforementioned, we will identify and analyze security requirements involved in this case study helping of security repository and mobile grid security uses cases. For all possible

use cases defined for this application, we are only going to consider three use cases (due to space constraints), defined in Table 1, which we are going to work with in the following tasks.

Initially our security repository contains several generic security use cases that we can adapt to our necessities (behavior, relations, restrictions, etc.), set of diagrams of security use cases and misuse which we can reuse modifying the relations, adding news security use cases and restrictions until adapting to the application requirements. Also, in the security repository, templates of threats, attacks, vulnerabilities, risk scenarios, and other security elements are defined. For example, the diagram of security use cases that we can use for building our own diagram of security use cases is shown in Figure 3 (an analysis more detailed as future work).

We describe a security scenario where we present use cases, misuse cases that can attack to the identified use cases, and the security use cases associated both with use cases and misuse cases for protecting the system of these misuse

Table 1. Use cases

Use Case Name	Login to the system
Goals/Description	Provide authentication mechanisms
Scenario example	All users log in to the grid system
Description	- A user launches the Grid application - The user provides username and password - The system checks the user data and permits or denies entry to the system

Use Case Name	Search for news
Goals/Description	A journalist can search for news material through the system interface in: 1. public sources 2. his organisation's historical archive 3. trusted commercial portals according to the subscriptions paid-for.
Scenario example	The journalist familiarizes himself with the topic
Description	- A user formulates a search query - The user selects sources to search from a list - The user submits the query

Use Case Name	Get query results
Goals/Description	Receive query results from available repositories
Scenario example	The Journalist receives a list with the results of the search query
Description	- The system returns results based on the metadata description of the stored material. - Results can be sorted according to the journalist's needs, such as thematic groups. - Visualization of results is based on the end user device capabilities (low resolution video for mobile devices)

cases, using the security use cases defined in the security repository.

Having identified these use cases, we can carry out a first iteration of our methodology, identifying the security requirements associated with these use cases and identifying and defining the rest of them in later iterations where a new refinement will be realized. Next, we will execute this process or set of tasks for analyzing all security requirements for the media domain in this case study.

Task 3.1: Identify Security Assets

On mobile Grid environments we can identify a set of assets that we must protect for obtaining a secure grid system, which are the following: User and system data (stored, transmitted); Identity information; Credentials (private keys, passwords); Accounting; CPU-/Storage-/Mobile devices-/Network-resources; General system.

In a first iteration of our case study, we define the most important assets related to use cases aforementioned that we must protect and that are the reference for the identification of threats, attacks and security use cases. These assets are:

Figure 3. Example of Grid security use cases inside of the security repository

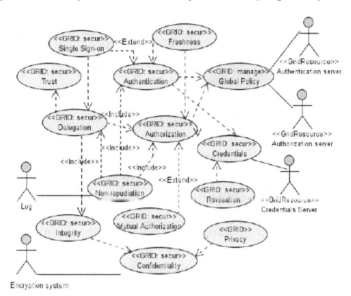

- Personal information about the journalist or editors: name, age, address, subscriptions, salaries.
- Media information used: photos, articles, recordings, videos, intellectual property rights.
- Exchange information: messages, queries, transactions.

Task 3.2: Identify Threats, Attacks and Risks

Examples of threats are unauthorized disclosure of information, attacks to the content of a message through wireless links, denial-of-service attacks, network authentication related attacks, physical node attacks, alteration of information, and so on. In Table 2 we can see the threats considered for the assets identified on mobile grid environments.

For our case study we can identify threats associated with security assets identified in previous task. The threats and attacks can be described with misuse cases as shown in Figure 4.

In our first iteration, we identify several possible types of threats to Information:

- Unauthorized access to grid system. In this scenario, the user wants login to the system, so that we must ensure authorized access.
- Unauthorized disclosure and alteration of information. The user can send information to the system or receive from the system, so that we must protect the information both transmitted or storage. Also we must protect the personal information that is transported through credentials.
- Unauthorized unavailability to resources. The user must have available resources anytime and anywhere.

In a first iteration we are going to consider these threats for the assets identified in task 3.1 as the most important that they damage and attack to our assets. We can show these threats in form of misuse cases and as these threats and misuse cases are common to grid environments and mobile computing, in our security repository will be defined and we can use for our application.

Table 2. Security threats on mobile grid environments

Assets	Threats
User and system data (stored, transmitted)	- Unauthorised access (stored data)
	- Eavesdropping (transmitted data)
	- Unauthorised publishing
	- Manipulation
	- Erroneous data
Identity information	- Eavesdropping
	- Manipulation
Credentials (private keys, pass-words)	- Theft / Spoofing (masquerade as a certain user, illegal use of software)
	- Publishing
Accounting	- Manipulation of log entries, CPU/memory usage, number and size of processes
	- Acquire information about competitor's work
CPU-/Storage-/Mobile devices-/Network-resources	- Misusage (e.g. Spambot)
	- Denial of Service
General System	- Security holes / exploits
	- Malicious / compromised resources
	- Backdoors, viruses, worms, Trojan horses

Figure 4. Use cases, misuse cases and security use cases for the case study

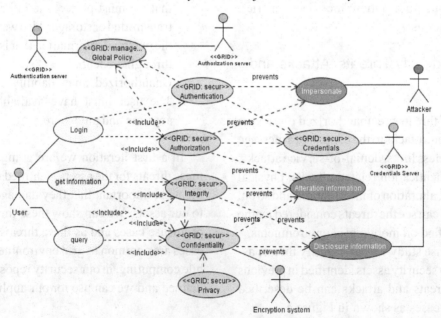

Task 3.3: Build Security Case Use and Misuse

Once we have identified and defined the treats, attacks, risks, and once we have a detailed definition of misuse cases and security use cases in our security repository, we can start to build the diagram of security use cases and misuse cases (diagram reduced) for this application. The Figure 4 shows the diagram of security use cases and misuse cases together with use cases defined in Table 1. We can see how a subset of the diagram of Mobile Grid security use cases shown in Figure 3 is used.

In Table 3 (stored in security repository) we can see the misuse cases specification for unauthorized modification of information which occurs, for example, when a mis-user attacks the content of a message, and also the misuse case specification for unauthorized interception of information which occurs when a misuser attacks the confidentiality of a message. These misuse cases have associated security use cases that define the sequence of steps that should be carried out to avoid misuse cases that they are associated with. Table 4 describes these security use cases that ensure message integrity preventing a misuser from corrupting a message and, message confidentiality preventing a misuser from having the means to intercept a message, respectively.

Once the diagram is built and the relations, constraints, stereotypes and tagged values are defined, we can obtain and specify the security requirements for this application.

Task 3.4: Assessment of Security

In Table 5 we define the impact and risk for two of these threats. For the time being, we are going to evaluate risk and impact with five possible values: Very Low, Low, Medium, High and Very High. The likelihood of a threat could be: Very Frequent (daily event), Frequent (monthly event), Normal (once a year), Rare (once in several years).

For alteration and disclosure of information we can see that if the information is sensitive (personal data, bank data), these treats represent a high risk for our system and we must ensure that attacks (modifying or altering information) do not attain their objectives. In this case we must strongly protect the information stored and transmitted between user and system. This assessment must be present in the next stages and activities and it must take into account when we design the security service oriented architecture.

CONCLUSION

The interest in incorporating mobile devices into Grid systems has arisen with two main purposes. The first one is to enrich users of these devices while the other is that of enriching the Grid's own infrastructure. Both benefit from this fact since, on the one hand, the Grid offers its services to mobile users to complete their work in a fast and simple way and, on the other hand, the mobile devices offer their limited resources, but millions of them, in any place and at any time, endorsed by the fast advance in the yield and capacity that is being carried out in mobile technology.

In many cases, constrained wireless networks are made up of devices that are physically constrained and therefore have little room for memory, batteries, and auxiliary chips. Security over the mobile platform is more critical due to the open nature of wireless networks. In addition, security is more difficult to implement into a mobile platform due to the limitations of resources in these devices.

Due to this difficulty when we want to incorporate mobile devices into a grid system and due to the fact that we must take into account security aspects throughout the life cycle, it is necessary to provide a systematic process to developers for building this kind of system considering grid characteristics, mobile computing and security aspects throughout the development process. This

Table 3. Misuse cases

Misuse Case	Modification of information
Attack	Attack on the content of a message (integrity).
Summary	The external attacker type gains access to the message exchanged between the journalist and the Grid system, and modifies the part of the message that contains the media information with the intention of changing its meaning by modifying some aspect of the information like authors, dates, or secrecy information.
Preconditions	
1)	The external attacker has physical access to the message.
2)	The external attacker has a clear knowledge of where the secrecy information is located within the message.
Interactions	
1 User Interactions	The journalist sends a query message for obtaining media information
2 Misuser Interactions	The external attacker intercepts it and identifies the part of the message to modify the media information and he/she forwards it on to media Grid
3 System Interactions	Media Grid receives the corrupted message and processes it incorrectly due to its altered semantic content. That is, it establishes that the journalist wishes as new media information that media information which had been modified by the attacker
Postconditions	
1)	Media grid will remain in a state of error with regard to the original intentions of the journalist.
2)	In the register of the system in which media grid was executed, the request received with an altered semantic content will be reflected.

Misuse Case	Interception of information
Attack	Attack on the confidentiality of a message from grid system to user
Summary	The external attacker type gains access to the message exchanged between the journalist and the Grid system, and reads a specific piece of information.
Preconditions	
1)	The external attacker has physical access to the message.
Interactions	
1 User Interactions	The journalist sends a query message for obtaining media information
2 System Interactions	Grid system receives the query message and processes it. Grid system returns the media information related with the query to the journalist
3 Misuser Interactions	The external attacker intercepts it and reads the part of the message that contains the media information and he/she forwards it on to journalist
4 User Interactions	The journalist wishes as new media information that media information which had been intercepted by the attacker.
Postconditions	
1)	Grid system will remain in a normal state and the journalist continues without realizing the interception of information by the attacker

process must always be flexible, scalable and dynamic, so that it adapts itself to the ever-changing necessities of mobile Grid systems.

In this article we have presented a methodology for designing and building a secure mobile grid system based on an iterative and incremental process. This methodology is composed of several stages and activities and in each one of them the stakeholders carry out their tasks. An important phase of the methodology is the security requirements analysis which we have proposed with a set of tasks to obtain security requirements for mobile grid systems based in security use cases. Considering a case study for media domain, we have applied the analysis activity for analyzing security requirements in this real application using techniques of uses cases, misuse cases, security use cases and risk assessment where we obtain a specification of security requirements of our system analyzed on several refinements.

Applying this set of tasks we have been able to incorporate security requirements into our analysis and into our system. The application of this case study has allowed us to improve and refine some tasks of the security requirements analysis activity.

As a future project we will define in depth all stages of the methodology and we will use our case study to apply the activities and tasks to analyzing and studying the obtained results so that they will be validated with the expected outcome. Also we will define the diagrams of security use cases that serve us as templates in our own diagrams of security use cases and misuse.

ACKNOWLEDGMENT

This research is part of the following projects: MISTICO (PBC-06-0082) and QUASIMODO (PAC08-0157-0668) financed by FEDER and by the "Consejería de Educación y Ciencia de la Junta de Comunidades de Castilla-La Mancha" (Spain), and ESFINGE (TIN2006-15175-C05-05) granted by the "Dirección General de Investigación del Ministerio de Educación y Ciencia" (Spain). Special acknowledgment to GREDIA (FP6-IST-034363) funded by European Commission.

REFERENCES

Anderson, R. (2001). *Security Engineering - A Guide to Building Dependable Distributed Systems*: John Wiley&Sons.

Baskerville, R. (1993). Information systems security design methods: implications for information systems development. *ACM Computing Surveys, 25*(4), 375 - 414.

Bradford, P. G., Grizzell, B. M., Jay, G. T., & Jenkins, J. T. (2007). Cap. 4. Pragmatic Security for Constrained Wireless Networks. In A. Publications (Ed.), *Security in Distributed, Grid, Mobile, and Pervasive Computing* (pp. 440). The University of Alabama, Tuscaloosa, USA.

Enterprise Grid Alliance Security Working Group. (2005, 8 July 2005). *Enterprise Grid Security Requirements Verison 1.0*

Foster, I., & Kesselman, C. (1999). Globus: A Toolkit-Based Grid Architecture. In *The Grid: Blueprint for a New Computing Infrastructure* (pp. 259-278): Morgan Kaufmann.

Foster, I., Kesselman, C., Nick, J. M., & Tuecke, S. (2002). Grid services for distributed system integration. *Computer, 35*(6), 37-46.

Foster, I., Kesselman, C., Tsudik, G., & Tuecke, S. (1998). *A Security Architecture for Computational Grids*. Paper presented at the 5th ACM Conference on Computer and Communications Security, San Francisco, USA.

Guan, T., Zaluska, E., & Roure, D. D. (2005). *A Grid Service Infrastructure for Mobile Devices*. Paper presented at the First International Conference on Semantics, Knowledge, an Grid (SKG 2005), Beijing, China.

Humphrey, M., Thompson, M. R., & Jackson, K. R. (2005). Security for Grids. *Lawrence Berkeley National Laboratory. Paper LBNL-54853.*

Jameel, H., Kalim, U., Sajjad, A., Lee, S., & Jeon, T. (2005, February 14-16). *Mobile-To-Grid Middleware: Bridging the gap between mobile and Grid environments.* Paper presented at the European Grid Conference EGC 2005, Amsterdam, The Netherlands.

Kwok-Yan, L., Xi-Bin, Z., Siu-Leung, C., Gu, M., & Jia-Guang, S. (2004). Enhancing Grid Security Infrastructure to Support Mobile Computing Nodes. *Lecture Notes in Computer Science, 2908/2003,* 42-54.

Litke, A., Skoutas, D., & Varvarigou, T. (2004, December). *Mobile Grid Computing: Changes and Challenges of Resourse Management in a Mobile Grid Environment.* Paper presented at the 5th International Conference on Practical Aspects of Knowledge Management (PAKM 2004).

Rosado, D. G., Fernández-Medina, E., López, J., & Piattini, M. (2008). *PSecGCM: Process for the development of Secure Grid Computing based Systems with Mobile devices.* Paper presented at the International Conference on Availability, Reliability and Security (ARES 2008), Barcelona, Spain.

Sajjad, A., Jameel, H., Kalim, U., Han, S. M., Lee, Y.-K., & Lee, S. (2005). *AutoMAGI - an Autonomic middleware for enabling Mobile Access to Grid Infrastructure.* Paper presented at the Joint International Conference on Autonomic and Autonomous Systems and International Conference on Networking and Services - (icas-icns'05).

Talukder, A., & Yavagal, R. (2006). Chapter 18: Security issues in mobile computing. In *Mobile Computing*: McGraw-Hill Professional.

Trusted Computing Group Administration. (2006). Securing Mobile Devices on Converged Networks.

Vivas, J. L., López, J., & Montenegro, J. A. (2007). Cap. 12. Grid Security Architecture: Requirements,fundamentals, standards, and models. In A. Publications (Ed.), *Security in Distributed, Grid, Mobile, and Pervasive Computing* (pp. 440). Tuscaloosa, USA.

Welch, V., Siebenlist, F., Foster, I., Bresnahan, J., Czajkowski, K., Gawor, J., et al. (2003, 22-24 June 2003). *Security for Grid services.* Paper presented at the 12th IEEE International Symposium on High Performance Distributed Computing (HPDC-12 '03).

This work was previously published in the International Journal of Grid and High Performance Computing, Vol. 1, Issue 3, edited by E. Udoh and F. Wang, pp. 1-17, copyright 2009 by IGI Publishing (an imprint of IGI Global).

Chapter 13
An MDA Compliant Approach for Designing Secure Data Warehouses

Rodolfo Villarroel
Universidad Católica del Maule, Chile

Eduardo Fernández-Medina
Universidad de Castilla-La Mancha, Spain

Juan Trujillo
Universidad de Alicante, Spain

Mario Piattini
Universidad de Castilla-La Mancha, Spain

ABSTRACT

This chapter presents an approach for designing secure Data Warehouses (DWs) that accomplish the conceptual modeling of secure DWs independently from the target platform where the DW has to be implemented, because our complete approach follows the Model Driven Architecture (MDA) and the Model Driven Security (MDS). In most of real world DW projects, the security aspects are issues that usually rely on the DBMS administrators. We argue that the design of these security aspects should be considered together with the conceptual modeling of DWs from the early stages of a DW project, and being able to attach user security information to the basic structures of a Multidimensional (MD) model. In this way, we would be able to generate this information in a semi or automatic way into a target platform and the final DW will better suits the user security requirements.

INTRODUCTION

The goal of information confidentiality is to ensure that users can only access to the information that they are allowed. In the case of multidimensional (MD) models, confidentiality is crucial, because business information that is very sensitive, can be discovered by executing a simple query. Several papers deal with the importance of security in the software development process. Ghosh, Howell, and Whittaker (2002) state that security must influence all aspects of design, implementation, and software tests. Hall and Chapman (2002) put forward ideas about how to build correct systems that fulfil not only the normal requirements but also the security ones. Nevertheless, security in databases and data warehouses is usually focused on the secure data storage, and not on their design. Thus, a methodology of data warehouse design based on the UML, with the addition of security aspects, would allow us to design DWs with the syntax and power of UML and with the new security characteristics ready to be used whenever the application has security requirements that demand them.

In this chapter, we present an approach for designing secure DWs as follows: we define the Model Driven Architecture (MDA) and Model Driven Security (MDS) compliant architecture of our approach, and we provide an Access Control and Audit (ACA) model for the conceptual MD modeling. Then, we extend the Unified Modeling Language (UML) with this ACA model, representing the security information (gathered in the ACA model) in the conceptual MD modeling, thereby allowing us to obtain secure MD models. By using this approach, makes possible to implement the secure MD models with any of the DBMS that are able to implement multilevel databases, such as Oracle Label Security and DB2 Universal Database, UDB.

The remainder of this chapter is structured as follows: Next section introduces related work; next, we present the MDA and MDS compliant architecture of our approach. Finally, we present the main conclusions.

RELATED WORK

As this chapter treats different research topics, the related work is organized as follows.

Multidimensional Modeling

Lately, several MD data models have been proposed. Some of them fall into the logical level (such as the well-known star-schema (Kimball & Ross, 2002). Others may be considered as formal models as they provide a formalism for the consideration of the main MD properties. A review of the most relevant logical and formal models can be found in Blaschka, Sapia, Höfling, and Dinter (1998) and Abelló, Samos, and Saltor (2001).

In this section, we will only make brief reference to the most relevant models that we consider "pure" conceptual MD models. These models provide a high level of abstraction for the main MD modeling properties at the conceptual level and are totally independent from implementation issues. One outstanding feature provided by these models is that they provide a set of graphical notations (such as the classical and well-known Extended Entity-Relationship model) which facilitates their use and reading. These are as follows: *The Dimensional-Fact (DF) Model* by Golfarelli, Maio, and Rizzi (1998), *The Multidimensional/ ER (M/ER) Model* by Sapia, Blaschka, Höfling, and Dinter (1998), *The starER Model* by Tryfona, Busborg, and Christiansen (1999), the *Yet Another Multidimensional Model (YAM²)* by Abelló et al. (2001), and the model proposed by Trujillo, Palomar, Gómez, and Song (2001). Unfortunately, none of these approaches for MD modeling considers security as an important issue in their conceptual models, and consequently they do not solve the problem of modeling security from the early stages of a DW project.

Security Integration into the Design Process

There are a few proposals which attempt to integrate security into conceptual modeling, such as the Semantic Data Model for Security (Smith, 1991) and the Multilevel Object Modeling Technique (Marks & Sell, 1996), but they are partial (since they do not cover the complete development process). More recent proposals are UMLSec (Jürjens, 2002) and SecureUML (Lodderstedt, Basin, & Doser, 2002) where UML is extended to develop secure systems. These approaches are interesting, but they only deal with information systems (IS) in general, whilst conceptual database and DW design are not considered. Moreover, a methodology and a set of models have been proposed (Fernández-Medina & Piattini, 2003) in order to design secure databases for implementation with Oracle9i Label Security (OLS). This approach, based on the UML, is relevant because it considers security aspects in all stages of the database development process, from requirement-gathering to implementation. Together with the previous methodology, the proposed Object Security Constraint Language (OSCL), based on the Object Constraint Language (OCL) of UML, allows us to specify security constraints in the conceptual and logical database design process, and to implement them in a specific database management system (DBMS), OLS. Nevertheless, the previous methodology and models do not consider the design of secure MD models for DWs, and therefore, are not appropriate for the representation of the peculiarities of DWs.

Access Control Models

Many proposals have been developed with the aim of protecting information against improper disclosure. All of them make use of the particularities of the systems they deal with, such as the types of objects, subjects, privileges, signs, and so on. For instance, there are authorization models for data archives, database systems, XML documents, distributed hypertext systems, Web services, multimedia documents, and workflows. Nevertheless, although many authorization models that allow a flexible and simple specification of authorizations have been proposed, they rely on the particular properties of the underlying data model. Thus, these authorization models cannot be easily extended to other data models, such as MD modeling.

Security and Access Control Models for Data Warehouses

The peculiarity of DWs and the MD model and its terms (facts, dimensions, classification hierarchies, and so on) used for both designing and querying DWs, makes it necessary to deal with specific access control and audit models for DWs.

In the literature, we can find several initiatives for the inclusion of security in DWs. Many of them are focused on interesting aspects related to access control, multilevel security, its applications to federated databases, applications using commercial tools, and so on. These initiatives refer to specific aspects that allow us to improve DW security in acquisition, storage, and access aspects. However, none of them considers the security aspects into all stages of the DW development cycle, nor does any examine the introduction of security in the conceptual MD design.

On the other hand, there are some interesting proposals which define authorization models for data warehouses, but they only deal with OLAP operations (e.g., roll-up or drill-down) accomplished with OLAP tools. So these are not conceived for their integration in MD modeling as part of the DW design process, and as a consequence, inconsistent security measures might well be defined. We believe that we should consider basic security measures for business DWs with a conceptual model from the early stages of a DW project. Then more specific security rules can be defined for particular groups of users in terms of data marts, views, and OLAP tools, or any other analysis tools, but which are consistent with the main security rules defined for the DW.

Finally, the work presented in Priebe & Pernul (2001) proposes the definition of basic security measures for main OLAP operations. To this end, authors propose the ADAPTed UML for specifying security measures on a UML class diagram which they use for the MD modeling of OLAP tools at the conceptual level. Although this is an interesting proposal that can be extended and improved, we consider two key aspects that should be given particular attention in this sense. The first of these is that the defined security measures are only based on the OLAP operations that users can carry out by using OLAP tools. The second is that its notation is simple, and rather than being a complete and formal model for data warehouses, we see it as a practical way of modeling simple OLAP scenarios. Some more complex elements of the MD model (e.g., the type of classification hierarchy) have a high impact on security measures, as in data warehouse systems users can access facts by navigating from different classification hierarchy paths, or then again access to facts or dimensions may be denied if users try to access a fine grain (low cardinality). What is more, one fact can be accessed if queried on its own, but access to the same fact can be absolutely forbidden if it is queried in combination with one dimension.

Finally, all the above-presented proposals only examine access control, but not audit; so the approach proposed in this chapter is the first one to consider both access model and audit in the multidimensional modeling of DWs at the conceptual level.

AN MDA AND MDS COMPLIANT APPROACH

Model Driven Architecture (MDA) is an Object Management Group standard that addresses the complete life cycle of designing, deploying, integrating, and managing applications. MDA (Kleppe, Warmer, & Bast, 2003) separates the specification of system functionality from the specification of the implementation of that functionality on a specific technology platform. Thus, MDA encourages specifying a Platform Independent Model (PIM) by using any specification language. Then, this PIM can be transformed into Platform Specific Models (PSM) in order to be executed on a concrete platform by transforming this PSM into the corresponding Code.

We have aligned our approach for the conceptual modeling of DWs with the MDA approach (see Figure 1). Our enriched PIM can be transformed into any logical model representing the multidimensionality of data (e.g., the star schema), and finally this logical model can be transformed into a particular DBMS (e.g., Oracle).

On the other hand, Model Driven Security (MDS) is a new approach (Basin, Doser, & Lodderstedt, 2003) for integrating security into the information systems design. This approach considers design models and security models, which are combined, leading to a new kind of model that is called security design model. Our approach has also been aligned with MDS (see Figure 1). We have considered a Raw PIM, which is the design model. This model does not contain security details, and is used for the conceptual modeling of DWs. Moreover, we have defined our ACA model, that is completely independent from the design model (and of course it is independent from the target platform, so in some sense is another PIM) and, in MDS terminology, is the security model. This independence is highly important, because we could use this security model together with other DW conceptual models. Combining both the design model and the security model, an enriched PIM is performed. This security design model is a DW conceptual model that also contains the security details that can be specified with our ACA model. The design model must usually be extended to be able to represent the security details.

Figure 1. Merging the UML extension and the ACA Model into one PIM

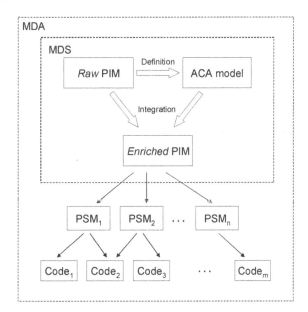

Therefore, this enriched PIM with all the security information is the model that will participate in the MDA architecture in the upcoming transformations.

Raw PIM. Next, we outline the approach, based on the UML, we use for DW conceptual modeling (Lujan-Mora, Trujillo, & Song, 2002; Trujillo et al., 2001). This approach has been specified by means of a UML profile that contains the necessary stereotypes in order to carry out the MD modeling at the conceptual level successfully. In this approach, structural properties of MD modeling are represented by means of a UML class diagram in which the information is clearly organized into facts (items of interest for an enterprise) and dimensions (context in which facts have to be analyzed).

Facts and dimensions are represented by means of fact classes (stereotype Fact) and dimension classes (stereotype Dimension) respectively. Fact classes are defined as composite classes in shared aggregation relationships of n dimension classes

(see Figure 2). The minimum multiplicity in the role of the dimension classes is 1 (all the facts must always be related to all dimensions). A fact is composed of measures or fact attributes. By default, all measures in the fact class are considered to be additive. With respect to dimensions, each level of a classification hierarchy is specified by a base class (stereotype Base). An association of base classes specifies the relationship between two levels of a classification hierarchy. Every base class must also contain an identifying attribute (OID) and a descriptor attribute (stereotype D). These attributes are necessary for an automatic generation process into commercial OLAP tools, as these tools store this information on their metadata.

Access Control and Audit (ACA) Model. Although there are many authorization models that allow a flexible and easy specification of authorizations, they rely on the particular properties of the underlying data model. As a result, these authorization models cannot be easily extended to other data models, such as the MD modeling.

Figure 2. Multidimensional modeling using the UML

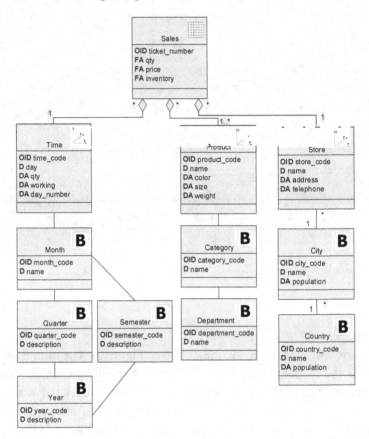

Access control is not a complete solution for securing a system as it must be coupled with auditing. Auditing requires the recording of all user requests and activities for their later analysis. Therefore, in our approach, we take both concepts into consideration for their integration in the conceptual MD modeling design.

Access control models are typically composed of a set of authorization rules that regulate accesses to objects. Each authorization rule usually specifies the *subject* to which the rule applies, the *object* to which the authorization refers, the *action* to which the rule refers, and the *sign* describing whether the rule permits or denies the access.

In order to regulate access to objects in a MD model, we have considered the Mandatory Access Control model (in the form of multilevel security

policies), which is based on the classification of subjects and objects in the system. So, our access control and audit model allows us to specify sensitivity information assignment rules for all elements of MD models (facts, dimensions, etc.), which define static and dynamic object classification. Moreover, our model allows us to define authorization rules that represent exceptions to the general multilevel rules, where the designer can specify different situations in which the multilevel rules are not sufficient. Finally, a set of audit rules, which represent the corresponding audit requirements, can be included in the model.

In multilevel policies, an access class is assigned to each object and subject. The most common access class is defined as a security level and a set of categories. The security level is an element of a hierarchically ordered set, such as Top Secret (TS), Secret (S), Confidential (C), and Unclassified (U), where, TS > S > C > U. The set of categories is a subset of an unordered set, whose elements reflect functional, or competence, areas. The access class is one element of a partially-ordered set of classes, where an access class c_1 dominates an access class c_2 iff the security level of c_1 is greater than or equal to that of c_2 and the categories of c_1 include those of c_2. We have considered a secrecy-based mandatory policy, so the two principles that must be satisfied to protect information confidentiality are: i) no-read-up (a subject is allowed a read-access to an object only if the access class of the subject dominates the access class of the object), and ii) no-write-down (a subject is allowed a write-access to an object only if the access class of the subject is dominated by the access class of the object).

In our model, we define an access class on the basis of three different but compatible ways of classifying users; by their security level, the user role they play and by the user compartments they belong to:

- **Security levels:** This indicates the clearance level of the user.
- **Security user roles:** Used by a company to organize users in a hierarchical role structure, according to the responsibilities of each type of work. Each user can play more than one role.
- **Security user compartments:** Also used by an organization to classify users into a set of horizontal compartments or groups, such as geographical location, area of work, and so on. Each user can belong to one or more compartments.

Therefore, in our model, the access class is one element of a partially ordered set of classes, where an access class c_1 dominates an access class c_2 iff the security level of c_1 is greater than or equal to that of c_2, the compartments of c_1 include those of

c_2, and at least one of the user roles of c_1 (or one of its ascendant) is defined for c_2.

Thus, for each object in the model, the user access requirements (security level, user roles, and user compartments) can be defined, thereby specifying with high accuracy which users can access each particular object.

Enriched PIM. The goal of this UML extension is to be able to design MD conceptual model, but classifying the information in order to define which properties has to own the user to be entitled to access the information. So, we have to consider three main stages:

- Defining precisely the organization of users that will have access to the MD system. We can define a precise level of granularity considering three ways of organizing users: Security hierarchy levels (which indicate the clearance level of the user), user Compartments (which indicate a horizontal classification of users), and user Roles (which indicate a hierarchical organization of users according to their roles or responsibilities within the organization)
- Classifying the information into the MD model. We can define for each element of the model (fact class, dimension class, fact attribute, etc.) its security information, specifying a sequence of security levels, a set of user compartments, and a set of user roles. We can also specify security constraints considering these security attributes. The security information and constraints indicate the security properties that users have to own to be able to access the information.
- Enforcing the mandatory access control. The typical operations that final users can execute in this type of systems are query operations. So, the mandatory access control has to be enforced for *read* operations. The access control rule for read operations is as follows: A user can access information only

if, a) the security level of the user is greater than or equal to the security level of the information, b) all the user compartments that have been defined for the information are owned by the user, and, c) at least one of the user roles that the information has defined, is played by the user.

In this chapter, we will only focus on the second stage by defining a UML extension that allows us to classify the security elements in a conceptual MD model and to specify security constraints.

According to Conallen (2000), an extension to the UML begins with a brief description and then lists and describes all the stereotypes, tagged values, and constraints of the extension. In addition to these elements, an extension contains a set of well-formedness rules. These rules are used to determine whether a model is semantically consistent with itself. According to this quote, we define our UML extension for secure conceptual MD modeling following the schema composed of these elements:

- **Description** (a brief description of the extension in natural language),
- **Prerequisite extensions** (this element indicates whether the current extension needs the existence of previous extensions),
- **Stereotypes / tagged values** (the definition of the stereotypes and / or tagged values),
- **Well-formedness rules** (the static semantics of the metaclasses are defined both in natural language and as a set of invariants defined by means of OCL expressions), and
- **Comments** (any additional comment, decision or example, usually written in natural language).

For the definition of the stereotypes, we follow the structure that is suggested in Gogolla & Henderson-Sellers (2002), which is composed of a name, the base metaclass, the description, the

tagged values and a list of constraints defined by means of OCL. For the definition of tagged values, the type of tagged values, the multiplicity, the description, and the default value are defined.

Basically, we have reuse the previous profile defined in Lujan-Mora et al. (2002), which allow us to design DWs from a conceptual perspective, and we have added the required elements that we need to specify the security aspects (Subjects, Objects, Actions, Sensitive Information Assignment Rules, Authorization Rules, and Audit Rules) considered in our ACA model. We define a set of tagged values, stereotypes, and constraints, which enables us to create secure MD models. Figure 3 shows an MD model with security information and constraints. We use several tagged values to allow us to model all our rules of the ACA model.

The MD model in Figure 3 includes a fact class (*Admission*), two dimensions (*Diagnosis* and *Patient*), two base classes (*Diagnosis_group* and *City*), and a class (*UserProfile*). *UserProfile* class (stereotype *UserProfile*) contains the information of all users who will have access to this multidimensional model. *Admission* fact class -stereotype *Fact*- contains all individual admissions of patients in one or more hospitals, and can be accessed by all users who have *secret* or *top secret* security levels -tagged value *SecurityLevels (SL) of classes*-, and play *health* or *administrative* roles -tagged value *SecurityRoles (SR) of classes*-. Note that the *cost* attribute can only be accessed by users who play *administrative* role -tagged value *SR of attributes*- *Patient* dimension contains the information of hospital patients, and can be accessed by all users who have *secret* security level—tagged value *SL*-, and play *health* or *administrative* roles—tagged value *SR*-. The *Address* attribute can only be accessed by users who play *administrative* role—tagged value *SR* of attributes-. *City* base class contains the information of cities, and it allows us to group patients by cities. Cities can be accessed by all users who have *confidential* security level—tagged value *SL*-. *Diagnosis* dimension contains the informa-

Figure 3. Example of MD model with security information and constraints

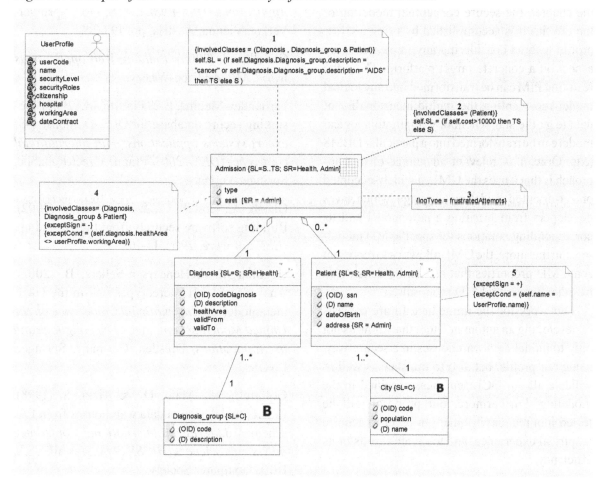

tion of each diagnosis, and can be accessed by users who play *health* role—tagged value *SR-*, and have *secret* security level—tagged value *SL-*. Finally, *Diagnosis_group* contains a set of general groups of diagnosis. Each group can be related to several diagnoses, but a diagnosis will always be related to a group. Diagnosis groups can be accessed by all users who have *confidential* security level—tagged value SLs-. Several security constraints have been specified by using the previously defined constraints, stereotypes, and tagged values.

Each security rule is first defined in natural language, then we specify the corresponding ACA rule, y finally we indicate the place this rule is specified in the secure MD conceptual model. For example:

Rule 1: For each instance of the fact class Admission, the security level will be at least Secret, and the security roles will be Health and Admin.

ACA rule: OBJECTS MDCL Admission SECINF SL Secret SR Health Admin

Secure MD Model: See Admission fact class and tagged-values SL and SR.

CONCLUSION

In this chapter, we have aligned our approach for the conceptual modeling of DWs with the MDA approach. Thus, as we have shown throughout the chapter, the secure conceptual modeling of the DW itself is accomplished by using a UML profile without considering any implementation aspect on a concrete target platform. Then, the resulting PIM can be transformed into any logical model representing the multidimensionality of data (e.g., the star schema), y finally this logical model can be transformed into a particular DBMS (e.g., Oracle). A relevant advantage of this approach is that it uses the UML, a widely-accepted object-oriented modeling language, which saves developers from learning a new model and its corresponding notations for specific MD modeling. Furthermore, the UML allows us to represent some MD properties that are hardly considered by other conceptual MD proposals.

Our work for the immediate future consists of developing an automated tool that allow us not only to model data warehouses in a secure way, using our profile, but also to translate as well as validate all our OCL sentences specified in the modeling. Furthermore, our proposal will be tested in a real environment in order to acquire empirical experience, and to obtain results of its efficiency.

REFERENCES

Abelló, A., Samos, J., & Saltor, F. (2001). A framework for the classification and description of multidimensional data models. *Proceedings of 12th International Conference on Database and Expert Systems Applications (DEXA'01)*, Springer-Verlag LNCS 2113, Munich, Germany, pp. 668-677.

Basin, D., Doser, J., & Lodderstedt, T. (2003). Model driven security: From UML models to access control infrastructures. ETH Zürich.

Blaschka, M., Sapia, C., Höfling, G., & Dinter, B. (1998). Finding your way through multidimensional data models. *Proceedings of 9th International Conference on Database and Expert Systems Applications (DEXA'98)*. LNCS, 1460, Springer-Verlag, Vienna, Austria, pp. 198-203.

Conallen, J. (2000). *Building Web applications with UML*. Addison-Wesley.

Fernández-Medina, E. & Piattini, M. (2003). Designing secure database for OLS. *Database and expert systems applications: 14th international conference (DEXA 2003)*, Prague, Czech Republic, Springer-Verlag.

Ghosh, A., Howell, C., & Whittaker, J. (2002). Building software securely from the ground up. *IEEE Software, 19*(1), 14-16.

Gogolla, M. & Henderson-Sellers, B. (2002). Analysis of UML stereotypes within the UML metamodel. *5th International Conference on the Unified Modeling Language - The Language and its Applications*, Dresden, Germany, Springer, LNCS.

Golfarelli, M., Maio, D., & Rizzi, S. (1998). Conceptual design of data warehouses from E/R schemes. *32th Hawaii International Conference on Systems Sciences (HICSS 1998)*, Hawaii, USA, IEEE Computer Society.

Hall, A., & Chapman, R. (2002). Correctness by construction: developing a commercial secure system. *IEEE Software, 19*(1), 18-25.

Jürjens, J. (2002). UMLsec: Extending UML for secure systems development. UML 2002 - The Unified Modeling Language, Model engineering, concepts and tools. Jézéquel, J., Hussmann, H. & Cook, S. Dresden, Germany, Springer: 412-425.

Kimball, R. & Ross, M. (2002). *The data warehousing toolkit*. 2nd ed. John Wiley.

Kleppe, A., Warmer, J. & Bast, W. (2003). *MDA explained. The model driven architecture: Practice and promise*. Addison-Wesley.

Lodderstedt, T., Basin, D. & Doser, J. (2002). *SecureUML: A UML-based modeling language for model-driven security*. 5th International Conference on the Unified Modeling Language (UML 2002), Dresden, Germany: Springer-Verlag.

Luján-Mora, S., Trujillo, J. & Song, I. Y. (2002). *Extending the UML for multidimensional modeling*. 5th International Conference on the Unified Modeling Language (UML 2002), Dresden, Germany: Springer-Verlag.

Marks, D., Sell, P., & Thuraisingham, B. (1996). MOMT: A multi-level object modeling technique for designing secure database applications. *Journal of Object-Oriented Programming, 9*(4), 22-29.

Priebe, T. & Pernul, G. (2001). *A pragmatic approach to conceptual modeling of OLAP security*. 20th International Conference on Conceptual Modeling (ER 2001). Yokohama, Japan: Springer-Verlag.

Sapia, C., Blaschka, M., Höfling, G., & Dinter, B. (1998). *Extending the E/R model for the multidimensional paradigm*. 1st International Workshop on Data Warehouse and Data Mining (DWDM'98). Singapore: Springer-Verlag.

Smith, G.W. (1991). Modeling security-relevant data semantics. *IEEE Transactions on Software Engineering, 17*(11), 1195-1203.

Trujillo, J., Palomar, M., Gómez, J., & Song, I. Y. (2001). Designing data warehouses with OO conceptual models. *IEEE Computer, Special issue on Data Warehouses,* (34), 66-75.

Tryfona, N., Busborg, F., & Christiansen, J. (1999). *starER: A conceptual model for data warehouse design*. ACM 2nd International Workshop on Data Warehousing and OLAP (DOLAP'99), Missouri, USA.

KEY TERMS

Access Control: Determines what one party will allow another one to do with respect to resources and objects mediated by the former. Access control models are typically composed of a set of authorization rules that regulate access to objects. Each authorization rule usually specifies the subject to which the rule applies, the object to which the authorization refers, the action to which the rule refers, and the sign describing whether the rule states a permission or a denial for the access.

Audit Process: Gathers data about activities in the system and analyzes it to discover security violations or diagnose their cause.

Data Warehouse (DW): A subject-oriented, integrated, time-variant, non-volatile collection of data in support of management's decision-making process.

Model Driven Architecture (MDA): An Object Management Group (OMG) standard that addresses the complete life cycle of designing, deploying, integrating, and managing applications.

Model Driven Security (MDS): A new approach for integrating security into the information systems design. This approach considers design models and security models, which are combined, leading to a new kind of models that is called security design model.

Multilevel Databases: Databases that contain objects with different levels of confidentiality and register subjects with different abilities.

Security: The capability of a software product to protect data and information in order to avoid that unauthorized individuals or systems are able to read and modify them and not to deny access to authorized staff.

UML Profile: A set of improvements that extend an existing UML type of diagram for a different use. These improvements are specified by means of the extendibility mechanism provided by UML (stereotypes, properties and constraints) in order to be able to adapt it to a new method or model.

Chapter 14
IPSec Overhead in Dual Stack IPv4/IPv6 Transition Mechanisms:
An Analytical Study

M. Mujinga
University of Fort Hare, South Africa

Hippolyte Muyingi
University of Fort Hare, South Africa

Alfredo Terzoli
Rhodes University, South Africa

G. S. V. Radha Krishna Rao
University of Fort Hare, South Africa

ABSTRACT

Internet protocol version 6 (IPv6) is the next generation Internet protocol proposed by the Internet Engineering Task Force (IETF) to supplant the current Internet protocol version 4 (IPv4). Lack of security below the application layer in IPv4 is one of the reasons why there is a need for a new IP. IPv6 has built-in support for the Internet protocol security protocol (IPSec). This chapter reports work done to evaluate implications of compulsory use of IPSec on dual stack IPv4/IPv6 environment.

INTRODUCTION AND BACKGROUND

The Internet protocol (IP) is the protocol that operates at the backbone of the Internet, and networking in general. The initial IP was first published in 1981, in RFC 791 [DARPA IP Spec., 1981] and is now generally known as IPv4. Internet protocol version 6 (IPv6) is the next generation Internet protocol proposed by the IETF in RFC

2460 (Deering & Hinden., 1998; Doraswamy & Harkins, 1999), published in 1998 to supplant IPv4. IP security (IPSec) is provided by a set of protocols, the main protocols being authentication header (AH) and encapsulating security payload (ESP) protocols (Kent & Atkinson, 1998). IPSec operates at the network layer in a way that is completely transparent to the applications, and much more powerful, because the applications do not need to have any knowledge of IPSec to be able to use it (Farrel, 2004). In IPv4, IPSec headers are inserted after the IPv4 header and before the next-layer protocol header. While with IPv6, this is applied in the form of additional extension headers (Loshin, 2003). This obviously increases the overhead of an IP datagram, and since this protocol is mandatory on IPv6, this overhead becomes increasingly significant.

There was some research done on the performance implications of IPSec deployment. In Ronan et al. (2004), the authors evaluated the performance overheads under a range of different bandwidth and different processors, on throughput and processor; single and dual, when communicating over a secured VPN on IPv4 infrastructure, using Linux 2.6.1 kernel. The findings showed that the overhead differs from one processor type to the other, and this was consistent when dual processors were used of the same type. The other work (Ariga et al., 2000) evaluated the performance of data transmissions with IPv4 and IPv6 networks. The results showed that IPSec obviously degrades the network performance in terms of throughput and end-to-end delay for the large data transmission and for the actual application. The authors concentrated on digital video (DV) transmission as the application. Their results showed that, for large data transmissions, when authentication and encryption are applied, the throughput degrades to 1/9 compared with the throughput without authentication or encryption.

Dual stack translation mechanism (DSTM) was our primary method in the IPv6 experiments; 6to4 in particular. 6to4 is a tunneling addressing

mechanism that enables communication between two IPv6 computers that live in an IPv4 environment (Carpenter & Moore, 2001). In this paper, we will investigate the cost in terms of performance when transmitting traffic on computer networks, with IPSec enabled on IPv4 and IPv6. Our research focuses on Windows IPv6 and IPSec implementations, and evaluates a variety of IP traffic over HTTP, FTP, TFTP, and ICMP protocols. We evaluated the additional frame overhead induced by IPSec on both IPv4 and IPv6 on these protocols, noting also its impact on average round-trip times. This is achieved by comparing traffic with IPSec on and IPSec off. The research we are conducting will give an insight into the quantitative expense, which the mandatory use of IPSec will bring into our networks, and we will give a model of how and when to use it on your network. Knowing when and how to deploy IPSec efficiently will help to save two of our most valued resources in the Internet community: the scarce and expensive bandwidth and computer processing power.

EXPERIMENTAL DETAILS

Our network consists of five computers, of which three are servers running Windows 2003 Server SP1 and two clients running Windows XP Professional SP 2. All nodes have Microsoft TCP/IP version 6 protocol stack enabled. We configured IPSec on the domain controller. We are using a third-party protocol analyzer for packet capturing and analysis.

All the computers used have the following system properties:

- CPU: 2.8 GHz
- RAM: 1.1 GB
- HD Size: 112 GB

Our experimental test bed consists of equipment with the specifications, as available in Table 1.

Table 1. List of experimental equipment

Hardware	Software
Domain Controller Server	Windows Server 2003 SP1
File Server	Windows XP Professional SP2
Web Server	Finisar Surveyor 5.5
2 Client computers	
10/100 Fast Ethernet Switch	

There were a number of tests that were carried out, and there are two main sections of tests, that is, those conducted to determine the traffic overhead and those conducted to determine the delay using the round-trip times and download times in the case of HTTP and FTP.

Frame Overhead

Frame overhead are bits that are added at regular intervals to a digital signal at the sending end or intermediary gateways of a digital link. We determined the frame overhead induced by applying different IPSec protocols and algorithms in our first set of experiments.

Round-Trip Time

Round-trip time (RTT) is a measure of the time it takes for a packet to travel from a computer, across a network to another computer, and back. RTT is computed by the sending side recording the clock when it transmits a packet, and then recording the clock again when an acknowledgment or a reply arrives. By subtracting the two values, we obtain a single estimate of the round-trip time. A collection of these values for a period of time gives the average RTT.

Download Time

The download time is the time it takes to download a file or a Web page from the remote server or computer to the local computer. We calculated this by subtracting the time the first frame of the downloaded file is received from the time the last frame is received.

APPLICATIONS/PROTOCOLS TESTED

ICMP

Internet control message protocol (ICMP) is a required protocol tightly integrated with IP. ICMP uses IP as if ICMP were a higher-level protocol, that is, ICMP messages are encapsulated in IP datagrams. ICMP is also not dependent on either TCP or UDP. Ping is an application that tests host responses over a network connection. Ping uses the network layer to send packets to a remote address. If there are network connectivity problems or the host has problems, the ping will fail, indicating that a problem exists. Additional tests may be needed at that point to determine the cause of the problem.

HTTP

The hypertext transfer protocol (HTTP) is an application-level protocol for distributed, collaborative, hypermedia information systems used to transfer data across the Internet. HTTP has been in use by the World Wide Web global information initiative since 1990. The current version of HTTP is HTTP/1.1. We used HTTP to test how IPSec performs on TCP.

FTP

File transfer protocol (FTP) is a procedure used to upload and download files to and from your FTP server. FTP is a special way to login to another Internet site for the purposes of retrieving and/or sending files, and is the best way of sending files from one computer to another over the Internet using TCP.

TFTP

Trivial file transfer protocol (TFTP) is a simple UDP-based protocol used for transferring files between computers. TFTP is used where user authentication and the need to view directories on remote computers are not required. Its two major uses are to bootstrap diskless machines that are being installed over the network, and to install images that reside in firmware. This type of communication also needs to be protected to improve network security.

FRAME STRUCTURE

IPv4

The minimum size of an IPv4 Ethernet frame is 64 bytes, which includes the minimum frame payload of 46 bytes plus the Ethernet header of 18 bytes, including 4 bytes for cyclical redundancy check (CRC). The maximum frame size for IPv4 Ethernet is 1518 bytes, given by an Ethernet maximum transmission unity (MTU) of 1,500 bytes plus the Ethernet header.

IPv6

An IPv4 Ethernet frame using 6to4 has a minimum size of 86 bytes, comprised of 68 bytes of frame payload plus 18 bytes of Ethernet header, including 4 bytes of CRC. There are fundamental differences on how IPSec affects IPv4 and IPv6. The default MTU size for IPv6 packets on an Ethernet is 1280 octets.

IPSec Transform Sets

An IPSec transform specifies a single IPSec security protocol (either AH or ESP) with its corresponding security algorithms and mode. Since our tests are based on a single network, that is, point–to-point communication within a site, we chose to use the transport mode for the tests. Therefore, all IPSec transform sets are based on transport mode IPSec that protects the IP payload only with the IP header visible. A transform set is a combination of individual IPSec transforms designed to enact a specific security policy for protecting a particular traffic flow. Table 2 shows the available IPSec transform sets in Windows Server 2003. Windows IPSec implementation provides two integrity algorithms: SHA1 and MD5, and two encryption algorithms: 3DES and DES. Hence, all our IPSec transform sets are based on these four algorithms and in transport mode.

There are 24 possible IPSec transform sets in Windows IPSec implementation, and we experimented with all of them on IPv4 and IPv6.

Test Considerations

Our tests were on both IP protocols, IPv4 and IPv6. For all tests we carried out plain benchmarking tests, that is, performance tests were performed without enabling IPSec and we used these results as a baseline for comparing with IPSec tests results as outlined in Kaeo and Van Herck (2006). IPv6 tests were carried out using 6to4 because it is applicable on the global Internet and intrasite networks, while intrasite automatic tunnel addressing protocol (ISATAP) provides IPv6 connectivity within an IPv4 intranet. However, we conducted preliminary experiments using ISATAP and realized that it has the same frame overhead impact as 6to4.

Table 2. IPSec transform sets in Windows Server 2003

Transform Set	AH algorithm	ESP Algorithm
AH Only		
1	AH-MD5	None
2	AH-SHA1	None
ESP Only		
3	None	ESP-SHA1
4	None	ESP-MD5
5	None	ESP-SHA1-3DES
6	None	ESP-MD5-3DES
7	None	ESP-SHA1-DES
8	None	ESP-MD5-DES
AH and ESP Encryption		
9	AH-MD5	ESP-DES
10	AH-MD5	ESP-DES
11	AH-SHA1	ESP-DES
12	AH-SHA1	ESP-DES
AH and ESP Integrity		
13	AH-MD5	ESP-SHA1
14	AH-MD5	ESP-MD5
15	AH-SHA1	ESP-SHA1
16	AH-SHA1	ESP-MD5
BOTH		
17	AH-MD5	ESP-SHA1-3DES
18	AH-MD5	ESP-MD5-3DES
19	AH-SHA1	ESP-SHA1-3DES
20	AH-SHA1	ESP-MD5-3DES
21	AH-MD5	ESP-SHA1-DES
22	AH-MD5	ESP-MD5-DES
23	AH-SHA1	ESP-SHA1-DES
24	AH-SHA1	ESP-MD5-DES

RESULTS AND DISCUSSION

Frame Overhead Tests on ICMP

The first protocol we measured IPSec frame overhead was ICMP, using the ping application on the different sizes of packets: 1 byte, 8 bytes, 32 bytes, 128 bytes, 512 bytes, 2,048 bytes, 8,192 bytes, 32,768 bytes, and 65,500 bytes, of which 1 to 512 bytes are nonfragmented packets and the rest are fragmented. We started the ping program on one client sending to the other client, while capturing the communication using the protocol analyzer on the sending computer. This procedure was conducted with IPSec off first and then IPSec on, using different transform sets on IPv4 and IPv6.

IPSec Overhead Tests on IPv4

The observations we made after capturing packets of different sizes is that AH, applied on its own, adds an additional 24 bytes to each packet sent on IPv4. Even if the packet is fragmented, only 24 bytes are added on the first fragment. These 24 bytes are made of the following sections of the AH header, as captured by our protocol analyzer.

1 byte – Next header
1 byte – Payload length
2 bytes – Reserved
4 bytes – Security parameters index
16 bytes – Authentication data

Table 3 shows the structure of the frame protected by AH protocol in transport mode, the sizes are in bytes. Table 4 shows the AH header sections.

The additional bytes due to IPSec headers are the same for all packet sizes, fragmented and nonfragmented. The overhead is the same irrespective of the hash function used, that is, MD5 or SHA1. ESP-only transform sets add an overhead of 36 bytes using both properties (in-

tegrity and encryption) of ESP. This is divided into the following sections:

- Security association identifier – 4 bytes
- Sequence number – 4 bytes
- Opaque transform data – 28 bytes

The overhead for applying ESP integrity only is 28 bytes, made up of

- Security association identifier – 4 bytes
- Sequence number – 4 bytes
- Opaque transform data – 20 bytes

The overhead for using both IPSec protocols is the summation of the overhead added by each protocol. For instance, the overhead of AH and ESP fully implemented is 60 bytes (24 AH and 36 ESP). We calculated the percentage impact of the overhead using the formula:

Percentage overhead =

$$\frac{\text{IPSec Frame Size - IPSec disabled Frame Size}}{\text{IPSec disabled Frame Size}} * 100$$

The additional bytes added by IPSec headers using different IPSec transforms sets are shown in Table 5.

Figure 1 shows the impact of each of the two security protocols enabled separately and both fully implemented. It compares the percentage of

Table 3. Ethernet frame protected by AH in transport mode

Ethernet header	IPv4 header	AH header	Data Variable	Ethernet Trail
14	20	24		4

Table 4. AH header format

Next header	Payload length	Reserved	SPI	Authentication data
1	1	2	4	16

the overhead discussed previously on the original packet transmitted with three different IPSec transform sets namely; AH only, ESP only, and AH and ESP both applied.

The overhead starts low on packet sizes of 1 byte, because some overhead bytes are used as padding bytes, which reduces the overall overhead of IPSec headers on the packets that need padding.

All packets less than 18 bytes require padding for them to be transmitted over the network and they all have a frame size of 64 bytes. That means the percentage of IPSec overhead increases from 1 byte and reaches the maximum on 18 bytes packet. Then it starts to fall on packet sizes of more than 18 bytes. By comparison, the overhead of 18-bytes

Table 5. IPSec Frame overhead bytes

Transform Set Description	Additional Bytes
AH only	24
ESP Integrity only	28
ESP Integrity and Encryption	36
AH and ESP Integrity	48
AH and ESP Encryption	52
AH and ESP	60

Figure 1. Impact of AH, ESP, and BOTH IPSec transform sets on IPv4 overhead

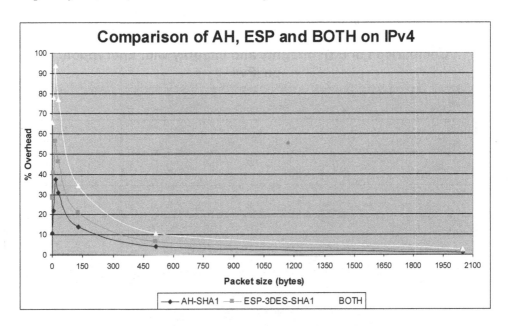

packets using the transform sets shown in Figure 1 is as follows; AH only gives 38%, ESP only gives 56%, and both protocols gives 94%. This shows that there is quite a significant increase in overhead when using ESP only compared to AH only on IPv4 on small packets.

The overhead of using both protocols on 18 bytes packets is 94%, which is the aggregate of AH and ESP overheads. The overhead falls sharply as packet size increases to the level of about 0.04% for packets of 65,000 bytes, because IPv4 IPSec headers are applied on the first fragment only. Hence, the additional overhead bytes are constant and they are spread over an increasing common denominator, that is, the cumulative size of all fragments. This trend applies to all three IPSec transform sets.

Understandably, AH only has a lower overhead as compared to ESP only, which in turn has a lower overhead compared to both protocols applied. Applying ESP only instead of AH only increases the overhead by 7.64% on average across all the packet sizes we experimented with. Using both protocols instead of ESP only increases

the overhead by 15.67% on average, and using both protocols instead of AH only increases the overhead by 23.31%.

The use of ESP protocol only in an IPSec transform gives two options of IPSec transform sets, namely; ESP with integrity only, and a complete ESP that has both integrity and encryption. Figure 2 shows the impact of these ESP transform sets.

ESP integrity using either MD5 or SHA1 algorithms results in the same overhead impact. The same applies for a complete ESP implementation that has integrity and encryption: irrespective of the algorithms used, the overhead is the same on ICMP packets. ESP integrity only overhead is relatively lower than that of ESP with integrity and encryption. Applying ESP integrity and encryption increases the overhead by almost 12% compared to ESP integrity only on smallest packet size that does not need padding, 18 bytes. On average the overhead increases by 5% from packet sizes of 1 byte to 65,500 bytes.

For all different IPSec transform sets on IPv4, the impact of the overhead relatively is the same on very large packets, for example, in our

Figure 2. Impact of ESP transform sets on IPv4 overhead

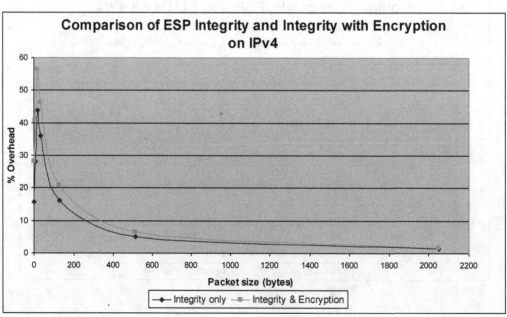

experiments, the impact of the overhead is almost constant at 0.04% across all different transform sets with packet size of 65,500 bytes.

IPSec Overhead on IPv6

IPSec overhead on IPv6 adds the same number of bytes (for IPSec headers) as IPv4 on all IPSec transform sets. Figure 3 shows the percentage impact of overhead on ICMP packets of different sizes. As was the case on IPv4, AH only has a lower overhead as compared to ESP only, which in turn has a lower overhead compared to both protocols applied. Unlike IPv4, there is no increase in the overhead on very small packets, because no padding bits are necessary when using IPv6. Since the minimum frame payload of IPv6 Ethernet exceeds the IPv4 Ethernet minimum payload. The impact of the overhead is higher from the first packet size of 1 byte, and it gradually decreases as the packet size increases. The first significant difference of how IPSec affects IPv6 as compared to that on IPv4 is that IPSec

headers are applied on all fragments, while on IPv4 they were applied on the first fragment only. This makes the overhead have a more significant impact on IPv6. Secondly, unlike the constant overhead percentage on packets of 65,500 bytes on IPv4 using different transform sets, IPv6 has a constant different value for each security policy from 32,768 bytes and larger.

On fragmented packets the IPSec protocol headers are applied on every fragment on IPv6 protocol; hence, the percentage overhead does not decrease sharply as it does on IPv4. Consequently, the overhead on large packets on IPv6 is higher than that on IPv4. Applying ESP only instead of AH only increases the overhead by 5.77% on average across all the packet sizes, while using both protocols instead of ESP only increases the overhead by 11.82% on average, and using both protocols instead of AH only increases the overhead by 17.59%.

Figure 4 shows the impact of two ESP only implementations of IPSec: ESP with integrity only and ESP with both integrity and encryption.

Figure 3. Impact of AH, ESP, and BOTH IPSec transform sets on IPv6 overhead

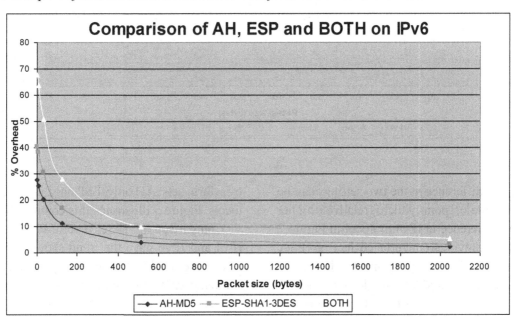

Figure 4. Impact of ESP transform sets on IPv6 overhead

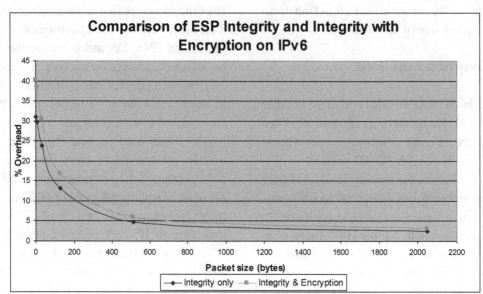

Figure 5. Comparison of IPSec transform sets on IPv4 and IPv6 overhead

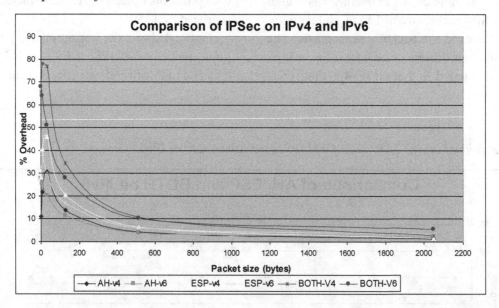

Significant difference in the two settings can be noticed on the last point, which is relatively higher than the difference in IPv4 protocol in Figure 2 due to the previously mentioned fact of IPSec headers applied on every fragment in IPv6.

We also compared how the IPSec overhead impacts on IPv4 and IPv6, using the default three transform sets: AH only, ESP only, and both protocols. Figure 5 illustrates this comparison.

Comparison of IPSec overhead impact on IPv4 and IPv6 gave the trend shown in Figure 5. The overhead has a higher impact on IPv4 as compared to IPv6 for smaller packets that are not fragmented. Comparing IPv4 and IPv6 average

Figure 6. Impact of IPSec on ICMP Average RTT on IPv4

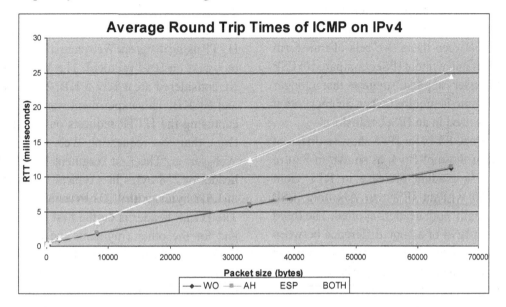

values shows that general IPSec have a higher overhead on IPv4 than IPv6. This can be attributed to the fact that IPSec headers' sizes are the same on both IP protocols, while there is a huge difference in the frame sizes of these IP protocols. IPv6 fragmented packets have a higher overhead as compared to IPv4, because in IPv4 the IPSec header is applied on the first fragment only, while in IPv6 it is applied on each fragment.

We noticed that the maximum frame size of 1,518 bytes is never exceeded in IPv4 even after turning IPSec on. The additional overhead of using IPSec headers will occupy part of the payload data; hence, reducing the payload of each fragment on fragmented IPv4 packets. This differs from how fragmented packets are handled in IPv6. In IPv6 the same payload data size is maintained and the additional bytes added by IPSec headers increase the frame size directly.

IPSec headers sizes are constant for both IPv4 and IPv6, but the way these headers are applied is different. Therefore, their effects are also different on both protocols. For instance, on IPv4 the overhead is applied on the first fragment only

where a packet needs fragmentation. This obviously means the burden of the overhead is higher on IPv6 than it is on IPv4. On both IP protocols, there is no difference in the frame size when using either SHA1 or MD5 for data integrity and DES or 3DES for data confidentiality.

Round-Trip Time Tests on ICMP

From the RTT values recorded when testing IPSec overhead, we also computed the average RTT for each IPSec transform set. Figure 6 shows the average RTT of ICMP messages on IPv4; the comparison includes the RTT of packets with IPSec disabled. Firstly, for all transform sets the RTT increases as packet sizes increases. This is because a larger packet obviously needs more time to reach its destination across the network and come back to the source. The graph shows that there is an insignificant difference between the RTT of transmissions with IPSec disabled and IPSec with AH only.

There is also an insignificant difference between the RTT of IPSec with ESP only and

IPSec with both headers implemented, especially on smaller packets, but the difference becomes slightly significant on very large packets. The huge difference between these two sets of transform sets: AH only and without IPSec compared to ESP and both headers applied, suggests that a longer processing time is required when an encryption algorithm is used in an IPSec transform.

The average RTTs for IPv6 shows a different picture from those of IPv4, as shown in Figure 7. There is a gradual increase in RTT from transmission without IPSec to AH only, ESP only, and finally both headers applied. The trend portrayed in IPv4 of a huge difference between transform sets with an encryption algorithm and those without an encryption algorithm does not apply in IPv6. This is because IPSec has ESP with null encryption in IPv6 while IPv4 ESP has functional encryption. Even though this is a case of ESP only, both IPSec protocols have a longer RTT as compared to AH only and disabled IPSec transmissions.

Frame Overhead Tests on HTTP

We conducted frame overhead tests of IPSec on HTTP using different Web page sizes that contain only text on IPv4 protocol. The Web page sizes we considered are 1 KB, 5 KB, 20 KB, 60 KB, and 100KB. This experiment was conducted by capturing the HTTP requests on the client machine that was requesting Web pages from the Web server. The first fragment has the HTTP header of 228 bytes in a typical Ethernet frame of 1,518 bytes, with 1,232 bytes of payload data. The HTTP header is on the first fragment only, and for the other fragments the HTTP header size is added to the payload. AH only adds an overhead of 24 bytes, ESP only adds 36 bytes, and with both protocols applied, the overhead is cumulative as was the case in ICMP. The first comparison shows the percentage overhead of the three main security policies: AH only, ESP only, and both applied, in Figure 8. The graph shows the impact of IPSec using the following transforms: AH with MD5 or SHA1, followed by ESP with both integrity and encryption, and lastly both

Figure 7. Impact of IPSec on ICMP Average RTT on IPv6

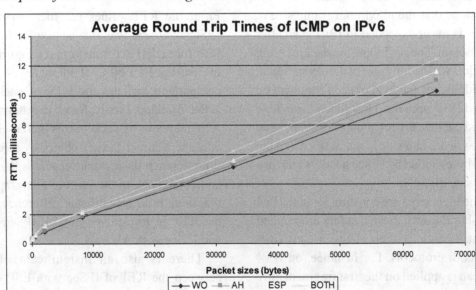

protocols applied. The overhead of AH is lower than that of ESP and both protocols because AH uses only one cryptographic algorithm to provide its security services while ESP uses two: one for integrity and the other for encryption.

The overhead is also higher on smaller Web pages as compared to larger pages. For AH, the overhead starts higher for a Web page of 1 KB and slightly drops for 5 KB Web pages, but for ESP and both it drops sharply because they add a larger overhead than AH. On the same note, ESP's overhead is lower than that of both protocols applied together.

On an average the overhead increases by almost 1 percentage point when using ESP instead of AH, and it further increases on an average by at least 1.5 percentage points. The overhead increases by a margin of 2.5 percentage points when both protocols are used instead of AH only. This is quite a significant impact and should be taken into account in deploying IPSec. The overhead starts higher on smaller packets but it drops as packet size increases and becomes almost constant. This is because IPSec protects every

fragment on fragmented packets; therefore, the same overhead is spread evenly on all the fragments, and on nonfragmented packets the impact is relatively higher. Comparing the two ESP-only transform-sets implementations of IPSec gives the picture in Figure 9.

Figure 9 shows that there is quite a huge difference in the IPSec overhead when using the two ESP-only transform sets on HTTP. ESP with integrity and encryption induce an additional 0.6 percentage point on average on the overhead as compared to ESP with integrity only

Figure 10 compares the impact of IPSec transform sets in the category of a full implementation of both protocols. There are three different implementations, namely AH and ESP encryption, AH and ESP integrity, and AH and ESP integrity and encryption. The graph shows that there is no huge differences in the overhead when these transform sets are applied separately. The overall overhead increases by almost 1 percentage point from the least expensive transform set to the most expensive set.

Figure 8. Impact of AH, ESP and BOTH transform sets on HTTP overhead

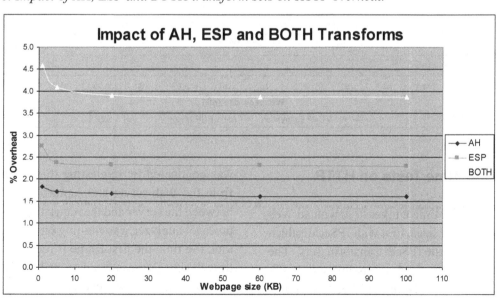

Figure 9. Impact of ESP transform sets on HTTP overhead

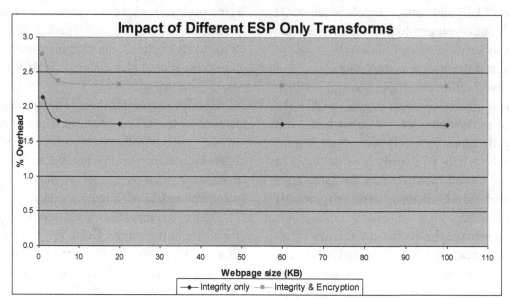

Figure 10. Impact of IPSec transform sets using on HTTP overhead

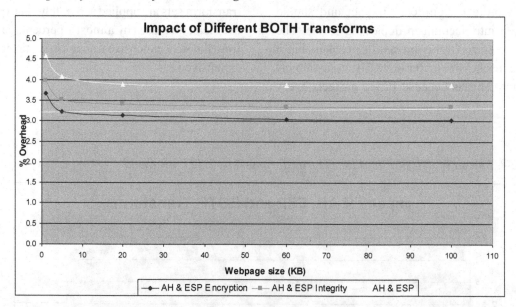

Download Time Tests on HTTP

We compared the time it takes to download Web pages of different sizes, first with IPSec disabled then with different IPSec transform sets. The Web page sizes we used are as follows: 1 KB, 5 KB, 20 KB, 60 KB, and 100 KB. This test was conducted by requesting these Web pages from the Web server and capturing the packets between the server and the requesting client. The protocol analyzer was running on the client. We took the time the first frame is received and the time the last frame is received, and the difference between the two was recorded as the download

Figure 11. Impact of different IPSec protocols on HTTP download times

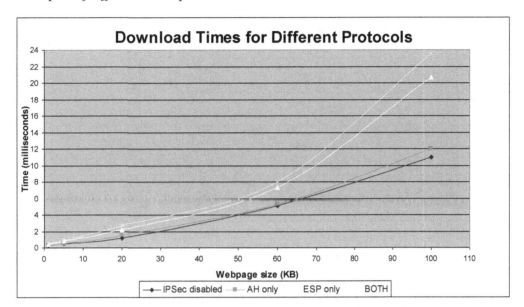

time. Even though the times were not uniform, the trend for different IPSec transform sets was relatively clear.

There was a slight difference between the download times of AH only transform sets using MD5 and SHA1. The average download time of all the Web page files tested shows that SHA1 has more average download time than MD5 by 1 second. Figure 11 shows the download times for different IPSec transform sets with different protocols. AH only transform uses SHA1 algorithm, ESP only transform uses 3DES and SHA1, and both protocols transform uses MD5 for AH and 3DES and SHA1 for ESP. These transform sets are compared against the download times of Web pages with IPSec disabled.

There is a small difference in the download times between the times without IPSec and IPSec using AH only transform set. There is a difference of 1.2 milliseconds in the average download times of the two sets. On the other hand, there is also a small difference between ESP only and both protocols transform sets' download times. For all transform sets, the download times in-

crease gradually from Web page size of 1 KB to 60 KB, but beyond this size the download times increase sharply. According to Sullivan (2005), the average size of the Web pages on the Internet is 60 KB. Figure 11 confirms the argument that as the more Web page sizes exceed 60 KB, the longer they take to download from the server; hence, performance is compromised. Therefore, in the case where IPSec is enabled using ESP only or both IPSec protocols, the cost in terms of performance is very significant for pages above 60 KB. The other reason why the download time increases sharply might be the use of an encryption algorithm, because in the sets without encryption the times do not increase that much.

Figure 12 shows the download times obtained when using the IPSec transform sets available when using ESP only. ESP integrity only transform was using MD5 algorithm, which has a slightly lower average download time than SHA1. The download times of ESP integrity only are higher than those of AH only using the same algorithm, if we compare ESP integrity only in Figure 12 and AH only in Figure 11.

Figure 12. Impact of ESP on HTTP download times

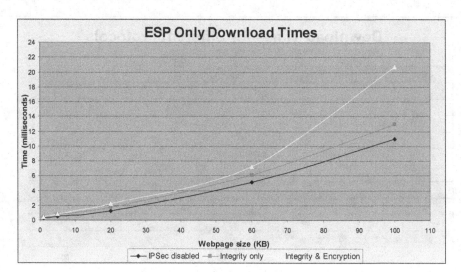

Figure 13. Impact of IPSec on HTTP download times using both protocols

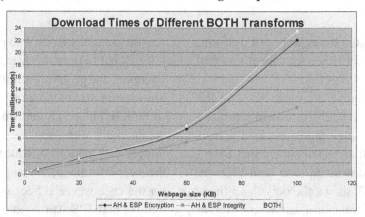

Figure 13 compares the download times of different IPSec transform sets of both protocols applied. The download times without IPSec encryption are significantly lower compared to encryption turned on, as can be seen in the graph. This is because encryption generally requires more processing time on the encrypting system, in our case on the Web server. This delays the transmission of a Web page request to the requesting client. There is a slight increase in download time from ESP encryption applied and both IPSec protocols fully implemented.

Frame Overhead Tests on FTP

Our tests included frame overhead tests of IPSec on FTP using different clear text file sizes. FTP tests were conducted using IPv4 protocol since there is no support for FTP on Windows IPv6 protocol. We considered the following sizes: 1 KB, 20 KB, 100 KB, 1 MB, 5 MB, and 10 MB, but in this section we will show sizes up to and including 1 MB only because the trend beyond 1 MB is constant. This experiment was conducted by capturing the FTP file requests on the client

Figure 14. Comparison of different IPSec protocols on FTP overhead

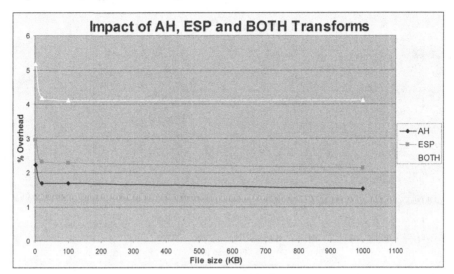

machine that was requesting files from the file server using a Web browser. The FTP packet fragment of 1,518 bytes consists of 1,460 bytes of data, and the rest are headers.

First we compared the impact of AH only, ESP only, and both protocol transforms on FTP, this shown in Figure 14. AH only adds an overhead of 24 bytes, ESP only adds 36 bytes, and with both protocols applied, the overhead is also cumulative as was the case in ICMP and HTTP. The transforms used in Figure 14 use the following algorithms: AH with MD5 or SHA1, ESP with both integrity and encryption, and lastly both protocols applied. For all transforms the overhead drops sharply from the file size of 1 KB to 20 KB because the frame size of a 1 KB FTP file (1,370 bytes, of IPSec both protocols transform set) is far lower than the fragment size (1,514 bytes); hence, the percentage of 24 bytes is higher on 1 KB compared to 20 KB fragments. This trend applies to all the three transform sets on the graph. On average AH only adds an overhead of almost 2%, ESP only adds an overhead of almost 2.5% and both protocols adds an average overhead of 4.5%, that is, the cumulative overhead of AH and ESP.

The overhead of fragmented packets is almost constant as file sizes increase because the IPSec

headers are applied on every transmitted fragment. AH overhead is lower than that of ESP and both protocols, as was the case on HTTP, because AH uses only one cryptographic algorithm to provide its security services while ESP uses two: one for integrity and the other for encryption.

When comparing the overhead of using different ESP transform sets of integrity only and integrity with encryption, we get the trend shown in Figure 15. On average, ESP integrity only adds an overhead of almost 2% on FTP, and ESP with both integrity and encryption adds an overhead of about 2.5%. The same trend shown in Figure 14 of the overhead remaining almost constant on fragmented packets applies also on ESP-only transform sets shown in Figure 15.

Figure 16 compares the overhead added by using different IPSec transform sets that utilize both IPSec protocols. It shows a significant increase in overhead when both IPSec protocols are fully implemented as compared to both protocols with partial ESP implementation.

The overhead increases by almost 1 percentage point. We noticed that there is a very small difference in download times when using DES for encryption and 3DES in ESP protocol, but this difference is really insignificant.

Figure 15. Impact of ESP transform sets on FTP overhead

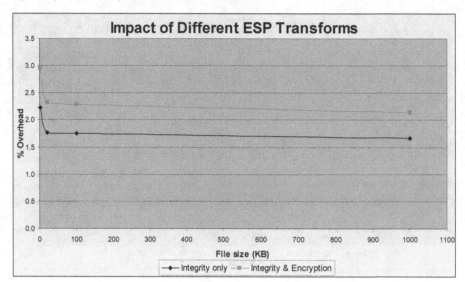

Figure 16. Impact of IPSec using both protocols on FTP overhead

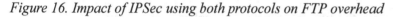
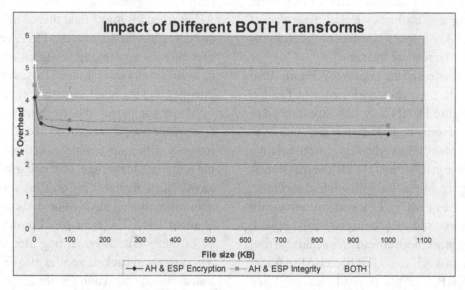

Download Times Tests on FTP

FTP download time tests were more uniform with a more clearly visible trend than that of HTTP tests. We used the following file sizes for this test: 1 KB, 20 KB, 100 KB, 5 MB, and 10 MB. We recorded the time it took to download all the frames of a particular download, that is, for the first frame and the last frame, and computed the difference, which we recorded as the download time. First we compared the times of IPSec disabled and IPSec using different protocols, as shown in Figure 17.

Figure 17 shows that there is the smallest of differences in download times between IPSec AH only and IPSec disabled. There is a difference of 4 milliseconds in the average values of these two sets, which is very insignificant. The other two

Figure 17. Impact of IPSec on FTP download times

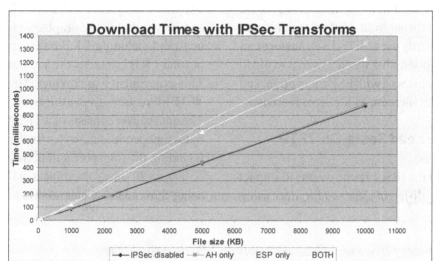

Figure 18. Impact of ESP transform sets on FTP download times

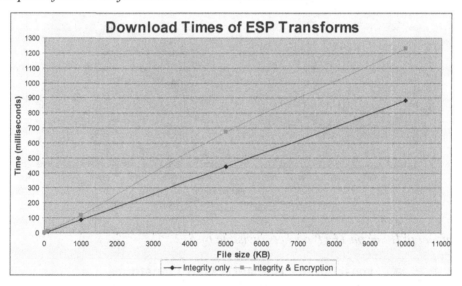

transforms, ESP only and both protocols, do have a small difference in their download times, but it is more significant than the first two sets. Unlike the trend in HTTP download times, FTP times increase gradually as the packet size increases. But still, there is significant differences between IPSec transform sets with ESP encryption and those without ESP encryption, confirming that ESP encryption needs more processing on the processing node.

Figure 18 compares the download times of FTP using ESP only transform sets. In ESP integrity only, we used SHA1 algorithms, and full ESP uses SHA1 and 3DES. On average there is a difference of 100 milliseconds between ESP with integrity only and ESP with both integrity and encryption; this is a very significant performance cost consideration when deploying IPSec.

When comparing download times that use a full implementation of IPSec with different set algorithms, we get the trend shown in Figure 19. The algorithms used in these transform sets are AH uses SHA1 through out, ESP encryption uses 3DES, and integrity uses MD5. The transform set without encryption also has a lower download time compared to those with ESP encryption, and download times increase as file sizes increase.

Frame Overhead Tests On TFTP

We also tested the IPSec frame overhead impact on TFTP using different clear text file sizes using IPv4. We considered the following sizes: 4 bytes, 14 bytes, 200 bytes, 1 KB, 20 KB, 100 KB, 1 MB, and 10 MB, but in the graphs we will show sizes up to and including 1 KB only because the trend beyond 1 KB is exactly the same as that of 1 KB. This experiment was conducted by capturing the TFTP file requests from a third-party TFTP server. The data packet consists of a TFTP header with 2 bytes for opcode and 2 bytes for the block number including the transport and network headers.

Figure 20 shows the impact of IPSec on TFTP using the transform sets of AH only, ESP only,

Figure 19. Impact of IPSec using both protocols on FTP download times

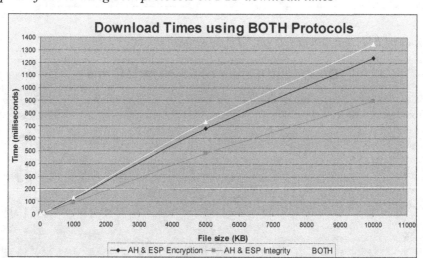

Figure 20. Impact of IPSec on TFTP packets divisible by 512

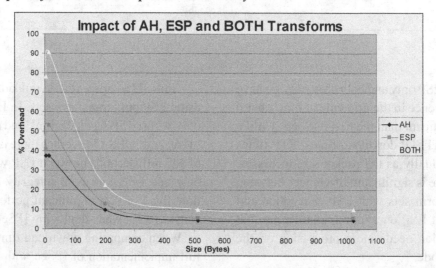

and both protocols, using packet sizes divisible by 512. IPSec headers added on TFTP traffic are of the same size as those added on FTP. For the packet sizes we tested, we chose 4 bytes, which is small enough to require padding, 14 bytes is the size that does not need padding, at which the overhead is at its maximum. Theoretically, the overhead starts low on packet sizes of 1 byte, in our case 4 bytes, because some overhead bytes are used as padding bytes, which reduces the overall overhead of IPSec headers on the packets that need padding. All packets less than 14 bytes require padding for them to be transmitted over the network, and they all have a frame size of 64 bytes. That means the percentage of IPSec overhead increases from 4 bytes and reaches the maximum on a 14 bytes packet. Then it starts to fall on packet sizes of more than 14 bytes. As long as the packet size is increasing in blocks of 512 bytes, the overhead becomes constant on all packets between 512 bytes and 32 MB.

This trend does not apply on packet sizes that are not divisible by 512, as the overhead will be higher if a packet is fragmented due to the overhead in the last fragment, which is not proportional; hence, the trend changes to that shown in Figure 21. This means that the overhead is higher the lower the last fragment is to 512 bytes; otherwise, if divisible by 512 the overhead is at its lowest. And on the same note, the overhead is also the fewer the number of blocks or fragments.

Figure 21 shows the comparison of the trend for IPSec overhead for packets divisible and not divisible by 512 bytes. We used the following sizes: 4 bytes, 14 bytes, 200 bytes, 512 bytes, 580 bytes, 1024 bytes, and 1400 bytes.

CONCLUSION

Our experiments showed that the impact of IPSec overhead on all protocols we tested is higher for smaller packets as compared to larger packets for both IPv4 and IPv6, except in cases where the packet is small enough for padding bits in IPv4. This is because part of IPSec overhead is used to replace the padding bits that were otherwise needed in the absence of IPSec. We also noticed that the use of both IPSec protocols increases the overhead cumulatively as the overhead of each protocol.

Figure 21. Impact of IPSec on TFTP packets not divisible by 512

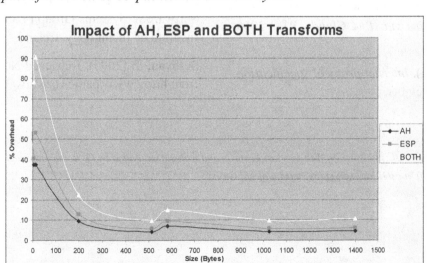

The tests also showed that irrespective of the integrity algorithm used in both AH and ESP protocols, between SHA1 and MD5, the IPSec header size does not change for all IPSec transform sets tested. Hence, the percentage overhead for both algorithms is the same. But they affect the round-trip time and download time differently. The use of SHA1 increases the round-trip time and download time because SHA1 is more secure than MD5.

The use of 3DES or DES algorithms for encryption in ESP protocol does apply the same overhead on both IPv4 and IPv6. But they differ on the round-trip time and download time in that 3DES increases the above two metrics because it is more secure than DES; hence, they are implemented differently.

REFERENCES

Ariga, S., Nagahashi, K., Minami, M., Esaki, H., & Murai, J. (2000, July 18-21). Performance evaluation of data transmission using IPSec over IPv6 networks. In *INET 2000 Proceedings — The Internet Global Summit: Global Distributed Intelligence for Everyone, the 10th Annual Internet Society Conference*, Pacifico Yokohama Conference Center, Yokohama, Japan.

Carpenter, B., & Moore, K. (2001). *Connection of IPv6 domains via IPv4 Clouds*. RFC 3056, February.

DARPA. (1981). *Internet protocol specification*. RFC 791, September.

Deering, S., & Hinden, R. (1998). *Internet protocol, version 6 specification*. RFC 2460, December.

Doraswamy, N., & Harkins, D. (1999). IPSec: *The new security standard for the Internet, intranets, and virtual private networks*. Englewood, NJ: Prentice Hall PTR.

Farrel, A. (2004). *The Internet and its protocols: A comparative approach*. Amsterdam: Morgan Kaufmann.

Kaeo, M., & Van Herck, T. (2006). *Methodology for benchmarking IPSec devices*. Internet-Draft (draft-ietf-bmwg-ipsec-meth-00), November 2005, Expires: May 5.

Kent, S., & Atkinson, R. (1998). *IP authentication header*. RFC 2402, November.

Kent, S., & Atkinson, R. (1998). *IP encapsulating security payload*. RFC 2406, November.

Kent, S., & Atkinson, R. (1998). *Security architecture for the Internet protocol*. RFC 2401, November.

Loshin, P. (2003). *IPv6: Theory, protocol, and practice* (2nd ed.). Amsterdam: Morgan Kaufmann.

Ronan, J., et al. (2004, March). *Performance implications of IPSec deployment*. Telecommunications Software & Systems Group (TSSG), Waterford Institute of Technology, Ireland.

Sullivan, T. (2005). Retrieved November 2005, from http://www.pantos.org/atw/35654.html

This work was previously published in Web Services Security and E-Business, edited by G. Radhamani and G. Rao, pp. 337-362, copyright 2007 by IGI Publishing (an imprint of IGI Global).

Chapter 15
An Approach for Intentional Modeling of Web Services Security Risk Assessment

Subhas C. Misra
Carleton University, Canada

Vinod Kumar
Carleton University, Canada

Uma Kumar
Carleton University, Canada

ABSTRACT

In this chapter, we provide a conceptual modeling approach for Web services security risk assessment that is based on the identification and analysis of stakeholder intentions. There are no similar approaches for modeling Web services security risk assessment in the existing pieces of literature. The approach is, thus, novel in this domain. The approach is helpful for performing means-end analysis, thereby, uncovering the structural origin of security risks in WS, and how the root-causes of such risks can be controlled from the early stages of the projects. The approach addresses "why" the process is the way it is by exploring the strategic dependencies between the actors of a security system, and analyzing the motivations, intents, and rationales behind the different entities and activities in constituting the system.

INTRODUCTION

The area of *Web services* (WS) has currently emerged as an approach for integrating Web-based applications. To facilitate this, several standards have been proposed, for example, simple object access protocol (SOAP) for data transfer, Web service definition language (WSDL) for providing a description of different available services, and extensible markup language (XML) for tagging data in such a way that users can create their customized applications. In the WS world, information can be transmitted between two service end points using SOAP messages. Security in WS has, therefore, gained importance, as the WS-based systems are susceptible to attacks by malicious users. For example, malicious users have the potential to intrude into the integrity and confidentiality of messages transmitted using SOAP. Several mechanisms are commonly available to address these security issues. An example is the use of secure socket layer (SSL), and transport layer security (TLS) to provide authentication, integrity, and confidentiality of information. Transport layer security can be provided using IPSec. Several pieces of literature are available in the area of architecting secured WS-based systems. A recent example is the work done by Gutierreze et al. (Gutierrez, Fernandez-Medina, & Piattini, 2005), who proposed an architecture-based process for the development of WS security. This process helps in identifying, defining, and analyzing the security requirements of a WS-based system using an architecture approach. Recently, different researchers have explored model-based assessment of security risk. (Alghathbar, Wijesekera, & Farkas, 2005; Dimitrakos, Ritchie, Raptis, & Stolen, 2002; Fernandez, Sorgente, & Larrondo-Petrie, 2005; Lodderstedt, Bastin, & Doser, 2002; Lund, Hogganvik, Seehusen, & Stolen, 2003; Swiderski & Snyder, 2004; Villarroel, Fernandez, Trujillo, & Piattini, 2005).

Fletcher et. al. (1995), Labuschangne (1999), and Martel (2002) have advocated that the field of security risk analysis has evolved through three generations. The *first generation* of risk analysis techniques date back to those associated with the advent of centralized mainframes. A brief overview of them can be had from Martel's thesis (Martel, 2002), and Labuschagne's paper (Labuschagne, 1999). Most of these approaches are checklist based, ad hoc, and assume that the risk scenarios are static and they do not change. There are different commercial tools available that support these ad hoc approaches (e.g., @RISK, and RiskPAC (Labuschagne, 1999)).

The *second generation* of risk analysis tools and techniques emerged with the growth of LANs, and distributed computing. COBRA Risk Consultant (COBRA, 2005) and Tivoli Secure Way Risk Manager (TSRM) (Tivoli, 2005) are two examples. While the former supports ISO 17799 compliant risk analysis, the later supports enterprise-wide risk management, whereby organizations are able to correlate security information from different sources in an enterprise. The second generation of the risk analysis techniques and tools are concerned more with the combined effects of threats rather than individual elements of threat. These techniques and tools attempt to view security from a holistic viewpoint of equipment, software, and data.

The *third generation* is what we have currently. Today security is no longer limited to local area networks, and individual standalone networks and data. Current security needs are cross-organizational because of interorganizational communication via the Internet, and extranets for organization-to-organization communication. Today data of one enterprise is transmitted over several third-party networks. Additionally, there are new types of attacks that emerge everyday. Martel (2002) provides an approach for risk analysis of current day security issues. She proposed a model wherein a global risk value is dynamically determined for a specific asset/exposure pair with the changes in the environment. Discussions of other such third-generation risk analysis approaches can be found in Swiderski and Snyder (2004) Dimitrakos et al. (2002), Lund et al. (2003), Lodderstedt et al. (2002), Fernandez et al. (2005), Villarroel et al. (2005), and Alghathbar et al. (2005). They are not individually elaborated over here, but most of them work based on dataflow diagramming and UML profiling approaches. These approaches help to address "what" the requirements are, and not "why" those requirements are needed. A critical comparative analysis has been done by rigorous review of the different existing pieces of literature, the summary of which is listed in Table 1.

In this chapter, we present a new approach for modeling information systems security risk assessment. The approach is based on the analysis of the strategic dependencies between the actors of a system. The purpose of this chapter is to introduce an approach that can help in modeling issues while performing WS security risk assessment. In this chapter, we have outlined the approach, and illustrated it with an example. We have not considered all possible aspects of WS security in this chapter. Therefore, we encourage further evaluation of the approach for modeling different scenarios possible in WS security.

BACKGROUND

Several risk assessment methodologies tailored towards specific domains are available in the existing pieces of literature (Aagedal, Braber, Dimitrakos, Gran, Raptis, & Stolen, 2002). For instance, SEISMED is a methodology that provides a set of guidelines on IT security risk analysis for health care IT personnel, and ODESSA is a methodology that provides health care data security. There are several other risk assessment methodologies in the domain of health care that are used for specific purposes, viz., ISHTAR, RAMME, CPRI, and TRA (Aagedal et al., 2002). Several attempts have been made for over a decade to make the existing schemes align into one framework that is acceptable to all for testing IT security functionality. The Common Criteria (CC) project successfully aligns the criteria followed by Europe, Canada, and America (Common Criteria Organization, 2002). Gradually, it is replacing all regional and national criteria with a common set followed worldwide and accepted by the International Standard Organization (ISO). However, CC does not provide any specific methodology for risk analysis. On the other hand, a new project, CORAS, run during 2001-2003, provides a concrete methodology focusing on the IT security risk assessment process (Aagedal et al., 2002).

Other methodologies (projects) in related areas include surety analysis (SA), control objectives for information and related technology (COBIT), and CCTA risk analysis and management methodology (CRAMM). SA provides a methodology based on the creation of an explicit model

Table 1. Comparative analysis of the traditional security modeling approaches (in general) and the stated approach (Misra, Kumar, & Kumar, 2005a)

	Traditional Modeling Approaches	**Proposed approach**
1.	Model late phase security requirements.	Models early phase security requirements.
2.	Indicate: "what" steps a process consists of, and "how" those steps to be done.	Indicates: "why" the process is the way it is.
3.	Do not capture the motivations, intents and rationales behind the activities.	Captures the motivations, intents, and rationales behind the activities.
4.	Do not capture the intentional structure of a process and the organization that embeds it.	Captures the intentional structure of a process and he organization that embeds it.
5.	Process performers are concerned with models that describe "hows". Process managers are concerned with models that indicate "whats".	Process engineers are concerned with models that describe "whys" as they are concerned with modifying the processes.
6.	Model functional security requirements.	Models non-functional security requirements.
7.	They cannot reason about the opportunities and vulnerabilities of the system under consideration.	It helps to incorporate the issues of trust, vulnerability, change, and risk explicitly in the process of systems analysis and design.

that includes various aspects of the behavior of a system (Sandia National Laboratories, 2002). RSDS is a tool-supported methodology that has been applied in the analysis of various reactive systems in the domain of chemical process control and automated manufacturing (Reactive System Design Support, 2002). COBIT project addresses the good management practices for security and control in IT for worldwide endorsement by various organizations (Control Objectives for Information and Related Technology, 2002). CRAMM is a risk analysis methodology that was developed with an aim of providing a structured approach to manage computer security for all systems (Barber & Davey, 1992).

We now present the three projects, and their related works on security, that had a major influence on our modeling approach.

CORAS

The most influential of the projects for our work is the CORAS methodology (Vraalsen Braber, Hogganvik, Lund, & Stolen, 2004), which bases itself on the following risk-management methodologies: hazard and operability (HazOp), fault tree analysis (FTA), failure mode and effect criticality analysis (FMECA), Markov analysis, and CRAMM. These methodologies are, to a great extent, complementary to one another. As we adopt ideas of CORAS in our approach, we, in turn, partially adopt the ideas of these methodologies. CORAS project introduced a unified modeling language (UML) Version 2.0 profile for security risk assessment. The profile includes a metamodel that describes different security risk components (e.g., assets, and vulnerabilities), and relations between them. Also, the profile includes mapping of the components to UML modeling elements. To perform a high-quality risk assessment, one should clearly understand the organization of the system being assessed. Description of the target system should be done in the first stage of the risk management process.

As CORAS uses UML to model security-related elements in order to achieve uniformity, CORAS suggests using UML to describe other aspects of the system. However, according to CORAS project, security-related elements should be depicted in separate diagrams that do not include other structural elements of the target system.

SecureUML

SecureUML is a modeling language based on UML. It helps in the model-driven development of secure systems. The approach bases on role-based access control. This approach helps to improve the productivity while developing secure distributed systems. SecureUML can integrate the specification of access control into application models (Lodderstedt et al., 2002).

Tropos

Tropos is an agent-oriented software engineering methodology that is capable of modeling both the organizational aspects of a system, and the late and early phase requirements of the system itself. It has been shown by Mouratidis et al. (Mouratidis, Giorgini, Manson, & Philip,2002), and Mouratidis et al. (Mouratidis, Giorgini, & Manson, 2003) how the extensions of Tropos methodology can be used to accommodate different security concerns of the system under development in the requirements analysis phase.

INTENTIONAL MODELING

Issues of Traditional Conceptual Modeling Techniques

As stated earlier, most of the recent initiatives conducted in the area of model-based security risk are based on dataflow diagramming, and UML profiling. We now briefly review some of those pieces of work, some of which were already mentioned in the earlier sections, while providing an overview of work done in the area of security.

Swiderski, and Snyder (2004) describe how dataflow-diagramming techniques can be used for threat modeling. Dimitrakos et al. (2002) proposed a model-based security risk analysis technique that uses UML for modeling security risk. Lund et al. (2003) proposed a UML profile for use in security assessment. Lodderstedt et al. (2002) proposed SecureUML, a UML-based modeling language for use in the area of security modeling. Similar other recent works in the uses of UML on the area of security modeling have been proposed by Fernandez et al. (2005), Villarroel et al. (2005), and Alghathbar et al. (2005). However, each of these conventional works has the following *issues*:

- Traditional conceptual security modeling techniques help to model the late phase requirements. However, they do not model early phase requirements.
- Such techniques indicate "what" steps a security process consists of, and "how" those steps are to be done. They do not indicate "why" a security process is the way it is.
- The traditional techniques do not capture the motivations, intents, and rationales behind the security activities.
- Those techniques do not capture the intentional structure of a security process, and the organization that embeds it.
- The traditional modeling techniques model functional requirements of a security process. They do not model nonfunctional requirements.
- The traditional modeling techniques cannot reason about the opportunities and vulnerabilities. They do not help to incorporate the issues of trust, vulnerability, change, and risk explicitly in the process of security systems analysis and design.

To address these issues, we proposed an agent-oriented security risk modeling approach (Misra, Kumar, & Kumar, 2005b). Our approach helps to explore the strategic dependencies between the actors of a security system being modeled. This helps to uncover the structural origin of security issues in a system. This approach extends the concept of i* (Chung, Nixon, Yu, & Mylopoulos, 2000; Donzelli & Bresciani, 2003; Gans, Jarke, Kethers, Lakemeyer, Ellrich, Funken, & Meister, 2001; Misra et al., 2005a; Misra et al., 2005b; Misra, Kumar & Kumar, 2005c; Misra, Kumar & Kumar, 2005d; Misra, Kumar & Kumar, 2005e; Misra, Kumar & Kumar, 2005f; Yu & Mylopoulos, 1994; Yu, 1999) for use in the domain of security modeling. In particular, our approach helps for security risk identification and analysis. This approach is further described.

The stated approach is demonstrated with the help of a *case study* as described next. The case study is hypothetical, and is amalgamated modification of the examples used in Giorgini et al. (Giorgini, Massacci, & Mylopoulos, 2003), and Yu and Liu (2000).

Case Study

The last few years have seen an upsurge in electronic commerce and electronic banking. Most of the major vendors supporting electronic payments are concerned about offering their customers an assurance of security of their personal sensitive information entered online. Let us consider a simple example of one such company, X, and see how it secures its online business of selling product Y.

Customers of company X are offered the ability to buy their products online using a smart card. Customers have the option of either walking to one of the satellite counters of the company, giving their card to the merchant, who can then use the cards to process the payment, or the customers can themselves enter or swipe the card using an input device (e.g., a card reader). To prevent the card information from being eavesdropped, the sensitive information is encrypted using the SSL protocol. However, such an encryption mechanism does not necessarily protect the customer-sensitive information to be stolen manually by the merchants. On the other hand, it might so happen that the information supplied by the customer is fraudulent.

Company X issues a smart card, uniquely to each of its customers, that they can either use at the card reader in a suitable terminal, or that they can use to enter their information manually. The cards issued to the customers are manufactured by a third-party vendor of company X. Similarly, the hardware and software supporting the entire system are built by another third-party vendor. The sensitive data is owned by a separate division of company X.

Although there are different scenarios that can be generated from this case study, in the interest of brevity, we will show only a few of them to illustrate our approach. Similarly, as will be seen next, there are many scenarios that are uncovered through the modeling exercise, but are not explicitly stated in the case study statement. Such instances resonate the usefulness of such a modeling exercise.

Recommendation: The Intentional Modeling Approach

The concepts associated with modeling actor dependencies have their roots in requirements engineering (RE). RE methodologies can be used to model organizational goals, processes, relationships, and actors. In order to perform very good quality risk assessment, one is required to understand the organization clearly.

In this section, we discuss the actor dependency concept using i* (see, for example, Chung et al., 2000; Donzelli & Bresciani, 2003; Gans et al., 2001; Misra et al., 2005a; Misra et al., 2005b; Misra et al., 2005c; Misra et al., 2005d; Misra et al., 2005e; Misra et al., 2005f; Sutcliffe

& Minocha, 1999; and Yu, 1999, to learn more about this area of research and its applicability to various domains). Although i* is a "brain-child" of software RE research, it can be used as a powerful tool to model organizational tasks, processes, actors, and goals. The framework allows requirements engineers to model, in detail, current processes, and to modify them in order to optimize, improve, and increase enterprise productivity. All these benefits could be obtained quite early, even when the project is yet to start. i* explores "why" processes are performed in the existing way. Moreover, it is much easier to obtain real and understandable requirements using i* modeling. Expected behavior of the software, and its rationale, could also be modeled using i*. Furthermore, i* does not take directly into account precision, completeness, and consistency as UML does. In contrast, i* principally takes into account the actors' interests, goals, rationale, tasks, and concerns.

In this work, we have used i* to model both requirements and risk management elements that help managers to identify, monitor, analyze, and control risks, all from the point of view of project goals. i* provides a qualitative analysis of project viability under several scenarios. In our context, this analysis will allow for verifying that all required actions to control risks have been taken into account (i.e., if project goals can be satisfied in all the studied scenarios). For any project, requirements can be modeled as goals and softgoals to be reached during project development.

In order to model and solve this problem, two actor-dependency diagrams are used: the strategic dependency model (SD), and the strategic rationale model (SR). In the interest of brevity, only brief introductions of SD and SR are provided.

SD diagrams are used to model dependencies between actors, while SR diagrams are used to model, internally, why each actor has those dependencies. In other words, SD describes dependencies at a higher level of abstraction than

SR, since SR shows an internal description of an actor, and supports those dependencies.

All dependencies comprise of a "depender," a "dependee," and a "dependum." "Depender" depends on a "dependee" to get "dependum." The most important elements in SD diagrams are

- **Goal dependency:** It is used to model when one actor depends on another to make a tangible condition come true. Dependee has freedom to choose how to achieve this goal.
- **Task dependency:** It is used to model when one actor depends on another to perform an activity. In this case, there is an implicit (usually not shown) depender's goal, which explains why this task must be performed.
- **Resource dependency:** It is used to model when one actor depends on another for the availability of an entity. Depender assumes that obtaining this resource will be straightforward.
- **Softgoal dependency:** It is used to model when one actor depends on another to real-

ize a fuzzy condition. In this case, *fuzzy* means there is no clear criteria for such a condition to be true. In this case, dependee collaborates, but depender will decide how to achieve the softgoal.

Figure 1 is an example of an SD model. It represents the dependencies between actors of a smart card payment system supporting Web services. Goal dependency "Account be Managed" indicates that Cardholder needs his account to be managed, and it is up to Data Owner how to manage the account. Data Owner, from the other side, expects payment from the Card Holder that is represented by resource dependency "Payment" between the two actors. Dependency "Read/Write on Card Correctly" is a softgoal dependency, as it is hard to determine what "correctly" means. Task dependency "Transmit Data" indicates data owner needs terminal owner to transmit data; terminal owner does not have freedom for completing the task.

Actors can be modeled as a generalized relationship among agents, position and role (Dubois,

Figure 1. SD diagram for a Web services-based card payment System

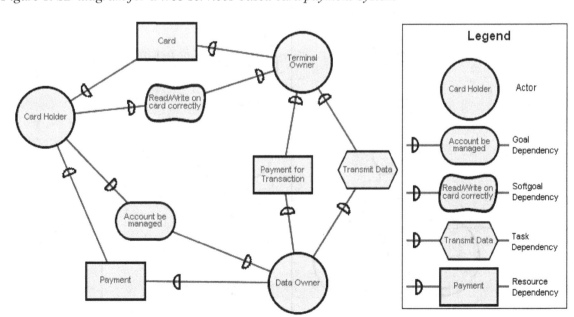

Yu, & Petit, 1998). In general, agents represent physical manifestation of actors. Agents occupy a *position* in SD diagrams. In fact, a *position* is a generalization of an agent. Furthermore, positioned agents can have or cover several roles. Figure 2 shows an example of different types of actors.

SR diagrams focus inside actors. In fact, SR diagrams show both external and internal information. External information is modeled using the same elements of SD diagrams (e.g., goals, softgoals, resources, and tasks). Internal information is represented basically using the same elements but arranged hierarchically in either a *means-end* or a *task-decomposition* relationship.

Internal elements of SR respond to external dependency relationships among actors. In general, external goals, tasks, softgoals, and resources are attached to internal tasks. Internal tasks might be decomposed into subtasks, subgoals, and subsoftgoals (task-decomposition relation-

ships). Moreover, internal goals might depend on other subtasks (means-end relationships). Finally, internal softgoals might obtain either negative or positive contribution from tasks and other subsoftgoals.

Figure 3 illustrates the SR diagram for various actors of our Web services-based card payment system case. Card holder has an internal goal, "Buy goods with a smart card." S/he uses a card to do this. So s/he has internal task "Use a Card." The goal "Buy goods with a smart card" and the task "Use a card" are linked with means-ends link. Terminal owner has a major task, "Process transaction." The task is divided into two separate subtasks: "Read/write on card" and "Read write DB," related with the task "Process transaction" by task decomposition links. "Read/write on card" is associated with the card holder. The external softgoal, "Read/write on card correctly," depends on this task. The external task, "Read\write central DB," as well is softgoal "Send data

Figure 2. Example of different types of actors

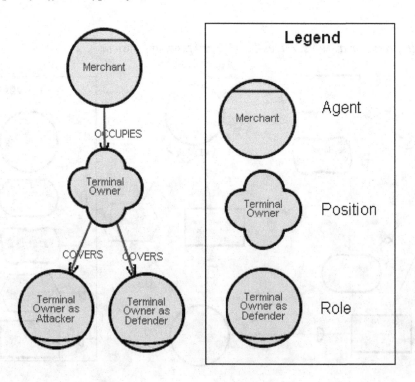

correctly" is dependency going from data owner to terminal owner. However, a more detailed view presents us that both "Read/write central DB" and "Send data correctly" depend on the internal task of terminal owner "Read write on DB." The dependencies between internal and external elements of SR Diagram allow performing more detailed modeling.

In any security risk management process, there are two main tasks: (a) the identification of the security risks and vulnerabilities, and their analysis, and (b) their evaluation to identify their

potential for damage. We now show how we can address these two concerns in our approach.

To conduct an attack, an attacker must exploit vulnerabilities. Thus, exploitations of vulnerabilities are subtasks of the task associated with the attack, and they are linked with task decomposition links. We note task elements corresponding to the exploitation of vulnerabilities by letter "V" on the right of the element, as shown in Figure 4.

If one actor depends on another actor who is an attacker, the attacker may provide a number of attacks to make the dependency not viable

Figure 3. SR diagram for a Web services-based card payment system

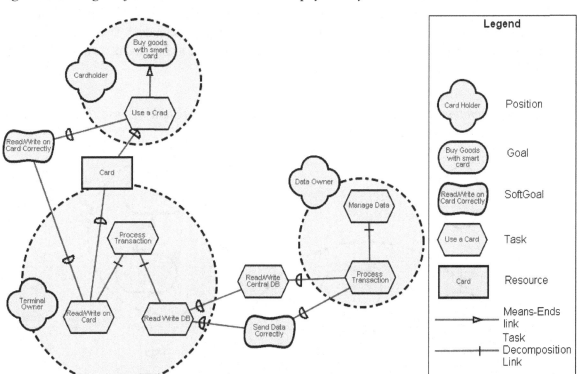

Figure 4. Representation of task elements corresponding to the exploitation vulnerabilities in the Web services-based card payment system

Making a dependency not viable is depicted by a contribution link connecting to the dependum. The links originate from the tasks associated with the attacks. For attacks that make dependency totally unviable, the link is labeled as a *break* link. This can be seen in the example in Figure 5.

The next important step in any risk management process is to determine the values of risks. In our approach, we have seen that a risk is associated with an attack. To estimate a risk value, we need to estimate possible frequency of the attack associated with the risk. Then we need to take into consideration values of all the assets that can be affected by the attack.

If we use discrete risk values, we can represent risk values by the exclamation mark ("!") at the top of a task element associated with an attack. For example, three exclamation marks depict that risk value is high, whereas one exclamation mark

depicts that the risk value is low. Figure 6 shows an example of how risk value is depicted.

If continuous risk values are used, the values can be depicted as numbers on the top of the corresponding task element.

If we want to assign value to an asset or a security feature, we assign a value to the corresponding goal or softgoal. We represent values on the top of i* goal and softgoal elements. If we use discreet values, we represent values as star marks ("*"). We draw more for assets and security features having larger value. If we use continuous value, we represent them as numbers.

To protect their assets, in other words, to reduce security risks, actors may want to provide countermeasures against possible attacks. An actor who provides defensive measures plays a role "Actor as a defender." The countermeasures are represented as internal tasks of defending ac-

Figure 5. Representation of attacks that make the dependency totally unviable in our Web services-based card payment system example. The link is labeled as a break link.

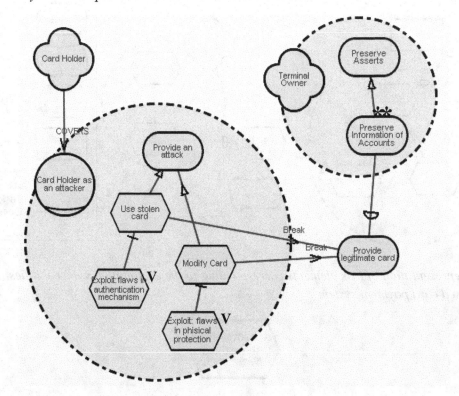

tors. The aim of treatment measure is to fix some vulnerability, and thus to reduce the impact or the frequency of the attack. To show that a treatment measure is aimed at fixing vulnerability, we draw a negative contribution link connecting the task representing the treatment measure with the task representing exploitation of the vulnerability. Figure 7 illustrates how treatment measures are depicted in SR diagram.

Figure 6. Depiction of risk values

CONCLUSION AND FUTURE TRENDS

We have described an approach that can be used for reasoning opportunities, vulnerabilities, threats, and risks that are associated with WS-based security systems.

There have been several initiatives undertaken to model security risks from different perspectives. So far, most of the pieces of literature describe different strategies for modeling as per the security requirements of a system under development. The development of a system from the perspective of the intentions of the actors of the system, and how they interact between each other, is interesting and necessary for a comprehensive management of security risks of a system. The actor dependency-based approach that we have illustrated in this chapter is helpful to address

Figure 7. Depiction of treatment measures in an SR diagram in our Web services-based card payment system example.

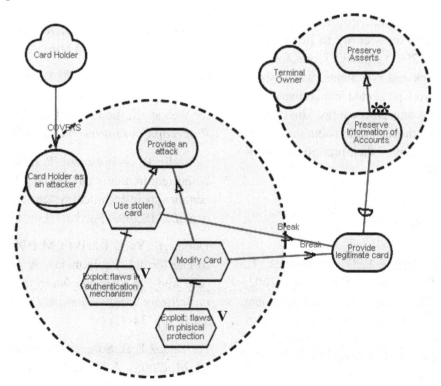

this need. However, this approach is developed considering the general security risks of a system. We believe that this approach can, as well, be used for modeling all aspects of security risk issues that might occur. However, it is necessary to consider specific cases of WS security, and analyze how well the presented approach in this chapter can help in addressing the modeling of those cases. Addressing all possible security issues is complex. Different issues need to be considered from different perspectives. Therefore, we believe that the aspect of intentional modeling of WS security has the potential for its growth as an independent field. We also believe that intensive work in this area has the strong potential to lead to the development of a new modeling language for use in the area of WS security.

ACKNOWLEDGMENT

The authors thank the anonymous referees for their valuable comments, which helped to strengthen the quality of this chapter. The authors also thank the referees and the audience of the 3rd International Workshop on Security in Information Systems (WOSIS 2005), Miami, Florida, for their valuable feedback and comments, where some portions of the work presented in this chapter appeared in the workshop proceedings. This chapter was written from the inspiration obtained by the authors while presenting their preliminary work in WOSIS 2005.

REFERENCES

Aagedal, J. O., Braber, F. D., Dimitrakos, T., Gran, B. A., Raptis, D., & Stolen, K., (2002, September 17-20). Model-based risk assessment to improve enterprise security. In *Proceedings of the Fifth International Enterprise Distributed Object Computing Conference (EDOC 2002)*, Lausanne, Switzerland.

Alghathbar, K., Wijesekera, D., & Farkas, C. (2005). Return on security investment (ROSI): A practical quantitative model. In *Proceedings of International Workshop on Security in Information Systems*, Miami, FL, USA (pp. 239-252).

Barber, B., & Davey, J. (1992). The use of the CCTA risk analysis and management methodology (CRAMM) in health information systems. In *Medinfo 92*, Amsterdam, North Holland (pp. 1589-1593).

Chung, L., Nixon, B. A., Yu, E., & Mylopoulos, J. (2000). *Non-functional requirements in software engineering*. Kluwer Academic Publishers, USA. ISBN 0792386663.

COBRA. (2005). *COBRA risk consultant*. Retrieved August 21, 2006, from http://www.riskworld.net/

Common Criteria Organization. (2002). *Common criteria for information technology security evaluation*. Retrieved August 21, 2006, from http://www.commoncriteria.org

Control Objectives for Information and Related Technology. (2002). *COBIT*. Retrieved from http://www.isaca.org/ct-denld.htm

Dimitrakos, T., Ritchie, B., Raptis, D., & Stolen, K. (2002). Model-based security risk analysis for Web applications: The CORAS approach. In *Proceedings of Euroweb 2002*, Oxford, U.K.

Donzelli, P., & Bresciani, P. (2003). An agent-based requirements engineering framework for complex socio-technical systems. In *Proceedings of SELMAS 2003*, Portland, OR, USA.

Dubois, E., Yu, E.,0 & Petit, M. (1998). From early to late formal requirements: A process control case study. In *Proc. 9th International Workshop on Software Specification and Design*, Ise-Shima, Japan (pp. 34-42).

Fernandez, E. B., Sorgente, T., & Larrondo-Petrie, M. M. (2005). A UML-based methodology for secure systems: The design stage. In *Proceedings of International Workshop on Security in Information Systems*, Miami, FL (pp. 207-216).

Fletcher, S., Jansen, R., Lim, J., Halbgenacher, R., Murphy, M., & Flyss, G. (1995). Software system risk assessment and assurance. In *Proceedings of the New Security Paradigms Workshop*, San Diego, CA.

Gans, G., Jarke, M., Kethers, S., Lakemeyer, G., Ellrich, L., Funken, C., & Meister, M. (2001). Requirements modeling for organization networks: A (dis)trust-based approach. In *Proceedings of the 5th IEEE International Symposium on Requirements Engineering*, Toronto, Canada.

Giorgini, P., Massacci, F., & Mylopoulos, J. (2003). *Requirement engineering meets security: A case study on modelling secure electronic transactions by VISA and Mastercard* (Technical Report DIT-03-027). Informatica e Telecomunicazioni, University of Trento, Italy.

Gutierrez, C., Fernandez-Medina, E., & Piattini, M. (2005). Towards a process for Web services security. In *Proceedings of the 3ʳᵈ International Workshop on Security in Information Systems* (WOSIS 2005), Miami, FL (pp. 298-308).

Labuschagne, L. (1999). *Risk analysis generations — The evolution of risk analysis*. Retrieved January 29, 2002, from http://csweb.rau.ac.za/deth/research/article_page.htm

Lodderstedt, T., Bastin, D., & Doser, J. (2002). SecureUML: A UML-based modeling language for model-driven security. In *Proceedings of the 5ᵗʰ International Conference on Unified Modeling Language,* Dresden, Germany.

Lund, M. S., Barber, F. D., Stolen K., & Vraalsen, F. (2004). *A UML profile for the identification and analysis of security risks during structured brainstorming* (Report # STF40 A03067). SINTEF, Norway.

Lund, M. S., Hogganvik, I., Seehusen, F., & Stolen, K. (2003). *UML profile for security assessment* (Report # STF40 A03066). SINTEF Telecom and Informatics, Norway.

Martel, S. (2002). A New Model for Computer Network Security Risk Analysis. MA.Sc. thesis. Carleton University, Canada.

Misra, S. C., Kumar, V., & Kumar, U. (2005a). How can i* complement UML for modeling organizations? In *Proceedings of the 18ᵗʰ IEEE Canadian Conference on Electrical and Computer Engineering* (CCECE 2005), Saskatoon, Saskatchewan, Canada (pp. 2319-2321).

Misra, S. C., Kumar, V., & Kumar, U. (2005b, May 24-25). An approach for modeling information systems security risk assessment. In *Proceedings of the 3ʳᵈ International Workshop on Security in Information Systems* (WOSIS 2005), Miami, FL, USA (pp. 253-262).

Misra, S.C., Kumar, V., & Kumar, U. (2005c, May 25-28). A strategic modeling technique for change management in organizations undergoing BPR. In *Proceedings of the 7ᵗʰ International Conference on Enterprise Information Systems (ICEIS 2005)* (Vol. 3, pp. 447-450). Miami, FL.

Misra, S. C., Kumar, V., & Kumar, U. (2005d, May 25-28). Modeling strategic actor relationships to support risk analysis and control in software projects. In *Proceedings of the 7ᵗʰ International Conference on Enterprise Information Systems (ICEIS 2005*, Miami, FL (Vol. 3, pp. 288-293).

Misra, S. C., Kumar, V., & Kumar, U. (2005e, May 1-4). Goal-oriented or scenario-based requirements engineering (RE) technique: What should a practitioner select? In *Proceedings of the 18ᵗʰ IEEE Canadian Conference on Electrical and Computer Engineering (CCECE 2005),* Saskatoon, Saskatchewan, Canada (pp. 2314-2318).

Misra, S. C., Kumar, V., & Kumar, U. (2005f, April 20-22). Strategic modeling of risk management in industries undergoing BPR. In *Proceedings of the 8th International Conference on Business Information Systems (BIS 2005)*, Poznan, Poland (pp. 85-103).

Mouratidis, H., Giorgini, P., Manson, G., & Philip, I. (2002). A natural extension of tropos methodology for modelling security. In *Proceedings of the Agent Oriented Methodologies Workshop (OOPSLA 2002)*, Seattle, WA.

Mouratidis, H., Giorgini, P., & Manson, G. (2003). An ontology for modelling security: The tropos approach. *Lecture Notes in Computer Science, 2773*, 1387-1394. USA: Springer-Verlag.

Sandia National Laboratories. (2002). *Surety analysis*. Retrieved from http://www.sandia.gov

Schechter, S. E. (2004). *Computer security and risk: A quantitative approach*. PhD thesis, Computer Science, Harvard University.

Standards Australia. (1999). *AS/NZS 4360: Risk management*. Standards Australia. Standard. AS/NZS 4360.

Sutcliffe, A. G., & Minocha, S. (1999). Linking business modeling to socio-technical system design. In *Proceedings of CaiSE'99* (pp. 73-87). Heidelberg, Germany.

Swiderski, F., & Snyder, W. (2004). *Threat modeling*. USA: Microsoft Press.

Tivoli. (2005). *Tivioli secure way risk manager*. Retrieved March 14, 2003, from http://www-306.ibm.com/software/tivoli/products/security-compliance-mgr/

Villarroel, R., Fernandez, E., Trujillo, J., & Piattini, M. (2005). Towards a UML 2.0/OCL extension for designing secure data warehouses. In *Proceedings of International Workshop on Security in Information Systems*, Miami, FL, USA (pp. 217-228).

Vraalsen, F., Braber, F. D., Hogganvik, I., Lund, S., & Stolen, K. (2004). *The CORAS tool-supported methodology* (SINTEF Report. Report # STF90A04015). SINTEF ICT, Norway.

Yu, E. (1999). Strategic modeling for enterprise integration. In *Proceedings of the 16th World Congress of International Federation of Automatic Control*, Beijing, China (pp. 127-132). Pergamon, Elsevier Sciences.

Yu, E., & Liu, L. (2000). Modelling trust in the i* strategic actors framework. In *Proceedings of the 3rd International Workshop on Deception, Fraud, and Trust in Agent Societies*, Barcelona, Catalonia, Spain.

Yu, E. S. K., & Mylopoulos, J. (1994, May 16-21). Understanding "why" in software process modeling, analysis, and design. In *Proceedings of the 16th International Conference in Software Engineering*, Sorrento, Italy (pp. 548-565).

Compilation of References

Aagedal, J. O., Braber, F. D., Dimitrakos, T., Gran, B. A., Raptis, D., & Stolen, K., (2002, September 17-20). Model-based risk assessment to improve enterprise security. In *Proceedings of the Fifth International Enterprise Distributed Object Computing Conference (EDOC 2002)*, Lausanne, Switzerland.

Abdul-Rahman, A., & Hailes, S. (2000). Supporting Trust in Virtual Communities. In *Proceedings of the Hawaii's International Conference on Systems Sciences*, Maui, Hawaii.

Abelló, A., Samos, J., & Saltor, F. (2001). A framework for the classification and description of multidimensional data models. *Proceedings of 12th International Conference on Database and Expert Systems Applications (DEXA'01)*, Springer-Verlag LNCS 2113, Munich, Germany, pp. 668-677.

Accorsi, R. (2006). On the relationship of privacy and secure remote logging in dynamic systems. In *Proceedings of the international information security conference*. (pp. 329-39). Boston: Springer-Verlag.

Accorsi, R. (2008). *Automated counterexample-driven audits of authentic system records*. Thesis.

Accorsi, R., & Stocker, T. (2008). Automated privacy audits based on pruning of log data. In *Proceedings of the international workshop on security and privacy in enterprise computing*. Washington, DC: IEEE Computer Society.

Agarwal, S., & Sprick, B. (2005). Specification of Access Control and Certification Policies for Semantic Web Services. In K. Bauknecht, B. Pröll, & H. Werthner (Eds.), *EC-Web* (Vol. 3590, pp. 348-357). Berlin: Springer.

Agrawal, R., Gunopulos, D., & Leymann, F. (1998). Mining process models from workflow logs. In *Advances in Database Technology — EDBT'98* (pp. 467-483).

Agreiter, B., Alam, M., Hafner, M., Seifert, J. P., & Zhang, X. (2007). Model driven configuration of secure operating systems for mobile applications in health care. In J. Sztipanovits, R. Breu, E. Ammenwerth, R. Bajcsy, J. Mitchell, & A. Pretschner (Eds.), *Workshop on model-based trustworthy health information systems*.

Alam, M., Breu, R., & Hafner, M. (2007). Model-Driven security engineering for trust management in SECTET. *Journal of Software*, *2*(1), 47–59. doi:10.4304/jsw.2.1.47-59

Alam, M., Hafner, M., & Breu, R. (2008). Constraint based role based access control in the SECTET-framework. *Journal of Computer Security*, *16*(2), 223–260.

Alberts, C., & Dorofee, A. (2002). *Managing information security risks: the OCTAVE approach*. Upper Saddle River, NJ: Pearson Education.

Alexander, J., Box, D., Cabrera, L. F., Chappell, D., Daniels, G., et al. (2006a). *Web Services Transfer (WS-Transfer)*. W3C. Retrieved April 20, 2009 from http://www.w3.org/Submission/WS-Transfer/

Alexander, J., Box, D., Cabrera, L. F., Chappell, D., Daniels, G., et al. (2006b). *Web Services Enumeration (WS-Enumeration)*. W3C. Retrieved April 20, 2009 from http://www.w3.org/Submission/WS-Enumeration/

Alghathbar, K., Wijesekera, D., & Farkas, C. (2005). Return on security investment (ROSI): A practical quantitative model. In *Proceedings of International*

Workshop on Security in Information Systems, Miami, FL, USA (pp. 239-252).

Al-Kahtani, M. A., & Sandhu, R. (2003). Induced Role Hierarchies with Attribute-Based RBAC. In *Proceedings of the 9th ACM Symposium on Access Control Models and Technologies*, (pp. 142-148). New York: ACM Press.

Alonso, G., Casati, F., Kuno, H., & Machiraju, V. (2004). *Web services: Concepts, architectures and applications.* Berlin: Springer.

Alonso, R., & Larrucea, X. (2008). ISOAS: Through an Independent SOA Security Specification. In *Proceedings of the 7th International Conference on Composition-Based Software Systems*, (pp. 92-100). Washington, DC: IEEE Computer Society.

Alves, A., Arkin, A., Askary, S., Barreto, C., Bloch, B., et al. (2007). *Web services business process execution language version 2.0. OASIS.* Retrieved April 20, 2009 from http://docs.oasis-open.org/wsbpel/2.0/OS/wsbpel-v2.0-OS.html

Anderson, A. (2005). *Core and hierarchical role based access control (RBAC) profile of XACML v2.0. OASIS.* Retrieved April 20, 2009 from http://docs.oasis-open.org/xacml/2.0/access_control-xacml-2.0-rbac-profile1-spec-os.pdf

Anderson, A. (2005). *Hierarchical resource profile of XACML v2.0.* OASIS. Retrieved April 20, 2009 from http://docs.oasis-open.org/xacml/2.0/access_control-xacml-2.0-hier-profile-spec-os.pdf

Anderson, A. (2005). *Multilple resource profile of XACML v2.0.* OASIS. Retrieved April 20, 2009 from http://docs.oasis-open.org/xacml/2.0/access_control-xacml-2.0-mult-profile-spec-os.pdf

Anderson, A. (2005). *XML Digital Signature profile of XACML v2.0.* OASIS. Retrieved April 20, 2009 from http://docs.oasis-open.org/xacml/2.0/access_control-xacml-2.0-dsig-profile-spec-os.pdf

Anderson, A. (2006). Web services policies. *Security & Privacy, 4*(3), 84–87. doi:10.1109/MSP.2006.81

Anderson, A., & Lockhart, H. (2005). *SAML 2.0 profile of XACML v2.0.* OASIS. Retrieved April 20, 2009 from http://docs.oasis-open.org/xacml/2.0/access_control-xacml-2.0-saml-profile-spec-os.pdf

Anderson, R. (2001). *Security Engineering - A Guide to Building Dependable Distributed Systems*: John Wiley&Sons.

Anderson, R., & Long, C. (2001). *Security engineering: A guide to building dependable distributed systems.* Hoboken, NJ: Wiley & Sons.

Anley, C. (2002). Advanced SQL injection in SQL server applications. *NGS Software Insight Security Research.*

Apache Axis2 Architecture Guide. (2006). The Apache Software Foundation.

Apvrille, A., & Pourzandi, M. (2005). Secure software development by example. *IEEE Security and Privacy, 3*(4), 10–17. doi:10.1109/MSP.2005.103

Arenas, A., Aziz, B., Bicarregui, J., Matthews, B., & Yang, E. Y. (2008). Modelling security properties in a grid-based operating system with anti-goals. In *ARES '08: Proceedings of the 2008 third international conference on availability, reliability and security.* Washington, DC: IEEE Computer Society.

Ariga, S., Nagahashi, K., Minami, M., Esaki, H., & Murai, J. (2000, July 18-21). Performance evaluation of data transmission using IPSec over IPv6 networks. In *INET 2000 Proceedings — The Internet Global Summit: Global Distributed Intelligence for Everyone, the 10th Annual Internet Society Conference*, Pacifico Yokohama Conference Center, Yokohama, Japan.

Arkin, A., Askari, S., Fordin, S., Jekeli, W., Kawaguchi, K., et al. (2002). *Web services choreography interface (WSCI) 1.0.* W3C. Retrieved April 20, 2009 from http://www.w3.org/TR/wsci/

Arora, A., Cohen, J., Davis, J., Dutch, M., Golovinsky, E., et al. (2005). *The WS-management catalog.* Dell. Retrieved April 20, 2009 from http://www.dell.com/downloads/global/corporate/standards/ws_management_catalog.pdf

Arsanjani, A. (2004). *Service-oriented modeling and architecture*. Technical report, SOA and Web services Center of Excellence, IBM. Retrieved April 20, 2009, from http://www.ibm.com/developerworks/webservices/library/ws-soa-design1/

Arsanjani, A., Borges, B. & Holley, K. (2004). Service-Oriented Architecture. *DM Direct.* (6), 32.

Arsanjani, A., Ghosh, S., Allam, A., Abdollah, T., Ganapathy, S., & Holley, K. (2008). SOMA: A method for developing service-oriented solutions. *IBM Systems Journal, 3*(47), 377–396.

Arsanjani, A., Zhang, L. J., Allam, A., & Channabasava-iah, K. (2007, March 28). *Design a SOA solution using a reference architecture*. Armonk, NY: IBM. Retrieved April 20, 2009, from http://www.ibm.com/developer-works/library/ar-archtemp/

Askarov, A., Hedin, D., & Sabelfeld, A. (2008). Cryptographically-masked flows. *Journal of Theoretical Computer Science, 402*(2-3), 82–101. doi:10.1016/j.tcs.2008.04.028

Atkinson, C., Brenner, D., Falcone, G., & Juhasz, M. (2008). Specifying high-assurance services. *Computer, IEEE, 8*(41), 64–71.

Aura, T., Nikander, P., & Leiwo, J. (2001). *DOS-Resistant Authentication with Client Puzzles, (. LNCS, 2133,* 170–177.

Avgeriou, P., & Zdun, U. (2005). Architectural patterns revisited: A pattern language. In *Proceedings of EuroP-LoP*, (pp. 1-39).

Bajaj, S., Della-Libera, G., Dixon, B., & Hondo, M. Hur, M., et al. (2003). *WS-federation: active requestor profile version 1.0*. Armonk, NY: IBM. Retrieved April 20, 2009 from http://download.boulder.ibm.com/ibmdl/pub/software/dw/specs/ws-fedact/ws-fedact.pdf

Bajaj, S., Dixon, B., Dusche, M., Hondo, M., Hur, M., et al. (2003). *WS-federation: passive requestor profile version 1.0*. Armonk, NY: IBM. Retrieved April 20, 2009 from http://download.boulder.ibm.com/ibmdl/pub/software/dw/specs/ws-fedpass/ws-fedpass.pdf

Baldwin, A., Beres, Y., Shiu, S., & Kearney, P. (2006). A model-based approach to trust, security and assurance. *BT Technology Journal, 24*(4), 53–68. doi:10.1007/s10550-006-0097-7

Balinger, K., Bissett, B., Box, D., Curbera, F., Ferguson, D., et al. (2006). *Web Services Metadata Exchange (WS-MetadataExchange) 1.1*. Retrieved April 20, 2009 from http://specs.xmlsoap.org/ws/2004/09/mex/WS-MetadataExchange.pdf

Banks, T. (2006).*Web services resource framework (WSRF) – primer vl.2. OASIS*. Retrieved April 20, 2009 from http://docs.oasis-open.org/wsrf/wsrf-primer-1.2-primer-cd-02.pdf

Barber, B., & Davey, J. (1992). The use of the CCTA risk analysis and management methodology (CRAMM) in health information systems. In *Medinfo 92,* Amsterdam, North Holland (pp. 1589-1593).

Barbon, F., Traverso, P., Pistore, M., & Trainotti, M. (2006). *Run-Time Monitoring of Instances and Classes of Web Service Compositions.* Paper presented at the Web Services, 2006. ICWS '06. International Conference on.

Baresi, L., Ghezzi, C., & Guinea, S. (2004). *Smart monitors for composed services.* Paper presented at the Proceedings of the 2nd international conference on Service oriented computing.

Barros, A., Dumas, M., & Oaks, P. (2005). *A Critical Overview of WS-CDL*: BPTrends.

Bartel, M., Boyer, J., Fox, B., LaMacchia, B., & Simon, E. (2002). *XML-Signature Syntax and Processing*. W3C Recommendation.

Basin, D., Doser, J., & Lodderstedt, T. (2006). Model driven security: From UML models to access control infrastructures. *ACM Transactions on Software Engineering and Methodology, 15*(1), 39–91. doi:10.1145/1125808.1125810

Baskerville, R. (1993). Information systems security design methods: implications for information systems development. *ACM Computing Surveys, 25*(4), 375 - 414.

Battle, S. (2006). Gloze: XML to RDF and back again. In *First Jena user conference*.

Bauer, A., & Jürjens, J. (2008). Security protocols, properties, and their monitoring. In *SESS '08: Proceedings of the fourth international workshop on software engineering for secure systems*. New York: ACM.

BEA WebLogic enterprise security version 4.2, SP02 documentation. (2009). Oracle/BEA. Retrieved April 20, 2009 from http://e-docs.bea.com/wles/docs42/index.html

BEA. *Specifying SOAP Handlers for a Web Service*: BEA WEBLOGIC WORKSHOP HELP.

Beatty, J., Kakivaya, G., Kemp, D., Kuehnel, T., Lovering, B., et al. (2005). *Web Services Dynamic Discovery (WS-Discovery)*. Redmond, WA: Microsoft Corporation. Retrieved April 20, 2009 from http://specs.xmlsoap.org/ws/2005/04/discovery/ws-discovery.pdf

Beeri, C., Eyal, A., Milo, T., & Pilberg, A. (2007). *Monitoring business processes with queries*. Paper presented at the Proceedings of the 33rd international conference on Very large data bases.

Bell, D. E., & La Padula, L. J. (1973). *Secure Computer Systems: Mathematical Foundations*, (MITRE Technical Report 2547, Vol. I, ESD–TR–73–278–I). Bedford, MA: The MITRE Corporation.

Berglund, A., Boag, S., Chamberlin, D., Fernández, M. F., Kay, M., Robie, J., & Siméon, J. (2007). *XML Path Language (XPath) 2.0*. W3C. Retrieved April 20, 2009 from http://www.w3.org/TR/xpath20/

Bertino, E., Castano, S., Ferrari, E., & Mesiti, M. (2000). Specifying and enforcing access control policies for xml document sources. *World Wide Web (Bussum), 3*(3), 139–151. doi:10.1023/A:1019289831564

Bertino, E., Jajodia, S., & Samarati, P. (1999). A Flexible Authorization Mechanism for Relational Data Management Systems. *ACM Transactions on Information Systems, 17*(2), 101–140. doi:10.1145/306686.306687

Bertot, Y., & Castéran, P. (2004). Interactive Theorem Proving and Program Development. In *Coq'Art: The Calculus of Inductive Constructions*. Berlin: Springer-Verlag.

Best, B., Jürjens, J., & Nuseibeh, B. (2007). Model-Based security engineering of distributed information systems using UMLsec. In *ICSE '07: Proceedings of the 29th international conference on software engineering*. Washington, DC: IEEE Computer Society.

Bhargavan, K., Fournet, C. & Gordan, A.D. (2008). Verifying Policy-Based Web Services Security. In *ACM conference on Computer and communications security*, (Vol. 30, pp. 268-277). New York: ACM.

Bhargavan, K., Fournet, C., Gordon, A. D., & O'Shea, G. (2005). An Advisor for Web Services Security Policies. In *SWS '05: Proceedings of the 2005 Workshop on Secure Web Services*, (pp. 1-9). New York: ACM Press.

Bhargavan, K., Fournet, C., Gordon, A. D., & Tse, S. (2006). Verified interoperable implementations of security protocols. In *Computer security foundations workshop, 2006 19th IEEE*.

Bialkowski, J., & Heineman, K. (2004). *Application vulnerability description language 1.0*. OASIS. Retrieved April 20, 2009 from http://www.oasis-open.org/committees/download.php/7145/AVDL%20Specification%20V1.pdf

Bianculli, D., & Ghezzi, C. (2007). *Monitoring conversational web services*. Paper presented at the 2nd international workshop on Service oriented software engineering: in conjunction with the 6th ESEC/FSE joint meeting.

Biba, K. J. (1977). *Integrity Considerations for Secure Computer Systems*, (Technical Report TR-3153). Bedford, MA: MITRE Corp.

Bilal, M., Thomas, J. P., Thomas, M., & Abraham, S. (2005). *Fair BPEL processes transaction using non-repudiation protocols*. Paper presented at the 2005 IEEE International Conference on Services Computing.

Biron, P. V., & Malhotra, A. (2004). *XML Schema Part 2: Datatypes Second Edition*. Retrieved April 20, 2009 from http://www.w3.org/TR/2004/REC-xmlschema-2-20041028/

Bishop, M. (2003). *Computer Security: Art and Science*. Reading, MA: Addison-Wesley Professional.

Bishop, M. (2005). *Introduction to computer security*. Reading, MA: Addison-Wesley.

Blaschka, M., Sapia, C., Höfling, G., & Dinter, B. (1998). Finding your way through multidimensional data models. *Proceedings of 9th International Conference on Database and Expert Systems Applications (DEXA'98)*. LNCS, 1460, Springer-Verlag, Vienna, Austria, pp. 198-203.

Blaze, M., Feigenbaum, J., & Lacy, J. (1996) Decentralized Trust Management. In *Proceedings of the IEEE Symposium on Security and Privacy*, (pp. 164 - 173). Washington, DC: IEEE Computer Society

Blobel, B., & Pharow, P. (2007). A model driven approach for the german health telematics architectural framework and security infrastructure. *International Journal of Medical Informatics*, 76(2-3), 169–175. doi:10.1016/j.ijmedinf.2006.05.044

Blobel, B., & Roger-France, F. (2001). A systematic approach for analysis and design of secure health information systems. *International Journal of Medical Informatics*, 62(1), 51–78. doi:10.1016/S1386-5056(01)00147-2

Blobel, B., Nordberg, R., Davis, J. M., & Pharow, P. (2006). Modelling privilege management and access control. *International Journal of Medical Informatics*, 75(8), 597–623. doi:10.1016/j.ijmedinf.2005.08.010

Boag, S., Chamberlin, D., Fernández, M. F., Florescu, D., Robie, J., & Siméon, J. (2007). *XQuery 1.0: An XML Query Language*. Retrieved April 20, 2009 from http://www.w3.org/TR/xquery/

Boehm, B. W. (1981). *Software engineering economics*. Englewood Cliffs, NJ: Prentice-Hall.

Boehm, O., Caumanns, J., Franke, M., & Pfaff, O. (2008). Federated Authentication and Authorization: A Case Study. In *Proceedings of the 12th International IEEE Enterprise Distributed Object Computing Conference*, (pp. 356 - 362). Washington, DC: IEEE Computer Society.

Bohring, H., & Auer, S. (2005). Mapping XML to OWL Ontologies. In K. P. Jantke, K.-P. Fähnrich, & W. S. Wittig (Eds.), *Leipziger informatik-tage,* (Vol. 72, p. 147-156). GI.

Bonatti, P., De Capitani Di Vimercati, S., & Samarati, P. (2000). A Modular Approach to Composing Access Control Policies. In *Proceedings of the 7th ACM Conference on Computer and Communication Security (CCS 2000)*, (pp.164 - 173). New York: ACM Press.

Bonatti, P., De Capitani Di Vimercati, S., & Samarati, P. (2002). An Algebra for Composing Access Control Policies. *ACM Transactions on Information and System Security*, 5(1), 1–35. doi:10.1145/504909.504910

Booth, D., & Liu, C. K. (2007). *Web Services Description Language (WSDL) Version 2.0 Part 0: Primer*. W3C. Retrieved April 20, 2009 from http://www.w3.org/TR/wsdl20-primer/

Box, D., Cabrera, L. F., Critchley, C., Curbera, F., Ferguson, D., et al. (2006). *Web Services Eventing (WS-Eventing)*. W3C. Retrieved April 20, 2009 from http://www.w3.org/Submission/WS-Eventing/

Boyer, J., Eastlake, D., & Reagle, J. (2002, July). *XML-Signature Syntax and Processing (Recom- mendation)*. W3C. Retrieved from http://www.w3.org/TR/xml-exc-c14n/

Bradford, P. G., Grizzell, B. M., Jay, G. T., & Jenkins, J. T. (2007). Cap. 4. Pragmatic Security for Constrained Wireless Networks. In A. Publications (Ed.), *Security in Distributed, Grid, Mobile, and Pervasive Computing* (pp. 440). The University of Alabama, Tuscaloosa, USA.

Bray, T., Hollander, D., Layman, A., & Tobin, R. (2006). *Namespaces in XML 1.0 (second edition). World Wide Web Consortium*. Retrieved April 20, 2009, from http://www.w3.org/TR/REC-xml-names/

Bray, T., Paoli, J., Sperberg-McQueen, C. M., Maler, E., Yergeau, F., & Cowan, J. (2006). *Extensible markup language (xml) 1.1 (second edition)*. Retrieved April 20, 2009, from http://www.w3.org/TR/xml11/

Braz, F., Fernandez, E. B., & VanHilst, M. (2008). Eliciting security requirements through misuse activities. In *Proceedings of the 2nd Int. Workshop on Secure Systems*

Methodologies using Patterns (SPattern'07), in conjunction with the 4th International Conference on Trust, Privacy & Security in Digital Busines (TrustBus'08), (pp. 328-333).

Brehm, N., & Marx Gómez, J. (2005): Secure Web service-based Resource Sharing in ERP Networks. *International Journal on Information Privacy and Security (JIPS).*

Brehm, N., & Marx Gómez, J. (2007). Web Service-based specification and implementation of functional components in Federated ERP-Systems. In *10th International Conference on Business Information Systems,* Poznan, Poland.

Brehm, N., Lübke, D., & Marx Gómez, J. (2007). Federated Enterprise Resource Planning (FERP) Systems. In P. Saha (Ed.), *Handbook of Enterprise Systems Architecture in Practice* (pp. 290-305). Hershey, PA: IGI Global.

Brehm, N., Mahmoud, T., Marx Gómez, J., & Memari, A. (2008). Towards Intelligent Discovery for Enterprise Architecture Services (IDEAS). *Journal of Enterprise Architecture, 4*(3), 26–36.

Brehm, N., Marx Gómez, J., & Rautenstrauch, C. (2006). An ERP solution based on web services and peer-to-peer networks for small and medium enterprises. *International Journal of Information Systems and Change Management (IJISCM).*

Breu, R., Burger, K., Hafner, M., & Popp, G. (2004). Towards a Systematic Development of Secure Systems. *Information Systems Security, 13*(3), 5–13. doi:10.1201/1086/44530.13.3.20040701/83064.2

Breu, R., Hafner, M., Innerhofer-Oberperfler, F., & Wozak, F. (2008). Model-Driven Security Engineering of Service Oriented Systems. In R. Kaschek, C. Kop, C. Steinberger, & G. Fliedl (Eds.), *Information Systems and e-Business Technologies,* (pp. 59-71). Berlin: Springer.

Breu, R., Innerhofer-Oberperfler, F., & Yautsiukhin, A. (2008). Quantitative assessment of enterprise security system. International Workshop on Privacy and Assurance. In *Proceedings of the The Third International Conference on Availability, Reliability and Security, ARES 2008,* March 4-7, 2008, Technical University of Catalonia, Barcelona, Spain (pp. 921-928). Washington, DC: IEEE Computer Society.

Breu, R., Innerhofer-Oberperfler, F., Mitterer, M., Schabetsberger, T., & Wozak, F. (2008). Model-Based Security Analysis of Health Care Networks. In *Proc. eHealth2008* (pp. 93-100). Vienna, Austria: OCG.

Brewer, D. F. C & Nash, M.J. (1989). The Chinese Wall security policy. *Security and Privacy, 1989 Proceedings., 1989 IEEE Symposium on (1989)*, Oakland, CA (pp. 206-214).

BSI. (2004). *IT Baseline Protection Manual.* Retrieved 11 21, 2008, from http://www.bsi.bund.de/english/gshb/index.htm

Bucchiarone, A., & Gnesi, S. (2006). *A Survey on Services Composition Languages and Models.* Paper presented at the International Workshop on Web Services Modeling and Testing (WS-MaTe 2006).

Buckley, I., Fernandez, E. B., Rossi, G., & Madjadi, S. (2009, July). Web Services reliability patterns. In *21st International Conference on Software Engineering and Knowledge Engineering (SEKE'2009).*

Buecker, A., Ashley, P., Borrett, M., Lu, M., Muppidi, S., & Readshaw, N. (2007). *Understanding SOA Design and Implementation.* Redmond, WA: IBM Redbooks.

Bullard, V., & Vanbenepe, W. (2006). *Web services distributed management: Management using web services (MUWS 1.1) part 1.* OASIS. Retrieved April 20, 2009 from http://www.oasis-open.org/committees/download.php/20576/wsdm-muws1-1.1-spec-os-01.pdf

Buschmann, F., Meunier, R., Rohnert, H., Sommerland, P., & Stal, M. (1996). *Pattern-oriented software architecture: A system of patterns.* New York: Wiley.

Business process execution language for web services. (2002). Armonk, NY: IBM. http://www.ibm.com/developerworks/webservices/library/specification/ws-bpel/

Butler, M., Hoare, T., & Ferreira, C. (2005). A Trace Semantics for Long-Running Transactions. In *Communicating Sequential Processes* (pp. 133-150).

Cahill, C. P., & Hughes, J. (2005, March). *Security Assertion Markup Language (SAML) v2.0.* Retrieved from http://docs.oasis-open.org/security/saml/v2.0/saml-core-2.0-os.pdf

Cantor, S., Hirsch, F., Kemp, J., Philpott, R., & Maler, E. (2005). *Bindings for the OASIS Security Assertion Markup Language (SAML) V2.0.* OASIS. Retrieved April 20, 2009 from http://docs.oasis-open.org/security/saml/v2.0/saml-bindings-2.0-os.pdf

Cantor, S., Kemp, J., Philpott, R., & Maler, E. (2005). *Assertions and Protocols for the OASIS Security Assertion Markup Language (SAML) V2.0.* OASIS. Retrieved April 20, 2009 from http://docs.oasis-open.org/security/saml/v2.0/saml-core-2.0-os.pdf

Cantor, S., Moreh, J., Philpott, R., & Maler, E. (2005). *Metadata for the OASIS security assertion markup language (SAML) V2.0.* OASIS. Retrieved April 20, 2009 from http://docs.oasis-open.org/security/saml/v2.0/saml-metadata-2.0-os.pdf

Carbo, J., Molina, J., & Davila, J. (2002). Comparing Predictions of SPORAS vs. a Fuzzy Reputation Agent Sys-tem. In *Third International Conference on Fuzzy Sets and Fuzzy Systems*, Interlaken, (pp. 147–153).

Carpenter, B., & Moore, K. (2001). *Connection of IPv6 domains via IPv4 Clouds.* RFC 3056, February.

Carter, J., Bitting, E., & Ghorbani, A. (2002). Reputation Formalization for an Information-Sharing Multi-Agent Sytem. *Computational Intelligence*, *18*(2), 515–534. doi:10.1111/1467-8640.t01-1-00201

Carter, S. (2007). *The New Language of Business: SOA & Web 2.0.* Armonk, NY: IBM Press.

Chandramouli, R. (2003). A Policy Validation Framework for Enterprise Authorization Specification. In *Proceedings of the 19th Annual Computer Security Applications Conference,* (pp. 319 - 328). Washington, DC: IEEE Computer Society.

Chappell, D., & Liu, L. (2006). *Web Services Brokered Notification 1.3 (WS-Brokered Notification).* OASIS.

Retrieved April 20, 2009 from http://docs.oasis-open.org/wsn/wsn-ws_brokered_notification-1.3-spec-os.pdf

Chess, B., & McGraw, G. (2004). Static analysis for security. *IEEE Security and Privacy*, *2*(6), 76–79. doi:10.1109/MSP.2004.111

Chinnici, R., & Haas, H. Lewis, A. A., Moreau, J.-J., Orchard, D. & Weerawarana, S. (2007). *Web Services Description Language (WSDL) Version 2.0 Part 2: Adjuncts.* W3C. Retrieved April 20, 2009 from http://www.w3.org/TR/wsdl20-adjuncts/

Chinnici, R., Moreau, J.-J., Ryman, A., & Weerawarana, S. (2006, March). *Web Services Description Language (WSDL) 2.0.* Retrieved from http://www.w3.org/TR/wsdl20/

Chiusano, J. (2003). *UDDI and ebXML registry: a co-existence paradigm, Booz Allen Hamilton.* Retrieved April 20, 2009 from http://lists.oasis-open.org/archives/regrep/200304/pdf00000.pdf

Christensen, E., Curbera, F., Meredith, G., & Weerawarana, S. (2001). *Web Services Description Language (WSDL) 1.1.* W3C. Retrieved April 20, 2009 from http://www.w3.org/TR/wsdl

Chung, L., Nixon, B. A., Yu, E., & Mylopoulos, J. (2000). *Non-functional requirements in software engineering.* Kluwer Academic Publishers, USA. ISBN 0792386663.

Clark, D. D., & Wilson, D. R. (1987), A Comparison of Commercial and Military Computer Security Policies. In *Proceedings of IEEE Symposium on Security and Privacy,* (pp. 184–194).

Clark, J., & DeRose, S. (1999). *XML Path Language (XPath) Version 1.0.* W3C Recommendation.

Clark, J., & DeRose, S. (2006, June). *XML Path Langauage (XPath) 2.0* (W3C Recommendation). Retrieved from http://www.w3.org/TR/xpath/

Clement, L., Hately, A., Riegen, C. V., & Rogers, T. (2004). *Universal Description Discovery and Integration (UDDI), version 3.0.2.* OASIS Standard 200502. Retrieved from http://www.uddi.orge/pub/uddi-v3.htm

Clement, L., Hately, A., von Riegen, C., & Rogers, T. (2004). *UDDI Version 3.0.2, UDDI Spec technical committee draft*. OASIS. Retrieved April 20, 2009 from http://www.uddi.org/pubs/uddi_v3.htm

Clement, L., Hately, A., von Riegen, C., & Rogers, T. (2005, February). *Universal Description, Discovery and Integration (UDDI) V3.0.2*. Retrieved from http://uddi.org/pubs/uddi-v3.0.2-20041019.htm

COBRA. (2005). *COBRA risk consultant*. Retrieved August 21, 2006, from http://www.riskworld.net/

Coffey, T., Saidha, P. (1996). Non-repudiation with mandatory proof of receipt. *ACMCCR: Computer Communication Review, 26*.

Cole, G. (2006). *OASIS service provisioning markup language (SPML) version 2*. OASIS. Retrieved April 20, 2009 from http://xml.coverpages.org/SPMLv2-OS.pdf

Common Criteria Editorial Board (2006). *Common Criteria for Information Technology Security Evaluation*, Version 3.1.

Common Criteria Organization. (2002). *Common criteria for information technology security evaluation*. Retrieved August 21, 2006, from http://www.commoncriteria.org

Conallen, J. (2000). *Building Web applications with UML*. Addison-Wesley.

Congress of the United States of America. (2002). *Sarbanes-Oxley Act of 2002*. Available from http://www.access.gpo.gov/

Congress of the United States of America.(1996). *Health Insurance Portability and Accountability Act of 1996*. Available from http://www.hhs.gov/ocr/hipaa/

Control Objectives for Information and Related Technology. (2002). *COBIT*. Retrieved from http://www.isaca.org/ct-denld.htm

Cover, R. (2002). *Web Services Inspection Language (WSIL)*. Retrieved from http://xml.coverpages.org/wsil.html

Cowan, J., & Tobin, R. (2004). *XML Information Set* (2nd Ed.). W3C. Retrieved April 20, 2009 from http://www.w3.org/TR/xml-infoset/

Crampton, J., Lim, H. W., & Paterson, K. G. (2007). What can Identity-Based Cryptography Offer to Web Services. In [New York: ACM Press.]. *Proceedings of SWS, 07*, 26–36. doi:10.1145/1314418.1314424

Crispo, B., Nair, S. K., Djordjevic, I., & Dimitrakos, T. (2007). Secure Web Service Federation Management Using TPM Virtualization. In *Proceedings of the 2007 ACM workshop on Secure Web Services*, (pp. 73-82). New York: ACM.

Crook, R., Ince, D., Lin, L., & Nuseibeh, B. (2002). Security requirements engineering: When anti-requirements hit the fan. In *Requirements engineering, 2002 proceedings IEEE joint international conference on*.

Cruz, S. M. S., Campos, M. L. M., Pires, P. F., & Campos, L. M. (2004). *Monitoring e-business Web services usage through a log based architecture*. Paper presented at the IEEE International Conference on Web Services.

Damiani, E., di Vimercati, S. D. C., Paraboschi, S., & Samarati, P. (2002). A fine-grained access control system for XML documents. *ACM Transactions on Information and System Security, 5*(2), 169–202. doi:10.1145/505586.505590

DARPA. (1981). *Internet protocol specification*. RFC 791, September.

Davidson, J. A. (1995). *Asymmetric isolation*. Paper presented at Computer Security Applications Conference, 1996, 12th Annual (pp. 44-54), San Diego, CA.

Davis, D., Karmarkar, A., Pilz, G., & Yalçinalp, Ü. (2007). *Web services reliable messaging policy assertion (WS-RM Policy) version 1*. OASIS. Retrieved April 20, 2009 from http://docs.oasis-open.org/ws-rx/wsrmp/200702/wsrmp-1.1-spec-os-01.pdf

Davis, D., Karmarkar, A., Pilz, G., Winkler, S., & Yalçinalp, Ü. (2007). *WS-ReliableMessaging (WS-1 ReliableMessaging) version 1.1*. OASIS. Retrieved April

20, 2009 from http://docs.oasis-open.org/ws-rx/wsrm/wsrm-1.1-spec-os-01.pdf

DCSSI Advisory Office. (2005). *EBIOS - Expression of Needs and Identification of Security Objectives.* Retrieved 11 21, 2008, http://www.ssi.gouv.fr/en/confidence/ebiospresentation.html den Braber, F., Hogganvik, I., Lund, M., Stølen, K., & Vraalsen, F. (2007). Model-based security analysis in seven steps-a guided tour to the CORAS method. *BT Technology Journal, 25* (1), 101-117.

De Pauw, W., Hoch, R., & Huang, Y. (2007). *Discovering Conversations in Web Services Using Semantic Correlation Analysis.* Paper presented at the IEEE International Conference on Web Services, ICWS 2007.

De Pauw, W., Krasikov, S., & Morar, F. J. (2006). *Execution patterns for visualizing web services.* Paper presented at the Proceedings of the 2006 ACM symposium on Software visualization.

Deering, S., & Hinden, R. (1998). *Internet protocol, version 6 specification.* RFC 2460, December.

Delessy, N., & Fernandez, E. B. (2008). A pattern-driven security process for SOA applications. In *Procs. of the Third International Conference on Availability, Reliability and Security (ARES 2008)*, Barcelona, Spain, March 4-7, (pp. 416-421).

Della-Libera, G., Gudgin, M., Hallam-Baker, P., Hondo, M., Granqvist, H., Kaler, C., et al. (2005, July). *Web Services Security Policy Language (WS-SecurityPolicy) V1.1 specification.* Retrieved from ftp://www6.software.ibm.com/software/developer/library/ws-secpol.pdf

DeLooze, L. (2008). Providing Web Service Security in a federated Environment. [Washington, DC: IEEE Educational Activities Department.]. *IEEE Security and Privacy, 5*(1), 73–75. doi:10.1109/MSP.2007.16

Demchenko, Y., Gommans, L., de Laat, C., & Oudenaarde, B. (2005). *Web services and grid security vulnerabilities and threats analysis and model.* Paper presented at the The 6th IEEE/ACM International Workshop on Grid Computing.

Denker, G., Kagal, L., Finin, T. W., Paolucci, M., & Sycara, K. P. (2003). Security for DAML Web Services: Annotation and Matchmaking. In D. Fensel, K. P. Sycara, & J. Mylopoulos (Eds.), *International Semantic Web Conference* (Vol. 2870, p. 335-350). Berlin: Springer.

DeRose, S. J., Daniel, R., Maler, E., & Marsh, J. (2003). *XPointer xmlns() Scheme.* W3C. Retrieved April 20, 2009 from http://www.w3.org/TR/xptr-xmlns/

DeRose, S., Maler, E., & Daniel, R. (2002). *XPointer xpointer() Scheme.* W3C. Retrieved April 20, 2009 from http://www.w3.org/TR/xptr-xpointer/

DeRose, S., Maler, E., & Orchard, D. (2001). *XML Linking Language (XLink), Version 1.0.* Retrieved April 20, 2009 from http://www.w3.org/TR/xlink/

Deubler, M., Grünbauer, J., Jürjens, J., & Wimmel, G. (2004). Sound development of secure service-based systems. In *Proceedings of the 2nd international conference on service oriented computing.*

Devanbu, P. T., & Stubblebine, S. (2000). Software engineering for security: A roadmap. In *ICSE '00: Proceedings of the conference on the future of software engineering.* New York: ACM.

Devdass, R., & Gandhirajan, A. (2008). *Securing web services using TransactionMinder.* Retrieved April 20, 2009 from http://www.developer.com/lang/article.php/3108551

Dietzold, S., & Auer, S. (2006, June). Access Control on RDF Triple Stores from a Semantic Wiki Perspective. In C. Bizer, S. Auer, & L. Miller (Eds.), (Vol. 183).

Dimitrakos, T., Ritchie, B., Raptis, D., & Stolen, K. (2002). Model-based security risk analysis for Web applications: The CORAS approach. In *Proceedings of Euroweb 2002*, Oxford, U.K.

Dimitrakos, T., Ritchie, B., Raptis, D., Aagedal, J., Braber, F. D., Stølen, K., et al. (2002). Integrating model-based security risk management into ebusiness systems development: The CORAS approach. In *I3E '02: Proceedings of the IFIP conference on towards the knowledge society.* Amsterdam: Kluwer, B.V.

Donzelli, P., & Bresciani, P. (2003). An agent-based requirements engineering framework for complex socio-technical systems. In *Proceedings of SELMAS* 2003, Portland, OR, USA.

Doraswamy, N., & Harkins, D. (1999). IPSec: *The new security standard for the Internet, intranets, and virtual private networks*. Englewood, NJ: Prentice Hall PTR.

dos Santos Mello, R., & Heuser, C. A. (2005). BInXS: A Process for Integration of XML Schemata. In O. Pastor & J. F. e Cunha (Eds.), *Caise*, (Vol. 3520, p. 151-166). Berlin: Springer.

Dreibelbis, A., Milman, I., Van Run, P., Hechler, E., Oberhofer, M., & Wolfson, D. (2008) Enterprise Master Data Management: An SOA Approach to Managing Core Information. IBM Press.

Du, W. (2006). *Cross-Site Scripting (XSS) Attack Lab*. Laboratory for Computer Security Education, Syracuse University, Syracuse, NY.

Dubois, E., Yu, E., & Petit, M. (1998). From early to late formal requirements: A process control case study. In *Proc. 9th International Workshop on Software Specification and Design*, Ise-Shima, Japan (pp. 34-42).

Dwibedi, R. (2005). XPath injection in XML databases. from http://palisade.plynt.com/issues/2005Jul/xpath-injection/

Eastlake, D., & Reagle, J. (2002, October). *XML Encryption Syntax and Processing* (Recommendation). W3C. Retrieved from http://www.w3.org/TR/xmldsig-core/

Eastlake, D., Reagle, J., Imamura, T., Dillaway, B., & Simon, E. (2002). *XML Encryption Syntax and Processing*. W3C Recommendation .

Eastlake, D., Reagle, J., Solo, D., Hirsch, F., & Roessler, T. (2008). *XML signature syntax and processing* (2nd Ed.). W3C. Retrieved April 20, 2009 from http://www.w3.org/TR/xmldsig-core/

Eckert, C., & Marek, D. (1997). Developing secure applications: A systematic approach. In *SEC'97: Proceedings of the IFIP TC11 13 international conference on information security (SEC '97) on information security*

in research and business. Boca Raton, FL: Chapman Hall, Ltd.

Egea, M., Basin, D., Clavel, M., & Doser, J. (2007). A metamodel-based approach for analyzing security-design models. In *Lecture notes in computer science*. (pp. 420-35). Berlin: Springer.

Elliott Bell, D. (1994). Modeling the Multipolicy Machine. In *Proceedings of the New security Paradigm Workshop*, (pp. 2-9). Washington, DC: IEEE Computer Society Press.

Enterprise Grid Alliance Security Working Group. (2005, 8 July 2005). *Enterprise Grid Security Requirements Verison 1.0*

Entrust secure transaction platform. (2004). Entrust. Retrieved April 20, 2009 from http://www.entrust.com/web-services-security/.

Epstein, J., Masumoto, S., & McGraw, G. (2006). Software security and SOA: Danger, Will Robinson. [Washington, DC: IEEE Educational Activities Department.]. *IEEE Security and Privacy, 4*(1), 80. doi:10.1109/MSP.2006.23

Erl, T. (2005). *Service-Oriented Architecture*. Delhi, India: Dorling Kindersley (India) Pvt. Ltd.

Estefan, J. A., Laskey, K., McCabe, F. G., & Thornton, D. (2008). *Reference Architecture for Service Oriented Architecture Version 1.0*. Public Review Draft 1, OASIS Service Oriented Architecture Reference Model TC. Retrieved January 19, 2009, http://docs.oasis-open.org/soa-rm/soa-ra/v1.0/soa-ra-pr-01.pdf

EU 6 Framework Program (2006). *SERENITY Project*. Retrieved from http://www.serenity-project.org/

EU 7 Framework Program (2008). *MASTER Project*. Retrieved from www.master-fp7.eu

European Commission. (2005). *eEurope 2005*. Retrieved November 21, 2008, from http://ec.europa.eu/information_society/eeurope/2005/

Extended Backus-Naur Form (EBNF). (1996). Retrieved from http://www.iso.ch/iso/iso_catalogue/catalogue_tc/catalogue_detail.htm?csnumber=26153

eXtensible rights markup language (XrML) 2.0 specification. (2001). ContentGuard. Retrieved March 12, 2009 from http://www.xrml.org/get_XrML.asp

Fallside, D. C., & Walmsley, P. (2004). *XML Schema Part 0: Primer*, (2nd Ed.). Retrieved April 20, 2009 from http://www.w3.org/TR/2004/REC-xmlschema-0-20041028/

Farkas, C., & Huhns, M. N. (2008). Securing Enterprise Applications: Service-Oriented Security (SOS). In *Proceedings of the 10th IEEE Conference on E-Commerce Technology and the 5th IEEE Conference on Enterprise Computing, E-Commerce and E-Services*, (pp. 428-431) Washington, DC: IEEE Computer Society.

Farkas, C., Jain, A., Wijesekera, D., Singhal, A., & Thuraisingham, B. (2006, May). Semantic-Aware Data Protection in Web Services. In *Proceedings of the IEEE Web Services Security Symposium*, (pp. 52-63). West Lafayette, IN: CERIAS.

Farrel, A. (2004). *The Internet and its protocols: A comparative approach*. Amsterdam: Morgan Kaufmann.

Feingold, M. & Jeyaraman. (2007). *Web services coordination (WS-Coordination) version 1.1*. OASIS. Retrieved April 20, 2009 from http://docs.oasis-open.org/ws-tx/wstx-wscoor-1.1-spec-errata-os.pdf

Ferdinand, M., Zirpins, C., & Trastour, D. (2004). Lifting XML Schema to OWL. In N. Koch, P. Fraternali, & M. Wirsing (Eds.), *Web engineering - 4th international conference, icwe 2004, munich, germany, july 26-30, 2004, proceedings*, (pp. 354-358). Heidelberg: Springer.

Ferguson, D. F., & Stockton, M. L. (2005). Service-oriented architecture: Programming model and product architecture. *IBM Systems Journal*, 4(44), 753–780.

Fernandez, E. B. (2009). Security patterns and a methodology to apply them. In G. Spanoudakis & A. Maña (Eds.), *Security and Dependability for Ambient Intelligence*. Berlin: Springer.

Fernandez, E. B., & Hawkins, J. C. (1997). Determining role rights from use cases. In *RBAC '97: Proceedings of the second ACM workshop on role-based access control*. New York: ACM.

Fernandez, E. B., & Larrondo-Petrie, M. M. (2006). Developing secure architectures for middleware systems. In *Proceedings of XXXII Conferencia Latinoamericana de Informática (CLEI 2006)*.

Fernandez, E. B., Cholmondeley, P., & Zimmermann, O. (2007). Extending a Secure System Development Methodology to SOA. In *DEXA '07: Proceedings of the 18th International Conference on Database and Expert, 2007*. Regensburg, Germany: IEEE Computer Society.

Fernandez, E. B., Larrondo-Petrie, M. M., Sorgente, T., & VanHilst, M. (2006). A methodology to develop secure systems using patterns. In H. Mouratidis and P. Giorgini (Eds.), *Integrating security and software engineering: Advances and future vision*, (pp. 107-126). Hershey, PA: Idea Group.

Fernandez, E. B., Pelaez, J. C., & Larrondo-Petrie, M. M. (2007). Attack Patterns: A New Forensic and Design Tool. In *IFIP International Federation for Information Processing: Advances in Digital Forensics III*. 242/2007, (pp. 345-357). Boston: Springer.

Fernandez, E. B., Sorgente, T., & Larrondo-Petrie, M. M. (2005). A UML-based methodology for secure systems: The design stage. In *Proceedings of International Workshop on Security in Information Systems*, Miami, FL (pp. 207-216).

Fernandez, E. B., VanHilst, M., Larrondo-Petrie, M. M., & Huang, S. (2006) Defining security requirements through misuse actions. In S. F. Ochoa & G.-C. Roman (Eds.), *International Federation for Information Processing Advanced Software Engineering: Expanding the Frontiers of Software Technology* (pp. 123-137). Berlin: Springer.

Fernández-Medina, E. & Piattini, M. (2003). Designing secure database for OLS. *Database and expert systems applications: 14th international conference (DEXA 2003)*, Prague, Czech Republic, Springer-Verlag.

Ferraiolo, D. F., & Kuhn, D. R. (1992). *Role Based Access Control*. Paper presented at 15th National Computer Security Conference, (pp. 554-563).

Ferris, C., & Langworthy, D. (2005). *Web Services Reliable Messaging Protocol.*

Feuerlicht, J. G., & Meesathit, S. (2005). Towards software development methodology for web services. In H. Fusita, & M. Mejri (Eds.), *New trends in software methodologies, tools and techniques: Proceedings of the fourth SoMeT-W05,* (pp. 263-277). Amsterdam: IOS Press.

Firesmith, D. (2003). Engineering Security Requirements. *Journal of Object Technology, 2*(1), 53–68.

Flechais, I., Mascolo, C., & Sasse, M. A. (2007). Integrating security and usability into the requirements and design process. *International Journal of Electronic Security and Digital Forensics, 1*(1), 12–26. doi:10.1504/IJESDF.2007.013589

Fletcher, S., Jansen, R., Lim, J., Halbgenacher, R., Murphy, M., & Flyss, G. (1995). Software system risk assessment and assurance. In *Proceedings of the New Security Paradigms Workshop*, San Diego, CA.

Forum Sentry SOA gateway. (2009). Forum Systems. Retrieved April 20, 2009 from http://www.forumsys.com/products/soagateway.php

Foster, I., & Kesselman, C. (1999). Globus: A Toolkit-Based Grid Architecture. In *The Grid: Blueprint for a New Computing Infrastructure* (pp. 259-278): Morgan Kaufmann.

Foster, I., Kesselman, C., Nick, J. M., & Tuecke, S. (2002). Grid services for distributed system integration. *Computer, 35*(6), 37-46.

Foster, I., Kesselman, C., Tsudik, G., & Tuecke, S. (1998). *A Security Architecture for Computational Grids.* Paper presented at the 5th ACM Conference on Computer and Communications Security, San Francisco, USA.

Fox, J., Mouratidis, H., & Jürjens, J. (2006). Towards a comprehensive framework for secure systems development. In *Lecture notes in computer science,* (pp. 48-62). Berlin: Springer.

Franklin, M. (2006). A survey of keyx evolving cryptosystems. *International Journal of Security and Networks, 1*(1/2), 46–53. doi:10.1504/IJSN.2006.010822

Freund, T., & Little, M. (2007). *Web services business activity (WS-BusinessActivity) version 1.1.* OASIS. Retrieved April 20, 2009 from http://docs.oasis-open.org/ws-tx/wstx-wsba-1.1-spec-errata-os.pdf

FTP data security and compliance. (2009). Forum Systems. Retrieved April 20, 2009 from http://www.forumsys.com/products/ftpgateway/features.php.

Fuger, S., Najmi, F., & Stojanovic, N. (2005a). *ebXML registry services and protocols version 3.0.* OASIS. Retrieved April 20, 2009 from http://docs.oasis-open.org/regrep/v3.0/specs/regrep-rs-3.0-os.pdf

Gajek, S., Liao, L., & Schwenk, J. (2007). Breaking and fixing the inline approach. *Workshop on Secure Web Services* (pp. 37-43). Washington, DC: ACM Press.

Gajek, S., Liao, L., & Schwenk, J. (2007). *Towards a Formal Semantic of XML Signature.* Paper presented at the W3C Workshop Next Steps for XML Signature and XML Encryption, Mountain View, USA.

Gamma, E., Helm, R., Johnson, R., & Vlissides, J. (1994). *Design patterns –Elements of reusable object-oriented software.* Upper-Saddle River, NJ: Addison-Wesley.

Gans, G., Jarke, M., Kethers, S., Lakemeyer, G., Ellrich, L., Funken, C., & Meister, M. (2001). Requirements modeling for organization networks: A (dis)trust-based approach. In *Proceedings of the 5th IEEE International Symposium on Requirements Engineering*, Toronto, Canada.

Ghosh, A., Howell, C., & Whittaker, J. (2002). Building software securely from the ground up. *IEEE Software, 19*(1), 14-16.

Giorgini, P., Massacci, F., & Mylopoulos, J. (2003). *Requirement engineering meets security: A case study on modelling secure electronic transactions by VISA and Mastercard* (Technical Report DIT-03-027). Informatica e Telecomunicazioni, University of Trento, Italy.

Giorgini, P., Massacci, F., Mylopoulos, J., & Zannone, N. (2005). Modeling security requirements through ownership, permission and delegation. In *Requirements engineering, 2005 proceedings 13th IEEE international conference on.*

Gogolla, M. & Henderson-Sellers, B. (2002). Analysis of UML stereotypes within the UML metamodel. *5th International Conference on the Unified Modeling Language - The Language and its Applications*, Dresden, Germany, Springer, LNCS.

Golfarelli, M., Maio, D., & Rizzi, S. (1998). Conceptual design of data warehouses from E/R schemes. *32th Hawaii International Conference on Systems Sciences (HICSS 1998)*, Hawaii, USA, IEEE Computer Society.

Gollmann, D. (2000). On the verification of cryptographic protocols: A tale of two committees. *Electronic Notes in Theoretical Computer Science, 32*, 42–58. doi:10.1016/S1571-0661(04)00094-5

Goubault-Larrecq, J., & Parrennes, F. (2005). Cryptographic protocol analysis on real C code. In *Verification, model checking, and abstract interpretation*. Berlin: Springer.

Graham, S., & Treadwell, J. (2006). *Web Services Resource Properties 1.2 (WS-ResourceProperties)*. OASIS. Retrieved April 20, 2009 from http://docs.oasis-open.org/wsrf/wsrf-ws_resource_properties-1.2-spec-os.pdf

Graham, S., Hull, D., & Murray, B. (2006). *Web Services Base Notification1.3 (WS-Base Notification)*. OASIS. Retrieved April 20, 2009 from http://docs.oasis-open.org/wsn/wsn-ws_base_notification-1.3-spec-os.pdf

Graham, S., Karmarkar, A., Mischkinsky, J., Robinson, I., & Sedukhin, I. (2006). *Web services resource 1.2 (WS-Resource)*. OASIS. Retrieved April 20, 2009 from http://docs.oasis-open.org/wsrf/wsrf-ws_resource-1.2-spec-os.pdf

Grandison, T. (2003). *Trust Specification and Analysis for Internet Applications*. Ph.D. Thesis, Imperial College of Science Technology and Medicine, Department of Computing, London.

Gross, T. (2003). Security Analysis of the SAML Single Sign-on Browser/Artifact Profile. In *Proceedings of the 19th Annual Computer Security Applications Conference*, (pp. 298). Washington, DC: IEEE Computer Society.

Grosso, P., Maler, E., Marsh, J., & Walsh, N. (2003). *XPointer Framework*. W3C. Retrieved April 20, 2009 from http://www.w3.org/TR/xptr-framework/

Gruschka, N., & Luttenberger, N. (2006). Protecting Web Services from DoS Attacks by SOAP Message Validation. In *Proceedings of the IFIP TC-11 21st International Information Security Conference*, (pp. 171-182), Karlstad, Sweden.

Gruschka, N., Jensen, M., & Luttenberger, N. (2007). A Stateful Web Service Firewall for BPEL. In *Proceedings of the IEEE International Conference on Web Services* (pp. 142-149), Salt Lake City, UT.

Gruschka, N., Luttenberger, N., & Herkenhöner, R. (2006). Event-based SOAP Message Validation for WS-SecurityPolicy-enriched Web Services. In *Proceedings of the 2006 International Conference on Semantic Web & Web Services* (pp. 80-86), Las Vegas, NV.

Guan, T., Zaluska, E., & Roure, D. D. (2005). *A Grid Service Infrastructure for Mobile Devices*. Paper presented at the First International Conference on Semantics, Knowledge, an Grid (SKG 2005), Beijing, China.

Gudgin, M., Hadley, M., & Rogers, T. (2006). *Web Services Addressing 1.0 – Core*. W3C. Retrieved April 20, 2009 from http://www.w3.org/TR/ws-addr-core/

Gudgin, M., Hadley, M., & Rogers, T. (2006). *Web Services Addressing 1.0 – SOAP Binding*. W3C. Retrieved April 20, 2009 from http://www.w3.org/TR/2006/REC-ws-addr-soap-20060509/

Gudgin, M., Hadley, M., Mendelsohn, N., Moreau, J., Nielsen, H. F., Karmarkar, A., & Lafon, Y. (2007). *Simple Object Access Protocol (SOAP) version 1.2*. Retrieved from http://www.w3.org/TR/soap/

Gudgin, M., Hadley, M., Rogers, T., & Yalçinalp, Ü. (2006a). *Web Services Addressing 1.0 - WSDL Binding*. W3C. Retrieved April 20, 2009 from http://www.w3.org/TR/ws-addr-wsdl/

Gudgin, M., Hadley, M., Rogers, T., & Yalçinalp, Ü. (2006b). *Web Services Addressing 1.0 – Metadata*. W3C. Retrieved April 20, 2009 from http://www.w3.org/TR/ws-addr-metadata/

Gudgin, M., Mendelsohn, N., Nottingham, M., & Ruellan, H. (2005). *SOAP Message Transmission Optimization Mechanism*. W3C. Retrieved April 20, 2009 from http://www.w3.org/TR/soap12-mtom/

Gürgens, S., & Peralta, R. (2000). Validation of cryptographic protocols by efficient automated testing. In *Proceedings of the thirteenth international florida artificial intelligence research society conference*. AAAI Press.

Gürgens, S., Ochsenschlager, P., & Rudolph, C. (2005). On a formal framework for security properties. *Computer Standards & Interfaces, 27*, 457–466. doi:10.1016/j.csi.2005.01.004

Gunestas, M., Wijesekera, D., & Elkhodary, A. (2009). *An Evidence Generation Model for Web Services*. Paper presented at the IEEE International Conference on System of Systems Engineering (SoSE '09).

Gunestas, M., Wijesekera, D., & Singhal, A. (2008). *Forensic Web Services*. Paper presented at the Fourth Annual IFIP WG 11.9 International Conference on Digital Forensics.

Gutierrez, C. A., Fernandez-Medina, E., & Piattini, M. (2006). PWSSec: Process for web services security. In *IEEE Proceedings of the International Conference on Web Services*, (pp. 213-222).

Gutierrez, C., Fernandez-Medina, E. & Piattini M. (2007). Web Services-Based Security Requirement Elicitation. *IEICE transactions on information and systems, 90*(9), 1374-1387.

Gutiérrez, C., Fernández-Medina, E., & Piattini, M. (2004). A Survey of Web Services Security. In *ICCSA 2004*, (LNCS Vol. 3043, pp. 968–977). Berlin: Springer-Verlag.

Gutierrez, C., Fernandez-Medina, E., & Piattini, M. (2005). Towards a process for Web services security. In *Proceedings of the 3rd International Workshop on Security in Information Systems* (WOSIS 2005), Miami, FL (pp. 298-308).

Gutiérrez, C., Fernández-Medina, E., & Piattini, M. (2006). PWSSec: Process for Web Services Security. In

IEEE International Conference on Web Services 2006, Chicago, USA.

Hafner, M., & Breu, R. (2008). *Security Engineering for Service oriented Architectures*. Berlin: Springer.

Hafner, M., Agreiter, B., Breu, R., & Nowak, A. (2006). SECTET - An Extensible Framework for the Realization of Secure Inter-Organizational Workflows. *Internet Research, 16*(5), 491–506. doi:10.1108/10662240610710978

Hafner, M., Memon, M., & Alam, M. (2008). Modeling and enforcing advanced access control policies in healthcare systems with sectet. In *Models in software engineering*.

Haldar, V., Chandra, D., & Franz, M. (2005). Dynamic Taint Propagation for Java. In *Proceedings of the 21st Annual Computer Security Applications Conference*, (pp. 303-311).

Haley, C. B., Laney, R., Moffett, J. D., & Nuseibeh, B. (2008). Security requirements engineering: A framework for representation and analysis. *Transactions on Software Engineering, 34*(1), 133–153. doi:10.1109/TSE.2007.70754

Hall, A., & Chapman, R. (2002). Correctness by construction: developing a commercial secure system. *IEEE Software, 19*(1), 18-25.

Hallam-Baker, P., & Mysore, S. H. (2005). *XML key management specification (XKMS 2.0) version 2.0*. W3C. Retrieved April 20, 2009 from http://www.w3.org/TR/xkms2/

Hallam-Baker, P., & Mysore, S. H. (2005). *XML Key Management Specification (XKMS 2.0) Bindings Version 2.0*. Retrieved June 28, 2005 from http://www.w3.org/TR/xkms2-bindings/

Haneberg, D., Reif, W., & Stenzel, K. (2002). A method for secure smartcard applications. In *AMAST '02: Proceedings of the 9th international conference on algebraic methodology and software technology*. London, UK: Springer-Verlag.

Hartman, B., Flinn, D. J., Beznosov, K., & Kawamoto, S. (2003). *Mastering Web Services Security.* Indiana: Wiley Publishing, Inc.

Hashizume, K. & Fernandez, E. B. (submitted). *The XML Signature pattern.*

Hashizume, K., Fernandez, E. B. & Huang, S. (submitted). *The WS-Security pattern.*

Hayes, P., & McBride, B. (2004, February). *W3C Recommendation, RDF Semantics.* Retrieved from http://www.w3.org/TR/rdf-mt/

Herzberg, A., & Yoffe, I. (2007). *The Delivery and Evidences Layer* (No. Report 2007/139). Retrieved from Cryptology ePrint Archive.

Hirsch, F., Philpott, R., & Maler, E. (2005). *[Saml05f] OASIS, Security and Privacy Considerations for the OASIS Security Assertion Markup Language (SAML) V2.0.* OASIS. Retrieved April 20, 2009 from http://docs.oasis-open.org/security/saml/v2.0/saml-sec-consider-2.0-os.pdf

Höhn, S., & Jürjens, J. (2008). Rubacon: Automated support for model-based compliance engineering. In *ICSE '08: Proceedings of the 30th international conference on software engineering.* New York: ACM.

Holgersson, J., & Soderstrom, E. (2005). *Web service security - vulnerabilities and threats within the context of WS-security.*

Hosmer, H. (1992). Metapolicies I. *ACM SIGSAC Review, 10*(2-3), 18–43. doi:10.1145/147092.147097

Houmb, S. H., Georg, G., France, R., Bieman, J., & Jürjens, J. (2005). Cost-Benefit trade-off analysis using BBN for aspect-oriented risk-driven development. In *Engineering of complex computer systems, 2005 ICECCS 2005 proceedings 10th IEEE international conference on.*

Hu, V. C., Martin, E., Hwang, J., & Xie, T. (2007). Conformance Checking of Access Control Policies Specified in XACML. In *Proceedings of the 31st Annual International Computer Software and Applications Conference –* (Vol. 02, pp. 275-280). Washington, DC: IEEE Computer Society.

Hughes, J., Cantor, S., Hodges, J., Hirsch, F., Mishra, P., et al. (2005). *Profiles for the OASIS Security Assertion Markup Language (SAML) V2.0.* OASIS. Retrieved April 20, 2009 from http://docs.oasis-open.org/security/saml/v2.0/saml-profiles-2.0-os.pdf

Huhns, M. N., & Singh, M. P. (2005). Service-Oriented Computing: Key Concepts and Principles. *IEEE Internet Computing, 9*(1), 75–81. doi:10.1109/MIC.2005.21

Hultin, F., & Heldal, R. (2003). Bridging model-based and language-based security. In *Lecture notes in computer science.* (pp. 235 52). Berlin: Springer.

Humphrey, M., Thompson, M. R., & Jackson, K. R. (2005). Security for Grids. *Lawrence Berkeley National Laboratory. Paper LBNL-54853.*

Hutter, D. (2006). Possibilistic Information Flow Control in MAKS and Action Refinement. In *Energing Trends in Information and Communication Security,* (LNCS 3995, pp. 268-281). Berlin: Springer.

Hutter, D., & Volkamer, M. (2006). Information Flow Control to secure Dynamic Web-Service Composition. In *Proceedings of the 3rd International Conference on security in Pervasive Computing, SPC-2006,* York, UK, (LNCS Vol. 3934, pp.196-210). Berlin: Springer-Verlag.

IBM application security software and services. (2009) IBM. Retrieved April 20, 2009 from http://www-01.ibm.com/software/tivoli/governance/security/application-security.html.

IHE. (2006, November). *IT Infrastructure Technical Framework.* Retrieved November 21, 2008, from http://www.ihe.net/Technical_Framework/

Imamura, T., Dilaway, B., & Simon, E. (2002). *XML encryption syntax and processing.* W3C. Retrieved April 20, 2009 from http://www.w3.org/TR/xmlenc-core/

Information Technology Laboratory. National Institute of Standards and Technology (2001). *Federal information Processing Standards Publication FIPS.* PUB 140-2. Security Requirements For Cryptographic Modules.

Ingalsbe, (n.d.). Threat Modeling: Diving into the Deep End. *IEEE Software*, 25(1), 28–34.

InnerGuard. (2006). Cerebit. Retrieved April 20, 2009 from http://www.cerebit.com/Product_innerGuard.htm

Innerhofer-Oberperfler, F., & Breu, R. (2006). Using an enterprise architecture for it risk management. In *Proceedings of the ISSA 2006 Conference*, Johannesburg, South Africa.

Insecure.org. (1996). *Ping of Death*. Retrieved April 09, 2009 from http://www.insecure.org/sploits/ping-o-death.html

Integrated SOA governance - Improving business efficiency. (2004). SOA Software. Retrieved April 20, 2009 from http://www.soa.com

ISO. (2005). *ISO/IEC 15408:2005 Information technology -- Security techniques -- Evaluation criteria for IT security* (Common Criteria).

ISO. (2005). ISO/IEC 27001:2005 - Information technology -- Security techniques -- Information security management systems -- Requirements.

ISO. (2005). ISO/IEC 27002:2005 - Information technology -- Code of practice for information security management.

Iwasa, K., Durand, J., Rutt, T., Peel, M., Kunisetty, S., & Bunting, D. (2004). *Web services reliable messaging TC WS-Reliability 1.1*. OASIS. Retrieved April 20, 2009 from http://docs.oasis-open.org/wsrm/ws-reliability/v1.1/wsrm-ws_reliability-1.1-spec-os.pdf

Jaeger, T. (2001). Access Control in Configurable Systems. In *Secure Internet programming: security issues for mobile and distributed objects*, (LNCS, Vol. 1603, pp. 289-316). Berlin: Springer-Verlag.

Jain, A., & Farkas, C. (2006). Secure Resource Description Framework: an Access Control Model. In *SACMAT '06: Proceedings of the eleventh ACM symposium on Access control models and technologies* (pp. 121-129). New York: ACM Press.

Jajodia, S., Samarati, P., Sapino, M. L., & Subrahmanian, V. S. (2001). A Unified Framework for Supporting Multiple Access Control Policies. *ACM Transactions on Database Systems, 26*(2), 214–260. doi:10.1145/383891.383894

Jameel, H., Kalim, U., Sajjad, A., Lee, S., & Jeon, T. (2005, February 14-16). *Mobile-To-Grid Middleware: Bridging the gap between mobile and Grid environments*. Paper presented at the European Grid Conference EGC 2005, Amsterdam, The Netherlands.

Jayaram, K. R., & Mathur, A. P. (2005). Software engineering for secure software - state of the art: A survey. *CERIAS and SERC SERC-TR-279, September 19Th*.

Jensen, M., & Gruschka, N. (2008). Flooding Attack Issues of Web Services and Service-Oriented Architectures. In *Proceedings of the Workshop on Security for Web Services and Service-Oriented Architectures* (pp. 117-122), Munich, Germany. Berlin: Springer.

Jensen, M., & Schwenk, J. (2009). The Accountability Problem of Flooding Attacks in Service-Oriented Architectures. In *Proceedings of the IEEE International Conference on Availability, Reliability, and Security,* (pp. 25-32), Fukuoka, Japan. Washington, DC: IEEE Computer Society.

Jensen, M., Gruschka, N., & Luttenberger, N. (2008). The Impact of Flooding Attacks on Network-based Services. In *Proceedings of the IEEE International Conference on Availability, Reliability, and Security,* (pp. 509-513), Barcelona, Spain. Washington, DC: IEEE Computer Society.

Jensen, M., Gruschka, N., Herkenhöner, R., & Luttenberger, N. (2007). SOA web services: New technologies - new standards - new attacks. In *Proceedings of the 5th IEEE european conference on web services (ECOWS)*.

Jian, Y. (2005). []: IEEE Computer Society Press.]. *Monitoring the Macroscopic Effect of DDoS Flooding Attacks, 2*, 324–335.

Jianyin, Z., Sen, S., & Fangchun, Y. (2006). *Detecting Race Conditions in Web Services*. Paper presented at the Telecommunications, 2006. AICT-ICIW '06. International Conference on Internet and Web Applications and Services/Advanced International Conference on.

Johnson, M. W. *Monitoring and Diagnosing Applications with ARM 4.0*: IBM Corporation.

Jordan, D., Evdemon, J., Alves, A., Arkin, A., Askary, S., Barreto, C., et al. (2007). *Web Services Business Process Execution Language Version 2.0 (WS-BPEL 2.0)*. OASIS Standard.

Jøsang, A., Ismail, R., & Boyd, C. (2007). A Survey of Trust and Reputation Systems for Online Service Provision Decision Support Systems. *Decision Support Systems, 43*(2), 618–644. doi:10.1016/j.dss.2005.05.019

Jürjens, J. (2000). Secure information flow for concurrent processes. In *Lecture notes in computer science,* (pp. 395-409). Berlin: Springer.

Jürjens, J. (2001). Secrecy-Preserving refinement. In *Lecture notes in computer science,* (pp. 135-52). Berlin: Springer.

Jürjens, J. (2001). Towards development of secure systems using UMLsec. In *Lecture notes in computer science,* (pp. 187-200). Berlin: Springer.

Jürjens, J. (2002). UMLsec: Extending UML for secure systems development. In *UML '02: Proceedings of the 5th international conference on the unified modeling language.* London: Springer-Verlag.

Jürjens, J. (2005). *Secure systems development with UML.* Berlin: Springer.

Jürjens, J. (2005). Sound methods and effective tools for model-based security engineering with UML. In *ICSE 2005 proceedings 27th international conference on software engineering.*

Jürjens, J. (2006). Security analysis of crypto-based java programs using automated theorem provers. In *ASE '06: Proceedings of the 21st IEEE/ACM international conference on automated software engineering.* Washington, DC: IEEE Computer Society.

Jürjens, J. (2009). A domain-specific language for cryptographic protocols based on streams. *Journal of Logic and Algebraic Programming, 54–73.* doi:10.1016/j. jlap.2008.08.006

Jürjens, J., & Rumm, R. (2008). Model-Based security analysis of the german health card architecture. *Methods of Information in Medicine, 47*(5), 409–416.

Jürjens, J., & Shabalin, P. (2007). Tools for secure systems development with UML. *Int. J. Softw. Tools Technol. Transf., 9*(5), 527–544. doi:10.1007/s10009-007-0048-8

Jürjens, J., & Wimmel, G. (2001). Security modelling for electronic commerce: The common electronic purse specifications. In *I3E '01: Proceedings of the IFIP conference on towards the e-society.* Amsterdam: Kluwer, B.V.

Jürjens, J., & Wimmel, G. (2002). Specification-Based test generation for security-critical systems using mutations. In *Lecture notes in computer science,* (pp. 471-82). Berlin: Springer.

Jürjens, J., & Yampolskiy, M. (2005). Code security analysis with assertions. In *ASE '05: Proceedings of the 20th IEEE/ACM international conference on automated software engineering.* New York: ACM.

Jurca, R., Binder, W., & Faltings, B. (2007). Reliable QoS Monitoring Based on Client Feedback. In *16th International Conference on the World Wide Web*, Banff, Alberta, Canada.

Juric, M. B. (2006). *Business Process Execution Language for Web Services* (Second Edition ed.). Birmingham, UK: Packt Publishing.

Kaeo, M., & Van Herck, T. (2006). *Methodology for benchmarking IPSec devices.* Internet-Draft (draft-ietf-bmwg-ipsec-meth-00), November 2005, Expires: May 5.

Kagal, L., Paoucci, M., Srinivasan, N., Denker, G., Finin, T., & Sycara, K. (2004, July). Authorization and Privacy for Semantic Web Services. [Special Issue on Semantic Web Services]. *IEEE Intelligent Systems, 19*(4), 50–56. doi:10.1109/MIS.2004.23

Kaiser (2007). Toward the realization of policy-oriented enterprise management. *IEEE Computer, 8*(40), 57-63.

Kaler, C., & Nadalin, A. (2005). *Web Services Security Policy Language (WS-SecurityPolicy) 1.1.* OASIS Standard.

Kanneganti, R., & Chodavarapu, P. (2008). SOA Security. Manning Publications.

Kaushik, S., Wijesekera, D., & Ammann, P. (2005). Policy-based dissemination of partial Web-Ontologies. In *SWS '05: Proceedings of the 2005 Workshop on Secure Web Services,* (pp. 43-52). New York: ACM Press.

Kavantzas, N., Burdett, D., Ritzinger, G., Fletcher, T., Lafon, Y., & Barreto, C. (2005). *Web services choreography description language version 1.0.* W3C. Retrieved April 20, 2009 from http://www.w3.org/TR/ws-cdl-10/

Kearney, P., & Brügger, L. (2007). A risk-driven security analysis method and modelling language. *BT Technology Journal, 25*(1), 141–153. doi:10.1007/s10550-007-0016-6

Keller, A., & Ludwig, H. (2003). The WSLA Framework: Specifying and Monitoring Service Level Agreements for Web Services. *Journal of Network and Systems Management, 11*(1), 57–81. doi:10.1023/A:1022445108617

Kemp, J., Cantor, S., Mishra, P., Philpott, R., & Maler, E. (2005). *Authentication Context for the OASIS Security Assertion Markup Language (SAML) V2.0.* OASIS. Retrieved April 20, 2009 from http://docs.oasis-open.org/security/saml/v2.0/saml-authn-context-2.0-os.pdf

Kemp, J., Cantor, S., Mishra, P., Philpott, R., & Maler, E. (2005). *Assertions and Protocols for the OASIS Security Assertion Markup Language (SAML) version 2.0.* OASIS Standard 200503. Retrieved from http://xml.coverpages.org/ni2005-03-14-a.html

Kent, S., & Atkinson, R. (1998). *IP authentication header.* RFC2402, November.

Kent, S., & Atkinson, R. (1998). *IP encapsulating security payload.* RFC2406, November.

Kent, S., & Atkinson, R. (1998). *Security architecture for the Internet protocol.* RFC 2401, November.

Khalaf, R., Mukhi, N., & Weerawarana, S. (2003). *Service-Oriented Composition in BPEL4WS.* Paper presented at the Twelfth International World Wide Web Conference, Budapest, Hungary.

Kimball, R. & Ross, M. (2002). *The data warehousing toolkit.* 2nd ed. John Wiley.

King, S. T., & Chen, P. M. (2003). *Backtracking Intrusions.* Paper presented at the 2003 Symposium on Operating Systems Principles (SOSP).

Kleijnen, S., & Raju, S. (2003). An Open Web Services Architecture. *Queue, 1*(1), 38–46. doi:10.1145/637958.637961

Kleppe, A., Warmer, J. & Bast, W. (2003). *MDA explained. The model driven architecture: Practice and promise.* Addison-Wesley.

Klyne, G., & Carroll, J. (2004, February). *W3C Recommendation, RDF Concepts and Abstract Syntax.* Retrieved from http://www.w3.org/TR/rdf-concepts/

Kobryn, C. (2000). Modeling components and frameworks with UML. *Communications of the ACM, 10*(43), 31–38. doi:10.1145/352183.352199

Koch, M., & Parisi-Presicce, F. (2006). UML specification of access control policies and their formal verification. *Software and Systems Modeling, 5*(4), 429–447. doi:10.1007/s10270-006-0030-z

Koshutanski, H., & Massacci, F. (2003). An Access Control Framework for Business Processes for Web Services. In *Proceedings of the 2003 ACM workshop on XML security* (pp. 15-24). New York: ACM Press.

Krafzig, D., Banke, K., & Slama, D. (2004). *Enterprise SOA: Service-Oriented architecture best practices.* Upper Saddle River, NJ: Prentice Hall PTR.

Krawczyk, H. (2001). The Order of Encryption and Authentication for Protecting Communications (or: How Secure is SSL?). In *Advances in Cryptology - CRYPTO 2001: 21st Annual International Cryptology Conference,* Santa Barbara, CA (LNCS Vol. 3934). Berlin: Springer-Verlag.

Kremer, S., Markowitch, O., & Zhou, J. (2002). An Intensive Survey of Non-repudiation protocols. *Computer Communications, 25*(17), 1606–1621. doi:10.1016/S0140-3664(02)00049-X

Kudo, M., & Hada, S. (2000). XML document security based on provisional authorization. In *CCS'00: Proceedings of the 7th ACM Conference on Computer and Communications Security,* (pp. 87-96). New York: ACM Press.

Kwok-Yan, L., Xi-Bin, Z., Siu-Leung, C., Gu, M., & Jia-Guang, S. (2004). Enhancing Grid Security Infrastructure to Support Mobile Computing Nodes. *Lecture Notes in Computer Science, 2908/2003,* 42-54.

Labuschagne, L. (1999). *Risk analysis generations — The evolution of risk analysis.* Retrieved January 29, 2002, from http://csweb.rau.ac.za/deth/research/article_page.htm

Lamport, L., & Schneider, F. (1984). The 'hoare logic' of CSP and all that. *ACM Transactions on Programming Languages and Systems, 6*(2), 281–296. doi:10.1145/2993.357247

Larmouth, J. (2003). *XML Common Biometric Format.* OASIS. Retrieved April 20, 2009 from http://www.oasis-open.org/committees/tc_home.php?wg_abbrev=xcbf

Lawrence, K., & Kaler, C. (2004). *Web services security: SOAP message security 1.1 (WS-Security 2004).* Retrieved 1 February 2006, from http://www.oasis-open.org/committees/download.php/16790/wss-v1.1-spec-os-SOAPMessageSecurity.pdf

Lawrence, K., & Kaler, C. (2006). *Web services security: Kerberos token profile 1.1.* OASIS. Retrieved April 20, 2009 from http://www.oasis-open.org/committees/download.php/16788/wss-v1.1-spec-os-KerberosTokenProfile.pdf

Lawrence, K., & Kaler, C. (2006). *Web Services Security: SAML Token Profile 1.1.* OASIS. Retrieved April 20, 2009 from http://www.oasis-open.org/committees/download.php/16768/wss-v1.1-spec-os-SAMLTokenProfile.pdf

Lawrence, K., & Kaler, C. (2006). *Web services security: username token profile 1.1.* OASIS. Retrieved April 20, 2009 from http://www.oasis-open.org/committees/download.php/16782/wss-v1.1-spec-os-UsernameTokenProfile.pdf

Lawrence, K., & Kaler, C. (2006). *Web Services Security: X.509 Certificate Token Profile 1.1.* OASIS. Retrieved April 20, 2009 from http://www.oasis-open.org/committees/download.php/16785/wss-v1.1-spec-os-x509TokenProfile.pdf

Lawton, G. G. (n.d.). Web 2.0 Creates Security Challenges. *Computer, 40*(10), 13–16.

Lee, E. (Ed.). (2005). *Web Service Implementation Methodology.* OASIS. Retrieved April 20, 2009 from http://www.oasis-open.org/committees/download.php/13420/fwsi im 1.0 guidlines doc wd publicReviewDraft_files

Leiwo, J., Nikander, P., & Aura, T. (2000). Towards Network Denial of Service Resistant Protocols. In *Proc. of the 15th International Information Security Conference,* (pp. 301-310).

Lenzerini, M. (2002). Data integration: a theoretical perspective. In *Pods '02: Proceedings of the twenty-first ACM sigmod-sigact-sigart symposium on principles of database systems,* (pp. 233-246). New York: ACM Press.

Li, J., & Karp, A. H. (2007). Access Control for the Service Oriented Architecture. In *Proceedings of the 2007 ACM workshop on Secure Web Services,* (pp. 9-17). New York: ACM.

Li, N., & Wang, Q. (2008). Beyond separation of duty: An algebra for specifying high-level security policies. *Journal of the ACM, 55*(3), 12. doi:10.1145/1379759.1379760

Li, N., Feigenbaum, J., & Grosof, B. (1999). A Logic-Based Knowledge Representation for Authorization with Delegation. In *Proceedings of the 12th IEEE Computer Security Foundations Workshop* (pp.162-174). Washington, DC: IEEE Computer Society.

Lindstrom, P. (2004). *Attacking and Defending Web Service.* A Spire Research Report.

Litke, A., Skoutas, D., & Varvarigou, T. (2004, December). *Mobile Grid Computing: Changes and Challenges of Resourse Management in a Mobile Grid Environment.* Paper presented at the 5th International Conference on

Practical Aspects of Knowledge Management (PAKM 2004).

Little, M., & Wilkinson, A. (2007). *Web services atomic transaction (WS-AtomicTransaction) version 1.1.* OASIS. Retrieved April 20, 2009 from http://docs.oasis-open. org/ws-tx/wstx-wsat-1.1-spec-os/wstx-wsat-1.1-spec-os.html

Little, M., Newcomer, E., & Pavlik, G. (2007). *Web services context specification (WS-Context) version 1.0.* OASIS. Retrieved April 20, 2009 from http://docs.oasis-open.org/ws-caf/ws-context/v1.0/wsctx.html

Liu, F., Wang, G., Chou, W., Fazal, L., & Li, L. (2006). *TARGET: Two-way Web Service Router Gateway.* Paper presented at the Web Services, 2006. ICWS '06. International Conference on.

Liu, P., & Chen, Z. (2004) An Access Control Model for Web Services in Business Process. In *Proceedings of the 2004 IEEE/WIC/ACM International Conference on Web Intelligence,* (pp. 292-298). Washington, DC: IEEE Computer Society

Livshits, B. (2006, December). *Improving software security with precise static and runtime analysis.* Thesis.

Lockhart, H., Andersen, S., Bohren, J., Sverdlov, Y., Hondo, M., et al. (2006). *Web services federation language (WS-Federation) version 1.1.* Armonk, NY: IBM. Retrieved April 20, 2009 from http://download.boulder. ibm.com/ibmdl/pub/software/dw/specs/ws-fed/WS-Federation-V1-1B.pdf?S_TACT=105AGX04&S_CMP=LP

Lodderstedt, T., Bastin, D., & Doser, J. (2002). SecureUML: A UML-based modeling language for model-driven security. In *Proceedings of the 5th International Conference on Unified Modeling Language,* Dresden, Germany.

Lopez, J., Oppliger, R., & Pernul, G. (2004). Authentication and Authorization Infrastructures (AAIs): A Comparative Survey. *Computers & Security, 23,* 578–590. doi:10.1016/j.cose.2004.06.013

Loscocco, P. A., Smalley, S. D., Muckelbauer, P. A., Taylor, R. C., Turner, S. J., & Farrell, J. F. (1989). The Inevita-bility of Failure: The Flawed Assumption of Security in Modern Computing Environments. In *Proceedings of the 21st National Information Systems Security Conference,* (pp. 303-314).

Loshin, P. (2003). *IPv6: Theory, protocol, and practice* (2nd ed.). Amsterdam: Morgan Kaufmann.

Lotz, V. (1997). Threat scenarios as a means to formally develop secure systems. *Journal of Computer Security, 5,* 31–67.

Luján-Mora, S., Trujillo, J. & Song, I. Y. (2002). *Extending the UML for multidimensional modeling.* 5th International Conference on the Unified Modeling Language (UML 2002), Dresden, Germany: Springer-Verlag.

Lund, M. S., Barber, F. D., Stolen K., & Vraalsen, F. (2004). *A UML profile for the identification and analysis of security risks during structured brainstorming* (Report # STF40 A03067). SINTEF, Norway.

Lund, M. S., Hogganvik, I., Seehusen, F., & Stolen, K. (2003). *UML profile for security assessment* (Report # STF40 A03066). SINTEF Telecom and Informatics, Norway.

Lyon, G. (2006). *Top 100 network security tools* [Web page]. Retrieved April 20, 2009, from http://sectools. org/

Maarof, M. A., & Krishna, K. (2002). An hybrid trust management model for multi agent systems based trading society. In *Proceedings of the International Workshop on Communication Software Engineering IWCSE'2002,* Marrakech, Morocco.

Maidl, M., Gilmore, S., Haenel, V., & Kloul, L. (2005). Choreographing security and performance analysis for web services. In *Lecture notes in computer science,* (pp. 200-14). Berlin: Springer.

Maña, A., & Pujol, G. (2008). Towards Formal Specification of Abstract Security Properties. In *Proceedings of The Third International Conference on Availability, Reliability and Security,* Barcelona, Spain. Washington, DC: IEEE Computer Society Press.

Maña, A., Montenegro, J. A., Rudolph, C., & Vivas, J. L. (2003). A business process-driven approach to security engineering. In *DEXA '03: Proceedings of the 14th international workshop on database and expert systems applications.* Washington, DC: IEEE Computer Society.

Maña, A., Presenza, D., Piñuela, A., Serrano, D., Soria, P., & Sotiriou, D. (2007). *Specification of SERENITY Architecture*, (Serenity Public Report A6.D3.1.)

Maña, A., Rudolph, C., Spanoudakis, G., Lotz, V., Massacci, F., Melideo, M., et al. (2007). Security engineering for ambient intelligence: A manifesto. In *Integrating security and software engineering: Advances and future vision.* (pp. 244-70).

Maña, A., Rudolph, C., Spanoudakis, G., Lotz, V., Massacci, F., Melideo, M., & López-Cobo, J. M. (2006). *Security Engineering for Ambient Intelligence: A Manifesto.* In P. Giorgini & H. Mouratidis (Eds.) *Integrating Security and Software Engineering.* Hershey, PA: IDEA Group.

Maña, A., Sánchez, F., Serrano, D., & Muñoz, A. (2006b). *Building Secure Ambient Intelligence Scenarios.* Paper presented at Eighteenth International Conference on Software Engineering and Knowledge Engineering (SEKE06), San Francisco Bay, USA.

Mandia, K., & Prosise, C. (2001). *Incident Response: Investigating Computer Crime.* New York: McGraw-Hill, Inc.

Manson, G., Mouratidis, H., & Giorgini, P. (2003). Integrating security and systems engineering: Towards the modelling of secure information systems. In *Lecture notes in computer science.* Berlin: Springer.

Marks, D., Sell, P., & Thuraisingham, B. (1996). MOMT: A multi-level object modeling technique for designing secure database applications. *Journal of Object-Oriented Programming, 9*(4), 22-29.

Marks, E. (2008). *Service-Oriented Architecture (SOA) Governance for the Services Driven Enterprise.* New York: Wiley.

Marks, E., & Bell, M. (2006). *Service-Oriented Architecture: A Planning and Implementation Guide for Business and Technology.* Hoboken, NJ: John Wiley & Sons.

Marsh, J., Orchard, D., & Veillard, D. (2006). *XML Inclusions (XInclude) Version 1.0 (2nd Ed.).* W3C. Retrieved April 20, 2009 from http://www.w3.org/TR/xinclude/

Martel, S. (2002). A New Model for Computer Network Security Risk Analysis. MA.Sc. thesis. Carleton University, Canada.

Martin, M., Livshits, B., & Lam, M. (2005). Finding application errors and security flaws using PQL: A program query language. In *20Th annual ACM conference on objects-oriented programming, systems, languages and applications.*

Massacci, F., Mylopoulos, J., & Zannone, N. (2007). Computer-Aided support for secure tropos. *Automated Software Engineering, 14*(3), 341–364. doi:10.1007/s10515-007-0013-5

Mathe, J., Duncavage, S., Werner, J., Malin, B., Ledeczi, A., & Sztipanovits, J. (2007). Implementing a model-based design environment for clinical information systems. In *Workshop on model-based trustworthy health information systems.*

Maximilien, E. M., & Singh, M. P. (2001). Reputation and endorsement for web services. *ACM SIGecom Exchanges, 3*(1), 24–31. doi:10.1145/844331.844335

Maximilien, E. M., & Singh, M. P. (2002). Conceptual model of web service reputation. *SIGMOD Record, 31*(4), 36–41. doi:10.1145/637411.637417

Maximilien, E. M., & Singh, M. P. (2004). Toward autonomic web services trust and selection. In *Proceedings of the 2nd international Conference on Service Oriented Computing.* New York: ACM Press.

Maximilien, E. M., & Singh, M. P. (2005). Agent-based trust model involving multiple qualities. In *Proceedings of the 4th international Joint Conference on Autonomous Agents and Multiagent Systems.* Utrecht, Netherlands: ACM Press.

McGuinness, D. L., & van Harmelen, F. (2004, February). *OWL Web Ontology Language Overview*. Retrieved from http://www.w3.org/TR/owl-features/

McIntosh, M., & Austel, P. (2005). XML signature element wrapping attacks and countermeasures. In *Proceedings of the 2005 workshop on Secure web services*, (pp. 20-27). New York: ACM Press.

McIntosh, M., Gudgin, M., Morrison, K. S., & Barbir, A. (2007). *Basic Security Profile Version 1.0.* Web Services Interoperability Organization (WS-I).

McLean, J. (1988) The Algebra of Security. In *Proceedings of the 1988 IEEE Computer Society Symposium on Security and Privacy*, Oakland, CA, (pp.2-7). Washington, DC: IEEE Computer Society.

Mell, P., Scarfone, K., & Romanosky, S. (2007). *CVSS: A complete guide to the common vulnerability scoring system.*

Méry, D., & Merz, S. (2007). Specification and refinement of access control. *Journal of Universal Computer Science, 13*(8), 1073–1093.

Microsoft aims to bridge your trust with new strategy. (2002). Retrieved April 20, 2009 from http://articles.techrepublic.com.com/5100-10878_11-1054084.html

Misra, S. C., Kumar, V., & Kumar, U. (2005). How can i* complement UML for modeling organizations? In *Proceedings of the 18th IEEE Canadian Conference on Electrical and Computer Engineering* (CCECE 2005), Saskatoon, Saskatchewan, Canada (pp. 2319-2321).

Misra, S. C., Kumar, V., & Kumar, U. (2005, April 20-22). Strategic modeling of risk management in industries undergoing BPR. In *Proceedings of the 8th International Conference on Business Information Systems (BIS 2005)*, Poznan, Poland (pp. 85-103).

Misra, S. C., Kumar, V., & Kumar, U. (2005, May 1-4). Goal-oriented or scenario-based requirements engineering (RE) technique: What should a practitioner select? In *Proceedings of the 18th IEEE Canadian Conference on Electrical and Computer Engineering (CCECE 2005)*, Saskatoon, Saskatchewan, Canada (pp. 2314-2318).

Misra, S. C., Kumar, V., & Kumar, U. (2005, May 24-25). An approach for modeling information systems security risk assessment. In *Proceedings of the 3rd International Workshop on Security in Information Systems* (WOSIS 2005), Miami, FL, USA (pp. 253-262).

Misra, S. C., Kumar, V., & Kumar, U. (2005, May 25-28). Modeling strategic actor relationships to support risk analysis and control in software projects. In *Proceedings of the 7th International Conference on Enterprise Information Systems (ICEIS 2005*, Miami, FL (Vol. 3, pp. 288-293).

Misra, S.C., Kumar, V., & Kumar, U. (2005, May 25-28). A strategic modeling technique for change management in organizations undergoing BPR. In *Proceedings of the 7th International Conference on Enterprise Information Systems (ICEIS 2005)* (Vol. 3, pp. 447-450). Miami, FL.

Mitra, N., & Lafon, Y. (2007). *SOAP Version 1.2 Part 0: Primer* (2nd Ed.). W3C. Retrieved April 20, 2009 from http://www.w3.org/TR/soap12-part0/

Mitra, T. (2005). *A case for SOA governance*. Armonk, NY: IBM. Retrieved April 20, 2009 from http://www.ibm.com/developerworks/webservices/library/ws-soa-govern/

MITRE. (2007). *Open vulnerability and assessment language (OVAL).*

Moebius, N., Haneberg, D., Reif, W., & Schellhorn, G. (2007). A modeling framework for the development of provably secure e-commerce applications. In *ICSEA '07: Proceedings of the international conference on software engineering advances.* Washington, DC: IEEE Computer Society.

Montangero, C., Buchholtz, M., Gilmore, S., & Haenel, V. (2005). End-To-End integrated security and performance analysis on the DEGAS choreographer platform. In *Lecture notes in computer science,* (pp. 286-301). Berlin: Springer.

Morrison, K. S., & Hirsh, F. (2006). *WS-I security challenges: threats and countermeasures,* WS-I Working Group Draft. Retrieved April 20, 2009 from http://www.ws-i.org/Profiles/BasicSecurity/SecurityChallenges-1.0.pdf

Moses, T. (2005). *Privacy policy profile of XACML v2.0*. OASIS. Retrieved April 20, 2009 from http://docs.oasis-open.org/xacml/2.0/access_control-xacml-2.0-privacy_profile-spec-os.pdf

Moses, T. (2005, February). *Extensible Access Control Markup Language (XACML) Version 2.0*. Retrieved from http://docs.oasis-open.org/xacml/2.0/access-control-xacml-2.0-core-spec-os.pdf

Mouratidis, H., Giorgini, P., & Manson, G. (2003). An ontology for modelling security: The tropos approach. *Lecture Notes in Computer Science, 2773*, 1387-1394. USA: Springer-Verlag.

Mouratidis, H., Giorgini, P., Manson, G., & Philip, I. (2002). A natural extension of tropos methodology for modelling security. In *Proceedings of the Agent Oriented Methodologies Workshop (OOPSLA 2002)*, Seattle, WA.

Myagmar, S. Lee, A. & Yurcik, W. (2005). Threat Modeling as a Basis for Security requirements. In *Proc. Symp. Requirements Engineering for Information Security (SREIS 05)*. Retrieved from www.sreis.org/SREIS_05_Program/short30_myagmar.pdf

Mylopoulos, J., Giorgini, P., & Massacci, F. (2003). Requirement engineering meets security: A case study on modelling secure electronic transactions by VISA and mastercard. In *Lecture notes in computer science,* (pp. 263-76). Berlin: Springer.

Nadalin, A., & Kaler, C. (2006). *Web Services Federation Language (WS-Federation)*. Joint whitepaper of BEA Systems, Inc., BMC Software, CA, Inc., International Business Machines Corporation, Layer 7 Technologies, Microsoft Corporation, Inc., Novell, Inc. and VeriSign, Inc.

Nadalin, A., Goodner, A., & Gudgin, M. Barbir, A. & Granqvist, H. (2007). *WS-SecureConversation 1.3*. OASIS. Retrieved April 20, 2009 from http://docs.oasis-open.org/ws-sx/ws-secureconversation/v1.3/ws-secureconversation.html

Nadalin, A., Goodner, A., & Gudgin, M. Barbir, A. & Granqvist, H. (2007). *WS-SecurityPolicy 1.2*. OASIS.

Retrieved April 20, 2009 from http://docs.oasis-open.org/ws-sx/ws-securitypolicy/v1.2/ws-securitypolicy.html

Nadalin, A., Goodner, A., & Gudgin, M. Barbir, A. & Granqvist, H. (2007). *WS-Trust 1.3*. OASIS. Retrieved April 20, 2009 from http://docs.oasis-open.org/ws-sx/ws-trust/v1.3/ws-trust.html

Nadalin, A., Goodner, M., Gudgin, M., Barbir, A., & Granqvist, H. (2007). *Web Services Trust Language (WS-Trust)*. OASIS Standard.

Nadalin, A., Kaler, C., Monzillo, R., & Hallam-Baker, P. (2006). *Web Services Security: SOAP Message Security 1.1 (WS-Security 2004)*. OASIS Standard.

Nadalin, A., Kaler, C., Monzillo, R., & Hallam-Baker, P. (2007). *Web Services Security: SOAP Message Security 1.1 (WS-Security 2004) OASIS Standard 200703*. Retrieved from http://www.oasis-open.org/committees/download.php/3281/WSS-OAPMessageSecurity-17-082703-merged.pdf

Nadalin, A., Kaler, C., Phillip, H.-B., & Monzillo, R. (2004, March). *Web Services Security, SOAP Message Security 1.1*. Retrieved from http://docs.oasis-open.org/wss/v1.1/wss-v1.1-spec-pr-SOAPMessageSecurity-01.pdf

Nagaratnam, N., Nadalin, A., Hondo, M., McIntosh, M., & Austel, P. (2005). Business-driven application security: from modeling to managing secure applications. *IBM Systems Journal, 44*(4), 847–867.

Newcomer, E. (2002). *Understanding Web Services: XML, WSDL, SOAP, and UDDI*. Reading, MA: Addison-Wesley Professional.

NICTIZ. (n.d.). *National IT Institute for Healthcare in the Netherlands*. Retrieved 11 21, 2008, from http://www.nictiz.nl/

Nishchal, B., & Kazerooni, S. (2007). *Web Services Vulnerabilities*: Security Compass.

OASIS Web Services Atomic Transaction (WS-Atomic Transaction). (2008). Retrieved from http://www.oasis-open.org/committees/tc_home.php?wg_abbrev=wsbpel

OASIS Web Services Business Activity (WS-Business-Activity). (2008). Retrieved from http://www.oasis-open.org/committees/tc_home.php?wg_abbrev=wsbpel

OASIS Web Services Coordination (WS-Coordination). (2008). Retrieved from http://docs.oasis-open.or/wstx/wscoor/2006/06

OASIS. (2006, October 12). *Reference model for service oriented architecture V1.0.* Retrieved April 21, 2009, from http://docs.oasis-open.org/soa-rm/v1.0/soa-rm.pdf

Obradovic, G. (2003). Threat Modeling and Data Sensitivity Classification for Information Security Risk Analysis. *Presentation at Data Protection '03.*

OMG. (2009). *Business Process Modeling Notation (BPMN) Information.* Retrieved January 6, 2009, from http://www.bpmn.org/

Onieva, J. A., Jianying, Z., Carbonell, M., & Lopez, J. (2003). *Intermediary non-repudiation protocols.* Paper presented at the IEEE International Conference on E-Commerce.

Oracle management pack for SOA. (2009). Oracle. Retrieved April 20, 2009 from http://www.oracle.com/technologies/soa/management-pack-soa.html, 2007.

Oracle web services manager. (2009). Oracle. Retrieved April 20, 2009 from http://www.oracle.com/appserver/web-services-manager.html

Ostrom, E. (1998). A Behavioral Approach to the Rational-Choice Theory of Collective Action. *The American Political Science Review, 92*(1), 1–22. doi:10.2307/2585925

Ou, X., Boyer, W., & McQueen, M. (2006). A scalable approach to attack graph generation. In *CCS '06: Proceedings of the 13th ACM conference on computer and communications security.* New York: ACM.

Paolucci, M., Kawamura, T., Payne, T. R., & Sycara, K. P. (2002). Semantic Matching of Web Services Capabilities. In *Iswc '02: Proceedings of the first international semantic web conference on the semantic web* (pp. 333-347). London: Springer-Verlag.

Papazoglou, M. P. (2008). *Web services: Principles and technology.* Old Tappan, NJ: Pearson/Prentice Hall.

Papazoglou, M. P., & Van den Heuvel, W.-J. (2007). Service Oriented Architectures: Approaches, Technologies, and Research Issues. *The VLDB Journal, 16*(3), 389–415. doi:10.1007/s00778-007-0044-3

Parducci, B., Lockhart, H., Levinson, R., Clark, J. B., & McRae, M. (2008). *eXtensible Access Control Markup Language (XACML) version 2.0.* OASIS Standard 200502. Retrieved from http://www.oasis-open.org/committees/tc_home.php?wg_abbrev=xacml

Pauls, K., Kolarczyk, S., Koch, M., & Löhr, K. (2006). Sectool – supporting requirements engineering for access control. In *Lecture notes in computer science,* (pp. 254-67). Berlin: Springer.

Peltier, T. (2001). *Information security risk analysis.* Boca Raton, FL: Auerbach.

Pfleeger, C. P., & Pfleeger, S. L. Security in Computing. 3rd ed., Pearson Education, Prentice Hall NJ, 2003

Piattini, M., & Fernández-Medina, E. (2004). Extending OCL for secure database development. In *Lecture notes in computer science,* (pp. 380-94). Berlin: Springer.

Pironti, A., & Sisto, R. (2008). Soundness conditions for message encoding abstractions in formal security protocol models. In *ARES '08: Proceedings of the 2008 third international conference on availability, reliability and security.* Washington, DC: IEEE Computer Society.

Pistore, M., Bertoli, P., Barbon, F., Shaparau, D., & Traverso, P. (2004). *Planning and Monitoring Web Service Composition.* Paper presented at the ICAPS'04 Workshop on Planning and Scheduling for Web and Grid Services.

Pope, N., Carlos, J., & Drees, S. (2007). *Digital Signature Service Core Protocols, Elements, and Bindings Version 1.0.* OASIS. Retrieved April 20, 2009 from http://docs.oasis-open.org/dss/v1.0/oasis-dss-core-spec-v1.0-os.pdf

Priebe, T. & Pernul, G. (2001). *A pragmatic approach to conceptual modeling of OLAP security.* 20th International Conference on Conceptual Modeling (ER 2001). Yokohama, Japan: Springer-Verlag.

Progress Actional SOA governance. (2009). Progress Software. Retrieved April 20, 2009 from http://www.actional.com/solutions/soa-governance/

Progress Software IONA Artix. (2009). Progress Software. Retrieved April 20, 2009 from http://www.iona.com/products/artix/welcome.htm

Prud'hommeaux, E., & Seaborne, A. (2008). *SPARQL Query Language for RDF.*

Qin, L., & Atluri, V. (2003). Concept-level access control for the Semantic Web. In *Xmlsec'03: Proceedings of the 2003 acm workshop on xml security,* (pp. 94-103). New York: ACM Press.

Rahaman, M. A., & Schaad, A. (2007). SOAP-based Secure Conversation and Collaboration. In *Proceedings of the IEEE International Conference on Web Services* (pp. 471-480), Salt Lake City, UT. Washington, DC: IEEE Computer Society.

Rahaman, M. A., Schaad, A., & Rits, M. (2006). Towards secure SOAP message exchange in a SOA. In *SWS '06: Proceedings of the 3rd ACM workshop on Secure web services,* (pp. 77-84). New York: ACM Press.

Rahm, E., & Bernstein, P. A. (2001). A survey of approaches to automatic schema matching. *The VLDB Journal, 10*(4), 334–350. doi:10.1007/s007780100057

Ramsaroop, P., & Ball, M. (2000). The Bank of Health: A Model for More Useful Patient records. *M.D. Computing, 17*(4), 45–48.

Ray, I., France, R., Li, N., & Georg, G. (2004). An aspect-based approach to modeling access control concerns. *Information and Software Technology, 46*(9), 575–587. doi:10.1016/j.infsof.2003.10.007

Reactivity web services management. (2007). Cisco Systems. Retrieved April 20, 2009 from http://www.cisco.com/cdc_content_elements/acquisitions/reactivity/download/reactivity_uc_web_services_management.pdf

Reddivari, P., Finin, T., & Joshi, A. (2007, January). Policy-Based Access Control for an RDF Store. In *Proceedings of the IJCAI-07 Workshop on Semantic Web for Collaborative Knowledge Acquisition.*

Redwine, S. (2007). *Introduction to modeling tools for software security.*

Reichert, M., Rinderle, S., Kreher, U., Acker, H., Lauer, M., & Dadam, P. (2006). ADEPT next generation process management technology — tool demonstration. In *Caise'06 forum.* Luxembourg.

Reif, G., Gall, H., & Jazayeri, M. (2005). WEESA: Web Engineering for Semantic Web Applications. In *Proceedings of the 14th International Conference on World Wide Web,* (pp. 722-729). New York: ACM Press.

Reistad, B., Murray, B., Davis, D., Robinson, I., McCollum, R., et al. (2006). *Web services resource transfer (WS-RT) version 1.0.* HP, Intel, IBM & Microsoft. Retrieved April 20, 2009 from http://download.boulder.ibm.com/ibmdl/pub/software/dw/specs/ws-rt/ws-rt-spec.pdf

Rembert, A. J. (2006). *Comprehensive workflow mining.* Paper presented at the Proceedings of the 44th annual Southeast regional conference.

Robinson, P., Cook, N., & Shrivastava, S. (2005). *Implementing fair non-repudiable interactions with Web services.* Paper presented at the Ninth IEEE International EDOC Enterprise Computing Conference.

Rohati products oveview. (2008). Rohati. Retrieved April 20, 2009 from http://www.rohati.com/products/index.php

Ronan, J., et al. (2004, March). *Performance implications of IPSec deployment.* Telecommunications Software & Systems Group (TSSG), Waterford Institute of Technology, Ireland.

Rosado, D. G., Fernández-Medina, E., López, J., & Piattini, M. (2008). *PSecGCM: Process for the development of Secure Grid Computing based Systems with Mobile devices.* Paper presented at the International Conference on Availability, Reliability and Security (ARES 2008), Barcelona, Spain.

Rosado, D. G., Fernandez-Medina, E., Piattini, M., & Gutierrez, C. (2006). A study of security architectural patterns. In *ARES '06: Proceedings of the first international conference on availability, reliability and security.* Washington, DC: IEEE Computer Society.

Rosenberg, J., & Remy, D. (2004). *Securing Web Services with WS-Security: Demystifying WS-Security, WS-Policy, SAML, XML Signature, and XML Encryption.* Sams.

Roth, H., Schiefer, J., & Schatten, A. (2006). *Probing and Monitoring of WSBPEL Processes with Web Services.* Paper presented at the E-Commerce Technology, 2006. The 8th IEEE International Conference on and Enterprise Computing, E-Commerce, and E-Services, The 3rd IEEE International Conference on.

Rouached, M., & Godart, C. (2006). *Analysis of Composite Web Services Using Logging Facilities.* Paper presented at the Second International Workshop on Engineering Service-Oriented Applications: Design and Composition (WESOA'06).

Rouached, M., Gaaloul, W., van der Aalst, W., Bhiri, S., & Godart, C. (2006). Web Service Mining and Verification of Properties: An Approach Based on Event Calculus. In *On the Move to Meaningful Internet Systems 2006: CoopIS, DOA, GADA, and ODBASE* (pp. 408-425).

Sabater, J., & Sierra, C. (2002). Reputation and Social Network Analysis in Multi-Agent Systems. In *Proceedings of the First International Joint Conference on Autonomous Agents and Multiagent Systems (AAMAS-02),* Bologna, Italy, (pp. 475–482).

Sabelfeld, A., & Myers, A. C. (2003). Language-Based Information Flow Security. *IEEE Journal on Selected Areas in Communications, 21*(1), 1–15. doi:10.1109/JSAC.2002.806121

Sahai, A., Machiraju, V., Sayal, M., van Moorsel, A., & Casati, F. (2002). Automated SLA Monitoring for Web Services. In *Proceedings Management Technologies for E-Commerce and E-Business Applications: 13th IFIP/IEEE International Workshop on Distributed Systems: Operations and Management, DSOM 2002, Montreal, Canada, October 21-23,* (pp. 28-41).

Sahai, A., Machiraju, V., Sayal, M., van Moorsel, A., & Casati, F. (2002). Automated SLA Monitoring for Web Services. In *Management Technologies for E-Commerce and E-Business Applications: 13th IFIP/IEEE International Workshop on Distributed Systems: Operations and Management, DSOM 2002, Montreal, Canada, October 21-23, 2002. Proceedings* (pp. 28-41).

Sajjad, A., Jameel, H., Kalim, U., Han, S. M., Lee, Y.-K., & Lee, S. (2005). *AutoMAGI - an Autonomic middleware for enabling Mobile Access to Grid Infrastructure.* Paper presented at the Joint International Conference on Autonomic and Autonomous Systems and International Conference on Networking and Services - (icas-icns'05).

Saltzer, J. H., & Schroeder, M. D. (1975). The protection of information in computer systems. In *IEEE, proceedings.*

Sanchez-Cid, F., & Maña, A. (2008). SERENITY pattern-based software development life-cycle. In *Proceedings of the 19th International. Conference on Database and Expert Systems Application (DEXA),* (pp. 305-309). Washington, DC: IEEE.

Sandhu, R. S., & Samarati, P. (1994, September). Access control: Principles and practice. *IEEE Communications Magazine, 32*(9), 40–49. doi:10.1109/35.312842

Sandhu, R., Coyne, E. J., Feinstein, H., & Youman, C. (1996, February). Role-based access control models. *IEEE Computer, 29,* 38–47.

Sandia National Laboratories. (2002). *Surety analysis.* Retrieved from http://www.sandia.gov

Santen, T. (2006). Stepwise development of secure systems. In *Lecture notes in computer science,* (pp. 142-55). Berlin: Springer.

Santen, T., Heisel, M., & Pfitzmann, A. (2002). Confidentiality-Preserving refinement is compositional - sometimes. In *ESORICS '02: Proceedings of the 7th european symposium on research in computer security.* London: Springer-Verlag.

Sapia, C., Blaschka, M., Höfling, G., & Dinter, B. (1998). *Extending the E/R model for the multidimen-*

sional paradigm. 1st International Workshop on Data Warehouse and Data Mining (DWDM'98). Singapore: Springer-Verlag.

Schabetsberger, T., Ammenwerth, E., Breu, R., Hoerbst, A., Goebel, G., & Penz, R. (2006). E-Health Approach to Link-up Actors in the Health Care System of Austria. *Studies in Health Technology and Informatics*, (124): 415–420.

Schechter, S. E. (2004). *Computer security and risk: A quantitative approach.* PhD thesis, Computer Science, Harvard University.

Schmidt, D., Stal, M., Rohnert, H., & Buschmann, F. (2000). Patterns for concurrent and networked objects. In *Pattern-oriented software architecture,* (vol. 2). Hoboken, NJ: J. Wiley.

Schneider, F. B. (1998). *Trust in cyberspace.* National Academy Press.

Schneider, F. B., Morrisett, G., & Harper, R. (2000). A Language-Based Approach to Security. *Informatics – 10 Years Back, 10 Years Ahead, (LNCS).* Heidelberg, Germany: Springer-Verlag.

Schneier, B., & Kelsey. (1999). Security audit logs to support computer forensics. *ACM Transactions on Information and System Security*, 2(2), 159–176. doi:10.1145/317087.317089

Schuba, C. L., Krsul, I. V., Kuhn, M. G., Spafford, E. H., Sundaram, A., & Zamboni, D. (1996). Analysis of a Denial of Service Attack on TCP. In *Proceedings of the 1997 IEEE Symposium on Security and Privacy*, (pp. 208–223). Washington, DC: IEEE Computer Society.

Schumacher, M., Fernandez, E. B., Hybertson, D., Buschmann, F., & Sommerlad, P. (2006). *Security Patterns: Integrating security and systems engineering.* Hoboken, NJ: J. Wiley.

Seaborne, A. (2004, January 9). *RDQL - A Query Language for RDF (Member Submission).* Tech. Rep. W3C.

Securent overview. (2007). Securent. Retrieved April 20, 2009 from http://www.securent.com/products/overview/

Security for REST Web Services. (2006, February 20). *Security for REST Web Services.* Retrieved December 11, 2008, from http://radio.weblogs.com/0111797/2006/02/20.html

Security in a web services world: a proposed architecture and roadmap. (2002). Retrieved April 20, 2009 from http://www-106.ibm.com/developerworks/webservices/library/ws-secmap/

Seehusen, F., & Stølen, K. (2006). Information flow property preserving transformation of UML interaction diagrams. In *SACMAT '06: Proceedings of the eleventh ACM symposium on access control models and technologies.* New York: ACM.

Sen, S., & Sajja, N. (2002). Robustness of Reputation-based Trust: Booblean Case. In *Proceedings of the First International Joint Conference on Autonomous Agents and Multiagent Systems (AAMAS-2002),* Bologna, Italy, (pp. 288–293).

Shabalin, P., & Jürjens, J. (2004). Automated verification of UMLsec models for security requirements. In *Lecture notes in computer science,* (pp. 365-79). Berlin: Springer.

Shabo, A. (2006). A Global Socio-Economic-Medico-Legal Model for the Sustainability of Longitudinal Electronic Health Records. Part 1. *Methods of Information in Medicine*, 45(3), 240–245.

Shah, S. (2007). Web 2.0 Security: Defending Ajax, RIA, and SOA. Course Technology PTR.

Shanmugasundaram, K., Memon, N., Savant, A., & Bronnimann, H. (2003). *ForNet: A Distributed Forensics Network.* Paper presented at the Second International Workshop on Mathematical Methods, Models and Architectures for Computer Networks Security, St. Petersburg, Russia.

Sidharth, N., & Liu, J. (2007). IAPF: A Framework for Enhancing Web Services Security. In *Proceedings of the 31st Annual International Computer Software and Applications Conference (COMPSAC 2007),* (Vol. 01, pp. 23-30). Washington, DC: IEEE Computer Society.

Sindre, G., & Opdahl, A. L. (2005). Eliciting security requirements with misuse cases. *Requir. Eng., 10*(1), 34–44. doi:10.1007/s00766-004-0194-4

Singhal, A., Winograd, T., & Scarfone, K. (2007). *Guide to Web Services Security.* NIST Special Publication 800-95

Sinha, S. K., & Benameur, A. (2008). A formal solution to rewriting attacks on SOAP messages. In *Proceedings of the ACM workshop on Secure web services* (pp. 53-60). New York: ACM.

Siveroni, I., Zisman, A., & Spanoudakis, G. (2008). Property specification and static verification of UML models. In *ARES '08: Proceedings of the 2008 third international conference on availability, reliability and security.* Washington, DC: IEEE Computer Society.

Smith, G.W. (1991). Modeling security-relevant data semantics. *IEEE Transactions on Software Engineering, 17*(11), 1195-1203.

Sohr, K., Mustafa, T., Bao, X., & Ahn, G.-J. (2008). Enforcing Role-Based Access Control Policies in Web Services with UML and OCL. In *Proceedings of the 2008 Annual Computer Security Applications Conference,* (pp. 257-266). Washington, DC: IEEE Computer Society.

Spanoudakis, G., Kloukinas, C., & Androutsopoulos, K. (2007). Towards security monitoring patterns. In *SAC '07: Proceedings of the 2007 ACM symposium on applied computing.* New York: ACM.

Spanoudakis, G., Maña, A., Kokolakis, S., Rudolph, C., & Lotz, V. (2009). *The Serenity Book.* Berlin: Springer-Verlag.

Srinath, P., Chathura, H., Jaliya, E., Eran, C., Ajith, R., Deepal, J., et al. (2006). *Axis2, Middleware for Next Generation Web Services.* Paper presented at the International Conference on Web Services (ICWS '06).

Srinivasan, L., & Banks, T. (2006). *Web Services Resource Lifetime 1.2 (WS-ResourceLifetime).* OASIS. Retrieved April 20, 2009 from http://docs.oasis-open.org/wsrf/wsrf-ws_resource_lifetime-1.2-spec-os.pdf

Stal, M. (2006). Using architectural patterns and blueprints for Service-Oriented Architecture. *Software IEEE, 2*(23), 54–61. doi:10.1109/MS.2006.60

Stamos, A. (2005). *Attacking Web Services.* DC: The OWASP Foundation.

Standards Australia. (1999). *AS/NZS 4360: Risk management.* Standards Australia. Standard. AS/NZS 4360.

Steffen, B., & Narayan, P. (2007). Full life-cycle support for end-to-end processes. *IEEE Computer, 40*(11), 64–73.

Stoica, A., & Farkas, C. (2002). Secure XML Views. In E. Gudes & S. Shenoi (Eds.), *Dbsec* (Vol. 256, p. 133-146). Amsterdam: Kluwer.

Stojanovic, Z., & Dahanayake, A. (2004). *Service-Oriented Software System Engineering.* Hershey, PA: Idea Group Publishing.

Sullivan, T. (2005). Retrieved November 2005, from http://www.pantos.org/atw/35654.html

Sun identity management. (2008). Sun. Retrieved April 20, 2009 from http://www.sun.com/software/products/identity/ds_solutions_your_environment.pdf

Sutcliffe, A. G., & Minocha, S. (1999). Linking business modeling to socio-technical system design. In *Proceedings of CaiSE'99* (pp. 73-87). Heidelberg, Germany.

Swiderski, F., & Snyder, W. (2004). *Threat modeling.* Redmond, WA: Microsoft Press.

Talukder, A., & Yavagal, R. (2006). Chapter 18: Security issues in mobile computing. In *Mobile Computing*: McGraw-Hill Professional.

Tang, K., Chen, S., Zic, J., & Levy, D. (2007). Performance Evaluation and Modeling of Web Services Security. In *Proceedings of the 2007 IEEE International Conference on Web Services (ICWS 2007),* (pp. 431-438). Washington, DC: IEEE Computer Society.

Technology, G. X. S. *A service oriented network for high performance B2B.* (2006). GXS Technology. Retrieved April 20, 2009 from http://www.gxs.com/products/technology/tradingGrid_tech.htm

Thompson, H. (2005). Application penetration testing. *IEEE Security and Privacy, 3*(1), 66–69. doi:10.1109/MSP.2005.3

Thompson, H. S., Beech, D., Maloney, M., & Mendelsohn, N. (2004). *XML Schema Part 1: Structure,* (2ⁿᵈ Ed.). Retrieved April 20, 2009 from http://www.w3.org/TR/2004/REC-xmlschema-1-20041028/

Threat Management –Web 2.0 Security Threats (2007, April). A Trend Micro White Paper I. Retrieved August 03, 2008 from http://us.trendmicro.com/imperia/md/content/us/pdf/threats/securitylibrary/trend_micro_web_2.0_threats_white_paper_apr07.pdf

Threat Risk Modeling (n.d.). Retrieved August 1, 2008, from http://www.owasp.org/index.php/Threat_Risk_Modeling

Thuraisingham, B., She, W., & I-Ling, Y. (2007) . Delegation-Based Security Model for Web Services. In *Proceedings of the 10ᵗʰ IEEE High Assurance Systems Engineering Symposium,* (pp. 82-91). Washington, DC: IEEE Computer Society.

Tivoli. (2005). *Tivoli secure way risk manager.* Retrieved March 14, 2003, from http://www-306.ibm.com/software/tivoli/products/security-compliance-mgr/

Trujillo, J., Palomar, M., Gómez, J., & Song, I. Y. (2001). Designing data warehouses with OO conceptual models. *IEEE Computer, Special issue on Data Warehouses,* (34), 66-75.

Trusted Computing Group Administration. (2006). Securing Mobile Devices on Converged Networks.

Tryfona, N., Busborg, F., & Christiansen, J. (1999). *starER: A conceptual model for data warehouse design.* ACM 2nd International Workshop on Data Warehousing and OLAP (DOLAP'99), Missouri, USA.

Turner, D. (2008). *Symantec global internet security threat report: Trends for July-December 2007.*

UMLsec group. (2009). *Security analysis tool* [Web page]. Retrieved January 12, 2009, from http://www.umlsec.org

Vakali, A., & Pallis, G. (2007). Web Data Management Practices: Emerging Techniques and Technologies. IGI Publishing.

Validation testing report: Sarvega XML Guardian Gateway & XML Speedway Accelerator. (2004). Retrieved April 20, 2009 from http://www.itslabs.com/tests/its04003.jhtml

Vampenepe, W., Graham, S., & Niblett, P. (2006). *Web Services Topics 1.3 (WS-Topics).* OASIS. Retrieved April 20, 2009 from http://docs.oasis-open.org/wsn/wsn-ws_topics 1.3 spec os.pdf

VanHilst, M., Fernandez, E. B., & Braz, F. (in press). A multidimensional classification for users of security patterns. *Journal of Research and Practice in Information Technology.*

Varadan, R., Channabasavaiah, K., Simpson, S., Holley, K., & Allam, A. (2008). Increasing business flexibility and soa adoption through effective soa governance. *IBM Systems Journal,* 47.

Vedamuthu, A. S. (2007). *Web Services Description Language (WSDL) Version 2.0 SOAP 1.1 Binding.* W3C. Retrieved April 20, 2009 from http://www.w3.org/TR/wsdl20-soap11-binding/

Vedamuthu, A. S., Orchard, D., Hirsch, F., Hondo, M., Yendluri, P., et al. (2007). *Web Services Policy 1.5 – Framework.* W3C. Retrieved April 20, 2009 from http://www.w3.org/TR/ws-policy/

Vedamuthu, A. S., Orchard, D., Hirsch, F., Hondo, M., Yendluri, P., et al. (2007). *Web Services Policy 1.5 – Attachment.* W3C. Retrieved April 20, 2009 from http://www.w3.org/TR/2007/REC-ws-policy-attach-20070904/

Ventuneac, M., Coffey, T., & Salomie, I. (2003). A Policy-Based Security Framework for Web-Enabled Applications. In *Proceedings of the 1ˢᵗ International Symposium on Information and Communication Technologies,* (pp. 487-492). Dublin: Trinity College.

Verma, M. (2004). *XML Security: Control Information Access with XACML.* Retrieved from http://www.ibm.com/developerworks/xml/library/x-xacml/

Verma, M. (2005). *Web Services Transactions*. Armonk, NY: IBM Publications.

Viega, J., & Epstein, J. (2006). Why applying Standards to Web Services is not Enough. *IEEE Security and Privacy, 4*(4), 25–31. doi:10.1109/MSP.2006.110

Villarroel, R., Fernandez, E., Trujillo, J., & Piattini, M. (2005). Towards a UML 2.0/OCL extension for designing secure data warehouses. In *Proceedings of International Workshop on Security in Information Systems*, Miami, FL, USA (pp. 217-228).

Vinoski, S. (2003). Integration with web services. *IEEE Internet Computing, 7*(6), 75–77. doi:10.1109/MIC.2003.1250587

Vivas, J. L., López, J., & Montenegro, J. A. (2007). Cap. 12. Grid Security Architecture: Requirements, fundamentals, standards, and models. In A. Publications (Ed.), *Security in Distributed, Grid, Mobile, and Pervasive Computing* (pp. 440). Tuscaloosa, USA.

Voelter, M., Schmid, A., & Wolff, E. (2002). *Server component patterns: Component infrastructures illustrated with EJB*. West Sussex, UK: Wiley.

Vordel, X. M. L. *Firewall: Threat protection for XML applications.* (2007). Vordel. Retrieved April 20, 2009 from http://www.vordel.com/products/vx_firewall/index.html

Vorobiev, A., & Jun, H. (2006). *Security Attack Ontology for Web Services*. Paper presented at the Second International Conference on Semantics, Knowledge and Grid (SKG '06).

Vraalsen, F., Braber, F. D., Hogganvik, I., Lund, S., & Stolen, K. (2004). *The CORAS tool-supported methodology* (SINTEF Report. Report # STF90A04015). SINTEF ICT, Norway.

Wang, W., & Daniels, T. E. (2005). *Building evidence graphs for network forensics analysis*. Paper presented at the 21st Annual Computer Security Applications Conference.

Washizaki, H., Fernandez, E. B., Maruyama, H., Kubo, A. & Yoshioka, N. (submitted). *Precise classification of software patterns.*

Web Service Enhancements. (WSE 3.0). (2005, November). Retrieved from http://msdn.microsoft.com/webservices/webservices/building/wse/default.aspx

Web Service Security Specifications. (n.d.). Retrieved from http://www.oasis-open.org/

Web services for management (WS-Management) 1.0. (2008). Distributed Management Task Force. Retrieved April 20, 2009 from http://www.dmtf.org/standards/published_documents/DSP0226_1.0.0.pdf

Weblayers. (2005). *Whitepaper: SOA Governance*, (pp. 9).

WebSphere DataPower XML Security Gateway XS40. (2004). IBM. Retrieved April 20, 2009 from http://www-01.ibm.com/software/integration/datapower/xs40/

Weerawarana, S., Curbera, F., Leymann, F., Storey, T., & Ferguson, D. F. (2005). *Web Services Platform Architecture: SOAP, WSDL, WS-Policy, WS-Addressing, WS-BPEL, WS-Reliable Messaging, and More*. Upper Saddle River, NJ: Prentice Hall PTR.

Welch, V., Siebenlist, F., Foster, I., Bresnahan, J., Czajkowski, K., Gawor, J., et al. (2003, 22-24 June 2003). *Security for Grid services.* Paper presented at the 12th IEEE International Symposium on High Performance Distributed Computing (HPDC-12 '03).

Whittle, J., Wijesekera, D., & Hartong, M. (2008). Executable misuse cases for modeling security concerns. In *ICSE '08: Proceedings of the 30th international conference on software engineering*. New York: ACM.

Williams, J. (n.d.). *The trinity of RIA security explained.* Retrieved August 09, 2008, from http://www.theregister.co.uk/2008/04/08/ria_security/

Wilson, K., & Sedukhin, I. (2006). *Web services distributed management: management web services (WSDM-MOWS) 1.1.* OASIS. Retrieved April 20, 2009 from http://www.oasis-open.org/committees/download.php/20574/wsdm-mows-1.1-spec-os-01.pdf

Wolff, B., Brucker, A. D., & Doser, J. (2006). A model transformation semantics and analysis methodology for secureuml. In *Lecture notes in computer science,* (pp. 306-20). Berlin: Springer.

Woo, T., & Lam, S. (1993). Authorizations in Distributed Systems: A New Approach. *Journal of Computer Security, 2*(2,3), 107-136.

Woodside, M., Petriu, D. C., Petriu, D. B., Xu, J., Israr, T., & Georg, G. (2009). Performance analysis of security aspects by weaving scenarios extracted from UML models. *Journal of Systems and Software, 82*(1), 56–74. doi:10.1016/j.jss.2008.03.067

Wozak, F., Ammenwerth, E., Breu, M., Penz, R., Schabetsberger, T., Vogl, R., et al. (2006). Medical Data GRIDs as approach towards secure cross enterprise document sharing (based on IHE XDS). *Ubiquity: Technologies for Better Health in Aging Societies: Proc. MIE2006,* (pp. 377-383). Amsterdam: IOS Press.

WS-Federation Spec. (2003, July 18). *WS- Federation Specification.* Retrieved November 20, 2008, from http://www.ibm.com/developerworks/library/specification/ws-fed/

WS-Policy Attachment Spec. (2007, September 4). *Web Services Policy Attachment.* Retrieved November 20, 2008, from http://www.w3.org/TR/ws-policy-attach/

WS-Policy Spec. (2006, April 25). *Web Services Policy 1.2 - Framework (WS-Policy).* Retrieved November 20, 2008, from http://www.w3.org/Submission/WS-Policy/

WS-Security appnotes. (2002). IBM and Microsoft. Retrieved April 20, 2009 from http://www-106.ibm.com/developerworks/webservices/library/ws-secapp

WS-Security Policy Spec. (2007, July 1). *WS-Security Policy 1.2.* Retrieved November 20, 2008, from http://docs.oasis-open.org/ws-sx/ws-securitypolicy/200702/ws-securitypolicy-1.2-spec-os.html

WS-Security Spec. (2006, February 1). *WS-Security.* Retrieved November 20, 2008, from http://www.oasis-open.org/committees/download.php/16790/wss-v1.1-spec-os-SOAPMessageSecurity.pdf

XACML 2.0 Specification. (n.d.). Retrieved from http://oasis-open.org/

XML Firewall and VPN. (2008). Layer7 Technologies. Retrieved April 20, 2009 from http://www.layer7tech.com/products/page.html?id=70

Xtradyne, W. *S-DBC - the XML firewall.* (2005). Xtradyne. Retrieved April 20, 2009 from http://www.xtradyne.com/products/ws-dbc/xml-firewall-intro.htm

Yee, G., & Korba, L. (2005). Negotiated Security Policies for E-Services and Web Services. In *Proceedings of the IEEE International Conference on Web Services (ICWS' 05),* (pp. 605 - 612). Washington, DC: IEEE Computer Society.

Yendluri, P. (2000). *RosettaNet Implementation Framework (RNIF) 2.0.* Retrieved from http://www.rosettanet.org/rosettanet/Doc/0/TA0508VV3E7KLCRIDD1B-MU6N38/RNIF2.1.pdf

Yoshioka, N., Honiden, S., & Finkelstein, A. (2004). Security patterns: A method for constructing secure and efficient inter-company coordination systems. In *EDOC '04: Proceedings of the enterprise distributed object computing conference, eighth IEEE international.* Washington, DC: IEEE Computer Society.

Yskout, K., Scandariato, R., Win, B. D., & Joosen, W. (2008). Transforming security requirements into architecture. In *ARES '08: Proceedings of the 2008 third international conference on availability, reliability and security.* Washington, DC: IEEE Computer Society.

Yu, B., & Singh, M. P. (2001). Towards a Probabilistic Model of Distributed Reputation Management. In *Proceedings of the Fourth Workshop on Deception, Fraud and Trust in Agent Societies,* Montreal, Canada, (pp. 125–137).

Yu, B., & Singh, M. P. (2002). An Evidential Model of Distributed Reputation Management. In *Proceedings of the First International Joint Conference on Autonomous Agents and Multiagent Systems (AAMAS-02),* Bologna, Italy, (pp. 294–301).

Yu, E. (1999). Strategic modeling for enterprise integration. In *Proceedings of the 16th World Congress of International Federation of Automatic Control,* Beijing, China (pp. 127-132). Pergamon, Elsevier Sciences.

Yu, E. S. K., & Mylopoulos, J. (1994, May 16-21). Understanding "why" in software process modeling, analysis, and design. In *Proceedings of the 16th International Conference in Software Engineering*, Sorrento, Italy (pp. 548-565).

Yu, E., & Elahi, G. (2008). A goal oriented approach for modeling and analyzing security trade-offs. In *Lecture notes in computer science*, (pp. 375-90). Berlin: Springer.

Yu, E., & Liu, L. (2000). Modelling trust in the i* strategic actors framework. In *Proceedings of the 3rd International Workshop on Deception, Fraud, and Trust in Agent Societies*, Barcelona, Catalonia, Spain.

Yu, W., Aravind, D., & Supthaweesuk, P. (2006). Software vulnerability analysis for web services software systems. In *Computers and communications, 2006 ISCC '06 proceedings 11th IEEE symposium on*.

Yu, Y., Jürjens, J., & Mylopoulos, J. (2008). Traceability for the maintenance of secure software. In *24Th IEEE international conference on software maintenance*.

Yuhong, Y., Pencole, Y., Cordier, M. O., & Grastien, A. (2005). *Monitoring Web service networks in a model-based approach*. Paper presented at the Web Services, 2005. ECOWS 2005. Third IEEE European Conference on.

Zacharia, G. (1999), *Collaborative Reputation Mechanisms for Online Communities*. Master thesis, Massachusetts Institute of Technology.

Zaha, J. M., Dumas, M., ter Hofstede, A. H. M., Barros, A., & Decker, G. (2008). Bridging Global and Local Models of Service-Oriented Systems. *Systems, Man, and Cybernetics, Part C: Applications and Reviews . IEEE Transactions on*, 38(3), 302–318.

Zdun, U., Hentrich, C., & van der Aalst, W. M. P. (2006). A survey of patterns for Service-Oriented Architectures. *International Journal of Internet Protocol Technology*, 3(1), 132–143.

Zhang, G., Baumeister, H., Koch, N., & Knapp, A. (2005). Aspect-Oriented modeling of access control in web applications. In *Proc. 6Th int. Workshop on aspect oriented modeling, AOSD*.

Zhou, J., & Gollman, D. (1996). *A fair non-repudiation protocol*. Paper presented at the Proceedings of the 1996 IEEE Symposium on Security and Privacy.

About the Contributors

Carlos A. Gutiérrez has more than 10 years of professional experience, currently being in the position of IT & e-Business project manager at Correos Telecom (Madrid, Spain). He is also assistant professor of Software Engineering at the University of Castilla - La Mancha (Ciudad Real, Spain). Gutiérrez obtained his doctoral degree in computer sciences at the University of Castilla - La Mancha and his MSc in Computer Sciences at the Autonomous University of Madrid. He is Expert in e-Business from the Technical University of Madrid, holds a postgraduate in Business Administration from the Madrid Chamber of Commerce and is PMP and ITIL foundations-certified. Gutiérrez participates at the ALARCOS Research Group of the Department of Computer Science at the University of Castilla – La Mancha. His main research interests are security engineering, software security architectures and security in distributed systems.

Eduardo Fernández-Medina holds a PhD. and an MSc. in Computer Science from the University of Sevilla. He is Associate Professor at the Escuela Superior de Informática of the University of Castilla-La Mancha at Ciudad Real (Spain), his research activity being in the field of security in information systems, and particularly in security in business processes, databases, datawarehouses, and web services. Fernández-Medina is co-editor of several books and chapter books on these subjects, and has several dozens of papers in national and international conferences (BPM, UML, ER, ESORICS, TRUSTBUS, etc.). He is author of several manuscripts in national and international journals (Decision Support Systems, Information Systems, ACM Sigmod Record, Information Software Technology, Computers & Security, Computer Standards and Interfaces, etc.). He is a member of the Alarcos research group of the Department of Computer Science at the University of Castilla-La Mancha, in Ciudad Real, Spain, and he leads the subgroup of security in the Alarcos Research Group.

Mario Piattini has an MSc and PhD in Computer Science from the Technical University of Madrid and an MSc in Psychology from the UNED. He is a Certified Information System Auditor, Certified Information Security Manager and Certified in the Governance of Enterprise IT by ISACA (Information System Audit and Control Association), CSQE by the American Society for Quality (ASQ). He is a professor in the Department of Information Systems and Technologies at the University of Castilla-La Mancha, in Ciudad Real, Spain. Author of several books and papers on software and security engineering, he leads the ALARCOS research group of the Department of Information Systems and Technologies at the University of Castilla-La Mancha, in Ciudad Real, Spain.

* * *

Rafael Accorsi is a post-doc at the University of Freiburg, Germany. He received the Ph.D. degree in Computer Science in 2008 from the University of Freiburg, the M.Sc. degree with a double major in Computer Science and Logic in 2000 from the University of Amsterdam, Holland, and the B.Sc. degree in Computer Science in 1998 from the University of Pelotas, Brazil. His research interests are generally in the area of security and privacy in distributed systems. Specifically, runtime and a posteriori enforcement of policies

Nico Brehm studied computer science at the University of Applied Sciences "Hochschule Harz" in Wernigerode (Germany). He worked as research assistant at the computer science departments of the universities of Magdeburg (Germany) and Oldenburg (Germany). In 2009 he received his PhD degree for his work "Federated ERP systems based on Web Services" from the University of Oldenburg. His research work is now focused on Service-oriented Architectures, Web Service technology and Reputation Systems. He also founded his own company where he is connecting the theoretical concepts of the reputation systems domain with E-Commerce platforms applied in practice.

Ruth Breu is full professor at the Institute of Computer Science at University of Innsbruck and head of the research group Quality Engineering since 2002. Prior to that she was a researcher at the Technische Universität München and Universität Passau and spent several years in industry working as a software engineering consultant. Quality Engineering focuses on foundations of model-based software development, in particular in the areas of security engineering, IT management, model-based quality assurance and workflow management. The research group currently has about 30 members and cooperates with industry partners such as Siemens, Swiss Re and Telekom Austria.

Ingrid Buckley is a Ph.D. student pursuing a degree in Computer Science at Florida Atlantic University under the direction of Prof. E.B. Fernandez. Ingrid holds a M.Sc. in Computer Science from FAU, focusing on reliability and security features for critical infrastructure systems. She is an active member of the Security Research Group of the CS department of FAU. She is a member of the Golden Key and Upsilon Pi Epsilon International Honor Societies, a recipient of the LACCEI scholarship and several awards for academic achievements. A participant in the PIRE program at the Universidad Nacional de La Plata in Argentina, she worked there on reliability and fault tolerance mechanisms. She is the author of a paper on web services reliability standards, accepted for the SEKE 2009 Conference.

Csilla Farkas is an Associate Professor in the Department of Computer Science and Engineering and Director of the Center for Information Assurance Engineering at the University of South Carolina. Csilla Farkas received her Ph.D. from George Mason University, Fairfax. In her dissertation she studied the inference and aggregation problems in multilevel secure relational databases. Dr. Farkas' current research interests include information assurance, data inference problem, security and privacy on the Semantic Web, and security and reliability of Service Oriented Architecture. Dr. Farkas is a recipient of the National Science Foundation Career award. The topic of her award is "Semantic Web: Interoperation vs. Security – A New Paradigm of Confidentiality Threats." Dr. Farkas actively participates in international scientific communities as program committee member and reviewer.

Eduardo B. Fernandez (Eduardo Fernandez-Buglioni) is a professor in the Department of Computer Science and Engineering at Florida Atlantic University in Boca Raton, Florida. He has published numerous papers on authorization models, object-oriented analysis and design, and security patterns. He has written four books on these subjects, the most recent being a book on security patterns. He has lectured all over the world at both academic and industrial meetings. He has created and taught several graduate and undergraduate courses and industrial tutorials. His current interests include security patterns and web services security and fault tolerance. He holds a MS degree in Electrical Engineering from Purdue University and a Ph.D. in Computer Science from UCLA. He is a Senior Member of the IEEE, and a Member of ACM. He is an active consultant for industry, including assignments with IBM, Allied Signal, Motorola, Lucent, and others. More details can be found at http://www.cse.fau.edu/~ed

Nils Gruschka studied computer science at the Christian-Albrechts-University of Kiel, Germany, and received his Ph.D. in 2008. His thesis presents methods for Web Service protection using efficient Web Service message validation. Currently he works as a research scientist at NEC Laboratories Europe in the field of Web Service security. Nils is a member of the ACM and GI.

Murat Gunestas is a captain at General Directorate of Security in Ankara, Turkey. He is also PhD candidate in Information Technology at George Mason University with support of Turkish Government. His dissertation topic is about forensics implementation on Service Oriented Architectures. His general research interests include web services security, computer and network forensics, and component-based software engineering. He has Bachelor degree in Security Science and MS degree in Software Engineering. He developed software for General Directorate of Security by 2003 and lead software teams afterwards. He currently holds software project lead position at the same department along with appointments of deploying appropriate security policies.

Michael Hafner is a senior researcher with the group "Quality Engineering" at the University of Innsbruck. He is leading a team of doctoral students with research interests in model driven security engineering placing a special emphasis on the engineering of large-scale service oriented systems. He was responsible for the design and the realization of the SECTET framework, a model-driven security infrastructure for SOA applications which is being used in industry projects. He is the author of the book "Security Engineering for Service-Oriented Architectures". Dr. Hafner has served on the program committee of several ACM and IEEE conferences and workshops. Prior to joining the University of Innsbruck where he obtained his doctoral degree in computer sciences in 2007 and a master's degree in international business administration in 1997, he gained industry experience in the automotive and the telecommunications sector as a technical consultant on systems integration with one of the "big five" consulting companies.

Keiko Hashizume is a MS student completing her thesis under the direction of Prof. E.B.Fernandez. She received her Bachelors degree in System Engineering from Universidad de Lima in Peru. She is a scholar of LACCEI (Latin American and Caribbean Consortium of Engineering Institutions). Keiko's research interest at FAU is Security in Web Services. Presently, she is working on developing patterns for security web services standards such as XML Encryption, XML Signature, and WS-Security. She is the author of three papers on these topics.

Sebastian Höhn works as a Researcher at the Albert-Ludwig University, Freiburg (Germany). He graduated in 2004 from the Technical University Munich in Computer Science and Computer linguistics.

Currently he is involved in research projects regarding secure business process management; compliance engineering; security and dependability. Several publications in the area of usable security; secure configuration management; and business process engineering. In cooperation with Hitachi and NII, Japan, he is developing methodologies for business process rewriting, with the goal of automated enforcement of security and compliance requirements arising from the new regulation based on SOX and HIPPA.

Frank Innerhofer-Oberperfler is leading the competence cluster IT-Governance at the Research Group Quality Engineering of the Institute of Computer Science at the University of Innsbruck. He is currently working on his PhD in Business Administration. His main research interests are in the fields of IT-Governance, IT-Risk Management, Information Security Management and Enterprise Modelling. He gained industry experience working as an independent software and web developer, as a system engineer at a IT-Infrastructure Provider and as a security consultant.

Amit Jain is a Semantic Security scientist with Belief Networks Inc in Charleston, SC. He received his M.E and PhD from University of South Carolina, Columbia. His dissertation is titled "Security on the Web: A Semantic-Aware Authorization Framework for Secure Data Sharing." In his PhD, he studied the problem of data leakage during data exchange in distributed systems due to inferences and dependence of authorizations models on data structure and syntax. He received his Bachelors of Engineering from Bangalore University in India. He has experience in Semantic data integration, Information Security, and Autonomous Agents. His current research interests include Web Services, Grid, & Semantic Web Security Protocols, Ontology & Knowledge Management Systems, Semantic Intelligence, and Natural Language Processing. He loves to travel and has travelled around the world. In his spare time he likes to read books and spend time with his family.

Meiko Jensen studied computer science at the Christian-Albrechts-University of Kiel, Germany, and received his degree in computer science (a german diploma) in 2007. Currently he is a Ph.D. student, researching in the field of Web Service security, and is particularly interested in service composition security, XML security, security modeling, and attacks on Web Services. Meiko is a member of ACM and GI.

Jan Jürjens is a Senior Lecturer at Open University (UK), Royal Society Industrial Fellow at Microsoft Research Cambridge (MSRC), non-stipendiary Research Fellow at Robinson College (Univ. Cambridge). Supervising 2 Postdocs, 8 PhD students. PI in projects with MSRC, BT, EPSRC, Royal Society. Research director of Integrated Project in EU FP7 FET Programme. PhD Computing, Oxford University. Author of "Secure Systems Development with UML" (Springer, 2004) and 80 publications mostly on secure software engineering. Founding chair, WG "Formal Methods and Software Engineering for Safety and Security", German Computer Society (GI). Member, IFIP Working Group 1.7 "Theoretical Foundations of Security Analysis and Design".

Anne V.D.M. Kayem is currently a post-doctoral researcher at the German Research Centre for Artificial Intelligence (Bremen, Germany). She holds a Bachelors degree and Masters degree in Computer Science from the University of Yaoundé I, Cameroon, and a PhD degree in Computer Science from Queen's University (Kingston, Canada). Her PhD thesis was centered on the topic of "Adaptive Cryptographic Access Control for Dynamic Data Sharing Environments". Her research interests are in the general area of information security with a focus on cryptographic access control, language-based security, and security in service oriented architectures. She has been a member of IEEE, ACM, and SIAM since July 2006.

Maria M. Larrondo-Petrie is Professor and Associate Dean in the College of Engineering and Computer Science at Florida Atlantic University. Her research in Software Engineering focuses on analysis, modeling, security, and visualization of complex systems and on integrating formal and informal methods. She has received almost $3M in research funding from the Department of Defense, Department of Information Systems Assurance, National Science Foundation, NATO, IBM, and the South Florida Water Management District. She is Vice President of the International Federation of Engineering Education Societies, and Executive Director of the Latin American and Caribbean Consortium of Engineering Institutions.

Lutz Lowis received his first degree in computer science from the University of Applied Sciences Furtwangen. Since 2004, he is a scientific assistant at the University of Freiburg's Department of Telematics, where in his PhD thesis he developed a new vulnerability analysis method on top of attack trees and FMEA concepts. Besides vulnerability analysis with a focus on SOA-based business processes, Lutz is interested in vulnerability classifications and how vulnerability information can be beneficial not only regarding the technical, but also the economic aspects of risk management. He has published on risk management in service-oriented architectures, and earlier works include the use of Trusted Computing remote attestation for the secure selection of remote services.

Sudeep Mallick is a Principal Researcher with SETLabs, INFOSYS TECHNOLOGIES LTD. During his over 10 years' experience in the IT field, he has worked in various capacities such as technical architect, technology evangelist and researcher and has several years of experience in implementing IT projects that involves J2EE technologies, SOA and web services. He has several international publications to his credit in the areas of software engineering, software architecture, SOA and XML technologies and is also the co-author of a book on Enterprise IT Architecture. His current research interests include SOA Governance, parallel computing, HPC and Cloud Computing and can be contacted at sudeepm@infosys.com

Antonio Maña received his MSc and PhD degrees in Computer Engineering from the University of Málaga in 1994 and 2003, respectively. In 1995 he joined the Department of Computer Science of the University of Málaga where he is currently Associate Professor. His current research activities include security and software engineering, information and network security, application of smart cards to digital contents commerce, software protection and DRM. He has more than 60 peer-reviewed publications. He has participated in several EU funded projects and is currently the Scientific Director of the FP6 SERENITY project and the UMAs principal investigator of FP6 GST and GREDIA projects. Prof. Maña is member of the Editorial Board of the Intl. Journal of Electronic Security and Digital Forensics (IJESDF) and reviewer for several other international journals. He is member of different professional and scientific societies and workgroups and is actively involved in the organisation of research and educational activities.

Jorge Marx Gómez studied computer engineering and industrial engineering at the University of Applied Science of Berlin (Technische Fachhochschule). He was a lecturer and researcher at the Otto-von-Guericke-Universität Magdeburg where he also obtained a PhD degree in business information systems with the work Computer-based Approaches to Forecast Returns of Scrapped Products to Recycling. In 2004 he received his habilitation for the work Automated Environmental Reporting through Material Flow Networks at the Otto-von-Guericke-Universität Magdeburg. From 2002 till 2003 he was a visiting professor for business informatics at the Technical University of Clausthal. In 2005 he became a full professor of business information systems at the Carl von Ossietzky University Oldenburg. His research interests include Very Large Business Applications, Federated ERP-Systems, Data Warehousing, Business Intelligence, Enterprise Systems Engineering, Enterprise Tomography and System Landscape Engineering.

Markus Mitterer has gained a Master of Business Administration and a Master in Computer Science at the University of Innsbruck. In his diploma thesis at the Institute of Computer Science he focused on the security analysis of health care networks. Markus Mitterer is now working as an IT and business consultant.

Antonio Muñoz is currently a PhD student and a research assistant in the GISUM group at the University of Malaga. He holds an MSc degree in Computer Science and a Postgraduate Master degree in Software Engineer and Artificial Intelligence, both of them from the University of Malaga. His principal research interests are in the area of Agent technology, Digital Rights Management Systems and security engineering. Antonio is involved in the EU Sixth Framework Programme project Ubisec, Serenity, and in the EU Seventh Framework Programme project OKKAM.

Deepti Parachuri is a Junior Research Associate with SETLabs, INFOSYS TECHNOLOGIES LTD. She holds a masters degree in computer science from Indian Institute of Technology, Madras. She has been actively involved in various publications and conferences. She has several international publications to her credit in the areas of software engineering, Semantic Web services, SOA and XML technologies. Her current research interests include SOA Governance, Service identification and Semantic web services and can be contacted at Deepti_parachuri@infosys.com.

Gimena Puyol was born in Buenos aires (Argetina) on 12th January, 1978. Gimena is a PhD student in computer science at University of Malaga. She receives her B.s. degree on Computer Science Engineer at 2006 and her M.s. degree on Software Engineering and Artificial Intelligence Master at 2007, both at University of Malaga. Currently, Gimena is member of the security area of the GISUM research team. She is evolved in the research projects: SERENITY - System Engineering for Security and Dependability (UE sixth framework programme, IST-027587), OKKAM - Enabling the Web of Entities – A scalable and sustainable solution for systematic and global identifier reuse in decentralized information environments (UE Seventh framework programme, IST-215032) y MISTICO-MECHANICS – Definición de un modelo de madurez integrado de seguridad de las TICs para pequeñas y medianas empresas (supported by Junta de Comunidades de Castilla-La Mancha, PBC06-0082-8542). Her principal research interests are in the area of security in AmI, study of the description and reasoning of the security properties through formal methods and delegation of attribute and privileges.

Anoop Singhal is currently a Senior Computer Scientist in the Computer Security Division at NIST. His research interests are in web services and network security, intrusion detection and large scale data mining systems. He has several years of research experience at NIST, George Mason University and AT&T Bell Labs. As a Distinguished Member of Technical Staff at Bell Labs he has led several software projects in the area of Databases and Data Mining Systems, Web Services and Network Management Systems. He is a senior member of IEEE and he has published more than 25 papers in leading conferences and journals. He received his Ph.D. in Computer Science from Ohio State University, Columbus Ohio. He has given talks and presented papers in computer security conferences such as ACSAC, RSA and IFIP DBSEC.

Michael VanHilst is an assistant professor in the Department of Computer Science and Engineering at Florida Atlantic University. His research interests include software development methods, process improvement, and computer security. He has 20 years of industry experience including for HP, IBM, and NASA. He was recently VP of Technology for a firewall development company. Dr. VanHilst received his PhD in Computer Science from the University of Washington, and holds 3 prior degrees from MIT. He is a member of the ACM and IEEE Computer Society.

Duminda Wijesekera is an associate professor in the Department of Computer Science at George Mason University, Fairfax, Virginia. During various times, his research interests have been in security, multimedia, networks, secure signaling (telecom, railway and SCADA), avionics, missile systems, web and theoretical computer science. He holds courtesy appointments at the Center for Secure Information Systems (CSIS) and the Center for Command, Control and Coordination (C4I) at George Mason University, and the Potomac Institute of Policy Studies in Arlington, VA. Prior to GMU he was at Honeywell Military Avionics, Army High Performance Research Center at the University of Minnesota, and the University of Wisconsin. His doctorates are in Computer Science and Logic from the University of Minnesota and Cornell University in 1997 and 1990 respectively.

Index